Essays in Presidential Rhetoric
Second Edition

Edited by
Theodore Windt

and

Beth Ingold

Kendall/Hunt
Publishing Company
Dubuque, Iowa

Copyright © 1983, 1987 by Kendall/Hunt Publishing Company

Library of Congress Catalog Card Number: 86–83058

ISBN 0–8403–4241–1

Printed in the United States of America
10 9 8 7 6 5 4 3 2

Contents

Preface to the Second Edition

We concluded the introduction to the first edition of *Essays in Presidential Rhetoric* by saying that we hoped the next edition could be expanded to include new studies in the discipline of presidential rhetoric. Happily, we are able to do so, even though our editing task was made more difficult by the sheer volume of excellent studies that have appeared during the past three years. In choosing which essays to include in this edition, we were again not concerned with essays about campaigning for the presidency, nor with studies whose principal purposes were to contribute additional scholarship to the field of rhetoric and communications or to the task of rhetorical criticism. Our concerns were to select essays that illuminate the role rhetoric plays in a presidential administration, the ways in which various Presidents have used rhetoric, comparative studies of rhetorical activities by contemporary Presidents, and especially studies of how the use of rhetoric has enhanced or diminished a President's ability to exercise his powers. We view rhetoric as one instrument of political power available to a President. We believe that power is the central dynamic of politics, and in this media age, we further believe that rhetoric is the central dynamic of presidential power.

The second edition is expanded from the twenty essays of the first edition to twenty-seven essays written by scholars in rhetoric, communications, and political science. We have replaced several essays in the original edition with newer essays on the same topic because these more recently published essays seem to address the themes of this book more directly. In several cases, we have included essays not previously published.

The volume is divided into eight parts. The introductory essay outlines the discipline of presidential rhetoric, summarizes the research done by rhetorical scholars from 1960 to the present, and proposes an agenda for future research in the rhetorical presidency.

The four essays that comprise the Overview section give perspective to the contemporary presidency. The authors of "The Rise of the Rhetorical Presidency" chart the developments that have led to the prominence of rhetoric in recent administrations. Karlyn Kohrs Campbell and Kathleen Hall Jamieson analyze the principal themes of inaugural addresses in an exceptionally perceptive scholarly exercise in generic criticism. Dan F. Hahn and J. Justin Gustainis provide a topology of strategies and tactics used by Presidents to defend against attacks on their policies. Theodore Windt describes how three Presidents have attacked the media. These historical and comparative studies should set the stage for the individual studies of Presidents that follow, from Kennedy to Reagan. The topics of these essays—ranging from the intensive study of single speeches to the study of rhetorical movements of Presidents to get legislation passed—and the methods for analysis and evaluation are as varied as the authors and their interests. These essays do not cover all the major rhetorical activities by recent Presidents, but we hope provide insight into many of those activities.

Essays in Presidential Rhetoric is intended not only as a collection of scholarly rhetorical criticism of presidential speeches, but also as a companion to the anthology, *Presidential Rhetoric: 1961 to the Present* (3rd edition, Dubuque: Kendall/Hunt, 1983). Most of the speeches by Presidents from Kennedy to Reagan that are referred to in this volume are anthologized in *Presidential Rhetoric*. Taken together, we believe the two books form the foundation for the disciplined study of contemporary presidential rhetoric.

Neither this edition nor the first edition of *Essays in Presidential Rhetoric* would have been possible without the scholars who provided the essays and without the generous cooperation of Dr. R. Gordon Hoxie, President of the Center for the Study of the Presidency and Editor of *Presidential Studies Quarterly*. The Center has become the leader in the study of the Presidency through its meetings, conferences, and publications. And Dr. Hoxie, as Editor of the *Quarterly,* has been especially sympathetic to studies in presidential rhetoric.

One final note. As we were completing the final editing of this volume, we learned of the death of Dr. Harold F. Harding, one of the two people to whom this collection is dedicated. Dr. Harding had long been concerned about the quality of presidential speeches and their effects on the American people. As editor of the *Quarterly Journal of Speech* in the late nineteen-forties, he inaugurated the practice of devoting a significant part of one issue of the *Journal* after an election to analysis of campaign speeches. In the nineteen-sixties, he pioneered in offering graduate courses in presidential campaign rhetoric at Ohio State University. Indeed, it was in one of those courses that the senior editor of this volume became interested in this subject. Later, Dr. Harding directed his doctoral dissertation, became his colleague at the University of Texas at El Paso, and remained his life-long friend. In the truest sense, he was a gentleman and a scholar. His death is both a professional and personal loss.

Theodore Windt
Beth Ingold
Pittsburgh, Pennsylvania

Acknowledgments

We wish to express our appreciation to the following officers of professional organizations for their permissions to reprint essays from the journals published by their respective organizations:

R. Gordon Hoxie, President of the Center for the Study of the Presidency publisher of *Presidential Studies Quarterly.*

William Work, Executive Secretary of the Speech Communication Association publisher of the *Quarterly Journal of Speech* and *Communication Monographs.*

John I. Sisco, former Executive Secretary of the Southern Speech Communication Association publisher of the *Southern Speech Communication Journal.*

Howard Dorgan, present Executive Secretary of the Southern Speech Communication Association publisher of the *Southern Speech Communication Journal.*

Caroline Drummond, Executive Secretary of the Eastern Communication Association publisher of *Communication Quarterly.*

Gary D. Keele, Executive Secretary of the Western Speech Communication Association publisher of the *Western Journal of Speech Communication.*

James F. Weaver, Executive Secretary of the Central States Speech Association publisher of the *Central States Speech Journal.*

Of course, our greatest appreciation is extended to the authors of these essays who granted approval to reprinting their work in this volume.

T. W.
B. I.

INTRODUCTION

Presidential Rhetoric: Definition of a Discipline of Study[1]

Theodore Windt

In the life of the human spirit, words are action, much more so than many of us realize who live in countries where freedom of expression is taken for granted. The leaders of totalitarian nations understand this very well. The proof is that words are precisely the action for which dissidents in those countries are being persecuted.
President Jimmy Carter, 1977.

In modern times the word "rhetoric" has fallen into such ill-repute that it may seem disrespectful to use it in the same breath with the presidency. In his *Political Dictionary* William Safire wrote that rhetoric once "the study of persuasive presentation of argument" now has come to mean "bombast, high-flying oratory."[2] When they think of "rhetorical," some old enough to remember conjure up images of Senator Everett Dirksen who was known on occasion to use more ornamentation in his speeches than his subjects required. But the derogation of rhetoric has gone beyond the simple equating of rhetoric with excessive lyricism. People who present arguments with which we disagree are castigated for engaging in "mere" rhetoric, especially if we cannot come up with good arguments to counter theirs. Journalists and politicians frequently wish to draw metaphysical distinctions between *rhetoric* and *reality,* as if the former is false or misleading while the latter is true and accurate. Usually, however, rhetoric is treated as some kind of artificiality of argument or subterfuge intended to make the worse case appear the better. In his 1960 Acceptance Speech at the Democratic National Convention, John F. Kennedy attacked rhetoric no less than three times. He warned Democrats not "to be lulled by good intentions and high rhetoric." He said he would not promise "more harsh rhetoric about the men in the Kremlin as a substitute for policy." He stated he would run on the Democratic platform because "our ends will not be won by rhetoric."[3] Given the repeated use of the word, rhetoric, in such derogatory ways, one who does not know better would probably agree with DeQuincey who once remarked that rhetoric has only two connotations: ostentatious ornament and fallacious argument.[4]

For the professional student of rhetoric, these charges are old hat. They have been around at least since Plato's attacks on rhetoricians and their profession in his dialogues, the *Gorgias* and *Phaedrus.*[5] And in this the sixth year of the age of "The Great Communicator," who has relied upon rhetoric as a central means for governing, we can imagine that few are still disposed to dismiss rhetoric as hollow or empty. Nonetheless, it may be appropriate to begin this essay on presidential rhetoric by returning to Aristotle, who composed the most thorough treatise on the subject, as a means for rescuing the legitimate idea of rhetoric that Safire noted and for presenting a broader perspective from which to view presidential speech-making and rhetoric.

1. Rhetoric as Public Persuasion

The study of rhetoric is the study of *public persuasion on significant public issues*. Oratory is its most conspicuous form though most modern scholars as well as some ancients (Isocrates, in particular) include all forms of persuasive discourse—both written and spoken—within the province of rhetoric. Aristotle defined it as "the faculty of observing in any given case the available means of persuasion."[6] Thus, rhetoric deals with the construction of persuasive arguments, the arrangement of these arguments in the most effective way, and the presentation of them as forcefully as possible. But about what matters do we argue? What issues lend themselves inherently to persuasive discourse?

> [R]hetoric . . . draws upon the regular materials of debate. The duty of rhetoric is to deal with such matters as we deliberate upon without the arts or systems [of exact knowledge] to guide us, in the hearing of persons who cannot take in at a glance a complicated argument [popular audiences], or follow a long chain of reasoning [philosophic or scientific arguments]. The subjects of our deliberation are such as seem to present us with alternative possibilities. . . . [7]

Two essential attributes of rhetoric come from this section: (1) rhetoric deals with issues in the realm of probability rather than issues about which we can be certain; and (2) rhetoric is concerned with public persuasion and therefore requires a knowledge of the audience to which the discourse is directed and an adaptation of ideas to that audience. By concentrating on political rhetoric, let us briefly explore these ideas.

Rhetoric deals with probabilities, with issues that "present us with alternative possibilities." In political rhetoric Aristotle wrote that the politician is concerned with five persistent subjects: (1) ways and means; (2) war and peace; (3) national defense; (4) imports and exports; and (5) legislation.[8] These remain—more than twenty centuries later—the central topics about which politicians and the public deliberate. To be more specific, we may cite several contemporary issues of 1986 that fall into one or more of these categories. Should we spend more money for national defense at the expense of programs for the social good of the nation? Is a "nuclear freeze" the best and most practical way to lessen the chances of nuclear war between the United States and the Soviet Union? Should we impose higher tariffs, or quotas on foreign-made steel to salvage our domestic steel industries? These are only a few of the many contemporary policy questions that admit of no certain answer, even among experts. Each is debatable. Each presents us with alternative possibilities. Each is a pertinent public issue that must be decided.

And how do we go about deciding? We argue the merits and demerits of each. A politician who has to vote on one of these issues will marshall the best evidence to support a position, develop the most persuasive arguments for it, and present them in the appropriate forum as forcefully as possible. Those who hold different positions will go through the same process. Eventually, a decision will be made and then approved or disapproved by the public. Of course, this description is simplified and to some degree, idealistic. There will be "tradeoffs," behind-the-scenes bargaining, pressures brought to bear by interest groups that are effected by the decisions. Nonetheless, for whatever political reasons decisions are made, politicians will eventually have to meet the rhetorical requirements of persuading their constituencies to support them or—at the very least—justifying those decisions to constituencies.

2. The Modes of Persuasion

What then are the modes of persuasion from which politicians choose their arguments? Aristotle said there were essentially three: *logos, ethos,* and *pathos,* or appeals to reason, appeals based on the character or reputation or prestige of the persuader, and psychological or emotional appeals.

By *logos* Aristotle meant the construction of reasonable arguments to support a position or course of action. One cannot persuade others without giving reasons—be they valid or specious. People want reasons for what they believe and for what they do or are called upon to do. But the concept of *logos* should not be confused with formal logic in either its academic or philosophic senses, nor with a rigid system testing validity or invalidity of premises. Rhetorical reasoning is drawn from personal beliefs, the public's beliefs and values, laws, customs, inferences from evidence, and a host of other sources. In developing rhetorical reasoning, the political persuader has a two-fold purpose: (1) to develop the best arguments possible to support a position; and (2) to choose among such arguments those that will be most appealing to the constituencies the persuader seeks to influence and convince.

By *ethos* Aristotle meant the character, prestige, authority, and credibility of the speaker as another mode of persuasion. Somewhere Emerson wrote that *what* you are speaks so loudly I can't hear what you are saying. In the persuasive process the audience always takes into account who is speaking. People

defer to those they recognize as authorities. They respect those who have character, even if they disagree with them. They believe those who have credibility
with them. But *ethos* refers not only to the personal characteristics that cause
people to trust others. In public life, the office one holds confers prestige, authority, and credibility upon one.[9] A politician's career may be marked by how
effectively these conferred attributes are used or abused.

By *pathos* Aristotle apparently meant two things: the personal emotions
that influence people to act or believe, and the psychology of different groups
that may make up target constituencies (psychological differences attributed
to age, sex, occupation, and so on). We would not be human if we did not take
our emotions into account when deciding and acting, and speakers would be
remiss were they not to do the same when trying to persuade an audience. We
act out of needs and desires, hopes and fears, anger and compassion, self-
interest and regard for the public interest. Emotions and reason are not antagonistic nor mutually exclusive of one another. We become agitated or pas-
sionate about one issue or another because we believe we have good reasons
to do so. If speakers want constituencies to support legislation to end discrimination against one group of people, they will attempt to arouse anger over
incidents of blatant prejudice and attempt to arouse compassion for those who
suffer unjustly.

Aristotle also meant that one who would persuade others must understand
the psychology of audiences or constituencies. As Donald C. Bryant aptly observed: rhetoric is the art of adjusting "ideas to people and people to ideas."[10]
In this sense, rhetoric is an integral part of the democratic process. John Bunzel
summarized the various interests a politician must balance:

> a political leader must have the consent of a plurality of the voting public. He must
> convince enough people that his approximate solutions on a wide variety of issues
> are better or at least more acceptable than those of his opponent. To stay in office
> the politician must become the champion, articulator, and follower of enough spe-
> cific issues involving the differences and divisions within society to insure his election
> or re-election. He must continually be able to create new coalitions of support when
> his former basis of power weakens. He must have a system of communications that
> will inform him of the constantly changing demands of his followers and at the same
> time let his supporters know his own position and action. He must commit himself
> to the norms, values, and traditions of the society he serves and play according to
> the rules of the political world he inhabits.[11]

Thus, political language and political rhetoric are:

> always a function of the context from which [they issue], of the disparate needs
> and interests of the audience involved, of their respective modes of perception. The
> realistic study of political language and its meanings is necessarily in probing not
> only of dictionaries, nor of word counts, but of the diverse responses to particular
> modes of expession of audiences in disparate social settings.[12]

Political language—the essential currency of political rhetoric—has dual essences and purposes. It is expressive in the sense that politicians try to clarify (or, on occasion, obscure) their positions on issues constituencies are relatively interested in. It is impressive in the sense that politicians are always adjusting their language, their rhetoric to meet the "norms, values, and traditions" of those constituencies. A natural tension, thus, always exists between the expressive elements and the impressive elements. This linguistic and creative tension is the defining feature of democratic rhetoric and separates such speakers or persuaders from the demagogues and the doctrinaire ideologues. Demagogues are interested only in their audiences—usually in arousing their most base passions—with little concern for the validity or consistency of the ideas they are voicing. Their eyes are on the audience only. Doctrinaire ideologues pursue the purity of thought through purely expressive language—so convinced are they that their ideas are true and just—and care little to nothing about audiences. Political rhetoric in a democratic society serves the humanizing and practical functions of adjusting people to ideas, adjusting policies to politics. Thus, speakers or persuaders who would denounce rhetoric as "high," "mere," or "only" will do so only through skillfully constructed rhetorical arguments of their own and at their own risk.

But how does rhetoric fit into the essential functions of government—the exercise and distribution of power? And how specifically does persuasion relate to the office of the presidency?

3. Power and the Rhetorical Presidency

The central theme of this essay and this collection of essays was stated by Richard Neustadt: "Presidential *power* is the power to persuade."[13] Power and persuasion are inextricably tied together in making the contemporary presidency function effectively. But different kinds of persuasion are necessary to use different kinds of power. What powers, then, constitute presidential power?

A President has three general areas or resources of power available to him. First, he has *constitutional* or *legal* power granted by the Constitution or conferred by law. Sections two and three of Article II of the Constitution outline the President's responsibilities as chief executive, as Commander-in-Chief in wartime, and as chief administrative officer of the United States. Generally, these powers are called his powers to *command*. In our textbook version of the separation of powers among the three branches of government, we all too often believe that these powers reserved for the President require only that he command certain things within his constitutional province to happen, and they happen by virtue of these constitutional powers. However, that is not always the case. The Executive branch of government now is a huge bureaucracy, and officials in charge of certain departments or agencies sometimes feel more responsibility to those departments or agencies than to the President.[14] Therefore, the President sometimes has to persuade those officials privately that the course he has set for a department is indeed the course that the department should steer. The problem any modern President faces is the same problem confronted by the head of any large bureaucracy: how to make the bureaucracy function effectively?[15] Persuasion plays a not insignificant role in solving this problem.

Also, embedded in the President's constitutional powers is an inherent power: the power of *interpretation*. Laws and legal decisions are written in language and language can be ambiguous. For example, what exactly did the Supreme Court mean in *Brown vs. the Board of Education* when it said that desegregation should proceed "with all deliberate speed?" Some Presidents have sought to act *deliberately*, while others have chosen to act with *speed*. In the case of desegregation, the interpretation has varied from President to President. What is recognized by scholars of the presidency is that the executive has an enormous resource of power in the power of interpretation. Edward S. Corwin remarked: "Indeed, the very kernel of the power to interpret a statute preparatory to its enforcement is the power to determine whether a prosecution or other positive act shall be attempted under it."[16] However, when a President interprets a statute or section of the Constitution in a manner that Congress or interest groups perceive as inappropriate to the letter or intention of the law, that act of interpretation creates the possibility of a rhetorical situation in which a President may have to justify his interpretation *vis-a-vis* other interpretations; that is, he may have to persuade others that his interpretation is correct and appropriate. President Nixon sought to distinguish between *de jure* and *de facto* segregation in order to justify his opposition to busing as a means for desegregation. Or to use a better known case, President Nixon argued repeatedly that the constitutional principles of confidentiality and executive privilege prevented him from turning over the executive tape recordings concerning Watergate to the courts. Eventually, of course, the Supreme Court ruled that his interpretation did not have a constitutional standing in that case. But the important point is that the President's constitutional powers carry with them the power to interpret those powers, and for a President to act upon that interpretation requires that he persuade others that his interpretation is correct—a rhetorical task.

The *second* major area or resource of power available to a President lies in his role as *legislative leader* and *head of his party*. Each year, the President places before Congress his legislative agenda for the year in his State of the Union address. But the President cannot command Congress to enact his policies. Members of Congress must be persuaded. And a President's ability to persuade Congress to enact policies (especially domestic policies) rests on his political and persuasive abilities to marshall majorities for different bills. The decline of the party system has diminished the President's ability to exercise control over his party in Congress, which is one reason why recent Presidents have taken their case to the people to get them to put pressure on their representatives and senators to enact presidential policies. Furthermore, when control of Congress is divided between the two parties, the President often is required by political necessity to appeal to the public for its support against the opposing party. Thus, presidential popularity and presidential public persuasion become essential ingredients in the exercise of political power.

The *third* and final resource of power is *public opinion.* Indeed, it is the power upon which all other powers rest, for persuasion is how public opinion is formed, changed, influenced, and molded. The discipline of presidential rhetoric is concerned with the study of presidential public persuasion as it affects the ability of a President to exercise the powers of the office. It is a study of "how Presidents gain, maintain, or lose public support."[17] The raw materials for this study are the speeches of a President, press conferences, messages to Congress; in sum, the public statements by a President. But such studies must also include an analysis and understanding of the target constituencies a President seeks to influence and why, his uses of television and the mass media, and an inquiry into a variety of other rhetorical weapons in his political arsenal that he uses to reach and persuade those in the public who either comprise his support or pose opposition to him. Furthermore, such studies must be placed in the over-all context of the policies and politics of the administration to determine how the uses of rhetoric have influenced or directed that administration. Scholars of presidential rhetoric, therefore, study the *context* of rhetorical events, the *rhetorical act* itself in all its manifestations (including the timing of a speech or press conference, the forum for the act, etc.), and the *effects* of the address or media meeting on policies, the administration, and its opponents. Presidential rhetoric, then, is only one of the powers available to the President, but in a democracy it may well be the fundamental power upon which all others rest.

4. The Rise of Studies in Presidential Rhetoric

Twenty-five years ago, Richard Neustadt published *Presidential Power: The Politics of Leadership,* and its importance became quickly apparent. Scholars recognized that Neustadt offered a new approach to the study of presidential power quite different from the descriptive and institutional studies that had dominated political science in the past. "Presidential *power*," Neustadt remarked, "is the power to persuade." With this definition, he placed the locus of presidential power in the President-as-persuader instead of residing solely in the formal, legal or political powers of the office. *Presidential Power* soon became a benchmark inquiry into the presidency and took its proper place along side Corwin's *The President: Office and Powers* and Rossiter's *The American Presidency* in the bookcase of classics on the subject.[18]

For rhetoricians, Neustadt's volume was a god-send. It began to locate the scholarly place of presidential rhetoric within the discipline of presidential studies. But Neustadt's perspective on persuasion was too narrowly drawn for rhetoricians. For the most part, Neustadt focused on inter-governmental persuasion and persuasion within the executive branch. Rhetoricians brought their own unique approaches to persuasion by asking: *How does a President persuade the public?* With this distinctively rhetorical perspective, rhetoricians insisted that public persuasion was an important and even essential part of any study of presidential performance and politics. And to that end, beginning in the early nineteen-seventies, rhetorical studies of the presidency began to appear, thus giving the materials for an academic foundation to the fledgling discipline of presidential rhetoric. Some were written by rhetoricians, others by historians, political scientists, and journalists. In 1979, the Speech Communication Association of America established a Task Force on Presidential Communication to examine presidential rhetoric as a means through which "a chief executive executes the powers of his office. . . ."[19] In 1980, Sidney Blumenthal published *The Permanent Campaign* in which he argued that persuasion is now central to governing; in fact, that campaign techniques are now merged with the methods of governing to run the presidency.[20] A year later, two major books—Larry J. Sabato's *The Rise of Political Consultants* and David Changell's *The New Kingmakers*—heralded the replacement of party politicians by political consultants who use modern communication technologies to transform traditional campaign politics.[21]

In 1981, *Presidential Studies Quarterly* published "The Rise of the Rhetorical Presidency," in which the authors contended that the very nature of the presidency has undergone a significant transformation in function and execution from a constitutional, administrative office to an executive, rhetorical office. They attributed this change to three influences: (1) the modern doctrine of activist leadership among twentieth-century Presidents; (2) the advances in communication technologies, especially in the mass media; and (3) the modern presidential campaign.[22] The "rhetorical presidency" added another dimension to rhetorical studies beyond the analysis and criticism of presidential speeches and campaigns to the influence—both theoretical and practical—of rhetoric on the nature and conduct of the office itself. With all this writing about presidential uses of public persuasion, it is time to draw much of it together by summarizing the research that has already been done, and by setting the agenda for future research in this area of presidential power.

The remainder of this essay summarizes the scholarship in modern presidential rhetoric that has been conducted in journals of rhetoric and communication and then outlines what kinds of additional research needs to be done. The first section deals with a catalogue of the different kinds of research that has been published from 1960 to the present in the national and regional journals of speech and communications on the subject of contemporary presidential rhetoric.[23] This survey is limited to this period because it coincides with the explosion of scholarly work in other academic fields on the presidency, because it coincides with the rise of television which allows the President to go directly to the people more often, and because the "rhetorical presidency" developed and became dominant during this time. The second section asks: Where do we go from here? In it, I will outline some topics for students of presidential persuasion in answer to the following questions: What kind of research agenda is now needed? How might we go about doing this research?

In his essay, "Studying the Presidency: Where and How Do We Go From Here?" Norman C. Thomas listed six areas of inquiry into the presidency that warrant continued scholarly attention. One of these is directly germane to the subject of this work:

> A third domain that has scarcely been investigated is that of the president's relationships with public opinion, and how the latter informs and affects the former, and vice versa. John Mueller's study of presidential popularity over time is the principal work in this area, but it relies on Gallup Poll data which does not probe the respondents' reasons for their assessments of the president. In studying the chief executive in a democratic society, the dynamics of the interaction between that individual and the public should be a subject of primary concern.[24]

Since Professor Thomas did not examine scholarship by rhetoricians in his essay, his conclusions need amendment, and the remaining sections of this essay are intended to provide them. Nonetheless, his general thesis that presidential rhetoric, "a subject of primary concern," has scarcely been investigated rigorously is generally compatible with the conclusions of this essay. At this time, there is no full-dress treatment of the nature and scope of presidential rhetoric. Indeed, presidential rhetoric remains a field in which some basic spadework has been done, but one in which much more plowing and planting is needed. What then can one say about the current status of research in presidential rhetoric?

5. Four Categories of Research

Contemporary studies in presidential rhetoric are primarily *critical* and fall into four categories: criticism of single presidential speeches, criticism of rhetorical movements, development and criticism of genres of presidential speeches, and miscellaneous articles on various ancillary topics.

Single speeches. More than half the articles published by rhetorical critics during this period concern a single presidential speech. Two types draw major attention: inaugural addresses and "crisis" speeches. Over the course of history, the inaugural address has been transformed from an attempt "to show how the actions of the new administration would conform to Constitutional and republican principles" to an attempt "to articulate the unspoken desires of the people by holding out a vision for their fulfillment."[25] Inaugural addresses are ceremonial addresses concerned with the rhetorical topics of public virtue and public vice ("Ask not what your country can do for you"—public vice; "ask what you can do for your country"—public virtue). They point to certain fundamental values a President espouses and believes the public should cultivate. But inaugural addresses are still ceremonial addresses in which policy concerns are secondary to values, desires, and visions for the future. They stand in relationship to policy speeches, especially the State of the Union addresses, as the Declaration of Independence stands in relation to the Constitution.

By "crisis" speeches, scholars mean those in which a President declares a crisis or those speeches critics believe confronted or created crises. Such analyses have ranged from Kennedy's Cuban missile crisis speech through Johnson's Gulf of Tonkin speech to Carter's attempts to persuade the public that an energy crisis existed. And critics have been drawn to a limited number of these. For example, President Nixon's November 3, 1969 speech on Vietnam incited no less than four separate critiques by eminent rhetorical critics.[26] Judging from these critical works, one would observe that rhetoricians are in many respects still bound to the "great speech" theory of political rhetoric, though the emphasis has passed—due to television—from stylistic excellence to dramatic impact.

What conclusions can be drawn about this kind of research? First, the value of criticism of single speeches is both *intrinsic* and *extrinsic*. It is *intrinsic* in that such critiques ideally provide illumination into how a particular speech worked on intended audiences or failed to work. (It may be important to note here that the definition of "audiences" has changed with the advent of television. The "audience" for a presidential speech is not a group of people present for the speech—indeed, sometimes there is no physical audience present, as in the case of an address from the Oval Office. The "audiences" are target constituencies who see the speech on television and/or the media that reports the speech. Presidential speeches are fashioned, as most major political speeches are these days, to reach and influence these two "audiences," and often media is the more important audience.)[27] Criticism is extrinsic in the sense that these critiques should provide the raw materials for an enriched knowledge of how a particular President used his persuasive powers to get done what he wanted done or for the development of theories about presidential rhetoric. Unfortunately, little has been done to meet the *extrinsic* purposes. The discipline of presidential rhetoric is new. Therefore, many of these essays were written not as scholarly contributions to the on-going study of the presidency, but as contributions to the broad field of rhetorical criticism. Can some unity of purpose be found that would point to a shared perspective appropriate to developing a significant critical methodology? I think so. If one were to draw upon the essays written about President Nixon's November 3, 1969 speech on Vietnam, one would discover a series of critical questions pertinent to developing these methods.

1. *How are rhetorical strategies selected and adapted to persuade a target constituency (or constituencies) of the validity of the President's policy? And why were these chosen as strategies rather than others?*

2. *Is the speech internally consistent? If so, why? If not, why not? Is the speech consistent with other statements made by the President on the same or similar subjects? If not, why not?*

3. *Is the evidence cited by the President used truthfully, and is the rhetorical reality of the speech plausible?*

4. *What are the probable consequences of the speech to target constituencies that believe it, to adversaries who will oppose the President, to future policies, and to the development of our on-going political debates on the subject?*

5. *Why would supporters of the President believe the speech? Why would adversaries disbelieve it? And why would "waverers" be persuaded or not?*

6. *How does the speech fit into the political movement of which it is a part, or into the generic tradition from which it comes, or into the rhetorical biography of the President who gave it?*

Those questions, of course, point to the critic's major responsibilities: to make significant contributions to a better understanding of how public arguments and presidential speeches affect the President, his policies, and the continuous political debates about our national agenda and the direction of public policy. But to meet these responsibilities, critics should not only ask questions about the speech, its context and effects, but also about themselves. I suggest, at minimum, that critics occasionally reflect upon their own work by asking themselves the following three questions:

1. *What are my criteria for criticizing presidential speeches?*

2. *Do I apply the same criteria to speeches by Presidents of different ideologies, especially to those Presidents with whom I agree on policy?*

3. *If I find a presidential speech deficient in some respect, can I outline a better way of making the speech—taking into account what I know the President knows about the topic and the situation, what the President's political circumstances were at the time, and what options the President thought he had at the time?*

A second conclusion about these studies of single speeches must mention what has been neglected. Though a number of essays have been written on inaugural addresses, only one essay in our professional journals has been devoted to a modern State of the Union Address—Dan Hahn's essay on Johnson's 1965 State of the Union—the only speech mandated by the Constitution. With the great concentration on "crisis" speeches, particularly those on foreign crises, there has been a neglect of equally significant speeches on domestic "crises," especially those concerned with economic issues. Nonetheless, these early studies of presidential speeches have forged the beginning of a disciplined study of one aspect of presidential rhetoric.

Movement studies. Studies of rhetorical movements to build constituencies, to get legislation passed, to defend against continuing opposition on basic issues—all these give a broader scope to the idea of presidential rhetoric because they stress the continuity of rhetorical efforts in an administration and because they place individual speeches in their proper political context. Scholars who have used this approach usually dwell on the chronological/rhetorical progression of a political idea or policy, or on the various uses of arguments a President employs in pressing a single theme. Such studies now include Johnson's rhetorical development of the Great Society, Nixon and Agnew engaging in a rhetoric of polarization to expand their constituency, and Nixon defending against charges and rumors resulting from the Watergate investigations. These studies not only provide significant research in themselves; they also provide a valuable historical and political framework within which to analyze how presidents use rhetoric with other instruments of power to pursue policy and political goals. Such studies should be expanded into book-length form, as David Zarefsky has done with his recent book on President Johnson and the Great Society, to give real substance to the field of presidential rhetoric.

Genre studies. Genre studies concentrate on comparisons of what different Presidents have said on similar occasions, on similar themes, or what they have said to similar audiences. Scholars who use this method depend heavily on their knowledge of past rhetorical activities to examine contemporary rhetorical efforts. Yet, such studies remain in an infant state. Jackson Harrell, B. L. Ware, and Wil A. Linkugel merged the use of the genre of apologia with a movement approach to produce an insightful criticism of Nixon's early defense against charges emanating from the Watergate scandals. But given the circumstances that produced Nixon's rhetoric, we may hope that we shall not see these kinds of speeches or this kind of criticism again. For the most part, genre essays have been limited to "crisis" speeches attempting to isolate the lines of argument that define genre. Cannot this approach be extended to other kinds of speeches Presidents traditionally are called upon to give? If so, what will be needed is a greater emphasis on comparative studies, a stronger historical knowledge of presidential speeches, and a surer grasp of what critics mean by genre.

Miscellaneous research. Textual accuracy, speech preparation, quantitative research, arguments over the ethics of using speech-writers and consultants—all these and a multitude of other subjects comprise what should be called miscellaneous contributions to specific analyses of various aspects of presidential rhetoric. Many of these are valuable in-and-of-themselves, but their primary contributions to the discipline lie in the background information they provide for the analysis and evaluation of how Presidents use rhetoric to exercise power.

6. Research on the Rhetoric of Recent Presidents

If we look at the same research from a different angle, we see how much remains to be done. The gaps in our research about how individual Presidents used their rhetorical powers is at times staggering.

Let us begin with John F. Kennedy, whose rhetorical prowess has been so greatly celebrated and so little analyzed. Hardly anything has been published in professional journals about Kennedy's rhetoric, except for various articles about his campaign speeches and his inaugural address. In fact, scholars have produced about as much scholarship about President Ford as President Kennedy. There is no study by a rhetorician about how Kennedy justified or excused the Bay of Pigs disaster, or how he treated the Berlin Crisis, or how he dealt with the civil rights revolution during his administration. This is astonishing. Even as Kennedy's rhetoric set the themes used or abused by subsequent administrations, it has been subjected to precious little scholarly inquiry.[28]

Due primarily to the work of David Zarefsky, Lyndon Johnson's rhetoric has been more scrutinized than one would have imagined. Scholars have examined the rhetorical foundations of the Great Society, affirmative action and various aspects of his public handling of Vietnam. Still, analyses of Johnson's blunders during the Dominican Republic intervention, his responses to protest, his attempts to press the war and still maintain his constituencies—all these and a goodly number of other topics (not the least of which is a thorough examination of what role President Johnson believed informing the public should play in the exercise of presidential power) remain fertile ground for future critical plowing.

More articles have been written about Richard Nixon than any other recent President. Probably that is because his rhetoric is so psychologically fascinating and his politics so transparent. A full third, however, of published studies deal with Nixon's campaign rhetoric. The others are devoted principally to Vietnam or Watergate in one way or another. Nothing has been written in an intensive manner about how this staunch anti-communist rhetorically "opened the door" to China or negotiated the SALT I agreement and made it palatable to his conservative constituencies. Indeed, there is nothing in professional rhetoric and communication journals about either his trips to China or to the U.S.S.R. Equally important, little has been written about Nixon's domestic policy rhetoric—his law 'n order speeches, his attempts to pacify his southern constituencies by opposing busing, or his speeches on economic issues and environmental concerns. The Nixon administration was the first contemporary administration to have a fully developed approach to presidential rhetoric, to the use of media to enhance presidential speeches, to the recognition of television as the central "check" on presidential power.[29] Such meticulous attention to the rhetorical presidency during Nixon's tenure merits equally meticulous scholarly attention.

What can one say about President Ford's rhetoric? After William Safire's regretable remark that Ford is the only President in the twentieth century who never uttered a memorable phrase, one is surprised to learn that anything has been written about his rhetoric. But Hermann Stelzner's essay on the WIN campaign and Dan F. Hahn's examination of the rhetoric surrounding the Mayaguez incident as well as the 1982 panel of the Speech Communication Association meeting devoted to Ford's pardon of Nixon provide more scholarly materials than one would anticipate about this unanticipated, and in some circles, underestimated and undervalued President.

Only a few scholarly studies have been published about the rhetoric of President Carter and President Reagan. Part of the reason for the paucity of work about the former is that Carter was rhetorically inept; part of the reason for so few studies about the latter is that Reagan has been so dazzling and his administration so contemporary that scholars do not believe they have sufficient distance to judge his efforts.[30] Yet, Dan Hahn's long essay on Carter is exceptional, and at this writing, more published studies of Reagan are beginning to appear.

From this brief description of what has been published by scholars in rhetoric and communication, one can see that considerable work remains to be done.

7. A Research Agenda for Presidential Rhetoric

If this assessment of current research is anywhere close to the mark, where do we go from here? What should be the agenda for research and how might one go about addressing that agenda in a scholarly fashion? Already, I have indicated some specific research that needs to be done about particular Presidents and about specific issues within administrations. However, there are at least six broad areas of research that need to be addressed, six areas of theory and criticism that if properly pursued should yield a fruitful harvest of knowledge about the contemporary presidency. These six are certainly not exhaustive, but they seem important issues for scholarly and intellectual inquiry.

First, what is the nature and scope of presidential rhetoric, and what place does it play in the modern presidency? A number of studies have been written about the rhetoric of various presidents, but few mesh in concrete ways to develop coherent theories about what presidential rhetoric is, its function and scope. In the beginning of this essay, I have tried to mark the perimeters of presidential rhetoric as a field of study and to suggest its central role in the contemporary presidency, but I make no pretense that these markings are as exhaustive or detailed as the standards of scholarship demand. In neglecting theory, rhetoricians are not alone. Professor Thomas noted that among political scientists there is an "absence of a comprehensive theoretical framework" for studying the presidency "that reduces or even negates the value of most past and current research."[31] Such a theoretical framework is also needed for the rhetoric of a president lest our work be reduced or negated in value.

To paraphrase F. Scott Fitzgerald, the presidency is very different from other political offices. But what do these differences mean to the uses of rhetoric by a President? We know that on some occasions (primarily those involving foreign crises) the President can speak with a national voice and have the public rally behind him as they will rally behind no other public official. But what do we know beyond that?

In inquiring into the nature of presidential rhetoric, we should also be asking how should a President persuade? Implicit in the scholarly criticism of presidential speeches are standards each critic uses to praise or blame a President for what he has said or did not say. But only rarely have these implicit standards been explored within the community of scholars. Development of standards of analysis and evaluation become particularly important as critics examine the rhetorical activities of Presidents in office when partisan concerns may interfere with critical detachment. In other words, what standards can be used to evaluate a speech by a sitting President? These and a variety of other questions require much more work in the theory of presidential rhetoric. And if theoretical research into the nature and scope of presidential rhetoric is to proceed in an orderly manner, then inquiries must be made not only into how presidential rhetoric functions in a democratic society, but also how it should function to further democratic processes.

Second, what is the nature of presidential "ethos"? If presidential rhetoric is different in important respects from other forms of political discourse, one reason for those differences must reside in the nature of the office, the expectations placed on the office, and the perceptions about the person who occupies the office. What characteristics are attributed to the office? What expectations are aroused by a President? Thomas Cronin has initiated research in this area with his study of the "textbook presidency." His study, responses to it, as well as James David Barber's examination of the "climate of expectations," need to be incorporated into any theory about the nature of presidential *ethos*.[32]

In this connection, we need also to develop rhetorical biographies of Presidents and potential presidential candidates. In conducting this kind of research, one leans heavily on Professor Barber's concept of political style:

> These themes [character and world view] come together strongly in early adulthood, when the person moves from contemplation to responsible action and adopts a style. In most biographical accounts this period stands out in stark clarity—the time of emergency, the time a young man found himself. I call it his first independent political success. It was then he moved beyond the detailed guidance of his family; then his self-esteem was dramatically boosted; then he came forth as a person to be reckoned with by other people. The *way* he did that is profoundly important to him. Typically he grasps that style and hangs onto it. Much later, coming into the presidency, something in him remembers this earlier victory and reemphasizes the style that made it happen.[33]

In this connection, rhetoricians might be asking: Are there persistent and typical rhetorical devices that a President uses that form his predictable rhetorical methods? Furthermore, are there persistent and typical rhetorical methods that a presidential figure developed during his pre-presidential career that are so distinctive and so a part of his over-all political style that a critic can predict he will rely on them when he becomes President? Developing such rhetorical biographies may make understanding Presidents and the conduct of particular presidencies more cogent.

Third, are there distinctive rhetorical periods during an administration that predictably present particular rhetorical opportunities and hazards to a President? In their research into the relationship between the White House and media, Grossman and Kuman developed several different phases that these relations predictably pass through during a presidential administration.[34] The same is probably true with rhetorical relations. Richard Beal, one of President Reagan's advisers, stated: "The whole issue of running the Presidency in the modern age is control of the agenda."[35] If so, how does a President control it at different times over the course of four or even eight years? Kathleen Farrell and I roughed out four general periods for the first term of an administration:

1. The *rhetoric* phase during the first nine months when the President can be rhetorically pre-eminent over Congress if he does not make major mistakes.[36]
2. The *partisan* phase of the second year when the opposition party begins demanding results from presidential policies of the previous year, and culminating in the off-term elections which serve as a symbolic referendum on the direction of the administration.

3. The *window* phase of the third year when incumbents are not pressured by running for re-election in Congress, but are influenced by the results of the off-term elections, a time when the President can present new initiatives before the presidential campaign gets underway.
4. The *campaign agenda* phase of the fourth year when issues are developed and discussed primarily as campaign issues rather than as legislative issues to be negotiated with Congress.[37]

These phases are hardly definitive and do not even attempt to speculate about what rhetorical situations might arise during a second term of a presidency. Research is needed to see if we can predict rhetorical situations that a President might confront.

Fourth, how and to what extent do the presidency and media, especially television, influence one another, political discussions in the country, and the agenda-setting for national issues? With all that has been written about politics and media, media and politics over the past two decades, it may seem fatuous to list this topic as a major research project. Yet, it remains because our research is not conclusive and the dynamic between politics and media constantly changes as each adapts to each. Furthermore, technological advances in media have dramatically altered the rhetoric used by Presidents as well as the rhetorical context of politics discussions:

> The media and the modern presidency feed on each other. The media has found in the presidency a focal point on which to concentrate its peculiarly simplistic and dramatic interpretation of events; and the presidency has found a vehicle in the media that allows it to win public attention and with that attention the reality, but more often the pretense, of enhanced power. What this two-sided relationship signifies is a change in the rhetorical context in which the President now operates, the implications of which extend beyond the question of how much power the President has to the issue of how he attempts to govern. Constitutional government, which was established in contradistinction to government by assembly, now has become a kind of government by assembly, with TV 'speaking' to the President and the President responding to the moods that it creates.[38]

The technological media era of politics has created a new "checks and balances"—one never dreamed of by the Founding Fathers. Congress now serves principally as a *legislative* check on the presidency, and media news—primarily television—functions as a *rhetorical* check on presidential pronouncements. Media news vies with the President to establish the national agenda; reporters immediately give analysis and evaluation after a presidential address; press conferences provide an institutionalized grappling between the two.[39] Regardless of whether we think this relationship is proper or improper, valuable or dangerous, this rhetorical relationship is the new reality of checks and balances in American politics in this technological, televised age. Once this new reality was recognized, critics began taking sides. Some contended that media greatly damaged traditional politics through the distorted and simplistic presentation of issues, which may well be true; others described the President's access to television as severely damaging to the balances between the executive and legislative bodies, which may be equally true; and even others contend that the rise of instant media communications has made the public more informed, government more accountable, and politics more democratic, which may be as true as the other two conclusions.[40] Recently, however, the direction in research is changing to studies of how media and politics influence one another to how each seeks to create the reality—or unreality, as some prefer—in which decisions are made.[41] But further studies are needed, especially intensive case studies that concern themselves exclusively with the President's rhetoric and media's responses, to determine the content and contours of this new reality and the respective influences of the presidency and the media upon one another.

Fifth, what are the rhetorical differences between campaigning and governing? This has become an agitating issue among journalists and scholars. Sidney Blumenthal observed: "The permanent campaign is the political ideology of our age. It combines image-making with strategic calculation. Under the permanent campaign governing is turned into a perpetual campaign. Moreover, it remakes government into an instrument designed to sustain an elected official's public popularity. It is the engineering of consent with a vengeance."[42] Inherent in these observations, which are shared by a number of scholars as well as journalists, is the implicit belief that once a President enters office, popular persuasion should be set aside, or at least demoted in importance. Among those who write about the presidency there resides the notion that a campaign is necessarily partisan and persuasive, but once in office, they seem to believe, a President should become a statesman and rise above such things. Apparently, what is acceptable practice on the campaign trail is unacceptable in the Oval Office.

The mistake these writers commit is in not recognizing that the essentials of presidential power indeed rest on persuasion, although the persuasive situations are different when one is a candidate from when one is actually elected and attempting to govern. This area of research has hardly been touched in a systematic fashion in rhetorical circles. Even though some of the strategies and tactics overlap, it may be useful to suggest some major distinctions between campaigning and governing, even as they tend to merge:

1. The metaphor for campaigning is war; the metaphor for governing is diplomacy or negotiation.[43]
2. Campaigning aims at absolute victory over one's enemy within a specified period of time; governing aims at solving problems through compromise and passing legislation in which there are no final victories.

3. In a campaign the *enemy* is singular, visible, and constant; in governing the *opposition* is varied, sometimes ill-defined, and changing. The representative or senator who may oppose the President on one issue may be the very one whose support the President needs on another issue. Therefore, the treatment of adversaries, when governing, must be more genteel than when campaigning.

4. In a campaign one must demand loyalty from one's supporters and usually one gets it; in governing, supporters may have divided loyalties among their own beliefs, their own party, and their own constituencies, and one must determine which to appeal to in order to gain support from them.

5. In a campaign one forces an either/or choice and frames issues that way; in governing, there are more alternatives and the goal often is compromise.

6. Finally, a campaign involves confrontation or at least the appearance of confrontation politics; governing seeks accommodation.

If these distinctions between the two political arts are valid, then it follows that the rhetoric constructed to achieve the aims of each will be different also. A campaign rhetoric will be one of either/or choices, a war-like rhetoric rallying the faithful to defeat the enemy and achieve victory for the candidate. A governing rhetoric, at least theoretically, will be one of decorum stressing accommodation and compromise while still retaining partisan or ideological commitments. But if Blumenthal is correct—and I believe that in part he is—that campaigning techniques have now merged with those of governing, research is needed to assess what this merger means to not only to the politics of the Presidency, but to the political processes themselves.

Sixth, what is the nature of contemporary political language and how does the creation of new words, phrases, indeed new rhetorics affect our perceptions of issues, politicians, and political discussion? Language is the essential currency in the rhetorical exchange. "The use of words," Madison wrote in the thirty-seventh *Federalist Paper:*

> is to express ideas. Perspicuity, therefore, requires not only that the ideas should be distinctly formed, but that they should be expressed by words distinctly and exclusively appropriate to them. But no language is so copious as to supply words and phrases for every complex idea, or so correct as not to include many equivocally denoting different ideas. Hence it must happen that however accurately objects may be discriminated in themselves, and however accurately the discrimination may be considered, the definition of them may be rendered inaccurate by the inaccuracy of the terms in which it is delivered.[44]

The study of political rhetoric is fundamentally the study of political language, of its uses and abuses, of its impact on those who speak and those who hear. For in a democratic society, words establish the compact between the governor and the governed, a secular trust not to be taken lightly. In this age of media politics and the rhetorical presidency, the concerted and disciplined study of political language—and therefore of political arguments (rhetoric) which do not exist until dressed in language—must be a priority study for students of presidential rhetoric.

Madison pointed to a central point about political language: it is both expressive and impressive, both stable and fluid. We need to inquire in a scholarly fashion not only about the precision with which words are used by Presidents, but also about how those very words effect those who use them and those who hear them. Murray Edelman has begun conspicious investigations into these questions, but his research needs to be aided and augmented by others. Furthermore, media's modifications of political language through compressed reporting, their introduction of influential new political terms into our public vocabulary ("credibility gap" and "gender gap" come to mind) that become buzzwords for White House responses and public opinion surveys, and other mediating activities on language by journalists demand the sensitivity to language that Madison early recognized was important to our democratic system.

Finally, political rhetoric is often metaphysical. Presidential decisions are not announced in a vacuum. When a President makes a speech, he creates through his rhetoric a reality that he says requires him to act. He describes the world, as he sees it, in which we live. It may be a world in which the forces of freedom do moral combat with the forces of evil, or it may be a world of adversaries bent on seeking accommodation with one another despite their ideological differences. It may be a world of opportunity, or a world of dangerous crises. Whether this world-view or reality takes hold with the public depends on the persuasiveness of the Prresident's language and arguments to justify that world-view, and on whether others can present counter-realities with equal or greater persuasiveness.

We should be as clear on this point as we possibly can be. Events occur in the world, but they do not carry an inherent meaning with them. People assign meaning to those events. And that means not only assigning words to those events to describe them, but also constructing persuasive arguments to justify those meanings. It is rhetoric (persuasive arguments) that provides the medium for making that leap from *event* to *meaning*. In this sense, rhetoric is not only metaphysical, but epistemological as well. In the field of rhetoric and communications, the discussions over the relations of rhetoric to reality are the most lively, imaginative, and challenging discussions within the profession, and are uniquely pertinent to political rhetoric.[45]

The old truism that "to name something is to possess it" bears significant scholarly weight today for anyone who would embark upon the study of presidential rhetoric. After all, it is always with words that we begin any study of anything human. And perhaps, by beginning to understand the dynamics of contemporary political language, we may be beginning to understand the central dynamics of the democratic processes themselves.

8. Conclusion

Presidential rhetoric is a new discipline of study within the field of rhetoric and within presidential scholarship. Scholars in this discipline are concerned with how public language and public arguments influence the exercise of presidential power. The principal goals of these studies are descriptive and critical works that help in understanding the contemporary American presidency and proscriptive studies of how the rhetorical presidency functions and should function. And continuing these studies is important for three reasons.

First, persuasion is central to the exercise of power, especially to presidential power. Elmer Cornwell, Jr. remarked:

> The President's prime weapon for influencing policy-making is his ability to command and influence a national audience. Since little is likely to be done constitutionally to strengthen the President's hand, his ability to lead and mold public opinion, for all its inherent limitations, remains his prime reliance.[46]

Furthermore, with the advent of television and the President's immediate access to it and thus to the American people, the President can gain the rhetorical initiative over his opponents: "The President's ability to place his views before the public is important primarily because he can usually set the terms of the national debate—and anyone who can set the terms of a debate can win it."[47] Thus does presidential rhetoric become a major source in the exercise of power.

Second, presidential rhetoric is a means of legitimation. H. Mark Roelofs wrote that: "Words may well be the essence of politics generally; they are certainly the essence of legitimation politics."[48] The persuasive process—the rhetorical process, that is—is at the center of this legitimizing function. By participating in the rhetorical dialogue between governor and governed, the President symbolically reaffirms his commitment to the "channel through which the subservient grant their governors powers to rule."[49]

Finally, rhetoric is at the center of democratic politics. If we do not engage in national debates marshalling persuasive arguments for one position over another, how then are we to decide issues? A totalitarian society has no use for rhetoric, for persuasion, for debate. Compliance with laws and authorities is enforced through coercion either by the state police or through confinement. Democratic decision-making requires debates and argument for a reasonable society, and rhetoric—imperfect instrument though it be, as imperfect as the fallible humans who use it—serves this function and thus may serve as the last fragile bulwark against chaos or know-nothingness.

In this essay, I have sought to describe the state of the discipline of presidential rhetoric and to outline six areas of inquiry that mandate critical attention. Perhaps, Lyndon Johnson best summarized much of what this essay and my work in presidential rhetoric is all about, when he asked:

> How does a public leader find just the right word or the right way to say no more and no less than he means to say—bearing in mind that anything he says may topple governments and may involve the lives of innocent men?
>
> How does that leader speak the right phrase, in the right way, under the right conditions, to suit the accuracies and contingencies of the moment when he is discussing questions of policy, so that he does not stir a thousand misinterpretations and leave the wrong connotation or impression?
>
> How does he reach the immediate audience and how does he communicate with millions of others who are out there listening from afar?

"The President," Johnson concluded, "often ponders these questions and searches for the right course."[50]

So should we all, especially those of us who labor in the vineyard of presidential rhetoric and presidential studies.

Notes

1. Part of this essay was first presented at the Temple University Conference on Political Discourse in March, 1983. Shorter versions have been published in the *Central States Speech Journal* (Spring, 1984), pp. 24–34 and in *Presidential Studies Quarterly* (Winter, 1986), pp. 102–116.
2. William Safire, *Safire's Political Dictionary* (New York: Ballantine Books, 1978), p. 611.
3. From an audio tape of Senator Kennedy's Acceptance Speech at the Democratic National Convention, 1960.
4. Cited by Everett Lee Hunt in "Plato And Aristotle on Rhetoric and Rhetoricians," *Historical Studies of Rhetoric and Rhetoricians,* ed. by Raymond F. Howes (Ithaca: Cornell University Press, 1961), p. 50.
5. Dean Hunt presented the major arguments Plato amassed against rhetoric as a guide to knowledge and as an instrument to decide public issues. These platonic arguments have been repeated with few variations throughout the centuries. Hunt also included Aristotle's defense of rhetoric which rhetoricians have used throughout the centuries. See *ibid.*, pp. 19–70.
6. *Rhetoric and Poetics of Aristotle,* trans. by W. Rhys Roberts (New York: Modern Library, 1954), 1355b, p. 24. For a good introduction to the idea of rhetoric as well as to central rhetorical categories, see Donald Lemen Clark, *Rhetoric in Greco-Roman Education* (New York: Columbia University Press, 1957). See especially his chapters "What the Ancients Meant by Rhetoric," (pp. 24–58) and "The Precepts of Rhetoric," (pp. 67–143). See also, Larry Arnhart, *Aristotle on Political Reasoning: A Commentary On the "Rhetoric"* (DeKalb, Ill.: Northern Illinois University Press, 1981).

7. *Ibid.,* 1357a, p. 27.
8. *Ibid.,* 1359b, p. 35.
9. See Theodore O. Windt, "The Classical Concept of *Ethos:* A Perspective," *Pennsylvania Speech Annual* (September, 1964), p. 46–49, and Theodore Otto Windt, Jr., "The Presidency and Speeches on International Crises: Repeating the Rhetorical Past," *Speaker and Gavel* (1973), p. 8–9.
10. Donald C. Bryant, "Rhetoric: Its Function and Its Scope," *Quarterly Journal of Speech* (December, 1953) p. 413.
11. John Bunzel, *Anti-Politics in America* (New York: Alfred A. Knopf, 1967), p. 13.
12. Murray Edelman, *The Symbolic Uses of Politics* (Urbana: University of Illinois Press, 1964), p. 130.
13. Richard E. Neustadt, *Presidential Power. The Politics of Leadership* (New York: John Wiley & Sons, 1961), p. 10.
14. John Ehrlichman, former Domestic Council chief under President Nixon, noted: "I was fond of saying that our problems stemmed from the fact that Cabinet officers went out and married the natives. And that's . . . what happened. You'd send a guy over to a department and you'd make him Secretary of Transportation, let's say, and then he'd say, 'Mr. President . . . I'm your man, Mr. President.' And then from that moment forward, he was that department's advocate back to the White House." Mr. Ehrlichman concluded: "[T]hey were continually playing back their departmental position and they were departmental advocates. They . . . had ceased to think as the President thought. . . ." Seminar with John Ehrlichman on the Nixon presidency, University of Pittsburgh, September 28, 1978.

    For an example of this problem, see the discussion of the politics of civil rights in the Justice Department under Nixon in 1969–70 in Rowland Evans, Jr. and Robert D. Novak, *Nixon in the White House* (New York: Random House, 1971), pp. 141–159.
15. Neustadt quotes President Truman as saying: "I sit here all day trying to persuade people to do the things they ought to have sense enough to do without my persuading them. . . . That's all the powers of the President amount to." *Presidential Power,* pp. 9–10.
16. Edward S. Corwin, *The President: Office and Powers 1787–1957* 4th Revised Edition (New York: New York University Press, 1957), p. 121. On the power of interpretation, see especially pp. 120–139.
17. "Introduction," *Presidential Rhetoric: 1961 to the Present,* ed by Theodore Windt, 34d edition (Dubuque: Kendall/Hunt, 1983), p. 2.
18. Neustadt's influence on the conception of presidential power has borne fruit in the number of scholarly articles about presidential rhetoric being published in rhetoric journals and particularly in *Presidential Studies Quarterly,* as well as in such recent volumes as George C. Edwards III's *The Public President. The Pursuit of Popular Support* (New York: St. Martin's Press, 1983), Samuel Kernell's *Going Public: New Strategies of Presidential Leadership* (Washington: Congressional 1986), and *The President and the Public,* ed. by Craig Allen Smith and Kathy B. Smith (Lanham: University Press of America, 1985).
19. Patricia D. Witherspoon, "A Proposal to Establish an SCA Tasks Force on Presidential Communication," 1979. The Task Force was established the next year.
20. Sidney Blumenthal, *The Permanent Campaign* (New York: Simon and Schuster, 1980).

21. Larry J. Sabato, *The Rise of Political Consultants* (New York: Basic Books, 1981) and David Chagall, *The New Kingmakers* (New York: Harcourt Brace Jovanovich, 1981. What seems to have kicked off this study of consultants is the rather naive, but sensational book by Joe McGinnis, *The Selling of the President 1968* (New York: Trident, 1969).

22. James W. Ceaser, Glen E. Thurow, Jeffrey Tulis and Joseph M. Bessette, "The Rise of the Rhetorical Presidency," *Presidential Studies Quarterly* (Spring, 1981), pp. 158–171.

23. In the selected bibliography attached to this essay I have cited only essays about the uses of rhetoric by incumbents. It is interesting to note that more than half the essays published in professional speech journals about presidential rhetoric deal with campaign rhetoric.

24. N. C. Thomas, "Studying the Presidency: Where and How Do We Go From Here?" *Presidential Studies Quarterly* (Fall, 1977), p. 173.

25. "The Rise of the Rhetorical Presidency," p. 9. On the development of themes of inaugural addresses, see Edward W. Chester, "Beyond the Rhetoric: A New Look at Presidential Inaugural Addresses," *Presidential Studies Quarterly* (Fall, 1980), pp. 571–582; and Karlyn Kohrs Campbell and Kathleen Hall Jamieson, "Inaugurating the Presidency," *Presidential Studies Quarterly* (Spring, 1985), pp. 394–411.

26. Karlyn Kohrs Campbell, "An Exercise in the Rhetoric of Mythical America," *Critiques of Contemporary Rhetoric* (Belmont: Wadsworth, 1972), pp. 39–58; Robert P. Newman, "Under the Veneer: Nixon's Vietnam Speech of November 3, 1969," *Quarterly Journal of Speech.* (April, 1970), pp. 113–128; Herman G. Stelzner, "The Quest Story and Nixon's November 3, 1969 Address," *Quarterly Journal of Speech* (April 1974), pp. 163–172; and Forbes Hill, "Conventional Wisdom— Traditional Form: The President's Message of November 3, 1969," *Quarterly Journal of Speech* (December, 1972), pp. 373–386. See also an exchange between Campbell and Hill about proper goals for such criticism in the same issue of the *Journal*, pp. 451–460.

27. For the 1976 presidential campaign, President Ford's consultants sought to put the idea of "audience" in perspective: "*[F]or the general election, Presidential campaign events are not significant in terms of their impact on the people who attend. These people are mainly important as backdrops for the television viewer. During the general election, all Presidential travel must be planned for its impact of those who learn about it through the media.*" *President Ford's Campaign Handbook.*

28. Critics have primarily focused on Kennedy's speeches during the 1960 primaries and the general election, and his Inaugural Address.

29. See Jeb Stuart Magruder, *An American Life: One Man's Road to Watergate* (New York Atheneum, 1974), esp. pp. 3–11, 53–145; William Safire, *Before the Fall. An Inside View of the Pre-Watergate White House* (New York: Belmont Tower Books, 1975), esp. pp. 307–387; Raymond Price, *With Nixon* (New York: Viking Press, 1977); Herbert G. Klein, *Making It Perfectly Clear* (Garden City: Doubleday & Co., 1980); John Tebbel and Sarah Miles Watts, *The Press and the Presidency. From George Washington to Ronald Reagan* (New York: Oxford University Press, 1985), pp. 501–521.

30. If John Kennedy's 1960 campaign was a textbook campaign, the first six years of the Reagan administration present a graduate school text on how to run the rhetorical presidency. The methods used by this administration will be and should be

studied intensively by every serious scholar of the presidency as a landmark case in how rhetoric can be used in pursuing political goals.

31. "Studying the Presidency," p. 169.
32. See Thomas Cronin, "The Textbook Presidency and Political Science," *Perspectives on the Presidency,* ed. by Stanley Bach and George T. Sulzner (Lexington: D. C. Heath, 1974), pp. 54–74; Douglas J. Hoekstra, "The 'Textbook' Presidency Revisited," *Presidential Studies Quarterly* (Spring, 1982), pp. 159–167; James David Barber, *The Presidential Character* (Englewood Cliffs: Prentice Hall, 1977); Eric B. Herzik and Mary L. Dodson, "Public Expectations and the Presidency: Barber's 'Climate of Expectations' Examined," *Presidential Studies Quarterly* (Fall, 1982), pp. 485–490.
33. *The Presidential Character,* p. 10.
34. Michael Baruch Grossman and Martha Joynt Kumar, "The White House and the News Media: The Phases of Their Relationship," *Political Science Quarterly* (Spring, 1979), pp. 37–53.
35. Quoted in Sidney Blumenthal, "Marketing the President," *New York Times Magazine* (September 13, 1981), p. 110. Cf. Paul C. Light, *The President's Agenda* (Baltimore: The Johns Hopkins University Press, 1981).
36. On President Reagan's advisers' approach to this initial stage, see Sidney Blumenthal, "Marketing the President," *New York Times Magazine* (September 13, 1981), p. 110.
37. Theodore Windt with Kathleen Farrell, "Presidential Rhetoric and Presidential Power: The Reagan Initiatives," *Essays in Presidential Rhetoric,* ed. Theodore Windt with Beth Ingold, 1st edition (Dubuque: Kendall/Hunt, 1983), pp. 310–322. Cf. Theodore Otto Windt, Jr., "Ronald Reagan's Rhetoric: An Update," *Speaker and Gavel* (Summer, 1982), pp. 47–54; and Beth A. J. Ingold and Theodore Otto Windt, Jr., "Trying to 'Stay the Course': President Reagan's Rhetoric During the 1982 Election," *Presidential Studies Quarterly* (Winter, 1984), pp. 87–97.
38. "The Rise of the Rhetorical Presidency," pp. 12–13.
39. Carolyn Smith of ABC-TV News is currently completing a doctoral dissertation on the rhetoric of presidential press conferences concentrating on those of President Reagan during his first term.
40. Cf. Robert Cirino, *Don't Blame the People* (New York: Random House, 1971); Newton N. Minow, John Barlow Martin and Lee M. Mitchell, *Presidential Television* (New York: Basic Books, 1973).
41. Cf. C. Don Livingston, "The Televised Presidency," *Presidential Studies Quarterly* (Winter, 1986), pp. 22–30; Dan Nimmo and James E. Combs, *Mediated Political Realities* (New York: Longman, 1983); Kathleen Hall Jamieson and Karlyn Kohrs Campbell, *The Interplay of Influence: Mass Media & Their Publics in News, Advertising, Politics* (Belmont: Wadsworth Publishing, 1983).
42. *The Permanent Campaign,* p. 23.
43. "Political campaigning is warfare with hardware. War and politics are related in techniques and goals. Both involve a collision of organizations seeking absolute victory; both are fought by the tactics of applied weaponry; and both are won by the grand strategy best combining factors of time plus the ability to win confrontations—surmounting hostile pressure while imposing decision upon the enemy." Herbert M. Baus and William B. Ross, *Politics Battle Plan* (New York: Macmillan Co., 1968), p. 2. Cf. Jeff Greenfield, *The Real Campaign* (New York: Summit Books, 1982).
44. *The Federalist Papers,* with an introduction, table of contents, and index of ideas by Clinton Rossiter (New York: Mentor Books, 1961), p. 229. For recent works

on political language, see Paul E. Corcoran, *Political Language and Rhetoric* (Austin: The University of Texas Press, 1979); Fred Dallmayr, *Language and Politics* (Notre Dame: University of Notre Dame Press, 1984); *Language and Politics* (New York: New York University Press, 1984) Roderick P. Hart, *Verbal Style and the Presidency: A Computer-Based Analysis* (Orlando: Academic Press, 1984).

45. For a summary of the major research and arguments, as well as an unique perspective, on the relation of rhetoric to *social*—not specifically political—reality, see Richard A. Cherwitz and James W. Hikins, *Communication and Knowledge: An Investigation in Rhetorical Epistemology* (Columbia: University of South Carolina Press, 1986).

46. Elmer E. Cornwell, Jr., *Presidential Leadership of Public Opinion* (Bloomington: Indiana University Press, 1965), p. 303.

47. George E. Reedy, *The Twilight of the Presidency* (New York: World Publishing Co., 1970), pp. 41–42.

48. H. Mark Roelofs, "The Gettysburg Address: An Exercise in Presidential Legitimation," *Presidential Studies Quarterly* (Summer, 1978), p. 235.

49. *Ibid.*, p. 227.

50. Lyndon B. Johnson, "The President and the Media," *Presidential Rhetoric: 1961 to the Present*, p. 107.

Selected Bibliography

This bibliography is a compilation of works from speech and communication journals as well as *Presidential Studies Quarterly*, which has assumed the leadership from communications journals in publishing essays in this area of study. This bibliography does not include any critical essays about campaign rhetoric for the presidency. But it may be interesting to note that about half the professional articles in rhetoric and communications journals that deal with the contemporary presidency concern themselves with campaign rhetoric rather than the rhetoric of governing.

The following abbreviations are used in this bibliography: *QJS (Quarterly Journal of Speech)*, *CM (Communication Monographs)*, *CQ (Communication Quarterly)*, *WJSC (Western Journal of Speech Communication)*, *CSSJ (Central States Speech Journal)*, *SSCJ (Southern Speech Communication Journal)*, *SG (Speaker and Gavel)*. *PSQ* refers to *Presidential Studies Quarterly*. [Normally this acronym refers to *Political Science Quarterly*].

Inaugural addresses: Karlyn Kohrs Campbell and Kathleen Hall Jamieson, "Inaugurating the Presidency," *PSQ* (Spring 1985), pp. 394–411; Edward W. Chester, "Beyond the Rhetoric: A New Look at Presidential Inaugural Addresses," *PSQ* X (Fall, 1980), pp. 571–582; Donald L. Wolfarth, "John F. Kennedy in the Tradition of Inaugural Addresses," *QJS* XLVII (April, 1981), pp. 124–132; Edward P. Kenney, "Another Look at Kennedy's Inaugural Address," *CQ* XIII (November, 1965), pp. 17–19; Dan F. Hahn, "Ask Not What a Youngster Can Do For You: Kennedy's Inaugural Address," *PSQ*

XII (Fall, 1982), pp. 610–614; Edward P. J. Corbett, "Analysis of the Style of John F. Kennedy's Inaugural Address," *Classical Rhetoric for the Modern Student* 2nd ed. (New York: Oxford University Press, 1971), pp. 554–565; "The John F. Kennedy Inauguration Speech: Function and Importance of Its 'Address System,' " *Rhetoric Society Quarterly* XII (Fall, 1982), pp. 239–250; Robert W. Smith, "The 'Second' Inaugural of Lyndon Baines Johnson: A Definitive Text," *CM* XXXIV (March, 1967), pp. 102–108; Robert L. Scott, "Rhetoric That Postures: An Intrinsic Reading of Richard M. Nixon's Inaugural Address," *WJSC* XXXIV (Winter, 1970), pp. 46–52; Barbara Ann Harris, "The Inaugural of Richard Milhous Nixon: A Reply to Robert L. Scott," *WJSC* XXXIV (Summer, 1970) and Scott's reply to Harris in the same issue, pp. 235–236; Anthony Hillbruner, "Archetype and Signature: Nixon and the 1973 Inaugural," *CSSJ* XXV (Fall, 1974), pp. 169–181; Ernest G. Bormann, "A Fantasy Theme Analysis of Television Coverage of the Hostage Release and the Reagan Inaugural," *QJS* SLVIII (May, 1982), pp. 133–145. Bert Bradley, "Jefferson and Reagan: The Rhetoric of Two Inaugurals," *SSCJ* XLVIII (1983), pp. 119–136. Gregg Phifer, "The Two Inaugurals: A Second Look," *SSCJ* XLVIII (1983), pp. 378–385.

Crisis speeches: Richard A. Cherwitz; "Lyndon Johnson and the 'Crisis' of Tonkin Gulf: A President's Justification of War," *WJSC* SLI (Spring, 1978), pp. 93–104; John H. Patton, "An End and a Beginning: Lyndon B. Johnson's Decisive Speech of March 31, 1968," *CQ* XXI (Summer, 1973), pp. 33–41; Richard B. Gregg and Gerald A. Hauser, "Richard Nixon's April 30, 1969 Address on Cambodia: The 'Ceremony of Confrontation,' " *CM* XL (August, 1973), p. 167–181; Theodore Otto Windt, Jr., "The Presidency and Speeches on International Crises: Repeating the Rhetorical Past," *SG* II (1973), pp. 6–14; Barry Brummett, "Presidential Substance: The Address of August 15, 1973," *WJSC* XXXIX (Fall, 1975), pp. 249–259; Gerald L. Wilson, "A Strategy of Explanation: Richard M. Nixon's August 8, 1974 Resignation Address," *CQ* XXIV (Summer, 1976), pp.14–20; Lawrence W. Rosenfield, "August 9, 1974: The Victimage of Richard Nixon," *CQ* XXIV (Fall, 1976), pp. 19–23; Ronald A. Sudol, "The Rhetoric of Strategic Retreat: Carter and the Panama Canal Debate," *QJS* LX (December, 1979), pp. 379–391; Dan F. Hahn, "Flailing the Profligate: Carter's Energy Sermon of 1979," *PSQ* X (Fall, 1980), pp. 583–587; James W. Pratt, "An Analysis of Three Crisis Speeches," *WJSC* XXXIV (Summer, 1970), pp. 194–204. David Zarefsky, "Civil Rights and Civil Conflict: Presidential Communication in Crisis," *CCSJ* XXXIV (1983), pp. 59–66.

Movement studies: Theodore Windt, "Seeking Detente with Superpowers: John F. Kennedy at American University," *Essays in Presidential Rhetoric,* pp. 71–84; David Zarefsky, "The Great Society as a Rhetorical Proposition," *QJS* LX (December, 1979), pp. 364–378; Zarefsky, "President Johnson's War on Poverty: The Rhetoric of Three 'Establishment' Movements," *CM* XLIV (November, 1977), pp. 352–373; Cal M. Logue and John H. Patton, "From Ambiguity to Dogma: The Rhetorical Symbols of Lyndon B. Johnson on Vietnam," *SSCJ* XLVII (Spring, 1982), pp. 310–319; Andrew A. King and Floyd Douglas Anderson, "Nixon, Agnew, and the 'Silent Majority': A Case Study in the Rhetoric of Polarization," *WJSC* XXXV (Fall, 1971), pp. 243–255; Jackson Harrell, B. L. Ware, and Wil A. Linkugel, "Failure of Apology in American Politics: Nixon on Watergate," *CM* XLII (November, 1975), pp. 245–262; Hermann G. Stelzner, "Ford's War on Inflation: A Metaphor That Did Not Cross," *CM* XLIV (November, 1977), pp. 284–297; F. Michael Smith, "Rhetorical Implications of the 'Aggression' Thesis in the Johnson Administration's Vietnam Argumentation," *CSSJ* XXII (Winter, 1972) pp. 217–224; William L. Benoit, "Richard M. Nixon's Rhetorical Strategies in his Public Statements on Watergate," *SSCJ* XLIII (Winter, 1982), pp. 192–211; Robert L. Ivie, "Images of Savagery in American Justifications of War," *CM* XLVII (November, 1982), pp. 279–294. David Zarefsky, Carol Miller-Tutzauer, and Frank E. Tutzauer, "Ronald Reagan's Safety Net for the Truly Needy: The Rhetorical Uses of Definition," *CSSJ* XXXV (1984), pp. 113–119. Robert L. Ivie, "Speaking 'Common Sense' about the Soviet Threat," *WJSC* XLVIII (1984), pp. 39–50. Craig Allen Smith and Kathy B. Smith, "Presidential Values and Public Priorities: Recurrent Patterns in Addresses to the Nation, 1963–1984," *PSQ* XV (1985), pp. 743–753.

Genre Studies: See Windt on "Crisis" rhetoric, Campbell and Jamieson on inaugural addresses, Harrell, Ware, and Linkugel on the apology genre. Robert L. King, "Transforming Scandal into Tragedy: A Rhetoric of Political Apology," *QJS* LXXI (1985), pp. 298–301. Robert A. Vartabedian, "Nixon's Vietnam Rhetoric: A Case Study of Apologia as Generic Paradox," *SSCJ* L (1985), pp. 366–381.

Biographical studies: James David Barber's work in this area sets the standards. See in particular Barber's "Adult Identity and Presidential Style: The Rhetorical Emphasis," *Daedalus* XCVII (Summer, 1968), pp. 938–968 and Barber's *The Presidential Character* (Englewood Cliffs: Prentice Hall, 1977). See also Roderick P. Hart, "Absolutism and Situation: Prolegomena to a Rhetorical Biography of Richard M. Nixon," *CM* XLIII (August, 1976), pp. 204–228; Ruth M. Gonchar and Dan F. Hahn, "The Rhetorical Predictability of Richard M. Nixon," *CQ* XIX (Fall, 1971), pp. 3–13. Gary C. Woodward, "Reagan as Roosevelt: The Elasticity of Pseudo-Populist Appeals," *CSSJ* XXXIV (1983), pp. 44–58. Sarah Russell Hawkins, "Archtypal Alloy: Reagan's Rhetorical Image," *CSSJ* XXXIV (1983), pp. 33–43.

Miscellaneous studies: Robert N. Hall, "Lyndon Johnson's Speech Preparation," *OJS* LI (April 1965), pp. 168–176; Ronald H. Carpenter and Robert V. Seltzer, "Nixon, Patton, and a Silent Majority Sentiment about the Viet

Nam War: The Cinematographic Bases of a Rhetorical Stance," *CSSJ* XXV (Summer, 1974), pp. 105–110; James W. Gibson and Patricia K. Felkins, "A Nixon Lexicon," *WJSC* XXXVII (Summer, 1974), pp. 190–198; David S. Kaufer, "The Ironist and Hypocrite as Presidential Symbols: A Nixon-Kennedy Analog," *CQ* XXVII (Fall, 1979), pp. 20–26; Walter R. Fisher, "Rhetorical Fiction and the Presidency," *QJS* LXVI (April, 1980), pp. 119–126. Roderick P. Hart, "The Language of the Modern Presidency," *PSQ* XIV (1984), pp. 249–264. William C. Spragens, "Kennedy Era Speechwriting, Public Relations and Public Opinion," *PSQ* XIV (1984), pp. 78–86. Craig Allen Smith, "The Audiences of the 'Rhetorical Presidency': An Analysis of President-Constituent Interactions, 1963–1981," *PSQ* XIII (1983), pp. 613–622.

OVERVIEW

The Rise of the Rhetorical Presidency

James W. Ceaser, Glen E. Thurow, Jeffrey Tulis
and Joseph M. Bessette

The Rise of the Rhetorical Presidency

One of the most revealing periods of President Carter's tenure in office—and perhaps of the modern presidency itself—occurred during the summer of 1979. Falling to a new low in the public's approval ratings and facing criticism from all quarters for his leadership, the President dramatically cancelled a scheduled televised speech on energy and gathered his advisors together for a so-called domestic summit. Discussions moved beyond energy and economics to a reappraisal of the nature of presidential leadership and to an analysis of what, for want of a better term, can only be called the state of the national consciousness. Having served already more than half of his term, the President came to the conclusion that he had been mistaken in his undertanding of the presidential office; he had, as he told David Broder, fallen into the trap of being "head of the government" rather than "leader of the people." As for the state of the national consciousness, the President concluded that the nation was experiencing a crisis of spirit or "malaise" that went deeper and was more ominous than the economic challenges at hand. Yet difficult as this problem of malaise was, the President believed it could be tackled—and by the very same means that would correct his own failures of leadership. By engaging in a rhetorical campaign to "wake up" the American people, the President hoped both to save his presidency and begin the long process of national moral revival. As a Washington Post front page headline proclaimed on the day preceding his newly scheduled national address: **CARTER SEEKING ORATORY TO MOVE AN ENTIRE NATION.**[1]

Looking back today at these unusual events, one must surely be surprised that all of this self-analysis and deep introspection was so quickly forgotten. True, the July 15th speech was no classic of American oratory; but it did receive an extraordinary amount of attention at the time and was commonly thought to mark a "turning point" in the Carter presidency, at least as measured by the President's own intentions. Yet just three months afterwards, no

Mr. Ceaser is Associate Professor of Government and Foreign Affairs at the University of Virginia.
Mr. Thurow is Professor of Political Science at the University of Dallas.
Mr. Tulis is Assistant Professor of Politics at Princeton University.
Mr. Bessette is Assistant Professor of Politics at The Catholic University of America.
Reprinted by permission of Center for the Study of the Presidency, publishers of *Presidential Studies Quarterly* Vol. XI, No. 2 (Spring 1981), pp. 158–171.

one in the administration was mentioning the crisis of malaise, and the President, after the Iranian hostage crisis, returned to the White House and began deliberately acting "presidential," which is to say more like "the head of the government" than the "leader of the people."

Were these events merely a peculiar "story" of the Carter presidency? Perhaps. On the other hand, it might be argued that they are revealing in an exaggerated form of a major institutional development in this century—the rise of the rhetorical presidency—and of some of the problems inherent in that development.

Popular or mass rhetoric, which Presidents once employed only rarely, now serves as one of their principal tools in attempting to govern the nation. What ever doubts Americans may now entertain about the limitations of presidential leadership, they do not consider it unfitting or inappropriate for presidents to attempt to "move" the public by programmatic speeches that exhort and set forth grand and ennobling views.

It was not always so. Prior to this century, popular leadership through rhetoric was suspect. Presidents rarely spoke directly to the people, preferring communications between the branches of the government. Washington seldom delivered more than one major speech per year of his administration, and that one—the Annual Address—was almost mandated by the Constitution and was addressed to Congress. Jefferson even ceased delivering the address in person, a precedent that continued until Woodrow Wilson's appearance before Congress in 1913. The spirit of these early presidents' examples was followed throughout the nineteenth century. The relatively few popular speeches that were made differed in character from today's addresses. Most were patriotic orations, some raised Constitutional issues, and several spoke to the conduct of war. Very few were domestic "policy speeches" of the sort so common today, and attempts to move the nation by means of an exalted picture of a perfect ideal were almost unknown. Indeed, in the conspicuous case where a president did "go to the people" in a "modern" sense—Andrew Johnson's speaking tour in the summer before the 1866 Congressional elections—the campaign not only failed, but was considered highly irregular.[2] It was not until well into the present century that presidential speeches addressed to the people became commonplace and presidents began to think that they were not effective leaders unless they constantly exhorted the public.[3]

Today, a president has an assembly-line of speechwriters efficiently producing words that enable him to say something on every conceivable occasion. Unless a president is deliberately "hiding" in the White House, a week scarcely goes by without at least one major news story devoted to coverage of a radio or TV speech, an address to Congress, a speech to a convention, a press conference, a news release, or some other presidential utterance. But more important even than the quantity of popular rhetoric is the fact that presidential speech and action increasingly reflect the opinion that speaking *is* governing. Speeches are written to become the events to which people react no less than "real" events themselves.

The use of rhetoric by some of our recent presidents is revealing of this development. During his campaign and throughout the first few months of his presidency, President Kennedy spoke continually of the existence of a national crisis and of the need for sacrifice and commitment, only to find it difficult at times to explain just what the crisis was and where the sacrifice and commitment were actually needed. Today, seen in perspective, much of Kennedy's talk about our "hour of national peril" has a nice ring but a hollow sound, as if it were fashioned to meet the imperatives of a certain rhetorical style and not those of the concrete situation he faced.[4] It seems to reflect the view expressed by a former Kennedy White House aide: "It will be less important in years to come for presidents to work out programs and serve as administrators than it will be for presidents through the means of television to serve as educational and psychic leaders."[5]

President Johnson followed with a steady stream of oratory that swelled popular expectations of governmental capacity to a level that even his apologists now concede far exceeded what government could possibly achieve. What Harry Macpherson, one of Johnson's chief aides and speechwriters, said of the goals of the Johnson administration characterizes perfectly the tone of its rhetoric:

> People were [seen to be] suffering from a sense of alienation from one another, of anomie, of powerlessness. This affected the well-to-do as much as it did the poor. Middle-class women, bored and friendless in the suburban afternoons; fathers, working at "meaningless" jobs, or slumped before the television set; sons and daughters desperate for "relevance"—all were in need of community beauty, and purpose, all were guilty because so many others were deprived while they, rich beyond their ancestors' dreams, were depressed. What would change all this was a creative public effort. . . .[6]

President Nixon sensed people's reaction to the feverish pitch of the mid-sixties and countered with an anti-rhetoric rhetoric that soberly promised to "lower our voices":

> In these difficult years, America has suffered from a fever of words; from inflated rhetoric that promises more than it can deliver; . . . from bombastic rhetoric that postures instead of persuading.[7]

But this calm and mature pose, typical of Nixon's political superego, could not contain his own desire to strike back at his detractors, and together with Vice-President Agnew, Nixon launched his own rhetorical counteroffensive. If they enjoyed, up to a point at least, a great deal of success with their oratory, it was because much of it had the self-contained purpose of calling into question the rhetoric of their liberal opponents. With Agnew in particular, the privilege of holding public office was less important for what it could allow him to do than for what it could allow him to say.

President Carter, the outsider who came to Washington promising to bring a simple honesty and decency to government, began his term speaking in a voice lowered to a point where many felt that it had become inaudible. By mid-term, falling in the polls and urged on by his media advisor, Gerald Rafshoon, the President began to look for more opportunities to display rhetorical forcefulness. And by the time of his July oratorical campaign he emerged with an assertive tone and vigorous body movement, his theme being the decline and revitalization of America:

> [We face] a crisis that strikes at the very heart and soul and spirit of our national will. We can see this crisis in the growing doubt about the meaning of our own lives and in the loss of unity of purpose for our nation. . . . The erosion of our confidence in the future is threatening to destroy the social and political fabric of America. . . . [What] we must do is to regenerate our sense of unity, joining hands with each other in a sense of commitment to a national purpose. . . . We must bring together the different elements in America—producers, consumers, labor, business—bring us all together from the battlefield of selfishness to a table of common purpose.[8]

In the face of no tangible crisis on the order of a war or domestic upheaval, Carter was seeking nevertheless to define a subtler crisis and, linking it to the pragmatic issues of energy politics, to lead a domestic cultural revival. As one of his aides claimed, "I think we have seen both the rebirth of the American spirit that he talks about and the rebirth of the Carter presidency as well."[9]

Much of this rhetoric is undoubtedly, as many say today, "mere rhetoric." The excess of speech has perhaps fed a cynicism about it that is the very opposite of the boundless faith in rhetoric that has been so far portrayed. Yet, despite this cynicism, it seems increasingly the case that for many who comment on and form opinions about the presidency, word rivals deed as the measure of presidential performance. The standard set for presidents has in large degree become an artifact of their own inflated rhetoric and one to which they frequently fall victim.[10] While part of this difficulty can be blamed on the ineptness of certain presidents' rhetorical strategies, it is also the case that presidents operate in a context that gives them much less discretion over their rhetoric than one might think. The problem is thus not one simply of individual rhetorics, but is rather an institutional dilemma for the modern presidency.

Beginning with the campaign, the candidates are obliged to demonstrate their leadership capacity through an ever growing number of rhetorical performances, with the potential impact of their words on future problems of governing often being the least of their concerns. The pressure to "say something" continues after the president has begun to govern. Presidents not only face the demand to explain what they have done and intend to do, but they also have come under increasing pressure to speak out on perceived crises and to minister to the moods and emotions of the populace. In the end, it may be the office of the presidency that is weakened by this form of leadership, puffed up by false expectations that bear little relationship to the practical tasks of governing and undermined by the resulting cynicism.[11]

How did the rhetorical presidency come into existence? What are its strengths and weaknesses? Can presidents escape its burdens, and to what extent should they try to do so? These are some of the important questions that need addressing.

I

The rise of the rhetorical presidency has been primarily the result of three factors: 1) a modern doctrine of presidential leadership, 2) the modern mass media, and 3) the modern presidential campaign. Of these three, doctrine is probably the most important.

As strange as it may seem to us today, the Framers of our Constitution looked with great suspicion on popular rhetoric. Their fear was that mass oratory, whether crudely demogogic or highly inspirational, would undermine the rational and enlightened self-interest of the citizenry which their system was designed to foster and on which it was thought to depend for its stability. The Framers' well-known mistrust of "pure" democracy by an assembly— and by extension, of the kind of representative government that looked only to public opinion as its guide—was not based, as is generally supposed, on a simple doubt about the people's capacity to govern, but on a more complex case concerning the evils that would result from the interplay between the public and popular orators.

In democracies, they reasoned, political success and fame are won by those orators who most skillfully give expression to transient, often inchoate, public opinion.[12] Governing by this means, if indeed it can be called governing, leads to constant instability as leaders compete with each other to tap the latest mood passing through the public. The paradox of government by mood is that it fosters neither democratic accountability nor statesmanly efficiency. Freed from the necessity to consult public opinion, understood as "the cool and deliberate sense of the community," popular orators would be so chained to public opinion, understood as "mood," that discretion and flexibility essential to statesmanship would be undermined.[13]

The Founders were not so impractical as to think that popular rhetoric could be entirely avoided in a republican system. But the government they designed was intended to minimize reliance on popular oratory and to establish institutions which could operate effectively without the immediate support of transient opinion. All of the powers of governing were to be given, not directly to the people, but to their representatives. These representatives would find themselves in a tri-partite government in which the various tasks of governing would be clearly discernable and assigned, and in which they would be forced to deal with knowledgeable and determined men not easily impressed by facile oratory. As part of their solution, the Founders were counting on the large size of the nation, which at the time erected a communication barrier that would mute the impact of national popular rhetoric, whether written or oral. Beyond this, the Founders instituted a presidential selection system that was designed to preclude active campaigning by the candidates. As for the presidency itself, the Founders discouraged any idea that the President should serve as a leader of the people who would stir mass opinion by rhetoric; their conception was rather that of a constitutional officer who would rely for his authority on the formal powers granted by the Constitution and on the informal authority that would flow from the office's strategic position.

These limitations on popular rhetoric did not mean, however, that presidents were expected to govern in silence. Ceremonial occasions presented a proper forum for reminding the public of the nation's basic principles; and communications to Congress, explicitly provided for by the Constitution, offered a mechanism by which the people also could be informed on matters of policy. Yet this intra-branch rhetoric, though public, was not meant to be popular. Addressed in the first instance to a body of informed representatives, it would possess a reasoned and deliberative character; and insofar as some in the public would read these speeches and state papers, they would implicitly be called on to raise their understanding to the level of characteristic of deliberative speech.

Nineteenth century politics in America did not, of course, follow exactly the Founders' model of an essentially nonrhetorical regime. Campaigns quickly changed from their intended place as quiet affairs into spirited events replete with fanfare and highly charged popular rhetoric, though it is important to observe that the rhetoric was produced not by the candidates but by surrogates arranged for by the parties. Moreover, certain presidents—most notably Jackson and Lincoln—used their communications with Congress and some of their speeches and proclamations to address the people more or less directly. Yet the amount of nineteenth century presidential rhetoric that even loosely could be called popular is very little indeed, and the presidency remained, with some slight alterations, a Constitutional office rather than the seat of popular leadership.[14]

The Inaugural and the Annual Address (now called the State of the Union) were the principal speeches of a President given wide dissemination. The character of the Inaugural Address illustrates the general character of presidential popular speech during the period. Given on a formal occasion, it tended to follow a pattern which was set by Jefferson's First Inaugural Address in which he delivered an exposition of the principles of the union and its republican character. Although Jefferson's speech might in one sense be considered a partisan document, in fact he sought to be conciliatory towards his opponents. More important still, he presented his case not as an attempt to win support for the particular policies of a party but rather as an effort to instruct the people in, and fortify their attachment to, true republican political principles. The form of inaugural address perfected by Jefferson proved a lasting model throughout the century. Although subsequent addresses did not often match the eloquence or understanding of Jefferson's—Lincoln's Second Inaugural, of course, being the most conspicuous exception—they consistently attempted to show how the actions of the new administrations would conform to Constitutional and republican principles.

Against this tradition Woodrow Wilson gave the Inaugural Address (and presidential speech generally) a new theme. Instead of showing how the policies of the incoming administration reflected the principles of our form of government, Wilson sought to articulate the unspoken desires of the people by holding out a vision of their fulfillment. Presidential speech, in Wilson's view, should articulate what is "in our hearts" and not necessarily what is in our Constitution.[15]

Theodore Roosevelt had presaged this change by his remarkable ability to capture the nation's attention through his understanding of the character of the new mass press and through his artful manipulation of the national press corps.[16] It was Wilson, however, who brought popular speech to the forefront of American politics by his dramatic appearance before Congress—breaking more than a century's precedent of presidential nonattendance—and by his famous speaking tour on behalf of the League of Nations. Most importantly, Wilson articulated the doctrinal foundation of the rhetorical presidency and thereby provided an alternative theoretical model to that of the Founders. In Wilson's view, the greatest power in modern democratic regimes lay potentially with the popular leader who could sway or—to use his word—"interpret" the wishes of the people. After some indecision Wilson finally concluded that the presidency was the institution best suited to assume this role: "There is but one national voice in the country and that is the voice of the President." And it is the "voice" that is most important for governing: "It is natural that orators should be the leaders of a self-governing people. . . ."[17]

The Wilsonian concept of the rhetorical presidency consists of two interfused elements. First, the President should employ oratory to create an active public opinion that, if necessary, will pressure the Congress into accepting his program: "He [the President] has no means of compelling Congress except through public opinion."[18] In advancing policy, deliberative, intrabranch rhetoric thus becomes secondary to popular rhetoric, and the President "speaks" to Congress not directly but through his popular addresses. Second, in order to reach and move the public, the character of the rhetoric must tap the public's feelings and articulate its wishes. Rhetoric does not instill old and established principles as much as it seeks to infuse a sense of vision into the President's particular legislative program.

> A nation is led by a man who . . . speaks, not the rumors of the street, but a new principle for a new age; a man in whose ears the voices of the nation do not sound like the accidental and discordant notes that come from the voice of a mob, but concurrent and concordant like the united voices of a chorus, whose many meanings, spoken by melodious tongues, unite in his understanding in a single meaning and reveal to him a single vision, so that he can speak what no man else knows, the common meaning of the common voice.[19]

Much the same idea, though stripped of some of its eloquence, was expressed by President Carter in his Convention acceptance speech when he promised to be a President "who is not isolated from the people, but who feels your pain and shares your dreams and takes his strength and his wisdom and his courage from you."[20] Presidents have not always found it easy to bring these two elements—policy and mood—together. Carter's "malaise" address of July 1979 again illustrates the point. The first half of the speech portrayed a national malaise of sweeping and profound proportions; the second half incongruously implied that we could secure our redemption by conserving energy and taxing the oil companies.

The Wilsonian concept of presidential leadership was echoed in FDR's claim that the presidency is "pre-eminently a place of moral leadership" and subsequently canonized in the scholarly literature by Clinton Rossiter's characterization of the presidency as the nation's "trumpet."[21] To be sure, not all presidents since Wilson have embraced this grandiloquent conception of their role, but as a doctrine the rhetorical presidency has become the predominant model. What these metaphorical terms like "voice of the nation," "moral leader" and "trumpet" all suggest is a form of presidential speech that soars above the realm of calm and deliberate discussion of reasons of state or appeals to enlightened self-interest. Rather, the picture of leadership that emerges under the influence of this doctrine is one that constantly exhorts in the name of a common purpose and a spirit of idealism.

If the doctrine of the rhetorical presidency leaves us today with the occasional feeling that it is hollow or outworn, it is not because of a decline in its influence but beause of the inevitable consequences of its ascendancy. Presidents such as Wilson, Franklin Roosevelt and John Kennedy found in the doctrine a novelty which they could exploit to win attention—if not always success—for their program. Exercised against the prevailing expectation of moral leadership, however, presidents may find that the doctrine is sometimes more of a burden than an opportunity. Presidents can speak and exhort, but will anyone genuinely heed what they say?

The events leading up to President Carter's address of July 1979 are instructive. Late in June of that year the President received a memo from his chief domestic policy advisor, Stuart Eizenstat, recommending what has become by now the standard use of the rhetorical presidency:

> Every day you need to be dealing with—and publicly be seen as dealing with—the major energy problems now facing us. . . . You have a variety of speeches scheduled after your return. . . . Each of those occasions should be used to talk about energy. . . . The windfall tax campaign was successful because of your repeated discussion of it during a short time. With strong steps we can mobilize the nation around a real crisis and with a clear enemy.[22]

But on the day before his originally scheduled TV address, the President decided to cancel it because, in columnist David Broder's words, "He believed that neither the country nor the Congress would heed or respond to another energy speech—the fifth of his term—from him."[23] If a nationally televised presidential address, itself once a dramatic event, must be cancelled as a way of recapturing a sense of drama, one wonders what expedient presidents will turn to next.

II

The second factor that accounts for the rise of the rhetorical presidency is the modern mass media. The media did not create the rhetorical presidency— doctrine did—but it facilitated its development and has given to it some of its special characteristics. The mass media, meaning here primarily radio and television, must be understood first from the perspective of its technical capacities. It has given the President the means by which to communicate directly and instantaneously with a large national audience, thus tearing down the communications barrier on which the Founders had relied to insulate representative institutions from direct contact with the populace. Besides increasing the size of the President's audience, the mass media has changed the mode by which he communicates with the public, replacing the written with the spoken word delivered in a dramatic visible performance. The written word formerly provided a partial screen or check against the most simplistic argumentations, as it allowed more control of the text by the reader and limited the audience to those with the most interest in politics.

One might reply, of course, that presidents today produce more written documents than ever before and that all of their speeches are recorded and transcribed. But this matters little as few in the public ever bother to peruse, let alone read, the President's words. Significant messages are delivered today in speeches, and presidents understand that it is the visible performance, not the tangible text, that creates the public impression. Under the constant demand for new information that characterizes audiences of the media age, what is not seen or heard today does not exist. Presidents accordingly feel the pressure to speak more and to engage in what Eizenstat called "campaigns" to keep their message before the public. Words come to have an ephemeral quality to them, and the more the President speaks the less value can be put on any one speech he delivers. One of the great ironies of the modern presidency is that as the President relies more on rhetoric to govern, he finds it more difficult to deliver a truly important speech, one that will stand by itself and continue to shape events.

The influence of the mass media on presidential rhetoric is not limited to its technical capacities. The mass media has also created a new power center in American politics in the form of television news. If the tehnical aspect of the media has given the President an advantage or an opportunity, the existence of television news often serves as a rival or an impediment. Journalists are filters in the communication process, deciding what portions of the President's non-televised speeches they will show and how their arguments will be interpreted. When presidents speak in public today, their most important audience is not the one they are personally addressing, but rather the public as it is reached through the brief cuts aired on the news. Speeches accordingly tend to be written so that any segment can be taken to stand by itself—as a self-contained lead. Argument gives way to aphorism.

The direct impact of the news' interpretation of the President's words is perhaps less important for presidential rhetoric than the indirect influence that derives from the character of news itself. Television news not only carries the messages of governing officials to the people; it also selects the issues that are presented to the government for "action" of some sort. "Real" expressions of mass opinion, which in the past were sporadic, are replaced by the news' continuous "sophisticated" analyses that serve as a surrogate audience, speaking to the government and supposedly representing to it what the people are saying and thinking. Driven by its own inner dynamic to find and sustain exciting issues and to present them in dramatic terms, news creates—or gives the impression of creating—national moods and currents of opinion which appear to call for some form of action by the government and especially by the President.

The media and the modern presidency feed on each other. The media has found in the presidency a focal point on which to concentrate its peculiarly simplistic and dramatic interpretation of events; and the presidency has found a vehicle in the media that allows it to win public attention and with that attention the reality, but more often the pretense, of enhanced power.[24] What this two-sided relationship signifies is a change in the rhetorical context in which the President now operates, the implications of which extend beyond the question of how much power the President has to the issue of how he attempts to govern. Constitutional government, which was etablished in contradistinction to government by assembly, now has become a kind of government by assembly, with TV "speaking" to the President and the President responding to the demands and moods that it creates. The new government by assembly—operating without a genuine assembling of the people—makes it increasingly difficult for presidents to present an appearance of stability and to allow time for policies to mature and for events to respond to their measures. Instead, the President is under more pressure to act—or to appear to act—to respond to the moods generated by the news.

Partly as result of these pressures from the media for more and more presidential speech, a major new staff capacity has been added to the White House to enable the President to produce the large number of speeches and messages that he speaks or writes. While not a major cause of the rhetorical presidency, like any staff capacity its existence becomes a reason for its continual use. Once known as "ghosts" and hidden in the presidential closet, rhetoric-makers today have come out into the full light of day and are openly employed under the title of speechwriters.[25] We have perhaps passed beyond the point of naïveté where we shudder at exposés which reveal that the personal convictions of the President are written by someone else, but it is worth noting the paradox that at a time when presidents are judged more by their rhetoric, they play less of a role in its actual formulation. If, as Francis Bacon once wrote, only writing makes a man exact, the incoherence of much presidential policymaking may owe something to the fact that presidents do so little of their own writing and sometimes schedule more speeches than they can possibly supervise closely.[26] Certain rapid shifts that occurred during 1978 in President Carter's pronounced foreign policy, which Senator Kennedy attempted to make into an important campaign issue, are attributable to different viewpoints of the authors of his speeches, which the President either did not want or did not have the time to integrate.[27] An institutionalized speechwriting staff may bring to presidential speeches interests of its own that conflict with presidential policy or, to the extent that the staff becomes divorced from the President's chief political advisors, it may be incapable of resisting pressure from others for the inclusion of remarks in speeches at the expense of presidential coherence. Finally the speechwriting task has come more and more to be influenced by pollsters and admen whose understanding of rhetoric derives from the premises of modern advertising and its offshoot, political consulting. Such influence is even more visible in the modern presidential campaign.

III

The modern presidential campaign is the third factor that accounts for the rise of the rhetorical presidency. The roots of the modern campaign go back to Wilson and the Progressives and to many of the same ideas that helped to create the rhetorical presidency. Prior to 1912, the parties were largely responsible for conducting the campaigns, and the candidates, with few exceptions, restricted their communications to letters of acceptance of the nomination. Wilson was the first victorious presidential candidate to have engaged in a full-scale speaking tour during the campaign. In his view, it was essential that the candidates replace the parties as the main rhetorical instruments of the campaign. This change would serve not only to downgrade the influence of traditional parties but also to prepare the people for the new kind of presidency that he hoped to establish. Indeed, with Wilson the distinction between campaigning and governing is blurred, as both involve the same essential function of persuading through popular oratory.

Although Wilson himself did not campaign extensively in the pre-convention period, he supported the idea of a preconvention campaign and pushed for nomination by national primaries. His ideal of a truly open presidential nomination campaign in which all candidates must take the "outside" route was not fully realized, however, until after the reforms that followed the 1968 election. Over the past two campaigns and in this one, we have seen the development of one of the most peculiarly irresponsible rhetorical processes ever devised. For a period of two years before the 1980 conventions, the various contenders had little else to offer except their rhetoric. Undisciplined by the responsibility of matching word to deed, they sought to create events out of their speeches, all the while operating under the constant media-created pressure to say something new. As their goal was to win power, and as that goal, especially in the pre-convention period, was remote, candidates could easily afford to disregard the impact of their speech on the demands of governing and instead craft their rhetoric with a view merely to persuading.

Scholars of the electoral process, interested in such issues as accountability and democratic voting theory, have sought to determine just how much of the candidates' rhetoric goes into spelling out stands on issues as compared to other kinds of appeals, *e.g.* character or vaguely formed interpretation of events. If there is an operative normative theory to some of these inquiries, it is based on the premise that it would be desirable for the voters to know the candidate's stand on the full range of issues and to make up their minds on the basis of a rational calculation of their position as it compares to those of the candidates.[28] However, if one does not focus exclusively in campaigns but tries to see campaigns as part of the total process of governing, there is cause for wondering whether what is ideal from the standpoint of democratic voting theory is very helpful for promoting effective governing: too many specific commitments might, if taken seriously, undermine a necessary degree of discretion, or, if blatantly ignored, add to public cynicism. It is the empirical findings of such research that are, perhaps, of most interest, and here one discovers two contrasting tendencies.

Benjamin Page has shown that candidates devote very little time in their speeches to spelling out anything like concrete policy stands; instead most of their effort goes into general interpretations of past records and highly ambiguous statements about future goals.[29] On the other hand, Jeff Fischel has found that the number of specific promises that candidates make over the course of a campaign has been increasing dramatically since 1952.[30] This paradox is easily explicable if one bears in mind that while candidates may discuss very little of substance in their speeches, they speak (and write) much more than they ever did in the past and thus accumulate more pledges. This research suggests, then, that we have the worst of both worlds—vague and uninstructive speeches on the one hand and more and more specific promises on the other. In this result one finds the perfect marriage of media and special interest politics.

It may also be that the distinctions scholars make in regard to "issue stands" and "image making" are increasingly irrelevant. For the candidates and their political consultants the campaign is often seen as a whole, with the most sophisticated campaigns today being run on the premise that the candidates must tap and express a popular mood. Issues and images are both fit into this general theme. As Jimmy Carter remarked in 1976, "Insofar as my political campaign has been successful, it is because I have learned from our people and have accurately reflected their concerns, their frustrations and their desires."[31] Reflecting but not necessarily educating the people's moods has in some instances been the order of the day. The old case against the political consultants and admen—that they build up an image of the candidate's person—largely underestimates their impact. Today, they are definitely in the "business" of dealing with "issues" no less than images, and both frequently are subordinated to mood.

Actually, the efforts that candidates do make in some of their speeches to address the issues are often passed over and ignored in the media. Although it may take the public a long time to learn the candidates' basic themes—and many never learn them—the reporters covering the campaign often tire of repetitive stories and resist putting comments from formal speeches on the air. As Thomas Patterson has shown, the press, and especially television news coverage, looks for the "new" in the campaigns, and thus tends to cover those comments of candidates that are made in impromptu sessions. Indeed, journalists attempt to stimulate "campaign issues"—e.g., off the cuff responses to charges or to contemporary news events—rather than to cover what the candidates seek to communicate in their own rhetoric.[32] This form of news coverage may well help us learn something about the candidates' "character" or ability to think in public, but it hardly does very much to encourage among the people a respect for the formal rhetorical mode. That speeches might, if heard, be a helpful way of judging candidates, however, is suggested by the importance of the one main campaign speech that the public can view in its entirety—the campaign acceptance speech.

The presidential campaign is important for the kinds of inflated expectations it raises, but it is even more important for the effects it has on the process of governing. So formative has the campaign become of our tastes for oratory and of our conception of leadership that presidential speech and governing have come more and more to imitate the model of the campaign. In a dramatic reversal, campaigns set the tone for governing rather than governing for campaigns. This trend, which is becoming more embedded in public expectations, is furthered by another dynamic that works on the President and his staff. Both may think of the campaign as their finest hour, to the extent that its techniques become internalized in their conception of governing. As pollster Pat Caddell advised Carter at the beginning of his term, "governing with public approval requires a continuing political campaign."[33] And in a memo that led up to the Camp David speech, Caddell suggested that "Carter should return to the style that had marked his campaign for the presidency, at least in its early stages: to address the nation's mood and to touch on the 'intangible' problems in our society."[34] Some of the President's political advisors, Vice President Mondale among them, opposed the whole idea of a campaign while holding office. But the political consultants stood together and won the day. As Gerald Rafshoon told Elizabeth Drew, "It was important for the President to be 'relevant,' which meant showing people he understood what was bothering them."[35]

The growing intrusion of the mentality of the campaign consultants into the governing process recalls the ancient philosophical battle between the original founders of the art of rhetoric—the sophists—and the political scientists. When rhetoric was first discovered as a teachable art in Ancient Greece, its masters emphasized its purely persuasive powers; and because rhetoric claimed to be able to instruct politicians on how to win power, it quickly began to pass itself off as the most important kind of political education. As Carnes Lord has stated, ". . . by encouraging the supposition that the exericise of political responsibility requires little substantive knowledge beyond rhetorical expertise itself, rhetoric as taught by the sophists tended to make men oblivious of the very need for a science of politics." The threat that the art of rhetoric so defined posed to political science, yet the evident necessity of politicians to use rhetoric, led Aristotle to write a rhetoric of his own. It was designed to recast the nature of the discipline so as to emphasize, within the realm of the potentially persuasive, the role of rational argumentation and to encourage politicians "to view rhetoric not as an instrument of personal aggrandizement in the sophistic manner, but rather as an instrument of responsible or prudent statesmanship."[36] This view, which came to constitute the rhetorical tradition of the West through its central place in a liberal arts education, exerted a powerful influence on our founding. Many of the Framers, as Gordon Wood has pointed out, were schooled in this tradition of rhetoric, and one of our presidents, John Quincy Adams, wrote a treatise on rhetoric that reflected many of its premises.[37] Clearly, however, under the impact of the modern campaign, this tradition has lost ground to a modern-day version of the sophistic tradition. Under the tutelage of political consultants and pollsters, the understanding of rhetoric as mere persuasion has come to be almost second nature to many of our politicians. The devolution of governing into campaigning is thus even more ominous than it first appeared, for it represents not just a change in the purpose of speeches but a decay in the standard of speech itself.

IV

President Carter's formulation of July, 1979, that a President should be "the leader of the people" rather than "the head of the government," was a perfect expression of his support for the doctrine of the rhetorical presidency. Acting explicitly on this doctrine, the President pledged to spend more time with the people and launched a campaign of speeches, largely inspirational in tone, that were designed to mobilize a popular constituency which supposedly would translate into higher opinion ratings and more power in Washington. The evident failure of this campaign, however, should perhaps have given the President pause about the effectiveness of his newly discovered conception of his office. For all the momentary attention lavished on the President's words, they did not succeed—nor come close to succeeding—in creating a "rebirth of the American spirit." Nor is this surprising.

As the very name implies, the rhetorical presidency is based on words, not power. When connected in a practical way with the exercise of power, speech can be effective, but when used merely to generate public support it is apt to fail. However much attention and enthusiasm a President can momentarily garner, there is little assurance that the Congress will accede. As Henry Fairlie once observed, "There is in fact very little that the people can do to assist a President while he is in office; brought together at a general election, they are dispersed between elections; brought together in the evening by a television address, they are dispersed the next day."[38] Although a President may sometimes find that he can make the greatest public impression by attacking Congress for failing to pass his preferred programs, or by attributing such failures to archaic procedures or undue influence and power of special interests, such appeals are not likely to win friends in that body which still retains ultimate authority over legislation. Moreover, to the extent that Presidents *can* pressure Congress through popular appeals, such a strategy, like crying "wolf," is likely to work less well the more often it is used.

The inflated expectations engendered by the rhetorical presidency have by now become a matter of serious concern among those who study the presidency. In response to this problem, a growing number of scholars have begun to argue that Presidents should remove themselves from much of the day-to-day management of government and reserve themselves for crisis management.[39] If this argument means only that Presidents should not immerse themselves in details or spread themselves too thinly, no one could quarrel with it. But if it means that the President should abandon the articulation of a broad legislative program or avoid general management of the bureaucracy at a time when the bureaucracy is becoming more and more unmanageable, then the argument is misguided. If the President does not give coherence to policy or enforce discipline on the executive branch, who will? Certainly not Congress. The President remains our only national officer who, as Jefferson once said, "commands a view of the whole ground."[40] A retrenched presidency that cedes much of its authority to others and merely reacts to crisis is hardly the answer to our difficulties. Nor is it the only possible response to the doctrine of the rhetorical presidency. Advocates of the retrenched presidency contend that to reduce the expectations on the office, its authority must be diminished. But the high expectations for the office are not the result of its authority, but rather of the inflated conception of presidential leadership that governs our thinking. It is the publicly proclaimed pretensions of presidential power, not the power itself, that is the source of the problem.

The roots of the rhetorical presidency stretch so deeply into our political structure and national consciousness that talk of change may seem futile; and yet, the evident failures of the current doctrine, together with the growing scholarly debate over the crisis of the presidency, suggest that the moment has arrived for a discussion of alternatives. It should not be forgotten that the foundations of the rhetorical presidency were deliberately laid by Woodrow Wilson and that other presidents might establish new doctrines. If a sensible reform of the institution is ever possible, the key will be found in reversing the order of President Carter's formulation of July 1979—that is, in restoring the President to his natural place as the head of government, and subordinating his awkward role of an itinerant leader of the people. But how could such change take place, and what would the contours of the office look like?

First, since the modern campaign is the source of so many of the problems of the presidency, it is evident that no reform of the office can hope to succeed without a change in the selection process. The operative theoretical principle that must govern this change is that the selection process should be thought of not as an end in itself, but as a means of promoting, or at least not undermining, the character of the presidential office. Construed in practical terms this principle translates into a call for electoral reform that would reduce the duration of the campaign, especially in the pre-convention period. The elimination or dramatic reduction in the number of presidential primaries and the return of the power of selection to the parties would be helpful. This change would not eliminate the campaign, but it would reduce its public phase to a shorter period and thus focus public attention on the speechmaking that takes place after the nomination. Indeed, as Thomas Patterson has recently shown, the longer campaigns of recent years have *not* increased the level of public knowledge of the candidates' stands; and the psychology of mass attention may well be such that, after a certain point, there is an inverse relationship between information and learning.[41] Rhetorical performances may lose their drama as they become simply another in a long and expected series.

Second, Presidents should reduce the number of their speeches. As they speak less, there is at least the chance that their words will carry more weight; and if their words carry more weight, then perhaps more thought will be given to speech that can sensibly direct action. What applies to speeches applies equally to press conferences. Press conferences without cameras would probably allow for a more detailed exchange of information between the President and the press corps and avoid the pressures on the President (and the journalists) to make each news conference dramatic and newsworthy.[42] Written messages might replace many presently oral performances, and personal television appearances would be reserved for truly important issues of public concern.

Third, it is obvious that a reduction in the quantity of rhetoric itself is not enough; its character must also change. To avoid inspirational rhetoric does not mean that the President must abandon firm principles, practical ideals or even a political poetry that connects this generation with the moorings of our political system. Indeed, such a rhetoric is perfectly consistent with the dignity of a head of state and the character of our political order. In respect to policy, however, Presidents must recapture the capacity to address the nation's enlightened self-interest no less than its sense of idealism and the related capacity to approach Congress directly rather than through the people.

The gravest problem of the rhetorical presidency, however, goes deeper than any issue confined to presidential practice. It extends to the basic questions of how our nation can be governed. No one would deny that Presidents need to hold up America's basic principles and on occasion mobilize the public to meet genuine challenges. Indeed, in a liberal system of government that frees men's acquisitive instincts and allows them to devote their energies to individual material improvement, there is room on occasion for Presidents to lift up the public's vision to something beyond the clash of interests. But under the influence of the rhetorical presidency, we have seen an ever-increasing reliance on inspirational rhetoric to deal with the normal problems of politics. If there is a place for such rhetoric, it is necessary also to be aware of its danger and of the corresponding need to keep it within limits. By itself, rhetoric does not possess the power to make citizens devote themselves selflessly to the common weal, particularly where the basic principles of society protect and encourage men's independent and private activities. The Founders of our country created a complex representative government designed to foster a knowledgeable concern for the common good in the concrete circumstances of political life that would be difficult, if not impossible, to elicit directly from a people led by orators. What the continued use of inspirational rhetoric fosters is not a simple credibility problem, but a deep tension between the publicly articulated understanding of the nature of our politics and the actual springs that move the system. No wonder, then, that some politicians, deceived by their own rhetoric, find it difficult to come to terms with the job of governing a nation of complex multiple interests. Far from reinforcing our country's principles and protecting its institutions, the rhetorical presidency leads us to neglect our principles for our hopes and to ignore the benefits and needs of our institutions for a fleeting sense of oneness with our leaders.

Notes

1. *The Washington Post,* July 14, 15, and 16, 1979.
2. For a discussion of Johnson's "swing around the circle," see Albert Castel, *The Presidency of Andrew Johnson* (Lawrence, Kans.: Regents Press, 1979).
3. Joseph Kallenbach, *The American Chief Executive* (New York: Harper & Row, 1966), pp. 333–340.
4. *Public Papers of the Presidents, John F. Kennedy 1961* (Washington, D.C.: U.S. Government Printing Office, 1961), p. 19; see also Henry Fairlie, *The Kennedy Promise: The Politics of Expectation* (Garden City, N.J.: Doubleday, 1973).
5. Cited in Thomas E. Cronin, *The State of the Presidency* (Boston: Little, Brown, 1975), p. 72. The identification of the aide is not revealed.
6. Harry McPherson, *A Political Education* (Boston: Little, Brown, 1972), p. 301–2.
7. *The Public Papers of the Presidents, Richard Nixon 1969* (Washington, D.C.: U.S. Government Printing Office, 1969), p. 2.
8. President Carter, Speeches of July 15, 1979, (National Television Address) and July 16, 1979, (Detroit). *Presidential Documents, Annual Index,* 1979, p. 1237 and 1248.
9. *The Washington Post,* July 17, 1979, p. A14.
10. See for example, Theodore Lowi, *The End of Liberalism* (New York: Norton, 1969), p. 182.
11. In discussing matters that "force" presidents to make decisions by specified dates, Richard Neustadt concludes: "It is hardly to be wondered at that during Truman's years such matters became focal points for policy development, especially in the domestic sphere." See Richard Neustadt, "Presidency and Legislation: Planning the Presidents Program" *American Political Science Review* (Dcember 1955), p. 1021. It is also interesting to note here that in reference to John Kennedy's decision to implement the moon shot program, Theodore Sorensen has implied that the decision was largely made "because we felt we were in need of some display of action." See Theodore Sorensen, Kennedy Library oral history.

12. Alexander Hamilton, James Madison and John Jay, *The Federalist Papers*, ed., Clinton Rossiter (New York: New American Library, 1962), p. 360 (#58).
13. *Ibid.*, p. 384 (#63).
14. See Marvin R. Weisbord, *Campaigning for President* (Washington: Public Affairs Press, 1964), pp. 1–55; Arthur Schlesinger, *Introduction to Schlesinger and Israel*, eds., *The State of the Union Messages of the President* (New York: Chelsea House, 1966).
15. Woodrow Wilson, *Papers*, ed. Arthur S. Link (Princeton, N.J.: Princeton University Press, 1978) vol. 27, p. 150.
16. Elmer Cornwell, Jr., *Presidential Leadership and Public Opinion* (Bloomington, Ind.: Indiana University Press, 1965), pp. 1–30.
17. Woodrow Wilson, *Constitutional Government in the United States* (New York: Columbia University Press, 1908), p. 67; Woodrow Wilson, Congressional Government (Cambridge, Mass.: Riverside Press, 1885), p. 209.
18. Wilson, *Constitutional Government*, p. 65.
19. Wilson, *Papers*, ed. Link, Vol. 19, p. 42.
20. *Congressional Quarterly Almanac*, 1976, pp. 852–53.
21. Kallenbach, p. 253; and Clinton Rossiter, *The American Presidency* (New York: Harcourt Brace, 1960), p. 34.
22. *The Washington Post*, July 10, 1979.
23. *The Washington Post*, July 14, 1979, p. A1.
24. See Michael J. Robinson, "Television and American Politics, 1956–1976," *The Public Interest* (Summer 1977), pp. 3–39; Michael Baruch Grossman and Martha Joynt Kumar, *Portraying the President: The White House and the News Media* (Baltimore, Md.: Johns Hopkins University Press, 1981); and Robert Entman, "The Imperial Media," in Arnold J. Meltsner, ed., *Politics and the Oval Office* (Washington, D.C.: Institute for Contemporary Studies, 1981).
25. For a review of the transformation of speechwriters from secret aides to openly identified advisers, see Marie Hochmuth Nichols; *Rhetoric and Criticism*, (Baton Rouge: Louisiana State University Press, 1963), pp. 35–48.
26. Francis Bacon, *A Selection of His Works*, ed. by Sidney Warhaft (Indianapolis: Odyssey Press, 1965), p. 42.
27. James Fallows, Personal Inteview, March 10, 1979. Also see James Fallows, "The Passionless Presidency" and "The Passionless Presidency, Part II," *Atlantic*, May and June, 1979.
28. Benjamin I. Page, *Choices and Echoes in Presidential Elections* (Chicago: University of Chicago Press, 1979), pp. 10–61.
29. *Ibid.*, pp. 152–192.
30. Jeffrey Fishel, "From Campaign Promise to Presidential Performance," A paper prepared for a Colloquium at the Woodrow Wilson Center, June 20, 1979.
31. *The Campaign of 1976 Jimmy Carter* (Washington, D.C.: U.S. Government Printing Office, 1976), vol. 2, p. 274.
32. See Thomas Patterson, *The Mass Media Election* (New York: Praeger, 1980).
33. Patrick H. Caddell, "Initial Working Paper on Political Strategy," mimeo. Dec. 10, 1976.
34. Elizabeth Drew, "Phase: In Search of a Definition," *The New Yorker Magazine*, Aug. 27, 1979, p. 49–73.
35. *Ibid.*, p. 59.
36. Carnes Lord, "On Aristotle's Rhetoric," conference paper delivered at the White Burkett Miller Center, July 1979.

37. John Quincy Adams, *Lectures on Rhetoric and Oratory* (Cambridge, Mass., 1810).
38. Cited in Cronin, p. 73.
39. See David Broder's column, "Making the Presidency Man-sized," *The Washington Post,* Dec. 5, 1979, p. A27. Broder summarizes the consensus of a conference on the presidency held at the White Burkett Miller Center of Public Affairs at the University of Virginia.
40. Richardson, p. 3.
41. Patterson, pp. 67–75 and 173–181.
42. See Cornwell, op. cit., for the history of the press conference. In a series of forums on the press conference sponsored by the White Burkett Miller Center, most of the reporters present who have covered the president were of the opinion that, while television conferences were helpful on occasion, they often were superficial and did not allow for a genuine and in-depth exchange with the president. Most felt that greater use of the "reporters around the desk" format would improve the reading public's knowledge of the president.

Inaugurating the Presidency

Karlyn Kohrs Campbell and Kathleen Hall Jamieson

The presidential inaugural address is a discourse whose significance all recognize but few praise. Arthur Schlesinger, Jr., for example, acknowledges that, during inaugural addresses, "the nation listens for a moment as one people to the words of the man they have chosen for the highest office in the land,"[1] but he finds little merit in them: "even in the field of political oratory, the inaugural address is an inferior art form. It is rarely an occasion for original thought or stimulating reflection. The platitude quotient tends to be high, the rhetoric stately and self-serving, the ritual obsessive, and the surprises few."[2]

Conceivably, inaugurals simply mirror the alleged mediocrity of American presidents. But, if so, why is this form of presidential rhetoric deprecated while others are praised? More plausibly, at least from a rhetorical perspective, presidential inaugurals are maligned because they are misunderstood. Resolving this misunderstanding requires addressing an issue in criticism: Can inaugural addresses be treated as a group? Are they a distinct type, a rhetorical genre?[3]

Conventional wisdom and ordinarily language treat them as a class. Critics have intuitively taken them to be a distinct rhetorical type, but generalizing about them has been difficult. Despite apparent dissimilarities among them, we hold that they form a distinct rhetorical category or genre, and in this essay we attempt to identify the elements that constitute this genre. In so doing, we shall account for the recurrent and the variable in these speeches, explain the unique functions of the presidential inaugural, and illuminate the power of those inaugural addresses widely regarded as eloquent.

Inaugurals are a subspecies of the kind of discourse which Aristotle called epideictic, a form of rhetoric that praises or blames on ceremonial occasions,[4] addresses an audience that evaluates the rhetor's skill (1354b.2–4), recalls the past and speculates about the future while focusing on the present (1358b.18–20), employs a noble, dignified, literary style (1414a.15), and amplifies or rehearses admitted facts (1368a.27).

More recently, in a work on rhetoric in the Catholic Church, John O'Malley notes that epideictic rhetoric has a unique problem of invention, that is, a problem in discovering and developing appropriate lines of argument. Unlike forensic (courtroom) or deliberative (legislative) speeches which deal "with more immediate and pressing issues" for which "classical theory proposed *topoi* or commonplaces, . . . [t]he occasional or ceremonial nature of

Ms. Campbell is Professor of Communication Studies at the University of Kansas.
Ms. Jamieson is Professor of Speech Communication at the University of Texas.

Reprinted by permission of the Center for the Study of the Presidency, publishers of *Presidential Studies Quarterly* Vol. XV, No. 2 (Spring, 1985), pp. 394–411.

epideictic often deprived it of obviously immediate issues."[5] As a result, *memoria* or recollection of a shared past is an exceptionally important resource for epideictic speeches. O'Malley also calls attention to the distinctively contemplative character of this genre when he remarks that "epideictic wants as far as possible to present us with works and deeds, . . . not for metaphysical analysis but quite literally for viewing . . . 'to look,' to 'view,' to 'gaze upon,' and to 'contemplate.' . . ."[6] Harry Caplan adds that in epideictic rhetoric the speaker tries by means of his art simply "to impress his ideas upon [the audience], without action as a goal."[7]

Presidential inaugurals are epideictic speeches because they are delivered on ceremonial occasions, fuse past and future in present contemplation, affirm or praise the shared principles that will guide the incoming administration, ask the audience to "gaze upon" traditional values, employ an elegant, literary language, and rely on "heightening of effect," that is, on amplification and reaffirmation of what is already known and believed. The special character of the presidential inaugural address is defined by these general epideictic features and by the nature of the inauguration ceremony. Inauguration is a rite of passage, a ritual of transition in which the newly-elected President is invested in the office of the Presidency.[8] The fusion of epideictic features with the requirements of this rite of investiture creates the distinct rhetorical type that is the presidential inaugural address.

Investiture necessitates participation in a formal ceremony in which a duly constituted authority confers the right to play a certain role or to take a certain position before appropriate witnesses. The ceremony usually involves a demonstration by the candidate for investiture of her or his suitability for such elevation. In the inauguration ceremony, the President must swear an oath specified by the Constitution[9] before "the people" as witnesses and demonstrate by rhetorical enactment his worthiness, his capacity to be the President. More specifically, the President must show that he understands the principles of a democratic-republican system of government and the limits it imposes on executive power, and he must manifest rhetorically his ability to lead and to be the symbolic head of state who is President of all the people.

The general qualities of epideictic rhetoric, modified by the nature of presidential investiture, generate a constellation of five interrelated elements which differentiate the presidential inaugural address from other types of epideictic rhetoric.[10] The presidential inaugural 1) unifies the audience by reconstituting its members as "the people" who can witness and ratify this ceremony; 2) rehearses communal values drawn from the past; 3) sets forth the political principles that will govern the new administration; 4) demonstrates that the President appreciates the requirements and limitations of his executive functions; and 5) achieves these ends through means appropriate to epideictic address, i.e., while urging contemplation not action, focusing on the present while incorporating past and future, and praising the institution of the Presidency and the values and form of the government of which it is a part.

Epideictic "timelessness" is the key element in the dynamic which constitutes the presidential inaugural. The time of the inaugurals is the eternal present, the mythic time that Mircea Eliade calls *illud tempus,* time out of time. Eliade writes: "Every ritual has the character of happening *now,* at this very moment. The time of the event that the ritual commemorates or re-enacts is made *present,* 're-presented' so to speak, however far back it may have been in ordinary reckoning."[11] An *illud tempus* has two distinguishing characteristics. It represents a universe of eternally subsisting relations, here the relationship between the ruler and the people, and it has the potential to be re-enacted, to be made present. Unlike historical time, an *illud tempus* can be re-enacted, made present once again, at any moment. This special sense of the present is central to the generic character of the inaugural because the address is about an institution and form of government fashioned to transcend any given moment. The timelessness of the inaugural address affirms and ensures the continuity of the constitutional system, the immortality of the Presidency as an institution, and it is reflected in its contemplative tone and by the absence of calls to specific and immediate action.

In order to transcend the historical present, inaugurals reconstitute an existing community, rehearse the past, affirm traditional values, and articulate timely and timeless principles that will govern the administration of the incoming President. Inaugurals manifest their locus in the eternal present in their dignified, literary style which heightens experience, prompts contemplation, and speaks to "the people" through all time. The quality of epideictic timelessness to which inaugurals aspire is captured by Franklin Roosevelt in his 1941 inaugural: "to us there has come a time, in the midst of swift happenings, to pause for a moment and take stock—to recall what our place in history has been, and to rediscover what we are and what we may be. . . ."[12] Epideictic qualities inform the other elements which form the presidential inaugural address.

Reconstituting "the People"

Before the audience can witness and ratify the ascent to power, it must be unified and reconstituted as "the people." John Adams illustrates the reconstituting power of historical re-enactment when he rehearses the founding of the nation: "In this dangerous crisis [under the Articles of Confederation] the people of America were not abandoned by their usual good sense, presence of mind, resolution, or integrity. Measures were pursued to concert a plan to form a more perfect union . . ." (10). Jefferson reveals his desire to construct a single people out of partisan division when he says: "We have called by different names brethren of the same principles. We are all Republicans. We are all Federalists" (16). More recently, after a close election and a divisive campaign, Kennedy in 1961 begins: "We observe today not a victory of party, but a celebration of freedom . . ." (269). As one would expect, explicit appeals for unity are most common in inaugural addresses that follow a divisive campaign or a contested electoral outcome.[13]

Partisan politicking is not the only source of division. Occasionally a major crisis or war creates disharmony that must be set aside if the President is to govern all the people. Acknowledging the disunity created by the Civil War, in 1801 McKinley declares: "We are reunited. Sectionalism has disappeared. Division on public questions can no longer be traced by the war maps of 1861" (180). In 1917, in the face of U.S. entry into World War I, Wilson affirms the importance of unity: "it is imperative that we should stand together. We are being forged into a new unity amidst the fires that now blaze throughout the world" (205).

Once the audience has been united as "the people" it can perform its role in the inaugural ceremony. The inaugural addresses themselves attest to the witnessing role of "the people." For example, in 1889 Benjamin Harrison says:

> There is no constitutional or legal requirement that the president shall take the oath of office in the presence of the people, but there is so manifest an appropriateness in the public induction to office of the chief executive of the nation that from the beginning of the Government the people, to whose service the official oath concentrates the officer, have been called to witness the solemn ceremonial (155).

Similar statements appear in many others. John Quincy Adams says: "I appear, my fellow citizens, in your presence and in that of heaven to bind myself . . ." (51). "In the presence of this vast assemblage of my countrymen," says Cleveland, "I am about to supplement and seal by the oath which I have taken to manifestation of the will of a great and free people" (151). "I, too, am a witness," notes Eisenhower, "today testifying in your name to the principles and purposes to which we, as a people, are pledged" (263).[14]

Without the presence of "the people," the rite of presidential investiture cannot be completed. The people ratify the president's formal ascent to power by witnessing his enactment of his role, acknowledging his oath, and accepting the principles he lays down to guide his administration. Benjamin Harrison recognizes the interdependence of President and people in this inaugural act: "The oath taken in the presence of the people becomes a mutual covenant. . . . My promise is spoken; yours unspoken, but not the less real and solemn. The people of every State have here their representatives. Surely I do not misinterpret the spirit of the occasion when I assume that the whole body of the people covenant with me and with each other today to support and defend the Constitution of the Union of the States, to yield willing obedience to all the laws and each to every other citizen his equal civil and political rights" (155).

That the inaugural address is an adjunct to or an extention of the oath of office is demonstrated dramatically in the shortest inaugural, Washington's second. After describing himself as "called upon by the voice of my country" to "this distinguished honor," Washington says: "Previous to the execution of any official act of the President the Constitution requires an oath of office. This oath I am now about to take, and in your presence: That if it shall be found during my administration of the Government I have in any instance violated willingly or knowingly the injunctions thereof, I may (besides incurring constitutional punishment) be subject to the upbraidings of all who are now witnesses of the present solemn ceremony" (7). Although it consists entirely of a presidential affirmation of the constitutional oath, this inaugural also recognizes the witnessing role of the audience in the rite of investiture. That the inaugural address is an extension of the oath of office is certified by many of these speeches.[15] However, one of the more eloquent inaugurals derives its power in part from its construction as an extension of the oath of office and its invitation to participate in a mutual covenant. In 1961 each assertion or promise articulated by Kennedy is phrased as a mutual pledge made by the leader and the people. His litany of mutual pledges culminates in the claim: "In your hands, my fellow citizens, more than mine, will rest the final success or failure of our course" (271). Finally, he explicitly invites audience participation when he asks: "Will you join in that historic effort?" (271). By casting his speech as an extension of the oath of office and by inviting the audience to join him in making these pledges, Kennedy underscores the ritualistic character of the occasion.

The force of Lincoln's first inaugural also derives, in part, from its invitation to audience participation. Lincoln makes us peculiarly aware that contemplation is a precursor of action.[16] After offering his interpretation of constitutional principles, Lincoln says:

> That there are persons in one section or another who seek to destroy the Union at all events and are glad of any pretext to do it I will neither affirm nor deny; but if there be such, I need address no word to them. To those, however, who really love the Union may I not speak?
>
> Before entering upon so grave a matter as the destruction of our national fabric, with all its benefits, its memories, and its hopes, would it not be wise to ascertain precisely why we do it? Will you hazard so desperately a step while there is any possibility that any of the ills you fly from have no real existence? Will you, while the certain ills you fly to are greater than all the real ones you fly from, will you risk the commission of so fearful a mistake? (120)

His conclusion draws participation from contemplation: "My countrymen, one and all, think calmly and *well* upon this whole subject" (122), and, in the line paraphrased by Kennedy, he says: "In *your* hands, my dissatisfied fellow-countrymen, and not in *mine,* is the momentous issue of civil war" (122). One reason that Lincoln's first inaugural is a great address is that the audience is asked to participate actively in contemplating the meaning of the constitutional principles Lincoln has laid down and in judging whether those principles warrant secession.[17]

Each of the other elements forming the presidential inaugural facilitates the President's task of reconstituting his listeners as "the people." The traditional values rehearsed by the President are selected and framed in ways that unify the audience. Thus, for example, following a campaign replete with charges that he was an atheist, Jefferson's inaugural consoles his former adversaries with assurances that he, too, recognizes the power of the deity, in his words, "acknowledging and adoring an overruling Providence . . ." (16) "that Infinite Power which rules the destinies of the universe . . ." (17). So, too, the founders are eulogized in early inaugurals but disappear as the Civil War approaches. Since Garrison and other abolitionists had widely publicized the slaveholding of the founders, public veneration of them would ally the President with those who favored slavery and invite the enmity of its opponents. Van Buren's exceptional reference in 1837 to Washington and the other founders—"him who above all others contributed to establish it [the Republic] on the field of battle and those whose expanded intellect and patriotism constructed, improved, and perfected the inestimable institutions under which we live . . ." (65) can be explained by Van Buren's explicitly pro-slavery stand.[18] When an appeal that was once a unifying recollection of past heroes interfered with the process of reconstituting the audience into a unified people, it was abandoned.

Just as recollection of the past and rehearsal of traditional values should be non-controversial and unifying, so, too, recommitment to constitutional principles unifies by assuring those who did not vote for this President that he will, nevertheless, scrupulously protect their rights. The need to unify the audience and to speak in the epideictic present also influence the language in which presidents articulate the principles that will govern their administrations.

Rehearsing Traditional Values

To demonstrate his qualifications for the office, the President must venerate the past and show that the traditions of the institution continue unbroken in him. He must affirm that he will transmit the institution of the Presidency intact to his successors. Consequently, the language of conservation, preservation, maintenance, and renewal pervades the inaugurals. What we conserve and renew is often sanctified as our "creed," our "faith," or our "sacred trust." Cleveland's statement in 1885 is illustrative: "On this auspicious occasion we may well renew the pledge of our devotion to the Constitution, which, launched by the founders of the republic and consecrated by their prayers and patriotic devotion, has for almost a century borne the hopes and aspirations of a great people through prosperity and peace and through the shock of foreign conflicts and the perils of domestic strife and vicissitudes" (151).

Presidential use of the principles, policies, and presidencies of the past suggest that, in the inaugural address, *memoria* (shared recollection of the past) is a key source of *inventio* (development of lines of argument). Lincoln's final appeal in his first inaugural is illustrative of the rhetorical power and resources of the past: "The mystic chords of memory, stretching from every battlefield and patriot grave to every leaving heart and hearthstone all over this broad land, will yet swell the chorus of the Union, when again touched, as surely they will be, by the better angels of our nature" (123). Coolidge puts it more simply: "We cannot continue these brilliant successes in the future, unless we continue to learn from the past" (215). Such use of the past is also consistent with the ritualistic process of "re-presenting" beginnings, origins, and universal relationships.

The past is conserved by honoring past Presidents. Washington is praised by John and John Quincy Adams, Jefferson, Taylor, and Van Buren; Monroe and Jackson refer to their illustrious predecessors; Lincoln speaks of the distinguished citizens who have administered the executive branch. The past is also conserved by reaffirming the wisdom of past policies. Cleveland, for example, praises policies of Washington, Jefferson, and Monroe (152); McKinley praises the policy of "keeping ourselves free from entanglement, either as allies or foes" (17).

The past is also used analogically to affirm that just as we overcame difficulties in the past, so, too, will we now. The venerated past assures us that the nation has a future. Thus, in 1932, in the face of severe economic problems, Franklin Roosevelt says: "Compared with the perils which our forefathers conquered because they believed and were not afraid, we have still much to be thankful for" (232), and in 1941 he reminds us of the difficult tasks that confronted Washington and Lincoln (243).

In the world of the inaugural address, we have inherited our character as a people; accordingly, veneration of the past not only unifies the audience but warrants present and future action, as recurring references to "no entangling alliances" illustrates. A more recent example is found in Ronald Reagan's 1981 inaugural in which Reagan paraphrases a statement Jefferson made in 1801. Jefferson said: "Sometimes it is said that man can not be trusted with the government of himself. Can he, then, be trusted with the government of others?" (16) Reagan said: "But if no one among us is capable of governing himself, then who among us has the capacity to govern someone else?"[19]

As Reagan's use of Jefferson illustrates, a president must go beyond the rehearsal of traditional values and veneration of the past to enunciate a political philosophy that will inform the incoming administration. Because rhetorical scholars have focused on the specific political principles of individual inaugurals, they have failed to note that although these principles vary from inaugural to inaugural, all inaugurals not only lay down political principles but present and develop such principles in predictable ways.

Enunciating Political Principles

In numerous inaugurals, Presidents testify that they feel obliged to specify the principles that will govern their tenure in office. Jefferson's 1801 statement exemplifies this: "About to enter, my fellow-citizens, on the exercise of duties which comprehend everything dear and valuable to you, it is proper you should understand what I deem the essential principles of our Government, and consequently those which ought to shape its Administration . . ." (16). In keeping with the epideictic character of inaugurals, when specific policies are proposed, it is for contemplation, not action. Policy proposals are not an end in themselves but illustrations of the political philosophy of the President. This contemplative, expository function differentiates policy proposals embedded in inaugurals from those in State of the Union addresses, where there is a call to immediate action.[20]

So, for instance, in a relatively detailed address Polk discusses "our revenue laws and the levy of taxes," but this discussion is an illustration of the principle that "no more money shall be collected than the necessities of an economical administration shall require" (93). Similarly, he airs his views on the national debt to illustrate the principle that: "Melancholy is the condition of that people whose government can be sustained only by a system which periodically transfers large amounts from the labor of the many to the coffers of the few. Such a system is incompatible with the ends for which our Republican Government was instituted" (93).

Because Taft conceives the inaugural address as a vehicle for articulating policy proposals, his speech provides a rigorous test of this claim. He says: "The office of an inaugural address is to give a summary outline of the main policies of the new administration, so far as they can be anticipated" (189). But his tedious list of recommendations functions not as a call for specific, immediate action, but as evidence of continuity and of loyalty to the Constitution. He says, for example, "I have had the honor to be one of the advisers of my distinguished predecessor, and as such, to hold up his hands in the reforms he has initiated. . . . To render the reforms lasting, however, . . . further legislative and executive action are needed" (189). Such reforms ("the suppression of the lawlessness and abuses of power of the great combinations of capital invested in railroads and in industrial enterprises carrying on interstate commerce") are defined as means of maintaining the democratic character of the government.

However, the rite of investiture demands that the President do more than rehearse traditional values and enunciate a political philosophy. He must also enact his role as President.

Enacting the Presidency

The audience, unified into "the people" witnesses the investiture of the President. To complete and ratify the President's ascent to power, the inaugural demonstrates rhetorically that this person can function as a leader within the constitutionally established limits of executive power and that he can perform the public, symbolic role of President of all the people.

The inaugural address is performative. It evinces presidential leadership by the very fact of its delivery. As President, the speaker appropriates the country's history and assumes the right to tell us what that history means; as President, the speaker constitutes his hearers as "the people," and as President, the speaker asks the audience to join him in a mutual covenant to commit themselves to the political philosophy he enunciates.

Franklin Roosevelt's first inaugural dramatically underscores his role as leader and the need for executive action. He speaks of "a leadership of frankness and vigor" and says: "I am convinced that you will again give the support to leadership in these critical days" (231). "This Nation asks for action, and action now" (232). "Through this program of action we address ourselves to putting our own national house in order . . ." (233) and "With this pledge taken, I assume unhesitatingly the leadership of this great army of our people . . ." (233). However, Roosevelt is aware that he is testing the limits of executive power. He says: "It is to be hoped that the normal balance of executive and legislative authority may be wholly adequate to meet the unprecedented task before us. But it may be that an unprecedented demand and need for undelayed action may call for temporary departure from that normal balance of public procedure. I am prepared under my constitutional duty to recommend the measures that a stricken nation . . . may require. . . . I shall ask Congress for the one remaining instrument to meet the crisis—broad Executive power to wage a war against the emergency, as great as the power that would be given to me if we were in fact invaded by a foreign foe" (234). What is crucial here is that his leadership is constitutional; special powers would be conferred by Congress; and those powers would be analogous to the extraordinary powers exercised by previous Presidents in similarly extreme circumstances.

An abiding fear of the misuse of executive power pervades our national history. For example, Washington's opponents accused him of wanting to be king; Jackson was called King Andrew[21] and Van Buren King Martin; Teddy Roosevelt was attacked in cartoons captioned: "Theodore Roosevelt for ever and ever"; Lincoln's abolition of habeas corpus and Franklin Roosevelt's use of presidential power and his third and fourth terms were damned as monarchical, or worse, as despotic. The American Revolution was fought, as the Declaration of Independence reminds us, in reaction to "repeated injuries and usurpations, all having in direct object the establishment of an absolute Tyranny over these States. . . ." To allay the fear that the President is a despot in democratic clothing, an incoming President must assure the citizenry that he does not covet power for its own sake and that he recognizes and respects constitutional limits on his authority.

There is a paradox in the generic requirement that the President demonstrate his capacity for effective leadership while acknowledging constitutional limitations. To the extent that he presents himself as a strong leader, he risks being seen as an incipient tyrant. By contrast, should he emphasize the limits on his power, he risks being seen as an inept or enfeebled leader. Eloquent presidents walk this tightrope with agility as Lincoln does in his first inaugural when he responds to the fear that he will use executive power to abolish slavery. He says: "I have no purpose, directly or indirectly to interfere with the institution of slavery in the State where it exists" (117). He attests that this is a consistent position by citing statements from his campaign speeches and a plank from the Republican party platform, material he characterizes as "the most conclusive evidence of which the case is susceptible" (117–118). Addressing abolitionist revulsion against the fugitive slave law, he quotes Article 4 of the Constitution and avers that the law is merely an extension of that article, a part of the Constitution he has just sworn to uphold. He adds: "I take the official oath to-day with no mental reservations and with no purpose to construe the Constitution or Laws by any hypercritical rules" (118).

In recognizing the limits on executive power, inaugurals not only affirm the balance of powers and locate presidential power in the mandate of the people, they also offer evidence of humility. The new President humbly acknowledges his deficiencies, humbly accepts the burdens of office, and humbly invokes God's blessings. The precedent for evincing humility was set by Washington in his first inaugural when he said: "the magnitude and difficulty of the trust to which the voice of my country called me, being sufficient to awaken in the wisest and most experienced of her citizens a distrustful scrutiny into his qualifications, could not but overwhelm with despondence one who ought to be peculiarly conscious of his own deficiencies . . ." (3). Washington's attitude is echoed in Carter's 1977 remark: "Your strength can compensate for my weakness, and your wisdom can help to minimize my mistakes."[22]

Inaugurals typically place the President and the nation under God, and this, too, is part of the process of acknowledging limits. By calling upon God, the President subordinates himself to a higher power. References to God are not perfunctory. The God of the inaugurals is a personal God who is actively involved in affairs of state, an "Almighty Being whose power regulates the destiny of nations," in the words of Madison (27), a God "who led our fathers," in the words of Jefferson (22), a God who protects us, according to Monroe (38), a God revealed in our history, according to Cleveland (153), and a God who punishes us, according to Lincoln: "He gives to both North and South this terrible war as the woe due to those by whom the offense came . . ." (126). The President enacts the presidential role by placing himself and the nation in God's hands. It is only when the President is fully invested in office that he has the power and authority to place the nation "under God." For this reason, prayers or prayerlike statements occur near or at the end of inaugurals. This explains why Eisenhower calls the prayer he delivers prior to his first inaugural "a private prayer." Although he has taken the oath of office, he is not yet fully invested as the President and lacks the authority to represent the nation before God.

The placement of prayers or prayerlike statements is a subtle indication that the address is an integral part of the rite of investiture. However, some inaugurals articulate the notion that the President becomes the President through delivering the inaugural address. For example, William Henry Harrison concludes his 1841 speech this way: "Fellow citizens, being fully invested with that high office to which the partiality of my countrymen has called me, I now take affectionate leave of you" (86).[23]

If delivery of the inaugural is to function as part of the investiture, the President must speak in his role as President. An inaugural would not fulfill this function if the address were preoccupied with the personality or personal history of the incoming President.[24] When evidence is drawn from the President's personal past, it must reveal something about the Presidency or about the people or the nation. Personal narrative is inappropriate in a rhetorical genre designed for the formal display of the President as the President. The role of personal material in an inaugural differentiates it from campaign oratory in which a high level of self-disclosure and self-aggrandizement is not only appropriate but expected. It also distinguishes the inaugural address from other presidential rhetoric.[25]

The most dramatic example of inappropriate personal material appears in the final paragraph of Grant's second inaugural. Here is how he concludes: "Notwithstanding this, throughout the war, and from my candidacy for my present office in 1868 to the close of the last Presidential campaign, I have been the subject of abuse and slander scarcely ever equalled in political history, which to-day I feel that I can afford to disregard in view of your verdict, which I gratefully accept as my vindication" (135). Grant's statement was criticized by his contemporaries and has been criticized by historians for its unbecoming self-preoccupation. The statement tells us about Grant the person, not about the presidency or about Grant the President, and in so doing, the statement calls into question Grant's ability to fulfill the symbolic role of President of all the people.

By contrast, Franklin Roosevelt uses his personal past effectively. In his fourth inaugural in 1945, he says: "I remember that my old schoolmaster, Dr. Peabody, said, in days that seemed to us then to be secure and untroubled: 'Things in life will not always run smoothly. Sometimes we will be rising toward the heights—then all will seem to reverse itself and start downward. The great fact to remember is that the trend of civilization itself is forever upward; that a line drawn through the peaks and valleys of the centuries always has an upward trend" (247). It is wartime; this statement brings hope out of tribution and becomes the basis for Roosevelt's claim that although the Constitution is a firm base, it is still a document open to improvement. The lesson of his mentor allows him to say something he could not have asserted directly as effectively.

By contrast, Carter's use of a statement by his former high school teacher illustrates a potential pitfall in using personal material. Immediately after thanking Ford for all he had done to heal the divisions in the nation, Carter said: "In this outward and physical ceremony, we attest once again to the inner and spiritual strength of our Nation. As my high school teacher, Miss Julia Coleman, used to say, 'We must adjust to changing times and still hold to unchanging principles.' "[26] As we have argued, the first duty of the President in an inaugural is to reconstitute his audience as "the people." Carter is attempting here to forge an American community out of his listeners. However, only certain people have the standing to do that, and Miss Julia Coleman, however able she may have been as a high school teacher, is not one of them. Had Carter made her the voice of the people expressing a timeless truth, Coleman's aphorism might have been appropriate later in the inaugural. Despite Coleman's lack of authority, her adage might have fulfilled this requirement had it been an unusual, penetrating, immediately intelligible, vivid statement of the relationship between change and continuity. However, even such a claim is questionable. In Carter's statement we have the rhetorical equivalent of what would have occurred had Kennedy said, "To paraphrase my old headmaster,[27] 'ask not what your country can do for you. . . .' "

The presidential inaugural address is part of the process by which the President is invested in office. As a result, the audience expects him to enact his role: to demonstrate his ability to lead, to recognize the limits of executive power, to speak and act in a presidential, rather than a personal role. As President, he can unify his audience as "the people" and lay down the principles that will guide his administration. Finally, the President must demonstrate an understanding of the epideictic demands of a ritualistic occasion.

Fulfilling Epideictic Requirements

The qualities Aristotle ascribes to epideictic discourse are rhetorical qualities appropriate to rituals or ceremonies. All presidential inaugurals are speeches of display inviting the audience to evaluate the rhetor's skill in enacting his role. All praise or blame, affirm traditional values, heighten what is known or believed, use elegant, noble language and focus on the eternal present. Great inaugurals heighten the nuances of the relationship between the people and the President and respond to situational exigencies in a fashion more subtle than their more pedestrian peers. Frequently praised inaugurals include Washington's first, Jefferson's first, Lincoln's first and second, Franklin Roosevelt's first, and that of Kennedy. Some add Theodore Roosevelt's first, Wilson's first, and Franklin Roosevelt's second.[28] These inaugurals share certain characteristics: (1) they reinvigorate as well as rehearse traditional values; (2) they create memorable phrases that tell us who we are as a people and what the presidency is as an institution; (3) they involve us actively in redefining the nation as embodied in the principles guiding the incoming administration; and (4) they address timely questions timelessly, or, in the words of William Faulkner, their "griefs grieve on universal bones."[29]

Great inaugurals capture complex, situationally resonant ideas in memorable phrases. We recall Jefferson's "peace, commerce, and honest friendship with all nations, entangling alliances with none" (17), Lincoln's "With malice toward none, with charity for all, with firmness in the right as God gives us to see the right, let us strive on to finish the work we are in, to bind up the nation's wounds, to care for him who shall have borne the battle and for his widow and his orphan, to do all which may achieve and cherish a just and lasting peace among ourselves and with all nations" (126). So, too, we remember Franklin Roosevelt's "So, first of all, let me assert my firm belief that the only thing we have to fear is fear itself" (231), and Kennedy's "And so, my fellow Americans, ask not what your country can do for you: Ask what you can do for your country" (271). Such phrases illustrate a rhetorical genius in reinvigorating traditional values; in them, familiar ideas become fresh and take on new meaning.

Stylistically and structurally, great presidential inaugurals are suited to contemplation. Through the use of parallelism, for example, Kennedy revives our traditional commitment to defend freedom when he says, "we shall pay any price, bear any burden, meet any hardship, support any friend, oppose any foe, in order to assure the survival and success of liberty" (269). The memorable antithesis, "Let us never negotiate out of fear. But let us never fear to negotiate" (270), is a vivid restatement of our traditional relationship to foreign nations, a relationship based on independence and interdependence. Kennedy's more famous antithesis asks us to contemplate a redefinition of who we are as a people, a redefinition based on sacrifice. By use of assonance, Kennedy underscores the nuclear peril when he speaks of "the steady spread of the deadly atom" (270). By arresting our attention, such literary devices invite us to ponder these ideas, ideas less suited to contemplation when stated in more mundane terms.

Inaugurals enable us to consider who and what we are as a people; great inaugurals invite us to see ourselves in a new light, to constitute ourselves as a people in a new way. In 1913, for example, Wilson says: "We have been proud of our industrial achievement, but we have not hitherto stopped thoughtfully enough to count the human cost. . . . We have come now to the sober second thought" (200). In 1865, Lincoln compels us to consider God's view of the conflict between the North and the South when he says: "Both read the same Bible and pray to the same God, and each invokes His aid against the other. . . . The prayers of both could not be answered. That of neither has been answered fully. The Almighty has His own purposes" (125–26). In 1961, Kennedy speaks of "a call to bear the burden of a long twilight struggle, year in, and year out, . . ." (271) a call that suggests *gotterdammerung* and denies easy victory or inevitable triumph.[30]

In a special and significant sense, the great inaugurals are timeless. They articulate a perspective that transcends the situation that parented them, and for this reason, they are often cited in subsequent inaugurals. For instance, although Lincoln's first inaugural encompasses the situation of a nation poised on the brink of civil war, Lincoln's message speaks to all situations in which the rights of constituent units are seen to clash with the powers of a central body. Likewise, although Franklin Roosevelt's first inaugural assures us that we, as a people led by Roosevelt, can surmount this economic crisis, it also assures us that Americans can surmount all material problems. Although Kennedy's inaugural reflects the history of the cold war, it also expresses the resoluteness required to sustain a struggle against a menacing ideology. Finally, George Washington's inaugural not only speaks to the immediate crisis but articulates what Arthur Schlesinger calls "a great strand that binds them [the inaugurals] together."[31] Washington said: "The preservation of the sacred fire of liberty and the destiny of the republican model of government are justly considered, perhaps as *deeply,* as *finally* staked on the experiment intrusted to the hands of the American people" (4–5).

The great inaugurals not only "re-present" this fundamental idea, they re-enact the process by which the President and the people "form a more perfect union." In recreating this mutual covenant, great inaugurals both reconstitute the audience as "the people" and they constitute us as a people in some new way: as those entrusted with the success or failure of the democratic experiment (Washington I), as members of a perpetual Union (Lincoln I), as a people whose spiritual strength can overcome material difficulties (Franklin Roosevelt I), as a people willing to sacrifice for an ideal (Kennedy), as a people capable of counting the costs of industrial development (Wilson I), as members of an international community (Theodore Roosevelt, Wilson II), as limited by the purposes of the Almighty (Lincoln II), as a nation dedicated to caring for all its citizens (Franklin Roosevelt II), as a people able to transcend political differences (Washington I, Jefferson I). Accordingly, the great inaugurals dramatically illustrate the processes of change within a continuous tradition. In them, the resources of epideictic ritual are yoked to political renewal.

We have identified five major elements that constitute the presidential inaugural. Our analysis suggests the processes by which a distinctive subspecies of epideictic discourse comes into being. Its broadest parameters are set by the general characteristics of epideictic rhetoric. A specific kind of ceremony or occasion refines the general further. In this case, the presidential inaugural is part of a rite of passage—investiture—a rite which establishes a special relationship between speaker and audience. The demands of investiture require a mutual covenant, a rehearsal of fundamental political values, an enunciation of political principles, and the enactment of the presidential persona.

The conventions of this rhetorical type also emerge because the Presidents we elect know the tradition and tend to study past inaugurals before presenting their own. So, for example, in 1809 in the sixth inaugural address, Madison says: "Unwilling to depart from examples of the most revered authority, I avail myself of the occasion now presented to express the profound impression made on me by the call of my country" (25).[32] As a result, presidential inaugurals are frequently quoted, such as those of Washington, Jefferson, and Franklin Roosevelt. This process of rhetorical introversion also casts light on some remarkable coincidences. Harding and Carter, for example, quote the same verse from Micah. Franklin Roosevelt and Carter quote a former teacher, Franklin Roosevelt and Kennedy have a rendezvous with destiny, Reagan paraphrases Jefferson, Nixon paraphrases Kennedy, Kennedy echoes Lincoln, Polk rephrases Jackson, Reagan echoes Kennedy. In other words, presidents recognize, capitalize on, and are constrained by the inaugurals of their predecessors which, taken together, form a tradition.

Thus, presidential inaugurals are shaped by their epideictic character, by inauguration as a rite of investiture, and by the inaugural tradition. However, presidential inaugurals vary, but simply saying that they vary is not enough. What makes the presidential inaugural a genre is that the variation is of a certain sort. Circumstances vary, of course, as do the personalities of the presidents, but the variation among inaugurals is predictable.

Inaugural addresses vary substantially because presidents choose to rehearse those aspects of our tradition which are consistent with the party or political philosophy they represent. Such selective emphasis is illustrated in Franklin Roosevelt's second inaugural, in which he says: "Instinctively we recognize a deeper need—the need to find through government the instrument of our united purpose to solve for the individual the everrising problems of a complex civilization. . . . In this we Americans were discovering no wholly new truth; we were writing a new chapter in our book of self-government. . . . The essential democracy of our Nation and the safety of our people depend not upon the absence of power, but upon lodging it with those whom the people can change or continue at stated intervals through an honest and free system of elections. . . . we have made the exercise of all power more democratic; for we have begun to bring private autocratic powers into their proper subordination to the people's government . . ." (237–38). Later, he adds: "Today we reconsecrate our country to long-cherished ideals in a suddenly changed civilization" (240). Similarly, in 1981, Ronald Reagan chose to emphasize facets of the system in order to affirm values consistent with his conservative political philosophy. He said: "Our government has no power except that granted it by the people. It is time to check and reverse the growth of government which shows signs of having grown beyond the consent of the governed."[33]

A major variation occurs in inaugurals delivered by incumbent Presidents. Because a covenant already exists between a re-elected President and "the people," the need to reconstitute the community is less urgent. Because the country is familiar with a sitting President's political philosophy, this requirement is also muted. Re-elected presidents tend to recommit themselves to principles articulated in their prior inaugurals or to highlight only those principles relevant to the agenda for the coming term. In this respect, subsequent inaugurals by the same President tend to be extensions, not replications, of earlier inaugurals.

The inaugural addresses themselves articulate the reason for this generic variation. For instance, although he is a President in the midst of the most serious of crises, Lincoln says: "At this second appearing to take the oath of the Presidential office there is less occasion for an extended address than there was at the first. Then a statement somewhat in detail of the course to be pursued seemed fitting and proper. Now, at the expiration of four years, during which public declarations have been constantly called forth on every point and phase of the great contest which still absorbs the attention and engrosses the energies of the nation, little that is new could be presented" (125).[34] Some presidents use the occasion of a subsequent inaugural to review the trials and successes of their earlier terms. In so doing, they rehearse the immediate past, a move rarely made in first inaugurals. When subsequent inaugurals develop specific policies, these are usually described as continuations of policies initiated in the previous term, continuations presumably endorsed by the President's re-election.

The special conditions faced by some Presidents cause some subsequent inaugurals to resemble first inaugurals. For example, in 1917 Wilson says: "This is not the time for retrospect. It is time rather to speak our thoughts and purposes concerning the present and the immediate future" (203). In the face of the events of World War I, he says: "We are provincials no longer. The tragic events of the thirty months of vital turmoil through which we have just passed have made us citizens of the world. There can be no turning back. Our own fortunes as a nation are involved whether we would have it so or not" (204). Circumstances constrain Wilson to constitute "the people" in a new way, as citizens of the world. Similarly, circumstances affect Franklin Roosevelt's choices in 1941. He says: "In this day the task of the people is to save the Nation and its institutions from disruptions from without" (243), a sharp divergence from the principles emphasized in 1933 and 1937.

The variability in inaugural addresses is evidence of an identifiable cluster of elements that fuse to form the essential inaugural act. Each apparent variation is an emphasis on or a development of one or more of the key elements we have described. As noted, Washington's second underscores the role of the audience as witnesses and the address as an extension of the oath of office. Jefferson's first is a call to unity through the enunciation of political principles; Lincoln's first is a dramatic appeal to the audience to join the mutual covenant between the President and the people; Lincoln's second is an exploration of what it means to say that this nation is "under God"; Theodore Roosevelt explores the meaning of our "sacred trust" as it applies to a people with an international role; Franklin Roosevelt's first explores the nature of executive leadership and the limits of executive power whereas his second constitutes the audience as a caring people; Wilson's first explores the meaning of our industrial development. Finally, Kennedy's address exploits the possibilities of the noble, dignified, literary language characteristic of the epideictic to such an extent that his address is sometimes attacked for stylistic excess.[35]

The presidential inaugural, then, must reconstitute "the people" as an audience which can witness the rite of investiture. The inaugural must rehearse communal values from the past, set forth the political principles that will guide the new administration, and demonstrate that the President can enact the presidential persona appropriately. Finally, the inaugural is an epideictic ritual which is formal, unifying, abstract, and eloquent, and at the core of this ritual lies epideictic timelessness—the fusion of the past and future of the nation in an eternal present in which we reaffirm what Franklin Roosevelt called "our covenant with ourselves" (247), that covenant between the executive and the nation that is the essence of democratic government.

Notes

1. Arthur Schlesinger, Jr., "Introduction," *The Chief Executive: Inaugural Addresses of the Presidents of the United States from George Washington to Lyndon B. Johnson* (New York: Crown Publishers, Inc., 1965), p. vi.
2. Schlesinger, *op. cit.*, p. vii.
3. We are concerned here exclusively with addresses delivered every four years following presidential elections. For an analysis of speeches by ascendant vice presidents, see Kathleen Hall Jamieson and Karlyn Kohrs Campbell, "Rhetorical Hybrids: Fusions of Generic Elements," *Quarterly Journal of Speech,* 68 (May 1982), pp. 146–57.
4. Aristotle, *Rhetoric* trans. W. Rhys Roberts (New York: The Modern Library, 1954), 1358b.12. Subsequent citations are in parenthesis in the text.
5. John W. O'Malley, *Praise and Blame in Renaissance Rome: Rhetoric, Doctrine, and Reform in the Sacred Orators of the Papal Court, c. 1450–1521* (Durham, N.C.: Duke University Press, 1979), p. 40.
6. O'Malley, p. 63.
7. Harry Caplan, "Introduction," *Rhetorica ad Herennium* (Cambridge: Harvard University Press, 1954), p. 173, cited in O'Malley, p. 39.
8. James L. Hoban, Jr., "Rhetorical Rituals of Rebirth," *Quarterly Journal of Speech,* 66 (October 1980), pp. 282–83.
9. According to historian John McCollister in his book *So Help Me God* (Bloomington, MN: Landmark Books, Inc., 1982), George Washington ad libbed the additional words "so help me God" in taking the oath of office although these words are not part of the oath specified in the Constitution, an addition which has become part of the convention of the ceremony. Cited by Francis X. Clines, "Presidents and Churchgoing, a Sensitive Subject," *New York Times,* 23 March 1982, p. 12Y.
10. The idea of a rhetorical genre as a constellation of elements governed by a dynamic principle is developed in Karlyn Kohrs Campbell and Kathleen Hall Jamieson, "Form and Genre in Rhetorical Criticism: An Introduction," in *Form and Genre: Shaping Rhetorical Action* ed. Karlyn Kohrs Campbell and Kathleen Hall Jamieson (Falls Church, Va.: Speech Communication Association, 1978), pp. 9–32.
11. Mircea Eliade, *Patterns in Comparative Religion,* trans. Rosemary Sheed (Cleveland: World, 1970), p. 392, cited in David Cole, *The Theatrical Event: A Mythos, A Vocabulary, A Perspective* (Middletown, Conn.: Wesleyan University Press, 1975), p. 8.
12. Davis Newton Lott, *The Presidents Speak: The Inaugural Addresses of the American Presidents from Washington to Nixon,* rev. ed. (New York: Holt, Rinehart and Winston, 1969), p. 243. Subsequent citations from inaugurals delivered through 1969 are found in parenthesis in the text.
13. See, for example, Buchanan's 1857 inaugural which followed an election held during the conflict between pro- and anti-slavery forces in "Bloody Kansas" (111); Hayes's

inaugural of 1877 (140–41); Cleveland's inaugural of 1885 (151); Benjamin Harrison's address in 1889 (162); Cleveland's speech in 1893 (168); and Nixon's address in 1969 (280), in addition to those cited in the text.

14. See, for instance, Lincoln's first (117), McKinley's first (171), and many others.

15. Van Buren speaks of "an avowal of the principles that will guide me . . ." (65); Buchanan repeats the oath at the beginning of his address (111); Cleveland refers to his speech as a supplement to the oath of office (151); Eisenhower says: "We are called as a people to give testimony in the sight of the world to our faith that the future shall belong to the free" (257); Lyndon Johnson says: "the oath I have taken before you and before God is not mine alone, but ours together" (275).

    For discussion of another rhetorical covenant pertinent to presidential discourse, see Roderick P. Hart, *The Political Pulpit* (West Lafayette, IN: Purdue University Press, 1977), pp. 43–65.

16. For a discussion of this dimension of epideictic rhetoric, see Chaim Perelman and L. Olbrechts-Tyteca, *The New Rhetoric: A Treatise on Argumentation,* trans. John Wilkinson and Purcell Weaver (Notre Dame: University of Notre Dame Press, 1969), pp. 49–51.

17. Garfield makes a moving plea which echoes that in Lincoln's first inaugural in 1881 when he says: "My countrymen, we do not now differ in our judgment concerning the controversies of past generations, and fifty years hence our children will not be divided in their opinion concerning our controversies. They will surely bless their fathers and their fathers' God that the Union was preserved, that slavery was overthrown, and that both races were made equal before the law. We may hasten or we may retard, but we can not prevent, the final reconciliation. Is it not possible for us now to make a truce with time by anticipating and accepting its inevitable verdict?" (146).

    In a footnote to his analysis of Nixon's first inaugural, Robert L. Scott calls attention to Nixon's excessive use of the pronoun "I." Such personal references, discussed below, not only violate the presidential persona that the speaker should assume, as Scott notes, they also tend to preclude the joint action through which the President and the people covenant together. See "Rhetoric That Postures: An Intrinsic Reading of Richard M. Nixon's Inaugural Address," *Western Speech,* 34 (Winter 1970), p. 47.

18. The extent to which the founders, including George Washington, were identified with pro-slavery positions is illustrated by John C. Calhoun's speech in the Senate on March 4, 1850 in which he said: "Nor can the Union be saved by invoking the name of the illustrious Southerner whose mortal remains repose on the western bank of the Potomac. He was one of us—a slaveholder and a planter. We have studied his history, and find nothing in it to justify submission to wrong." Cited in *American Public Addresses,* 1740–1952 ed. A. Craig Baird (New York: McGraw-Hill Book Company, Inc., 1956), p. 83.

19. Ronald Reagan, "Inaugural Address," *Vital Speeches of the Day,* 47 (15 February 1981), pp. 258–59.

20. Kathleen Hall Jamieson, *Critical Anthology of Public Speeches* (Chicago: Science Research Associates, 1978), pp. 28–30.

21. Marcus Cunliffe, *American Presidents and the Presidency* (New York: American Heritage Press, 1968), pp. 149, 152, 154–55, 158, 163, 172.

22. Carter's statement calls attention to the risks involved in confessing limitations, as this remark can be taken as evidence of an inability to lead forcefully.

23. In 1877, Rutherford Hayes expresses similar sentiments as he begins his address: "We have assembled to repeat the public ceremonial, begun by Washington, observed by all my predecessors, and now a time-honored custom, which marks the commencement of a new term of the Presidential office" (137).

24. See material from Scott cited in note 17 above.

25. A computer analysis of 380 presidential speeches by Roderick P. Hart generated an 8.01 level of self-reference (all first-person pronouns are counted). By contrast, the nine inaugurals in this sample generate a 1.00 level of self-reference. See "Persuasion and the Presidency," a paper presented at the Fourth Annual Conference on Discourse Analysis, Temple University, March 1983. A further refinement of self-referencing is made by Dan Hahn who notes that in 1977 Carter used "we" forty-three times, "our" thirty-six times, but "I" only six times in his inaugural. See "The Power of Rhetorical Form," a paper presented in the Fourth Annual Conference in Discourse Analysis, Temple University, March 1983, p. 6.

26. Jimmy Carter, "Inaugural Address," *Public Papers of the Presidents of the United States,* Jimmy Carter, 1977, Book I (Washington, D.C.: U.S. Government Printing Office, 1977), p. 1.

27. The Rev. George St. John, headmaster of Choate, the prep school in Wallingford, Conn., attended by John Kennedy, used to say to his students, "Ask not what your school can do for you; ask what you can do for your school." ("Walter Scott's Personality Parade," *Parade,* 15 December 1968, p. 2.)

28. Schlesinger, p. vii.

29. William Faulkner, "Nobel Prize Speech," *Famous American Speeches* ed. Stewart H. Benedict (New York: Dell, 1967), p. 223.

30. A number of other inaugurals include admonitions. See, for example, the inaugurals of Eisenhower in 1957 (264), Truman (252), and Harding (211).

31. Schlesinger, p. vii.

32. Eight years later in 1817, Monroe says: "In commencing the duties of the chief executive office it has been the practice of the distinguished men who have gone before me to explain the principles which would govern them in their respective Administrations. In following their venerated example my attention is naturally drawn to the great causes which have contributed in a principle degree to produce the present happy condition of the United States" (33).

33. Reagan, p. 259.

34. In 1805, Jefferson reports that his conscience tells him he has lived up to the principles he espoused four years earlier (19). In 1821, Monroe says: "If the person thus elected has served the preceding term, an opportunity is afforded him to review its principal occurrences and to give the explanation respecting them as in this judgment may be useful to his constituents" (41).

35. For example, Garry Wills writes: "The famous antitheses and alliterations of John Kennedy's rhetoric sound tinny now." (*The Kennedy Imprisonment: A Meditation on Power* [New York: Pocket Books, 1982], p. 312.

   More detailed treatments of the style of John Kennedy's inaugural include Edward P. J. Corbett, "Analysis of the Style of John F. Kennedy's Inaugural Address," *Classical Rhetoric for the Modern Student,* 2nd ed. (New York: Oxford University Press, 1971), pp. 554–65, and Sam Meyer, "The John F. Kennedy Inauguration Speech: Function and Importance of Its 'Address System,' " *Rhetoric Society Quarterly,* 12 (Fall 1982), pp. 239–50.

Defensive Tactics in Presidential Rhetoric: Contemporary *Topoi*

Dan F. Hahn and J. Justin Gustainis

Theodore Windt observed that "genre studies in presidential rhetoric remain in an infant state,"[1] and a survey of the relevant literature in speech communication supports his contention. Monographs in the field examining types of presidential speaking have been devoted to messages to Congress,[2] justifications of war,[3] crisis speeches,[4] and state of the union and inaugural addresses.[5]

One aspect of presidential rhetoric which has received relatively little consideration is the speech of self-defense, or apologia. Although studies of self-defense rhetoric date back to 1956,[6] the first extensive theoretical consideration of the form was provided by Ware and Linkugel in 1973.[7] Since then, the notion of apologia as a legitimate rhetoric genre has come to be accepted.[8] However, the study of the apology has seen only occasional application in presidential rhetoric.[9] In this essay we attempt to add to the development of typology of the tactics of presidential apologia, focusing upon contemporary presidents and those tactics which seem to support major presidential myths.

Earlier scholarship identified the apology as a speech wherein the speaker defended his or her character. Butler contended that apologies by President Harry Truman, then-Senator Richard Nixon and Senator Edward Kennedy all concerned "matters of a highly personal nature: their families, their moral codes, their character."[10] Ware and Linkugel conceived of the apology as a response to "an attack upon a person's character. . . ."[11] Kruse defined the apology as "public discourse produced whenever a prominent person attempts to repair his character if it has been directly or indirectly damaged. . . ."[12] This belief that the apology was a speech employed exclusively in defense of character went substantially unchallenged until Ryan argued that apology properly consists of two types of speeches: those defending character and those defending policy.[13] Ryan supported his claim by examining the ancient Greek conception of apology, which defined the term broadly, and by providing several examples of self-defense speeches which focused on policy.[14]

Mr. Hahn is Professor of Communication Arts and Sciences at Queens College.
Mr. Gustainis is Associate Professor of Communication at State University of New York—Plattsburgh.
This essay is published by permission of the authors.

We share Ryan's belief that the notion of the apology should include both self-defense and policy defense. In this essay, we attempt to identify major tactics of presidential apologia, utilizing personal and policy examples drawn primarily from contemporary speeches by Presidents Kennedy, Johnson, Nixon, Ford, Carter and Reagan. Once the tactics have been identified to the satisfaction of the profession, the next task will be the examination of apologetic strategy, *i.e.,* which tactics can/should be used in which crisis situations. While we make some few suggestions of tactic-strategy relations, those should be read as highly tentative. A full-blown examination of strategy needs to await the completion of the identification of tactics.

The presidency and the incumbent are so intermingled in the minds of many (possibly including the incumbent) that it is difficult to separate them.[15] Thus, *ipso facto,* any personal or policy attack upon the president can be perceived as an attack upon the office, and *vice versa.* Of the two, the presidency is obviously the more potent symbol. Therefore, it should not be surprising to discover that defensive presidential rhetoric relies heavily upon the myths (or convenient fictions) which bolster the prestige of the office. This means that presidential defenses are different from the defenses available to the rest of us; no one else can respond, "I did it because my role as Commander-in-Chief demanded it."

Presidential Myths

Joseph Campbell has contended that all people require "life-supporting illusions,"[16] and it is in that spirit and sense that we discuss presidential myths. The major function of myth is to define "the rights and privileges of groups and persons to particular positions of social power. . . ."[17] Political myths sanctify the establishment by identifying authority and legitimizing the use of power. In short, political myths serve "to validate the existing order, to show that it is right for the rulers to rule and for the governed to be governed."[18] Since political myths are concerned with power, it is no surprise that our most powerful office, the presidency, has become "a breeding ground of indestructible myth."[19]

From the myriad of available presidential myths, three are more important rhetorically because presidents spend more time affirming them: (1) all problems are caused by outgroups, (2) our leaders are benevolent heroes who will lead us out of danger, and (3) the function of the citizen is to sacrifice and work hard to do the bidding of the leader.[20] It will be noted that each of these myths supports the status quo, strengthening the power of the incumbent president (the major "identifier" of problems, "proposer" of solutions, and only representative of all the people).

Defensive rhetoric seems to heighten the importance of these myths because generally it is aimed at their maintenance. But before examining defensive presidential rhetoric, it is necessary to delineate more fully the nature of the myths.

Outgroups

All problems are caused by outgroups—Commies, outside agitators, bums, nervous Nellies, effete snobs, or merely the ubiquitous "they." Our problems are never caused by us. If we deploy troops abroad (Lebanon, for example) and they are fired upon, we never assume we might have provoked the violent reaction. Some "enemy" is blamed for the fighting. Domestically, racial problems are blamed on outside agitators, inflation upon greedy union leaders, and overweening dissent upon querulous critics in the press.

This comfortable myth allows leaders to transform the substantive question, "What should be done?," into the accusative, "Who caused the problem?" Concomitantly, it allows them to "solve" the problem by affixing blame rather than proposing solutions. In contemporary parlance, the outgroup myth allows the president to solve the politics of the problem while ignoring the problem.

The Hero

The first myth blends in well with the second, that our leaders are benevolent heroes who will lead us out of the danger posed by the outgroup. Thomas Cronin has documented the support for this myth, as expressed in political science texts written since F. D. R. expanded the power of the presidency: "The President is the most strategic policy maker in the government. His policy role is paramount in military and foreign affairs." "He reigns but he also rules; he symbolizes the people but he also runs their government." "He is . . . a kind of magnificent lion who can roam widely and do great deeds."[21]

Two dimensions of the "benevolent hero" aspect of the presidential myth are apparent: the Omnipotent dimension and the Moralistic-Benevolent dimension.[22] The Omnipotent dimension itself divides along two interacting lines. First, only the president is, or can be, the genuine architect of the United States public policy, and, by attacking problems frontally and aggressively, can be the engine of change to move this nation forward. (It should be noted here that actions the president initiates need not be successful; they just must be taken. Since the results of action are difficult to measure, practically any action is presumed to have been right.) Second, the president is the strategic catalyst in the American political system and the central figure in the international system. This second line expresses the importance of the president's centrality to the cosmos. As such, it provides justification for line one of the

Omnipotent dimension. That is, if the myth envisions the world revolving around the president, it follows that only the incumbent can shape its destiny and engineer its progress.

The Moralistic-Benevolent dimension develops similarly along two lines. First, the president must be the nation's personal and moral leader; by symbolizing the past and future greatness of America and radiating inspirational confidence, a president can pull the nation together while directing us toward the fulfillment of the American dream. Second, if only the right person is placed in the White House, all will be well; and, somehow, whoever is in the White House *is* the right person. This final self-reflexive line binds the others together, providing a self-fulfilling prophecy for the myth.[23]

The Citizens' Function

Finally, given acceptance of the notions of threat by outsiders and salvation by a benevolent hero, the third myth is obvious: the function of the citizen is to sacrifice and work hard to do the bidding of the leader. After all, a leader can only lead if there are followers following. The folklore supporting this myth is voluminous—"too many cooks spoil the broth," "too many chiefs, not enough Indians," etc.

Leaders reinforce the myth of the sacrificing followers with their rhetoric. Churchill offered Great Britain "blood, toil, sweat, and tears," and Kennedy reminded Americans to "ask not what your country can do for you; ask what you can do for your country." Indeed, one of the perceived weaknesses in Richard Nixon's first Inaugural address was "his reluctance to ask for sacrifice or new government programs to meet our mounting crisis. His appeal was to those who want to occupy that comfortable moral middle ground between ease and sacrifice."[24]

Defending via the Outgroup Myth

At least four interrelated tactics stem from the Outgroup Myth in defensive presidential rhetoric: (1) outgroup labeling, (2) strawman, (3) denial of means, and (4) counterattack. Before we discuss these tactics, two preliminary points should be made. First, use of the myths functions not only to defend the president but also to revalidate the myths. In rhetoric as elsewhere, nothing succeeds like success. Second, each use contains within it the seeds of its own destruction of its credibility, sometimes through internal conflict, but most often through conflict with one of the other two myths.

Tactic of Outgroup Labeling

The tactic of outgroup labeling is, at base, the deceptively simple tactic of naming—simple because the form seems to argue that naming is pure, utilitarian identification, unrelated to the persuasive functions of rhetoric; deceptive because, as Burke asserts, "the mere act of naming an object or situation decrees that it be singled out as such-and-such rather than as something-other."[25] Stylistically, naming invites assent rather than contemplation, providing the user with a seemingly innocuous method of locating the opposition outside the audience's latitude of acceptance.

In John F. Kennedy's Yale University Commencement Address in 1962, a defense of his proposed tax cut, he used outgroup labeling to distinguish his "realistic" position from his opponent's "mythic" one.[26] In the characterizing passages in the speech, he labeled his opponents positions as "truisms," "stereotypes," "stale phrases," "prefabricated . . . interpretations," "illusion," "platitude," "noise," "irrelevant," "misleading," "traditional labels," "worn-out slogans," "political," and "sterile acrimony." His own positions, by contrast, he labeled "new," "essential confrontations with reality," "truth," "careful," "dispassionate," "ways to separate false problems from real ones," "honest assessment," "sophisticated," "sensible," "clearheaded," "technical," and "sober." The unnamed opponents (by implication, anyone who opposed the Kennedy position) were clearly meant to be perceived as outside the acceptable limits of political dialogue, thus "outsiders" because of their policy stances rather than who they were.

F. Michael Smith has traced the evolution of President Johnson's Administration's labeling of North Vietnam as the "outsider" in the Vietnamese conflict. He notes that prior to U.S. escalation of the war in February of 1965 the Administration tended to describe the war as an "insurgency" or "insurrection." However, after the escalation, "No longer was North Vietnam an aggressor because she aided and directed an 'insurrection' in the South, rather North Vietnam officially metamorphasized into the major, and ultimately the only, cause of the fighting in Vietnam."[27] The shift eventually became so total that the Administration came to contend that if it were not for the North there would be no conflict in the South—i.e., the North was converted into an "outsider" solely responsible for the problem. When an "opponent" is transformed into THE ENEMY, the status of "outsider" is assured; henceforth, the outsider can be depicted as Johnson depicted the North Vietnamese—cunning, indiscriminate, excessive, and without human compassion.[28]

Nixon's use of naming as a strategy of defense is legion. Those who opposed his Vietnam war policy were accused of supplying aid and comfort to the enemy (thus implicitly identified as traitors); those responsible for campus disruptions were labeled bums; when Nixon was blamed for setting the tone which led to Watergate, he identified the lawlessness of anti-war dissenters as the responsible milieu-producing agency.[29]

Leaving aside President Ford's use of the Outsider myth in the Mayaguez affair, amply documented elsewhere,[30] his most interesting use of this tactic came in his response to the New York City budget crisis in 1975. It is interesting because the tactic usually isolates outsiders so that the government can act against them; in this case, Ford identified the causal agent as outsiders in order to justify governmental inaction.

Of course, Ford did not use the term "outsider" (almost no President does). Rather, he argued that the predicament of New York was "unique," i.e., outside the mainstream of urban management. Yet, that assessment is demonstrably wrong, and there are indications that he knew it was wrong. According to President Ford, "the New York City record of bad financial management is unique among municipalities throughout the United States."[31] But other passages from the same speech demonstrate that he recognized his own labeling error. For example, he also said, "the time has come for all Americans to consider how the problems of New York and the hard decisions they demand foreshadow and focus upon potential problems for all government—Federal, State and local—problems which demand equally hard decisions for them." Later, in arguing against the idea of a federal guarantee against default, he said, "Such a step would set a terrible precedent for the rest of the Nation. It would promise immediate rewards and eventual rescue to every other city that follows the tragic example of our largest city." Finally, he clearly said that others were imperiled when he claimed, "Other cities, other states as well as the Federal Government are not immune to the insidious disease from which New York is suffering."

It is true, of course, that our assessment that "unique" equals "outsider" in this case could be challenged. But it must be remembered that the speech was given in New York City and that those the President were blaming were among the immediate audience. The next day, when the President flew to California for a speaking tour, he was less inhibited. "He campaigned up and down California against the wastrels in New York, the shiftless everywhere waxing fat on the Federal food stamp program. He went back to 1906 to praise San Francisco for its self-reliance in rebuilding after the earthquake—wrongly, since San Francisco got Federal aid."[32] Considering all of this, Russell Baker concluded that Ford's New York crisis speech was "Not one of the Presidency's nobler days" and accused Ford of "demagoguery by omission."[33] We think Baker was wrong; if there was demagoguery here it was not by omission, but via the Outgroup Myth.

Of all recent presidents, Jimmy Carter seemed to utilize the Outsider Myth the least. However, there is a sense in which his whole 1976 campaign was based on this approach. That is, in 1976, running as an "outsider," he attempted to redefine "insider" and "outsider," so that those "inside" the government could be seen as "outside" the wishes, desires, and experiences of the voters. To distance himself from the capitol he emphasized that he had not been a part of the group in Washington that had created the mess; in fact, he wasn't even a lawyer. Further distancing was created by dressing casually, carrying his own suitcase, sometimes staying in the homes of supporters rather than in hotels and, in general, picturing himself as not only non-Washington but anti-Washington. "The people" were the true insiders and Washingtonians were "outsiders."

President Reagan's most obvious use of the Outsider Myth has been in his defense of the invasion of Grenada. The problems on that island were, he said, caused by Cuba and Russia. He claimed the captured weapons and communications equipment "makes it clear a Cuban occupation of the island had been planned" and that "Moscow assisted and encouraged the violence" there.[34] In order to keep the United States from being depicted as the outsiders, President Reagan soon stopped using his initial term for the action, "invasion," and substituted for it the term, "rescue mission," then chided the press when they continued to call it an invasion.[35] It is instructive to note that the change in appellation contradicted the change in justification. That is, the first Reagan pronouncement called the action an invasion and gave as the reason the rescue of American students; the subsequent Reagan position called it a "rescue mission" but gave as the reason the need to "restore democracy."[36] James Reston contends that Reagan's use of the Outsider Myth in Grenada is typical of Reagan: "This has been precisely Mr. Reagan's theme ever since he came to the White House and long before: that all the foreign problems of this country are the result of the wicked Russians and all its domestic problems the fault of the wicked Democrats."[37]

Thus, we have seen that every president from Kennedy through Reagan has utilized the Outsider Myth in defense situations. Fortunately for presidents, however, the entirety of presidential defense does not devolve upon the president. Surrogates in the government, sympathetic columnists, and common citizens are also participants, and they often can take stances the president either can not (for fear of looking foolish) or will not (for fear of endangering other programs). In fact, the tactic of outgroup labeling is best pursued by surrogates because it is a strategy which suggests that we should pity the president because of the unjustness of the accusation, yet pity does not coexist well with the Omnipotent Dimension of myth two, i.e., it is difficult to feel pity for one who is supposed to be omnipotent.

Surrogates were especially active in the Watergate case. Southern strategy coordinator Harry Dent identified *The Washington Post, The New York Times* and *Time Magazine* as publications which were "out to get the President and are making a trial out of the whole affair."[38] Presidential Special Consultant, Pat Buchanan, characterized as unpatriotic those who dared attack the president: "There now appears no damage to United States interests that is unacceptable and no political principle they will not rise readily above—to sink their teeth in the President of the United States."[39] Referring to the Ervin Committee, Senator Curtis of Nebraska charged, " 'publicity-seeking politicians' were out to 'get Nixon' in their pursuit of the Watergate scandal."[40] And New York's Senator Buckley, perhaps overly impressed by the avian terminology of the Vietnam conflict, averred, "It appears that the vultures are circling—hoping against hope to find the corpse of the Presidency."[41] It is interesting to note that, with the exception of Senator Curtis, the surrogates identified the target of the "outsiders" as "the president" or "the presidency," rather than as Richard Nixon.

In foreign policy defenses, surrogates continue to utilize the Domino Theory, although Administration spokespersons (with the exception of President Reagan) have tended to avoid that explanation since Vietnam. Thus, in the Grenada defense, Senator Rudy Boschwitz of Minnesota said, "if Grenada had fallen to Cuba, other Caribbean nations would have followed."[42] And a citizen, Sheldon Ritter, suggested we should follow up on Grenada with a little domino-pushing of our own:

> Bravo to President Reagan for taking prompt action against the Communists in Grenada! If President Eisenhower had done the same in Cuba when Castro expropriated American property, we would have been spared 20 years of trouble.
>
> Now we should stop being coy about our efforts to bring democracy back to Nicaragua and mount a full-scale effort to oust the Sandinistas and the Cubans from that beleaguered country. Castro will learn soon enough that the Soviets are not going to fight a nuclear war to save him or his troops in Central America, and the next step would be to restore democracy in Cuba itself.[43]

In foreign affairs, "outsiders" always are clearly "outsiders." In domestic relations, it is less clear. In the Watergate case, the outsiders were not only horrible outgroups but misleading friends. So, in addition to "I was attacked by those who hate me," a variant of outgroup labeling was adopted: "I was misled by those I trusted." Inherently, misleading people are outsiders even if, or perhaps especially when, they are former friends. Nixon himself enunciated the "I was misled" line: "Because of these continuing reassurances, because I believed the reports I was getting, because I had faith in the persons from whom I was getting them, I discounted the stories in the press that appeared to implicate members of my Administration. . . ."[44] For any number of reasons, this appears to be an unusually weak tactic. For one thing, in an hierarchical arrangement a superior is responsible for the activities of subordinates even if they "betray" the trust. As Vic Gold, Vice President Agnew's press agent, commented: "the idea that men of great power can be absolved of accountability for the actions of those to whom they delegate that power is a banality. . . ."[45]

Another weakness of this tactic is the obvious conflict between it and the Omnipotent Dimension of myth two, especially the often-utilized omnipotency contention that the president knows all. Writer Isaac Asimov noted this conflict in his reaction to the "I was misled" excuse:

> Those who clamored for peace in Vietnam over the past four years were constantly told that only the President had all the facts; that they should trust the President; that if they knew what the President knew they would keep quiet. Now President Nixon has assured the whole nation on television that he knew nothing about the Watergate scandal; that no one told him anything; that he was completely ignorant of it all. It would seem then that we have a President who knows everything, or knows nothing, according to how it suits his political interests.[46]

While the "misled" tactic does appear weak in the Watergate case, it is not clear whether it is inherently weak or if Nixon's "softness" toward former allies such as Haldeman and Erlichman unduly weakened the tactic.

The Strawman Tactic

The identification of outgroups blends subtly into the Strawman tactic, which is part defense, part counter-attack.

Bums, vultures and traitors obviously are undesirable types, but it often is the case that critics are not so clearly of the criminal typology. So the first step of the Strawman strategy is to redefine critics as enemies. President Johnson, in a curious, and curiously unattacked, perversion of democratic theory, established the standard for contemporary redefinition. In his view, democratic discussion passed the realm of legitimacy once the president had made his decision. From this standpoint, those who prior to the decision were engaging in the free exchange of debate became, after the decision, disloyal. The debate was over; no longer were they participating in a reaffirmation of the myth of democratic discussion; they now became attackers, "outsiders." Johnson said, "As our commitment in Vietnam required more men and more equipment, some voices were *raised* in opposition."[47] The raising of voices implies shouting, not rational debating. The President continued, "The administration was urged to disengage, to find an excuse to *abandon* the effort."[48] The peace advocates were thus depicted as turncoats, suggesting America abandon her commitments. Placing critics into the "outgroup" category makes it easier for the president to attack their motives rather than their arguments. The tactic is a typical *argumentum ad hominem* defense: debunk the attacker and you need not deal with the argument.

Surrogates may also be used to advance this strategy. In October, 1967, Senator Everett Dirkson was persuaded by Johnson to defend the president's Vietnam policies on the Senate floor and in the process to castigate Johnson's critics. He accused some of his fellow Senators of attacking the president directly and of endangering the American military personnel fighting in Vietnam.[49]

But if, for whatever reason, the redefining of critics as enemies is impossible or insufficient, the second portion of the Strawman tactic can be called into play: redefining their positions as evil. Johnson's defense of the Vietnam war included this ploy. In his speech of March 15, 1966, he created eight "questions" supposedly raised by opponents. The questions, however, did not reflect the real questions his critics were asking; he redefined his attackers' positions and criticisms.[50]

President Nixon was even more sophisticated in his use of redefinition, for he radicalized his opposition into two extremes, leaving the middle of the road, the Golden Mean, for himself.

> Nixon first identifies three or four paths which his thorough preparation and private sources demonstrated were open to him. He then negates all but the last, indicating as he does that these unacceptable, dread paths were the alternatives suggested by "Them," the amorphous enemy, his critics. Nixon negates, first, by the use of a "Straw Man," distorting his critics' position beyond the latitude of acceptance for the Nation's majority, and, second, by predicting the terrible consequences that would accrue from accepting those alternatives. His critics' position radicalized and his crystal ball having revealed the dread effects of those alternatives, Nixon then concludes that the path he has chosen is the right path because it is the only viable one available. His action is vindicated.[51]

Finally, the Strawman tactic can be used as a follow-up to the "I was misled" strategy through the simple expedient of sacrificing personnel, which is a form of rhetorical naming. Former associates are labeled "enemies" and then sacrificed ingloriously (as Nixon blandly put it, "The counsel to the President, John Dean, has also resigned.")[52] Nixon also sacrificed Haldeman and Ehrlichman, but not as traitors; he sacrificed them gallantly and grandly, like two great, devoted servants, "whose zeal exceeded their judgment and who may have done wrong in a cause they deeply believed to be right."[53] He could not call them traitors; they had been too close to him.

This tactic normally is very beneficial to the President.

> Presidents in trouble always score big with voters by firing men around them. This is because Americans believe Presidents are such good and sagacious men that if they get into trouble it can only be because bad men around them let them down or sold them out. Firing these men satisfies public yearning and pleases newspaper editors who become grateful for lovable old easy headlines like "President Cleans House."[54]

But Nixon's housecleaning did not achieve the desired result; the Watergate scandal dragged on. There are several possible explanations for this. One is that the firings were too few, too late, too unindignantly and grudgingly enacted. A second explanation is the some firings were too "soft" and did not identify villainy. Nixon's lack of vindictiveness against those sacrificed implied his complicity with them. It was observed at the time that Nixon "cannot denounce those former Cabinet members and White House aides because one or more of them may be able to corroborate part or all of the staggering indictment leveled against him. . . ."[55] He sacrificed them under political pressure rather than in moral indignation. It was "as if he had told us, back in 1952, that his funds were all in good order, but, to appease his critics and get on with the nation's business, he had sent Checkers off to be chloroformed."[56]

The Denial of Means Tactic

This third tactic in support of the outgroup myth is not completely rhetorical, but it has rhetorical manifestations and *is* entirely defensive. By denying the means of attack to one's enemies, one may silence criticism. Denial of means identifies the "outgroup" and allows the user to demonstrate the problem is being handled. The denial of parade permits to would-be demonstrators is a common non-Presidential example.

President Nixon utilized this tactic persistently. From the double-entry hiding of the U.S. bombing in Cambodia to the pronouncements on executive privilege in the Watergate case; from the tying of the special prosecutor's hands (and firing the first one) to the speeches which couched denial of culpability in generalities and ignored the details, Nixon seemed to operate on the principle that what they don't know can't hurt you. Of course, Nixon was unable to deny to his critics all the means of attack (he could not control or stop TV coverage of the Ervin hearings), and his resignation undoubtedly was hastened by that lack of control.

A more successful example of the denial of means tactic was in Reagan's refusal to allow the media to accompany the troops invading Grenada. As a result, the media, and the American people, were totally dependent upon the government for news concerning this military endeavor. But the public, perhaps because of the success of the mission, was not upset by this thwarting of freedom of the press. When NBC broadcast a criticism of the exclusion, their mail ran 10–1 against their position.[57]

Counterattack

While all of the foregoing are, in a sense, forms of counterattack, they do not exhaust the available tactics in the counterattack strategy.

One such tactic attempts to overcome the appearance of culpability by implying, "I didn't do it, but here's why it looks like I did." While there are numerous possibilities for developing this tactic, the most common seem to be "*they* are out to get me" and "journalistic misinterpretation." Thus, the Ervin Committee became a "they" for Richard Nixon. This approach attempts to divert attention from the question at hand to the motives of the questioners, from "is Nixon guilty?" to "Why is Ervin trying to assassinate the President's character?" The "journalistic misinterpretation" charge attempts to deflect the inquiry from "what did the President say?" to "what motivates the press to misquote the President?"

A second counterattack tactic takes the form of "I didn't do it; they did it." Thus, in September, 1972, Vice President Agnew "told reporters in Minneapolis that the apprehension of five men in the headquarters of the Democratic National Committee was a 'set-up' designed to embarrass the Republicans and damage their Presidential campaign."[58]

A recent example of "I didn't do it; they did it" can be found in the responses of the Reagan Administration to the charge of the Long Commission that failures in the processing of intelligence led to the slaughter of American Marines at the Beirut airport. According to a White House spokesman, "intelligence failures in connection with the Beirut bombing could be attributed to decisions taken by the Carter Administration."[59] But perhaps the best use (strategically, not morally) of the outgroup counterattack tactic may be credited to Franklin Roosevelt. During World War II Roosevelt read a news story which, he thought, would discourage women from joining the armed forces. In his anger at the piece, Roosevelt tried to have the Nazi Iron Cross awarded to the reporter who wrote it.[60]

Defending via the Omnipotent Dimension of the Benevolent Hero Myth

The Omnipotent Dimension of the Benevolent Hero Myth provides the president with four major defensive tactics: (1) dismissal, (2) disarmament, (3) redefinition and (4) co-opting of procedures.

The Tactic of Dismissal

The philosophy of the tactic of dismissal is to avoid addressing the charge. The methods of implementation include three varieties of the "I won't even dignify that with a response" tactic: (1) it's unimportant (and other things are more important), (2) it's exaggerated (beyond the realm of plausibility) and (3) it's a secret (and must be kept secret).

In his omnipotent role as the major identifier of societal problems, the President is in a unique position to dismiss questions and charges with the approach, "it's not important." In the Watergate case, however, President Nixon could not make this assertion bluntly because it was an unusual situation—unusual because it was not totally within the control of the President. So Nixon was reduced to implying the situation's unimportance through his (and his surrogates') characterizations of it. Thus, two days after the break-in, the President's Press Secretary, Ronald Ziegler, called it a "third rate burglary attempt."[61] By August of that year Attorney General Kleindienst was referring to it as a "simple burglary,"[62] and Nixon was characterizing it as "this very bizarre incident."[63] By December the government prosecutors were calling it "another street crime."[64] When, on May 9, 1973, President Nixon referred to Watergate as "this deplorable incident,"[65] James Reston commented, "This is the mildest use of the English language since somebody referred to the San Francisco earthquake as 'an unfortunate occurrence,' and it suggests that Mr. Nixon still hasn't identified the source or measured the magnitude of the tragedy."[66]

Reston's analysis to the contrary notwithstanding, it seems likely that President Nixon did have some measure of the magnitude of the tragedy and was trying to counter it with the tactic of dismissal. This conclusion seems to be supported by Nixon's subsequent references to the case—"murky, small, unimportant, vicious little things," "petty, little, indecent things that seem to obsess us," and "let the others wallow in Watergate."[67] Throughout, President Nixon employed language which was calculated to equate Watergate with a liquor store holdup.

President Reagan's use of the tactic of dismissal is implicit rather than explicit. That is, he does not explicitly say that something is not worth considering or unimportant or wrong; he merely dismisses it with a "there you go again" verbal wave of the hand. Thus, when asked how American action in Grenada differed from Soviet action in Afghanistan, he said, "Well, for heaven sakes, anyone who would link Afghanistan to this operation. . . ."[68]

Another variant of the "I won't even dignify that" tactic is "it's exaggerated beyond the realm of plausibility." The omnipotent hero is the only one who can see reality clearly, thus is the logical one to identify exaggeration. The undisputed king of this variant was plain-talking Harry Truman. When he took over the nation's steel mills in 1952, a reporter asked, "If it's okay to take over steel mills, would you also take over radio stations and newspapers?" Truman's answer was interpreted by the press as "Yes," and he subsequently was subjected to much villification in the media. At his next press conference, when asked about his position, Truman implemented the rhetoric of dismissal, saying, "That was a lot of hooey!"[69]

In the Watergate affair President Nixon did not utilize the implausibility variant directly, although his assertions that he was too busy with the business of government to be involved in day-to-day politicking were probably designed to effect the same result. And his surrogates were busy putting out the word that it was implausible that such a smart man would have approved such a dumb scheme. The logic so well fit the omnipotency myth that it was believed for a long time. Even James Reston, not a surrogate and hardly a friend of Nixon's, repeated the argument: "He is too intelligent to approve such risks in an election against George McGovern which was never in doubt. Also, in fairness to him, he is too smart to get involved in raising funds laundered through Mexico, or recruiting C.I.A. characters to bug Larry O'Brien's telephones."[70]

Another line of the "it's not plausible" variant builds upon the lack of hard evidence. It says, in effect, that if the charges were plausible there would be some evidence. Thus, Nixon complained, "A climate of sensationalism has developed in which even second- or third-hand hearsay charges are headlined as fact and repeated as fact."[71] Not only does the statement imply that no hard evidence exists, it attacks what evidence there is as flimsy and unsubstantial.

A final way which the "I won't even dignify that" tactic is operationalized is through the "secrecy with a rationale" variant. The logic here is: this is happening in a given crisis, and some of it is too secret to tell the public. So critics cannot justifiably attack—they do not have enough information. As Lyndon Johnson said about the Vietnam war, "Hundreds and hundreds of quiet diplomatic conversations . . . are being held,"[72] of which the public was unaware, but which were being directed to solving the problem.

This variant is designed to remove the user from the hurly-burly of attack and place the opponents at an informational disadvantage: Nixon on Watergate—"I can report today that there have been major developments in the case concerning which it would be improper to be more specific now, except to say that real progress has been made in finding the truth."[73] Exposure of Watergate might lead, the President implied, to the revealing of other *legal* but *secret* CIA operations which must be protected. Myth one thus is also affirmed: National security requires that secrecy protect government activities from some unspecified "horrible others."

President Nixon also connected the secrecy variation with the "other things are more important" approach when he said: "Neither do I believe I could enter into an endless course of explaining and rebutting a complex of point-by-point claims and charges arising out of conflicting testimony which may engage committees and courts for months or years to come, and still be able to carry out my duties as President."[74] Here the argument is not that things must be secret because of national security; rather, the secrecy is justified because it would take too long to ferret out the truth—longer than the matter justifies, especially in light of the many other important things the president must do.

President Reagan, faced with criticism of U.S. covert attacks on Nicaragua, replied, "I think covert actions have been a part of government and a part of government's responsibilities for as long as there's been a government . . . I do believe in the right of a country when it believes that its interests are best served to practice covert activity . . . you can't let your people know without letting the wrong people know. . . ."[75] In short, Reagan argues that government has not only the right but the responsibility to act in secret whenever it is to its advantage to do so.

In sum, secrecy with a rationale can include four premises: I can't tell you if it was done; I can't tell you why it was done; I can't tell you if I did it; and I can't tell you why I did it. All four premises attempt to dismiss charges against the President without answering them and all implicitly ask the citizens to trust the omnipotent leader—presaging myth three. If nothing else, the frequent use of secrecy with a rationale in modern presidential rhetoric may suggest that in contemporary society secrecy is becoming its own rationale.

The Tactic of Disarmament

Another way in which the omnipotent hero may deal with attacks is to attempt to disarm critics and questioners. The techniques for doing so include humor, pathos, assuming of responsibility, fairness and toughness. This tactic is a difficult one to use because it requires not only a subtle rhetorical style, but a finely-tuned sense of timing.

The tactic of humor exemplifies this need for style and timing. President John Kennedy could defuse a critic by poking fun, generally at himself, on the assumption that it is hard to criticize the person with whom you're laughing. When asked, for example, if he saw his role as a "splendid misery" (which is another way of asking Kennedy if he believed in the hero myth), he replied, "I have a nice home; the office is close by and the pay is good."[76]

President Reagan also is fond of defusing critics with humor. When he was criticized for suggesting that education reform would not require much additional money, he replied, "you can get credits toward graduation for cheerleading in some of our schools. Or how would you like to graduate by getting straight A's in bachelor life?"[77] While Reagan's humor is well received, some members of his Administration, such as James Watt, and Pat Buchanan, have not been as successful at defusing attacks with humor, perhaps because they have tended to use humor in attacking others rather than in the Kennedy-Reagan self-deprecatory way.

The second tactic of disarmament, pathos, has already been discussed in terms of Nixon's "pity me, I've been misled" approach. It seems to have failed there because of its inherent conflict with the idea of omnipotence. Theoretically, then, the tactic should be used only in international affairs, where the president does have equals, or near-equals. Even then, however, it should be followed immediately by a statement of moral outrage and a specific counteraction that is highly visible. Otherwise the tactic's inherent weakness may effect a boomerang.

Carter's handling of the Iranian hostage crisis is instructive here. He played on the pathos and the moral outrage, but there was no visible and specific counter-action until much later. Thus, Carter came to look weak and the early popularity which normally accrues to a President in times of crisis dwindled steadily away.

Far stronger is the third tactic, assuming responsibility. Kennedy's assumption of responsibility for the abortive Bay of Pigs invasion is instructive. He said: "Victory has 100 fathers and defeat is an orphan. . . . I am the responsible officer of the government."[78] Kennedy's popularity soared to 82% in the national polls. Rather than merely defending the myth of the benevolent hero, he had fulfilled it.

Yet the assumption of responsibility for error is, in theory, at odds with the idea of omnipotence—how can the omnipotent err? A president is not supposed to make mistakes, or so the myth goes. But the American people are tolerant, and they want to believe in their president. So when the president does err they expect an acceptance of responsibility and blame in the style of the hero, gracefully and grandly.

President Nixon admitted his responsibility for Watergate, but then presented a unique distinction between responsibility and blame. His pretense at accepting responsibility is discussed under the strategy of "Overt Denial" in the upcoming section on Dimension Two of the Hero myth.

President Reagan also has attempted to utilize this tactic. Responding to the criticism of the Long Commission examination of the cause of the loss of Marines in the Beirut bombing, Reagan concluded,

> I do not believe, therefore, that the local commanders on the ground, men who have already suffered quite enough, should be punished for not fully comprehending the nature of today's terrorist threat. If there is to be blame, it properly rests here in this office and with this President. And I accept responsibility for the bad as well as the good.[79]

Undoubtedly, this was a magnanimous gesture which had the effect of defusing criticism of the Marines. At the same time, it should be noted that the Long Commission's direct criticism of the president, to the effect that diplomacy should have been relied upon more, was not even mentioned by Mr. Reagan.

Fairness, the fourth disarmament tactic, is the strongest, for it calls upon powerful components of democratic myth, such as fair debate and equal chance at the bar of justice.

When President Johnson was criticized by the young, the liberal and the press, often in terms anathema to many Americans, he responded by saying: "I do not mean to say that I will remain altogether silent on the critical issues of our day. For just as strongly as I believe in other men's freedoms to disagree, so do I also believe in the President's freedom to attempt to persuade." After all, Johnson continued, even though "in these last days there have been questions about what we're doing in Vietnam," discussion has been allowed to occur, because "the strength of America can never be sapped by discussion, and we have no better nor stronger tradition than open debate—free debate in hours of danger."[80] The essential message of this tactic is that even though the omnipotent hero *knows* the correct course of action, no interference with the citizens' right of debate will be tolerated.

Likewise, President Nixon relied on the fairness tactic to support his reluctance to address the issues in Watergate: ". . . I was determined not to take precipitate action and to avoid if at all possible any action that would appear to reflect on innocent people."[81] This is the voice of the omnipotent hero—even if it weakens the case the innocent will not be implicated; of course, the case is thereby strengthened. The critics are disarmed; any further attack would be unfair to those innocent people.

By contrast, Jimmy Carter, who in his early days in the national spotlight was perceived as fair because he was perceived as a "nice person" and a "good Christian," eventually came to be perceived as unfair because of his relative inflexibility. The first direct evidence of Carter's inflexibility came in his response to criticism of his campaign rhetoric: "He tended to explain that his staff did not follow up or that an aide wrote a letter which Carter did not see or that Carter had forgotten an incident from the past or that he was unaware of some tactic in his campaign,"[82] or, if no answer seemed possible, he flashed his "mules eating briars smile"[83] and pressed on.

Toughness is the final tactic of disarmament. The basic ploy is, "If you think this made you mad, look at how mad I am." Thus, Nixon said, "I have expressed to the appropriate authorities my view that no individual holding, in the past or present, a position of major importance in the Administration should be given immunity from prosecution."[84] In the public eye it looked like Nixon was being tough. Of course, this was before his lawyers asserted that Nixon was immune from prosecution.

Even Jimmy Carter, generally perceived as a less-than-tough president, made occasional forays into toughness in an attempt to defend himself against the charge of "softness." This was most notable in his 1980 State of the Union Address.[85] He warned the Iranians, "If the American hostages are harmed, a severe price will be paid." And the message to the Russians concerning Afghanistan was, "While this invasion continues, we and the other nations of the world cannot continue business as usual with the Soviet Union." On the surface both of these appear to be tough messages, but they contain identical weaknesses—namely, the implication that if the perpetrators stop now all will be forgiven. If Iran returns the hostages they will not be punished for their "international terrorism," and if Russia withdraws we will overlook her "military aggression." Further, there was no indication in the speech that the conditions would change the next week. Carter did not draw a line in the dirt and tell the bullies not to cross it; rather, the message was that he would yell at them and threaten them until they chose to stop, then he would kiss and make up. No wonder President Carter continued to be perceived as weak.

Labeling

Two tactics of outgroup labeling (redefining critics as enemies and redefining their positions as evil) already have been discussed. In addition, there are three other tactics of labeling which derive from the omnipotent hero myth: (1) the Pollyanna principle, (2) actual redefinition, and (3) the truncating of history.

The Pollyanna principle says, simply, "look at all the good that came out of this mess," thus defining the evil as beneficial. It was the first defense employed by Kennedy after the Bay of Pigs fiasco. Speaking to the American Press Guild in Washington, Kennedy praised the efforts of the Cuban exiles in attempting an overthrow of tyranny and suggested that the United States would not rest until it had freed the Western Hemisphere from the disruptive force of Castro.[86] The speech was strong, positive and buoyant; its tone was in direct contrast to the disasterous events of the previous day. By opposing one day's policy failure with the next day's rhetorical strength, Kennedy fulfilled myths two and three (I am strong, I have acted, and we must work together).

Nixon, likewise, employed the Pollyanna principle, as when he told the nation, "If we learn the important lessons of Watergate . . . we can emerge from this experience a better and stronger nation."[87]

But perhaps the most Pollyannaish statement ever to come out of the White House was when President Carter dubbed the fiasco of the failed Iranian hostage rescue mission an "incomplete success."[88]

Actual redefinition is also a labeling tactic. Examples are common in the speeches given by Johnson and Nixon throughout the Vietnam War, in attempting to redefine the war as a noble effort. Johnson's redefinition attempted to place the war within the pantheon of American values:

men who believe they can change their destinies, will change their destinies.

Armed with that belief, they will be willing—yes, they will be eager—to make the sacrifices that freedom demands. They will be anxious to shoulder the responsibilities that are inseparably bound to freedom.

They will be able to look beyond the four essential freedoms, beyond the freedom to learn, to master new skills, to acquaint themselves with the lore of man and nature.

To the freedom to grow, to become the best that is within them to become, to cast off the yoke of discrimination and disease.

To the freedom to hope and to build on that hope lives of integrity and well-being.

That is what our struggle in Vietnam is all about tonight.[89]

When Nixon inherited the war he also inherited the need to redefine it as noble:

When men write the history of this nation, they will record that no people in the annals of time made greater sacrifices in a more selfless cause than the American people sacrificed for the right of 18 million people in a faraway land to avoid the imposition of Communist rule against their will and for the right of these people to determine their own future free of outside interference.[90]

As hindsight shows, this tactic was not completely successful. The Johnson-Nixon attempts at redefinition undoubtedly were hampered by television. It is easy to believe that war is noble when one is singing martial songs and saluting the flag, less so when one sees villages being sacked and civilians napalmed.

President Nixon also utilized actual redefinition in the Watergate case, in an attempt to "change the battleground from 'was the President involved in these sleazy political shenanigans?' to a loftier ' what liberties are we prepared to give up for national security?' "

President Ford's handling of the Mayaguez affair included a classic example of redefinition. Despite the fact that the boat was captured in the territorial waters of Cambodia, President Ford described its location as "on the high seas," thereby justifying his depiction of the capture as "piracy." These definitions were utilized despite the interpretation of his legal council, who had told him that "the ship's capture was not 'piracy.' Under international law, they said, Cambodia had a legal right to seize the ship after it steamed within the 12-mile limit which Cambodia claim[ed] as its territorial waters."[91]

Because President Ford consistently utilized the appellations he did about the Mayaguez, many people did not see those usages as redefinitions. Only those who knew international law noticed that his language fit the redefinition category. A more obvious case of redefinition, therefore, can be found in President Reagan's clever substitution of "the truly needy" for "the poor."[92]

The third tactic of labeling is "the truncating of history." It is very like the strawman approach—it does to history what the strawman does to argument.

That is, it presents a distorted or myopic version of events which distorts reality. With history seen as the president wants it seen, presidential policies become legitimized. Given the generally accepted historical record about the U.S. bombing of Cambodia, it is instructive to examine President Nixon's account of why the Cambodian "incursion" took place:

> Cambodia, a small country of seven million people, has been a neutral nation since the Geneva agreement of 1954—an agreement, incidentally, which was signed by the government of North Vietnam.
> American policy since then has been to scrupulously respect the neutrality of the Cambodian people. We have maintained a skeleton diplomatic mission of fewer than fifteen in Cambodia's capital, and then only since last August. For the previous four years, from 1965 to 1969, we did not have any diplomatic mission whatever in Cambodia. And for the past five years, we have provided no military assistance whatever and no economic assistance to Cambodia.
> North Vietnam, however, has not respected that neutrality.[93]

The President then went on to detail the ways in which North Vietnam had violated Cambodian neutrality. Given the ground laid by the truncated history, the only logical conclusion was that the U.S. should go in and "clean out" the Communist sanctuaries. But that seemingly logical conclusion was based on erroneous history *and Nixon knew it*. He knew it was a lie that America had "provided no military assistance." He knew that it was a lie that U.S. policy had been "to scrupulously respect the neutrality of the Cambodian people." This "history" was not only truncated—it was "trumped up."

But this would seem to be an unusual case; the truncating of history is probably not a tactic used consciously by most presidents. More often, the history presented probably represents the actual world-view of the speaker, and should be examined in this light. From this perspective, analysis of truncated history probably will reveal more valuable information about how the president perceives the world than about the crisis at hand.

That certainly seems the case in President Reagan's account of the reasons for the invasion of Grenada. While we do not have room here to detail all the misinformation flowing from the White House about that action, it can be generally stated that the Administration "inflated the number of Cuban military personnel in Grenada, made other misleading factual allegations to bolster President Reagan's unproven assertion that the invasion was necessary to prevent a Cuban military takeover, and exaggerated the evidence that Americans in Grenada have been in danger."[94] Examining the misleading reasoning, Ronald Steel concludes that the invasion reveals more about Ronald Reagan than about the situation in Grenada:

> the Administration had trouble keeping its stories straight. First it said it had to evacuate the students, although the Grenadian Government had offered to do so itself. Then it was to restore democracy. Now, we are told, it was to prevent the island from becoming a Soviet-Cuban base to export 'terrorism'—as if there were

any shortage of such bases already. The public is gullible, but not stupid. Ronald Reagan invaded because he did not like the Government and had the power to get rid of it.[95]

The Tactic of Co-opting Procedures

Simply stated, this tactic avers, "I didn't do it, but I'll find out who did." As such it frequently puts the president in the position of co-opting the investigatory functions of the bodies responsible for the area in question—the Attorney General's office, Congress, or independent regulatory commissions.

In the Watergate case, Nixon depicted himself as the chief prosecutor. "I'm finding out who is guilty," Nixon implied, as in this example: "Last June 17 while I was in Florida . . . I first learned from news reports of the Watergate break-in. . . . I immediately ordered an investigation by appropriate government authorities."[96] The hero reacts the way a hero should, through proper channels. Later, as these channels were seen as inadequate, the hero dispensed with them: "on March 21 I personally assumed the responsibility for coordinating intensive new inquiries into the matter and I personally ordered those conducting the investigations to get all the facts and to report them directly to me right here in this office."[97]

The pre-emptive purpose of this tactic was to get the culprits before the grand jury, the Ervin Committee of the special prosecutor did. The motive was to prove that Nixon was not hiding anything, that he was completely open and that he was acting in the mold of the omnipotent hero.

Interestingly, the president-turned-investigator with an "I'm not hiding anything" tactic may create conflict with the "secrecy with a rationale" defense. In that circumstance the co-opting strategy may come to read, "I didn't do it, but I'll find out who did . . . but I won't tell you who it was or why they did it."

Defending via the Moralistic-Benevolent Dimension of the Benevolent Hero Myth

The tactics of the Moralistic Dimension appear to be utilized less frequently than those of the Omnipotent Dimension, probably because politics is a story of power and America's foremost politician would rather defend with strength (omnipotence) than goodness (morality). Nonetheless, there are four tactics by which presidents can defend the Moralistic Dimension of their heroism: (1) Postponement, (2) Overt Denial, (3) Co-opting Goals and Arguments and (4) Admission with a Zinger.

The Tactic of Postponement

The purpose of this tactic is to allow the president to rise above the attack, or, at least, give a rationale obviating the necessity of responding to charges. This tactic (which says, in effect, it is unfair to make a judgment now) is strongest when coupled with a plea to the democratic ideal of fair play, of not judging before all the evidence is in.

Nixon did this by suggesting that the people should postpone judgment until the proper machinery of government decided if the accusations were justified:

> Charges are these days made rather easily, as we know, in our political process, and there is sometimes a tendency for us to convict the innocent . . . let us resolve tonight that until we hear the evidence, until those who have been charged have had a chance to present their case in a court of law, let's uphold the great American tradition that an individual, even a government official, is innocent until he's proven guilty.[98]

Other versions of the tactic of postponement include: "Let's let the future decide (whether I did wrong)," "Let's let a commission decide," and "Let's let the people decide."

This tactic is in inherent conflict with the Omnipotent Dimension—the president is supposed to know all. Further, the tactic is designed to evade criticism, and evasion is not moralistic. Also, the idea of postponement implies that eventually there should be a judgment; thus, it is in inherent conflict with "secrecy with a rationale," which implies that national security or some other good reason forbids the development of the evidence necessary for judgment.

The Tactic of Overt Denial

President Nixon began his Watergate defense with a flat denial of knowledge of Watergate plans and a denial that anyone on his staff had been involved. When it was no longer possible to deny the complicity of his aides, Nixon denied any personal knowledge of the entry, cover-up, offer of executive clemency, etc. Later, he denied *specific* approval of the illegal actions, denied *intent* to contribute to the climate in which the actions took place, and denied *intent* to place a security "cover" on the Watergate investigations.

Nixon denied guilt (but admitted error); he denied blame (but accepted responsibility). This last denial is rather interesting. Nixon asks: "Who then is to blame for what happened in this case?"[99] He answers the question negatively: "the easiest course would be for me to blame those to whom I delegated the responsibility to run the campaign."[100] Note the correlation—blame and responsibility cohere; but that would be "the cowardly thing to do. I will not place the blame on subordinates. . . ."[101] On whom then? "In any organization the man at the top must bear the responsibility."[102] "That responsibility, therefore, belongs here in this office. I accept it."[103] But what happened to blame? He ends: "And I pledge to you tonight from this office that I will do everything in my power to insure that the guilty are brought to justice. . . ."[104] But who are the guilty? Not "those to whom I delegated the responsibility to run the campaign." Who, then? William Sloan Coffin? How hollow and mythless sounds Nixon's analogy to Truman's "the buck stops here" phrase: "There can be no white wash at the White House."[105]

Analyzed through Burkeian terms, the Nixon responsibility—blame confusion proves to be an elegant cop-out. For those who have responsibility are "agents," capable of acting and thus of being blamed. Those who are denied responsibility are reduced to "agencies," carrying out the will of the agent and incapable of being blamed. If Nixon denies to his subordinates the characteristic of responsibility he also denies to them the characteristic of blame (or guilt). If he takes exclusive responsibility then he must take exclusive blame. To attempt, as he did, to take responsibility as agent and leave blame or guilt to mere agencies is to accept a no-risk responsibility, for the risk resides with the blame. All that can go with no-risk responsibility is credit. In attempting to be moralistic by taking the responsibility, Nixon actually was immoral in refusing to accept the concomitant blame.

Analogously, when Nixon was asked, "How much personal blame do you accept for the climate in the White House and of the re-election committee for the abuses of Watergate?," he replied, "I accept it all."[106] Yet, just one week earlier Nixon had gone to great lengths (ten paragraphs) to demonstrate that the climate "resulted from the assumption by those involved that their cause placed them beyond the reach of those rules that apply to other persons and that hold a free society together."[107] And did that assumption come from Nixon? No, "That attitude . . . became fashionable in the 1960s, as individuals and groups increasingly asserted the right to take the law into their own hands, insisting that their purposes represented a higher morality."[108] Nixon's rhetoric did not exemplify the moralistic-benevolent myth; it mocked it. Again we ask, shall we blame Richard Milhous Nixon or William Sloan Coffin?

Outright denial works well when it is not disproven. It maintains rhetorical distance between the attacker and the user. But when denial rings false (as history shows it did in Nixon's case), the strategy-gone-sour strikes at the heart of the moralistic hero myth; heros, after all, do not lie. How can citizens do the bidding of the hero (myth three) when they are not sure what the hero has or has not done, when they are not sure what will be labeled "inoperative" tomorrow?

The Tactic of Co-opting Goals and Arguments

The president's ability to co-opt the investigatory means of the opposition already has been discussed. But it is also possible to co-opt goals and arguments. One of Richard Nixon's favorite ploys was to say, in effect, "We agree on the goals; our only disagreement is on the means." He especially used this tactic in defending his Vietnam policies. His position was that his goals and the goals of his critics were the same: to end the war and bring American troops home. The opposition was characterized as wanting immediate, precipitate withdrawal, no matter what happened to Vietnam. Nixon depicted himself, on the other hand, as wanting to end the conflict with honor, with South Vietnam strong enough to defend herself and with peace that would last a generation.

President Johnson's "abdication" speech is another good example of co-opting the arguments of the opposition (which included stopping the bombing, scaling down the fighting and intensifying the diplomatic efforts). And to prove that his arguments had substance, that he was sincere in his efforts to effectuate peace, Johnson added these words: "Accordingly, I shall not seek, and I will not accept the nomination of my party for another term as your President."[109] It was a large price to pay in order to prove sincerity, but Johnson's credibility gap was such that anything less would have been ignored. Johnson's act may have been unwise, unpolitic and useless. But it was moral, benevolent and heroic.

The Tactic of Admission With a Zinger

This tactic employs such rationales as, "I did it because . . . ," "I did it but . . . ," and "I did it for. . . ." The important element is to emphasize the "zinger" which follows the "because," "but," or "for" to such an extent that the first part, "I did it," is largely forgotten. Skillfully employed, it provides the desired diversion. Lamely employed, it is an admission with a rationalization rather than a reason. The key to success with this strategy depends on the zing in the zinger.

A commonly-used tactic is "I did it because it was right." This approach often was employed to justify the Vietnam war—and often used in the negative, i.e., "not to have done it would have been morally wrong." To have let Vietnam fall into the hands of Communists would have been morally wrong, especially since the South Vietnamese did not want Communism, and Communists were outside invaders, and America had the power—thus, duty—to stop them. By the time the litany was completed the listener was supposed to possess amazement that anyone could consider the action immoral.

Closely aligned to this is the tactic, "I did it because I had to." Giving the Watergate tapes to the prosecutor, Nixon informed the nation, would destroy the presidency. So, not because he wanted to, but because he had to, the tapes would be kept secret. James Reston, although using somewhat different terminology, noted Nixon's historic use of this "alibi":

> President Nixon's latest explanation of his part in the Watergate scandal—which is quite different from his first two explanations—is that everything he did, or failed to do, was motivated by his concern for "national security."
>
> In his mind this is probably true, and this is precisely the problem. In fact, it is the main theme of his political life. Whenever he has been charged with dubious political or executive decisions, he has always justified them on the ground that, right or wrong, they were done in the name of "national security."[110]

The "national security" justification is thus one way for a president to complete the zinger. It is one way to say, "I had to."

A third zinger asserts "I did it because it was my responsibility to do it." At a time when Americans were wondering if Lieutenant William Calley was going to receive a fair trial, President Nixon "intruded" into the case in a manner which many thought inappropriate. His "it was my responsibility" defense included the rider, "and it worked":

> I believe that the system of military justice is a fair system, but a part of that system is the right of the President to review. I'm exercising that right and I think that reassured the country and that's one of the reasons that the country has cooled down on this case.[111]

In a democratic society, the president's responsibility may stem from "I did it because I was ordered to by the people." However, in American democracy the voice of the people is seldom specific enough for a leader to know what the orders are (despite the assertions of Reagan, and others, that they know what their "mandate" is, an attempt to exploit the myth of the national will), so in practice the tactic intertwines with "I'm right because the people support me." A case in point is President Johnson's assertion that his position on the war had triumphed: "I think that most of our citizens have, after a very penetrating debate, which is our democratic heritage, reached a common understanding on the meaning and on the objectives of that struggle."[112] The obtained unity justifies his action and proves him a moralistic-benevolent leader.

The most popular of the admission-zinger tactics is "I did it but others do it, too." Speaking of the Republican abuses of 1972 which came to light over the succeeding year, Nixon asserted, "both of our great parties have been guilty of such tactics."[113] The President's speech writer, Pat Buchanan, lamented, "Poor Liddy and Hunt. If only, like Ellsberg, they had dropped their stolen papers off at the national desk of the *New York Times,* instead of the campaign desk of Jeb Magruder, they might be sharing the Pulitzer Prize."[114] The impression to be left by the "you, too" argument is that it is the height of hypocrisy to attack the president for this when it has been going on for so long as to be standard operating procedure. But in the long run, the tactic may be self-defeating for the president, for, if the population became convinced that all politicians are untrustworthy, even the president's own moral standing will have been undermined, as well as the whole structure of political myths. Far from proving innocence, the tactic may actually indict the whole system.

Finally, a weak admission-zinger tactic, but one occasionally used, is "I did it but nobody was hurt by it." The president tends not to utilize this—it is too weak—but sometimes supporters do. A partisan of President Nixon from New York wrote: "there is no evidence tendered or available that the President profited to the extent of even a single ballot in his overwhelming re-election as a result of the Watergate transgressions."[115] And from Muncie, Indiana, came this argument: "no lives were lost, no one harmed, no bank robbed, or large amounts of money lost. And so far as we can detect, no one in particular was harmed. It is indeed getting boring."[116] Historical hindsight suggests the writer was wrong.

Defending via the Citizen's Duty Myth

This final myth suggests that if the problems at hand are caused by out-groups and if the president is acting strongly and morally to counter them, it is the duty of the citizen to follow and do the bidding of the hero-leader. Thus, the best hope that the president has of activating this myth is in convincing the audience that myths one and two apply to the current situation. If that is successful, myth three automatically will come into play; if not, no amount of exhortation is going to convince the people to follow.

Not only do the generalities of myths one and two support this myth, so do many of the specific tactics. Thus, if the president expresses moral outrage at being misled by trusted subordinates, the implication that no such misleading would originate in the Oval Office is implied. A successful attack on the press for misinterpretation leaves potential followers with only one source of information—the president. If the secrecy with a rationale argument is convincing, it activates a "trust me" syndrome in the population. If the people are convinced the president is being responsible, fair and tough, their loyalty is ensured. If they accept the truncation of history, they undoubtedly will accept the actions to which that truncation logically lead. If they agree with any of the zingers, they probably will forgive the admitted action. In addition to all of these interrelations with other tactics, there is a tactic peculiar to this myth.

The Tactic of Keeping Faith

In this tactic, the president asserts the importance of the faith of the citizens and pledges to prove worth of that faith. Nixon's development of this theme went as follows:

. . . I knew that in the final analysis the integrity of this office—public faith in the integrity of this office—would have to take priority over all personal considerations.

. . . in matters as sensitive as guarding the integrity of our democratic process, it is essential not only that rigorous legal and ethical standards be observed, but also that the public, you, have total confidence that they are being observed and enforced by those in authority, and particularly by the President of the United States.

. . . I want the American people, I want you, to know beyond the shadow of a doubt that during my term as President justice will be pursued fairly, fully and impartially, no matter who is involved.[117]

More than any other president, Mr. Carter tended to suffuse all of his rhetoric with the tactic of keeping faith. In a strange kind of way, Carter's use of language as self-fulfilling prophecies seems to have been related to his desire for and promise of trust and faith. That is, we are what we think we are; our feelings capture reality; our programs are as we describe them. We must trust ourselves, our feelings, our solutions. Then, as we see how well everything works, we will be able to trust each other and, eventually, even have faith in our government. Somehow, the key to his whole political approach was revealed and reflected in his language. It was, in a sense, the politics of biofeedback wherein trust and confidence flowed from actions, but successful actions flowed from trust and confidence. So the "logical" point at which to begin to repair the damage to public faith was the rhetorical. Hence the "trust me" campaign, the symbolism of his first year, the 1978 presentation of the liberation of the Panama Canal as an act of atonement, the malaise speech of 1979 and perhaps even his overall preference for the straightforward and banal rather than the eloquent.[118]

It was as though Carter set out to rebuild the national faith, substituting himself for George Washington and replacing the Constitution with the Coke commercial: "I'd like to build the world a home and furnish it with love, grow apple trees, and honey bees and snow white turtle doves." Like Coke, the aftertaste was cloyingly sweet, and Carter himself was seen as mushy, soft, simpering, a view based as much on his rhetoric as on his presidential actions and accomplishments.

Again, it must be emphasized that the tactic of keeping faith is useless by itself. It only can be useful as an appendage to the successful employment of myths one or two. For if the people ever get to the point of wondering who the enemy really is or of perceiving the President as an imposter, they may begin to see their citizen's duty as not to "follow the leader" but to "throw the rascal out."

Conclusion

American presidents often have complained, both privately and publicly about the verbal attacks to which they constantly are subjected while in office. It cannot be denied that presidents suffer much criticism—from political opponents, special interest groups, the media and diverse other sources. However, it also is manifest that presidents have an arsenal of rhetorical weapons with which to defend themselves and their policies. Naturally, the use of one or another of these techniques does not guarantee that a president will successfully weather a crisis. Success in a given instance would seem to depend on the issue at stake, the strength of the attackers and the attitude of the public as much as upon the president's defensive skills. To date, President Reagan has defended himself and his policies with great success. Presidents Carter and Nixon, on certain conspicuous occasions, were less successful.

Future research in the area of presidential defensive rhetoric might focus on the extent to which the tactics discussed in this essay reflect the behavior of presidents prior to John F. Kennedy. The American presidency, along with the set of myths surrounding it, has evolved gradually. Earlier conceptions of the presidency may well have called for different defensive choices on the part of the chief executive. It seems a reasonable assumption to suggest that a president's ability to defend self and policies will be greatly affected by the way the office is perceived by the public.

The most important remaining research, however, must come in two waves. First, a typology of tactics needs to be developed, including those we introduce here as well as all those introduced by others in the noted sources plus those yet to be identified. Second, once that typology has been developed, we need to move to the larger category of strategy, answering such questions as 1) when is a certain tactic appropriate and potentially workable, 2) what are the consequences of the various tactics, 3) which contextual circumstances alter the choice of tactics 4) which tactics are most efficacious to the president and least damaging to democracy? At that point, we can begin to talk about the possibility of having a theory of presidential apologia.

Notes

1. Theodore Otto Windt, Jr., "Presidential Rhetoric: Definition of a Field of Study," *Central States Speech Journal*, 35 (1984), 28.
2. John R. Johannes, "Executive Reports to Congress," *Journal of Communication*, 26 (1976), 53–61.
3. Robert L. Ivie, "Presidential Motives for War," *Quarterly Journal of Speech*, 60 (1974), 337–345.
4. James W. Pratt, "An Analysis of Three Crisis Speeches," *Western Journal of Speech Communication*, 34 (1970), 194–203; Theodore Otto Windt, Jr., "The

Presidency and Speeches of International Crises: Repeating the Rhetorical Past," *Speaker and Gavel,* 11 (1973), 6–14.

5. Donald Wolfarth, "John F. Kennedy in the Tradition of Inaugural Speeches," *Quarterly Journal of Speech,* 47 (1961), 124–132; Dante Germino, *The Inaugural Addresses of American Presidents: The Public Philosophy and Rhetoric* (Lanham, MD: University Press of America, 1984); Dan F. Hahn, "Archetype and Signature in Johnson's 1965 State of the Union Address," *Central States Speech Journal,* 34 (1984), 42–59; Dan F. Hahn and Justin Gustainis, "Anatomy of an Enigma: Jimmy Carter's 1980 State of the Union Address," *Communication Quarterly,* 33 (1985), 43–49; Karyln Kohrs Cambell and Kathleen Hall Jamieson, "Inaugurating the Presidency," *Presidential Studies Quarterly,* 15 (1985), 394–411.

6. James H. Jackson, "Clarence Darrow's 'Plea in Defense of Himself,'" *Western Speech,* 20 (1956), 185–195.

7. B. L. Ware and Wil A. Linkugel, "They Spoke in Defense of Themselves: On the Generic Criticism of Apologia," *Quarterly Journal of Speech,* 59 (1973), 273–283.

8. For a bibliography of studies in apologia, see Walter R. Fisher, "Genre: Concepts and Applications in Rhetorical Criticism," *Western Journal of Speech Communication,* 44 (1980), 288–299.

9. See L. W. Rosenfield, "A Case Study in Speech Criticism: The Nixon-Truman Analog," *Speech Monographs,* 35 (1968), 435–450; Richard A. Katula, "The Apology of Richard Nixon," *Today's Speech,* 23 (1975), 1–5; Gerald L. Wilson, "A Strategy of Explanation: Richard M. Nixon's August 8, 1974 Resignation Address," *Communication Quarterly,* 24 (1976), 14–20; William L. Benoit, "Richard M. Nixon's Rhetorical Strategies in His Public Statements on Watergate," *Southern Speech Communication Journal,* 47 (1982), 192–211; Jackson Harrell, B. L. Ware and Wil A. Linkugel, "Failure of Apology in American Politics: Nixon on Watergate," *Speech Monographs,* 42 (1975), 245–261.

10. Sherry Devereaux Butler, "The Apologia, 1971 Genre," *Southern Speech Communication Journal,* 36 (1972), p. 282.

11. Ware and Linkugel, p. 27.

12. Noreen W. Kruse, "Motivational Factors in Non-Denial Apologia," *Central States Speech Journal,* 28 (1977), p. 13.

13. Halford Ross Ryan, "*Kategoria* and *Apologia:* On Their Rhetorical Criticism as a Speech Set," *Quarterly Journal of Speech,* 68 (1972), p. 255.

14. Ryan, pp. 255–258.

15. Harrell, Ware and Linkugel, p. 247.

16. Joseph Campbell, *Myths to Live By* (New York: Bantam Books, 1972), p. 9.

17. Bronislaw Malinowski, as quoted in Max Gluckman, *Politics, Law and Ritual in Tribunal Society* (New York: Mentor, 1965), p. 54.

18. John Beattie, *Other Cultures* (New York: Free Press, 1964), p. 161.

19. Clinton Rossiter, as quoted in James D. Barber, *The Presidential Character* (Englewood Cliffs: Prentice-Hall, 1972), p. 7.

20. Murray Edelman, "Myths, Metaphors, and Political Conformity," *Psychiatry,* 30 (1967), 217–228. This article informs much of our discussion of these myths.

21. Thomas E. Cronin, "The Textbook Presidency and Political Science," *Congressional Record,* 116 (1970).

22. Edelman, p. 224.

23. Much of the language in this section, and to a lesser extent in the explanations of myths one and three, is taken from Dan Hahn and Ruth Gonchar, "Richard

Nixon and Presidential Mythology," *Journal of Applied Communications Research,* 1 (1973), pp. 25–48.

24. Robert Cathcart, "The Nixon Inaugural Address," in *Public Speaking as Dialogue: Readings and Essays,* edited by Jon L. Erickson and Robert F. Forston (Indianapolis: *Kendall-Hunt Publishing Co., 1979*), p. 130.

25. Kenneth Burke, *The Philosophy of Literary Form; Studies in Symbolic Action* (Baton Rouge: Louisiana State University Press, 1941), p. 4.

26. John F. Kennedy, "Commencement Address at Yale University, June 11, 1962," in Arthur L. Klein, Editor, *Spoken Arts Treasury of John F. Kennedy Addresses* (New Rochelle, New York: Spoken Arts, Inc., 1972), 63–70. All subsequent references from this source.

27. F. Michael Smith, "Rhetorical Implications of the Aggression Thesis in the Johnson Administration's Vietnam Argumentation," *Southern States Speech Journal,* 23 (1972), 218.

28. Cal M. Logue and John H. Patton, "From Ambiguity to Dogma: The Rhetorical Symbols of Lyndon B. Johnson in Vietnam," *The Southern Speech Communication Journal,* 47 (1982), 310–329.

29. Richard Nixon, "Prepared Text of Nixon's Watergate Speech," *Long Island Press,* August 16, 1973, p. 7.

30. Dan F. Hahn, "Corrupt Rhetoric: President Ford and the Mayaguez Affair," *Communication Quarterly,* 28 (1980), 38–43.

31. Gerald Ford, "Transcript of President's Talk on City Crisis, Questions Asked and His Response," *The New York Times,* October 30, 1975, p. 46. Subsequent quotes also from this source.

32. Anthony Lewis, "Good Old Gerry Ford," *The New York Times,* November 3, 1975, p. 35.

33. Russell Baker, "What We Are Cheering For," *The New York Times,* November 4, 1975, p. 35.

34. Ronald Reagan, "Transcript of Address by President on Lebanon and Grenada," *The New York Times,* October 28, 1983, p. A 10.

35. Francis X. Clines, "It Was a Rescue Mission, Reagan Says," *The New York Times,* November 4, 1983, p. A 16.

36. Ronald Steel, "Reveling in Military Power," *The New York Times,* October 30, 1983, p. E 19.

37. James Reston, "What Went Wrong?," *The New York Times,* October 30, 1983, p. E 19.

38. Tom Wicker, "Liberals, Demons and Nixon," *The New York Times,* July 29, 1973, p. E 13.

39. Patrick J. Buchanan, "Mr. Nixon as the Target," *The New York Times,* August 2, 1973, p. 35.

40. "Senator Defends Nixon," *The New York Times,* June 15, 1973, p. 19.

41. James L. Buckley, "The Benefit of Doubt," *The New York Times,* May 9, 1973, p. 47.

42. Steven V. Roberts, "Senate Leaders Want to Send Fact-Finding Group," *The New York Times,* October 30, 1983, p. A 23.

43. Sheldon Ritter, Letter to the Editor, *The New York Times,* October 30, 1983, p. E 20.

44. Richard Nixon, "Transcript of President's Broadcast Address to the Nation on the Watergate Affair," *The New York Times,* May 1, 1973, p. 31.

46. Isaac Asimov, Letter to the Editor, *The New York Times,* May 31, 1973, p. 40.

47. Lyndon Johnson, "Vietnam: Our Position Today," *Vital Speeches of the Day,* 33 (April 1, 1967), p. 354. (Emphasis ours.)

48. Lyndon Johnson, p. 354 (Emphasis ours.)

49. James L. Golden, Goodwin F. Berquist and William E. Coleman, *The Rhetoric of Western Thought,* 3rd ed. (Dubuque, IA: Kendall/Hunt Publishing Co., 1983), p. 10.

50. Lyndon Johnson, "Vietnam: The Cause of Freedom," *Vital Speeches of the Day,* 32 (March 15, 1966), pp. 323–324.

51. Ruth M. Gonchar and Dan F. Hahn, "The Rhetorical Predictability of Richard M. Nixon," *Today's Speech,* 19 (1971), p. 10.

52. Nixon, "Transcript of. . . ." May 1, 1973, p. 31.

53. Nixon, "Transcript of. . . ." May 1, 1973, p. 31.

54. Russell Baker, "Caper Comes to Crisis," *The New York Times,* April 24, 1973 p. 41.

55. William V. Shannon, "The Dangling Man," *The New York Times,* July 18, 1973, p. 33.

56. Garry Wills, "Richard Nixon's Seventh Crisis," *The New York Times Magazine,* July 8, 1973, p. 7.

57. Jonathan Friendly, "Press Voices Criticism of 'Off-the-Record War," *The New York Times,* November 4, 1983, p. A 16.

58. James T. Wooten, "Agnew Confirms His Faith in Nixon about Watergate," *The New York Times,* April 26, 1973, p. 34.

59. "White House Contends Carter Crippled C.I.A.," *The New York Times,* December, 29, 1983, p. A 15.

60. Hillier Krieghbaum, *Pressures on the Press* (New York: Thomas Y. Crowell Co., 1972), p. 10.

61. Anthony Ripley, "Simple Watergate 'Caper' Sends Ripples over U.S.," *The New York Times,* April 27, 1973, p. 14.

62. Ripley, p. 14.

63. R. W. Apple, Jr., "Nixon on Watergate: A Shrinking Defense," *The New York Times,* May 23, 1973, p. 29.

64. Walter Rugaber, "Still No Real Answers," *The New York Times,* February 4, 1973, p. E 3.

65. Richard Nixon, "Excerpts from Nixon Speech to G.O.P.," *The New York Times,* May 10, 1973, p. 36.

66. James Reston, "Mr. Nixon's 'Deplorable Incident,' " *The New York Times,* May 11, 1973, p. 39.

67. R. W. Apple, Jr., "Nixon's Remarks at Tanaka Dinner Indicate Tough Stand on His Watergate Critics," *The New York Times,* August 2, 1973, p. 19.

68. Ronald Reagan, "Transcript of the President's New Conference on Rumsfeld and Grenada," *The New York Times,* November 4, 1983, p. A 16.

69. Harry S. Truman, "The President's News Conference of April 24, 1952," *Public Papers of the Presidents of the United States: Harry S. Truman, 1952–53* (Washington, D.C.: Government Printing Office, 1966) p. 290.

70. James Reston, "After the Watergate," *The New York Times,* April 20, 1973, p. 33.

71. Richard Nixon, "Text of a Statement by the President on Allegations Surrounding Watergate Inquiry," *The New York Times,* May 23, 1973, p. 28.

72. Johnson, "Vietnam . . . ," April 1, 1967, p. 357.

73. Richard Nixon, "Text of Nixon's Statement," *The New York Times,* April 18, 1973, p. 1.

74. John Herbers, "Nixon and the Political Prospects," *The New York Times,* August 17, 1973, p. 8.
75. Ronald Reagan, "President's News Conference on Foreign and Domestic Issues," *The New York Times,* October 20, 1983, p. B 10.
76. Quoted in Arthur M. Schlesinger, Jr., *A Thousand Days: John F. Kennedy in the White House* (Boston: Houghton Mifflin Co., 1965), p. 679.
77. Ronald Reagan, "President's News Conference on Foreign and Domestic Matters," *The New York Times,* May 18, 1983, p. A 20.
78. "Meeting the Press," *The New York Times,* August 23, 1963, p. 36.
79. Ronald Reagan, "Transcript of President's News Conference on Attack of Marine Barracks," *The New York Times,* December 28, 1983, p. A 11.
80. Johnson, "Vietnam . . . ," March 15, 1966, pp. 322–323.
81. Nixon, "Transcript of . . . ," May 1, 1973, p. 31.
82. Thomas W. Ottenad, "Jimmy Carter: A Smile and a Shoeshine," *The Progressive,* May, 1976, p. 24.
83. James T. Wootern, "Center's Drive From Obscurity to the Front," *The New York Times,* March 15, 1976, p. 36.
84. Nixon, "Text of . . . ," April 18, 1973, p. 1.
85. Jimmy Carter, "Transcript of the President's State of the Union Address to Joint Session of Congress," *The New York Times,* January 24, 1980, p. A 12.
86. John F. Kennedy, "The Cuban Missile Crisis," in Windt, *Presidential Rhetoric* (Dubuque: Kendall/Hunt, 1983), pp. 36–40.
87. Nixon, "Prepared Text . . . ," August 16, 1973, p. 7.
88. Jimmy Carter, "Transcript of the President's News Conference on Foreign and Domestic Matters," *The New York Times,* May 1, 1980, p. A 12.
89. Johnson, "Vietnam . . . ," March 15, 1966, p. 322.
90. Richard Nixon, "The President's Address to the Nation on Television and Radio—April 20, 1970," in Richard Wilson, ed., *A New Road for America: Major Policy Statements, March 1970 to October, 1971* (Garden City, New York: Doubleday and Co., 1972), p. 31.
91. Jack Anderson, "Vietnam's Benefits," *The New York Post,* May 28, 1975, p. 41.
92. David Zarefsky, Carol Miller-Tutzauer and Frank E. Tutzauer, "Ronald Reagan's Safety Net for the Truly Needy: The Rhetorical Uses of Definition," *The Central States Speech Journal,* 35 (1984) 113–119.
93. Richard Nixon, "The President's Address to the Nation on Television and Radio—April 30, 1970," in *A New Road For America,* pp. 34–35.
94. Stuart Taylor, Jr., "In Wake of Invasion, Much Official Misinformation by U.S. Comes to Light," *The New York Times,* November 6, 1983, p. 20.
95. Ronald Steel, "Reveling in Military Power," *The New York Times,* October 30, 1983, p. E 19.
96. Nixon, "Transcript of . . . ," May 1, 1973, p. 31.
97. Nixon, "Transcript of . . . ," May 1, 1973, p. 31.
98. Nixon, "Transcript of . . . ," May 10, 1973, p. 36.
99. Nixon, "Excerpts from . . . ," May 1, 1973, p. 31.
100. Nixon, "Excerpts from . . . ," May 1, 1973, p. 31.
101. Nixon, "Excerpts from . . . ," May 1, 1973, p. 31.
102. Nixon, "Excerpts from . . . ," May 1, 1973, p. 31.
103. Nixon, "Excerpts from . . . ," May 1, 1972, p. 31.
104. Nixon, "Excerpts from . . . ," May 1, 1973, p. 31.
105. Nixon, "Excerpts from . . . ," May 1, 1973, p. 31.
106. Nixon, "Transcript of . . . ," August 23, 1973, p. 28.

107. Nixon, "Prepared Text . . . ," August 16, 1973, p. 7.
108. Nixon, "Prepared Text . . . ," August 16, 1973, p. 7.
109. Lyndon Johnson, "The Vietnam War; The President's Plans," *Vital Speeches of the Day,* 34 (April 15, 1968), p. 389.
110. James Reston, "Mr. Nixon's Historic Alibi," *The New York Times,* May 25, 1973, p. 35.
111. Richard Nixon, "Transcript of the President's News Conference on Foreign and Domestic Matters," *The New York Times,* April 30, 1971, p. 18.
112. Johnson, "Vietnam . . . ," April 1, 1967, p. 354.
113. Nixon, "Transcript of . . . ," May 1, 1973, p. 31.
114. Buchanan, p. 35.
115. Henry M. Shephard, letter to the Editor, *The New York Times,* May 25, 1973, p. 34.
116. William V. Shannon, "Fortunate Crisis," *The New York Times,* May 1, 1973, p. 43.
117. Nixon, "Transcript of . . . ," May 1, 1973, p. 31.
118. William Safire, "The New Foundation," *The New York Times,* January 25, 1979, p. E 21.

Different Realities: Three Presidential Attacks on the News Media

Theodore Windt

By early 1982 President Reagan's new economic program was in place. The twenty-five percent tax cut was in its second phase. Inflation was coming under control. Interest rates were falling. The rate of government spending was beginning to be curtailed. Only the rising federal deficit and increased unemployment remained major economic problems. Few people paid much attention to the deficit. But the news media, especially television, had begun to focus on the plight of the unemployed. It was within this context that another skirmish in the long war between Presidents and the press occurred.

In an interview with reporters from the *Daily Oklahoman* on March 16, 1982, President Reagan complained about the "lack of responsibility" on the part of television network news organizations. He said that one could not turn on the evening news without seeing an interview with someone who had recently lost his job. "Is it news," the President asked "that some fellow out in South Succotash someplace has just been laid off, that he should be interviewed nationwide?" He charged that such a "constant downbeat" in reporting economic news contributed "psychologically to slowing down a new recovery that is in the offing." And, he continued, such reporting had done a "pretty good job" of picturing him as "Scrooge to a lot of people." President Reagan concluded that such distorted reporting contributed to a negative psychology about his policies and about himself.[1]

Five days later, James Reston of *The New York Times* replied that it was indeed news when unemployment rose dramatically and that the news media had the responsibility to report it. He pointed out—as a sly dig to the President—that there was an actual Succotash, Rhode Island and unemployment had increased by two per cent there over the last year.[2]

With this exchange it seemed as if the contentious issue between the President and the press had once again been joined, and journalists braced for more attacks. But they did not come. Just as quickly as he had erupted against reporters, President Reagan broke off the skirmish. Perhaps he recalled the rueful observation of Lyndon Johnson to the effect that a politician cannot win a war of words with the media because they are on the air every night and the

This essay was presented at the 1984 Speech Communication Association of America convention for a panel on "The Presidency and the Press."

politician is not. The greater probability is that President Reagan and his advisers recognized that this brief outburst could develop into a full-blown issue and jeopardize the President's political goals, which would be counterproductive. And this particular President has always been more sophisticated in handling the media than they have been in handling him.[3] Nonetheless, the attack and the response have become standard between Presidents and the press. These two great powers often come in conflict with each other because they have two different responsibilities: one to govern, the other to report; one to lead, the other to criticize that leadership.

This essay is concerned with presidential attacks on contemporary news reporting. I have chosen three speeches from three different administrations, speeches that were devoted solely to criticizing reporting of presidential actions: Kennedy's speech to the American Newspaper Publishers Association in 1961; Johnson's speech before the National Association of Broadcasters in 1968; and Vice President Agnew's speech to Republicans in Des Moines in 1969.[4] In being concerned solely with the relationship of the press to politics, these speeches are unique. Equally important, these speeches represent in one way or another an attack on the *reality* held or created by news media. The major point of contention is *metaphysical*. President Kennedy contended that reporters and publishers did not understand the reality of the communist menace. President Johnson asked why television stations concentrated on the negative as opposed to the positive aspects of reality. Vice President Agnew charged that the news media were irresponsible when they broadcast a reality different from that presented by the President. In each case, all other arguments and criticism flowed from this central contention regarding political reality. And in each case, the administration believed that publishing or broadcasting something other than what the President had revealed or stated constituted a threat to the Republic. But we should remember that such criticism is not new to politics. On May 5, 1777 General George Washington wrote to the President of Congress:

> It is much to be wished, that our printers were more discreet in many of their publications. We see, almost in every paper, proclamations or accounts transmitted by the enemy, of an injurious nature. If some hint or caution could be given to them on the subject, it might be of material service.[5]

Recent Presidents have done more than "hint" or "caution."

Kennedy: The President and the Press

On April 17, 1961 fourteen hundred anti-Castro Cubans attempted to invade Cuba at the Bay of Pigs. They were quickly captured or killed with only a few escaping. Just as quickly the world learned that the Kennedy administration had armed and transported the Cubans, and had given both approval and active support to the abortive attempt to overthrow Castro. When this became known, both Republicans and Democrats, adversaries and allies criticized the invasion. Clearly, less than three months after he had assumed the presidency, President Kennedy had a full-scale military and political disaster on his hands. To repair, or at least contain, some of the damage done by the failed operation, President Kennedy delivered two major speeches, the second of which is the most important for our purposes here. But a brief summary of the first is necessary for a better understanding of the second.

On April 20, Kennedy sought to justify the invasion of Cuba in a hastily written speech before the American Society of Newspaper Editors. He opened the speech by saying that: "The President of a great democracy such as ours and the editors of great newspapers such as yours, owe a common obligation to the people: an obligation to present the facts, to present them with candor, and to present them in perspective."[6] He then tried to soothe his liberal critics ("Any unilateral American intervention, in the absence of an external attack upon ourselves or an ally, would have been contrary to our traditions and to our international obligations") and to reassure his conservative critics ("Should it ever appear that the inter-American doctrine of noninterference merely conceals or excuses a policy of nonaction—if the nations of this Hemisphere should fail to meet their commitments against outside Communist penetration—then I want it clearly understood that this Government will not hesitate in meeting its primary obligations which are the security of our Nation!").

From the ordeal of the invasion fiasco, Kennedy drew three lessons:

> *First,* it is clear that the forces of communism are not to be underestimated in Cuba or anywhere else in the world.
> *Second,* it is clear that this Nation . . . must take an even closer and more realistic look at the menace of external Communist intervention and domination in Cuba.
> *Third,* and finally, it is clearer than ever that we face a relentless struggle in every corner of the globe that goes far beyond the clash of armies or even nuclear armaments.

These harsh lessons were based on Kennedy's view of the reality of the communist threat to the United States, and he stated that view of the world in uncompromising terms:

> We dare not fail to see the insidious nature of this new and deeper struggle. We dare not fail to grasp the new concepts, the new tools, the new sense of urgency we will need to combat it—whether in Cuba or South Viet-Nam. And we dare not fail to realize that this struggle is taking place every day, without fanfare, in thousands of villages and markets—day and night—and in classrooms all over the globe.
> The message of Cuba, of Laos, of the rising din of Communist voices in Asia and Latin America—these messages are all the same. The complacent, the self-indulgent, the soft societies are about to be swept away with the debris of history.

Only the strong, only the industrious, only the courageous, *only the visionary who determine the real nature of our struggle can possibly survive.* (*Emphasis added.*)

It is not coincidental that the President used this platform before an audience of newspaper editors to lecture them and the country on his view of the critical reality of the cold war. Newspaper editors (and reporters), he believed, had not grasped the importance of this new reality, and he had to describe it vividly to them, a description of crisis so great that he would elaborate upon it and its consequences to the press in a speech a week later.

On April 27, Kennedy spoke before the American Newspaper Publishers Association and devoted his entire remarks to the relationship between the presidency and the press in light of the world-wide crisis facing the country. He stated that the United States faced an unprecedented threat to our security and our survival in every part of the world and in every sphere of human activity. This threat was new and unique to our history:

> Today no war has been declared—and however fierce the struggle may be, it may never be declared in the traditional fashion. Our way of life is under attack. Those who make themselves our enemy are advancing around the globe. The survival of our friends is in danger.

And he continued:

> [This new threat] requires a change in outlook, a change in tactics, a change in missions—by government, . . . *by every newspaper.* For we are opposed around the world by a monolithic and ruthless conspiracy that relies primarily on covert means for expanding its sphere of influence. . . . (*Emphasis added.*)

Thus, the world according to John F. Kennedy: a world in which the United States is locked in a deadly struggle with communism, a struggle so great and so extensive that our entire way of living requires radical changes and readjustments to insure the possibility of survival. It was within this extreme and perilous political reality that the President got to the heart of the matter of the relations between the President and the press.

The new reality of the communist attack on freedom demanded that newspapers change their outlook and their mission—according to Kennedy—and join the government in its crusade against communism:

> This deadly challenge imposes upon our society two requirements of direct concern both to the press and to the President—two requirements that may seem almost contradictory in tone, but which must be reconciled and fulfilled if we are to meet this national peril. I refer, *first,* to the need for far greater public information; and *second,* to the need for far greater official secrecy.

The uninitiated may ask how one can have "far greater public information" and at the same time have "far greater official secrecy," but that contradiction ("in tone" according to the President) seemed to bother Kennedy very little.

He denied that he intended to establish a new Office of War Information, despite the assertion that the country was involved in a new kind of war, or that he intended to impose government censorship. Instead, he called for self-restraint on the part of the news media. And again, he reiterated that restraint was essential to a country facing such an unprecedented peril:

> If the press is awaiting a declaration of war before it imposes the self-discipline of combat conditions, then I can only say that no war ever posed a greater threat to our security. If you are awaiting a finding of 'clear and present danger,' then I can only say that the danger has never been more clear and its presence has never been more imminent.

If the news media did not impose self-restraint, Kennedy predicted that publications might undermine American national security:

> For the facts of the matter are that this nation's foes have openly boasted of acquiring through our newspapers information they would otherwise hire agents to acquire through theft, bribery or espionage; that details of this nation's covert preparations to counter the enemy's covert operations have been available to every newspaper reader, friend and foe alike; that the size, the strength, the location and the nature of our forces and weapons and our plans and strategy for their use, have all been pinpointed in the press and other news media to a degree sufficient to satisfy any foreign power. . . .

Kennedy concluded with this recommendation to the publishers, and he did so more forthrightly than other recent Presidents: "Every newspaper now asks itself with respect to every story: 'Is it news?' All I suggest is that you add the question: 'Is it in the interest of national security?' " Kennedy assured the publishers that if the press agreed to voluntary self-discipline, his administration would cooperate "whole heartedly" in establishing specific new steps or machinery to help determine what stories were inconsistent with the national interest. Needless to say, the audience applauded only once during the speech.

Kennedy's speech is remarkable in the clarity with which he stated what most Presidents believe: the national interest must supersede constitutional liberties in times of peril. Had the country truly been at war, Kennedy's requests might not have sounded unreasonable. Indeed, publishers, editors, and reporters probably would have rushed to avoid compromising American national security and would have considered such actions their patriotic contributions to the war effort.

But there was no visible threat at the time of the speech to American national security. No Pearl Harbor had happened, not even a North Korean invasion of South Korea. What had happened was that the President had foolishly approved a stupid invasion of Cuba that had failed miserably and now the President had a political disaster on his hands. And what he seemed to be implying in the speech was that the press was somehow to blame for the disaster because it published information that he did not believe it should be publishing.

Therefore, because there existed little evidence of a direct threat to the United States in terms of specific and concrete actions taken by an enemy, Kennedy sought to create a new world reality of imminent dangers in which ideological angels do mortal combat with ideological demons. This apocalyptic rhetoric featured a world irreconcilably divided between communism and freedom with the enemy banging at the gates and where everyone within the gates should be united behind the President. It is within this political reality that Kennedy could call for self-restraint and self-discipline on the part of the press, even to the point of asking the press to relinquish its First Amendment rights. But to have Kennedy's recommendations taken seriously by the press required that it share his view of the reality of the struggle between communism and freedom. And that is where the speech began to fall apart.

Editorial responses were cautious and ranged the political gamut. William Randolph Hearst, Jr. ambiguously said: "Having been a war correspondent, I can well understand the need for security."[7] Benjamin M. McKelway, editor of the *Washington Star* and President of the Associated Press, stated: "I know of no responsible newspaper which would print material damaging to the interests of this country. The old problem is: What is it that is damaging to the interests of this country?"[8] *The New York Times* took an editorial stance that was soon adopted by most others: "For the preservation of our democratic society in this time of 'clear and present danger' it is more essential than ever that the people be fully informed of the problems and of the perils confronting them. This is a responsibility as much of the press as of the President."[9]

Nonetheless, the Publishers Association appointed a committee to study the questions, problems, and recommendations voiced by President Kennedy. On May 9, they held a seventy-minute meeting with the President and told him that they did not see an imminent peril so great as to merit restricting the First Amendment and therefore saw no need for machinery to assist the press in guarding vital security information. Felix McKnight, representing the American Society of Newspaper Editors, said the group believed that only a "declaration of a national emergency, or something like that" would warrant considering some kind of machinery for dealing with issues of national security and freedom of the press.[10] In other words, they rejected the rhetorical reality the President presented as the *raison d'etre* for self-censorship or "self-discipline."

According to memoirs written by close advisers, Kennedy was sorely disappointed with the response of the press. And he was never again to speak publicly at such length about his criticism of the press. Instead, he would cancel his subscription to *The New York Herald Tribune* when it offended him, and, as Sorensen reported, he would inform his friends in the press of stories which he liked and disliked through "phone calls, notes, and staff relays," would privately remind reporters of their responsibilities (as he saw them), and would seek to prevent "the publication of information harmful to the security of the United States" by requesting "newspapers to hold off printing stories their reporters had uncovered. . . ."[11] He thought the press had misunderstood him and the world around them. In fact, they had understood the President all too well and only had a different view of danger in the world from the view he held.

There are two footnotes to be added to this examination of this remarkable speech. First, during the cold war years the media had almost always behaved exactly as Kennedy had wished. Almost all major newspapers were overwhelmingly anti-communist, and generally vied with one another to see who could be more anti-communist and hard-line. Rarely did journalists in mainline publications give any attention to a searching examination of the cold war or the assumptions upon which American foreign policy was based. Even *The New York Times* had suppressed certain facts and a story on the Bay of Pigs before the invasion. In fact, what Kennedy was calling for—self-discipline and self-restraint—were already the standard practice.

Second, even as President Kennedy was meeting with the committee from the Publishers Association and berating *The New York Times* representative, he turned aside to Turner Catledge and said: "If you had printed more about the operation, you would have saved us from a colossal mistake."[12] Eighteen months later only a little more than a month before the Cuban Missile Crisis, Kennedy told Orvil Dryfoos of *The New York Times*: "I wish you had run everything on Cuba . . . I am just sorry you didn't tell it at the time."[13]

Johnson: The President and the Media

In an informal session before he began filming his memoirs for CBS, Lyndon Johnson was asked how politics had changed over the years from when he first entered Congress to the present day. Johnson answered with vehemence: "You guys. All you guys in the media. All of politics has changed because of you. You've broken all the machines and the ties between us in Congress and the city machines. You've given us a new kind of people."[14] Certainly, by 1971, the relationship between journalism and the President had changed dramatically. Television had jumped to the fore as the principal medium for news, eclipsing both newspaper and magazines. Television could bring events right into the living room of Americans with a dramatic vividness and verisimilitude unimagined before. And now people talked about "the media" instead of "the press."

Whether Johnson's anger was justified or not, he believed what he said. When Walter Cronkite returned from Vietnam and began his critical reports about our efforts there, Johnson is reported to have said that if he had lost

Cronkite, he had lost the war. Shortly thereafter, on March 31, 1968, Johnson announced that he would not seek re-election. The next day, President Johnson addressed the National Association of Broadcasters in Chicago. From the references to his speech the night before, this speech must have been written overnight. Though the speech has its share of political rationalizations (in that Johnson seemed to blame his failure as President more on his problems with communicating than on his policies themselves), this speech is one of the more thoughtful addresses by a President on the problems of television and contemporary presidential politics, and especially the problem of political reality.

Johnson began his discussion by saying the major problem confronting the President and the media was informing the public. He defined the rhetorical problems of the presidency in this electronic age succinctly and poignantly:

> How does a public leader find just the right word or the right way to say no more or no less than he means to say—bearing in mind that anything he says may topple governments and may involve the lives of innocent men?
>
> How does that leader speak the right phrase, in the right way, under the right conditions, to suit the accuracies and contingencies of the moment when he is discussing questions of policy, so that he does not stir a thousand misinterpretations and leave the wrong connotation or impression?
>
> How does he reach the immediate audience and how does he communicate with the millions of others who are out there listening from afar?

Though Johnson seemed to believe there was some "right" way, some magical words or phrases—form or style rather than content—that might have spared him the pain of stepping down from the presidency, Johnson's questions (when abstracted from his biographical and political context) ring true about the rhetorical problems a President must ponder and seek to solve. But in this day of electronic news, those are not the only problems.

From the rhetorical problems of the President, Johnson proceeded to the problems of electronic broadcasting (at least as he saw them) in relation to their effects on national politics. In different parts of his speech, Johnson addressed three important topics he wanted broadcasters to consider. First, the perennial question of accuracy:

> You of the broadcast industry have enormous power in your hands. You have the power to clarify and you have the power to confuse. Men in public life cannot remotely rival your opportunity—day after day, night after night, hour after hour on the hour . . . you shape the Nation's dialogue.
>
> The words that you choose, hopefully always accurate, and hopefully always just, are the words that are carried out for all of the people to hear.
>
> The commentary that you provide can give the real meaning to the issues of the day or it can distort them beyond all meaning. By your standards of what is news, you can cultivate wisdom—or you can nurture misguided passion.

Johnson recognized that the shift in reporting from printing the news to broadcasting it meant a shift in the meaning of accuracy in news. Accuracy now meant not so much the *accurate printing* of the exact statement by a President as *fair excerpting* in a news broadcast the essential meaning of a presidential speech. In this context, the standard for judging news becomes fairness as much as truth and falsehood, and often fairness is the more relevant question. After all, as Johnson pointed out, electronic news reporting frequently has to excerpt only a portion from a lengthy address instead of carrying the speech in its entirety, and thus that excerpt becomes the whole story of the speech. Since that excerpt is on film or tape, it is always exact, but the question is whether it is fair representation of what a President has said? Thus, the notion of accuracy in an electronic media age changes. The words can be exactly reproduced. But can they be reproduced in the exact context in which they were spoken or for which they were intended? The shift in the meaning of accuracy is a shift in meaning from reporting the message of a speech to the essential meaning of a speech. And then the standard for judgment shifts from truth and falsehood (did the President say what he is reported to have said?) to fairness and honesty (did the President mean what reporters in the broadcast medium say he meant? or was this excerpt from the speech representative of the meaning of the speech?). The questions Johnson posed are questions professionals still grapple with.

The second problem Johnson addressed concerned the nature and structure of television news. He rightfully pointed out that television news is more concerned with stories involving conflict than with stories involving cooperation:

> It occurred to me that the medium [television] may be somewhat better suited to conveying the actions of conflict than to dramatizing the words that leaders use in trying and hoping to end the conflict.
>
> Certainly, it is more 'dramatic' to show policemen and rioters locked in combat than to show men trying to cooperate with one another.
>
> The face of hatred and of bigotry comes through much more clearly—no matter what its color. The face of tolerance, I seem to find, is rarely 'newsworthy.' Perhaps this is because tolerance and progress are not dynamic events—such as riots and conflicts are events.
>
> Peace, in the news sense, is a 'condition.' War is an 'event.'

Johnson linked television's emphasis on conflict to the divisiveness that had plagued the country during the final years of his administration, implying that television was responsible for the turmoil and disruptions. It is precisely at this point that television news and the presidency collide. Television news does emphasize conflict and dissenting points of view. A President is constantly attempting to demonstrate that the public is united behind his policies. Television news does feed on the dramatic; after all, one house burning down is news while one hundred thousand houses not burning down is not news. A President does emphasize cooperation because that demonstrates that he is being successful in the stewardship of his office. A President, therefore, will blame, as Johnson did, television news for encouraging dissension and undermining the public interest. Representatives of the media will accuse the President of attempting to suppress dissent or of being isolated from the real public and what is happening to it. The conflict between the two institutions is inevitable in a democratic society and is irreconcilable.

The third and final criticism concentrated on the unique nature of electronic news:

> Your commentary carries an added element of uncertainty. Unlike the printed media, television writes on the wind. There is no accumulated record which the historian can examine later with a 20–20 vision of hindsight, asking these questions: 'How fair was he tonight? How impartial was he today? How honest was he all along?'

It is the nature of television to present vivid impressions with apparent verisimilitude, but the memory of those *impressions* is often more lasting than the exact words or events that occasioned them. Johnson must have been thinking of his own quandry: How does a President refute *impressions,* if he believes them to be incorrect or especially if he believes them to be unfair? In the conflict between the President and media, the choice of *what* to believe often comes down to a question of *who* to believe: a question of credibility. By 1968, Johnson had lost that battle with the media and the American public.

President Johnson's speech was interrupted by applause only once, little reported in the press, and largely forgotten. One purpose of Johnson's speech was to shift part of the blame for the consequences of the failures of his policies in Vietnam to television for reporting those failures instead of his successes. But despite this self-serving purpose, Johnson's speech represents one of the more thoughtful ruminations about the relationship of media to the presidency. Johnson correctly grasped the realities created by television news that, in turn, created new problems for a President attempting to impress his reality upon the public. Television as a news medium had emerged as a major force in American society during the Johnson administration, and Johnson had puzzled over how to react to its influence and, on occasion, its forceful presentation of events. On April 1, 1968, the day after he had announced he would not seek re-election, he was comfortable enough to ask pertinent questions about this medium in a civil manner.

Nixon/Agnew: The President Versus the Media

On November 13, 1969 Vice President Agnew addressed the Mid-West Regional Republican Committee Meeting in Des Moines, Iowa on the "importance of the television news medium to the American people." The speech may be fairly said to represent President Nixon's views. The speech had been written by one of President Nixon's major speech-writers, Patrick Buchanan, and it was read "line by line" by the President. Depending on whom one believes, the President either "toned it down" or "toughened it up."[15]

Agnew delivered the speech ten days after President Nixon had presented a major prime time address outlining his Vietnamization policy to end the war in Vietnam that he had inherited from Johnson. Nixon's address had been a resounding success, one of the most politically successful speeches in modern times. When the President concluded his address, each of the networks devoted time to discussions of the speech and Mr. Nixon's policies. Anchorpeople, reporters, and invited guests (ABC used Averell Harriman) participated in these discussions as they often had in the past following a presidential speech. Despite the precedent for this kind of analysis (which is by no means instant since reporters usually have a text of the speech well in advance and sometimes are briefed by officials about the speech beforehand), the Nixon administration rankled over it and decided to counter-attack. Nixon was not about to wait, as Kennedy had done, until he had a disaster on his hands to attack the press, nor was he to wait, as Johnson had done, until the media had contributed to his downfall. William Safire, one of Nixon's major speechwriters, pointedly described the purpose of Agnew's speech: "[It] was the opening gun . . . of a campaign to belittle, discredit, and generally wear down the credibility of the burr [the media] under Nixon's saddle."[16] It is equally clear that the President intended to treat the press as a powerful political opponent by attacking it before it could attack him.

Vice President Agnew's speech has been so celebrated that it has been critically chewed over by numerous writers.[17] And it would not serve much purpose here to delve into another analysis of it. The purpose of this essay can best be served through a brief catalogue of the charges Agnew leveled at the media for they comprise a direct, frontal, partisan attack on television news. Agnew saw the issue as a confrontation between the President and his power to govern and the news media and its power to oppose:

> When the President completed his address . . . his words and policies were subjected to instant analysis and querulous criticism. The audience of 70 million American gathered to hear the President of the United States was inherited by a small band of network commentators and self-appointed analysts, the majority of whom expressed in one way or another their hostility to what he had to say.

It was obvious that their minds were made up in advance. With this scathing indictment, Agnew proceeded to catalogue the network sins that caused them to oppose the President. These include the sins of being:

1. *Unprofessional.* "To guarantee in advance that the President's plea for national unity would be challenged, one network trotted out Averell Harriman for the occasion. Through the President's message he waited in the wings. When the President concluded, Mr. Harriman recited perfectly."

2. *Biased.* "But the President of the United States has a right to communicate directly with the people who elected him, and the people of this country have the right to make up their own minds and form their own opinions about a Presidential address without having a President's words and thoughts characterized through the prejudices of hostile critics before they can even be digested."

3. *Unrepresentative.* "The views of the majority of this fraternity do not— I repeat, do not—represent the views of America. That is why such a great gulf existed between how the nation received the President's address and how the networks reviewed it."

4. *Undemocratic.* Agnew used two lines of argument with this charge. He said that network news was controlled by a minority ("A small group of men, numbering no more than a dozen anchormen, commentators and executive producers") who through their powerful positions dominate the majority of Americans by deciding what the viewers will see, hear, and learn about national events. Second, he argued that the networks have this enormous concentrated power and yet are neither elected nor accountable. "The American people would rightly not tolerate this concentration of power in Government. Is it not fair and relevant to question its concentration in the hands of a tiny, enclosed fraternity of privileged men elected by no one and enjoying a monopoly sanctioned and licensed by Government?"

5. *Unfair specifically to President Nixon.* "When Winston Churchill rallied public opinion to stay the course against Hitler's Germany, he didn't have to contend with a gaggle of commentators raising doubts about whether he was reading public opinion right, or whether Britain had the stamina to see the war through. When President Kennedy rallied the nation in the Cuban missile crisis, his address to the people was not chewed over by a roundtable of critics who disparaged the course of action he'd asked America to follow."

The Nixon/Agnew attack on television journalists and the medium was the most thorough, biting, and direct challenge to the press in public of any contemporary administration. Nixon/Agnew pulled no punches. They said in public what previous Presidents usually only said in private. The week following this famous speech, Agnew was on the cover of both *Time* and *Newsweek,* and the speech and the charges it contained became the basis for innumerable editorials, rebuttals, seminars, academic theses, books, and other discussions. Furthermore, Agnew did not let up in his criticism but expanded it in subsequent speeches to include newspapers and public figures who would presume to criticize Nixon and his policies.[18]

Agnew encapsulized the reason why Presidents attack the press when he stated: "A raised eyebrow, an inflection of the voice, a caustic remark dropped in the middle of a broadcast can raise doubts in a million minds about the *veracity of a public official or the wisdom of a government policy.*" Indeed, these are the issues in the conflict between the President and the media: the veracity and wisdom of public policy and policymakers. Agnew turned the issue around by questioning the veracity and wisdom of television news reporting and the reporters who provide that news.

Summary and Conclusion

The three attacks on the media represent three different rhetorical approaches to the problems Presidents believe they have with the American media.[19]

President Kennedy's speech, as well as his speech a week earlier to the Newspaper Editors, was essentially defensive. Kennedy sought to contain the damage he had done to himself through the Bay of Pigs fiasco by blaming the press, indirectly and in part, for his problems. In the political heat of that time, he went so far as to recommend abridging the First Amendment through self-censorship of the press. His attack is a classic example of blaming the bearer of bad news for the bad news itself.[20]

President Johnson's address was delivered in the aftermath of his announcement that he would not seek re-election. Even though a spirit of resentfulness creeps into the speech, Johnson was in a reflective mood about what the power of electronic media had done and could do to the political processes. Despite the political overtones and personal hurt resonating throughout the speech, Johnson raised pertinent and troubling questions, questions that remain about the relationship between politics and media.[21]

The Nixon/Agnew attack took place in an entirely different context from either Kennedy's or Johnson's. And it took a quite different form. Nixon had just delivered a stunningly effective speech outlining and justifying the policies he would pursue in his search for peace in Vietnam. He had no political disaster on his hands, and he was still in the relative infancy of his administration. The Nixon/Agnew attack was directly political, animated by a view of the media as another political enemy to be vanquished. It was the opening rhetorical salvo in a campaign to belittle and discredit reporting and reporters, a campaign that worked rather effectively until Watergate swallowed up the administration.[22]

There is a difference in specific charges that Presidents have made against the print media and the electronic media. Against the print media, Presidents claim they are inaccurate in what they print or that they disclose unauthorized information. This was true of Kennedy's claims and remains true from the Pentagon Papers case forward. Against the electronic media, Presidents claim they are unfair and distort information. This has been the case since Johnson's and Agnew's claims and remains the case right through to President Reagan and his comments on South Succotash.

The major charge that Presidents have levelled against the press, however, is irresponsibility. To substantiate that charge Presidents have accused members of the press and the media as a whole of disclosing harmful information that may damage American national security, of distorting facts and information, of harboring personal and institutional biases against Presidents and against presidential policies, and—above all—of misleading the public and thereby eroding the popular support Presidents seek. Each of these accusations seems to assume that media are usurping the President's responsibilities and endangering the country in one way or another. What actually is at stake is public opinion. The President seeks unity. The media thrive on conflict. The President wants his version of reality accepted. The media print and broadcast different realities. The President acts and has to accept responsibility for his policies. The media have to report news and have to accept responsibility for the accuracy and fairness of that news, but the media do not accept the responsibility to propose policies to replace the President's, even as the stories they present may be critical of presidential policies. The President usually presents his version of political reality personally in major political speeches. Media—especially television news—often present different realities through stories, interviews with experts and partisan opponents, except when they are explicitly critical through editorials or commentaries. Even as these differences make for conflict between Presidents and the press, so too the similarities between the two intensify that conflict. Both contend they act in the public interest as no other political figure can and as no other private organization can. The President claims that he, unlike other politicians, is President of all the people. The media claim that they, unlike other private organizations, are devoted to the public's right to know. When they conflict with one another, they each contend that the other is intruding on their constitutional rights. The President claims he has the constitutional right and responsibility to govern, and the media contend that they have the constitutional right to report and publish. Little wonder, then, that in this global village in which Americans live, dominated as it is by media politics that the President and the press so often find themselves at loggerheads. They have different functions and therefore see the world differently. Thus, not only are the realities that motivate them different, so too are the realities they create through their speeches and their news stories. In a democratic society these differences are not only to be expected, but to be welcomed.

Notes

1. *Weekly Compilation of Presidential Documents* (March 21, 1982), pp. 3–4.
2. *The New York Times* (March 21, 1982), p. E 21. For other commentaries on Reagan's relations with the press, see: David Hoffman, "How Reagan Controls His Coverage At Home: The Candidate Packaged and Protected," *Washington Journalism Review* (September, 1984), pp. 36–41; Barbara Matusow, "How Reagan Controls His Coverage Abroad: The White House Writes the Lead," *ibid.,* pp. 42–46; "Accusing the Press: What Are Its Sins?" *Time* (December 12, 1983), pp. 76–93; "Gunsmoke and Sleeping Dogs: The Prez's Press at Midterm," *Columbia Journalism Review* (May/June, 1983), pp. 27–35; George Reedy, "There They Go Again," *ibid.,* pp. 35–36; Steven R. Weisman, "Can the Magic Prevail?" *The New York Times Magazine* (April 29, 1984); John Tebbel and Sarah Miles Watts, "Reagan: The Image Triumphant," *The Press and the Presidency* (New York: Oxford University Press, 1985), pp. 531–553.
3. See, for example, James Nathan Miller, "Ronald Reagan and the Techniques of Deception," *Atlantic Monthly* (February 1984), pp. 62–68.
4. Quotations from President Kennedy's speech and President Johnson's speech are taken from the texts as reprinted in *Presidential Rhetoric: 1961 to the Present,* 3rd edition, ed. by Theodore Windt (Dubuque: Kendall/Hunt, 1983), pp. 11–14 and pp. 106–111 respectively. Quotations from Vice President Agnew's speech are taken from the text as reprinted by Karlyn Kohrs Campbell in *Critiques of Contemporary Rhetoric* (Belmont; Wadsworth, 1972), pp. 79–87.
5. "Letter to the President of Congress," 5 May, 1777, *The Writings of George Washington,* ed. by Jared Sparks, Vol. IV (Boston: Russell, Odiorne, and Metcalf, 1834), p. 409.
6. "Lessons to be Learned from the Bay of Pigs Invasion," in Windt, p. 12. All subsequent quotations are from this reprint of the speech.
7. *The New York Times* (April 28, 1961), p. C 30.
8. *Ibid.*
9. *Ibid.*
10. *The New York Times* (May 10, 1961), p. 10.
11. Theodore C. Sorensen, *Kennedy* (New York: Harper and Row, 1965), pp. 319–320.
12. Clifton Daniel, "The Press and National Security, a lecture delivered on June 1, 1966 and reprinted in Appendix B of William McGaffin and Erwin Knoll, *Anything But the Truth* (New York: G. P. Putnam's Sons, 1968), p. 205. This speech contains Daniel's recollections about how and why *The New York Times* decided to suppress stories and information about the Bay of Pigs invasion.
13. *Ibid.*
14. Quoted in David Halberstam, *The Powers That Be* (New York: Alfred A. Knopf, 1979), p. 6.
15. Richard Nixon wrote: "A few days after the [November 3] speech, Pat Buchanan sent me a memorandum urging a direct attack on the network commentators and a few days later he submitted a speech draft that did so in very direct and articulate language. Ted Agnew's hard-hitting speeches had attracted a great deal of attention during the fall, and I decided that he was the right man to deliver this one. I toned down some of Buchanan's rhetoric and gave it to Agnew. We further moderated some sections that Agnew thought sounded strident, and then he edited it himself so that the final version would be his words. *RN: The Memoirs of Richard Nixon* (New York: Grosset & Dunlap, 1978), p. 411. But William Safire wrote "Pat Buchanan turned away from his news summaries long enough to belt out a

speech for the Vice President's Des Moines, Iowa, appearance on November 13. Agnew liked it. Buchanan went over the speech line by line with the President. Nixon read it all the way through without expression, as he does when he is excited, and Pat told me he commented: 'This really flicks the scab off, doesn't it?' The President then added a few lines, toughening it up. Only three drafts were written— very few for a major address. It retained its white-heat vitality." Safire, *Before the Fall* (New York: Belmont Tower Books, 1975), p. 352.

16. Safire, p. 352.
17. See Karlyn Kohrs Campbell, pp. 94–110; Theodore Otto Windt, Jr. "Administrative Rhetoric: An Undemocratic Response to Protest," *Communication Quarterly* (Summer, 1982), pp. 245–250; and Ben H. Bagdikian, "The Great Nixon-Agnew Media Con Game; or, A Few Plain Facts About the Politics of Newspapers," in *The Effete Conspiracy and Other Crimes of the Press* (New York: Harper and Row, 1972), pp. 143–149.
18. See his speech, "The Power of the Press," delivered before the Montgomery Chamber of Commerce, November 29, 1969 in *Frankly Speaking* (Washington: Public Affairs Press, 1970), pp. 78–85. After Agnew was forced to resign the Vice Presidency, he had a quite different view of the wisdom and veracity of public officials and public policy (at least in regard to him). See Spiro Agnew, *Go Quietly . . . Or Else* (New York: William Morrow, 1980).
19. For studies on perceptions of news media bias by Presidents and of presidential news management, see Harvey G. Zeidenstein, "White House Perceptions of News Media Bias," *Presidential Studies Quarterly* XIII (Summer, 1983), pp. 345–356; Harvey Zeidenstein, "News Media Perceptions of White House News Management," *Presidential Studies Quarterly* XIV (Summer, 1984), pp. 391–398. For a historical account of the relations between press and Presidents, see John Tebbel and Sarah Miles Watts, *The Press and the Presidency*. I believe the most reasonable and balanced account of the problems between the two is presented in Austin Ranney, *Channels of Power* (New York: Basic Books, 1983).
20. For Kennedy's views on the press and his attempts to influence it, see Sorensen, pp. 310–326; Halberstam, pp. 316–390; James Deakin, *Straight Stuff* (New York: William Morrow and Co., 1984), pp. 42–44, 85–86, 163–191; Pierre Salinger, *With Kennedy* (Garden City: Doubleday, 1966).
21. On Johnson and the press, see Halberstam, pp. 428–548; McGaffin and Knoll; Hugh Sidney, *A Very Personal Presidency* (New York: Atheneum, 1969).
22. On Nixon and the press, see Joseph C. Spear, *Presidents and the Press: The Nixon Legacy* (Cambridge: MIT Press, 1986); *President Nixon and the Press* (New York: Funk and Wagnalls, 1972); Herbert G. Klein, *Making It Perfectly Clear* (Garden City: Doubleday, 1980).

JOHN F. KENNEDY

Analysis of the Style of John F. Kennedy's Inaugural Address

Edward P. J. Corbett

"If, in the effective use of language, style is the man, style is the nation too; men, countries, and entire civilizations have been tested and judged by their literary tone."
John F. Kennedy

General Situation of the Speech

If we are to relate the style of the Inaugural Address to its content, we must take into account the subject matter, the occasion, the audience, and the ethos of the speaker. An inauguration is a solemn, ceremonial event, attended by certain traditions and rituals. A speech delivered on such an occasion is usually of the ceremonial variety, although there may be deliberative elements in it. What the people have come to expect is not so much a speech that lays down a specific program as a speech that sets a mood. In striking the keynote of the coming administration, the speaker will try to heal the wounds that may have been inflicted during the campaign, to remind the audience of a common heritage and a common purpose, to set forth, in a general way, the policies and objectives of the new administration, and to reassure the international community of the continuity and determination of the nation.

Since a ceremonial speech like this deals in generalities rather than in particulars, it can very easily slip off into platitude and pious cant. In seeking to please everyone with a "safe" speech, the speaker runs the risk of pleasing no one. In striving for that happy mean between the general and the specific, between the trite and the bizarre, and between the offensive and the fulsome, the speaker will have to draw on all his ingenuity to come up with a content and a form that will impress his audience without boring them.

Having characterized the kind of speech that is usually delivered at an inauguration, we might consider now the special situation that faced President Kennedy on that January morning in 1961. John Fitzgerald Kennedy was the youngest man and the first Catholic to be elected to the highest office in America, and he had been elected by a narrow margin of voters. His youth, his religious affiliation, and his narrow victory at the polls—all these combined

Mr. Corbett is Professor Emeritus of English, Ohio State University.

to establish some doubts about him in the minds of his own people and the people of other countries. Having created an image, during the campaign, of enormous vitality and considerable political shrewdness, this leader of the New Frontier had to fulfill his promise to push the country forward. Clearly, this was an occasion when a powerful ethical appeal would have to be exerted if the confidence and initiative of the people were to be aroused.

What about the audience for this address? There would be the immediate audience—the high dignitaries on the platform and the thousands of people gathered in the plaza in front of the Capitol building. Then there were the millions of people who would see and hear the speaker through the medium of television. And finally there would be the millions of people in foreign lands who would read accounts of the speech in their newspapers the next day. Taken together, this was a vast, heterogeneous audience, posing special problems for the speaker. As we have remarked before, the larger and more heterogeneous the audience is, the more difficult it is to adjust the discourse to fit the audience. In his content and his style, the President must strike some common denominator—but a common denominator that does not fall below the dignity that the occasion demands.

Having looked at the general situation that prevailed for the speech, let us now see how the President accommodated his means to his end. In this analysis, of course, we are going to investigate only the way in which the President accommodated his *style* to the subject matter, occasion, audience, and his own personality.

The Speech as a Whole

One of the first things that strikes the reader is the relative brevity of the speech—1343 words, which at the normal rate for public address would take between nine and ten minutes to deliver. When the President wrote this speech he could not have known that the "live" audience for the speech would be standing in the biting cold that followed a heavy snowstorm in the Washington area on the day before the inauguration. So the President had not made his speech brief out of consideration for his wind-chilled audience. In preparing the speech, however, he might have taken into consideration that it would be delivered at the end of some lengthy preliminary speech-making. But perhaps the consideration that mainly determined the brevity of the speech was the traditional nature of inaugural addresses. As we have observed, inaugural addresses usually deal in broad, undeveloped generalities. Principles, policies, and promises are enunciated without elaboration.

Paragraphs

The relative brevity of the speech is reflected in the paragraph and sentence structure. A glance at the printed text of the speech reveals a succession of short paragraphs. Of the twenty-seven paragraphs in the speech, ten have only one sentence; seven paragraphs are two sentences long; and another seven are three sentences long. The longest paragraphs (9 and 24) contain only four sentences. In terms of averages, there are 49.3 words per paragraph and 1.92 sentences per paragraph.

The President is trying to cover a lot of ground in this short speech. In order to do this, he enunciates his principles, promises, and policies in a litany of capsule paragraphs. The effect of these unelaborated paragraphs would have been slight if the President had not rendered many of those paragraphs memorable by the brilliance of his style.

Sentences: Length

Descending to the next smallest unit of discourse, the sentence, we note some interesting facts about the length and kinds of sentences. The two extremes of sentence length are represented by the sentence of eighty words (second sentence of paragraph 3) and the sentence of four words (third sentence of paragraph 20). The average length of the President's sentences is 25.8 words. But what is more revealing about the President's style is the variation above and below this average. Fourteen of the fifty-two sentences (27 per cent) in the speech are ten words or more *above* the average; but twenty-three sentences (44 per cent) are five words or more *below* the average. Although the President has a number of unusually long sentences—66 words (paragraph 10), 64 words (paragraph 22), 54 words (paragraphs 8 and 13)—an unusually high proportion of his sentences are composed of twenty words or less. Even by modern journalistic standards, a twenty-word sentence is short. This high proportion of short sentences matches the over-all brevity of the speech and the short paragraphs. Although the President displays an admirable variety in sentence-length, his heavy use of the short sentence does suggest that he had his *listening* audience in mind when he composed his speech. Another consideration that may have influenced the President in the use of short sentences is that short sentences help to create the effect of sententiousness that is appropriate for a ceremonial speech.

Sentences: Grammatical Types

Having noted a high proportion of relatively short sentences, we might expect that a majority of the sentences would be of the simple or compound type. But a close investigation of the grammatical types reveals that this is not so. Twenty (38.4 per cent) of the sentences are simple; only six (11.6 per cent) sentences are compound. But twenty-six sentences (exactly 50 per cent) are complex. Taken together, the simple and compound sentences constitute 50 per cent of the whole, but the predominant grammatical type is the complex sentence. What this reveals is that the President manages the expansion of his sentences mainly through the sophisticated pattern of subordination. A study of the sequence of sentences, however, shows how well the President has mixed the grammatical types in order to avoid monotony of structure. Only in a half dozen or so places in the speech does he string together two or more sentences of the same grammatical type.

Sentences: Rhetorical Types

When we study the rhetorical patterns of the speech, we note another interesting feature of President Kennedy's style. The predominant rhetorical structure is antithesis. This recurring structure was perhaps dictated by the fact that the speech deals mainly with comparisons of opposites (end–beginning, old–new, rich–poor, friend–enemy). He strikes the theme of the speech and the antithetical keynote in the first sentence: "We observe today *not a victory of party/ but a celebration of freedom*—symbolizing *an end/* as well as *a beginning*—signifying *renewal/* as well as *change.*" Additional examples of antithesis are not hard to find:

to friend and foe alike (paragraph 3)

United . . . Divided (paragraph 6)

To those old allies . . . To those new states (paragraphs 6, 7)

If a free society cannot help the many who are poor, it cannot save the few who are rich. (paragraph 8)

What problems unite us . . . those problems which divide us (paragraph 15)

And the most memorable line of the speech is cast in the form of an antithesis:

. . . Ask not what your country can do for you—ask what you can do for your country.

Most of these antitheses of thought are laid out in parallel grammatical structure. The recurring parallelism is appropriate here because although the President is pointing up opposites by his antitheses he wants to suggest that these opposites can be reconciled. Opposites can be reconciled only if they are co-ordinate, and one way to emphasize the co-ordinate value of opposites is to juxtapose them in a parallel grammatical structure.

The other use that the President makes of parallelism is for the purpose of specification or enumeration, as in these three examples:

> born in this century, tempered by war, disciplined by a hard and bitter peace, proud of our ancient heritage (paragraph 3)
>
> pay any price, bear any burden, meet any hardship, support any friend, oppose any foe (paragraph 4)
>
> Together let us explore the stars, conquer the deserts, eradicate disease, and encourage the arts and commerce (paragraph 17)

As we shall see when we come to study the figures of speech, there are additional schemes intertwined in many of these parallel and antithetical patterns.

Before concluding this section on rhetorical patterns, we shall point out some other features of style. If the student needed any evidence to justify his use of a co-ordinating conjunction at the beginning of the sentence, he could cite this speech. The President begins fourteen of his sentences (over 25 per cent) with a co-ordinating conjunction. There is, of course, ample precedent for this usage in modern prose and the prose of earlier centuries. But it is interesting to note how effective rhetorically this means of articulating sentences is in the President's speech. Let us look at just one example of this usage:

> We dare not tempt them with weakness. For only when our arms are sufficient beyond doubt can we be certain beyond doubt that they will never be employed. (paragraph 12)

Contrast the effect of this with the following:

> We dare not tempt them with weakness, for only when our arms are sufficient beyond doubt can we be certain beyond doubt that they will never be employed.

The content and rhetorical scheme of both sentences is exactly the same, and perhaps if one were *reading* the second sentence aloud he could produce the same effect as the first sentence has. But on the printed page, a special emphasis is achieved by setting off the second clause in a sentence by itself and by signaling the syllogistic relationship of the two clauses by the capitalized initial *For*. If the student analyzes the other uses of initial co-ordinating conjunctions, he will usually find some rhetorical purpose being served.

Sentences: Functional Types

The overwhelming majority of the sentences are declarative. This proportion is appropriate in a speech that is designed to inform and reassure the world about the objectives of the new administration. Occasionally, however, the President uses some other functional types of sentence. In paragraph 23, he uses two rhetorical questions ("Can we forge against these enemies a grand and global alliance, North and South, East and West, that can assure a more fruitful life for all mankind? Will you join in that historic effort?"). These questions occur at the point in the speech when the President is about to launch into his peroration. Up to this point the President has been declaring what he will do, what the American people will do. Now he wants to suggest what the international community can do to support his program of peace and prosperity. But he can only suggest—he cannot dictate or predict—what other countries will do. The rhetorical questions are phrased in such a way, however, that the natural answer to them is a resounding *Yes*.

The President groups together two other types of functional sentences—imperatives and hortatives. In paragraphs 25, 26, 27 (the concluding paragraphs of the speech), we see three sharp imperatives, using the verb *to ask,* which leave the citizens with a call to action. Up to this point, the audience have been mere listeners to this ceremonial discourse. Now the audience must be engaged actively. The imperatives point to the general line of action that they must take.

The series of fourteen hortative sentences ("Let us . . . Let both sides . . .") in paragraphs 14 through 20 also lays down a program of action, but the directives are softened by being cast in a hortatory form. (The Latin and Greek languages would have used the subjunctive mood of the verb to create this effect.) The President here is seeking to induce action, not command it. In other words, he wants to persuade rather than coerce.

Diction

The diction of the speech unobtrusively but unmistakably exerts an influence on the effect of the speech. The simplicity of the diction is perhaps not immediately noticeable, but when one studies it, one notes that there is almost no word that a moderately intelligent high-school graduate would have to look up in a dictionary. A closer study of the diction reveals a high proportion of monosyllabic words: some 951 words in the speech (71 per cent) are monosyllabic. In paragraphs 19 and 20, the proportion of monosyllabic words is as high as 80 per cent. Even in the peroration of the speech, where one might expect the orator to make use of the sonorous cadence that can be achieved with polysyllabic diction, one finds a high proportion of one-syllable words. This monosyllabism helps to account not only for the impression of simplicity but also for the note of strength in the speech—a note that people had come to associate with the vigor of this youthful public figure. In working over the drafts of the speech, the President must consciously have sought out simple, Anglo-Saxon words.

Having noted the high proportion of monosyllabic words, one might expect to find also a high proportion of concrete words. But this is not the case. Investigation of the nouns in the speech turns up many abstract words—words like *freedom, poverty, tyranny, loyalty, devotion, responsibility, aggression, subversion*. And most of this abstract diction in Latinate and polysyllabic. Aside from the figures of speech—which we will investigate later—there are surprisingly few concrete words—*huts, villages, stars, deserts, graves*. Whatever air of concreteness the speech has is created by the figures of speech. Perhaps the high proportion of abstract words is the natural consequence of the brief, unelaborated character of the speech. Once the President had decided to enunciate only the broad, general policy of his administration, it was almost inevitable that most of his substantive words would be abstract. What we have in this short speech really is a series of undeveloped topic sentences.

Another thing that accounts for the formal quality of this ceremonial speech is the occasional use of slightly archaic diction. We find the President using such words as *forebears* (twice), *host, anew, asunder, foe, adversary, writ*. Besides echoing the tone of Lincoln's *Gettysburg Address* ("Fourscore and seven years ago," "our fathers," "final resting-place," "hallow"), this quaint diction has Biblical overtones and a certain appropriateness to the old-new motif. The President reinforced the effect of this kind of diction by two quotations from the Old Testament and the folksy adage about riding the back of the tiger. The repetition of certain honorific key terms, like *pledge, citizens, peace* also helps to reinforce the reverential tone of the speech.

Figures of Speech: Schemes

First of all, let us look at some of the schemes—those patternings of words which represent departures from the ordinary way of speaking. Since we have already remarked about the pervasive parallelism and antithesis in the speech, we will concentrate here on some of the other schemes.

There are a number of schemes of repetition. The most notable of these is anaphora—repetition of the same words at the beginning of successive clauses. Anaphora is conspicuous in two key passages in the speech: the section (paragraphs 6–11) in which the President is making a series of pledges ("To those . . ."); and the section (paragraphs 15–18) in which the President is suggesting a course of action ("Let both sides . . ."). We have previously observed that these two sections make use of parallelism. The addition of *anaphora* to these passages performs two functions: it combines with the parallelism to mark off and emphasize the co-ordinateness of the series, and it helps to establish the rhythm of the passages. The speech has no example of the opposite scheme, epistrophe (repetition of the same word at the end of successive clauses), but it does have two examples of repetition of similar words in a medial position: "bear *any* burden, meet *any* hardship, support *any* friend, oppose *any* foe" (paragraph 4); "sufficient *beyond doubt* . . . certain *beyond doubt*" (paragraph 12).

The most remembered sentence in the speech—"ask not what your country can do for you—ask what you can do for your country"—contains a figure of repetition known as antimetabole (repetition of words in converse order). Another memorable utterance—"Let us never negotiate out of fear. But never fear to negotiate"—appears to be another example of antimetabole, but it is more accurately classified as polyptoton (repetition of words derived from the same root). Here we have different conjugates of the word *fear*—serving as a noun in the first clause and as an infinitive in the second clause. There is another example of polyptoton in paragraph 22 ("Not as a call to *battle,* though *embattled* we are")—although, as the editors of the *New Yorker* observed, there is a suggestion here too of the trope called paronomasia (play on words).

President Kennedy made sparing use of the scheme of repetition known as alliteration. There are only two instances of noticeable alliteration in the speech—"the *a*rea in which its *w*rit may *r*un" (paragraph 10); "to *l*ead the *l*and we *l*ove" (paragraph 27). Perhaps in accord with his personality, the President avoided frequent use of alliteration because of the soft, effeminate sound-effect often produced by this figure; the President was striving for a note of strength and vigor. One wonders, though, whether the President did not intend some sound-effect of appropriate harshness in the succession of *s* and *d* sounds in "before the dark powers of destruction unleashed by science engulf all humanity in planned or accidental self-destruction" (paragraph 11).

Let us look briefly at a few more schemes. In most of his parallel series, the President shows a preference for the hurried rhythms that can be achieved with asyndeton (omission of conjunctions)—e.g. "born in this century, tempered by war, disciplined by a hard and bitter peace, proud of our ancient heritage" (paragraph 3). The President makes little use of the scheme called anastrophe (unusual word order). In the entire speech, there is only one structure that is inverted: "*United,* there is little we cannot do in a host of cooperative ventures. *Divided,* there is little we can do" (paragraph 6). It is easy to see the special emphasis the President achieves here by placing the past participles in the initial position, even though these participles do not modify, as they normally do in this position, the subject of the main clause. One could regard this structure, however, as ellipsis rather than anastrophe. The closest the President comes to the figure known as climax is in paragraphs 25, 26, 27; but even here we have to strain a bit to find any element of rising importance in the series.

Figures of Speech: Tropes

Although the President makes rather skillful use of the schemes, he is less satisfactory in his use of tropes. There are a number of metaphors in the speech, and those metaphors represent, as we remarked earlier, the chief way in which the President introduces concreteness into the speech. But many of these metaphors—"the torch," "bonds of mass misery," "the chains of poverty," "corners of the earth," "the trumpet," "the glow from that fire"—are rather hackneyed. He achieves a little more freshness in some of his more subtle metaphors, like "iron tyranny," "destruction unleashed," "twilight struggle," "forge." Perhaps his most successful metaphor is the one in paragraph 19— "And if a beachhead of co-operation may push back the jungle of suspicion." By themselves, *beachhead* and *jungle* are rather shopworn metaphors, but they acquire a certain freshness by being combined in a complex metaphor.

The several uses of "hands" (part for the whole) and "arms" (genus for the species) can be looked upon as examples of synecdoche, but those tropes too are fairly trite. The use of "hand" in paragraph 13—"that uncertain balance of terror that stays the hand of mankind's final war"—should be classified as an instance of personification rather than of synecdoche. Perhaps the only other expression in the speech which might be read as an instance of personification is found in the last paragraph—"with history the final judge of our deeds."

Style of Delivery

Undoubtedly, a good deal of the effect of this speech was produced by the "style" of delivery. Those who watched the inauguration ceremonies on television may recall the President's clear, crisp, voice, the distinctive Bostonian accent, the mannerisms of the jabbing finger, the pauses, the inflections, the stresses. All of these features of voice and gesture helped to put the speech across; combined with the carefully worked-out style, they helped to communicate the President's message to the electorate and to the world. And perhaps it would be well for the student who has read this close analysis of the style to put the speech together again by listening to it on one of the many memorial records that were issued shortly after the President's assassination. Listening to a recording of the speech will make the student aware that this was a discourse designed for oral delivery, and it might prove interesting to note how much of the highly refined style of the speech comes through to the student once he has had the devices of style pointed out to him.

Concluding Remarks

The various stylistic devices we have been observing may be looked upon by some people as the ornamentation of the speech. These devices do "dress up" the speech, but if they are regarded as no more than ornamentation, they have failed to perform the functions that rhetoricians traditionally assigned to them. These formal devices should be one of the carriers of meaning. If the diction, the composition of words, and the figures of speech are not functioning to clarify, enliven, and emphasize the thought, if they are not exerting an ethical, emotional, or logical appeal, then indeed the style of a piece is so much sounding brass and tinkling cymbals, so much sound and fury signifying nothing.

It is not so important that the style of the speech be recognizable as the "Kennedy style" as it is that the style be seen as appropriate to the subject matter, the occasion, the purpose, and the audience. Just as Lincoln's *Gettysburg Address* was not particularly impressive to the audience who heard it in the National Cemetery on November 19, 1863, so Kennedy's Inaugural Address was not—if we may judge from the restrained applause that greeted it while it was being delivered—notably impressive to the audience who heard it in the snow-packed Capitol Plaza on January 20, 1961. It is only when we get a chance to read and reread Lincoln's and Kennedy's speeches that we realize what splendid performances they were. Only a close analysis such as we have engaged in can make us aware of the great care and deliberation President Kennedy devoted to the "expression" of his speech. So much eloquence did not come by chance. It had to come from calculated choices from among a number of possibilities.

We should now be in a better position to judge whether the President's choices were judicious. And we should be in a better position to predict whether future generations will judge this Inaugural Address to be one of the noblest utterances to issue from the lips of an American statesman.

Anger, Language and Politics: John F. Kennedy and the Steel Crisis

Richard Godden and Richard Maidment

The conflict that occurred between the Kennedy administration and the steel industry in April, 1962 was an interesting and revealing episode. Unhappily it has been increasingly overlooked as historical attention has been diverted either to the administration's conduct of foreign affairs or to the other more 'glamorous' areas of domestic policy, principally civil rights.[1] This is unfortunate because a series of questions concerning the behaviour of President Kennedy and his main advisers have never been raised, let alone satisfactorily answered. Why, for instance, was a price rise of less than 3.5% deemed to be a major political issue in 1962, requiring presidential intervention and an investigation into the practice of the steel industry by the F.B.I.? Yet in 1963 an increase in prices of similar proportions was all but ignored.[2] Why did the administration claim in 1962 that the price increase severely damaged the economy but a year later appeared to be unconcerned about the level of steel prices? Finally, and above all, why did President Kennedy take such personal offense at the behaviour of the steel industry's management? Apart from the famous "sons-of-bitches"[3] remark, which gained wide currency and was the cause of considerable damage to relations between the administration and the business community, Kennedy's reaction to the price increase was reported to have been a mixture of "incredulity and . . . anger."[4] According to a close friend and confidant, Benjamin Bradlee, Kennedy was visibly irritated and confessed that he had been given a "cold fucking" by the steel industry management.[5] So the portrait of Kennedy that emerges from this episode is hardly the conventional one of a cool detached politician with a developed sense of irony. Instead he appears to have been overwrought and somewhat rattled.

The standard and accepted explanation for Kennedy's behaviour is that the President was furious with the management of the steel industry for breaking their word.[6] The explanation is thus located in the realm of personality and individual ethics. The industry leaders, so we are told, were ill-mannered and had "duped" the president, who justifiably felt that his "trust had been abused"

Mr. Godden is Lecturer in American Literature at the University of Keele.
Mr. Maidment is Lecturer in American Politics at the University of Keele, England.
Reprinted by permission of Center for the Study of the Presidency, publishers of *Presidential Studies Quarterly* Vol. X, No. 3 (Summer 1980), pp. 317–331.

and therefore took it as a personal "affront."[7] We do not accept the thrust of the explanation. We do not believe that Kennedy was the vassal of his own undoubted anger at apparent industrial deceit. We wish to argue that Kennedy's concerns were self-consciously political in that the issues raised by the steel crisis threatened his public standing. The President was particularly sensitive to the potential damage that this affair could do to his reputation as a political mediator. What do we mean by mediator? Perhaps the answer will be apparent if we briefly recount the events which preceded April 11.

Late in 1961 the administration, principally through its Secretary of Labor, Arthur Goldberg, had been involved as a broker between the management and the unions of the steel industry over their triennial wage negotiations. Kennedy and Goldberg believed that they had convinced the union leadership to accept a modest wage increase on the barely articulated understanding that the companies would show a comparable restraint over pricing levels. However, if this understanding was audible to the administration it was not to the management side, for on April 10 the United States Steel Corporation posted a 3.5 percent increase which exceeded the administration's expectations. In response Kennedy organized a political onslaught on the industry's management; an act fraught with danger. Politicians in a liberal constitutional democracy do not declare war on an important element of their constituency unless they are obliged to. America's politicians do not impair their relations with the business community unless compelled to do so, and Kennedy's sense of personal pique is not a sufficiently compelling reason. Neither are the arguments offered by Schlesinger, Sorensen et al. that the administration was concerned about inflation, the balance of payments and collusion between the steel companies (for reasons outlined below.) We believe that the source of Kennedy's worry was that his credentials as a mediator would be irredeemably damaged and that consequently his political effectiveness would be considerably diminished, for the act of mediation between the component elements of a constituency is the central activity of a politician in a liberal political system. Therefore, the most damaging judgment to be made of a politician would be that he is an incompetent broker; that he is unable to fashion a deal or even worse that any deal he puts together will become unstuck. Who then would trust Kennedy or his good offices? The lack of trust, however, would have nothing to do with ethics but with competence, or rather its absence. We sustain our proposition about brokerage by turning to the medium in which the deal is made—to language as the agency and register of liberal collusion.

Liberalism, indeed any belief system, is not necessarily apparent in the reportage of fact, nor does it readily reveal itself to statistical analysis; it is a conceptual shadow most clear at the intersection of language and event. Where a speaker describes he will invariably prescribe, and his latent assumptions will infuse his most literal terms with a propositional quality. If ideology may be spoken of as habitual inflexion it ought to be peculiarly available to the stylistic analysis of particular speeches, read in the context of singular events.

Shadows, nuances, and implicitudes . . . such evidence is liable to vanish before it can be piled up. But the clear, the straight and the explicit too often offer only a mirage of concreteness. Unless some account of the awkward relationship between description and prescription is given, the critic is left with material which, although it feels like the real stuff, is a shadow—items without thought. The negotiation between ideas and things, items and thought is carried out most continuously, surreptitiously and even gracefully in everyday speech, where, without the tacit assumption that meanings are shared, prolixity would thwart all exchange. Of course, collective meanings can be as subtly variegated as the terms that embody them, but unless ideas and their linguistic vehicles are allowed a formative place within the substance of fact, reality will pass unnoticed. We find the language models of Saussure, Vološinov and Eco particularly helpful in locating this materiality. These are large claims to make on the evidence of a single domestic circumstance, but the decision to concentrate on one case study was largely methodological. The steel crisis offered itself as an ideal example.

Turning to the details of the crisis: On April 11, at a news conference, Kennedy stated the administration's case. He raised three principal objections to the actions of the steel industry. The first was that there was no sound economic rationale for the price increase.

> The facts of the matter are that there is no justification for an increase in steel prices. The recent settlement between the industry and the union, . . . was widely acknowledged to be noninflationary. . . . Steel output per man is rising so fast that labor costs per ton of steel can actually be expected to decline in the next 12 months. . . . The cost of the major raw materials, steel scrap and coal has also been declining. . . . The industry's cash dividends have exceeded $600 million in each of the last 5 years, and earnings in the first quarter of this year were estimated in the . . . Wall Street Journal to be among the highest in history.
>
> In short at a time when they could be exploring how more efficiency and better prices could be obtained . . . a few gigantic corporations have decided to increase prices in ruthless disregard to their public responsibilities.[8]

His second criticism was based on a suspicion that the steel companies had acted collusively. The first sentence of his opening statement referred to "Simultaneous and identical actions of United States Steel and other leading corporations."[9] Later in the press conference Kennedy stated:

> The Department of Justice is particularly anxious, in view of the very speedy action of the companies who have entirely different economic problems facing them than did United States Steel—the speed with which they moved, it seems to me, to require an examination of our present laws and whether they're being obeyed, by the Federal Trade Commission and particularly the Department of Justice. I'm very interested in the respective investigations that will be conducted in the House and Senate . . . .[10]

Finally Kennedy pointed to the damaging effects of the price increase:

> . . . [T]his rise in the cost of steel . . . would increase the cost of homes, autos, appliances, and most other items for every American family. It would increase the cost of machinery and tools to every American businessman and farmer. It would seriously handicap our efforts to prevent an inflationary spiral from eating up the pensions of our older citizens, and our new gains in purchasing power.
>
> It would add, Secretary McNamara informed me this morning, an estimated $1 billion to the cost of our defenses, at a time when every dollar is needed for national security and other purposes. It would make it more difficult for American goods to compete in foreign markets, more difficult to withstand competition from foreign exports, and thus more difficult to improve our balance of payments position, and stem the flow of gold.[11]

Kennedy rested his case on these three facts and then concluded his statement on a very bitter note:

> Some time ago I asked each American to consider what he would do for his country and I asked the steel companies. In the last 24 hours we had their answer.[12]

The question that we find intriguing is, do Kennedy's 'facts' explain his bitterness and anger, or for that matter, do they explain the transformation of a price increase into a political crisis? We do not think so.

Of all Kennedy's 'facts' the third—the consequence for the American economy—is the most persuasive, given the economic conditions that prevailed in 1962. Since February, 1961, the economy had been recovering from the 1960 recession. However, the recovery had been weak and had not materially improved the three most pressing economic problems, unemployment, the underutilisation of plant and machinery, and the balance of payments.[13] Inflation, to a lesser extent, was also a matter of concern. But what was most worrying to the administration were indications that the recovery, barely a year old, was already faltering. So the price increase did come at an inopportune moment. As the administration analysed it, steel was a "bellwether" industry and an increase in steel prices would inevitably have an adverse consequential effect on wage and price levels throughout the economy. This, the administration feared, would make American industry less competitive, exacerbate the balance of payments deficits, raise inflation rates, slow economic growth and so lower employment levels. Kennedy, like other presidents before and after him cherished a combination of low rates of unemployment and inflation with high economic growth and thus found the price increase politically unpalatable. So Kennedy's distaste for the increase was predictable and understandable, but it does not, by itself, explain his response to the steel companies because all presidents are accustomed both to politically difficult economic developments and to a lack of available remedies. They are the inevitable consequence of governing a market economy.

The principal characteristic of a market economy is that the decision making process on such issues as pricing and investment is decentralised and located in a multiplicity of structures which are, at least in the United States, overwhelmingly privately owned. The decisions that are taken by these structures are intended, of course, to further their own self defined interests. So the federal government's ability to affect the policies adopted by these structures is limited. The federal government, however, does attempt to create an economic climate, through fiscal and monetary policy, which it hopes will have a consequential effect on the nature of these decisions but the record of successive administrations is not marked by a continuing success. This is so, primarily, beause the functioning of a complex and sophisticated market economy by fiscal and monetary measures is inordinately difficult. To a lesser extent, the lack of success has also resulted from the reality that while corporations, unions and other industrial and financial institutions are affected by governmental economic policy, it is not the sole determinant of their individual decisions. Their decisions will be affected by a host of other factors, some of which may have considerably greater impact on them than the policies and preferences of the federal government. So presidents, their advisers and civil servants have become inured to their policies being thwarted and their desires being unfulfilled. They are reconciled to it. Thus President Kennedy's dislike of the increase in steel prices cannot by itself explain his abrasive response to the steel companies. The answer must lie elsewhere.

Perhaps the answer lies in Kennedy's second 'fact'; that implied collusion of the steel companies over the price increase. If the companies had colluded, they would not only have been guilty of breaking the law but also of breaking the rule of market economy. But despite an investigation by the F.B.I. no prosecution was brought by the government against the management of the companies concerned presumably because there was insufficient evidence to sustain it. So, what was the basis of Kennedy's suspicion? In response to a question asked at the press conference on April 11, Kennedy declared that

> . . . the suddenness by which every company in the last few hours, one by one as the morning went by, came in with their almost, if not identical, almost identical price increases . . . isn't really the way we expect the competitive private enterprise system to always work.[14]

Now this answer and Kennedy's opening statement contain a version of the market economy which would not do Adam Smith an injustice. In an economic universe where perfect competition reigned, "simultaneous and identical price increases" would indeed be a very sound cause for suspecting that something untoward had taken place. If the American steel industry had a structure of multiple competing units of comparable size and power then again the activities of the companies between April 10–11 would have aroused justifiable suspicion about collusion. But, of course, perfect competition did not reign in the steel industry. The various companies were not equal competitors. And steel was no different to any other major American industry. The industry was dominated by the United States Steel Corporation. In 1961, U.S. Steel was the third largest industrial corporation in the United States. It had thirty percent of the industry's total capacity and well over a third of capacity in particular steel products. Nor was the company's preeminence a recent development. From its creation in 1901 it had always been the largest producer and at various times in its existence had produced over fifty percent of the industry's output. It was thus the acknowledged price leader of the steel industry. When U.S. Steel set its prices the other companies in the industry followed.[15] As the Kefauver Committee noted in 1957 the pricing policies of U.S. Steel were affected by the "almost certain knowledge, based on years of experience, that its so-called leading competitors will make the same increase."[16] Thus the actions of Bethlehem, Republic, Youngstown Sheet and Tube, Jones and Laughlin, and Wheeling in following the lead of U.S. Steel on April 11 was not grounds for suspicion that these companies had acted in an illegal and complicit manner, but merely evidence that in the market for steel products, prices were 'administered' by U.S. Steel as they had been for the previous half century.[17] The rules of the market, as they pertained to steel and other major industries, thus were not being broken but quite to the contrary, they were being closely adhered to. The market that Kennedy was referring to had ceased to exist, at least for heavy industry, some considerable time ago. We are intrigued as to why this eluded him.

Closely related to Kennedy's imputation of collusion was his final 'fact' that the price increase was unwarranted. According to Kennedy "employment costs per unit of steel output" had not risen in the preceding three years and that tht cost of some raw materials had been declining. But Roger Blough, chairman of the board of U.S. Steel challenged these figures. Blough claimed that costs had risen by six per cent since 1958, the year of the previous general increase in steel prices and that even the proposed 3.5 percent increase would not restore the cost price relationship that had existed in 1958. The source of this dispute between the administration and U.S. Steel over the nature of costs in the industry, derived from the absence of a mutually agreed concept of productivity and its measurement. While we do not intend to discuss the varying notions of productivity in any detail, we believe it is important to note that the corporation's version of productivity was not idiosyncratic or self-serving. U.S. Steel also had a further and more persuasive argument to make in justifying the price rise. In 1961 it had announced profits of $190.2 million but this was some $114 million less than the previous year. This decline in profitability had grave consequences for the corporation's investment programme. In 1960 $117 million had been invested in new plant and machinery, but in 1961 that figure had declined precipitously to only $2.7 million. According to

William T. Hogan "The need for investment was a pressing one . . . to modernize the company's facilities. . . . Clearly something had to be done to restore the level of profitability of United States Steel . . . modern equipment had to be installed and this required higher profits for reinvestment, and they in turn required higher prices."[18] So U.S. Steel did have a case. The president's assertion that "there is no justification for an increase in steel prices" was somewhat misleading. It offered a rather distorted interpretation of the economic and financial conditions that prevailed in the steel industry. But what interests us is not the misleading nature of Kennedy's 'fact' but its failure to provide a convincing rationale for his personal intervention and attack on the steel companies in general and U.S. Steel in particular. There was no proven collusion between the companies and there was a case for a price rise. And while we do concede that the administration had some grounds for concern about the consequences of the price increase for the economy, it was a worry which was hardly worthy of translation into a political crisis. So why then did President Kennedy act in the manner that he did?

We return to the notion of political mediation and Kennedy's belief that his credentials as a political broker or mediator has been severely damaged. Perhaps we ought to make it clear that we are not dismissing the sense of personal outrage that the biographies of Kennedy and his administration normally allude to. We do not deny that it existed. Indeed it is very understandable that the president was irritated and felt that he had been used by the steel industry's management. But his irritation would have been contained within the Oval office and would not have surfaced in public. It certainly would not have taken the precise and concentrated manner with which the administration conducted itself during the steel crisis. It would have been most unlike Kennedy, a sophisticated and clever politician, to have started a conflict and a very bitter one, with a key element of his constituency, solely out of personal pique. The administration from the outset, fully realised the damage that this episode would wreak on its relations with the business community. Consequently, after the dust had settled, they had to spend a considerable amount of time and political energy on repairing their fences with the business world. The administration would not have endangered this relationship unless something very substantial was at stake, something that had little to do with economics and even less with personal anger.

As soon as he had heard about the price increase, Kennedy phoned David McDonald, president of the United Steelworkers. "Dave," he said, "you've been screwed and I've been screwed." The reference of this remark was that the administration, had persuaded the steelworkers leadership to sign a new contract which provided for a wage increase of 2.5 per cent, a figure deemed to be 'non-inflationary' by the administration. Kennedy and Goldberg believed that this fulfilled the first part of an unwritten and indeed unspoken agreement between the union, the industry's management and themselves. The second part of this implicit understanding was that the companies would then refrain from the general price increase. Thus, when Roger Blough informed Kennedy of U.S. Steel's intentions, both Goldberg and the President believed that the management side had broken the agreement and their word, a grave offence in the Washington code of political practice. But it is our case that the administration's onslaught against Blough and his allies did not occur because the management side had sinned. The administration's attack was not an act of retribution, but a dramatised act of self-protection. Kennedy realised that the credibility and standing of himself and his administration were at stake. Their ability to mediate was severely threatened. The administration had operated on certain understandings, which they believed to be shared by management and labour, only to discover that was not the case. Who then would subsequently trust the Kennedy administration's good-faith or competence, particularly where the dimensions of Kennedy's faith could so easily be cast as administrative incompetence. Unwritten words and conceptual contracts are scant documents to take to the industrial market place, and implicit understanding evidences little more than touching innocence when set against the profit motive. Retrospectively Kennedy's anger seems rhetorical; a device to distract attention from his own rather tenuous intrusion into industrial negotiations. The argument might run—he should have obtained signatures, agreed contracts and reached explicit understandings. Having failed to do so he casts the owners as conspirators to avoid accusations of executive ineptitude. The anger is therefore rhetorical and manipulative. Such an account recasts Schlesinger's Kennedy as the cynical politician of recent demythologizing political histories.[19]

Both versions mistake the materials of political brokerage and so misrepresent the broker. The conceptual, the implicit, the unwritten are as substantive to the steel issue as the industrial plant itself. It is perhaps a function of the liberal tradition and of liberal historiography that the ideological and the pragmatic are divorced, as a prelude to the characterization of politicians as anything from cool pragmatists to willful opportunists. The roles are opposed in name alone, since both validate a political world of "immediate issues" "practical decisions" "checks and balances" in which "conflicts" are "problems" and "solutions" are "engineered." It is our contention that Kennedy's anger is genuine, not because he has burned his tinkering fingers, but because he experiences an impasse at the centre of his political conviction. The authenticity of his obscenity is poignant because it points to the paucity of the tradition that Kennedy was elected to serve—a liberal tradition that delimits his imagination.

While thinking about and analysing the language in which liberal ideology is realized we grew increasingly aware of the need for a simple vocabulary. We failed to find one, and can only apologize if some of what follows treats linguists and their theories like fast litter. The need to signpost the emergence of a tentative critical position may explain why, in the cause of credibility, names, references and footnotes too often impede fluency. We hope, however, that the reader will be sustained by the simplicity of our basic interest in what happens when a politician talks. In order to understand this linguistic process and to locate its implications for the political process, we need some more general account of what happens when a word is used.

The Swiss linguist Ferdinand de Saussure argues that a sign unites not a "thing" and a "name," but a "concept" and a "sound image," these he calls "signifier" and "signified," expressing their relationship as "complicity."[20] His idea defeats the notion of two orders of reality, names and things. Words are granted a substance in and of themselves, since a speaker realizes materiality even as his signs are themselves materialized. The notion is hardly new, (Saussure was lecturing in the first decade of the century) nonetheless political commentators continue to allude to rhetoric and event as though they were antithetical, the former invariably veiling the latter. Talk of "veils," "mists" and "smokescreens" does not illuminate the political word, since it implies that the politician is detached, isolated in cynicism or ignorance: further, the wraith-like connotation of such language obscures the materiality of meaning. But what is the nature of that materiality? Umberto Eco takes it to be culturally determined and pursues a study of signs as a study of social forces. By his definition a sign should be renamed a "sign function," since it is not a fixed entity but a social process. Our need to verify the sign by discovering its referent as a physical entity—out there—derives from our unwillingness to regard perception as dependent upon previous verbal acts. Eco offers a simple parable: a man walking in the dark glimpses an imprecise shape on the pavement. What does it mean? When he has ordered his somewhat surprised sense, it is a "cat." He recognizes this because he has seen other cats. Consequently, a troublesome field of sensory stimuli is calmed by the cultural unit "cat," a sign that was prior to the adequate perceptual event.[21] Were it not the case that communicative signs depended for verification upon culturally shared ideas, "unicorns," not to mention "cold-wars," would be more problematic than they are. Implicit in the idea that a sign represents a real object of collective thought, rather than a real object per-se, is the political consequence that appeals to "The facts of the matter . . ." depend as much upon shared assumptions generated by the phrase, as upon inherent matter within fact: as Stawson put it, "mentioning or referring is not something an expression does; it is something someone *can* use an expression to do."[22]

If signs achieve their content through collectivity that content is necessarily ideological, since interested parties rather than objective dictionaries determine meaning. Vološinov claims that meanings enter a society's attention and its vocabulary because they impinge on the interests of a significant group. As a result the semantic item becomes the object of a sign; this object or signified he calls a "theme," a choice that illustrates his Marxist determination to ascribe the materiality of the sign to a continuous historical process:

> *The forms of signs are conditioned above all by the social organization of the participants involved and also by the immediate conditions of their interaction.* When these forms change so does the sign.[23]

This is most readily experienced at the level of particular dialogue, where "meaning belongs to a word in its position between speakers"[24] the speaker talks, offering meanings that are a register of his social, economic and cultural position; the recipient, in order to understand, lays down a set of complementary, answering and transposing words—matches word with "counterword"—as he orientates himself to the social and semantic position of the speaker. Words, therefore, are not only ideological but inherently argumentative. At the risk of repetition—Vološinov suggests the "multivalency" of meaning, a ubiquity that he sets within the "dialogic" nature of language, where dialogue awakens in signs their "inner dialectical quality" or "multiaccentuality." However, accents are different ways of saying the same thing, and a multitude of accents is liable to be noisy rather than significantly differentiated. Vološinov's version of meaning, for all its dynamism, does not sustain an account of the partiular workings of group interest within speech. Eco's *A Theory of Semiotics* is similarly deficient: the semiologist offers a convincing account of semantic stability as cultural coding, but fails to determine how the consensus which stabilizes meaning reaches its agreement:

> We can imagine all the cultural units as an enormous number of marbles contained in a box; by shaking the box we can form different connections and affinities among the marbles. The box would constitute an informational source provided with high entropy, and it would constitute the abstract model of semantic association in a free state. According to his disposition, his previous knowledge, his own idiosyncrasies, each person when faced with the sign-vehicle [centaur] could arrive at the unit "atomic bomb" or "Mickey Mouse."
>
> But we are looking for a semiotic model which justifies the *conventional* denotations and connotations attributed to a sign-vehicle. And so we should think of magnetized marbles which establish *a system of attraction and repulsion,* so that some are drawn to one another and others are not. . . . Still better, we could consider every cultural unit . . . as emitting given wave-lengths which put in tune with a limited (though possibly very large) number of other units. Except that we have to admit that the wave-lengths can change according to new messages emitted and that therefore the possibilities of attraction and repulsion change in time; in other words . . . that the components of meaning are not closed in number, frozen into a system of relevant units . . . but form an open series.[25]

The analogies are illuminating, but for our purposes lavish. Indeed, those wishing to account for Kennedy's anger on April 11, 1962 may take little but underconfidence from the notion of meaning as a "cultural code" vitiated and transformed by magnetic fields linked in a potentially infinite open series.

Nonetheless Eco's "abstract model" is useful in that it links idiosyncracy to culture. The fact that Kennedy's outburst over the big-steel men was not only idiosyncratic but untypical pushes explanation all too easily towards the biographical. Indeed, Kennedy's notoriously offending remark would seem to descend directly from Joseph Kennedy:

> My father always told me they were sons of bitches, but I never really believed him until now.

Whatever the felicities of phrasing, the bitchery of businessmen is a semantic choice made available to Kennedy through his participation in the shared assumptions, called by Eco "cultural codes." The linguist M. A. K. Halliday focuses this, and much else of what has been said, by defining the semantic field as a process of choices within which any text can be understood as "the paradigmatic environment of what might have been meant."[26] Such a context is disarmingly vast, but even if it leaves the political analyst in the awkward position of contemplating "what might have been meant," the presentation of meaning as a "potential," "dialogic," ideological," and culturally encoded environment will have served considerable purposes. It will not, of itself, provide a theory of interest, but within the context of specific events semantic biases may emerge.

On April 11, 1962 the big-steel men broke their word. We hope that our hasty and eclectic resume of the semantic process as continuing collective labour indicates that the breaking of some words does offense to more than the Washington codes of political practice. Certainly the administation was discomfited but it could say so (loudly) only because it sensed that the electorate was similarly discomfited. A collapse of industrial mediation in the economic field has implications for the semantic field in so far as price administration is semantic administration, since particular interests ascribe particular values to the sign-vehicle "steel." From Vološinov's perspective—three power groups enter a dialogue in which Kennedy plays broker; the dialogue is interrupted when a single group imposes a price increase which realizes *their* understanding of the financial situation. (As we have seen 3.5% is only one account of the economic climate.) Alice's question to Humpty Dumpty is pertinent:

> (Alice) The question is whether you can make words mean so many things.
> (Humpty Dumpty) The question is *who* is to be master.

In itself U.S. Steel's act, read as an imposition of "univocality" or "multiaccentuality," is politically irrelevant; after all, demogogic language is manifestly non dialectical and yet it frequently succeeds. The semantic and political point about Roger Blough's announcement is that it offends particular shared meanings within the liberal imagination. Kennedy's annoyance reflects an offense against general patterns of consciousness that are a key semantic/political element within his constituency. We are not referring to pressure groups or bodies of the electorate, but to structures of feeling, most probably shared by steel-owner, steel-worker and President alike. Kennedy's belief that Adam Smith is alive and well and that he should reside at Bethlehem convinces himself, his electorate and eventually the owners, not because of F.B.I. investigations, but because Adam Smith's market continues to operate within the liberal mind. Unless its exchanges can be located both as a shared assumption and as a material element in the crisis, Kennedy's reaction will appear illogical; the owner's reversal will seem incomprehensible and the electorate's position will remain inconsequential.

On March 31, immediately after the successful wage negotiations, Kennedy read a statement over the phone, "first to David McDonald, President, United Steel Workers of America, and then to R. Conrad Cooper, Executive Vice President, United States Steel Corporation."

> I know that I speak for every American in congratulating you on the early and responsible settlement in steel. The contract that you have agreed upon is a document of high industrial statesmanship.
> When I appealed to you and to the industry to begin negotiations early enough to avert any inventory build-up that would have had deterimental consequences for all, I did so with firm confidence that your union and the industry would serve the national interest. That confidence has been fully justified.[27]

His mode of address is formal and yet casual; a prepared statement delivered by the President's voice over a medium that nominally permits interruption and dialogue. The other textual options open to him—telegrams, letters and representatives—are less cohesively personal. The telephone was an ideal device, perhaps because it dramatized equanimity among negotiators: President (he who, "describes the public interest"), Employer (Big Business) and Employee (Organized Labour) have agreed a "contract" in which the mingling of voices affirms mutuality of meaning. (Spokesmen are spokesmen for their collective interests, but once agreements have been made spokesmen can afford to be men who speak to one another over the phone.) Such is the semantic amity that terms which generally draw distinctions are used to affirm unity: in the phrase "your union" the possessive-pronoun applies without strain to McDonald *and* to Cooper; likewise, "the industry" refers not to plant but to a "concept" or "theme" in which consumers, workers and owners are co-labourers.

Kennedy's confidence about the achievement of a shared understanding is reflected in his presentation of the "settlement" as "a document of high industrial statesmanship," a metaphoric transition which contains a semantic tour-de-force. Max Black, discussing metaphor, draws a useful distinction between the metaphoric terms or "focus," and the "frame"[28] in which the term occurs; this may be a sentence, a paragraph—indeed any segment of text over which the term exerts a connotative influence. He argues that "focus" and "frame" are interactive, so that in the sentence, "Man is a wolf," the focus "wolf" operates as "a system of associated commonplace," rather than as a current lexical meaning—that is to say, "man" is set within a network of rapacity, savagery, hunger, animalism, etc.: "wolf" does not stand in for "man," rather the focus organizes a frame in which a certain view of man may be taken. Likewise, when Kennedy speaks of the steel "settlement" as a document of state, that "document" is not a substitute for the agreement: it is a metaphor which permits a view of that agreement. Too often metaphors are read as decorative deviations from the literal; their meaning is thought to be available to paraphrase which restores a proper and primary intent. However, to speak of one thing in terms of another involves tension and persuasion rather than straight substitution (as Aristotle put it, "to metaphorisize well implies an intuitive perception of the similarity in dissimilars."[29]) If this is the case, the dissimilarity between industrial negotiations and the canons of statecraft is potentially as much a part of Kennedy's hypothetical "document(s)" as the similarities. How then can he assume that his listeners will hear his metaphor as apt rather than arguable? Much is at risk since "document" is part of a network of terms—"settlement," "contract," "statesmanship," "national interest"—and were "document" to fail "national interest" might be exposed. Nominally the issue is stylistic: does the metaphor work? But it must be remembered that orators do not impose meanings: meaning is a mutual act between consenting language users. However fanciful or inert, a politician's speech works (if work it does) only because his chosen audience labours with him. Complicity is prominent in metaphor which, because it operates on "a system of associated commonplace," effectively activates the politician's semantic constituency.

> Rhetoric does not develop in some empty space of pure thought, but in the give and take of common opinion. So metaphors and proverbs also draw from the storehouse of popular wisdom—at least, those that are 'established'.[30]

Contracts "not forced but chosen,"[31] have long enjoyed a special place in the popular wisdom of liberalism: they are the documents which affirm that free collective bargaining is going on in the market place—as such they resurrect Adam Smith. A testament to the power of contract over the liberal imagination is Article 1 Section 10 of the American Constitution, "No state shall . . . pass any . . . law impairing the obligation of contracts."

Not all metaphors work in this way. During the press-conference on April 11 Kennedy's discomfiture is metaphorically realized: discovering himself in a conceptually free market where price-leaders are nonetheless a fact of healthy economic life, he uses a troubled and troubling metaphor. U.S. Steel has announced its increase and the other major procedures are rapidly falling in line:

> THE PRESIDENT: I'm hopeful that there will be those who will not participate in this parade and will meet the principle of the private enterprise competitive system in which everyone tries to sell at the lowest price commensurate with their interest. And I'm hopeful that there will be some who decide that they shouldn't go in the wake of U.S. Steel.[32]

"Parade" and "wake" are metphors, though both might deny it. Kennedy had already used "parade" in response to an earlier question; by quoting himself and employing the indexical "this" he seeks to turn his metaphor into a referential term.[33] Likewise, "the wake of U.S. Steel," in a press-conference that has featured discussion of military cuts, appears an uncomplicated analogy. U.S. Steel is a major company whose product is a staple of the ship-building industry; to speak of the company as a military vessel seems therefore almost conventional. However, both metaphors, and the network between them, are highly problematic. A parade is generally a celebration, though it carries connotations of irresponsible frivolity and martial regularity; in the context of "wake" a parade could become funereal. The tension between the "semantic markers" dramatizes Kennedy's ideological position. For the Supreme Commander, facing international "crisis" in Berlin and Vietnam, U.S. Steel's price-leader threatens to cut a deathly wake through military expenditure. As economic broker to a liberal, oligopolistic, capitalist society he has his terms in a twist—the ideological account of the market as a source for liberal democracy requires that the market be free, but the market itself has a convention of administered prices, therefore its operatives are simultaneously democratic citizens *and* self-interested executives; a parade of such men is both a celebration *and* a frivolity. For the consumer "parade" might simply refer to an irresponsible collusion over prices, but American consumers (like their representatives) are concerned over military strength as well as their imaginative investments in Horatio Alger. Consequently, for President and electorate alike, the meaning of "parade" is unstable. To adapt Max Black's terms, the "frame" is not and cannot be "focused." Although "parade," like "document," can be seen depending upon "system(s) of associated commonplace," its relationship to them is speculative and uneasy.

We want to argue that Kennedy's confusion and anger is neither illogical nor biographical, rather it expresses a semantic shock reaching to the centre of a collective habit of imagination. Having fulfilled a broker's role in a vital economic contract, Kennedy learns that neither role nor contract was significant. He is left in a state of conceptual need, quite at a loss for a way to account for events. His shock is intimately registered in the instability of "parade/wake." Our descriptive phrasing derives from Paul Ricoeur's account of creative metaphor as a form of semantic dynamism:

> (The) gain in meaning is inseparable from the tension not just between the terms of the statement, but also between two interpretations—a literal interpretation restricted to the established values of words, and a metaphorical interpretation resulting from the 'twist' imposed on these words, in order to 'make sense' in terms of the statement as a whole. The resulting gain in meaning is thus not yet a *conceptual* gain, to the extent that the semantic innovation is not separable from the switching back and forth between the two readings, from their tension and from

the kind of stereoscopic vision this dynamism produces. We might say then that the semantic shock produces a conceptual need, but not as yet any knowledge by means of concepts.[34]

Plainly, political language cannot long afford such dynamism: since any mass audience contains a range of "interests," successful political speech must tap the social codes that distribute those interests cohesively. Although signs are "multivalent" and in a state of transition, the politician (indeed any interested party) must perform as though this were not entirely the case. To acknowledge that, "meaning belongs to a word in its position between speakers" might debilitate one's authority over that meaning. The speaker who works within the liberal tradition must maintain dialogic forms even as he dispenses stabilized meanings. While it would be misrepresentative to elect *one* model of liberal language, it does seem likely that an ideology which preserves "open markets" by means of "administered prices," is going to require of its spokesmen a difficult mix of stable and unstable meanings. Such semantic prestidigitation is less than magic, it happens every day:

Good morning. How are you?
I'm fine. How are you?

The exchange is typical. Constructed from ready-made phrases, it requires "no lapse of time" for judgment; its workings are something like the workings of red on a set of traffic-lights—"red" means "stop" and in so doing unifies diverse social and national groups. Nonetheless, "Good morning," is only nominally a signal; differences of phrasing, timing and emphasis allow those who exchange greetings to make distinctive points within the format. The convention is stable and its sources are unquestioned, but the user has had his say. If one were seeking a liberal model of political discourse one might start with the coercive freedoms of, "Good morning. How are you?" Such a study would concentrate on the phatic aspect of language, where an active sharing of meaning displaces the recognition of differences:

The phatic function plays a very important part in all forms of communication: rites, solemn occasions, ceremonies, speeches, harangues; family conversations or amorous exchanges, in which the content of the communication is less important than the fact of being there and affirming one's membership of the group.

The same words, the same gestures are replaced: the same stories are reiterated. This makes communication absurd and unbearable to the outsider, but renders it euphoric for the 'participant' who 'is involved'—and unpleasant if and when he ceases to be involved.[35]

Such language may seem redundant from the outside, but it allows "the participant" to rest from the dialogic labour of offering "counter signs:" he rests secure in the phatic flow, with the conventionalized confidence that he can forecast what will be said and agree with it—a confidence that involves the gentle effort of self-fulfilling prophecy. The phatic is the place of collusion and so would seem the ideal starting point for a typology of liberal rhetorical ploys. The work is yet to do.

Our current aim is more modest; we seek only to relate Kennedy's reactions on April 11 and 12, 1962 to the collective pressures latent in the role of brokerage: but that reaction and those pressures direct us to the phatic relation between Kennedy and his audience. For example, during his press conferences on steel Kennedy repeatedly appeals to facts; his figures are economically partial but as sign vehicles for certain assumptions *about* facts they are impeccable. The economist may assess accuracy but the semiologist C. S. Peirce offers a different measure for the meaning of "Steel output per man . . . labour costs per ton of steel . . . The cost of the major raw materials . . . the February 28th Wall Street Journal."[36] For Peirce signs are of three kinds—iconic (in which the signifier imitates the signified); indexical (in which the signifier corresponds factually to the signified) and symbolic (in which the signifier is imputed to relate to the signified via laws, conventions and habits.)[37] His distinctions express degrees of motivation among signs and are of interest for the analysis of liberal language. A speaker who seeks (rather than imposes) univocality will often work with highly motivated signs. An appeal to facts and figures encourages the listener to assume that he and the speaker see things in the same way and share a past experience that is concrete. Consequently, citations from the Wall Street Journal have an eccentrically phatic function. Nonetheless, as we have seen, "mentioning is not something an expression does, it is something someone can use as expression to do;" consequently the whole idea of referring (exemplified by icons and indices) is just *that*, an idea, whose force depends upon the culture in which it is mooted. American politicians often sound pragmatic; after the manner of William James they are, "Men who are strongly of a fact loving temperament,"[38] because in an empiricist tradition there is little more phatic than fact. When Kennedy tells a pressman; "Secretary McNamara informed me this morning . . ." of an estimated $1 billion increase in defence costs, he dramatizes the power of the figure and the fixer in the American political tradition.

Persons as diverse as John Stuart Mill, James, Chomsky and Secretary McNamara insist that the way to truth is direct, and that the measurement of facts should everywhere be employed against the idealism of ideas. Just as Locke wanted a greater use of illustration in dictionaries, so Chomsky divides utterances into propositions whose truth value can be tested against outer states of affairs: for Locke the model is the Naturalist who "treat(s) of Plants and Animals this way,"[39] while for Chomsky a "picture theory" of language assures words a real and fixed meaning existing in a finite and known universe.[40] As John Stuart Mill put it:

> When I use a name for a purpose of expressing a belief it is a belief concerning the thing itself, not concerning my idea about it. When I say, "the sun is the cause of the day," I do not mean that . . . thinking of the sun makes me think of the day. I mean that a certain physical fact, which is called the sun's presence (and which, in the ultimate analysis, resolves itself into sensations, not ideas) causes another physical fact, which is called day. . . . Names therefore, shall always be spoken of in this work as the names of things themselves, and not merely as our idea of things.[41]

Kennedy's approach to the big-steel men is well glossed in Mill's acount of the sun: by offering facts in all their sources and immediacies Kennedy implies that, "in the ultimate analysis," the steel-crisis "resolves itself into sensations, not ideas." Even as the politician plays pragmatist, turning issues into fact, so he assures his audience that they share a world in which the profit motive can be measured and indexed, and where he who indexes may become an icon. As surely as the Wall Street Journal embodies one aspect of capitalism; so Kennedy, with the agencies of measurement at his finger tips, exemplifies how, for him as for his audience, beliefs are "really rules for action."[42] Instigating "nocturnal activities" by the F.B.I. may seem over active but, as the President put it, "We wanted to get the facts."[43] And where the facts pertain to a semantic ghost living in the market place, it is perhaps wiser to be forceful than subtle.

Retrospectively, many of the factual details offered by Kennedy sound redundant, but this very redundancy commits the listener to phatic confidence:

> And in fact, the Acting Commissioner of the Bureau of Labor Statistics informed me this morning that, and I quote, "employment costs per unit of steel output in 1961 were essentially the same as they were in 1958."[44]

The sentence might more gracefully have run:

> 'And in fact, Robert J. Myers told me that employment costs per unit of steel output in 1961 were essentially the same as they were in 1958.'

But much would have been sacrificed. The initial "And," an ungrammatical use of the conjunction which is typical of Kennedy's speeches, turns sentences and paragraphs into a sequence of linked propositions: grammatical units designed for argument are modified for the presentation of information. The substitution of a proper name for a professional function, along with the use of "told," could only have weakened this intent; while, "and I quote," which subordinates the voice of the policy maker to the voice of the statistician, affirms the vitality of "objective-fact" within the decision making process. After this kind of analysis it may be possible to argue that the ungainly rhythm of the sentence (punched full of interruption) realizes a phatic meaning for the audience, glossable as—'Man working; using our ways of working.' It is this kind of meaning, located in the pragmatic process, that Blough's alternative figures, directed as they are to content, cannot touch.

It would have disconcerted Alice, as doubtless it disconcerted Roger Blough, to watch the many meanings of a fact become singular. Humpty Dumpty might have explained that semantic singularity exists only where agreed by speaker and audience. To which we would add that such semantic contracts are a politician's constituency, since it is within their mutualities that he discovers and creates his own credibility. The steel crisis seems, to us, from available historical and political perspectives, incredible. Kennedy's anger and his apparent economic naivete look inexplicable until one sets them within the unwritten and often unspoken assumptions of his tradition; implicitudes which rest at the intersection of language and event, informing facts and figures with a conceptual shadow in whose absence no fact or figure can be spoken of as existing. The technical apparatus of linguistics and semiology seemed the best way of locating this awkward "environment of what have been meant," as the missing and formative element in what *was* said and meant. If our argument throws some light on the activity of politicians, we would hope that its method could usefully be developed, through other case studies, so that a way of listening critically to political rhetoric, in the liberal idiom, might emerge.

Notes

1. The steel crisis has not attracted a great deal of scholarly attention. The most useful accounts of the episode are to be found in: J. Heath, *JFK and the Business Community* (Chicago, University of Chicago Press, 1969); R. Hoopes, *The Steel Crisis* (New York, Harper & Row, 1963); G. McConnell, *Steel and the Presidency, 1962* (New York, Norton, 1963). The steel crisis is also described by A. M. Schlesinger, *A Thousand Days: John F. Kennedy in the White House* (Boston, Houghton Mifflin 1965), pp. 635–640; A. M. Schlesinger, *Robert Kennedy and his Times* (London, Andre Deutsch, 1968), pp. 401–408; T. Sorensen, *Kennedy* (London, Pan, 1965), pp. 491–508.
2. The price increases in 1963 were of a selective nature rather than the across the board type of 1962, but they amounted to a similar percentage increase. See W. T. Hogan, *Economic History of the Iron and Steel Industry in the United States,* Vol. 5 (Toronto, Heath, 1971) p. 2085.
3. Kennedy was reported to have said: "My father always told me they were sons of bitches, but I never really believed him until now." R. J. Whalen, *The Founding Father: The Story of Joseph P. Kennedy* (London, Hutchinson, 1964), p. 467.
4. Schlesinger, *Thousand Days,* p. 635.
5. B. C. Bradlee, *Conversations with Kennedy* (New York, Norton, 1975), p. 102.
6. See Schlesinger, *Thousand Days:* Sorensen, *Kennedy.*
7. Sorensen, *Kennedy,* p. 497.
8. John F. Kennedy, *Public Papers of the Presidents, 1962* (Washington, Government Printing Office, 1963), p. 316.
9. Kennedy, *Public Papers, 1962,* p. 315.
10. Kennedy, *Public Papers, 1962,* p. 318.
11. Kennedy, *Public Papers, 1962,* p. 316.
12. Kennedy, *Public Papers, 1962,* p. 317.

13. See S. E. Harris, *Economics of the Kennedy Years* (New York, Harper & Row, 1964), p. 61; J. L. Sundquist, *Politics and Policy: The Eisenhower, Kennedy and Johnson Years* (Washington, Brookings, 1968), p. 39.
14. Kennedy, *Public Papers*, 1962, p. 320.
15. W. T. Hogan, *Economic History of the Iron and Steel Industry*, Vol. 4. (Toronto, Heath, 1971), pp. 1647–1686; S. N. Whitney *Antitrust Politics: American Experience in Twenty Industries* Vol. 1 (New York, Twentieth Century Fund, 1958), pp. 253–329.
16. Report of the Antitrust and Monopoly Subcommittee of the Senate Judiciary Subcommittee, U.S. Senate Report 1387, March 13, 1958.
17. The term "administered price" was coined by the economist Gardner Means in the 1930s, but popularised by the Kefauver Committee who interpreted to mean prices, "which are administratively set, administratively maintained, and are insensitive to change in their markets e.g. they are maintained when demand falls off through a curtailment in output. . . ." Quoted in J. B. Corman, *Kefauver: A Political Biography* (New York, Oxford University Press, 1971), p. 303.
18. Hogan, *Economic History of the Iron and Steel Industry*, Vol. 5, p. 2083.
19. See as typical examples of revisionist writing on Kennedy as a cynical politician: Bruce Miroff, *Pragmatic Illusions: The Presidential Politics of John F. Kennedy* (New York, David McKay, 1976); Lewis J. Paper, *The Promise and the Performance: The Leadership of John F. Kennedy* (New York, Crown, 1976); Richard J. Walton, *Cold War and Counterrevolution: The Foreign Policy of John F. Kennedy* (New York, Viking Press, 1972).
20. F. de Saussure, *Course in General Linguistics*, trans. W. Baskin (London, McGraw Hill, 1966), pp. 65–67.
21. U. Eco, *A Theory of Semiotics* (London, Macmillan, 1977), p. 165.
22. Eco, *A Theory of Semiotics*, p. 163.
23. V. N. Volosinov, *Marxism and the Philosophy of Language* (London, Seminar Press, 1973), p. 21.
24. V. N. Volosinov, *Marxism and the Philosophy of Language*, p. 102.
25. Eco, *A Theory of Semiotics*, p. 124.
26. M. A. K. Halliday, *Language as Social Semiotic* (London, Arnold, 1978), p. 137.
27. Kennedy, *Public Papers*, 1962, p. 284.
28. M. Black, *Models and Metaphors* (Ithaca, Cornell U.P.), p. 47.
29. Aristotle, *Aristotle's Art of Poetry* (London, Oxford U.P., 1948), p. 62.
30. P. Ricoeur, *The Rule of Metaphor*, trans. R. Czerny (London, Routledge & Kegan Paul, 1978), p. 30.
31. Kennedy, *Public Papers, 1962*, p. 284.
32. Kennedy, *Public Papers*, 1962, p. 321.
33. Arguably indexical signs like 'this-that,' 'here-there' work more in the manner of a pointing finger or a directorial arrow than words. For example, if a speaker were suddenly to say, 'I disagree with this!' anyone overhearing him would probably try to invent something to which 'this' referred—an unstated thought; an earlier sentence missed by the listener; an offensive object or person not in sight. "This" summons referents into being because we expect it to point to something. See Eco, *A Theory of Semiotics*, pp. 115–121.
34. P. Ricoeur, *The Rule of Metaphor*, p. 33.
35. P. Guiraud, *Semiology*, trans. G. Gross (London, Routledge & Kegan Paul, 1975), p. 8.
36. Kennedy, *Public Papers, 1962*, p. 316.

37. T. A. Sebeok provides a useful summary of Peirce's distinctions in, "Semiotics: A Survey of the State of the Art," collected in his, *Contributions to the Doctrine of the Sign* (Bloomington, Indiana University Press, 1976), pp. 1–45.
38. W. James, Lecture II of *Pragmatism: A New Name for Some Old Ways of Thinking,* collected in P. Miller, *American Thought: Civil War to World War I* (New York, Holt, Rinehart & Winston, 1964), p. 177.
39. J. Locke, *An Essay Concerning Human Understanding of Words,* collected in, F. Ryland, *Locke on Words* (London, W. Swann, Sonnenschein & Co., 1882), p. 250.
40. See R. Rommetveit, *On Message Structure: A Framework for the Study of Language and Communication* (London, Wiley, 1974). His critique of Chomsky is usefully glossed by Astri Heen Wold in *Decoding Oral Language* (London, Academic Press, 1978), p. 27–37.
41. J. S. Mill, *A System of Logic* (London, Longmans Green, 1868), p. 24.
42. William James quoting C. S. Peirce. See P. Miller, *American Thought,* p. 166.
43. Kennedy, *Public Papers, 1962,* p. 335.
44. Kennedy, *Public Papers, 1962,* p. 316.

The Presidency and Speeches on International Crises: Repeating the Rhetorical Past

Theodore Windt

1.

Over a century ago Alexis de Tocqueville made an acute observation about the American political orator that is apt today:

> He . . . presents to the mind of his auditors a succession of great general truths (which he himself comprehends and expresses only confusedly) and of petty minutiae, which he is but too able to discover and point out. The inhabitants of the United States seem themselves to consider [speech-making] in this light; and they show their long experience of parliamentary life, not by abstaining from making bad speeches, but by courageously submitting to hear them made. They are resigned to it as to an evil they know to be inevitable.[1]

If the people tolerate bad speeches as one of the many evils they have to bear, many journalists and scholars do not feel such a theological burden. During the first term of Mr. Nixon's administration we were treated to a series of essays that showed scorn for the rhetorical devices he and his spokesmen use.[2] The result of this criticism has been extraordinary. During those four years the rhetoric of the administration—frequently apart from any policy—became a major issue. *How various members of the administration, especially Vice President Agnew, spoke about policies became as important in the minds of many as what they said.* In fact, critics sometimes condemned the administration as much for its rhetoric as for its policies. These criticisms have their value. However, they are often predicated on the romantic assumption that a speech is a unique personal experience. Most critics *imply* that the lines of argument used by President Nixon and Vice President Agnew are unique to them.

The basic assumptions of this essay are that Presidential speeches are repetitive, that the lines of argument a President chooses come from the office of Presidency and from tradition, that genres of Presidential speeches exist which every President uses. Aside from particular policies, what President Nixon has done rhetorically is to rely on lines of argument that other modern Presidents have used in similar situations.[3] To substantiate these assumptions,

Mr. Windt is Associate Professor of Rhetoric at the University of Pittsburgh.
Reprinted by permission of the author from *Speaker and Gavel* Vol. II, No. 1 (1973), pp. 6–14.

I want to examine a particular genre of Presidential rhetoric: speeches on international crises. But if I am correct in arguing that these speeches come primarily from the office and from tradition, especially from the mystique surrounding the Presidency, rather than from a particular man, I must first examine the nature of crises and the *ethos* of the office of Presidency.

The nature of crises. "Crisis" is one of those words that became popular during the Kennedy years as an inflated description of the making of hard decisions. If one reads Sorensen's or Schlesinger's account of the Kennedy administration, he will soon learn about the Laos crisis, the Berlin crisis, the balance of payments crisis, the Cuban missile crisis, the steel crisis, the crisis in the Congo, and so on and on. Richard Nixon followed this trend, as is his habit, by entitling his remarkable autobiography, *Six Crises.* But what are the characteristics of crises pertinent to this essay?

First, *political crises are primarily rhetorical.*[4] The President announces to the people, usually over national television, that a situation critical to the United States exists. He contends that the situation requires that he act decisively and calls upon the public to support him fully. Invariably, the policy he advocates is elevated from a political decision to an issue involving world peace (in foreign affairs) or an issue synonymous with the public interest (in domestic affairs). The so-called steel crisis would not have been a domestic crisis to the public had not President Kennedy attacked the $6 per ton increase by U.S. Steel with such vehemence in his press conference of April 11, 1962. Perhaps, the events of August 2 and 4, 1964, in the Gulf of Tonkin would have remained as minor as they were had not the President interrupted a television show to denounce the attacks on American ships and to order reprisals. Situations do not create crises. Rather, the President's perception of the situation and the rhetoric he uses to describe it mark an event as a crisis. Because the President has immediate access to television and because neither Congress nor the public has alternative sources of information that can *quickly* verify or question the President's account of the facts, a President usually can implement a policy with a minimum of opposition.

The second characteristic of a crisis is that the President can depend on tremendous public support for whatever policy he pursues in a situation he has deemed "critical." Nelson Polsby observed: "Invariably, the popular response to a President during international crises is favorable, regardless of the wisdom of the policies he pursues."[5] Letters and telegrams will range from 2–1 upwards in support of the President. People support the President overwhelmingly in these situations because they see the President as the personification of the country.

Thus, a crisis that does not involve an external military attack on the United States is a political event rhetorically created by the President in which the public predictably rallies to his defense.

The Ethos of the Presidency. The American Presidency, originally intended as a democratic executive office, has evolved into an elected monarchy, a striking example of Caesarism. The multitude of writings about the office has created a reverence for the Presidency to the point that the office and the man who occupies it are frequently confused with the true destiny of the nation.

In the popular mythology, and even in scholarly circles, the President is different from any other political official. More is expected of him even as less is suspected about him. He personifies American government. He is "President of all the people."[6] In the words of Clinton Rossiter: "He reigns, but he also rules; he symbolizes the people, but he also runs their government."[7] There is a reverence that surrounds the Presidency, and much of this reverence comes from the fact that people believe that the President has superior information and knowledge about national affairs. James MacGreagor Burns and Jack W. Peltason, certainly not unsophisticated scholars of the Presidency, wax romantic about this aspect of the Presidency:

> The President has not only the authority but the capacity to act. For example, he has at his command unmatched sources of information. To his desk comes facts channeled from the entire world. Diplomatic missions, military observers, undercover agents, personal agents, technical experts gather tons of material which are analyzed by experts in the State Department and elsewhere. Since the President draws on the informed thinking of hundreds of specialists, *his pronouncements have a tone of authority.*[8]

Inherent in these descriptions of the President, regardless of who he is, is a predisposition to believe the President, a predisposition that does not exist in the same extreme degree for any other official. In the words so often used in letters to newspapers, "the President knows best." The psychology persistent here makes the President's decisions seem wise and prudent even when they turn out to be stupid. The aura of reverence shapes a will to believe the President when he speaks, and places the burden of disproving any Presidential statement upon those who disagree

2.

When a man assumes the office of President, he quickly learns that his rhetorical options are limited by precedent, tradition, and expediency. In the sense that literary forms are stylized, so too are Presidential speeches. Genres of Presidential rhetoric exist. My purpose in this essay is to examine one genre of Presidential speeches through a comparison of speeches by a liberal Democrat and a conservative Republican on international affairs. John F. Kennedy's speech on the Cuban missile crisis and Richard M. Nixon's speech on the invasion of Cambodia provide the raw materials for this comparison.

Presidential speeches about international crises begin with an assertation of the President's control over the facts of the situation and an acknowledgment that the New Facts which occasion the speech constitute a New Situation—a crisis for the United States. President Kennedy opened his address with these ominous words:

> This Government, as promised, has maintained the closest surveillance of the Soviet military buildup on the island of Cuba. Within the past week, unmistakable evidence has established the fact that a series of offensive missile sites is now in preparation on that imprisoned island. The purpose of these bases can be none other than to provide a nuclear strike capability against the Western Hemisphere.[9]

President Nixon began his speech in like manner:

> Ten days ago, in my report to the Nation on Vietnam, I announced a decision to withdraw an additional 150,000 Americans from Vietnam over the next year. I said then that I was making that decision despite our concern over increased enemy activity in Laos, in Cambodia, and in South Vietnam.
>
> At that time, I warned that if I concluded that increased enemy activity in any of these areas endangered the lives of Americans remaining in Vietnam, I would not hesitate to take strong and effective measures to deal with that situation.
>
> Despite that warning, North Vietnam has increased its military aggression in all these areas, and particularly in Cambodia.
>
> After full consultation with the National Security Council, Ambassador Bunker, General Abrams, and my other advisers, I have concluded that the actions of the enemy in the last 10 days clearly endanger the lives of Americans who are in Vietnam now and would constitute an unacceptable risk to those who will be there after withdrawal of another 150,000.[10]

Such authoritative statements of Presidential control over the situation are intended to draw upon what Thomas Cronin has called the public's image of the "President as Superman."[11] The President possesses "unmistakable evidence" or has been advised by high-ranking experts about the New Situation. He, therefore, understands the New Situation better than anyone else. At this point, political leadership is personalized; the course of national policy is rhetorically concentrated in one man. Each President emphasized that he was keeping his compact with the people (and thus to identify this policy as the people's policy) to study the situation carefully and to report to the people once a decision had been made. Under study mandated by the President's compact with the people New Facts emerged. These New Facts pointed to a New Situation and thus constituted a crisis demanding decisive action.

Having established his mastery of the New Situation, each President then turned to a narration of the New Facts. Kennnedy told the public about the Soviet missile build-up in Cuba. Nixon, using a chart as well as words, described the increased North Vietnamese military activity in Cambodia. Intertwined in this narration is the second major line of argument: a comparison between the patience and honesty with which the United States handled the

Old Situation versus the enemy's record of duplicity and secrecy in creating the New Situation. Kennedy recounted in detail how he had tried to learn the truth about the Soviet missiles in Cuba only to realize that Foreign Minister Gromyko among others was lying to him. He concluded: "Neither the United States of America nor the world community of nations can tolerate deliberate deception and offensive threats on the part of any nation, large or small." President Nixon recounted that the United States had continually respected the sovereignty of Cambodia while the North Vietnamese had persistently used Cambodia as a sanctuary for more than five years. He concluded: "North Vietnam in the last 2 weeks has stripped away all pretense of respecting the sovereignty or the neutrality of Cambodia. Thousands of their soldiers are invading the country from the sanctuaries. . . ." The purpose of this line of argument is to introduce a devil-angel interpretation into the narration of facts. The enemy is duplistic and secretive; the United States is open and trusting. Melodrama replaces politics as each President delves into the sinister motives of the enemy even as he accentuates the pure motives of the United States.

To intensify the either-or/devil-angel nature of the New Situation created by the enemy, each President reminded the public that this incident was only one in the continual battle between the Free World and the Communist World. President Nixon stated late in his address that he would not take the "easy political path" in resolving a conflict that transcended his personal political ambitions because the United States would be obliged:

> to desert 18 million South Vietnamese people, who have put their trust in us and to expose them to the same slaughter and savagery which the leaders of North Vietnam inflicted on hundreds of thousands of North Vietnamese who chose freedom when the Communists took over North Vietnam in 1954; to get peace at any price now, even though I know that a peace of humiliation for the United States would lead to bigger war or surrender later.

In speaking directly to the Cuban people, Kennedy also drew upon major melodramatic features of the anti-communist ideology as an implicit reason for intervention:

> And I have watched and the American people have watched with deep sorrow how your nationalist revolution was betrayed, and how your fatherland fell under foreign domination. Now your leaders are no longer Cuban leaders inspired by Cuban ideals. They are puppets and agents of an international conspiracy which has turned Cuba against your friends and neighbors in the Americas. . . .

Each President elevated his particular policy to a struggle between the Free World and the Communist World, one in which ideological angels do mortal and moral combat with ideological devils. Melodrama. Each drew upon the language and assumptions permeating the anti-communist ideology of the public.[12] Nixon spoke disparagingly about "peace at any price" as a consequence of dissenting from his policy. Kennedy reminded his hearers that they ought to have learned their lesson about thwarting aggression from the events of the nineteen-thirties, an obvious reference to Munich and "peace at any price."

Understanding this part of the rhetoric is crucial to interpreting responses to Presidential speeches on international crises. Insofar as the people believe that the particular issue is truly an ideological issue between the Free World and the Communist World or that any decisive action is preferable to any inaction, they will be disposed to support the President. Insofar as people no longer believe that the issue is ideological or insofar as they ask that action be deferred until more facts are presented from contrary sources, they will not be disposed to support the President.

Sometime during the course of his arguments the President announces what policy he has decided upon. President Nixon listed alternatives to his policy—a rhetorical habit he has aquired as a means for anticipating objections. After rejecting two policies, Nixon announced that he was sending American and South Vietnamese forces into selected areas of Cambodia. President Kennedy did not discuss what other options were open to him, but rather concentrated on describing the quarantine of Cuba and the seven *initial* steps to be taken by the United States against Cuba. Each President argued briefly that the policy was enacted through the power of the President as Commander-in-Chief and instituted primarily to protect American lives. Kennedy went into more specific detail about how American lives were endangered than did Nixon.

Even as each President announced his policy, he also attempted to shift the issue from its obvious military and political context to an ethical context; that is, from the consequences of war to a question of American character. Nixon asked plainly whether the United States was a "pitiful, helpless giant?" He asked: "Does the richest and strongest nation in the history of the world have the character to meet a direct challenge by a group which rejects every effort to win a just peace, ignores our warning, tramples on solemn agreements, violates the neutrality of an unarmed people, and uses our prisoners as hostages?" Kennedy also stressed the necessity for testing American character:

> Let no one doubt that this is a difficult and dangerous effort on which we have set out. No one can foresee precisely what course it will take or what costs or casualties will be incurred. Many months of sacrifice and self-discipline lie ahead, months in which both our patience and our will will be tested, months in which many threats and denunciations will keep us aware of our dangers.
>
> The path we have chosen for the present is full of hazards, as all paths are, but it is the one most consistent with our character and courage as a nation and our commitments around the world. The cost of freedom is always high, but Americans have always paid it.

Thus a political decision is transformed for a third time. It began as a simple, if potentially dangerous, American policy in response to a President's perception of extreme danger to American vital interests. Then, it became a melodramatic test between the Free World and the Communist World, between Good and Evil, between pure motives and sinister motives. Finally, it evolved rhetorically into a mark of character and honor for the American people to support the President's decision. This last transformation is the "bear any burden, pay any price" part of the appeal. The essence of the problem, according to two Presidents, is no longer political or military, but ethical. Those who support the President have character and courage for that is what standing steadfast with him in his (and now our) hour of crisis means; those who oppose him lack these virtues. Deliberative rhetoric gives way first to melodrama and then to epidiectic.

Finally, each President indulged in snatches of Newspeak. War is peace; peace is war. Kennedy described the military blockade of Cuba as a "quarantine," denied that this act of war was actually an act of war, but insisted instead that the blockade was a step toward "peace and freedom."[13] Nixon forthrightly denied that the invasion of Cambodia by American and South Vietnamese troops was an invasion. "This is not an invasion of Cambodia," he stated. No, it was not if one believes what President Nixon said: "We take this action not for the purpose of expanding the war into Cambodia but for the purpose of ending the war in Vietnam and winning the just peace we all desire." Thus, the American people—at least those accustomed to Newspeak—can rationalize the possibility of nuclear war or rationalize the expansion of the American-Vietnamese War into Cambodia. They can do so because political language has become so distorted and mangled that words have lost traditional or even legal meanings. They can do so because they are so sincerely committed to another symbolic battle with Communism. They can do so because they want to prove dramatistically that they have character and courage in the wake of this latest threat. They can do so in order to demonstrate their patriotic support of the President of the United States. They can do so because the President has enacted a policy that they cannot change. They can do so because they have no alternative. War is peace; peace is war.

The purpose of these three basic lines of arguments in "Crisis Rhetoric" is to unify the people behind a particular policy announced by the President. In more succinct form, President Roosevelt used these three arguments when he asked Congress to declare war on the Japanese on December 8, 1941. President Truman outlined in detail these same three arguments in his announcement of the Truman Doctrine of March 12, 1947. In each case, the policy has been enacted; the rhetoric is primarily explanatory. In the words of Senator Vandenberg the purpose of "Crisis Rhetoric" is "to scare hell out of the country." The effect of this genre is to limit, if not destroy, reasonable public discussion of policy. The President draws upon his enormous prestige to squelch or discredit dissent. He continually casts his policy in abstract or analogical

terms, thereby hoping to shift attention away from the very real possible consequences of his act to the circumstances that produced it. The need to confront, rout, or destroy the evil enemy overrides practical considerations. For
the public it is an either/or choice. Either you support the President or you
do not. Either you are on the side of the Free World or you are not. Either
you have courage and character or you do not. What the President is asking,
covertly or overtly, is "What kind of citizen are you?" A profound existential
question. But he does not want one to ponder that question because he readily
provides an absolute answer. Those who support him and his policy are courageous, possess character, and are loyal Americans. Those who oppose him
are none of these and may be worse.

The problems of answering these speeches are obvious. The opponent is
constantly open to *ad hominem* attacks because those are the terms in which
the President has cast the issue. Thus, an opponent of a Presidential policy in
foreign affairs must first *attack the terms for argument before he can begin
to argue the merits of the particular policy.* He must demonstrate to the
American public that his dissent from the President's policy is not an act of
cowardice or disloyalty or conceit. He must immediately present contrary evidence that is believable to the American public. He must convince people that
the issue is not as simple as the President has presented it. He must show that
the other side had reasons for doing what it did, even if he disapproves of those
actions. He must, in fact, attempt to lift the issue out of the right/wrong-
angel/devil moral context in which the President has placed the problem. The
prospects for effective opoposition are not favorable. George Reedy, former
assistant to President Johnson, concluded: "The President's ability to place
his views before the public is important primarily because he can usually set
the terms of the national debate—and anyone who can set the terms of debate
can win it."[14] In essence, when a President employs "Crisis Rhetoric," the
question before the public is not whether the policy is a reasonable one or not,
but rather whether one supports the President or not.

3.

In this essay I have attempted to outline the major lines of argument used
by Presidents in situations they declare to be crises. First, the President tells
the people that a dangerous new situation exists that requires that he act decisively. Second, he states that this new situation is only one more in an on-
going greater battle between incompatible ideologies. Finally, he calls for the
public to realize that the enactment of his policy and support for it are moral
acts. In such speeches the policy is not proposed but declared. The President
does not ask for debate but for support. And the rhetoric accompanying these
situations is one of declaration, not one of discussion.

During the debates about the Federal constitution, Mr. Pickney stated that he supported a strong Federal Executive, but he feared that extending to the President the powers over war and peace "would render the Executive a monarchy, of the worst kind, to wit an elective one."[15] Mr. Pickney's worst fears have come true. Successive Presidents' greater control over the powers of war and peace have made the Presidency into an elected monarchy, into Caesarism, in international affairs. "Crisis rhetoric" has become a potent force in consolidating this power.

The result of this generic form of rhetoric is that the President *qua* monarch enjoys considerable support on occasions that he deems critical. Using this genre of persuasion the President demands that the people forfeit their right to judge for themselves the propriety of a policy. He calls upon the people to invest in the President more wisdom than most Presidents exhibit. He speaks the name of freedom even as he works to undermine freedom of speech. He speaks about reasonableness even as he casts potential opponents in positions that are *a priori* unreasonable.

In situations the President perceives as critical, the President sees himself as Caesar and therefore uses an aristocratic form of rhetoric to justify his declarations of action. This perception and this use of rhetorical forms are unsuitable to a democratic society.

Notes

1. Alexis de Tocqueville, *Democracy in America,* The Henry Reeve Text as revised by Francis Bowen now further corrected and edited with a historical essay, editorial notes and bibliographies by Phillips Bradley, Vol. 2 (New York: Vintage Books, 1945), p. 97.
2. *Cf.* David Halberstam, "American Notes. Mr. Nixon Meets the Language," *Harpers* (July, 1970), 30–31; Lynn Hinds and Carolyn Smith, "Nixspeak. The Rhetoric of Opposites," *Nation* (February 18, 1970), 172–174; Jeff Greenfield, "A Short Course in Nixon's Rhetoric," *The Village Voice* (January 13, 1972), col. 1, 1, 70–71; Hermann G. Stelzner, "The Quest Story and Nixon's November 3, 1969 Address," *Quarterly Journal of Speech* (April, 1971); and Ruth M. Gonchar and Dan F. Hahn, "The Predictable Strategies of Richard Nixon," a paper delivered at the Speech Communication Association Convention, New Orleans, Louisana, December 29, 1970.
3. In *Nixon Agonistes* Gary Wills notes the similarities between Nixon's first Inaugural Address and Kennedy's Inaugural Address even to the point of stylistic similarities. See *Nixon Agonistes* (New York: Houghton Mifflin Co., 1970), pp. 402–404. Scholars of the Presidency are not surprised to learn that Presidents, often so different in ideology and temperament, use the same lines of argument to justify their policies. In fact, Presidents or their aides often admit that they model Presidential addresses after some previous President. To analyze fairly a Presidential speech, I would argue, requires that the critic understand the historial model upon which it is based.

4. One of my graduate students has developed this idea more fully than space allows me in this essay. Cf. Richard E. Vatz, "The Myth of the Rhetorical Situation," *Philosophy and Rhetoric* (Summer,1973), 154–161.

5. Quoted in Thomas E. Cronin, "The Textbook Presidency and Political Science," prepared for delivery at the 66th Annual Meeting of the American Political Science Association, Los Angeles, California, September 7–12, 1970, 5. Cf. John E. Mueller, "Presidential Popularity from Truman to Johnson" *The American Political Science Review* (March, 1970), 18–34. Using public opinion polls, Mueller demonstrates that on occasions which Presidents call "critical' public support increases dramatically.

6. Andrew Jackson was the first President to proclaim himself President of all the people. That conception of the Presidency apparently was not in the minds of the writers of the Constitution.

7. Clinton Rossiter, *The American Presidency,* rev. ed. (New York: New American Library, 1960), p. 17.

8. James M. Burns and Jack W. Peltason, *Government by the People,* 5th ed. (Englewood Cliffs, N.J.: Prentice Hall, Inc., 1964), pp. 434–435. Emphasis added.

9. All quotations from Kennedy's Speech on the missile crisis are taken from the transcript of the speech as published in *The Burden and the Glory,* ed. by Allan Nevins (New York: Harper and Row, 1964), pp. 89–95.

10. All quotations from Nixon's speech on the Cambodian invasion are from the transcript of the speech published in *Weekly Compilation of Presidential Documents* (May 4, 1970), 596–601.

11. Thomas E. Cronin, "Superman, Our Textbook President," *Washington Monthly* (October, 1970), 48.

12. For one analysis of the language and symbols of the anti-communist mythology, see Michael Parenti, *The Anti-Communist Impulse* (New York: Random House, 1969).

13. All of the accounts that I have read of the Cuban missile crisis suggest that Kennedy realized that what he was doing might lead to nuclear war.

14. George Reedy, *The Twilight of the Presidency* (New York, 1970), pp. 41–42.

15. James Madison, *Notes of Debates in the Federal Convention of 1787* (New York, 1966), p. 45.

Seeking Détente with Superpowers: John F. Kennedy at American University

Theodore Windt

In *To Move a Nation* Roger Hilsman chronicled the delicate rhetorical and political maneuvers in 1962–1963 the State Department engaged in as it sought to send a signal to the People's Republic of China that the U.S. was willing to be more flexible in its policies toward that country if China would reciprocate.[1] More ambitiously, the Kennedy administration sought to change basic assumptions about American-Chinese relations. John Foster Dulles, Secretary of State under President Eisenhower, had assumed that the Communist regime in China was a "passing and not a perpetual phase" and that it was the responsibility of the United States "to do all that we can to contribute to that passing."[2] The Kennedy administration, according to Hilsman, had ceased to base policy on those assumptions, and believed a new, realistic approach would include understanding that the Communist regime was in firm control of the mainland and that there was little likelihood it would be overthrown. Such a major change in assumptions about foreign policy with a major power required a public announcement and justification. But how to do it?

Hilsman, by then Assistant Secretary of State for Far Eastern Affairs, became the principal spokesman for this change. He chose to speak at the Commonwealth Club of San Francisco on December 13, 1963. The symbolism of this setting was important because San Francisco with its large Chinese-American population is a traditional place for speech on China policy and because Dulles had made the "last full statement on the subject in 1957" in that city.[3] Hilsman's speech aimed at being firm, flexible, and dispassionate. He later wrote:

> By firmness, we meant firmness in our support for our friends and allies, including the people and government of the Republic of China on Taiwan; firmness in our determination to maintain our strength in Asia and firmness in our determination to meet aggression wherever it occurred. By flexibility, we meant a willingness to seek and carry out initiatives that seemed promising and to negotiate with anyone who sincerely wanted to negotiate, including the Chinese Communists. And by dispassion, we meant analyzing our problems and our policies coolly, without emotion, to discover our own best interests—appealing to the American people to substitute rationality in China policy for the emotionalism of which . . . there had been too much.[4]

135

Though the speech got mixed reviews in the press, it did not change policy, at least, not at that time.[5]

The experiences Hilsman recounted serve as an introduction to the subject of this essay: how does an American President go about announcing a change in assumptions to one of the adversary superpowers as a prelude to changes in policy? And how does he attempt to persuade the American public to accept those changes, especially when there are vested political and/or psychological interests in maintaining the status quo? Hilsman provides a skeletal outline for such a rhetoric:

1. An appropriate symbolic setting must be chosen to emphasize the importance of the announcement.
2. The President must persuade the public that the old assumptions are irrational or unrealistic and that the new assumptions are rational and realistic as well as in the best interests of the United States.
3. The President must signal our adversary that the United States is willing to negotiate certain issues based on the new assumptions.
4. The President must reassure the American people as well as interested outside parties that we will not compromise American national security nor essential agreements with allied governments.
5. The President must act in a concrete way to symbolize that some policy changes will come from these new assumptions.

President John Kennedy's dramatic move toward détente with the Soviet Union in the summer of 1963 provides an example of how one President went about changing the rhetoric and policies toward that country. It resulted in the limited nuclear test ban treaty. And it changed American policy from confrontation to détente, a policy that was to last through the next four Presidents.

"The Strategy of Peace"

The Cuban missile crisis had a sobering effect on President Kennedy. In a variety of ways the President sought to ease tensions between the U.S. and the U.S.S.R. Finally, he decided on a major speech on the topic of peace and decided also that he would announce a unilateral suspension of atomic testing in the atmosphere. Sorensen wrote:

The final step was the American University speech itself, the first Presidential speech in eighteen years to succeed in reaching beyond the cold war. The address had originated in a Presidential decision earlier in the spring to make a speech about 'peace.' His motives were many. It was, first of all, an expression of his deep personal concern. He had not elaborated his views on this topic since his 1961 address to the UN. He thought it desirable to make clear his hopes for East-West agreement as a backdrop to his European trip in June. He valued in particular an April 30 letter from Norman Cousins. Cousins suggested that the exposition of a peaceful posture prior to the May meeting of the Soviet Communist Party Central Committee, even if it could not deter an expected new rash of attacks on U.S. policy, might at least make those attacks sound hollow and hypocritical outside the Communist world. That meeting had been postponed until June, and the June 10 commencement at American University appeared to be the first appropriate forum on the President's schedule.[6]

Sorensen worked on the speech and cleared it with the necessary Cabinet officials. Appropriate Soviet officials in Moscow and Washington as well as the White House correspondents were briefed in advance that the speech was to be of major importance.[7]

Symbolic setting for the speech. On June 10, 1963 President John F. Kennedy received an honorary degree from American University and delivered his speech, "The Strategy of Peace." The setting was most appropriate for the message he bore.

When a President delivers a major speech on a university campus, his role changes perceptibly. He becomes not only leader of the nation, but *teacher* of the nation. All the trappings of the occasion contribute to this change. He is attired in academic regalia. Leaders of the university—administrators, faculty, and outstanding students—share the platform with him, symbolically conferring intellectual approval on him. The academic atmosphere of disinterest permeates the event. Specific and immediate concerns fade as larger issues are discussed. The search for enduring principles that will guide one in day-to-day activities becomes paramount.[8] Indeed, Kennedy recognized the symbolism of the setting when he opened his speech by saying:

'There are few earthly things more beautiful than a university,' wrote John Masefield, in his tribute to English universities—and his words are equally true today. He did not refer to spires and towers, to campus greens and ivied walls. He admired the splendid beauty of the university, he said, because it was 'a place where those who hate ignorance may strive to know, where those who perceive truth may strive to make others see.'

I have, therefore, chosen this time and this place to discuss a topic on which ignorance too often abounds and the truth is too rarely perceived—yet it is the most important topic on earth: world peace.[9]

Furthermore, commencement is an occasion to look to the future which was precisely what Kennedy intended to do in his speech. The commencement exercises mark a major change in the graduates' lives. The era of being a student ends; life in the real world begins. So, too, in Kennedy's speech: old Soviet-American antagonisms must ease; new relations must be developed. Finally, the audience at commencement is made up primarily of young people. They symbolize the future. And the speaker will emphasize that the ideas he proposes will make the future safer and better for them. In sum, such a setting is ideal for the President to assume his role as teacher of the nation and to present fresh new ideas for the country.

Flexibility. Kennedy's purpose in this speech, according to Sorensen, was to reach beyond the cold war rhetoric that had prevailed for 18 years. Equally important, the President intended to prepare the American people for a series of negotiations which eventually would lead to the ratification of the limited nuclear test ban treaty. To be effective Kennedy had to discredit the strident anti-communist perceptions of American-Soviet relations that had pervaded those relations for almost two decades. In other words, Kennedy had to establish a new political context within which to view the new initiatives—especially the unilateral cessation of atmospheric nuclear tests and negotiations for the test ban treaty—so as to marshall public support. A new political context requires a new political language. It is that new language that creates new "pictures in our heads" and thus a new linguistic lens through which to view events and policies.[10]

Early in his speech, Kennedy asked his audience (and the nation as well) to re-examine its attitudes "toward the possibilities of peace, toward the Soviet Union, toward the course of the cold war and toward freedom and peace here at home." The first three would occupy the bulk of the speech and are most pertinent to the subject at hand. Kennedy interwove three lines of argument throughout the speech: (1) *specific definitions of the new attitudes he wished Americans to cultivate;* (2) *incentives for adopting these attitudes;* and (3) *negative consequences for maintaining the old, out-moded anti-communist attitudes.* His organizational and stylistic pattern was a *negative/positive* approach. Part of this pattern is revealed in his answer to his rhetorical question of what kind of peace we seek:

> Not a Pax Americana enforced on the world by American weapons of war. Not the peace of the grave or the security of the slave. I am talking about genuine peace, the kind of peace that makes life on earth worth living, the kind that enables men and nations to grow and to hope and to build a better life for their children—not merely peace for Americans but peace for all men and women—not merely peace in our time but peace for all time.

Kennedy continued by citing 3 major incentives for seeking peace: (1) "Total war makes no sense in an age when great powers can maintain large and relatively invulnerable nuclear forces and refuse to surrender without resort to those forces." (2) Stockpiling nuclear weapons "is not the only, much less the most efficient, means of assuring peace." (3) Peace is "the necessary rational end of rational men." These incentives infuse the rest of the speech as Kennedy continued to discuss the 3 major topics of his speech.

Kennedy began his re-examination of our attitudes with the idea of peace itself.

> Too many of us think it impossible. Too many think it unreal. But that is a dangerous, defeatist belief. It leads to the conclusion that war is inevitable—that mankind is doomed—that we are gripped by forces we cannot control.
>
> We need not accept that view. Our problems are manmade—therefore, they can be solved by man. No problem of human destiny is beyond human beings. Man's reason and spirit have often solved the seemingly unsolvable—and we believe they can do it again.

But Kennedy needed to be more precise about what kind of peace he sought. Beginning negatively, he stated that he was not "referring to the absolute, infinite concept of universal peace and good will of which some fantasist and fanatics dream." No, his kind of peace would be a more limited, more practical, more positive peace "based not on a sudden revolution in human nature but on a gradual evolution in human institutions—on a series of concrete actions and effective agreements which are in the interest of all concerned." This definition of limited steps toward peace dovetailed neatly with the specific, limited proposals he would announce near the end of his address.

But if we were to seek peace, we would also have to change our attitudes toward the Soviet Union, the second topic of the address. Kennedy began by deploring the distorted view Russians have of the United States, but used that to warn Americans against falling into the same trap of seeing "conflict as inevitable, accommodation as impossible, and communication as nothing more than an exchange of threats." Instead of these negative and unproductive attitudes, Kennedy sought to emphasize our common human traits:

> No government or social system is so evil that its people must be considered as lacking in virtue. As Americans, we find communism profoundly repugnant as a negation of personal freedom and dignity. But we can still hail the Russian people for their many achievements—in science and space, in economic and industrial growth, in culture and in acts of courage.
>
> Among the many traits the peoples of our two countries have in common, none is stronger than our mutual abhorrence of war.

So, to change attitudes toward the Soviet Union Kennedy sought to shift focus from ideological differences that divide the two nations and will continue to human traits shared by the two peoples that must be the foundation for resolving some outstanding issues. In the rhetoric of seeking accommodation with adversaries this separation between a political system and its people is standard.[11] Kennedy re-enforced this distinction as well as the shift in emphasis in what is the most eloquent paragraph of the speech:

> So, let us not be blind to our differences—but let us also direct attention to our common interests and to the means by which those differences can be resolved. And if we cannot end now our differences, at least we can help make the world safe for diversity. For, in the final analysis, our most basic common link is that we all inhabit this small planet. We all breathe the same air. We all cherish our children's future. And we are all mortal.

Certainly, if the U.S. were to seek peace cooperatively with the Soviet Union, a new view of Russians would have to be created. In emphasizing the human bonds that unite us rather than the ideological differences that separate us, President Kennedy found a realistic common ground upon which to begin building that cooperative effort.

Kennedy's charge to change our attitudes toward the Cold War comes almost as an anti-climax within the speech since everything that precedes it draws the listener to that logical conclusion. If we are to seek peace in a cooperative spirit, then it necessarily follows that the Cold War must thaw. And so the President said: "Let us examine our attitude toward the cold war, remembering that we are not engaged in a debate, seeking to pile up debating points. We are not here distributing blame or pointing the finger of judgment. We must deal with the world as it is, and not as it might have been had the history of the last 18 years been different." To achieve these ends, Kennedy stated that our weapons must be controlled, our military forces committed to "peace and disciplined in self-restraint," and our diplomats instructed "to avoid unnecessary irritants and purely rhetorical hostility."

This entire section of the speech—perhaps the most important part of the speech—was intended to achieve what Hilsman called flexibility, the signal to the Soviets that the U.S. was willing to negotiate from a new set of assumptions. However, sending a signal to the Soviets was a far easier task than changing American attitudes.

Every President who offers dramatically new directions for policy (especially foreign policy) must attack and discredit the old linguistic lens, the old slogans, the old rhetoric if he is to have any chance of implementing his new policies. "For the most part we do not first see, and then define," Walter Lippmann wisely observed, "we define first and then see. In the great blooming, buzzing confusion of the outer world we pick out what our culture has already defined for us, and we tend to perceive that which we have picked out in the form stereotyped for us by our culture."[12] Thus, President Kennedy sought to re-define relations between the United States and the Soviet Union so the American people would *see* differently. In treating each of the three major topics of his address, Kennedy contrasted the old definitions with the new and argued that continuation of acting upon the old definitions would be futile or injurious whereas acting upon the new definitions would be realistic and bring a sliver of hope to the world.

Firmness. As Hilsman pointed out, flexibility in such a situation always has to be tempered by firmness. By this Hilsman meant that certain commitments had to be re-affirmed. As Kennedy stated in his speech, "we merely invite discouragement and incredulity" by seeking universal peace and good will immediately. Moreover, such a dramatic change, as the one advocated by the President, so changes perceptions—if effective—that it may leave the auditor confused and disoriented. Thus, Kennedy sought to stress his firmness toward the Soviet Union in two ways: (1) by pointing to the differences that still separate the two nations; and (2) by reaffirming existing American alliances with countries that might be affected by the flexibility he had called for.

Kennedy scored the Soviets for their distorted view of the West and for their aggressive intentions toward other nations. Yet, in both cases the President drew clear lessons from these Soviet faults that lent credence to his call for greater cooperation between the two countries. Early in the speech as he was asking Americans to re-examine their attitudes toward the Soviet Union, the President prefaced his argument by noting the distorted view Soviets have of the West:

> It is discouraging to think that their leaders may actually believe what their propagandists write. It is discouraging to read a recent authoritative Soviet text on *Military Strategy* and find, on page after page, wholly baseless and incredible claims—such as the allegation that 'American imperialist circles are preparing to unleash different types of wars . . . that there is a very real threat of a preventive war being unleashed by American imperialists against the Soviet Union . . . [and that] the political aims of the American imperialists are to enslave economically and politically the European and other capitalist countries . . . [and] to achieve world domination . . . by means of aggressive wars.'

Even as Kennedy cited this quotation as typical of misperceptions, he warned the American public "not to fall into the same trap as the Soviets, not to see only a distorted and desperate view of the other side." Later, Kennedy placed responsibility for world unrest on the Communists: "The Communist drive to impose their political and economic system on others is the primary cause of world tension today." But, the peace could be assured, Kennedy concluded, if we embarked upon "a new effort to achieve world law—a new context for world discussion," which would be achieved through "increased understanding between the Soviets and ourselves," through "increased contact and communication."

In developing his argument in this fashion, Kennedy accomplishes several tasks at once. First, he demonstrates that he is not näive about the Soviet system and the difficulties to be confronted in seeking cooperation with the

Soviet leaders. Second, he re-enforces the distinction between the Communist system (that is aggressive and the major cause of world tensions) and the Soviet people (who are human and the base for a cooperative effort between the two countries.) Third, he uses these hard-line statements as incentives for changing American attitudes and seeking greater cooperation with the Soviet Union. Thus, firmness is tempered by flexibility.

In re-affirming American commitments with her allies, however, there can be no compromise:

> Speaking of other nations, I wish to make one point clear. We are bound to many nations by alliances. Those alliances exist because our concern and theirs substantially overlap. Our commitment to defend Western Europe and West Berlin, for example, stands undiminished because of the identity of our vital interest. The United States will make no deal with the Soviet Union at the expense of other nations and other peoples, not merely because they are our partners, but also because their interests and ours converge.

Thus, the rearrangement of perspectives about the Soviet Union does not compel a rearrangement of existing commitments to allies. In this area, Kennedy exhibits the firmness essential to maintaining stability within the Atlantic Alliance.

Rationality. It is a commonplace in political rhetoric for the speaker to present himself as rational and his opponents as emotional just as it is another commonplace to describe one's own proposals as truth and opposing proposals as "mere rhetoric." These commonplaces are used even as the advocate becomes emotional about his own rationality, even as he skillfully constructs rhetorical arguments to denounce the use of rhetoric by others.

Throughout the address Kennedy presented his definitions of what kind of attitudes Americans ought to adopt as rational and positive and contrasted them with the old attitudes that were persistently described as irrational. Those who think peace cannot be achieved are described as indulging in "dangerous, defeatist" thinking.[13] Those who would continue with the old assumptions about confrontation with the Soviets are described as indulging in a "distorted and desperate view of the other side." The President, moreover, predicted that the consequences of not changing our attitudes would be catastrophic in this nuclear age: the ultimate irrationality. Peace becomes then, as Kennedy said early in the speech, "the necessary rational end of rational men."

Symbolic acts. Persuasive arguments alone are seldom enough to change deep-rooted ideas or attitudes either among friends or adversaries. Specific acts of good faith are needed to demonstrate to friend and foe alike that one means what one says. Such actions within a rhetorical context are symbolic, confirming the sincere intent of the speaker. Thus, President Kennedy announced two important decisions near the end of the speech:

First: Chairman Khrushchev, Prime Minister Macmillan, and I have agreed that high-level discussions will shortly begin in Moscow looking toward early agreement on a comprehensive test ban treaty. Our hopes must be tempered with the caution of history—but with our hopes go the hopes of all mankind.

Second: To make clear our good faith and solemn convictions on the matter, I now declare that the United States does not propose to conduct nuclear tests in the atmosphere so long as other states do not do so. We will not be the first to resume. Such a declaration is no substitute for a formal binding treaty, but I hope it will help us achieve one.

The first announcement symbolized the beginning of Soviet-American cooperation, though on a small scale—a beginning, nonetheless. The second demonstrated American willingness to take the initiative in making such cooperation as basis for more progressive relations between the two nations.[14] The importance of these announcements lay in their symbolism for they did not weaken or harm our national security in any perceptible fashion as Amitai Etzioni later pointed out:

Although [halting nuclear testing in the atmosphere] was dramatic, it was basically a psychological gesture. It did not limit American arms. At the time the U.S. could deliver five times the firepower of the Soviet Union, and its missiles were better protected. The U.S. had conducted about twice as many tests as the U.S.S.R., and needed a one-or-two-year pause to digest the information.

Moreover, American experts agreed that even after two years there was little to be gained from additional testing. Any necessary tests could be conducted underground. Thus, in effect, the President used the termination of testing as a psychological gesture.[15]

Indeed, the Soviets responded positively to these symbolic acts. The next day, they removed their objection to sending observers to Yemen, a Western proposal they had previously blocked. On June 15, Premier Khrushchev made a speech favorable to the Kennedy initiatives and announced that he had ordered a halt to production of strategic bombers.[16] The moves toward détente were underway.

Follow-through. Though Kennedy's speech generally met with favorable editorial response (especially in Europe), it did not have the immediate impact intended.[17] Part of the reason for this lay in an event beyond the President's control. The next day (June 11) Governor George Wallace fulfilled a campaign promise to try to stop school desegregation by blocking the entrance to the University of Alabama when black students tried to enroll. That evening President Kennedy spoke to the nation justifying his decision to send National Guardsmen to insure the enrollment of black students. In addition, he proposed a new civil rights bill outlawing segregation in public accommodations facilities. Thus, this dramatic confrontation between federal authority and the governor became *the* major news story of the week putting the Kennedy peace initiatives on the back pages.

Furthermore, the President left Washington on June 23 for a triumphant tour of Europe. His first stop was in West Germany to reassure its people that his overtures for peaceful settlement of outstanding differences between the U.S. and U.S.S.R. would not endanger German security.[18] His appearances were intended to reaffirm symbolically American commitments to West Germany even as his statements reassured them that he intended to remain firm in those commitments.

However, in one of his speeches, he got carried away. Speaking in the shadow of the infamous Berlin Wall in the Rudolph Wilde Platz, Kennedy orated:

> Two thousand years ago the proudest boast was *'civis Romanus sum.'* Today, in the world of freedom, the proudest boast is *'Ich bin ein Berliner.'*
>
> There are many people in the world who really don't understand, or say they don't, what is the great issue between the free world and the Communist world. Let them come to Berlin. There are some who say that communism is the wave of the future. Let them come to Berlin. And there are some who say in Europe and elsewhere we can work with the Communists. Let them come to Berlin. And there are even a few who say that it is true that communism is an evil system, but it permits us to make economic progress. *Lass sie nach Berlin kommen.* Let them come to Berlin.[19]

This attempt at firmness surely went beyond what the occasion required, and it was a direct contradiction of what the President had said at American University. After all, it was Kennedy himself who had said—only 16 days before—that communism permits some economic progress and that "we can work with the Communists." The speech was unfortunate in that it could have torpedoed the earlier peaceful initiatives.[20] On the other hand, it shored up Kennedy's image for firmness in dealing with the Soviets. Apparently, it is this kind of hard-line approach that a President must take after advocating accommodation with an adversary in order to persuade allies and opponents at home that he will not "sell out" American interests.

The Test Ban Treaty. On July 25, 1963 the limited nuclear test ban treaty was concluded and initialed in Moscow. The next day President Kennedy spoke on national radio and television about the significance of the treaty. The speech was intended to marshall public support for the treaty and to present the President's major arguments to the Senate as it began deliberations over ratification of the treaty. In sum, the President was attempting to set the terms for argument knowing full well that whoever sets those terms can usually win the argument.[21]

Kennedy advanced four major reasons or incentives for ratifying the treaty:

> "First, this treaty can be a step towards reduced world tension and broader areas of agreement."
>
> "Second, this treaty can be a step towards freeing the world from the fears and dangers of radioactive fallout."

"Third, this treaty can be a step toward preventing the spread of nuclear weapons to nations not now possessing them."

"Fourth and finally, this treaty can limit the nuclear arms race in ways which, on balance, will strengthen our Nation's security far more than the continuation of unrestricted testing."[22]

Each of these was argued by balancing firmness with flexibility. For example, when Kennedy argued the first advantage of the treaty, he stated:

The Moscow talks have reached no agreement on any other subject, nor is this treaty conditioned on any other matter. Under Secretary Harriman made it clear that any nonaggression arrangements across the division in Europe would require full consultation with our allies and full attention to their interests. He also made clear our strong preference for a more comprehensive treaty banning all tests everywhere, and our ultimate hope for general and complete disarmament. The Soviet Government, however, is still unwilling to accept the inspection such goals require.

* * *

But the difficulty of predicting the next step is no reason to be reluctant about this step. Nuclear test ban negotiations have long been a symbol of East-West disagreement. If this treaty can also be a symbol—if it can symbolize the end of one era and the beginning of another—if both sides can by this treaty gain confidence and experience in peaceful collaboration—then this short and simple treaty may well become an historic mark in man's age-old pursuit of peace.

Kennedy concluded the speech by remarking on the symbolic nature of the treaty:

According to the ancient Chinese proverb, 'A journey of a thousand miles must begin with a single step.'

My fellow Americans, let us take that first step. Let us, if we can step back from the shadows of war and seek out the way of peace. And if that journey is a thousand miles, or even more, let history record that we, in this land, at this time, took the first step.

Thus Kennedy established the ultimate grounds for argument: ratification of the treaty is a step toward peace; failure to ratify may, by implication, be a step away from peace and perhaps toward greater tensions between the U.S. and the U.S.S.R. These grounds are quite favorable grounds upon which to wage battle for the President's position.

On September 24, 1963 by a vote of 80 to 19 the Senate of the U.S. ratified the limited nuclear test ban treaty.[23]

Conclusion. Chairman Nikita Khrushchev called Kennedy's speech at American University "the best speech by any President since Roosevelt."[24] Truly, it was the best speech by Kennedy during his administration. But it was only part of an over-all rhetorical effort to change public attitudes toward reaching détente with the Soviet Union. Kennedy used a deductive rhetorical approach. That is, he began with the principles upon which the U.S. should seek accommodation with the U.S.S.R., spelled out in full in the American

University speech. The speech is a mixture of firmness, flexibility and rationality. The specific issues to be negotiated are relegated to the conclusion of the speech and are to be seen in light of the principles enunciated.

The major problem he faced was assuring both the American public and our allies in Europe that he was as firm in his commitments to national interests and allies as he was in his call for flexibility in dealing with the Soviets. The European trip and his tough "Ich Bin Ein Berliner" speech were intended to give those assurances.

Using the unique Presidential pulpit on the eve of Senate debate over ratification, Kennedy established the firmest possible ground for advantage in those debates. He gave his supporters arguments to use for ratification as well as arguments to use against opponents. And the treaty was ratified.

In sum, President Kennedy's rhetorical efforts to change assumptions about policy differences on outstanding issues ushered in the era of détente. It was a masterful performance, and one that will be emulated by other Presidents seeking to change attitudes on controversial issues facing the American public.

Notes

1. Roger Hilsman, *To Move a Nation. The Politics of Foreign Policy in the Administration of John F. Kennedy* (New York: Dell Publishing Co., 1967), pp. 340–357.
2. *Ibid.*, p. 351.
3. *Ibid.*, p. 350.
4. *Ibid.*, p. 351
5. *Ibid.*, pp. 356–357. Of course, by the time the speech was delivered, Lyndon Johnson had become President and was attempting to bring the Executive branch under control and probably had precious little time for a major change in policy toward China.
6. Theodore C. Sorensen, *Kennedy* (New York: Harper and Row, 1965), p. 730. Sorensen contends that Soviet opposition to "on-site" inspections provided the major stumbling block to negotiations over limiting nuclear testing. Frequently, this opposition to inspections was used in American cold war rhetoric as demonstrative proof of the closed nature of the Soviet society. But it had been an on-going argument between the two nations with each country shifting positions as it suited each. See Allen W. Dulles, "Disarmament in the Atomic Age," *Foreign Affairs* 25 (January, 1947), pp. 204–217.
7. *Ibid.*, p. 731.
8. The announcement of major policy changes in a university setting is not unusual. On June 5, 1947 Secretary of State George Marshall launched the European Recovery Program (the Marshall Plan) at commencement exercises at Harvard. President Johnson unveiled his "Great Society" at the University of Michigan graduation on May 22, 1964. Indeed, Johnson emphasized the symbolism of the event when he remarked: "I have come today from the turmoil of your Capitol to the tranquility of your campus to speak about the future of your country."

9. John F. Kennedy, "Peace," in *Presidential Rhetoric: 1961–1980* ed. by Theodore Windt, 2nd edition (Dubuque: Kendall/Hunt Publishing Company, 1980), p. 41. All subsequent quotations from Kennedy's speech are taken from this volume. To appreciate fully the change in assumptions and language Kennedy was attempting, one should compare this speech with President Truman's speech on aid to Greece and Turkey (later called the "Truman Doctrine") delivered to Congress on March 12, 1947. Truman's speech, as much as any other, helped to establish the strident anti-communist language and rhetoric that would prevail until Kennedy attacked it directly in his American University speech. One should also consult Charles E. Osgood, *An Alternative to War or Surrender* (Urbana: University of Illinois Press, 1962), p. 139 *passim*.

10. *Cf.* Walter Lippmann, *Public Opinion* (New York: Pelican Books, 1946), pp. 59–96.

11. During his 1959 visit to the United States Chairman Nikita S. Khrushchev persisted in making the same distinction as he sought peaceful coexistence with the United States. See the collection of his American speeches in *Khrushchev in America* (New York: Crosscurrents Press, 1960) and especially his address to the American people over national radio and television, pp. 198–207. *Cf.* my unpublished doctoral dissertation, *The Rhetoric of Peaceful Coexistence: A Criticism of Selected American Speeches by Nikita Khrushchev* (Columbus: Ohio State University, 1965).

12. Lippmann, p. 61. See also Amitai Etzioni, "The Kennedy Experiment," *Psychology Today* 3 (December, 1969), pp. 43–45, 62–63.

13. In this instance, Kennedy appropriated the language of the "right" to use against the "right." William Safire defined "defeatist" as an "attack word against those urging caution, or withdrawal from what they consider indefensible positions." See Safire, *Safire's Political Dictionary* (New York: Ballantine Books, 1978), p. 161.

14. Khrushchev's agreement to participate in these discussions arrived only a day before the speech was delivered.

15. Amitai Etzioni, "Can JFK Peace Psychology Tactics Work for Nixon?" *Washington Post* (December 7, 1969), p. C 2.

16. *Ibid.*

17. Sorensen, p. 733.

18. See in particular Kennedy's news conference at the Foreign Ministry in Bonn on June 24 and his "Address in the Assembly Hall at the Paulskirche in Frankfurt," June 25 in *Public Papers of the Presidents of the United States. John F. Kennedy 1963* (Washington: Government Printing Office, 1964), pp. 505–511, 516–521.

19. "Ich Bin Ein Berliner," in Windt, p. 50.

20. Schlesinger described the speech as "true but unwontedly harsh." Arthur M. Schlesinger, Jr., *A Thousand Days. John F. Kennedy in the White House* (Boston: Houghton Mifflin Company, 1965), p. 884. Schlesinger's literary evaluation of the speech is less useful and less insightful than O'Donnell's and Powers': "Kennedy's fighting speech in Berlin . . . actually was a grave political risk, and he knew it. Such a heated tribute to West Berlin's resistance to Communism could have undone all the success of his appeal for peace and understanding with the Soviets in his American University speech two weeks earlier." Furthermore, they added: "When [Kennedy] reached City Hall, and saw the huge mob of people waiting for a few words of hope and encouragement, he had to speak out to them passionately to give them reassurance that they desperately wanted to hear, even if it meant the ruin of his cherished ambition to make a nuclear test ban treaty." They concluded that it was fortunate that Khrushchev "decided to ignore the City Hall

speech and to accept the Free University speech [a speech given later that afternoon and in which Kennedy modified his views given at the Wall and returned to the themes of the American University speech], and went ahead with his endorsement of the atmospheric test ban treaty." Kenneth P. O'Donnell and David F. Powers with Joe McCarthy, *Johnny We Hardly Knew Ye. Memories of John Fitzgerald Kennedy* (New York: Pocket Books, 1973), pp. 417–418.

21. George E. Reedy, *The Twilight of the Presidency* (New York: World Publishing Co., 1970), pp. 41–42. The "terms for argument" set the stage for public discussion. And the words one chooses creates those terms. Even as a President may choose certain words and arguments advantageous to his case, so too he may choose other words and arguments not as a means for defeating opponents, but as a means for establishing a common ground for the beginning of reasonable discussion of issues.

   Chairman Nikita S. Khrushchev recognized this need for a common diplomatic language when he prepared for his 1959 visit to the United States. In his press conference on August 5, 1959, he said he wanted "to find a common language and a common understanding on the questions which we should settle." *Nikita Sergeyevich Khrushchev. On the Occasion of his Visit to the United States* (New York: International Arts and Sciences Press, 1959), p. 31. Much of the specific language of Khrushchev's speeches in the U.S. was an attempt to establish this common language laying a basis for a common ground of understanding.

   Kennedy's American University speech had presented to the Soviets this kind of common language.

22. "Radio and Television address to the American People on the Nuclear Test Ban Treaty," *Public Papers,* pp. 601–606.

23. For one discussion (among many) of the politics of the treaty, see Sorensen, pp. 734–746.

24. Sorensen, p. 733.

LYNDON B. JOHNSON

The Great Society as a Rhetorical Proposition

David Zarefsky

Mention Lyndon Johnson's Great Society and one of two images is likely to come to mind. For the political conservative, the dominant image is of "throwing dollars after problems" in the arrogant belief that no social evil is so intractable that it will not yield in the face of Federal attention and funds. For the liberal, the dominant image probably is of a cornucopia of programs, ranging from "Medicare for the old, educational assistance for the young, tax rebates for business, a higher minimum wage for labor," to "auto safety for drivers, pensions for the retired, fair labeling for consumers, conservation for the hikers and the campers, and more and more and more."[1] Both images are oversimplifications, however. They construe the Great Society as only a slogan or stereotype, not as a conceptually coherent set of programs of appeals. There *was* such a conceptual core to the Great Society, and it was revealed in a series of speeches by President Johnson during 1964 and 1965. To advocate this core of ideas involved the President in a rhetorical problem, which his choice of appeals permitted him to solve. The Great Society, taken as a whole, can be seen as a "rhetorical proposition": an assertion advanced in response to a problem in persuasion. This essay consists of an account of the development of the Great Society idea, an explication of its central themes, and a discussion of the rhetorical problem and how it was resolved.

Development of the Idea

The phrase "great society" surfaced in a series of presidential statements during the spring of 1964. Lyndon Johnson, in need of a slogan to describe the goals of his domestic program, had tried "better deal" with little apparent success. In a fund-raising dinner in Chicago on 23 April, he said, "[W]e have been called upon to build a great society of the highest order."[2] The next day, he told the League of Women Voters in Pittsburgh, "The goal of my administration is to work for a greater society, and try to unite men of good will in both parties to build a greater society, not just here but throughout the world."[3] On 30 April, he told the 1964 Campaign Conference of Democratic Women that the great society was "the grandest design of all—a design which creates

Mr. Zarefsky is Associate Professor of Communication Studies at Northwestern University.
Reprinted by permission from *Quarterly Journal of Speech* 65 (December 1979), pp. 364–378.

a state whose only reason for existence is the welfare and the happiness of its people."[4] On 4 May he implored labor leaders, "Help us as we build the great society America can, and will, be."[5] Similar appeals were made to the Advertising Council on 6 May, to students at Ohio University on 7 May, to the New Jersey State Democratic Committee on 10 May, and in remarks accepting honorary membership in the National Forensic League on 12 May.[6] None of these usages of the phrase, however, received much attention. It was the University of Michigan commencement address on 22 May, which the White House described as "the first speech devoted almost entirely to defining the concept of a Great Society,"[7] which attracted widespread interest.

Early drafts of this speech had been written by Douglas Cater, Richard Goodwin, and Horace Busby. The final draft was prepared by Goodwin and Bill Moyers, who, in a memorandum to the President, explained that the speech was designed to impress thinking people with the President's concern for "the *future problems of America,*" that it "talks about *new themes* instead of repeating themes . . . you have talked about in the past," and that "from the momentum of this speech we may be able to go ahead and develop *the outlines of a Johnson program for 1965.*"[8] Another memorandum added that a university audience was chosen specifically for this speech because Johnson's experience during the Depression had convinced him of the power of youth to reshape the country.[9]

In the aftermath of the Ann Arbor speech, the origins of the phrase aroused considerable speculation. It had been used in 1381 by an English organization to combat feudalism, in 1776 by Adam Smith to refer to the global economic community, and, most prominently, as the title of the 1914 book by Graham Wallas, a Fabian Socialist who proposed an interconnected-world community.[10] It is unlikely, however, that Johnson's writers sought to allude to these previous usages. In a retrospective memorandum, Press Secretary George Reedy explained that the Ann Arbor speech had been called to the attention of the press by Goodwin. Reedy added, "There was considerable press discussion speculating that the phrase originated from the title of a book by a British, Fabian socialist named Wallace (or Wallas?). Personally, I doubt it. I think it was just a phrase in a speech which caught on and then was promoted vigorously by Moyers and Goodwin."[11]

Although the Ann Arbor speech is most often identified with the "great society" phrase, the same essential ideas were repeated the next week in a commencement address at the University of Texas and in speeches throughout the next year. Reference is made to the "great society," for example, in both the 1965 State of the Union Message and in Johnson's Inaugural Address.

The Central Themes

Despite the widespread publicity given the phrase, its precise meaning seemed difficult to discern. The President sometimes used the slogan as a summary term for his domestic programs, sometimes as an overarching goal or vision with transcended specific programs. Moreover, presidential statements typically defined the term, not conceptually, but only by enumeration of some of its particulars. For example, the third draft of the Ann Arbor speech, written by Goodwin and Jack Valenti, characterized it as "the Society where no child will go unfed; and no youngster will go unschooled"; "where no man who wants a job will fail to find it"; "where education is blind to color and employment is unaware of race"; "where there is a narrowing of prejudice and an enlargement of peace"; "where men are more concerned with the quality of their goals than the quantity of their goods."[12] These phrases seem to suggest a vision of a utopian future without specifying the details of what it is or how it will be obtained. As delivered, the speech shortened the enumeration considerably, but without providing any greater conceptual coherence.

Nevertheless, a reading of the President's speeches during 1964 and 1965 does suggest central themes of the Great Society. One theme was a strong emphasis on the *quality* of life, an emphasis which typically was contrasted with purely quantitative and materialistic measures of national well-being. The contrast was drawn most strikingly in the 1965 State of the Union address, in which the President said, "The Great Society asks not how much, but how good; not only how to create wealth but how to use it; not only how fast we are going, but where we are headed," and added, "It proposes as the first test for a nation: the quality of its people." In the same speech, the President declared his intention to "seek to establish a harmony between man and society which will allow each of us to enlarge the meaning of his life and all of us to elevate the quality of our civilization."[13]

Similar ideas could be found in other speeches. In the University of Texas Commencement Address, Johnson characterized the Great Society as one "where man's spirit finds fulfillment in the works of his mind."[14] In the University of Michigan speech, he contrasted the Great Society with a society that was merely rich or powerful, and stated, "The purpose of protecting the life of our Nation and preserving the liberty of our citizens is to pursue the happiness of our people."[15] Contrasting the Great Society with one unmotivated by considerations of quality, the President declared in his Inaugural Address, "I do not believe that the Great Society is the ordered, changeless, and sterile battalion of the ants. It is the excitement of becoming—always becoming, trying, probing, falling, resting, and trying again—but always trying and always gaining."[16]

One sign of a society inspired by quality is its ability not to be overwhelmed by change but to shape and direct the forces of change. This idea is discussed in the University of Texas speech, in which the President contrasted the Great Society with "a legacy of despair and degradation, where a man's hopes are overwhelmed by change that he cannot control."[17] At the suggestion of Chester Bowles, Johnson made the management of change a major theme in his Inaugural Address, declaring, "Is our world gone? We say farewell. Is a new world coming? We welcome it, and will bend it to the hopes of man."[18]

This view of the Great Society as a striving for quality was premised upon material prosperity. In the mid-1960's, especially after the tax cut, permanent prosperity had been accepted as within the realm of the United States economy. Freed from purely material concerns, citizens could revise their aspirations upward toward a vision of quality. Buoyed by their economic success, they believed that success in social intervention also was possible; the President asserted at Ann Arbor, "We have the power to shape the civilization that we want."[19] And, since economic expansion automatically would increase Federal revenues, the Great Society could be financed through this "fiscal dividend" and by cutting back on obsolete programs. Quality would be achieved not through individual sacrifice but through the rewards of economic growth.

A vision of quality also required long-range thinking and planning. Although efforts toward the goal must begin at once, the goal could be realized only in the long run. Johnson implored his audience at a fund-raising dinner in Chicago, "So let us, as party and people, think not only of the next election, but let us think tonight and plan for the next generation."[20] The preparation of the Ann Arbor speech likewise was guided by a concern for long-range planning and by the belief that "unless the President looks *far into the future* and considers these consequences, it is unlikely there will be effective national planning for the decades ahead."[21] This combination of immediate action and a long-range goal allowed the President both to claim that his objectives were attainable and to avert charges of failure when they were not met at once.

A second theme of the Great Society was the need for special efforts in behalf of individuals and groups who were relatively immune to the effects of macroeconomic policy—the beginnings of the idea of affirmative action. Unlike the merely "rich" or "powerful" society, the Great Society would provide for the needs of all its people. The idea was developed most fully in the President's 1965 commencement speech at Howard University, in which he called for the achievement of equality "not just . . . as a right and a theory but equality as a fact and equality as a result." Using language drafted by Richard Goodwin, the President explained himself by invoking the metaphor of a race: "You do not take a person who, for years, has been hobbled by chains and liberate him, bring him up to the starting line of a race and then say, 'you are free to compete with all the others,' and still justly believe that you have been completely fair."[22] Special action was needed, then, to offset the debilitating effects of the past.[23]

The same idea also appears in other presidential statements. In his February, 1964, health message, Johnson had declared, "But our remaining agenda is long, and it will be unfinished until each American enjoys the full benefits of modern medical knowledge."[24] In the poverty message, after noting that the tax cut would create new jobs—exits from poverty—Johnson had insisted, "But we must also strike down all the barriers which keep many from using those exits."[25] The voting rights message of March, 1965, contains the statement, "to exercise these privileges [of citizenship] takes much more than just legal right," and the pledge, "So we want to open the gates to opportunity. But we are also going to give all our people, black and white, the help that they need to walk through those gates."[26] What these messages have in common is the belief that, for certain groups of people, opportunities in the abstract are not meaningful. True opportunity requires special action to insure that people are able to benefit from what society makes available.

The final central theme of the Great Society involved the role of government as stimulus and guarantor in meeting the goals described above. Although the goals were discussed as if they should be shared by all, it was assumed that the private sector alone could not achieve them—not because of perversity or disinclination but because of lack of sensitivity to and experience with the problems. Sensitizing the people was the job of government, and particularly of the President. Preparation of the Ann Arbor speech, for example, reflected the belief that *the President alone has power to match responsibility and means to match motives.*"[27] Although government could not do the job alone, it could serve as the catalyst to focus the resources of the private sector. That such a role was appropriate was argued by Johnson both in the Ann Arbor speech and in his remarks to the Campaign Conference of Democratic Women, to whom he said that promoting "the welfare and happiness of its people" was the only *raison d'être* of the state.[28] Likewise, Johnson's 1964 State of the Union message had explained, "This budget, and this year's legislative program, are designed to help each and every American citizen fulfill his basic hopes."[29] And the poverty message had proclaimed, "Today, for the first time in our history, we have the power to strike away the barriers to full participation in our society. Having the power, we have the duty."[30] The government's decision to emphasize a social problem would guarantee that public attention would be focused upon it, and the stimulus provided by government would attract private energies and resources. With all sectors of society working in concert, impressive gains could be achieved for a relatively small outlay of public funds.

Advocacy of these three themes served important functions for Johnson. He was able to present himself, in aide Jack Valenti's words, as "just as human, as compassionate, as strong in his views about the lost, as President Kennedy was"[31]—an important objective since Johnson assumed office with only a small proportion of the public believing that they knew him well[32] and with his dominant image from the Senate being that of a Southern conservative. Johnson also was able to espouse a set of programs and themes which would command the support of Kennedy admirers, but which clearly went beyond what Kennedy had been able to accomplish. He also was able to develop a broad coalition of interests on whose political support he would wish to draw. Although it was strategically useful for Johnson to espouse these themes, it should not be supposed that he was less than genuine in his advocacy. Many of the programs of the Great Society responded to problems he had known in his own youth or had pursued in his early political experience during the New Deal.

Rhetorical Problems and Choices

The idea of the Great Society might have been embodied in the general goals described above, but progress toward those goals required specific legislation on a variety of topics. Many of the legislative initiatives can be grouped into one or two categories. Some, such as Medicare and Federal aid to education, had been proposed for several years but had been stymied by failure to resolve or overcome a troublesome issue—the fear of socialized medicine in the former, the church-state issue in the latter. Success depended, therefore, on the ability to fund a combination of appeals which would bypass or remove the obstacle. It was a problem of argument selection, involving both the crafting of legislative proposals and the choice of how to describe them and on what basis to promote them.

Other measures, such as the War on Poverty and aid to the cities, involved subjects which had no pre-existing informed or aroused public. Although writing about another topic, Mechanic explained the difficulty facing these programs: "[T]he needs of one social group or another are communicated by the ability of that group, or that of its advocates, to arouse an emotional response in those holding the powers of decision."[33] But most of the direct beneficiaries of these programs—the poor and slum dwellers, for example—would score low on most indices of political participation. At the local level, they had few advocates; big-city mayors were more sensitive to the competing demands of ethnic or neighborhood blocs, who were more vocal politically. And, because the ideas were new, the usual gestation period, during which interest groups might organize in their behalf, was absent. The legislative proposals, rather than responding to public clamor, had been developed by task forces of professionals consulting directly with the Administration.[34] The need, therefore, was to arouse attention to the problems and to mobilize support for the Johnson programs. Complicating the task was the fact that the electorate generally was not sanguine about the prospects for success. In the Spring of 1964 the Gallup poll reported that 83 percent of its sample felt that poverty could not be cured[35] and that the Biblical injunction, "The poor ye shall always have with you," was valid. The 88th Congress, presumably, mirrored these sentiments; the 1963 session had been particularly difficult for Kennedy and nothing suggested that 1964 would be easier for Johnson. Even after the landslide election of 1964, Johnson said he was uncertain of his ability to control the Congress. Following a "honeymoon" period, he thought, the legislative branch always would assert its independence of the executive.[36]

President Johnson referred to his proposals as "a program of action to clear up an agenda of social reform almost as old as this century and to begin the urgent work of preparing the agenda for tomorrow."[37] But adoption of the program was no foregone conclusion. The President's major task was one of persuasion, mobilizing public and Congressional support for his legislation.[38] To this end, he and his advisers made numerous public speeches, engaged in interpersonal persuasion, and made strategic choices about the contents of the bills to be sent to Congress. Some of the rhetorical choices were unique to particular bills. Poverty and Model Cities, for example, were defended as local demonstration projects offering big payoffs at low cost. But three rhetorical tactics were used in the service of many programs: stress on conservative themes, use of moralistic rhetoric, and development of crucial distinctions in order to evade politically difficult choices.

Conservative Themes

One important means to obtain Congressional support for the Great Society was to depict the proposals in such a way that they might attract the support of fiscal conservatives, and particularly Southern Democrats worried about expansion of the power of the Federal government. Such a description, the administration hoped, would enlarge the ranks of supporters by enough votes to gain passage of the bills and begin to develop a broad base of public support. To this end, the Administration stressed conservative themes.

One such theme was the frugality of the programs, both because of their low initial cost and because they would save money in the long run. In his first State of the Union message, Johnson startled the Congress with the news that his proposals could be implemented "with an actual reduction in Federal expenditures and Federal employment," because of his insistence on "closing down obsolete installations, by curtailing less urgent programs, by cutting back where cutting back seems to be wise, by insisting on a dollar's worth for a dollar spent."[39] Initial costs of the programs would be financed by savings elsewhere in the budget. Johnson urged his Cabinet to find possible savings in outmoded programs, because "the Congress and the American people will provide the budgetary means to build the Great Society *only* if we take positive steps to show that we are spending only where we legitimately need to spend."[40]

In the long run, the programs would pay for themselves. By "making taxpayers out of taxeaters," they would bring additional tax revenues to the Treasury and also would save numerous welfare costs. For example, in his first State of the Union message, Johnson asserted that spending $1,000 to train an unemployable youth would bring a $40,000 eventual return.[41] In his consumer message, the President explained, "All these proposals for consumer protection would cost us as taxpayers only a small fraction of what they would save us as consumers."[42] In the education message, implying that failure to spend on education would require spending on welfare and corrections, Johnson observed, "We now spend about $450 a year per child in our public schools. But we spend $1,800 a year to keep a delinquent youth in a detention home, $2,500 a year for a family on relief, $3,500 a year for a criminal in state prison."[43]

In another appeal to conservatives, the Administration denied that the Great Society was a series of programs to benefit only special interests. Although affirmative action currently is understood, in some measure, as redistributing opportunities—benefiting the disadvantaged at the expense of the privileged—that understanding is not evident in the lexicon of 1964 and 1965. In the early planning of a possible antipoverty bill, Robert J. Lampman had advised Walter Heller, "Probably a politically acceptable program must avoid completely any use of the term 'inequality' or of the term '*redistribution*' of income or wealth."[44] Indeed, the President scrupulously avoided such references, maintaining instead that *everybody* would benefit from the programs he espoused. In his first State of the Union message, he explained that all people would benefit from Medicare, that all communities would benefit from training programs and from new construction, and that all taxpayers would benefit from the proposed tax cut.[45] He was even more explicit in the poverty message, explaining, "Our history has proved that each time we broaden the base of abundance, giving more people the chance to produce and consume, we create new industry, higher production, increased earnings and better income for all." He drew the conclusion, "Giving new opportunity to those who have little will enrich the lives of all the rest."[46] Since, Johnson's argument ran, the Great Society would contribute overall to economic growth, gains for the deprived need not come at the expense of the well-to-do. Rather than redividing the pie, the social reform programs would *enlarge* the pie. This claim was likely to appeal to legislators who were dubious about how they and their nonpoor constituents would benefit from the Great Society.

Perhaps the best way to summarize the conservative themes was to say that the new social programs were "businesslike." Often businessmen were consulted in the shaping and development of the programs. In the instance of the War on Poverty, Shriver was able to claim "more inputs from businessmen than any other group" and to assert that his program was "based on sound business principles" of opportunity, initiative, investment, and growth.[47] An unsigned memorandum entitled "Why Should Conservatives Support the War on Poverty?" contains all of these themes. The new program is claimed to be businesslike because of the long-run savings; capable of success because "we have the resources, the technology, and the will"; American because "it preserves our basic national principles of equal opportunity, local initiative, voluntary services, Federal-state-local cooperation, and of public and private cooperation" and because "it is one our most effective tools in the war against Communism"; and prudent because "it does not mean massive new spending; every cent is included in the President's budget, and comes from cutting back low priority and unnecessary other Government expenses."[48]

Scott has noted that radical rhetoric often reveals a conservative voice, that the advocate of change often depicts the goal as a return to the promise of the past and as consistent with the heritage of the past.[49] This tendency certainly is evident in the rhetoric of the Great Society, and it is easy to see why. It permitted President Johnson to co-opt conservatives in the Congress and the country into support for his programs of social reform. Having no organized and articulate liberal interest group in behalf of his measures, Johnson was able to neutralize his potential opposition and thereby increase his chances for success.

The Moral Imperative

The legislative programs of the Great Society often were described in moralistic language about rights and responsibilities, with exhortation emphasizing the urgency of the problem and the imperative of action. Moral considerations, of course, transcend the norms of political conflict among competing interests; they subsume the processes of bargaining and coalition building.[50] Since public opinion was not aroused to support the Great Society programs in advance, a moral appeal might be a speedy way to develop a broad base of support.

Civil rights furnished the most obvious example of moral exhortation. In his address to Congress appealing for the Voting Rights Act, Johnson specifically stated, "There is no moral issue,"[51] implying, not that it was an amoral question, but that the command of morality was plain. In his Howard University address, he called for measures specifically directed at Negro poverty in order to correct "the one huge wrong of the American Nation."[52] But other programs, too, were described in terms of moral imperative—even when the moral principle was far broader in scope than the specific legislation proposed. For example, Johnson appealed for the Elementary and Secondary Education Act on the grounds that education should be a right. He asked the Congress to "declare a national goal of *Full Educational Opportunity*. Every child must be encouraged to get as much education as he has the ability to take."[53] The act itself, however, as the President characterized it in his memoirs, was "a foundation on which the country could work toward educational achievement."[54] Likewise, the President asked for Medicare legislation—a specific program to pay a portion of the medical bills of the aged—and regarded it as recognition "that good medical care is a right, not just a privilege."[55] In appealing for support for the poverty program, Johnson told the Advertising Council, "It is almost insulting to urge you to enlist in this war for just economic motivations. This is a moral challenge that goes to the very root of our civilization."[56] Indeed, Interior Secretary Stewart Udall testified in Congress that the antipoverty effort might serve as Willam James's desired moral equivalent of war.[57]

Although President Kennedy had been advised that a forthcoming poverty program "*ought to be presented quite frankly in terms of the obligations which a prosperous majority owes to a submerged and desperately poor minority,*"[58] and although President Johnson did employ this theme, he was careful not to make it his sole defense. For example, in response to Johnson's instruction, Moyers informed Adam Yarmolinsky, who was drafting the poverty message, that "there needs to be more logic and less rhetoric in outlining *why* we must wage war on poverty. He [Johnson] wants it to appeal to the mind as well as the heart." In amplifying this theme, Moyers explained, "He wants to point out—with facts and figures—how the obligation to help the poor goes beyond even the fundamental moral obligation we have; in other words, eliminating poverty will have what substantial effects on the total American economy."[59]

A more subtle form of moral exhortation was developed by selecting military terms and images to describe the poverty program.[60] In the early planning, no particular name had been selected. Kennedy's Council of Economic Advisers was thought to be leaning toward "Widening Participation in Prosperity," but other proposed titles included "Human Conservation and Development," "Access to Opportunity," and "Attack on Poverty." CEA Chairman Walter Heller concluded that he was "in the market for a more effective title."[61] It was in the State of the Union address of 8 January 1964 that President Johnson declared "unconditional war on poverty," and the references to *war* were quite frequent thereafter. Not only was the program labeled a war, but a number of corollary images also were employed in public discourse. For example, Walter Reuther promised that the labor movement would "enlist . . .

in the war against poverty for the duration." The U. S. Conference of Mayors saw that the plan of battle was "to wheel up weapons and ammunition together for the first time for a coordinated, concerted, multifront offensive." Labor Secretary Willard Wirtz insisted that the war involved "a carefully worked out battle plan based less on praising the Lord than on passing the ammunition." Even opponents of the program used the military image, as when Senator John Tower described local control and representative government as the "first casualty of the war on poverty."[62]

According to the President, the military metaphor was selected in a meeting at his ranch at the end of 1963. In his memoirs, Johnson wrote, "The military image carried with it connotations of victories and defeats that could prove misleading. But I wanted to rally the nation, to sound a call to arms which would stir people in the government, in private industry, and on the campuses to lend their talents to a massive effort to eliminate the evil."[63]

The military image illustrates many of the rhetorical benefits to the Administration of an appeal based on moral imperative. First, it helped to unite the nation, subsuming partisan strife in a call for righteous sacrifice. Mayor Richard Daley of Chicago put the appeal succinctly in his Congressional testimony: "One characteristic of the American people when a war is declared is that all sides come together, and this is a war."[64] Second, it captured presumption for the Administration and shifted the burden of proof onto the opponents of Great Society legislation. When a nation is at war, it has acknowledged, by definition, the existence of a foe sufficiently threatening to warrant attack. The need for action is assumed and the persistent challenge of the enemy becomes prima facie evidence of the inadequacy of existing measures. By capturing presumption, the Administration was able to avoid having to prove that all existing remedies left substantial problems inherently unsolved—a burden of proof which, given the absence of supportive public opinion, might have been quite difficult to meet. And, third, the military image justified the centralized structure of the Office of Economic Opportunity, not as a way out of bureaucratic infighting between the Departments of Labor and Health, Education, and Welfare (which it was),[65] but as necessary for a chain of command. As Congressman Phil Landrum put it, "in recognizing this as a D-day, we are just setting up a general just like we set up General Eisenhower as commander of all the forces in World War II and had him directing all these different arms of strength."[66]

It might be objected that too much has been made of the value of the military symbolism and of moral exhortation in general.[67] To be sure, the nation has been called on to wage war against all manner of problems, ranging from street crime to waste in government. And President Jimmy Carter only recently called for a national energy program as the moral equivalent of war, with little apparent effect. But the Johnson Administration invoked the moral imperative at a particularly opportune time. Aroused by President Kennedy's untimely death, and feeling guilty for "not having worked more for tolerance toward others,"[68] the United States citizens longed for redemption through sacrifice. The moral appeal, among its other virtues, permitted audiences to conceive of the Great Society programs as memorials to the slain President. Before the military conflict in Vietnam called into question the values of patriotism and national honor, the Administration could assert the moral imperative to attack social problems, and thereby minister to the national need.

Critical Distinctions

The Great Society programs had to appear quite different from other measures on which opinion was sharply divided or there was strong disapproval. If new efforts, such as poverty and Model Cities, were made to seem similar to older, negatively-valued programs, their chances for attracting the needed legislative support would be slim. Accordingly, a primary rhetorical approach of the Administration was to argue that any basic similarities were far outweighed by essential differences.

The search for critical distinctions can be seen most clearly in the development of the Elementary and Secondary Education Act. Previous attempts at general aid to education had foundered on the fear of Federal control and on the complicated issue of the wisdom and frugality of aid to parochial schools. A task force headed by John Gardner, though developing no specific proposal, strongly advised against going "through one more agonizing tug of war over the church-state issue."[69] In a memorandum transmitted to the President, Commissioner of Education Francis Keppel warned, "The membership of the new Congress will presumably be more favorable to strengthening education in general, and particularly in the cities. But it will not ease the church-state problem." If the Administration proposed aid to parochial schools directly, it would be in a clear violation of the Constitution. But if it chose to press for aid to public schools only, there would be a bitter legislative and public battle, "leaving scars politically and perhaps creating divisiveness among the people along religious lines. The value of the gain to the public schools," Keppel advised, "would have to be considered in the light of the loss to the spirit of interfaith cooperation in other parts of the society, particularly with regards to civil rights."[70]

To escape this dilemma, Keppel suggested that the aid program be constructed by analogy to the concept of "impacted areas." The principle of Federal aid to school districts significantly affected by government activities (particularly by the presence in the area of military installations) had been long recognized. The definition of "impacted areas" was stretched to include areas with high concentrations of poverty, and aid was calculated according to the number of poor children in the district. This approach, which resulted in the distribution of funds to school districts most in need of aid, was also rhetorically valuable: it defined the aid as going really neither to public nor parochial schools, but to *children*. In his memoirs, Johnson claimed that the "child benefit theory" and a similar compromise, according to which schoolbooks would be owned by the public schools but borrowed by parochial school students, were the key factors in circumventing the church-state issue.[71] Likewise, since the specter of Federal control had not been raised with respect to impacted areas, the definition of the new program by analogy to that concept helped to vitiate the fear.

Drawing crucial distinctions also was important for other Great Society legislation. The proposed poverty program would be in trouble if it came to be seen as a measure primarily to aid Negroes. Even before black militancy and the summer riots prompted a nation-wide white backlash, many Southerners in Congress (whose support was thought essential for the poverty bill to pass) feared that the proposal would hasten unduly the pace of racial integration. The intensity of this fear is reflected in a memorandum in the White House files: "[A]pparently the [worry] that is being carefully cultivated throughout the Southern bloc is the fear that this is a deliberately disguised attempt to further racial integration, that it was suggested by the Negro leadership, and that it will in fact be implemented by devious individuals who believe in government by decree and not by the democratic legislative process."[72] Similar fears on the part of North Carolina and South Carolina Congressmen probably were responsible for the President's decision to scuttle Adam Yarmolinsky, who had been slated to be Sargent Shriver's deputy at the helm of OEO.[73] For the poverty program, the value of using civil rights as the basis for a moralistic appeal was outweighed by the adverse effect on the South of identifying a new program with the issue of race.

Whether in recognition of these pitfalls or out of sound political instinct, the President sought to distinguish the poverty program from civil rights measures. His highly publicized tours in the Spring of 1964, to promote the program, concentrated on Appalachia, where most of the poor were white. Willard Wirtz had argued that "for most Americans the strongest visual image of poverty is that of the miners and hill folk of Eastern Kentucky and West Virginia,"[74] and it was to the Administration's advantage to reinforce this image.

The poverty program was carefully distinguished also from traditional welfare programs. Welfare was almost universally unpopular, and if the new program were seen basically as another public assistance program, it probably would assume the same stigma. So the President portrayed the poverty program as the *antithesis* of traditional welfare. In speeches throughout 1964, Johnson insisted that the new program, unlike welfare, had the aim of "making taxpayers out of taxeaters."[75] In his remarks upon signing the Economic

Opportunity Act, he said, "We want to offer the forgotten fifth of our people opportunity and not doles," and pronounced that, "The days of the dole in our country are numbered."[76]

The same quest for critical distinctions is evident in the design of the Medicare legislation. Although the newly-elected 89th Congress was far more favorable to a Medicare bill than its predecessors had been, the Administration still was worried about the opposition that would be aroused if its program were associated with the dread term, "socialized medicine." The original Administration program, for this reason, envisioned primarily a program of hospital insurance, apparently on the theory that the American Medical Association hardly could charge that doctors were controlled by the government if coverage of doctors' costs were omitted altogether. The final bill was broader in scope than the original proposal (in part because of the AMA argument that the program was inadequate since it *omitted* doctors' fees),[77] but it remained essentially a reimbursement program that left physicians in control of their own fees. In retrospect it has been argued that the weakness of cost controls in Medicare and Medicaid has been a major factor in the inflation of medical care costs since 1965.[78] But at that time it seemed the wiser course to draft the program in such a way that the epithet of "socialized medicine" would be difficult to apply.

In each of these instances, the Administration was able to insulate the Great Society programs from potential opposition; by making crucial distinctions, Administration personnel were able to argue that Great Society programs were basically unlike the targets of opposition. With would-be antagonists neutralized, the Administration succeeded with less support than otherwise would have been needed. Furthermore, the Administation gained needed support simply in the act of making the distinctions. If these programs were basically unlike things that were bad, then it must mean that the new measures are good.

Conclusions

Kearns has written that the Johnson Administration regarded the passage of legislation as the criterion of success in its domestic program.[79] Johnson assumed that the values implicit in his vision of the future were desirable, and that the nation had the ability and means to achieve his goals. His implicit theory of rhetoric, therefore, viewed it as a process of selecting strategies and tactics which would comprise an effective public appeal. Although beyond the scope of this essay, it may be argued that Johnson's a priori judgments of value and ability, and the limited role he saw for rhetoric—as evidenced in this study of his domestic program—also help to explain the tragic course of United States policy in Vietnam.

By the President's own standard, however, he was immensely successful. Aid to education moved from initial bill to final passage in only three months, the poverty program in five, and Medicare in six. All told, eighty-nine major Administration bills were passed in 1965 alone, with the only two major defeats being Congress' refusal to repeal right-to-work laws or to grant home rule to the District of Columbia. Given the circumstances of divided or nonexistent constituencies coupled with potentially hostile opposition, the President's rhetorical success in gaining acceptance of his Great Society program is all the more impressive.

Though intellectuals occasionally criticized his "style," the President enjoyed widespread public approval during 1964 and 1965. Whether this approval was an endorsement of the overarching concepts of the Great Society is unclear; it may have reflected only the individual popularity of specific programs. This observation suggests that the President succeeded only partially in convincing the people of the merit of the Great Society, but achieved a measure of success great enough to satisfy his legislative needs in 1964 and 1965.

Few of the Great Society programs matched the promises which had been made for them. The discrepancy between promise and result led some critics to charge that the vision of a Great Society was utopian and impractical—a charge which Johnson himself vigorously denied.[80] To what extent the programs were conceptually flawed, to what degree the programs suffered from lack of presidential attention to the details of administration, or to what degree they were casualties of underfunding caused by the Vietnam war—these issues are arguable. To some extent, the initial choice of rhetorical tactics also may have invited long-run problems. The invocation of conservative themes, for example, made it difficult to expand programs beyond their initial funding levels, or to target them to the most severe areas of need. Moral exhortation and military imagery might well have inflated expectations and led to frustration when all did not turn out for the best. Some of the crucial distinctions could not be sustained in practice, and their collapse exposed the programs to familiar attacks they had sought to avoid. But in 1964 and 1965 these rhetorical choices were immensely successful.

Currently it is fashionable for political rhetors to stress the limits, not the possibilities, of what government can do in the realm of social policy. In the contemporary context, talk of building a Great Society seems naive at best, suspect at worst. Statements such as "we have the power to shape the civilization we want," from the Ann Arbor speech, or "Is a new world coming? We welcome it, and will bend it to the hopes of man," from the Inaugural Address, today suggest arrogance approaching hubris, to which some critics attribute economic and social disorder at home and military and diplomatic disaster abroad. The fifteen years since the Ann Arbor speech have introduced a discontinuity in public discourse, making obscure the fact that summoning the people through a vision of unlimited possibilities has been a recurrent appeal in the nation's rhetorical history. But there are cycles in the strength of these appeals, and at some time again it will be politically feasible and desirable for rhetors to appeal to an expansive vision of the future. At such time, rhetorical practioners should be able to profit from studying the vision of the Great Society offered by Lyndon Johnson.

Notes

1. Doris Kearns, *Lyndon Johnson and the American Dream* (New York: Harper and Row, 1976), p. 216.
2. *Public Papers of the Presidents: Lyndon B. Johnson, 1963–64* (Washington, D. C.: U. S. Government Printing Office, 1965), I, 529.
3. Ibid., I, 536.
4. Ibid., I, 597.
5. Ibid., I, 606.
6. Ibid., I, 609, 631, 675, 686.
7. Letter from Malcolm Kilduff to Jack H. Hamilton, 29 Jan. 1965, General File SP 3–28, Box 36, Lyndon Baines Johnson Library (hereafter LBJL).
8. Memorandum from Dick Goodwin and Bill Moyers to the President, 18 May 1964. Statements of Lyndon Baines Johnson, Box 14, LBJL.
9. Memorandum, unsigned and undated, "The President's Speech on the Great Society." Statements of Lyndon Baines Johnson, Box 14, LBJL.
10. Marvin E. Gettleman and David Mermelstein, eds., *The Great Society Reader: The Failure of American Liberalism* (New York: Random House, 1967), pp. 13–14.
11. Memorandum from George E. Reedy to Juanita Roberts, 13 Sept. 1968, Executive File SP 3–28, Box 36, LBJL. Reedy indicated that he had disapproved of the phrase "because it seems pompous and had too many overtones of Marxist-style planning."
12. Statements of Lyndon Baines Johnson, Box 14, LBJL.
13. *Public Papers of the Presidents: Lyndon B. Johnson, 1965* (Washington, D. C.: U. S. Government Printing Office, 1966), I, 4 and 1. The original draft by Richard Goodwin posed quality as the only test; Comptroller General Elmer B. Staats changed it to the *first* test. Goodwin had posed the three antitheses as "not/but"; Douglass Cater changed them to "not *only*/but." Statements of Lyndon Baines Johnson, Box 23, LBJL.
14. *Public Papers*: 1963–64, I, 728.
15. Ibid., I, 704. Johnson had made a virtually identical statement on 30 Apr. to the 1964 Campaign Conference for Democratic Women. See ibid., I, 597.
16. *Public Papers: 1965*, I, 73. This line was written by John Steinbeck. See cable from Eric F. Goldman to Mrs. Johnson, 16 Jan. 1965, Statements of Lyndon Baines Johnson, Box 25, LBJL.
17. *Public Papers: 1963–64*, I, 728.
18. *Public Papers: 1965,* I, 74. On the influence of Bowles, see Memorandum from Chester Bowles to the President, 24 Dec. 1964, Statements of Lyndon Baines Johnson, Box 25, LBJL; Personal-Confidential Letter from Bill Moyers to Chester

Bowles, 18 Jan. 1965, Statements of Lyndon Baines Johnson, Box 25, LBJL. Moyers wrote, "I hope you know that our theme of change in the Inaugural Address was inspired by your draft."

19. *Public Papers: 1963–64,* I, 706.

20. Ibid., I, 529.

21. Memorandum, unsigned and undated, "The President's Speech on the Great Society," Statements of Lyndon Baines Johnson, Box 14, LBJL.

22. *Public Papers: 1965,* II, 636.

23. Ibid., II, 636. Goodwin's draft, with nearly identical language, may be found in Statements of Lyndon Baines Johnson, Box 27, LBJL.

24. *Public Papers: 1963–64,* I, 276.

25. Ibid., I, 376.

26. *Public Papers: 1965,* I, 286.

27. Memorandum, unsigned and undated, "The President's Speech on the Great Society," Statements of Lyndon Baines Johnson, Box 14, LBJL.

28. *Public Papers: 1963–64,* I, 597, 704.

29. Ibid., I, 113.

30. Ibid., I, 379–80.

31. Memorandum from Jack Valenti to Theodore Sorensen, 24 Dec. 1963, Statements of Lyndon Baines Johnson, Box 11a, LBJL.

32. Kearns, p. 412, n. 3.

33. David Mechanic, "Ethics, Justice, and Medical Care Systems," *Annals of the American Academy of Political and Social Science,* 437 (May 1978), 76.

34. On the role of the task forces, see William E. Leuchtenberg, "The Genesis of the Great Society," *Reporter,* 21 April 1966, pp. 36–39.

35. Cited in Sargent Shriver, *Point of the Lance* (New York: Harper & Row, 1964), p. 107.

36. Johnson's fears to this effect are recounted in Eric F. Goldman, *The Tragedy of Lyndon Johnson* (New York: Knopf, 1969), pp. 259–60.

37. Lyndon Baines Johnson, *The Vantage Point: Perspectives of the Presidency, 1963–1969* (New York: Holt, Rinehart and Winston, 1971), p. 104.

38. Troublesome issues which blocked passage of some reforms and the absence of aroused public opinion about others, constitute the "exigencies" of the rhetorical situation, in the sense in which the term is used by Lloyd F. Bitzer in "The Rhetorical Situation," *Philosophy & Rhetoric,*1 (1968), 1–14.

39. *Public Papers: 1963–64,* I, 112 and 113.

40. Statement by the President on "The Great Society," Cabinet Meeting, 19 Nov. 1964, Executive File WE 9, Box 25, LBJL.

41. *Public Papers: 1963–64,* I, 114. This comparison was suggested by the Budget Bureau in its review of the draft for this speech. See Statements of Lyndon Baines Johnson, Box 11a, Folder V, LBJL.

42. *Public Papers: 1963–64,* I, 268.

43. Public Papers: 1965, I, 25. This comparison was suggested by Commissioner of Education Francis Keppel, whose draft added the claim, "If increased spending will help us to reduce the soaring costs of crime, delinquency and unemployment, it is by far the very best of investments." Keppel's memorandum was transmitted by Anthony Celebrezze to Bill Moyers. Executive File SP 2–3/1965/ED, Box 65, LBJL.

44. Memorandum from Robert J. Lampman to Walter W. Heller, 10 June 1963, Legislative Background, Economic Opportunity Act of 1964, War on Poverty, Box 1, LBJL.

45. *Public Papers: 1963–64*, I, 115.
46. Ibid., I, 377.
47. Speech by Sargent Shriver to National Chamber of Commerce Congressional Breakfast, 28 Apr. 1964, "Poverty—Speeches" folder, Richard Goodwin Files, Box 24, LBJL.
48. Memorandum, "Why Should Conservatives Support the War on Poverty?" 26 May 1964, Executive File WE 9, Box 25, LBJL. The memorandum was circulated by Bill Moyers to the President, Walter Jenkins, Jack Valenti, Lawrence O'Brien, Henry Hall Wilson, and Mike Manatos.
49. Robert L. Scott, "The Conservative Voice in Radical Rhetoric: A Common Response to Division," *Speech Monographs*, 40 (1973), 123–35.
50. For a discussion of the need to clothe policy arguments in moralistic language in order to attract public support, see Saul D. Alinsky, *Rules for Radicals* (New York: Random House, 1971), pp. 36–47.
51. *Public Papers: 1965*, I, 283.
52. Ibid., II, 640.
53. Ibid., I, 25–26.
54. Johnson, *Vantage Point*, p. 219.
55. Ibid., p. 220.
56. *Public Papers: 1963–64*, I, 611.
57. Stewart L. Udall, *Economic Opportunity Act of 1964*, Hearings, U. S. House Committee on Education and Labor, Subcommittee on the War on Poverty Program, 88th Cong., 2d sess. (Washington, D.C.: U.S. Government Printing Office, 1964), I. 36.
58. "Some Notes on a Program of 'Human Conservation,'" unsigned (marked in corner "C. L. Schultze"), 2 Nov. 1963, Legislative Background, Economic Opportunity Act of 1964, War on Poverty, Box 1, LBJL.
59. Memorandum from Bill Moyers to Adam Yarmolinsky, 28 Feb. 1964, Legislative Background, Economic Opportunity Act of 1964, War on Poverty, Box 2, LBJL.
60. For a more detailed analysis of the rhetoric surrounding the poverty program, see David Zarefsky, "President Johnson's War on Poverty: The Rhetoric of Three 'Establishment' Movements," *Communication Monographs*, 44 (1977), 352–73.
61. Memorandum from Walter W. Heller to the Secretary of Agriculture, the Secretary of Commerce, the Secretary of Labor, the Secretary of Health, Education and Welfare, the Director of the Bureau of the Budget, and the Administrator of the Housing and Home Finance Agency, 5 Nov. 1963, Legislative Background, Economic Opportunity Act of 1964, War on Poverty, Box 1, LBJL.
62. Walter P. Reuther, *Economic Opportunity Act of 1964*, Hearings, I, 422; Raymond R. Tucker, ibid., II, 787; W. Willard Wirtz, ibid., I, 184; John G. Tower, *U.S. Congressional Record*, 110 (22 July 1964), 16616.
63. Johnson, *Vantage Point*, p. 74.
64. Richard J. Daley, *Economic Opportunity Act of 1964*, Hearings, II, 763.
65. *Wall Street Journal* reporter Jonathan Spivak discussed the bureaucratic influences on the antipoverty strategy in "War-on-Poverty Planners Seek New Agency to Direct Program, Rise in Proposed Funds," *Wall Street Journal*, 3 Mar. 1964, p. 2. Walter Heller and Kermit Gordon urged the creation of a new agency as a means for transcending the conflict between Labor and Health, Education, and Welfare. See "The Office of Economic Opportunity During the Administration of President Lyndon B. Johnson," unpublished administrative history, p. 16, LBJL.
66. Phil Landrum, *Economic Opportunity Act of 1964*, Hearings, I, 190.

67. For a recent study suggesting the possible risks of the military metaphor, see Hermann G. Stelzner, "Ford's War on Inflation: A Metaphor That Did Not Cross," *Communication Monographs,* 44 (1977), 284–97.
68. This was the conclusion of a Harris Poll published on 30 Dec. 1963, and cited in Philip W. Borst, "President Johnson and the 89th Congress: A Functional Analysis of a System Under Stress," Diss. Claremont 1968, p.24.
69. Johnson, *Vantage Point,* p. 208.
70. Memorandum from Francis Keppel to Anthony J. Celebrezze (transmitted by Celebrezze to Bill Moyers, 1 Dec. 1964), Executive File SP 2–3/1965/ED, Box 65, LBJL.
71. Johnson, *Vantage Point,* pp. 208, 210. Johnson credited the latter compromise to Lawrence O'Brien, Douglass Cater, Wilbur Cohen, and Congressman Hugh Carey.
72. Memorandum from John W. Carley to Adam Yarmolinsky and Wilson McCarthy, 30 July 1964, "Poverty" folder, Bill Moyers Files, Box 39, LBJL.
73. This episode is described in Rowland Evans and Robert Novak, "The Yarmolinsky Affair," *Esquire,* Feb. 1965, pp. 80–82, 122–23.
74. Memorandum from W. Willard Wirtz to Bill Moyers, 29 Feb. 1964, Legislative Background, Economic Opportunity Act of 1964, War on Poverty, Box 2, LBJL.
75. *Public Papers: 1963–64,* I, 411, 480, 483.
76. Ibid., II, 989.
77. Johnson, *Vantage Point,* p. 215.
78. On the history particularly of Medicaid, see Robert Stevens and Rosemary Stevens, *Welfare Medicine in America: A Case Study of Medicaid* (New York: Free Press, 1974).
79. Kearns, p. 218.
80. Ibid., p. 211.

Lyndon Johnson Redefines "Equal Opportunity:" The Beginnings of Affirmative Action

David Zarefsky

Commitment to the value of "equal opportunity" has long characterized the American political creed. This value makes it possible to reconcile empirical inequalities in economic and social status with a normative belief in egalitarianism. If people differ in wealth, education, life style, or occupation, it does not matter; what is important is that they all begin with an equal chance. If chances are truly equal, one can rise as fast and as far as individual ability permits. Social inequalities can be explained as the result of applying unequal abilities to equal chances. The value of "equal opportunity," in other words, serves both to sustain faith in the chance for upward mobility and to rationalize existing inequalities.

Within the past fifteen years, however, the meaning of "equal opportunity" has undergone a profound transformation. Traditionally, it had been thought to be a *description* of the natural condition of society in the absence of government interference. The task of government, then, was to avoid imposing restrictions which discriminated against people in the allocation of opportunities. If the law favored one race over another, or even appeared to make race a salient consideration, it was suspected of interfering with equal opportunity. So, in the name of this goal, vestiges of preferential treatment disappeared during the early 1960's; even references to race or ethnic origin were deleted from educational and employment application forms. Now, however, equal opportunity is regarded as a *goal* to be achieved, in large part through government initiative; this is the idea of affirmative action. In order to achieve equal opportunity, special efforts—amounting in effect to preferential treatment—have been justified. References to race (and sex) reappear on application forms so that employers and educational institutions can "act affirmatively" to recruit qualified minorities. Originally seen as a means to redress discrimination against blacks, the idea of affirmative action has been extended to the problems of sex discrimination and discrimination against the handicapped. The Supreme Court's recent *Bakke* decision gave the concept

Reprinted by permission from *Central States Speech Journal* Vol. 31, No. 2 (Summer 1980), pp. 85–94.

implicit sanction. This transformation in the meaning of "equal opportunity" has had significant political consequences. Government intervention in the "opportunity structure," once *forbidden*, is now *mandated*.

For the rhetorical scholar, the significant question is *how* such a change in political values is proposed and widely accepted in a relatively brief time. Though he does not address the rhetorical behavior by which concepts are changed, Stephen Toulmin does suggest that the rationality of a concept depends upon its adaptability to change.[1] In *Atitudes Toward History*, Kenneth Burke refers to the practice of casuistic stretching, according to which the ambiguities of a situation are exploited in order to expand a concept's scope of reference.[2] In the process, of course, the meaning of the concept is somewhat altered. Perelman and Olbrechts-Tyteca offer a much more specific examination of how a concept is effectively "stretched." The key process at work is *dissociation*—separating a unitary concept into parts, identifying the old way of thinking with the less valued "part" and the reformulation with the more valued.[3] These insights may be summarized by stating that an effective way to change the meaning of concepts is to pour new wine into an old bottle—to leave the positive connotation of a term unchanged while its denotation undergoes substantial revision.[4]

The shift in the concept of "equal opportunity" from nondiscrimination to affirmative action provides a case study of this method for achieving conceptual change. The case study should illustrate the effectiveness of dissociation by exploring how it works in a given situation. Equally, demonstrating the effectiveness of dissociation should explain how Americans were persuaded to change their views of what "equal opportunity" meant while retaining their commitment to the value itself.

The process of dissociation is evident in one of the very first attempts to reformulate "equal opportunity" as "affirmative action"—the commencement address delivered by President Lyndon Johnson at predominantly black Howard University in 1965. This speech warrants more attention from rhetorical critics than it has received. What follows is a description of the rhetorical situation confronting Johnson at Howard University and an analysis of how he responded to the situation by dissociating the term "equal opportunity" both in that speech and in other addresses as well.

The Rhetorical Situation

The Howard University speech was delivered at a crucial time in the history of the civil rights movement. The recently proposed Voting Rights Act probably would be the last major piece of civil rights legislation. But the entire group of civil rights laws and judicial decisions really would attack only the formalized structure of racial discrimination in the South. They could do little to address the more subtle and complicated problems of *de facto* segregation and economic discrimination which existed throughout the nation, particularly in the urban centers of the North and West. Civil rights leaders, having largely succeeded in their battle against Jim Crow laws in the South, were preparing to make the Northern ghetto their next major target. Bayard Rustin summarized the course of the movement by writing, "It is now concerned not merely with removing the barriers to full *opportunity* but with achieving the fact of equality."[5]

These developments presented Johnson with the rhetorical problem of determining what stance to take. At one extreme, he might have insisted, in the idiom of the late 1970's, that with the passage of the Voting Rights Act we had reached the limits of what government could do. He might have chosen a course of "benign neglect" similar to that which Moynihan urged upon his successor. But such approaches were not in keeping with Johnson's belief in the efficacy of government to solve problems, nor would they have been politically wise. They would have produced an antagonism between the government and the civil rights movement, with the former only reacting to the initiatives of the latter. The civil rights movement was supported by most of the constituencies of the Democratic Party (except for the South). For this reason, it would be desirable for the Administration to ally itself with the movement, or better yet to "leapfrog" the movement by taking a stance in the direction in which the movement seemed headed but beyond the point at which it had arrived. Then it would be Lyndon Johnson who was recognized as the foremost civil rights leader in America, and the White House could initiate rather than merely respond.

Attempting to "leapfrog" the movement was rhetorically difficult. It was necessary, in Rainwater and Yancey's phrase, "to move toward a next step that would make it possible for the Negro Americans to realize the gains that the laws made possible."[6] But such a step would involve special efforts or programs in behalf of black Americans, and preferential treatment seemed at odds with the very goal of nondiscrimination to which the civil rights laws were addressed. Therefore, Johnson would need somehow to resolve this seeming inconsistency and to defend measures aimed particularly for blacks.

For a speech delivered in such a complex situation, the Howard University address of 1965 was planned almost haphazardly. It was not a speaking engagement which the President had planned months in advance; in fact, his aide Jack Valenti in March had declined the invitation to speak at Howard. University President James M. Nabrit was anxious for Johnson to appear, however, and offered to revise the commencement program in any way that would accommodate him. When, in May, Johnson approved the Howard commencement on a list of places he would like to go, his action produced a plaintive memorandum from Mary Rawlins to Valenti. Noting that the President previously had declined the invitation, Rawlins asked, "So, what to do here now?" The handwritten reply was "Punt."[7] The decision to deliver the speech was not made final until May 25, only ten days prior to the commencement occasion.

The speech was drafted by Richard Goodwin and Daniel P. Moynihan. Moynihan had been concerned for some time with the inability of civil rights laws by themselves to rid the country of racial discrimination, and had been working toward a view of what more was needed. In April of 1964, he had attended a planning conference sponsored by *Daedalus* and the American Academy of Arts and Sciences, at which he suggested that the question of compensatory preferential treatment for blacks should be given serious attention. Like the other conference participants, however, he was unclear as to how preferential treatment "could be rationalized in traditional political rhetoric."[8] In March of 1965, as Assistant Secretary of Labor, he had written a report on the condition of the Negro family, proposing a national policy to promote family stability. The report was circulated during the spring to approximately eighty people within the government and formed the basis for the section of the Howard speech which dealt with the black family.[9]

Goodwin and Moynihan worked until early in the morning on June 4, the day of the commencement exercise, in drafting the final version of the speech. For this reason, there was no time to seek comments and reactions from pertinent government departments and agencies. Rainwater and Yancey, though describing the speech as basically a "Presidential act," report that three civil rights leaders were consulted and approved of the speech in advance—Martin Luther King, Jr., Roy Wilkins, and Whitney Young.[10]

Dissociation in the Howard University Address

Johnson began the commencement speech[11] by paying tribute to the Negro revolution of the 1950's and early 1960's. He mentioned the Supreme Court decision in *Brown v. Board of Education*, the passage of three civil rights laws, and the impending passage of the Voting Rights Act as measures of its success. The outcome of this movement was to tumble the barriers to freedom for the American Negro.

But legal freedom, Johnson argued, was not sufficient to end the separation of the races or the unequal conditions experienced by blacks. As the President put it, "it is not enough just to open the gates of opportunity. All our citizens must have the ability to walk through those gates." For this purpose the traditional idea of equal opportunity was inadequate. Giving theoretically equal opportunities to persons in unequal circumstances still would produce inequalities in treatment. And the inequalities could not be attributed to differences in individual ability (as the traditional view required), because "ability is stretched or stunted by the family you live with, and the neighborhood you live in, by the school you go to and the poverty or the richness of your surroundings." Johnson was faced, then, with a positively-valued term — "equal opportunity" — whose traditional meaning was insufficient for his purposes. It was at this point that Johnson effectively redefined the concept of "equal opportunity" through the process of dissociation.

Perelman and Olbrechts-Tyteca describe the dissociation of concepts as a process of separating a unitary concept into parts through the use of philosophical pairs. A philosophical pair consists of two terms thought to be in opposition (such as "theory" and "practice"), of which one is generally recognized to be preferable to the other (after all, of what use is a theory that does not work in practice?). The originally unitary idea is then equated with the less preferred member of the philosophical pair and the speaker's reformulation of the idea, with the more preferred term. In this way dissociation serves as a means of redefinition, so that the original term, with all its heritage and connotations, takes on a different referential meaning.[12] Schematically, the process of dissociation might be represented in the following stages: (1) Prior to argument, B generally is taken to be the *equivalent* of A, so that A is regarded as isomorphic with B; (2) B is argued to be only some aspect of A, and a relatively undesirable aspect—such as only the "means" to an end, only the "letter" of A, only an "accidental" feature of A, or only the "appearance" of A; (3) by contrast, a new term C is argued to be the more desirable aspect—it is the "true end" of A, the "spirit" of A, the "essential" feature of A, or the "reality" of A; (4) hence, A effectively is redefined as designating C rather than B. Dissociations are employed when the formerly unitary term comes to appear self-contradictory or to lead to unacceptable results.

In the Howard University speech, Johnson sought to dissociate the concept of "equal opportunity," as the means to resolve his rhetorical problem. The dissociation is explicit: "We seek not just freedom but opportunity—not just legal equity but human ability—not just equality as a right and a theory but equality as a fact and a result." The dissociation also is suggested by the statement, "Thus it is not enough just to open the gates of opportunity. All our citizens must have the ability to walk through those gates." The philosophical pairs of right/fact, theory/result, and, more broadly, appearance/reality were employed. Applying the schema above, the process of reasoning was as follows: (1) "Equal opportunity" customarily means the absence of legally sanctioned racial discrimination; (2) but the removal of these legal barriers is only the appearance of equal opportunity—equality "as a right and a theory;" (3) true equality of opportunity—equality "as a fact and a result"—comes only when all citizens "have the ability to walk through those gates;" (4) since opportunities can be equal only when all citizens have this ability, then special programs to improve the circumstances of blacks were not really examples of preferential treatment but steps toward equal opportunity.

How did Johnson defend this redefinition? Goodwin's first draft of the speech provided the basic formula: by analogy to a race. "You do not take a man," Goodwin wrote, "who, for years, has been hobbled by chains, liberate him, bring him to the starting line of a race, saying 'you are free to compete with all the others,' and still justly believe you have been completely fair."[13] Goodwin's draft generally reflects the language used by the President in the final delivery.

Removal of legal discrimination was analogous to permitting persons previously excluded from the race to come to the starting line and compete against the others. Yet the legacy of discrimination disabled them from a chance to succeed in the race, because of the problems and pathologies Johnson described. They were in the same position as the "person who, for years, has been hobbled by chains" who had no chance to succeed because he lacked the ability to run. The intuitive unfairness of the race would transfer by analogy to the equation of equal opportunity with merely the absence of legally sanctioned racial discrimination. If that equation were also unfair, then elimination of officially approved discrimination must be only the *appearance* of equal opportunity, not true equality.

By this method of reasoning, an alternate criterion for equal opportunity was implicit in the speech. If opportunities truly were equal, not just in a formal but in a material sense, then the laws of randomization would dictate that each group's percentage of successes ("winners" in the race) should be roughly proportional to its percentage of the population ("entrants" in the race). A disproportionate ratio of winners to entrants becomes *prima facie* evidence that opportunities really were not equal in the first place, and this evidence justified special measures in behalf of those groups with a disproportionately low number of winners. In this way the society could "move beyond opportunity to achievement" and "shatter forever not only the barriers of law and public practice but the walls which bound the condition of man by the color of his skin." The extensiveness of the redefinition can be seen in the fact that, whereas *initial conditions* (the chance to enter the race) traditionally had defined equality of opportunity now *terminal conditions* (the outcomes of the race) were the indicators.

As if to provide further support for this redefinition, Johnson praised the achievement of the Howard graduates (their success in the race) but insisted that their accomplishment was atypical of "the great majority of Negro Americans" for whom "the walls are rising and the gulf is widening." Statistics regarding Negro unemployment, poverty, infant mortality, and residential segregation were offered to describe the problem. The programs of the

Great Society were addressed generally to economic and social concerns, but they were not designed for the specific needs of blacks.[14] Consequently, they would not be able to overcome the legacy of "ancient brutality, past injustice, and present prejudice" circumscribing the Negro American. Here the President referred to the concentrations of Negroes in slums and to the high incidence of family breakdown, which "flows from centuries of oppression and persecution of the Negro man." While the Administration did not have all the answers, Johnson announced his intention to call a White House Conference of scholars and experts, whose goal would be to find ways "to move beyond opportunity to achievement" and thereby "to end the one huge wrong of the American Nation."

Other Examples of Dissociation

The Howard University commencement address was the most explicit redefinition of "equal opportunity" through the process of dissociation, but it was not an isolated example. Johnson's other statements on a variety of domestic issues during 1964 and 1965 reveal the same processes at work. What the rhetorical scholar would call redefinition through dissociation was a recurrent rhetorical choice made by the President.

For example, in his nationally televised message on voting rights in March of 1965, the President foreshadowed the idea of affirmative action which he would develop more fully at Howard in June. Noting that "to exercise these privileges [of citizenship] takes much more than just legal right," he had added, "so we want to open the gates to opportunity. But we are also going to give all our people, black and white, the help that they need to walk through those gates."[15] This help would come to be a part of the definition of "true" opportunity.

The early discussion of the poverty program reveals a similar process of redefinition through dissociation. Macroeconomic policy succeeded in promoting growth and creating jobs, but the existence of jobs hardly provided "economic opportunity" to those without the skills and training necessary to qualify for them. Availability of jobs was analogous to permission to compete in the race; inadequate training and skills, to the chains which hobbled the racer. A true opportunity to escape from poverty therefore required special programs of education and training to give the poor a chance to succeed. As Johnson explained to Congress in his special message on poverty, "Our new tax cut will create millions of new jobs—new exits from poverty. But we must also strike down all the barriers which keep many from using those exists." He added, "The war on poverty is not a struggle simply to support people, to make them dependent on the generosity of others. It is a struggle to give people a chance."[16] The implied premise is that what was needed was a chance not just to be at the starting line but to succeed in the race.

Likewise, the Elementary and Secondary Education Act was defended through dissociation of the term, "opportunity." In his message to the Congress, Johnson proposed "that we declare a natural goal of *Full Educational Opportunity*. Every child must be encouraged to get as much education as he has the ability to take."[17] The pattern of reasoning was familiar. School attendance by itself was not "full" opportunity. School systems which enrolled many children from low-income families, particularly in inner city areas, lacked the financial base to provide for educational quality. Graduates of these school districts, though they received a diploma which entitled them to enter the economic and social "race," still were at a disadvantage analogous to that of the "person who, for years, has been hobbled by chains." To achieve *full* opportunity, special programs would be needed to redress the economic imbalance among school districts. For this purpose the concept of aid to "impacted areas" (by which federal aid was given to school districts significantly impacted by the presence of federal installations, such as military bases) was extended so that a district with a significant percentage of low-income children could be described as "impacted."[18]

In short, while the redefinition of "equal opportunity" to justify affirmative action was most obvious in the Howard University speech, it was a persistent rhetorical feature of the Great Society. In her recent biography of Johnson, Doris Kearns asserts, "Johnson seemed to mean something more than equality of opportunity, that no one should be deprived of the essentials of a decent life. Everyone should be not only guaranteed an equal chance but insured against the possibility of total defeat."[19] Such insurance could be provided only if individuals had a real—not merely apparent—chance to succeed. This point of view permeated the Executive Branch. In proposing language for the first State of the Union message, in January, 1964, the Budget Bureau had suggested, "The task of Government, therefore, is to assure all its citizens an opportunity to meet their minimum needs."[20] In an early draft of the 1964 University of Michigan commencement address, in which Johnson explicated the notion of the Great Society, Richard Goodwin boldly had asserted, "Before this decade is over, no American will be handicapped by his race, his color, or his beliefs," but went on to caution, "once those barriers are down we must make sure that on the other side is a nation where freedom from the wants of the body brings fulfillment of the needs of the spirit."[21] And in a memorandum to the President, Secretary of Labor Willard Wirtz advised "that a great deal of what I understand you want to do—and the country wants to do—could be effectively presented as a Program for Full Opportunity. Having a chance is most of what life is about." Wirtz added, "This approach could cover the Health, Medicare, Conservation, Agriculture, Civil Rights, Business, and other domestic fronts."[22] The line of reasoning always was the same. Although macro-level measures provided for the general well-being of society, there were people who, left behind by these measures, did not have a real opportunity to partake of the benefits of American life. The Johnson domestic program was an effort to provide not just the shadow but the substance of equal opportunity.

The Impact of Johnson's Dissociation

The Howard University speech evoked intense, and surprisingly hostile, reaction. Rainwater and Yancey suggest that some government officials anticipated "the unpleasant prospect of Southern newsmen and public figures seeking to twist the argument to substantiate their fears of the inferiority of Negroes." There was some reaction along these lines, but there also was a backlash among civil rights leaders who believed that a discussion of such issues as family breakdown would serve only to support the view that blacks were responsible for their own plight and that self-help rather than social action was called for.[23] In retrospect, it is not difficult to explain this hostile reaction. Although the redefinition of "equal opportunity" was clear and direct, the recommended policy outcomes were vague. The Howard University speech had been primarily an attempt to describe a problem and the principles which should guide its solution, without proposing specific remedial measures. Accordingly, it was possible to interpret the speech as calling for special programs to redistribute opportunities, or for intervention in the personal lifestyles of blacks, or for black self-help. If civil rights leaders interpreted the speech as an attack on black life-styles or as a call for governmental retreat until blacks stabilized their own family structure, it is understandable that they would be enraged. But if the speech provoked antagonism from civil rights leaders, with whom the President sought to ally, then there was little gain in continuing to espouse its ideas. The promised White House Conference was downgraded to a planning and produced unspectacular results. Seldom, if ever, did Johnson again articulate the redefinition of "equal opportunity" so clearly and forthrightly. He thereby missed the chance to link his theoretical discussion at Howard with specific policy proposals.

It is not at all certain, however, that Johnson himself was fully committed to the concept of affirmative action, the Howard University address notwithstanding. In a speech to civil rights leaders in 1964, for example, he had declared, "None of the provisions in this bill [the Civil Rights Act] of 1964 would create preferential treatment for one race or another. This would be a direct violation of the bill itself."[24] How could this statement be reconciled with the expansive vision of the Howard University speech? Johnson's civil rights program, and indeed the whole of the Great Society, was based on the premise of sustained economic growth. In a constantly growing economy, remedying discrimination does not require redistributing existing opportunities because the system always is creating new ones. Hence, special programs for blacks do not really constitute "preferential" treatment. The privileged are not discriminated against; it is simply a matter of preparing the underprivileged for the new opportunities opening to them.

As often happens, however, the idea of affirmative action became functionally autonomous of the context in which it was devised. The underlying logic of the Howard University speech (if not the speech itself) won wide acceptance in the late 1960's and early 1970's, and was institutionalized in a variety of legal and political forms. It was only later, under assumptions of scarcity, that a careful hearing would be given the argument that affirmative action meant giving minorities and women, for example, preferential treatment in the competition for a *fixed* supply of opportunities, and that this preferential treatment was discrimination against white males.

While the recent debate over "reverse discrimination" is beyond the scope of this paper, what has happened to the concept of affirmative action is worthy of brief note. Defining equal opportunity as an equal proportion of winners to entrants in the race required the measurement of achievement on a *group* basis. But that approach seemed inconsistent with the traditional belief in meritocracy—achievement as a matter of *individual* ability. The opposition between focusing on groups and on individuals has led to much of the current controversy. If the *Bakke* decision is a reliable sign, it appears that the dispute again may be resolved by dissociation. Instead of regarding affirmative action as synonymous with all forms of preferential treatment, the latter notion has itself been dissociated—so that *goals* for the hiring of minorities, for instance, are legitimate forms of preference, whereas, *quotas* are corrupt forms. It was on this basis that the Court simultaneously ruled against the University of California at Davis and yet upheld the concept of affirmative action.

Certainly the current controversy points to the need to study the process of dissociation in public discourse and the need to understand the genesis of affirmative action as a response to rhetorical problem. Both needs can be satisfied in large part by examining the Presidential rhetoric of Lyndon Johnson.

Notes

1. *Human Understanding Vol. I: The Collective Use and Evolution of Concepts.* (Princeton, New Jersey: Princeton University Press, 1972), p. 84.
2. (1937; rpt. Boston, Massachusetts: Beacon Press, 1959), pp. 229–232.

3. Chaim Perelman and L. Olbrechts-Tyteca, *The New Rhetoric*, trans. John Wilkinson and Purcell Weaver (Notre Dame, Indiana: Universty of Notre Dame Press, 1969), pp. 415–426. The concept of dissociation is explored throughout pp. 411–459.
4. Charles L. Stevenson characterizes the linkage of favorable (or unfavorable) connotation with a new referent as "persuasive definition." See his *Ethics and Language* (New Haven, Connecticut: Yale University Press, 1944), pp. 206–226.
5. "From Protest to Politics: The Future of the Civil Rights Movement," *Commentary*, 39 (February, 1965), 27.
6. Lee Rainwater and William L. Yancey. *The Moynihan Report and the Politics of Controversy* (Cambridge, Massachusetts: M. I. T. Press, 1967), p. 15.
7. These details are described in several memoranda. The original invitation was declined in a letter from Jack Valenti to James M. Nabrit, Jr., 10 March, 1965. An unsigned memorandum to Valenti, 24 May, 1965, reports Nabrit's willingness to rearrange the program to accommodate the President. The quoted document is a memorandum from Mary Rawlins to Jack Valenti, n.d. Johnson's final decision to attend the Howard commencement was made in response to a 25 May memorandum from Valenti. All these documents are in Statements of Lyndon Baines Johnson, Box 27, Lyndon Baines Johnson Library.
8. Rainwater and Yancey, pp. 22–24.
9. Moynihan's report subsequently was published under the title *The Negro Family: The Case for National Action* (Washington, D. C.: U. S. Government Printing Office, 1965). A text also is reprinted in Rainwater and Yancey, pp. 39–124. On the use of this report as background for the speech, see Memorandum from Dorothy Territo for the Record, n.d., Statements of Lyndon Baines Johnson, Box 27, Lyndon Baines Johnson Library; Rainwater and Yancey, pp. 1–37, passim.
10. Rainwater and Yancey, p. 4.
11. The text of the speech may be found in *Public Papers of the Presidents: Lyndon B. Johnson, 1965* (Washington, D. C.: U. S. Government Printing Office, 1966), II, 635–640.
12. Perelman and Olbrechts-Tyteca, pp. 411–459, passim. In a recent essay, Hans-Martin Sass has referred to attempts at dissociation as "ideational politics," calling attention to the political interests involved in redefinition. See Hans-Martin Sass, "Ideational Politics and the Word Tolerance," *Philosophy and Rhetoric*, 11 (Spring, 1978), 98–113.
13. Richard Goodwin Draft #1, Statements of Lyndon Baines Johnson, Box 27, Lyndon Baines Johnson Library. The President used nearly identical language in the speech. He changed "man" to "person," but it is likely that this change was innocuous rather than an attempt to eliminate what some people today might regard as a sexist reference.
14. In fact, it was rhetorically desirable that the Great Society be portrayed as the *antithesis* of a special program for blacks. See David Zarefsky, "The Great Society as a Rhetorical Proposition," *Quarterly Journal of Speech*, 65 (December, 1979), 364–378.
15. "Special Message to the Congress: The American Promise," *Public Papers of the Presidents: Lyndon B. Johnson, 1965*, I, p. 286.
16. "Special Message to the Congress Proposing a Nationwide War on the Sources of Poverty," *Public Papers of the Presidents: Lyndon B. Johnson, 1963–64*, I, p. 376. Essentially similar language was proposed in a draft of this speech by Walter Heller, Chairman of the Council of Economic Advisers. After referring to the exits from poverty opened by the tax cut, Heller had written, "open exits mean little to those who cannot move. They mean little to those who are trapped in the web of

poverty by . . . conditions which are hardly touched by prosperity and growth."
Executive File SP 2–3/1964/WE, Box 64, Lyndon Baines Johnson Library.

17. "Special Message to the Congress: 'Toward Full Educational Opportunity,' " *Public Papers of the Presidents: Lyndon B. Johnson, 1965*, I, pp. 25–26.

18. The use of the impacted-areas concept for this purpose also was a way to avoid the controversy over federal aid to parochial schools, as was explained in a memorandum from Francis Keppel to Anthony J. Celebrezze (transmitted by Celebrezze to Bill Moyers, 1 December, 1964), Executive File SP 2–3/1965/ED, Box 65, Lyndon Baines Johnson Library.

19. *Lyndon Johnson and the American Dream* (New York: Harper and Row, 1976), pp. 215–216.

20. Statements of Lyndon Baines Johnson, Box 11a, Folder V, Lyndon Baines Johnson Library.

21. Richard Goodwin draft, Statements of Lyndon Baines Johnson, Box 14, Lyndon Baines Johnson Library.

22. Memorandum from W. Willard Wirtz to the President, 13 November, 1964, Executive File SP 2–4/1965, Box 17, Lyndon Baines Johnson Library.

23. These reactions are described in Rainwater and Yancey, pp. 32–33. Rainwater and Yancey offer an excellent study of the diffusion of the ideas of the Moynihan report and the Howard University speech, emphasizing particularly the role of the press in shaping public perceptions of the speech and report. See especially chapters 5, 8, 15.

24. "Remarks to a Group of Civil Rights Leaders, April 29, 1964," *Public Papers of the Presidents: Lyndon B. Johnson, 1963–64*, I, p. 589.

Lyndon Johnson and the "Crisis" of Tonkin Gulf: A President's Justification of War

Richard A. Cherwitz

United States Foreign Affairs in the 1960's were characterized by the expansion of presidential power used to support a policy of unilateral military interventions into third world nations. The President, acting as Commander-in-Chief, on numerous occasions in the decade of the 1960's embroiled the U.S. in conflicts with other nations. This occurred because the Congress generally acquiesced in the assumption of a stronger policy-making role by the chief executive. As Hans J. Morgenthau and other political observers have noted, more and more power accumulated in the hands of the president in the 1960's, while Congress was reduced to virtual impotence in the making of foreign policy.[1]

One of the most unpopular episodes of such executive initiative was the Vietnam war. Although the conflict in Indochina spanned three decades, involving more than four presidents, Lyndon Johnson deserves special attention when discussing the theme of the expanding power of the executive. Undoubtedly one of the more flagrant examples of the President's control of foreign policy was the incident in the Tonkin Gulf in 1964—an event which has often been cited as the basis for the U.S. policy of massive escalation in Vietnam.[2]

Scholarly interest in the Gulf of Tonkin and the more general subject of executive control has been limited substantially to the efforts of a few historians and political scientists. Consequently one aspect of this episode which has not been extensively explored is Johnson's use of discourse which preceded, accompanied, and followed the implementation of policy in 1964. The purpose of this paper is to examine President Lyndon Johnson's speeches of August 4 and 5, 1964. This essay begins with an historical account of the situation, followed by an examination of the rhetorical strategies used by President Johnson. Finally, this investigation analyzes the effect of Johnson's rhetoric, offering support for the following two propositions: (1) Johnson's rhetoric created an international crisis; and (2) Johnson's rhetoric limited the foreign policy alternatives of the United States in Vietnam.

Mr. Cherwitz is Assistant Professor of Speech Communication at the University of Texas at Austin.
Reprinted by permission from *Western Journal of Speech Communication* Vol. 41, No. 2 (Spring 1978), pp. 93–104.

The Rhetorical Situation: Tonkin Gulf as a Pretext

Although differing opinion still exists concerning the nature of events between July 13 and August 5, 1964, historians agree on several points. The United States *Maddox* had been ordered by the Department of Defense to activate North Vietnamese radar and monitor its communications. In carrying out her mission, she twice approached a North Vietnamese island attacked two days before by American supplied vessels operated by the South Vietnamese. On August 2 the *Maddox* was chased out to sea by North Vietnamese vessels. Shortly thereafter, the *Maddox* fired at three approaching patrol boats. Similar activities were reported on August 4. At about 10:00 p.m. the destroyer *Maddox* and her sister ship, *Turner Joy,* radioed that they were under attack from North Vietnamese torpedo boats.

Although historical accounts differ as to whether or not President Johnson authorized or was aware of these spying missions, testimony of White House authorities confirms that his intelligence sources immediately relayed the accounts of the naval encounters of August 2 and 4.[3] Within hours of the arrival of this information, Johnson ordered the initiation of strategic bombing over North Vietnam.

These circumstances led many historians in the late 1960's and early 1970's to raise several pertinent questions concerning the *authenticity* of the reported chain of events. Richard Barnet, for example, argues that "There is considerable question as to the location of the encounter and its exact character (the destroyers were undamaged)."[4] Historian William Miller provides further credence to the claim of distortion: "To ensure an enduring demonstration, the administration early in August, 1964, contrived the so-called Tonkin Gulf incident involving a debated attack by North Vietnamese vessels on two American war ships, on a provocative spying mission."[5]

While the accounts of these two historians tend to indicate presidential fabrication, primary source material is lacking to document such allegations. Almost all available historical material, including the Pentagon Papers, reveals that the incidents were real. Yet careful scrutiny of the record uncovers a more rhetorically oriented, and perhaps interrelated question. Did the attacks provide a *prima facie* case for the retaliatory air raids ordered within hours by the President or were they merely used rhetorically as a pretext for Johnson's much earlier decision to become involved in Vietnam?

The preponderance of evidence indicates that the Administration was preparing for bombing and other tactical operations in Vietnam long before the Tonkin incident.[6] Moreover, the exact wording of the Tonkin Gulf Resolution had been framed months prior to the reported chain of events.[7] Hence, even to the extent that one accepts the accuracy of the events of August, it is hard to understand why retaliatory bombing was chosen by the Johnson Administration as the most appropriate response to the naval encounter.

Administration actions prior to the Tonkin Gulf incident were clearly rhetorical in that they were designed to acquire public and congressional support. Johnson's use of discourse following the Gulf of Tonkin became the means by which he gathered support for the policies he had been unable to implement prior to August.

The *New York Times* version of the "Pentagon Papers" reveals that during the six months preceding the Tonkin Gulf incident in August, 1964, the United States had been conducting clandestine military attacks against North Vietnam "while planning to obtain a Congressional resolution that the Administration regarded as the equivalent of a declaration of war."[8] These clandestine military maneuvers had reached such proportions by August, 1964, that "Thai pilots flying American T–28 fighter planes apparently bombed and strafed North Vietnamese villages near the Laotian border on August 1 and 2."[9]

In addition, United States' bombing in August would have been nearly impossible in the absence of the large scale contingency planning that commenced months earlier. Neil Sheehan, editor of the *Pentagon Papers,* explains: "Although a firm decision to begin sustained bombing of North Vietnam was not made until months later, the Administration was able to order retaliatory air strikes on less than six hours' notice during the Tonkin incident only because planning had progressed so far that a list of targets was available for immediate choice."[10] The *Pentagon Papers* underscore how the bombing policy chosen in August was not *uniquely* designed as a response to the events in Tonkin Gulf. In fact, these papers go so far as to note that "the target list had been drawn up in May, along with a draft of Congressional resolution, also as part of a proposed scenario culminating in air raids on North Vietnam."[11]

Clearly most of this evidence is circumstantial. Yet some historians allude to Johnson's frustration concerning the lack of public and congressional support for a stepped-up policy in Vietnam.[12] For that reason, even as the Pentagon prepared for military responses in the months prior to the Tonkin incident, Johnson knew that such operations would remain only hypothetical, unless he could build a *prima facie* case for the public and congress.[13] It is not surprising, therefore, that when Johnson went to the people and congress concerning the Tonkin Gulf attack, he did *not* mention such prior military preparation or the exact mission of the *Turner Joy* and *Maddox.* Instead, he chose to build a case for retaliation on the merits of the attack itself—events which as I will show later were characterized in Johnson's speeches as a major crisis.

The fact that the Tonkin Gulf incident was a pretext for military involvement is perhaps best understood in light of Johnson's quickness to act even before final accounts of the incident were firmed up. As Joseph Goulden notes: "The Johnson Administration claimed that it had 'incontrovertible' evidence that the August fourth attack had occurred before Johnson approved the air raids. Yet even as bombers flew over North Vietnam, the Pentagon 'urgently' pleaded with Pacific commanders for substantiating evidence."[14]

Although there is not an abundance of primary historical evidence concerning the accounts of the Gulf of Tonkin incident, it seems relatively clear that the events of August were used as a dramatic pretext for the implementation of earlier designed policies of the Johnson Administration. The Gulf of Tonkin events gave Johnson a desperately needed opportunity to muster support for his military plan in Vietnam. In other words, the events in Tonkin Gulf provided Johnson the rhetorical opportunity to justify previously formulated plans and decisions regarding the U.S. expanded military posture in Vietnam—plans which could not be persuasively justified prior to August, 1964. As Stavens, Barnet, and Raskins contend: "The U.S. was prepared to widen the war unilaterally, and justify it on the basis that the North was infiltrating troops into the South. *But the infiltration argument, aside from its gross falsity, lacked the glamour attendant upon a surprise or shock attack.*"[15]

In marked contrast, the Tonkin Gulf incidents afforded the administration the "rationale" necessary to present a persuasive case to the public and congress for intervening in Vietnam. Unlike the infiltration argument, which Stavens *et al.* argue was "grey, dreary, and continuous, requiring research and explanation," the events in Tonkin Gulf were more glamorous and convincing. "The death of Americans, the sinking of a U.S. ship on the high seas," they contend, "was dramatic, shocking and unique. It was the stuff of headlines."[16] They conclude: "The immediate dispatch of U.S. airplanes to bomb the North in response to the death of innocent American soldiers on the sinking of an innocent American ship could tap the romantic impulse of the American public and drum up sufficient support for a wider war. In 1964 the problem was how to widen the war in a legitimate way. Tonkin furnished the answer: it was provocation."[17]

If indeed Johnson used Tonkin Gulf as a persuasive strategy for implementing previously designed policies not unique to the incident itself, the question for the rhetorical critic becomes how and why was the tactic successful in rallying American public opinion and Congressional support behind a more grandiose war plan? Moreover, why was this support so extensive (e.g., Johnson's popularity in the polls increased and the resolution was passed with but a couple of dissenting votes) when in fact no American ships were sunk and no American lives were lost, and the attackers suffered comparatively heavy casualties?[18]

Johnson's Rhetorical Strategies

The answer to these questions may in part be explained by the President's discourse following the events of early August. Johnson spoke on three occasions. On August 4 he addressed the American public over radio and television. The following day he sent a message to a joint session of Congress. Later that same day he spoke at Syracuse University. An analysis of all three speeches reveals several recurring rhetorical techniques.

First, all three messages were thematically predicated upon action already taken by the Executive as Commander-in-Chief. In each case, President Johnson opened the address by explaining that he had ordered air raids on North Vietnam. In this sense, each discourse pivoted around the theme of retaliation, revealing a rhetoric of justification. In his address to the American public, Johnson included within one sentence both an account of the North Vietnamese attack and his decision to respond with military force. "As President and Commander in Chief it is my duty to the American people to report that renewed hostile actions have today required me to order the military forces of the United States to take action in reply."[19] Similarly, Johnson wrote congress: "The North Vietnamese regime had conducted further deliberate attacks against the United States naval vessels operating in international waters, and I had therefore directed air action against gunboat and supporting facilities used in these hostile operations."[20] By closely associating a description of the attack and America's military reply, Johnson was able to magnify and internationalize a local incident, providing the Congress and American public a strong case of justification.

Second, Johnson's discourse was typified by explanation and use of facts based on dubious evidence. In each of the three addresses Johnson succinctly described the North Vietnamese attack. He did not, however, explain the circumstances leading to the naval barrage. Moreover, he left unmentioned the very rationale for the presence of the *Maddox* and *Turner Joy* in the Tonkin Gulf. Rather, through circumstantial evidence, that is, just mentioning the occurrence of the attacks, he dramatized the events as a "deliberate attack against the United States."[21]

Third, Johnson's vivid and descriptive language contributed to the dramatization. In all three speeches he used the words "hostile" and "deliberate" repeatedly. For example, in his address to the nation Johnson spoke of "repeated attacks" by "hostile vessels" using "torpedoes." This attack, declared the President was an "act of aggression."[22] Couched in this language was the threat or danger of direct aggression against the United States and its people. This language contributed to an overall impression of crisis.

Complementing this vividness was Johnson's parallel structuring of sentences designed to impress upon the nation the severity of the situation. In his address delivered at Syracuse University on the fifth of August, Johnson portrayed the seriousness of the Tonkin incident through short, terse sentences, climaxing in the "rationale" for United States retaliation:

The attacks were deliberate.
The attacks were unprovoked.
The attacks have been answered.[23]

Furthermore, Johnson's hyphenated insertion of powerful adjectives compounded the dramatization of events. "Aggression—deliberate, willful, systematic aggression—has unmasked its face to the rest of the world. The world remembers—the world must never forget—that aggression unchallenged is aggression unleashed."[24] Immediately following this vivid account of the attack, the President attempted to justify his actions: "We of the United States have not forgotten. That is why we have answered the aggression with action."[25] Johnson's use of vivid language, coupled with short, abrupt sentences and repetition, cast for Congress and the public an atmosphere of emergency.

A fourth rhetorical device was Johnson's magnification of local events through appeals to global and more philosophical principles. Although the Tonkin incident transpired thousands of miles from the United States mainland, the President was able to highlight the severity of the events, giving them a sense of international importance, by associating them with a broader doctrine striking closer to home. Thus, on August 4 Johnson reasoned with the American public: "In the larger sense this new act of aggression, aimed at our own forces, again brings home to all of us in the United States the importance of the struggle for peace and security in Southeast Asia."[26] This strategy allowed Johnson to bring the crisis into the homes of every American citizen. By capturing the essence of the attack in devil/God terms (e.g., aggression/peace), Johnson succeeded in making the incident more global, dramatic, and real.

Johnson's philosophical appeal was also evident in his ideological description of the attack as "communist subversion and aggression."[27] The President must have realized that attaching an ideological label to a local event would further dramatize the crisis. For that reason, his remarks to Congress included a detailed historical account of events in Southeast Asia. From this account, Johnson extrapolated that the Communists were violating laws and using terrorist and aggressive techniques to destroy security in Indochina. Johnson's rhetoric, therefore, went far beyond the immediacy of the naval attacks in Tonkin Gulf. This was not just a jungle war, declared Johnson, but a struggle for freedom on every front of human activity.[28] One sensed in these remarks the President's overriding concern for the land war in Southeast Asia. In this regard, the events of Tonkin Gulf appeared throughout Johnson's rhetoric as a mere pretext for the engagement of American troops in Southeast Asia. His use of ideological appeals not only aided in the dramatization of local events, but also supported his more fundamental concern for containing communism in Indochina.

A final rhetorical ingredient present in all three speeches was the development of personal credibility. In order to capture the intensity and severity of the crisis, thereby justifying his action, Johnson offered ethical proof. He made frequent references to his official sanction and authority as president. Johnson prefaced his accounts of United States response with the phrase "as President and Commander-in-Chief." This strategy allowed him to convey to the American people both a sense of authenticity regarding the reported events and a high degree of credibility concerning his actions.

This reference to official sanction and authority was further developed by Johnson's frequent description of the need to act quickly and swiftly in foreign affairs. Knowing that the American public was inclined to support the President in actions requiring prompt decision-making, Johnson was able to use his appeal to authority as basis for justifying his initial instigation of action, followed by a rhetorical explanation. In other words, Johnson used his office as a means of both evidencing the severity of the crisis and providing sufficient rationale for his circumvention of the collective decision-making process.

The Effects of Johnson's Rhetoric

As stated earlier, the purpose of this investigation was to show that Johnson's discourse resulted in the perception of an international crisis, thus reducing the foreign policy alternatives available to the United States. While it would be naive to assume that these propositions can be absolutely documented, it is possible, nevertheless, to advance certain theories, which in conjunction with Johnson's rhetorical techniques lend credence to the hypotheses provided.

Precipitation of a Crisis

Although physical moves are usually associated with crisis during conflicts between two nations, it is often the president's rhetoric that draws attention to the situation, and defines it in such a way that the nation's response is clearly implied. In other words, the rhetoric employed to describe an event gives that event its significance. As Richard Vatz observes: "Rhetors choose or do not choose to make salient situations, facts, events, etc. This may be the *sine qua non* of rhetoric: After salience is created the situation must be translated into meaning. When political commentators talk about issues they are talking about situations made salient, not something that became important because of its intrinsic importance."[29]

This analysis may be applied to the Gulf of Tonkin situation in 1964 where the President was able to use discourse to create a crisis. In other words, through discourse, the President was able to draw attention to this circumstance, making it salient enough to persuade Congress to intervene in Vietnam. As Windt states: "Political crises are primarily rhetorical. The President announces to the people that a situation critical to the U.S. exists. Situations do not create crises. Rather, the President's perception of the situation and the rhetoric he uses to describe it mark an event as a crisis."[30]

This phenomenon is grounded in the President's use of language. Language is a cause, not an effect, of meaning. It is antecedent, not subsequent, to the situation's impact. Murray Edelman elaborates about the importance of language in this way: "Language does not mirror objective 'reality' but rather creates it by organizing meaningful perceptions abstracted from a complex bewildering world. Political events can become infused with strong affect stemming from psychic tension, from perceptions of economic, military or other threats or opportunities and from interactions between social and psychological responses. These political 'events' are largely creations of the language used to describe them."[31] He continues: "Mass publics respond to currently conspicuous political symbols: not to facts, and not to moral codes embedded in the character or soul, but to the gestures and speeches that make up the drama of the state."[32]

The American public and Congress in 1964 did not base their beliefs and perceptions on observation or empirical evidence available to them, but rather derived their views from cuings read into the events of Tonkin Gulf. The objective situation did not trigger salience. Instead the process of symbolization (in which words were chosen by the President to refer to certain ideas and facts) established salience. In short, a social reality was constructed vis-a-vis a linguistic interaction between the President and the public.[33]

In addition, the President's choice of information sources further helped to establish salience in 1964. Johnson's very selection of issues to address why the Tonkin Gulf events were perceived as a "crisis." Once a choice among issues is communicated, for example, "an event is automatically imbued with salience."[34] Thus, when a speaker decides to address a particular question, he/she is communicating to the audience a sense of importance regarding that issue. As Chaim Perelman comments: "By the very fact of selecting certain elements and presenting them to an audience, their importance and pertinency to the discussion are implied."[35] For that reason, when President Johnson addressed the American public in 1964 concerning the supposed events in Tonkin Gulf, his very selection of the topic and decision to address the nation over national radio and television conveyed a sense of urgency and importance.

Limitation of Alternatives

Although the United States had several options to employ as a response to the Gulf of Tonkin in 1964, the President was able to gain support for only one through his communication to the American public and Congress. This is in part explained by the principle of consensus building articulated by Stanley Hoffmann.[36] According to his theory, in times of crisis the president can rally the nation behind his policies through exploitation of the mass media. This may also explain why the United States became involved in the most unpopular conflict in its history; for in times of emergency, people tend to rally behind their leader no matter how ineffective his decisions may be. We assume, for instance, that the president's facts are better than ours, and that he is in a superior position to assess policies. In short, his communicative power may have the effect of convincing the country that only one policy option exists—his own. Windt notes: "Because the President has immediate access to television and because neither congress nor the public has alternative sources of information that can quickly verify or question the President's account of the facts, a President usually can implement a policy with a minimum of opposition."[37]

This same phenomenon may be generalized to presidential messages to Congress. In the Gulf of Tonkin, the President used a *fait accompli* to minimize policy alternatives. After taking the initial military move, President Johnson turned to Congress and in so many words said, "you must provide money and men to support the commitment already made." Congress, of course, has virtually no alternative. Rather than sacrificing policy and prestige, it followed the President's lead, thus initiating a policy of escalation. As Windt concludes: "Perhaps, the events of August 2 and 4, 1964, in the Gulf of Tonkin would have remained as minor as they were had not the President interrupted a television show to denounce the attacks on American ships and to order reprisals."[38]

The President's ability to minimize policy options through actions followed by discourse can be further explained by the relationship between the rhetorical power and institutional nature of the executive office. As Richard Neustadt reveals: "The status and authority inherent in his office reinforces his logic and his charm. A president's authority and status give him great advantages with the men he would persuade."[39] And as Windt notes: "In the words so often used in letters to newspapers, 'the President knows best.' The psychology persistent here makes the President's decisions seem wise and prudent when they turn out to be stupid."[40] The reverence we accord the President, argues Windt, "shapes a will to believe him when he speaks, and places the burden of disproving any Presidential statement upon those who disagree."[41]

In retrospect, Johnson was able to limit policy alternatives following the Gulf of Tonkin crisis by taking action *first* and then supporting his actions rhetorically. Through consensus building Johnson was able to foster a *fait accompli,* rendering Congress virtually impotent. In other words, Johnson employed the inherent rhetorical powers of the presidency to prevent Congressional disagreement. For that reason, Congress was forced to acquiesce in the assumption of a stronger policy-making role by the Executive.

Summary

Considering the effects of Johnson's speeches as a whole allows us to understand the nature and power of Presidential discourse in foreign affairs. From a purely *rhetorical* (as contrasted with an historical or political scientific) perspective, one might argue that President Lyndon Johnson's rhetorical choices *created,* or at least *defined* the situation in Tonkin Gulf. This seems probable given his strategies in the speeches of August 4 and 5, and the critical theory advanced by Vatz. In fact, the President's specific use of language coupled with the notion of a social construction of reality presented by Edelman, Windt, and Perelman support the claim that Johnson's rhetorical choices shaped the meanings people attached to the events of August 1964. Through such manipulation, the President was able to engineer public consensus. His precipitation of the crisis and limitation of foreign policy alternatives, therefore, were effects stemming directly from his rhetorical discourse.

Implications

This investigation has treated the Tonkin Gulf incident predominantly as an historical example of the so-called "Imperial Presidency." However, it would be a mistake to ignore the implications of this and other events of the 1960's and early 1970's for the current status of relations among the President, Congress, and the public. It can be argued, for example, that the rhetorical advantages available to Johnson over twelve years ago have been reduced, or, in essence, that the "Imperial Presidency" has come to an end. Admittedly, the attitudes of the public and Congress have changed since 1964. The passage of the War Powers Act provides one illustration of this desire to change the rhetorical situation and reduce the opportunities of the President to unilaterally shape policy decisions during emergencies. Yet even the passage of this act does not *inherently* preclude the possibility that through his rhetorical choices a future Executive will be able to create a situation comparable to that of Tonkin Gulf. It is this very potential that led Arthur M. Schlesinger to conclude that the War Powers Act merely institutionalizes the present imbalance of power by specifying a period of time during which the President need not consult with the congress in the formulation and execution of foreign policy.[42] The President thus retains the ability to present the public and congress with a *fait accompli*. And as the Tonkin Gulf crisis indicates, even a few short hours is ample time for the President to take steps, the impact of which may be felt for years. Thus, while attitudes have changed since 1964, the very existence of institutions and structures (e.g., the President's powers as Commander-in-Chief, his unique access to the media, his ability to unilaterally initiate executive agreements, etc.) must not lead us to conclude confidently that the "Imperial Presidency" is dead and that there will be no more Vietnams.

Notes

1. See, for example: Hans J. Morgenthau, *A New Foreign Policy for the U.S.* (Chicago: Univ. of Chicago Press, 1970), pp. 111–39. For a more specific commentary on this subject, see: Henry S. Commager, "Can We Limit Presidential Power," *New Republic,* April 6, 1968, pp. 15–18, and Frank Church, "Making Foreign Policy," *Current History,* January 1968, pp. 6–12.
2. See, for example, Richard J. Barnet, *Intervention and Revolution* (New York: World, 1968), p. 217.
3. This conclusion seems to be reasonable given Barnet's research. See also: William Miller, *A New History of the U.S.* (New York: Dell, 1968), p. 474.
4. Barnet, p. 217.
5. Miller, p. 474.
6. Neil Sheehan, *The Pentagon Papers* (New York: The New York Times, 1971), pp. 234–35.
7. Sheehan, p. 235.
8. Sheehan, p. 234.
9. Sheehan, p. 234.
10. Sheehan, p. 235.
11. Sheehan, p. 235.
12. An interesting psychological examination of Johnson is made by Doris Kearns, *Lyndon Johnson and the American Dream* (New York: Harper and Row, 1976). A more explicit reference to this fact, however, is made by Ralph Stavins, Richard Barnet, and Marcus Raskins, *Washington Plans An Aggressive War* (New York: Random House, 1971), p. 98.
13. Stavins, Barnet, and Raskins, p. 98.
14. Joseph Goulden, *Truth is the First Casualty* (Chicago: Rand McNally, 1969), p. 240.
15. Stavins, Barnet, and Raskins, p. 98. (Author's italics.)
16. Stavins, Barnet, and Raskins, p. 98.
17. Stavins, Barnet, and Raskins, p. 98.
18. See, for example: Nelson Polsby and Aaron Wildavsky, *Presidential Elections* (New York: Charles Scribner's Sons, 1971), p. 81.
19. Lyndon B. Johnson, "Address to the Nation," in *Gulf of Tonkin Resolution,* ed. John Galloway (Madison: Associated Univ. Press, 1970), p. 169.

20. Lyndon B. Johnson, "Address to Congress," in *Gulf of Tonkin Resolution,* ed. John Galloway (Madison: Associated Univ. Press, 1970), p. 171.
21. Johnson, "Address to Congress," p. 171.
22. Johnson, "Address to the Nation," p. 169.
23. Lyndon B. Johnson, "Address to Syracuse University," in *Gulf of Tonkin Resolution,* ed. John Galloway (Madison: Associated Univ. Press, 1970), p. 174.
24. Johnson, "Address to Syracuse University," p. 175.
25. Johnson, "Address to Syracuse University," p. 175.
26. Johnson, "Address to the Nation," p. 169.
27. Johnson, "Address to Congress," p. 173.
28. Johnson, "Address to Congress." This line of thought is found on pp. 171–73.
29. Richard E. Vatz, "The Myth of the Rhetorical Situation," *Philosophy and Rhetoric,* 6 (1973), 160. See also: Robert L. Ivie, "Presidential Motives for War," *Quarterly Journal of Speech,* 60 (1974), 337–45.
30. Theodore Otto Windt, Jr., "The Presidency and Speeches of International Crisis: Repeating the Rhetorical Past," *Speaker and Gavel,* 11 (1973), 7.
31. Murray Edelman, *Politics as Symbolic Action* (Chicago: Markham, 1971), p. 67.
32. Edelman, p. 66.
33. For a more thorough discussion of the notion that linguistic interaction may yield the construction of a social reality, see: Peter L. Berger and Thomas Luckmann, *The Social Construction of Reality* (Garden City, N.Y.: Doubleday, 1967).
34. Vatz, p. 157.
35. Chaim Perelman and L. Olbrechts-Tyteca, *The New Rhetoric,* trans. John Wilkinson and Purcell Weaver (Notre Dame and London: Univ. of Notre Dame Press, 1969), pp. 116–17.
36. See, for example: Stanley Hoffmann, *Gulliver's Troubles* (New York: McGraw-Hill, 1968), pp. 254–66 and pp. 305–16.
37. Windt, p. 7.
38. Windt. p. 7.
39. Richard Neustadt, *Presidential Power* (New York: Wiley, 1960), p. 244. This point is also underscored by James Burns and Jack Peltason, *Government by the People,* 5th ed. (Englewood Cliffs, N.J.: Prentice Hall, 1964), pp. 434–35. According to them: "Since the President draws on the informed thinking of hundreds of specialists, his pronouncements have a tone of authority."
40. Windt, p. 8.
41. Windt, p. 8. He concludes on the same page: "There is a predisposition to believe the President, a predisposition that does not exist in the same degree for any other official."
42. See, for example: Arthur M. Schlesinger, Jr., "Congress and the Making of Foreign Policy," in *The Presidency Reappraised,* eds., Thomas E. Cronin and Rexford Tugwell (New York: Praeger, 1974), p. 106. Schlesinger argues that, "Had it been on the statute books in past years [he is talking about the 1972 War Powers Act] it would surely not have prevented Johnson from escalating the war in North Vietnam." In short he calls the act "a measure of inducing formal Congressional approval for warlike acts."

From Ambiguity to Dogma: The Rhetorical Symbols of Lyndon B. Johnson on Vietnam

Cal M. Logue and John H. Patton

Political leaders are dependent upon persuasion for their authority. This is especially true of Presidents. A "President," observes James Barber, is "subject to his subjects, forever in the position of supplicant for renewal of his license to rule. A President can so dissipate his real powers that he has nothing left but the shell of office."[1] Indeed, history is replete with examples of the dissipation of political power, perhaps none more telling than reflected in the rhetoric of Lyndon B. Johnson's defense of United States' policies in Vietnam from 1964–68.

The purpose of this essay is to describe and evaluate Johnson's use of certain key symbols designed to justify Vietnam policy, and to explain why these symbols ironically contributed to his loss of power.[2] Accordingly, we seek to answer four questions: (1) what crucial factors influenced Johnson's processes of invention about Vietnam?; (2) how did those factors manifest themselves in Johnson's language about Vietnam?; (3) how did critics redefine the President's assessment of the war?; (4) what theoretical and ethical implications evolve from an awareness of Johnson's rhetoric?

Personality and Experience in the Invention of Vietnam Policy

We begin with an assumption that rhetoric in the political realm is a public manifestation of the internal thoughts, feelings, and values of the person as these coincide with specific experiences. Only when we obtain some evidence about the interior workings of the person, however limited that may be, can we grasp the inclinations and trends which form the basis of a particular type of discourse. Certainly rhetoric is not solely a matter of internal conditions, however it is important to discover the individuality of the communicator. From our own scrutiny of Johnson's life and times we argue that there is a discernable correlation between the nature of his personality and experience and the sort of symbols upon which he chose to erect the structure of his Vietnam policy.

Mr. Logue is Professor of Speech Communication at the University of Georgia.
Mr. Patton is Associate Professor of Speech at Louisiana State University.
Reprinted by permission from *Southern Speech Communication Journal* 47 (Spring 1982), pp. 310–329.

The distinctiveness of Johnson's personality and his sense of history governed the origin of key symbols and the development of rhetorical forms in which he depicted the war. Moreover, once those forms were articulated, they tended to actualize and affirm important aspects of Johnson's self-concept. Johnson's verbilization of the war was an extension of what Kenneth Burke called one's own "frames of acceptance." "Rhetorical messages," Richard B. Gregg explained, "are comprised of levels of formings, which, through subconscious and conscious maneuvering, constitute a 'way of envisaging what it's all about'. It is just these 'ways of envisaging,' these summative manifestations of the processes of symbolic forming, that profoundly underlie all rhetorical invention and entreaty."[3]

Reactions by persons who observed Johnson and his statements help us understand how the President's public symbols were an offshoot of his personal "frames of acceptance." In reflecting about the war in Vietnam, whether in private consultations or in public statements, Johnson was constrained by two recurring forms of thought. First he was disposed to view complex human events in simplistic categorical frames of reference. Second Johnson was conditioned by experience and history for aggressive and resolute acts.

Johnson's private and public "envisaging" reflected a simplistic categorization of complex human dramas. Even when significant cultural differences in perception existed among participating agents, Johnson drew sharp distinctions between symbols of good versus evil. This process of categorical dichotomizing left little room for negotiation or compromise. In demonstrating how Johnson viewed international relationships, for example, Eric F. Goldman concluded that to the President "aggression is when one country won't let another one alone. Everybody knows when that is happening." According to Goldman, Johnson "had no carefully thought out conception of the workings of the international system." Rather, making international decisions was simply "like a Senate maneuver; you had to show that you were ready to play your cards."[4]

Meeting in 1965 in a crucial session with a few close advisors to decide what to do about Vietnam, Johnson depicted the choices categorically between whether to "get out" or "get in with more." Clearly to "get out" for Johnson would be a personal admission of defeat. Although the "American people . . . had little or no inkling" of it, stated James Deakin, "on Capitol Hill . . . there was no doubt" as to "Johnson's simplistic black-and-white view of the communist-capitalistic struggle, no doubt at all that he was a hawk."[5] When George Ball opposed escalating the United States' involvement in Vietnam, Johnson rejected that mode of thinking as a form of losing. "But, George," the President answered Ball, "is there another course in the national interest. . . ? I am concerned that we have very little alternative to what we are doing."[6] Even after his term as President had expired, Johnson repeated his conviction that the only workable solution at the time was to convince the "aggressor," whether on the battlefield or at the conference table, that he would be "broken."[7]

Johnson's "frames of acceptance" were also conditioned by experience and history to favor aggressive and "resolute" acts. Not to be bluffed, Johnson believed one should defend his own honor. Whereas Jack Valenti, a close advisor, found Johnson to be "tender," "sensitive," and "patient," he also judged his boss to be "terrorizing," "ruthless," "impatient," "bullying," "tough," "resolute," and "brutal." "Nothing," recalled Valenti, "could overcome his central will or rupture his sense of duty."[8] As early as 1964, William S. White determined that Johnson was "tough and compassionate, born to action." "The jugular approach in foreign affairs," contended Goldman, "fitted in easily with the L.B.J. tendency to go it alone." Doris Kearns extends our understanding of how Johnson's process of "envisaging" influenced his thinking on Vietnam. She notes, for example, Johnson's admiration for Harry Truman and Franklin Roosevelt as leaders who put successful programs into action. Indeed, in his Vietnam speeches Johnson tried to legitimize his own war policies as being "consistent" with the actions of George Washington, Franklin Roosevelt, John Kennedy, and "our ancestors" generally. Just as these persons had succeeded in many ways, Johnson wanted to prevail. He feared indecisiveness and failure. In his words, "everything I knew about history told me that if I got out of Vietnam and let Ho Chi Minh run through the streets of Saigon, then I'd be doing exactly what Chamberlain did in World War II. I'd be giving a big fat reward to aggression."[9]

Johnson was not inclined to bend under pressure, whether from at home or from abroad. During the war he acted resolutely so that observers would not perceive in him "a weakening will." Writing later about his handling of the war, Johnson said simply, "I . . . was not a 'peace at any price' man." He regretted only that he had not been even more assertive in "pledging" his "faith" in the war policy. "Looking back on early 1968," he stated, "I am convinced I made a mistake by not saying more about Vietnam in my State of the Union report on January 17, 1968. In that address I underscored how intensely our will was being tested . . . but I did not go into details concerning the build-up of enemy forces or warn of the early major combat I believed was in the offing."[10] That is also an accurate assessment of Johnson's rhetorical strategy throughout his term of office. Rather than present details of the war the President primarily condensed his arguments into a cluster of more abstract symbolic forms. In so doing he demonstrated a preference for what Edelman terms "condensation symbols" over "referential symbols."[11] Significantly, "condensation symbols" are closely linked to the subjective states of the person in contrast to "referential symbols" which aim at the reflection of external conditions. The nature of Johnson's persona and experience oriented him toward symbols which enabled him to believe in the appropriateness of his actions. In effect, Johnson's way of addressing the nation about Vietnam was also his means of depicting that policy to himself, the one reinforcing the other. The result was a fundamental confusion of audiences, making it almost impossible to recognize growing differences in public perceptions of his policy.

Political Policy in Rhetorical Forms

Based on his personal requirements for simple categories and resolute action it is reasonable to expect that President Johnson framed his foreign policy in a definable pattern of language consistent with his own "terministic screen," or way of viewing the world. Johnson substituted key symbols and the values they embody for substantive information concerning the historical background of the war, the nature and effectiveness of the South Vietnamese government, and United States' involvement. Specifically, Johnson's discourse revealed three dominent sets of symbols: *Peacemaker, Enemy, and Savior.* Each of the President's symbols reflected an ostensibly positive cluster of values and attitudes, giving their inherent ambiguity an initially positive tone.

Indeed, ambiguity in depicting political policy is commonplace. As John G. Pocock has observed, "It is the nature of . . . all political rhetoric which is designed to reconcile men pursuing different activities and a diversity of goals and values—that the same utterance will simultaneously perform a diversity of linguistic functions. . . ."[12] Nevertheless, the positive potency of symbols depends heavily on time and circumstance and without a sensitivity to changing conditions ambiguity initially favoring the user may turn feverishly against him. In that case we speak of dissolution, or what came to be known in the Vietnam years as the "credibility gap." Pocock's reminder about political discourse helps us understand the seeming paradox of how Johnson was able for a time to speak convincingly in ambiguous and potent symbols about what became an increasingly confusing national experience. In his case it is appropriate to ask, did the ambiguity of his political symbols work positively to reconcile or negatively to divide? With that in mind, let us turn to the President's symbols themselves.

Peacemaker

Lyndon Johnson used the persuasive power available in his status as President to depict his administration's foreign policy aim as peace, with himself cast in the role of peacemaker. Publicly, at least, the ideal of peace is held in high regard by Americans and others throughout the world. In a 1966 speech about the Vietnam war, Pope Paul VI, borrowing from Jesus' "Sermon on the Mount," promised, "Those who promote peace are blessed for they shall be called children of God."[13] Johnson claimed this blessing for himself.

Johnson's linguistic strategy was to display himself and his administration as totally dedicated to peace. Drawing on a fragile assumption imposed on Americans by politicians in the past, Johnson claimed the United States once again to be first-with-the-most: "We will never be second in the search for . . . a peaceful settlement in Vietnam." Johnson exclaimed, "I know that our peoples want peace, because we are a peace-loving nation." The President asserted his peace commitment with generalizations intensified to drown out questions from critics whom Secretary of State Dean Rusk reportedly called "quitters." Johnson talked of the "agony of men struggling toward peace." He would "press the search for peace to the corners of the earth." His language was frequently exaggerated: "We will discuss any problem, we will listen to any proposal, we will pursue any agreement, will take any action which might lessen the chance of war. . . ." When in 1966 Johnson was given the National Freedom Award, his words on that occasion again portrayed the United States as stalking peace: "We will seek peace every day by every honorable means." America, proclaimed the President, was ready to meet "at any place at any time," a phrase Johnson learned on playgrounds in Texas and one many Americans identified with courage and commitment, though usually in the context of aggression.[14]

To create an image of America searching for peace and to answer critics who challenged the veracity of his words, Johnson employed a sequence of abstractions. He stacked words on words meta-communicatively as a means of amplifying metaphoric generalizations: "We tried to open a window to peace. . . . Our offer stands. We mean every word of it. The window to peace is still open." "The door is always open to any settlement. . . ." The President appealed for sympathy and support by reserving for himself the largest role in the peace process: "For finally I must be the one to order guns to fire against the—against all the most inward pulls of my desire"; "There is no human being in all this world who wishes . . . peace to come to the world more than your President."[15]

Johnson symbolically compared "the battle field" and "the conference table," always depicting America sitting alone waiting anxiously for "discussions." The "other side," however, refused to come, though the American "government has labored with imagination and endurance to remove any barrier to peaceful settlement." Peace, according to the President, was as close as Hanoi's "willing[ness] to pick up the telephone." Indeed, on many occasions Johnson stated that talks could be "unconditional" and, later, "unconditional or conditional." But it would be absurd and dishonorable, Johnson ridiculed, for a peacemaker to "stop" its "half of the war" or "tie" its "hands" or to "walk on water." A rebuffed peacemaker mistrusts an aggressor as, metaphorically, "A burned child dreads the fire."[16]

The Enemy

The remoteness of Vietnam required that Johnson convince Americans that a serious threat did exist "over there." The unfamiliarity of the war also made American audiences more dependent upon their President for information and impressions about the conflict. Johnson explained the chief criterion he used to determine when war is justified, and introduced his second symbolic form: "At times of crisis before asking Americans to fight and die to resist aggression in a foreign land, every American President has finally had to answer this question: Is the aggression a threat. . . ?"[17]

In developing this theme, Johnson devoted some discourse to defining the enemy. The chief enemy was "Communism," an evil that for many Americans still evoked fear and concern. Johnson associated this familiar foe with an unknown threat, North Vietnam. "Communism" had been decried so often, however, that the President had to express this threat in a manner which would be attended and feared. Johnson's strategy was to describe Communist aggression in a series of condensation symbols about Vietnam. For example he often referred to the enemy as "Hanoi," thus de-emphasizing the fact that the fight was between what had been historically the "North" and "South" of the same country. "Hanoi," he said, will "persist in aggression; they insist on the surrender in South Vietnam to Communism." Johnson contrasted images of a northern aggressor with an innocent and vulnerable South: "North Vietnam has attacked the independent nation of South Vietnam. . . ." "Its goal is to conquer the South. . . ."; "We believe—we genuinely and sincerely believe that aggression just must not succeed there or again."[18]

Johnson further dramatized the enemy with earthy details, depicting the Communist as being cunning, indiscriminate, excessive, and without human compassion: "The aggression . . . takes the form of men and equipment coming down from the north on foot or in trucks, through jungle roads and trails or on small craft, moving silently through the water at night. . . . Well-organized assassination, kidnapping, intimidation of innocent citizens in remote villages." "Communist expansionism . . . is killing and kidnapping . . . ruthlessly attempting to bend a free people of its will"; "they explode their bombs in cities and villages, ripping the bodies of the helpless." Whether an audience believed these generalizations depended upon the rhetorical status they assigned the President, plus their general disposition toward such descriptions, for few specific supporting details were presented. After planting images of murderers and body-rippers, Johnson often allowed audiences to conclude for themselves what victory by the enemy would mean. Even his rhetorical questions continued the pattern of warning: "What would be the consequences of letting armed aggression against South Vietnam succeed? What would follow in the time ahead? What kind of world are they prepared to live in five months or five years from tonight? The stakes to us have seemed clear and have seemed high."[19]

Capitalizing again on the inherent ambiguity of political symbols, Johnson attempted to reconcile his war policy with his audiences' esteem for the role of peacemaker and their aversion to the thought of any tyrant. China and North Vietnam were characterized not only as menaces to South Vietnam but to freedom throughout the world.

Savior

By portraying the United States as peacemaker and North Vietnam and Communism generally as enemies, Johnson's analysis by definition placed the United States in the role of savior. At this point, Kenneth Burke's notion of the emancipatory appeal of symbolic forms is especially beneficial. He observes that "The appeal of the Symbol as 'emancipator' involved fundamentally a mere shifting of terms in this way: leisure for indolence, fool-hardiness for bravery, thrift for miserliness, improvidence for generosity, et cetera or vice versa."[20] While this sort of terminology is apparent in the other mythic-themes examined, it is particularly decisive in understanding how Johnson sought to create a savior image. A scene which depicts a cunning criminal attacking an innocent victim also demands a hero. Accordingly, Johnson cast America in this heroic role, with some lines suitable for the savior character reserved for himself as well.

The President legitimized war by creating a feeling of obligation, mixed with the sympathy one feels toward an underdog. Avoiding concrete data about the war, Johnson stressed by repetition pronouns and verbs connoting action, duty, and commitment to America's role as savior: "We are there because we have a promise to keep"; "We will not abandon our commitment . . ."; people rely on this "American promise" and "protection" and expect us to be "Guardians at the gate"; "We will stay because a just nation cannot leave to the cruelty of its enemies a people who have staked their lives and independence on America's solemn pledge . . ."; at stake is "the obligation of power."[21]

A primary role of the hero is to rescue, and Johnson seemed most comfortable talking about the brave deeds of Americans. Explaining and defending apparent contradictions in an admittedly "hard" and "difficult" war frequently frustrated him. Yet, words about heroic soldiers were less vulnerable to attack, so Johnson was less defensive, more secure, and more aggressive when communicating the savior-form. The hero image came quite naturally. Scorning those too timid to fight for peace, the Commander-in-Chief evoked feelings of pride and patriotism: "It requires more than speeches to resist the international enemies of freedom"; "We are not going to be . . . soft-headed and pudding-headed as to say that we will stop our half of the war and hope and pray that they stop theirs"; "Our commitment is being tested . . . on the anvil of war"; "Peace is not something that just happens. Peace does not come just because we wish for it. Peace must be fought for."[22]

Johnson constructed the savior-symbol from imagery native to his political origins. This form of message was seemingly more convincing because it sounded like the messenger. With this symbolic strategy Johnson could freely speak in war language suited to his own personal style. War words matched both the manner of the man and the authority of his office, creating a style of strong words about defeating Communists, a style highly effective with many Americans. Some of the savior-symbols in which Johnson condensed explosive feelings of pride, love, hate, victory, honor, duty, and safety include: "There is no human power capable of forcing us from Vietnam"; we will "fight for freedom. . . . As long as there are men who hate and destroy we must have the courage to resist. . . ."[23]

The savior-symbol was maintained both with referential detail and metaphoric flourish. For example, Johnson used statistics to hue feelings of heroism: "Tonight in Vietnam more than 200,000 of your young Americans stand there fighting for your freedom." In a brief speech on the *U.S.S. Enterprise,* Johnson delivered a ringing apostrophe to the Navy in honor of the war effort: "Your weapons and wings are the swords and shields of freedom. . . . Your planes . . . the watchwords of liberty." Here the statistical details are removed from the context of explanatory information and set in the realm of meritorious ideological principles. Notice that the precise connection between statistics and the theme of determination and deliverance is left unclear. The very ambiguity of that connection serves to perpetuate the life of the appeal.

In selecting these symbols Johnson identified a war even he called "confusing"[24] with larger, underlying themes familiar to and significant in American culture and values. In fact, the symbols of peacemaker, savior, and enemy generally are prized so highly in the United States that they can be accurately classified as rhetorical institutions. Because these symbols reside within the cultural experience of Americans—when skillfully tapped—they exert considerable influence on attitudes and actions. If employed carefully, the symbols of peacemaker, enemy, and savior become potent rhetorical instruments in conjunction with a variety of particular causes: pollution of the environment, poverty, minority rights, or military policy. A vast public audience, however, eventually had to be convinced that the President's "envisaging" was relevant to a war in a place many Americans had difficulty locating on a map. Indeed, the stage was set for a virtual domestic war of symbols.

Conflict Over the Symbolization of the War

As the war in Vietnam accelerated so did the dialectic between Lyndon Johnson and critics of the conflict, so much so that the war of words at home played a significant role in extinguishing the violence abroad. Public displeasure with the war went from a fragmented rhetoric of diverse voices to a pervasive confrontation which caused the nation to reexamine its motives and eventually to change its foreign policy. The stasis of this public debate was whether the war should be ended. This point of conflict refracted rhetorically into arguments about the worth of the war, and was reflected in the growing sense of incongruity about the symbols used to define the war.

Initially put on the defensive by the President's prestige and power, and by the martial mood of many countrymen, critics of the war were hard pressed to find means of attacking the administration without appearing to be treasonous. Murray Edelman explained why challenging an incumbent president on matters of foreign policy proved to be difficult. Persons tend to "accept the reassuring explanations of authorities" although they often "recognize that the reassurance is unwarranted, even exploitative. But the official explanations are bound to be dominant, for these political beliefs permit people to live with their political worlds and with themselves with a minimum of strain. The alternative means a politicized life of active protest and resistance, and few want it."[25] Late in 1965, the Gallup Poll confirmed Edelman's premise as it applied to Johnson's policy on Vietnam. When asked for their attitudes about the way Johnson was "handling the situation in Vietnam," 56% approved, 26% disapproved, and 18% expressed no opinion.[26]

After a period of general acceptance, however, the issue of Vietnam became an exception to Edelman's explanation. An increasing number of persons chose "a politicized life of active protest" against the war. Overt resistance arose because the President's envisaging of the United States as merely a peacemaker was to many so clearly at odds with reality. Protesters sought to redefine the war as it actually existed. The debate at home was waged over the way the war had been symbolized by the President and his administration.

Critics disputed the President's insistence that the country fought because of an honorable, peaceful intent. Believing the administration employed subterfuge in selling an unwarranted war, protesters directly attacked the President's symbolization of the conflict in terms of peacemaker, enemy, and savior. "Policymakers have distorted history," argued Senator George McGovern, and "misled the American public." Critics refuted the claim that the administration was motivated by any high obligation of power. They argued that American foreign policy was predicated on arrogance and inflated faith in its own wisdom. Poet Robert Lowell viewed that policy with "dismay and distrust," charging that the country was "in danger of imperceptibly becoming an explosive and suddenly chauvinistic nation." The National Council of

Churches explained that the national ego was puffed-up by the President's overly narrow analysis of alternatives as he perceived them: "The United States may affirm a too rigid identification of its self-judging course of action with righteousness, thus becoming blind to other courses of action which may achieve justice and peace." A higher purpose, the Council advised, would be, not destruction, but "love and reconciliation," "healing," and a willingness to "withdraw" from violence. A country with defendable values, they continued, "maintains" its "spiritual and ethical sensitivity," principles many citizens found to be inconsistent with Johnson's war plank. Offering similar warnings, Senator Robert Kennedy urged the administration not to be "fearful for our dignity and anxious for our prestige." Dr. Martin Luther King, Jr. also questioned the administration's emancipatory motivation and explanation of the war, and concluded that "we are the greatest military power and we don't need to prove our military power." Apparently commenting on the President's inflated pronouncements, Pope Paul VI advised against "exaggerated seeking after national self-interests." McGovern was less subtle in his assessment maintaining bluntly that "we fight in Vietnam . . . because of a highly questionable notion that this is the only honorable course," trying "to play God in Asia," when the real reason soldiers continue fighting is "to save the professional reputation of policy-planners."[27]

Opponents of Johnson's war policy advanced three major arguments: that it was a policy based on deceit, that it had a nationally corrupting influence, and that it was a failure. First, critics opposed the President's military peace formula as a devious strategem for staying in the fight. He hoped to rationalize his bloody foreign policy, they claimed, by fighting on in Vietnam while, at the same time, rhetorically promising peace at home. Thus, Johnson was accused of merely talking peace while actually making war. Senator Ernest Gruening, for example, warned that the President "is pushing us along the path to war, not to peace." "While orally calling for negotiations," insisted McGovern, "we are practicing military escalation and diplomatic rigidity." Johnson's administration was portrayed not as seeking an end to the violence but as obsessed with war. "It will do little good," argued Robert Kennedy, "to go to the conference table if discussions are simply used to mask continued escalation of the war. . . ." Quoting Tacitus, Kennedy laid bare the President's principle peace disguise: "We made a desert and we called it peace."[28]

Critics made a second accusation concerning what they felt was the President's callous attitude toward ending the fighting. Whereas Johnson claimed that he followed the honorable course of peacemaker and savior, critics attacked this idea by arguing that prolonging the conflict was actually corrupting American character. Rather than "honorable," "resolute," peacemaking, and heroic, critics called the war a "putrid mess," a "crime," "racist" action, and "evil," an aimless venture which "saps our spirit" and results in "hatred," "distrust, and despair." McGovern labeled the "deepening involvement . . . the most tragic diplomatic and moral failure in our national experience." The National Council of Churches charged that America was "seen as a predominantly white nation using our overwhelming military strength to kill more Asians." Perhaps King made the most damaging indictment of the increasingly troublesome war, contrasting the "evil" of war and its tragic imprint upon the human spirit with the potential for good possible in a policy of peace. Because of his "moral commitment to dignity and the worth of human personality," words generally foreign to Johnson's war vocabulary, King insisted that he "must cry out when" he saw "war escalated at any point." Instead of being "a moral example for the world," he continued, "we have . . . become morally and politically isolated as the result of our involvement in war. . . ." Breaking the President's war code for peace, King explained that "you can't have justice without peace, so it is more of a realization of the interrelatedness of racism and militarism and the need to attack both problems rather than leaving one."[29]

In addition to finding the President's public defense of the Vietnam War to be deceptive and immoral, opponents pointed out that the policy was not working. Rather than peace, there existed more and more killing and waste of America's material resources. "We have lost some 10,000," reminded McGovern at one point in the war; we have had "50,000 wounded, crippled, left armless or legless," while "the enemy, so-called," the Russians and Chinese, have "not put a single soldier into the war."[30] Rather than settling the problem, Kennedy argued, the President's decision to fight simply raised "the risk of wider war" and destroyed "the country and the people it was meant to save."[31] Kennedy suggested "more emphasis on social, political, economic, and agricultural progress for the peasants there."[32] Kennedy advised that "victory in a revolutionary war is won not by escalation but by de-escalation,"[33] a way of thinking quite different than Johnson's. The National Council of Churches advanced the contention that "massive military intervention and occupation were self-defeating means of establishing the basic objectives of peace and social change."[34] "We should never have stayed in. We should get out,"[35] advised Senator Wayne Morse.

As the protest rhetoric intensified and the war continued, the former presumption of Presidential credibility was eroded. By 1968, only 35% approved Johnson's "handling" of "the situation in Vietnam," while 50% disapproved and 15% expressed no opinion. Johnson's claim that the country's involvement in Vietnam was simply a matter of honorable soldiers defending innocent people from outside aggressors was no longer believed by most Americans. Indeed, even though by 1967 Johnson had been promoting his policies for many months, citizens still questioned why the United States was fighting in Vietnam. In May 1967, when Gallup inquired whether Americans had "a clear idea of what the Vietnam war is all about," i.e., "What are we fighting for?," 48% said yes, 48% no, and 4% no opinion. Significantly, in March of 1967, when Gallup asked whether "the Johnson Administration is or is not telling the public all they should know about the Vietnam war," only 24% replied "is," 65% said "is not," and 11% had no opinion.

The American people no longer were satisfied by Johnson's overly simplified explanation of what had become an expensive war in human lives and money. Citizens demanded more details about the war. When asked specifically by Gallup, "What exactly would you like to have the President tell the public about the war?," The questions most frequently mentioned were: "How many lives are being lost?" "What is the war costing?" "Many in the survey," stated Gallup, expressed "doubts about the number of United States forces killed and the number of enemy soldiers killed." By March, 1968, the option Johnson had rejected in 1965 in private consultation with his advisors had become readily acceptable to American people: Gallup found that 56% approved "gradually withdrawing" from Vietnam, 34% disapproved, and 10% had no opinion.[36]

Later, after Johnson had left the presidency, refusing to believe that Vietnam was the dominant cause of "divisiveness" in the country, he admitted that criticism had forced him to place a higher priority upon the stated concerns of the critics.[37] "The public was very much aware of the critical and well-publicized views of a few Senators and Congressmen regarding Vietnam," he wrote. "My biggest worry was not Vietnam itself; it was the divisiveness and pessimism at home." He had hoped in one more speech in March of 1968 "to help right the balance and provide better perspective." Finally, however, Johnson was convinced that he should not run again for president, confessing candidly that as long as he was associated with that office his words as a leader would be considered incredulous. Rather than negotiate policy, this strong-willed man chose to restore credibility to the presidency by vacating that high office. "Perhaps now that I was not a candidate," he concluded, "commentators in the press and television might regard issues and efforts more objectively, instead of concentrating on criticism and cynical speculation. For awhile the nation and the world would reflect on my words."[38]

Implications and Conclusions

Our discussion of Lyndon Johnson's selection of evocative symbols and development of rhetorical forms illuminates a number of larger theoretical and ethical issues. Johnson's case is illustrative (1) of the necessity of understanding the value structures, including relevant personal and historical factors, that contribute to the world-views of political leaders, (2) of the perpetual dangers of extreme egoism and isolation in politics, and (3) of the significance of failures to distinguish between *controlling* and *shaping* or *winning* public opinion. These themes emerge from what we have observed in Johnson's discourse, that is, the selection of key symbols based on an essentially private value system which perpetuated his sense of isolation from the public mind, and the development of a rhetorical form which undermined the possibility of community and negated the formation of public knowledge.

The symbols of peacemaker, savior, and enemy by which Johnson chose to characterize his policy evolved into a pattern of intense indignation, a rhetorical form conveying exclusiveness and the superiority of private values. In effect, the symbolic forms in Johnson's rhetoric contained the unstated, but crucial, assumptions that "because my intentions are virtuous, and because the values I endorse are good ones (who could argue against the motifs of peacemaker and savior?), then my claims should be accepted *ipso facto*." Sincerity and virtue—as defined solely by a reservoir of private, and therefore non-debatable, values and experiences—became the chief criteria for deciding public policy. Yet, the connections between the private and public realms were never established. The messianic form of peacemaker/enemy/savior committed the President to an intransigent stance of indignation and superiority which itself mitigated against making such connections. In fact, no real awareness of the necessity to develop reasons for the benefit of a public emerges. Even at the end of his administration Johnson failed to comprehend the nature and significance of Vietnam as a public issue.

The nature and function of Johnson's rhetorical forms thus reveal a classic version of what Wayne Booth terms "modernist dogma," a damaging perpetuation of the fact-value dichotomy. Booth argues that "the automatic reliance on the distinction between facts and values"[39] misconstrues the very nature of information on the one hand and simultaneously prevents the rhetoric of reason-giving as a movement toward assent from operating on the other hand. While much has been written about the "scientismic" (i.e., so-called "value-free facts") side of the dichotomy, less attention has been given to the equally misleading "irrationalist" form (i.e., the espousing of values as if cognitive, factual, and other rational considerations were unrelated). Significantly, in employing the symbols of peacemaker, savior, and enemy, Lyndon Johnson attempted to invoke traditional values unaccompanied by reasons and cognitive patterns which were necessary for gaining public assent. In his case the value positions announced were simply assumed to be self-sufficient, and in making this assumption Johnson chose to substitute one-half of the fact-value dichotomy for the other. Defense of policy, requiring an integration of facts and values into a coherent whole, was replaced by defensiveness of an essentially private and isolated value system, with evocative symbols being selectively patterned to establish marketable forms for public consumption.

The personal and political factors which influenced Johnson's thinking established a mind-set hostile to public and private criticism of his policy. He invented the symbols of peacemaker, savior, and enemy as ways of expressing values which ought to be taken, he believed, as ends-in-themselves. And it is precisely here that the ethical quality of rhetorical form, or absence thereof, can be detected. We can ask of Johnson, "What are the reasons which support the symbols you chose to depict Vietnam policy; what are the grounds for the values you espoused?" Johnson's choice of symbols and the rhetorical forms which developed not only worked against value-integration with larger structures of public knowledge but, perhaps more significantly, blocked the cognitive dimension of the ritual use of political symbols. Precisely because they were cast in the form of an isolated and exclusionary moral pronouncement Johnson's symbolic forms never supplied the cognitive material necessary for intelligible patterns of public understanding.

Thus, Lyndon Johnson engaged in misleading rhetoric about Vietnam not necessarily because he was mistaken about the means of his policy, but because he failed to address the fundamental question of ends, the question of "What goods are worthy of being considered ends in themselves." Without consideration of that question, political rhetoric degenerates into irrationalism and ultimately into dogma. In the final analysis, then, the case of Lyndon Johnson reveals the vital significance of frames of choice which govern the selection of symbols to portray policy, the relative ease with which those symbols can be combined into irrational and dogmatic forms under the guise of traditional values, and the necessity for presidents and other political leaders to be "subject to their subjects," or else risk the slow but certain loss of power.

Notes

1. *The Presidential Character,* second edition (Englewood Cliffs: Prentice-Hall, 1977), 17–18.
2. We attempt to enlarge upon previous studies that have examined (1) aspects of Johnson's motivation for war as part of a larger "terministic screen through which American Presidents assess international relations," (2) the rhetorical effects of his Gulf of Tonkin speeches on August 4 and 5, 1964, and (3) the development of Johnson's domestic program from a social movement framework; see: Robert L. Ivie, "Presidential Motives for War," *Quarterly Journal of Speech,* 60 (1974), 344; F. Michael Smith, "Rhetorical Implications of the 'Aggression' Thesis in the Johnson Administration's Vietnam Argumentation," *Central States Speech Journal,* 23 (1972), 217–24; Richard A. Cherwitz, "Lyndon Johnson and the 'Crisis' of Tonkin Gulf: A President's Justification of War," *Western Journal of Speech Communication,* 41 (1978), 93–104; David Zarefsky, "President Johnson's War on Poverty: The Rhetoric of Three 'Establishment' Movements," *Communication Quarterly,* 44 (1977) 352–73.

3. "Kenneth Burke's Prolegomena to the Study of the Rhetoric of Form," *Communication Quarterly,* 26 (1978), 13.
4. *Tragedy of Lyndon Johnson* (New York: Alfred A. Knopf, 1969), 379–80.
5. *Lyndon Johnson's Credibility Gap* (Washington, D.C.: Public Affairs, 1968), 9.
6. Quoted in Jack Valenti, *A Very Human President* (New York: W. W. Norton, 1975), 326–29.
7. Lyndon Baines Johnson, *Vantage Point Perspectives of the Presidency, 1963–1969* (New York: Holt, Rinehart, and Winston, 1971), 232, 371.
8. Valenti, *A Very Human President,* x, xiii; William S. White, *Professional: Lyndon B. Johnson* (Boston: Houghton Mifflin, 1964), 252, 264; Merle Miller, *Lyndon: An Oral Biography* (New York: Putnam, 1980); Goldman, *Tragedy of Lyndon Johnson,* 382.
9. Associated Press Luncheon Speech, *New York Times,* 21 April 1964; Speech on Receiving National Freedom Award, New York City, 24 Feb. 1966; Johns Hopkins University Speech, 8 April 1965; Doris Kearns, *Lyndon Johnson and the American Dream* (Harper and Row, Signet Books, 1976), 264.
10. Johnson, *Vantage Point,* 68, 377, 380.
11. *Symbolic Uses of Power* (Urbana: Univ. of Illinois Press, 1964), 6, 132.
12. *Politics, Language and Time* (New York: Atheneum, 1971), 17.
13. *New York Times,* 9 Dec. 1966.
14. Speech to National Farmers Union Convention, Minneapolis, *New York Times,* 19 March 1968; Jewish Labor Dinner Speech, New York City, 10 Dec. 1967; Speech on Board the *U.S.S. Enterprise,* San Diego, 12 Nov. 1967; News Conference in Washington, D.C., 29 July 1965; 8 April 1965; 21 March 1964; 24 Feb. 1966.
15. "Statement" issued in Johnson City, Texas, *New York Times,* 18 April 1965; State of Union Message to Congress, 13 Jan. 1966; Speech in Omaha, Nebraska, 1 July 1966; Address to Nation, 1 Nov. 1968; 21 April 1964.
16. Arlington Cemetery Address, *New York Times,* 31 May 1966; News Conference, Washington, D.C., 10 March 1967; Speech to American Cartoonists, 14 May 1964; 13 Jan. 1966; 8 April 1965; 29 July 1965.
17. Television interview with Ray Scherer, Dan Rather, and Frank Reynolds, *New York Times,* 20 Dec. 1967; National Legislative Council Speech, 30 Sept. 1967.
18. Statement on Resumption of Bombing, *New York Times,* 1 Feb. 1966; Remarks Upon Returning from Far East, 3 Nov. 1966; 8 April 1965; 29 July 1965; 1 July 1966.
19. *New York Times,* 31 May 1966; 30 Sept. 1967; 18 April 1965.
20. *Counter-Statement* (1931); reprinted (Berkeley: Univ. of California Press, 1968).
21. Woodrow Wilson School of Public and International Affairs Address, Princeton University, *New York Times,* 12 May 1966; Speech from White House by Telephone to American Alumni Council in White Sulphur Springs, West Va., 13 July 1966; 8 April 1965; 14 May 1965; 19 July 1965; 13 Jan. 1966; 1 July 1966.
22. *New York Times,* 24 Feb. 1966; 10 Nov. 1967; 31 May 1966; 20 Dec. 1967.
23. *New York Times,* 18 April 1965; 29 July 1965.
24. *New York Times,* 24 Feb. 1966; 12 Nov. 1967; 31 May 1966.
25. *Political Language: Words that Succeed and Policies that Fail* (New York: Academic Press, 1977), 150.
26. George H. Gallup, *Gallup Poll Public Opinion 1935–1971,* Vol. 3, 1959–1971 (New York: Random House, 1972), 1982.

27. U.S. Senate Speech, *New York Times,* 26 April 1967; Policy Statement, 10 Dec. 1966; U.S. Senate Speech, 3 March 1967; Recorded Interview, Louisville, Ky., 2 April 1967; 3 June 1964; 4 Dec. 1964; 9 Dec. 1966; 26 April 1967.
28. *New York Times,* 21 March 1964; 26 April 1967; 3 March 1967.
29. Letter to Johnson, *New York Times,* 3 June 1964; Atlanta Press Club Speech, 11 Nov. 1964; 4 Dec. 1964; 2 April 1967; 11 Nov. 1964; 2 April 1967.
30. *New York Times,* 26 April 1967.
31. Announcing candidacy for president, *New York Times,* 17 Mar. 1968.
32. Interview, *New York Times,* 26 Aug. 1964.
33. International Policy Academy Speech, Washington, D.C., *New York Times,* 10 July 1964.
34. *New York Times,* 10 Dec. 1966.
35. U.S. Senate Speech, *New York Times,* 21 March 1964.
36. *Gallup Poll Public Opinion,* 2105, 2068, 2058, 2115–2116.
37. Johnson, *Choices We Face* (New York: Bantam, 1969), 145–46.
38. Johnson, *Vantage Point,* 432.
39. Wayne C. Booth, *Modern Dogma and the Rhetoric of Assent* (Univ. of Notre Dame Press, 1974), 13.

RICHARD M. NIXON

Nixon, Agnew, and the "Silent Majority": A Case Study in the Rhetoric of Polarization

Andrew A. King and Floyd Douglas Anderson

Throughout his presidential campaign, Richard M. Nixon was a candidate without an enthusiastic constituency. Although conceded to be the strongest Republican hopeful, for the simple reason that he was acceptable to all wings of the party, he was no one's beau ideal. He was a compromise between the extremes.[1] In November of 1968, having won the election with a mere 43 percent of the vote, Nixon found himself still without a strongly supportive constituency. As early as October of 1967, however, he had shown an acute awareness of his lack of a popular base and had made an initial attempt to create one out of the diverse groups that compose the great center[2] of American society. In a speech before the National Association of Manufacturers, he had identified himself as a spokesman for the "broad and vital center"[3] of America. Months later, in his Acceptance Speech at Miami, he carried this identification further by naming his constituency as "the great majority of Americans, the forgotten Americans, the nonshouters, the nondemonstrators."[4] It was not until November of 1969, however, that Nixon finally consolidated this potential power base, the "Silent Majority," as his constituency.

Nixon was well aware that unification of the diverse elements comprising "the forgotten Americans"—"black" and "white," "native born and foreign born," "young and . . . old," workers and businessmen, public officials and soldiers[5]—could not be accomplished on ideological grounds. His years of political experience, however, had taught him that men who cannot unite on the basis of issues can nevertheless unite on the basis of a common enemy, a shared foe. Hence, the very President who had begun his term of office with a promise to "bring us together" resorted, instead, to a rhetoric of polarization, an intensification of the real differences that already divided the American people. Our intent in this paper is to demonstrate the accuracy of this assessment. We will (1) provide a brief working definition of polarization as a rhetorical phenomenon and (2) present an analysis of the strategies that Nixon has employed in creating, broadening, and mobilizing his constituency from his inauguration as President in 1969 through the 1970 election campaign.

Mr. King is Professor of Speech Communication at the University of Arizona.
Mr. Anderson is Associate Professor of Speech Communication at Suny College.
Reprinted by permission from *Western Speech* Vol. 35, No. 4 (Fall 1971), pp. 243–255.

The Rhetoric of Polarization: A Definition

Polarization, as a rhetorical phenomenon, may be defined as the process by which an extremely diversified public is coalesced into two or more highly contrasting, mutually exclusive groups sharing a high degree of internal solidarity in those beliefs which the persuader considers salient.[6] Polarization always exhibits two dimensions. On the one hand it implies a powerful feeling of solidarity—"strong group cohesiveness, unity, 'we feeling,' human homogenization."[7] On the other hand, polarization also presupposes the existence of a perceived "common foe" which the group must oppose if it is to preserve the fabric of beliefs out of which the persuader has woven its identity. At the outset a practitioner of a rhetoric of polarization must have available a core of potentially sympathetic individuals. Accordingly, he may not view uncommitted persons as neutral, but as either potential converts or "foes." His goal is to move persons out of the ranks of the uncommitted and force them to make a conscious choice between one of the two competing groups.[8]

A rhetoric of polarization always encompasses two principal strategies: a strategy of affirmation and a strategy of subversion.[9] A strategy of affirmation is concerned with a judicious selection of those images that will promote a strong sense of group identity. A strategy of subversion is concerned with a careful selection of those images that will undermine the *ethos* of competing groups, ideologies, or institutions. Strategies are implied by motives: a strategy of affirmation is implicit when a communicator's motive is to persuade potential believers to accept a new concept; a strategy of subversion is implicit when a communicator's motive is to weaken or destroy the credibility of a concept. Both strategies are always present, in varying degrees, in all rhetorical situations which may be termed "polarized." Clarification and exemplification of the complementary functioning of these strategies in effecting a "rhetoric of polarization" is the aim of the following critical analysis of Nixon's efforts to create a base of support during his first two years in office.

The Strategy of Affirmation

Throughout the first year of his presidency, Nixon was still in search of a means of transforming the "broad and vital center" into a cohesive group solidly backing his policies. Thus he was confronted with a situation that called for the affirmation of a new group identity which large numbers of potential believers would embrace. From the Miami Convention onward Nixon had made a concerted effort to affirm and revitalize the identity of those he termed "the forgotten Americans." He depicted these Americans, admittedly and unashamedly "rich in material goods," as the "good people," the "decent people," who "save," "pay their taxes," and "care."[10] But he also depicted them as victims who, because of their very willingness to sacrifice, are "deluged by Government programs for the unemployed, programs for the cities, programs for the poor"[11] and have thus "reaped . . . an ugly harvest of frustrations, violence and failure"[12] and have become "ragged in spirit . . . [leading] empty lives, wanting fulfillment."[13]

In order to elicit a mandate from these "forgotten Americans" Nixon had to provide them with a political "image" which they could perceive as being legitimate, coherent, and significant. The tactics he employed to accomplish this can be conveniently explained in terms of the concept of the "self-justifying image."[14] The concept of the "self-justifying image" (also frequently called the "self-fulfilling prophecy") is based on an old proposition in sociology that "ideas, even if false (like magic), still have consequences for action."[15] As a rhetorical tactic the "self-justifying image" implies a false symbolic depiction of a situation which, by the very nature of the behavior it evokes, makes the originally false conception come true, at least in its consequences. Thus, as Kenneth Boulding has observed, "If . . . there is a general image of an impending rise in the price of some commodity, people will rush to buy it, and this very behavior will bring about the expected rise."[16] Roy G. Francis provides an example of the principle:

> If a Negro, for example, moves into a neighborhood, will the property values decline? Well, if people believe their property values will decline then they tend to. Again, at one time people believed in essentially, a flat world. The objective reality of the roundness of the world (or its oval shape) was immaterial to the fact that people believed the world was flat. They confined their behavior to that kind of world. To all intents and purposes they lived in a flat world. It is in that sense that "if something is believed to be true, it is true in its consequences."[17]

This principle, as Don Martindale has observed, "operates throughout social life."[18] In the political sphere, for example, to provide a man who has hitherto felt isolated and individually powerless with a larger ready-made group identity (e.g., as a member of "the Great Silent Majority") is to prompt self-protective responses that will make the identity a reality.

Although the principle of the "self-justifying image" operates ubiquitously, its effective utilization in rhetorical discourse requires a knowledge of audience "images" that is almost unerring. Rhetorical discourse always creates an "image," a moral universe; it is not rooted in "fact" but in "definition." An audience's definition of a situation, which is an "expression of image," governs all its actions in regard to that situation.[19] Hence, as Fisher has hypothesized, rhetorical discourse will be persuasive to the extent that it provides the necessary "signs of consubstantiality":

> . . . rhetorical discourse will be persuasive to the extent that the image it creates regarding a subject corresponds with the image already held by the audience, the degree to which the image it implies of the audience corresponds with the self-images held by members of the audience, and the degree to which the image assumed in the message and its presentation . . . is attractive to the audience. . . .[20]

The growing division in the nation over the Vietnam War in late 1969, evidenced by the success of the October 15 moratorium and the impending November 15 demonstration, provided Nixon with the rhetorical situation he sought—a situation in which a rhetoric of affirmation was a "fitting response."[21] The spectacle of thousands of Americans marching in the streets indicated that the size and power of the peace groups were growing at an accelerating rate. In a nation perhaps even more tired of demonstrations than it was of the war, the threat of escalating monthly disruptions allowed Nixon to refract the images of domestic disorder that so deeply troubled large segments of "Middle America." In his now historic November 3 speech on Vietnam,[22] Nixon labeled the peace groups as "a vocal minority" determined to prevail "over reason and the will of the majority," thus jeopardizing the future of the United States as a free society.[23] In contrast, he appealed for the support of "the great silent majority of my fellow Americans" who remained loyal to the 200-year policy of allowing important decisions to be formulated by "leaders in the Congress and the White House elected by all the people."[24] Only with such solid backing of the President by the "great silent majority," Nixon insisted, could the small but vocal forces of "unreason" be prevented from imposing their will on the nation "by mounting demonstrations in the streets."[25]

The response to this speech probably exceeded Nixon's own expectations. The Gallup telephone poll, taken immediately following the speech, found 77 per cent approving.[26] The presidential performance poll showed a dramatic rise of 12 per cent over the previous month, boosting Nixon's support to a peak of 68 per cent.[27] Nixon's dichotomy between the loyal supporters of his administration and those whom his Vice-President had not long before labeled "an effete corps of impudent snobs"[28] had touched an exposed nerve of the center and right. The back of the moratorium was broken. Not until the Cambodian invasion was the peace movement able to rally its own disparate segments for a massive show of strength. Within a few weeks large sub-groups of the American population actively identified themselves as members of the "Silent Majority."[29] By providing the needed symbolic images, Nixon called the "Silent Majority" into being. His use of the phrase generated the illusory consciousness of a common identity among many traditionally hostile groups.

What was the social cement inherent in the name that enabled Nixon to ignore all of the usual interests that separate the banker from the plumber, the teacher from the industrialist, the liberal from the conservative, the hard-hat from the college president? By ignoring the very real differences—economic, educational, political, social—that exist among the diverse segments of "Middle America," and by focusing attention instead on the shared features of their respective "self-images" (i.e., non-shouters, non-demonstrators, taxpayers, respecters of law and order, etc.), Nixon manufactured a constituency. By defining the "Silent Majority" as a real entity, he prompted modes of behavior that made it a *"real fiction."*[30] His originally false depiction of the situation evoked new patterns of behavior which made that false conception come true, at least in its consequences.

The Strategy of Subversion

Sensitive to the power potential of his newly forged constituency, Nixon knew that he would have to go beyond the strategy of affirmation if he were to hold their loyalty and mobilize their strength in the future. To accomplish this he resorted to a strategy of subversion designed to materialize the "Silent Majority's" common foe.

In applying this second major strategy, Nixon tested the validity of the old rhetorical maxim that "Men who can unite on nothing else can unite on the basis of a foe shared by all."[31] At the core of this strategy was the exploitation of the fears and prejudices of the "Silent Majority." Nixon was by no means a novice at such exploitation. He had relied upon it in what Barnet Baskerville has termed his "irresponsible campaign tactics from 1946 to 1954." In those years Nixon had implied that his opponents and their associates were "Communists, crooks, or fellow-travellers."[32] As Dwight Eisenhower's running mate, he had called Stevenson "Adlai the Appeaser" and charged that he had earned "a Ph.D. from Dean Acheson's College of Cowardly Communist Containment."[33] By the late 1960's the fear of Communism had been muted, but Nixon's "forgotten Americans" were still plagued by very real anxieties resulting from the immense cultural explosions of the post-Eisenhower years. The so-called "new morality," the diffusion of the "drug culture" among all classes of the young, the premium youth place on ecstatic and mystical experiences, a revival of a new and ferocious ethnicity—all of these phenomena were utterly foreign to most Americans, who "began to fear they might become a nation of outsiders."[34] The most vocal peace movement in American history, "shoot-outs" in the great cities the "forgotten Americans" had abandoned as unlivable, clergymen who began to espouse the slogan "God is dead," virtual warfare on the campuses of many major universities, spontaneous assaults on police, increasing verbal attacks on business and technology—these, too, convinced the "Silent Majority" that they were in a near state of siege.

This widespread frustration and disunity created a unique rhetorical opportunity for Nixon. At the heart of any attempt to materialize a common foe lies the "projection device," whereby one seeks to transfer the internal ills of a people to a scapegoat, thus purifying them by dissociation. Kenneth Burke has called this device "especially medicinal":

> . . . if one can hand over his infirmities to a vessel, or "cause," outside the self, one can battle an external enemy instead of battling an enemy within. And the greater one's internal inadequacies, the greater the amount of evils one can load upon the back of "the enemy." . . .[35]

Rather than viewing these internal ills as symptoms of problems demanding remedies, Nixon chose to treat them as the work of "external enemies" who were actively spreading disease throughout the land. The whole situation was presented symptomatically rather than in terms of underlying causes which might suggest legitimate solutions. Such a line of argument was especially appealing to Nixon's "forgotten Americans" who wished to conduct their lives without basic change once the "external enemies" poisoning the country had been purged, and who also felt relief that the burden of guilt had been transferred from their own shoulders to those of a discernible enemy.

Throughout his first year and a half in office, Nixon, with the aid of his Vice-President, had sought frequently to materialize the "external enemy." The so-called "new morality" and the diffusion of the "drug culture" were presented not as symptoms of deeper problems within American society, but as the result of "the merchants of crime and corruption in American society," and of "the pill peddlers and the narcotics peddlers who are corrupting the lives of the children."[36] The "radical faculty" members guilty of "poisoning the student mind against the validity of our system"[37] were said to have produced campus radicals bent on the systematic destruction of our great universities.[38] Distrust of the President's policies were blamed on the small group of elitist journalists and television commentators from Washington and New York, "the most unrepresentative community in the entire United States,"[39] who had polluted the wellsprings of public information and in whose distorted sense of values "One minute of Eldridge Cleaver is worth 10 minutes of Roy Wilkins."[40] In active complicity were the Congressional critics of executive policy whom Agnew called "Hanoi's most successful—even if unintentional—apologists,"[41] as well as "the usual apologists" of the larger community, who, in what Nixon called their "self-righteous moral arrogance," were "ready to excuse any tactic in the name of 'progress.' "[42]

It was not until the off-year election campaign of 1970, however, that a suitable name—"Radical-Liberal"—broad enough to encompass all opponents and critics of presidential policy was devised. Early in the campaign Nixon announced the Republican hope to gain the seven seats needed to take control of the Senate, hold their own in the House, and keep their considerable majority of State Houses.[43] His principal tactic towards this end was to identify all of the administration's opponents as apologists for violence and disruption. The vehicle of this tactic was Spiro T. Agnew who, as Walter Cronkite has observed, was assigned a role "intended to play with the worst fears of the people in order to gain political advantage."[44] How Agnew aroused such fears is illustrated in the very characteristics that he ascribed to "Radical-Liberals." They were portrayed as "neo-isolationists in foreign policy . . . obstructionists in Congress at a time when America's need is for progressives who will cooperate with our President . . . social permissivists," persons who "resist anticrime bills . . . undercut the President abroad . . . excuse violence while they denounce the police . . . support fast withdrawal from Asia . . . pooh-pooh pornography and keep religion out of the schools" and were even "responsible for the erosion of decency" by applauding "sex, nudity, and four letter words in events ranging from Broadway musicals to orgiastic drug-steeped rock festivals."[45]

In early September, Agnew, accompanied by several of the President's personal speech writers (including Pat Buchanan and William Safire),[46] set out on a barnstorming campaign across the country denouncing opponents of presidential policy. During the first week Agnew announced that "Ten to 15 Senators can qualify for the [Radical-Liberal] designation from time to time,"[47] though he named only one full-fledged "Radical-Liberal," Senator Philip Hart of Michigan. As the month of September wore on, however, Agnew admitted one Democrat after another into membership in the "Radical-Liberal" club. Democratic Senators Quentin Burdick of North Dakota, Vance Hartke and Birch Bayh of Indiana, Joseph Tydings of Maryland, George S. McGovern of South Dakota, Albert Gore of Tennessee, and J. William Fulbright of Arkansas were not only called full-fledged "Radical-Liberals," but also "nattering nabobs of negativism" and "pusillanimous pussyfooters."[48] Illinois Democratic senatorial candidate Adlai Stevenson III was not only labeled a "Radical-Liberal," but was even accused of demeaning his great name when young Stevenson referred to the Chicago police during the 1968 Democratic Convention as "storm troopers in blue."[49] Senator Edward Kennedy was accused of "charging in from the far left of the political spectrum" in response to "those faithful navigators—the professional pollsters."[50]

Agnew's strongest sustained attack, however, was reserved for his fellow Republican, Senator Charles E. Goodell of New York, whom he scored as part of a group that is "viscerally antagonistic" to President Nixon's defense program,[51] as " 'too strange' a political bedfellow for the White House,"[52] and even as the "Christine Jorgensen of the Republican Party."[53]

Throughout his whirlwind campaign, Agnew did describe some of the real radicals, the "bombers of campus buildings" and the "assassins of police."[54] But almost invariably he sought to establish a link between "Weathermen or their ilk and liberal Democrats."[55] In a Republican banquet speech at Albuquerque he expostulated, "Make no mistake. This radicalism that infects our Congress *and* poisons our country is at best a bizarre mutation of Democratic liberalism."[56] As the campaign wore on, Agnew sought continually to forge this linkage. Campaigning on behalf of Lenore Romney in Saginaw, Michigan, Agnew told his audience that the demonstrators among them, who were attempting to interrupt him by shouting peace slogans and obscenities, were somehow associated with the Democratic incumbent, Senator Philip Hart. Indicating the knot of noisy demonstrators, Agnew told the group: "That's exactly what we're running against in this country today. With enemies like that, how can you lose?"[57] He then asserted that Mrs. Romney's election over Hart would "help rescue the Democratic Party from radical liberals so that America can stand safe and secure in this dangerous world."[58] At a rally in Belleville, Illinois, Agnew pointed directly at jeering youthful demonstrators and exhorted the crowd of adults to "sweep that kind of garbage out of our society."[59] He followed with a blanket indictment of Democrats who, he claimed, had "been stimulating and encouraging these people."[60] Perhaps Agnew's most explicit attempt to link liberals, and by extension all Democrats, with the militant elements in society came in an October 22 speech in Tucson, Arizona:

> For years the people I call radical liberals have politically consorted and cooed with militants and radicals in our society. For years they have sought to give respectability to lawless conduct by pointing to the unhappy lot or alleged lofty social objectives of lawbreakers. For years they assiduously sowed the seeds of disruption—and America from Maine to California is reaping the bitter harvest. . . . Men like Senators Kennedy and McGovern, and, of course, Hubert Humphrey, who once fawned upon militants and radicals, now suddenly take a hard line against the riotous conduct which their inflammatory rhetoric excused and indirectly invited.[61]

Nevertheless, by early October, it was apparent that Agnew's impact had palled. As Stewart Alsop suggested, Agnew's "famous alliterations . . . suddenly made him a national joke, greatly reducing his political impact."[62] In addition, the Democrats' use of the failure of the administration's economic policy had proved an effective counterweight to Agnew's "Radical-Liberal" attack.[63] At this point Richard Nixon, "arms swooping, fingers jabbing," exiled "Agnew into the provinces" and took "center stage himself."[64]

Though the style and substance of Nixon's speeches were his own, passages touched the same notes that Agnew had been playing for weeks. Thus, as *Newsweek* noted, "the Veep's 'pusillanimous pussyfooters' turned into senators who caused delay on crime bills; the 'nattering nabobs of negativism' were transposed by Mr. Nixon into the 'disrupters' who try to shout down 'the great silent majority' " and Agnew's "radiclibs" lost their specific designation but retained their group identity as all those "opposing the President on the major issues."[65]

Like Agnew, Nixon sought to link the Democratic liberals with lawlessness, pornography, violence, and obscenity. Also like Agnew, he attempted to use the youthful demonstrators who almost always appeared in his audiences to his own advantage. At a Republican rally in Teterboro, New Jersey, for example, Nixon delivered what he called the "Stump Speech" in an airport hangar. In the rear of the hangar, surrounded by police, was a small knot of radical youths. The demonstrators had been excluded from the hangar until "word was passed by the White House staff to admit 'about 50 of them.' "[66] About one-third of the way through the speech, the demonstrators began to chant: "ONE, TWO, THREE, FOUR, WE DON'T WANT YOUR F------ WAR," and "S--- ON NIXON, S--- ON NIXON."[67] Nixon responded in the following words:

> . . . Is that the voice of America? . . . I say to you it is not. It is a loud voice but, my friends, there is a way to answer: Don't answer with violence. Don't answer by shouting the same senseless words that they use.
>
> Answer in the powerful way that Americans have always answered. Let the majority of Americans speak up, speak up on Nov. 3, speak up with your votes. That is the way to answer.[68]

In speech after speech, Nixon sought to turn the presence of the youthful protestors to his own advantage. By simply pointing them out in the crowds, Nixon not only attempted to provide a *"material* reference"[69] for the highly abstract label, "Radical-Liberal," but also to establish some kind of linkage between the youthful demonstrators and liberal and Democratic candidates. The crucial test of this tactic offered itself late in the campaign when 900 demonstrators, many allegedly hurling rocks, eggs, bottles, and other missiles, massed at a Nixon-Murphy rally in San Jose, California, on October 29. The next evening, speaking at an elaborately prepared and well-staged political rally in Anaheim, California, Nixon used the interest generated by the battering of his motorcade to deliver a strong endorsement for Republican tickets across the country. "[W]hat we need," he said, "are men in the House and the Senate of the United States who . . . work and talk and vote for those measures that are necessary to stop the criminal element all year round."[70] Then, implying that Democratic candidates did not so "work and talk and vote," Nixon added: "I urge you to vote for those men who would stand with the President rather than against the President."[71] The next day in Phoenix, Arizona, in a speech later broadcast election eve over national television, Nixon blamed "creeping permissiveness—in our legislatures, in our courts, in our family life, in our universities" for eroding the strength of American society.[72] In an impassioned plea for the votes of his auditors, Nixon told them:

> The time has come to draw the line. The time has come for "The Great Silent Majority" of Americans of all ages, and of every political persuasion to stand up and be counted against the appeasers of the rock throwers and obscenity shouters.[73]

Assessment of Effects and Conclusion

In assessing the effectiveness of Nixon's rhetoric of polarization, it is surely not unfair to apply the ultimate political test: the returns of the 1970 off-year election. In the House, the Republicans actually lost but a small part of their power where they already had "ideological control with yardage to spare."[74] In the Senate, the Republicans registered a net gain of a single seat. Even so, there is merit in presidential adviser Robert Finch's claim that the Senate gain of six conservative senators from both parties "was offset by the loss of only two—George Murphy and Ralph Smith."[75] Both Albert Gore and Ralph Yarborough, Southern liberals, were replaced by conservatives William Brock and Lloyd Bentsen. In New York, the special object of Agnew's purge, Charles Goodell, was defeated by independent conservative James Buckley. And in Maryland "Radical-Liberal" Joe Tydings was beaten by Republican J. Glenn Beall. On the other hand, many whom Agnew had designated as "Radical-Liberals" won handsomely, and, to the administration's discomfiture, the Democrats gained eleven governorships, taking "important patronage . . . in . . . key statehouses"[76] from the Republicans. Kenneth Crawford interpreted the election as revealing "no great swing from left to right or vice versa."[77] *Time* assessed the Republicans' claims of success as "negative," asserting that at best they could boast that "they . . . held their losses below what a President's party normally loses in an off-year election"[78] and that the "Silent Majority" remained a fragile entity which "as in 1968" had "proved to be neither cohesive nor a majority in partisan terms."[79] On balance, the consensus appears to be that the overall success of the administration's rhetoric of polarization was modest at best.

What factors, then, account for the limited success of the administration's rhetoric of polarization? Nixon's strategy of affirmation must be conceded to have been effective: large numbers of Americans continue to identify with the "self-images" he created. The success of the strategy of subversion is more questionable. Persons actively identifying themselves as members of the "Silent Majority" could easily perceive the Nixon-Agnew configuration of militant youth, radical university professors, Black Power advocates, and "Eastern Establishment" journalists as a "common foe." But the identification that the administration sought to establish between liberal Democrats, such as Hartke, Hart, and Kennedy, and the "common foe" was more difficult for "Middle Americans" to accept. Perhaps the strong party identification of liberal Democrats prevented the administration from successfully linking them with those who had already been presented as an alien force. At any rate, the administration's strategy of subversion failed to provide the suitable "signs of consubstantiality": the images of liberal Democrats it sought to foster lacked a high degree of correspondence with the images already held by the electorate. Few will deny that polarization does exist; its effective utilization is quite another matter. Perhaps in a time of charges and countercharges, the administration's "anti-*ethos*" rhetoric represented only another voice in a Babel of strident voices.

Notes

1. Even hard-core Nixon men tended to express their support in terms that were less than ecstatic. For examples of this see Lewis Chester, Godfrey Hodgson, and Bruce Page, *An American Melodrama: The Presidential Campaign of 1968* (New York, 1969), p. 435.
2. We use the term "center" to designate that amorphous group which continues to give its allegiance to traditional values.
3. Quoted in Jules Witcover, "Is There Really a New Nixon?" *The Progressive,* Mar. 1968, p. 17.
4. Richard M. Nixon, "Acceptance Speech," *Vital Speeches,* 1 Sept. 1968, p. 674.
5. *Ibid.*
6. Several of the ideas and assumptions underlying this definition are generally consistent with those found in Walter W. Stevens, "Polarization, Social Facilitation, And Listening," *Western Speech,* 25 (1961), 170; Charles H. Woolbert, "The Audience," *Psychological Monographs,* 21, No. 4 (1916), 39; and John Waite Bowers and Donovan J. Ochs, *The Rhetoric of Agitation and Control* (Reading, Mass., 1970), pp. 17–28.
7. Stevens, p. 170.
8. Cf. Bowers and Ochs, p. 26.
9. Our definitions of these concepts and their subsequent critical applications represent in part an adaptation of Walter R. Fisher's "A Motive View of Communication," *Quarterly Journal of Speech,* 56 (1970), 131–39. Fisher's article presents, among other things, a framework for critical analysis. Our intent has not been to apply Fisher's comprehensive model, but rather to adopt certain portions that have particular relevance for our purpose in this essay.
10. Nixon, "Acceptance Speech," p. 675.
11. *Ibid.,* p. 676.
12. *Ibid.*
13. Richard M. Nixon, "Inaugural Address," *Vital Speeches,* 1 Feb. 1969, p. 226.
14. Our definition of this concept and much of our subsequent discussion is derived from the following sources: Roy G. Francis, "Talking About Bread," in *Perspectives on Communication,* ed. Carl E. Larson and Frank E. X. Dance (Milwaukee, 1968), p. 1; Kenneth E. Boulding, *The Image* (Ann Arbor, 1956), pp. 82–147; and Don Martindale, *The Nature and Types of Sociological Theory* (Boston, 1960), p. 426. Also, see William Isaac Thomas, "The Relation of Research to the Social Process," in *Essays on Research in the Social Sciences* (New York, 1934); William I. Thomas and Florian Znaniecki, *The Polish Peasant in Europe and America* (Boston, 1918–1920), 5 vols.; and Robert K. Merton, *Social Theory and Social Structure* (Glencoe, Ill., 1949).
15. Martindale, p. 426.
16. Boulding, p. 124.
17. Francis, p. 2.
18. Martindale, p. 426.
19. Fisher, p. 131.
20. *Ibid.*
21. See Lloyd F. Bitzer, "The Rhetorical Situation," *Philosophy and Rhetoric,* 1 (1968), 10.
22. For critical analyses of Nixon's November 3 speech see Robert P. Newman, "Under the Veneer: Nixon's Vietnam Speech of November 3, 1969," *Quarterly Journal of Speech,* 56 (1970), 168–78; and Hermann G. Stelzner, "The Quest Story and Nixon's November 3, 1969 Address," *ibid.,* 57 (1971), 163–72.

23. Richard M. Nixon, "A Vietnam Plan," *Vital Speeches,* 15 Nov. 1969, p. 69.
24. *Ibid.*
25. *Ibid.*
26. George Gallup, "Nixon Support Soars to 68%," *The Washington Post,* 24 Nov. 1969, p. A1.
27. *Ibid.*
28. For an analysis of the origin of this and other memorable Agnew phrases see Martin Mayer, "The Brilliance of Spiro Agnew," *Esquire,* May 1970, pp. 117–19 ff.
29. "The Politics of Polarization," *Time,* 21 Nov. 1969, pp. 16–17.
30. See Fisher, p. 132; also, Edwin Black, "Frame of Reference in Rhetoric and Fiction," in *Papers in Rhetoric and Poetic,* ed. Donald C. Bryant (Iowa City, 1965), pp. 26–35.
31. Kenneth Burke, "The Rhetoric of Hitler's 'Battle,' " in *The Philosophy of Literary Form* (Baton Rouge, 1941), p. 193.
32. Barnet Baskerville, "The New Nixon," *Quarterly Journal of Speech,* 43 (1957), 38. Also, see Baskerville's "The Illusion of Proof," *Western Speech,* 25 (1961), 236–42; and William Lee Miller, "The Debating Career of Richard M. Nixon," *The Reporter,* 19 Apr. 1956, pp. 11–17.
33. Baskerville, "The New Nixon," pp. 38–39.
34. Peter Schrag, "The Decline of the WASP," *Harper's,* Apr. 1970, p. 86.
35. Burke, pp. 202–03.
36. Nixon, "Acceptance Speech," p. 676.
37. "Agnew Talks About 'Those Agnew Speeches,' " *U.S. News & World Report,* 24 Aug. 1970, p. 34.
38. Richard M. Nixon, "Cambodia," *Vital Speeches,* 15 May 1970, p. 451.
39. Spiro T. Agnew, "Television News Coverage," *Vital Speeches,* 1 Dec. 1969, p. 99.
40. *Ibid.,* p. 100.
41. *Tucson Sunday Star Citizen,* 21 June 1970, p. A1.
42. Richard M. Nixon, "Campus Revolutionaries," *Vital Speeches,* 1 July 1969, p. 547.
43. "And Now, Looking Toward 1972," *Time,* 16 Nov. 1970, p. 15.
44. Oriana Fallaci, "What Does Walter Cronkite Really Think?" *Look,* 17 Nov. 1970, p. 60.
45. *Arizona Daily Star* (Tucson), 1 Oct. 1970, p. A5.
46. Stewart Alsop, "The Secret of Spiro T.," *Newsweek,* 28 Sept. 1970, p. 104.
47. "Agnew's Elastic List," *Time,* 28 Sept. 1970, p. 8.
48. "Agnew on the Warpath," *Life,* 16 Oct. 1970, p. 29.
49. *Ibid.,* p. 30.
50. Spiro T. Agnew, "New Mexico Republican Reception," Albuquerque, 15 Sept. 1970, p. 4 (mimeo copy from the Office of White House Press Secretary).
51. Spiro T. Agnew, "Navy League Dinner Address," New York, 27 Oct. 1970, p. 8, *ibid.*
52. *The New York Times,* 7 Oct. 1970, p. 1.
53. *The Washington Post,* 10 Oct. 1970, p. A2.
54. "Agnew's Elastic List," p. 9.
55. *Ibid.*
56. *Ibid.*
57. *The New York Times,* 17 Sept. 1970, p. 29.
58. *Ibid.*
59. *Ibid.,* 31 Oct. 1970, p. 12.
60. *Ibid.*

61. Spiro T. Agnew, "Arizona Republican Reception," Tucson, 22 Oct. 1970, p. 3 (mimeo copy supplied by station KVAT, Tucson).
62. Stewart Alsop, "The President's Too-Secret Weapon," *Newsweek*, 2 Nov. 1970, p. 124.
63. "The President Who Runs for Congress," *ibid.*, p. 24.
64. *Ibid.*
65. *Ibid.*, p. 25.
66. Alsop, "The President's Too-Secret Weapon," p. 124.
67. *Ibid.*
68. *The New York Times*, 18 Oct. 1970, p. 1.
69. As Kenneth Burke notes (*Philosophy of Literary Form*, p. 194), this tactic is "a burlesque of contemporary neo-positivism's ideal of meaning, which insists upon a *material* reference."
70. *The New York Times*, 31 Oct. 1970, p. 12.
71. *Ibid.*
72. *Ibid.*, 1 Nov. 1970, p. 66.
73. *Arizona Daily Citizen* (Tucson), 31 Oct. 1970, p. A1.
74. Robert Finch, *The President's Decision to Campaign—When and Why*, 9 Nov. 1970, p. 1 (mimeo copy prepared by the Office of the White House Press Secretary).
75. *Ibid.*
76. "And Now, Looking Toward 1972," p. 15.
77. Kenneth Crawford, "A Normal Mix-Up," *Newsweek*, 16 Nov. 1970, p. 48.
78. "And Now, Looking Toward 1972," p. 15.
79. "Issues That Lost, Men Who Won," *Time*, 16 Nov. 1970, p. 18.

Under the Veneer: Nixon's Vietnam Speech of November 3, 1969

Robert P. Newman

With the political honeymoon over, with his Congressional critics nipping at his heels and threatening fullscale attacks, and with a major outpouring of antiwar sentiment probable on the October 15 Moratorium, Richard M. Nixon announced, on October 13, 1969, that he would make a major address about Vietnam November 3. The advance notice was unusually long for presidential addresses; the stakes in the burgeoning combat were unusually high. Vietnam had broken his predecessor, and Richard Nixon did not care to let himself in for the same treatment.

Part of the tension in October was due to the President's earlier incautious remark that he would not allow his program to be influenced by demonstrations in the streets. This gratuitous irritant to the peace forces guaranteed a massive turnout for the October 15 Moratorium, and it was partially to defuse the Moratorium that the President announced his speech so early. In this effort, the early announcement was perhaps successful; the size of the October 15 turnout remained impressive, but its tone was muted. All but the most violent of the protesters cushioned their stance with an anticipation that on November 3, when the President could speak without appearing to have yielded to pressure, he would announce major steps to end the war.

Even after the Moratorium, announcement of the coming address had its effect on the peace movement. From October 15 until Nixon spoke, plans for the November antiwar events were affected by anticipation of the Presidential speech. Had the prognosis for the November 3 speech been unfavorable, the peace forces would have strained every nerve to mount their greatest effort in mid-November. But Presidential aides let it be known that Nixon had attended to the Moratorium, even though he did not approve it, and the Washington gossip mills were rife with predictions that, on November 3, the President would produce good news for peace. For two weeks, the doves relaxed. Perhaps, thought many, Nixon has really got the word, and the November push won't be necessary after all.

Every channel of public intelligence built up the significance of the November 3 effort. The President was known to be "almost totally preoccupied" with drafting the speech during the last two weeks of October.[1] Whether in

Mr. Newman is Professor of Rhetoric at the University of Pittsburgh.
Reprinted by permission from *Quarterly Journal of Speech* 56 (April 1970), pp. 168–178.

the White House, at Camp David, or on the road, he was writing, revising, reflecting. The speech had to "convey an authentic note of personal involve-ment," rather than appear as a run-of-the-mill ghost-written production; and for this reason, all ten drafts were pristine Nixon. Ray Price, one of the Pres-ident's top writers, had no idea what was in it: "I contributed nothing—not even a flourish."[2] Evans and Novak, executive-watchers of more than usual competence, noted on the day of the speech: "In stark contrast to his last major speech on Vietnam, almost six months ago, Mr. Nixon's talk tonight has been written by one hand alone—the President's hand."[3]

Buildup? On the night of November 3, Caesar himself could not have up-staged Richard Nixon.

In retrospect, expectations were so high that not even the Sermon on the Mount could have fulfilled them. The President had focused the spotlight so long and so carefully that only rhetorical perfection would have been equal to the occasion.

The Background

One of the first questions to be raised about a major address by Nixon, who for years was dogged with the nickname "Tricky Dick," would be "Is he sin-cere?" Nixon did not survive the political wars by the simple-minded morality of a country parson. He had scuttled Helen Gahagan Douglas, done in Alger Hiss, run interference for Eisenhower, fought Jack Kennedy to a virtual draw, and outlasted Barry Goldwater. He is a politician, which is to say that he has run a gauntlet the parameters of which are set, not by the Marquis of Queens-berry, but by the necessities of survival.[4] From such an old pol, some tem-porizing might be expected.

When, therefore, he claimed, on November 3, to have a plan for peace, which he must unfortunately keep secret due to the perverseness of the enemy, some skepticism was expressed. Did he mean it? Did he really have a secret plan? Did he intend to close out the war, or was this just another maneuver to justify the same old business?

The reaction of the peace forces was largely predictable. Few were more blunt than Nixon's erstwhile nemesis, Senator Kennedy, as quoted by the *Times:*

I do not wish to be harsh nor overly critical, but the time has come to say it: as a candidate, Richard Nixon promised us a plan for peace once elected; as chief ex-ecutive, President Nixon promised us a plan for peace for the last 10 months. Last night he spoke again of a plan—a secret plan for peace sometime. There now must be doubt whether there is in existence any plan to extricate America from this war in the best interest of America—for it is no plan to say that what we do depends upon what Hanoi does.[5]

But when it comes to judging the President's sincerity, by all the canons of truth, Mansfield of Montana and Fulbright of Arkansas are superior judges. After five years of dealing with LBJ, they can be counted on to smell a fraud. Both want rapid withdrawal from Vietnam. Both have registered profound opposition to the course of the war. When, after conferences with the President, and caveats about the pace of withdrawal, they nonetheless acknowledge that the President does intend to get out, one must believe them. Both want withdrawal to be programmed independently of what Hanoi does, but both accept as genuine the President's wish to wind down the war.[6]

Were the testimony of the two leading Democratic Senators not conclusive, the ever-watchful White House press contingent, and the major liberal columnists, might be cited in their support. James Reston, whom I shall quote later on matters less favorable to Nixon's cause, regarded Nixon's sincerity as "almost terrifying."[7] And Richard Harwood and Laurence Stern of *The Washington Post* accept as true "that the President, a veteran of the Korean War settlement, is intent on liquidating the American involvement in Vietnam under a veneer of tough talk."[8] The veneer is highly visible, for all to see; but under it is the intention of winding down the American part of the war in Vietnam. What he said, he meant.

But what is the shape of his commitment to withdrawal? Has he now, after all these years of supporting the anticommunist effort in Indochina, decided that it was a mistake and that we *should* withdraw? Or is he merely bowing to political expediency, withdrawing because he can do no other and still retain power? An understanding both of his rhetoric and of his politics depends on answers to these questions.

There are those who maintain that the President is nonideological, a consummate politician and nothing more. This view is concisely expressed by Edwin Newman of NBC News: "But Mr. Nixon is as he is, and it is as well for him, and perhaps for the country, that he is so little ideological. He is neither embarrassed nor bound by having written in 1964 that the war in Vietnam was a life and death struggle in which victory was essential to the survival of freedom, and by having said in Saigon in April, 1967, that the great issue in 1968 would 'not be how to negotiate defeat but how to bring more pressure to bear for victory.' "[9]

There is indeed much evidence in Nixon's recent behavior to indicate that the anticommunist cold war ideology which he so powerfully embraced has now been modified: the SALT talks are underway with apparently serious intent; economic and travel restrictions applied to China for twenty years have been relaxed, and we are talking to the Chinese in Warsaw; germ warfare has been disavowed; and the military budget is, for the first time in years, on the way down. Does all this add up to a new Nixon, one who can willingly disengage from Vietnam?

Nixon's massive, sustained, vigorous hostility to Ho Chi Minh and his movement simply cannot be wiped out overnight. It was, after all, Nixon who as early as 1954 did his best to launch an American expeditionary force against Ho Chi Minh and in support of the French. On April 16, 1954, Nixon appeared for an off-the-record session before the American Society of Newspaper Editors, meeting in Washington, and said that "if France stopped fighting in Indo-China and the situation demanded it the United States would have to send troops to fight the Communists in that area."[10] This 1954 speech was the first sign that the battle to maintain a noncommunist government in Saigon, whether of French colonials or of French-trained Vietnamese generals, was precisely Richard Nixon's battle. And consistently since, with no exceptions until the campaign of 1968, he has supported that battle.

One must approach the Nixon rhetoric, then, entertaining the hypothesis that he is disengaging reluctantly, that his heart is not in it, that only the pressure of public opinion has caused him to embrace what he for fifteen years rejected. And one of the strong reasons for believing that the President does have a plan to phase out this war rapidly is the possibility that by late 1970 even the American Legion will be tired of fighting.

A second approach to understanding the President's speech lies in reflection on the various audiences to whom he was speaking.

There were at least three domestic audiences of consequence. First, his friends: the conservative Republicans who voted him into office and the Wallaceites he is now courting, largely a hawkish group, for whom he had the message, "Do not despair. I'm not heeding the demonstrators. We have to withdraw, but we don't have to give away a thing to the Viet Cong." Second, the "silent majority," some of whom had voted for him and some of whom had voted for Humphrey, many of them fence-straddlers on the war, all of them open, as Nixon saw it, to the plea, "I am winding down this war, but in a methodical and reasonable way which you ought to support." Third, the convinced doves, to whom he said, "Knock it off. I am the President, and disengaging from Vietnam is my bag. I respect your right to dissent, but don't carry it too far." In this latter group the youth, to whom he addressed a specific appeal, probably fit.

Abroad, he was concerned first with the South Vietnamese and other American client states: "We'll keep the faith, we won't desert you, and if the VC get tough again, we'll match them." There was also a clear word for Hanoi and other communist states: "You are going to have to come to terms with Thieu, or we will hang on forever; and if you escalate, the whole ball game is off."

One vital task of criticism is to decide which audience, and which message, was paramount. One is aided in making this decision by the recent publication of a startling book by a Nixon staffer, Kevin Phillips, an assistant to the Attorney General. In *The Emerging Republican Majority,*[11] Phillips analyzes socioeconomic data to conclude that the white working-class voters who produced 9,906,473 votes for George Wallace in the last election can be turned into permanent Republicans. This can be done, says Phillips, by taking over the Wallace message (which rejects peacenik and Black demands) and peddling it with enough sophistication to retain the present registered Republican clientele. Since the conservative, middle-class sun belt cities are growing at the expense of the Democratic cities in the East, this combination will give the Republicans a permanent majority.

The President has not, obviously, endorsed the book; but it fairly represents the strategy with which he fought the last election, and no repudiation of Phillips has been forthcoming: he assisted Attorney General Mitchell until February 1970. And it was to precisely this group, the Wallaceites, that the "veneer of tough talk" was directed. Nixon's rhetorical strategy was thus influenced by a political strategy: placate the doves not at all, appeal to the patriotism of the silent majority, but above all, show the "lower-middle-class clerks in Queens, steelworkers in Youngstown, and retired police lieutenants in San Diego"[12] *that you are their champion.* This is the rhetoric of confrontation.

It is a rhetoric which the Nixon administration, up to now, has largely delegated to the Vice-President. Careful scrutiny of Nixon's text will provide support for the thesis that he sought confrontation. He made numerous references to humiliation, disaster, and defeat, all of which outcomes he projects on to his opponents; these are fighting words. They were incorporated in the speech against the better judgment of Henry Kissinger,[13] and, according to columnists Evans and Novak, against the advice of Republican leaders in Congress to "give the doves something": "Mr. Nixon rejected that advice because he consciously wanted to split off what he regards as a small minority of antiwar activists from his 'great silent majority' of Americans. He was striving for a polarization of opinion isolating the dissenters and thereby dooming the extremist-led Nov. 15 march on Washington."[14]

This divide-and-isolate strategy was not dictated by the circumstances. The substance of the President's plan could have been made palatable to many of his opponents. There were three crucial action programs: (1) avoid precipitate withdrawal; (2) keep the timetable secret; and (3) maintain a noncommunist government in Saigon. Given the division within the peace forces, who ranged from Friends to anarchists, he could easily have explained why the whole timetable could not be announced while announcing the next phase of withdrawal, which he did within six weeks anyway; he could have acknowledged the desirability of broadening the base of the Saigon government; and he could have put a higher priority on a cease fire. Had he done these things, he could have substantially alleviated the fears of many doves.

He not only failed to make these gestures of conciliation, he went far to agitate his opponents. He need not have injected the abrasive discussion of how the war started and how we got involved. He need not have talked as if all his opponents favored precipitate withdrawal. He need not have paraded before us again the controversial domino theory. He need not have done these things, that is, unless he had already decided to write off the dissenters and to start building his "emerging Republican majority" with Wallaceite support. But the decision was his. Anthony Lewis, Pulitizer Prize Winner of *The New York Times,* put it this way: "The puzzle is why he chose to speak as he did. He could so easily have expounded the same policy in less doom-laden rhetoric."[15]

The Argument

There were, according to the President, five questions on the minds of his listeners:

"How and why did America get involved in Vietnam in the first place?

"How has this Administration changed the policy of the previous Administration?

"What has really happened in the negotiations in Paris and the battlefront in Vietnam?

"What choices do we have if we are to end the war?

"What are the prospects for peace?"[16]

After a brief description of the "situation I found when I was inaugurated on Jan. 20th," he turns to what he claims is the "fundamental issue," why and how did we become involved in the first place. This is a surprising candidate for priority in any discussion today. One might have thought that the burning question was how to get out. The President's chief foreign policy advisors, his allies on Capitol Hill, and the memorandum he got from the Cabinet bureaucracy all urged him to skip discussions of the causes and manner of our involvement. Yet the history comes out with top billing. How and to what extent it is distorted is an interesting subject, but not our major concern here. This was a deliberate speech, and the President is arguing for a specific policy.

The substance of his policy argument, scattered throughout the speech, deals with four alternative plans for achieving disengagement. (The possibility of escalation is reserved as a club with which to scare the North Vietnamese into cooperating with Nixon's preferred plan for disengagement, but it is not offered as a full-fledged course of action in its own right.)

First, the President could "end the war at once by ordering the immediate withdrawal of all American forces. From a political standpoint, this would have been a popular and easy course to follow." But it is not Nixon's course; it is craven advice, and it draws his most concentrated fire.

It would, for one thing, constitute a defeat. Given Mr. Nixon's historic commitment to a noncommunist South Vietnam, and his visceral reaction to being bested by communists any time on any issue (as revealed in his auto-biographical *Six Crises*)[17] it is not surprising that he makes much of this argument. Even though, as he claims, he could blame the defeat on his predecessor, this would not be an honorable course.

Whether acknowledging defeat in Vietnam would be a wise course is another matter. Mr. Nixon's mentor, Eisenhower, recognized that, in the much more defensible war in Korea, we sustained a substantial defeat of MacArthur's objectives of rolling back the communists to the Yalu River. Most Americans seemed to approve a less-than-satisfactory settlement; avoidance of defeat did not then commend itself as the greatest good.

Similarly, in the abortive Bay of Pigs invasion, American-trained troops and American strategy suffered great humiliation. But, as Theodore Draper says of John F. Kennedy, "the President knew how to end the misery, without deception or whimpering, in a way that made him seem to grow in defeat."[18] The trauma of defeat varies with the character of the captain, as de Gaulle proved once again in Algeria. But then Nixon is no Kennedy or de Gaulle.

When one asks, "How can the anguish and terror of a loss in Vietnam be mitigated?" the answer has to be something other than the repeated stress on the necessity of avoiding defeat which we heard from President Nixon November 3. There is a case to be made for the honesty and therapeutic value of admitting that we were in over our heads, that we cannot police the whole world, that we really should not, as the military once told us, become involved in a ground war on the Asian continent.

Nixon does not reject immediate withdrawal solely on the basis of its intrinsic evil as a symbol of defeat. It would also lead to a train of undesirable consequences, all of which he ticks off as reasons for repudiating such a policy. It would damage the credibility of other American commitments; encourage communist aggressiveness everywhere; lead not only to the collapse of South Vietnam but all of Southeast Asia; result in horrendous massacres when the Viet Cong take over; and cause us to lose confidence in ourselves, with "inevitable remorse and divisive recrimination."

It might, indeed, do all of these things. These are consequences which need to be considered, *but they need to be considered only if immediate withdrawal is a serious alternative plan which the President needs to refute.* It is hard to see that it had such status. The sharpest challenge to his policy came from Senator Goodell and those who favored phased but definite withdrawal, with a specific deadline by which all American troops, or at least all combat troops, would be out. The call for immediate and total withdrawal came from a minority faction of the peace movement; and in rebutting it as if it were the most serious challenge to his preferred course, Nixon was drawing a red herring across the trail of his opponents, attacking a straw man whose demolition he could portray as destruction of the dissenters generally. This argumentative strategy seems to have succeeded with the silent majority; it festers and repels when one attends to his rhetoric carefully.

The second alternative plan for disengagement is negotiation. Mr. Nixon holds open some slight hope that this might still be the road out; but after a long and frustrating year of meeting with the enemy in Paris, he does not put much faith in it. In this he is undoubtedly correct. North Vietnam has not now, and is not likely to acquire, any faith in negotiated agreements. For those who can remove the distorting lenses of national self-righteousness, which of course always reveal the other party as culprit in scuttling international agreements, the evidence points overwhelmingly to a justification of Hanoi's attitude.[19] But this need not concern us here. Aside from the debater's points Mr. Nixon makes by detailing the substance of U.S. negotiating proposals, and his claim that "Hanoi has refused even to discuss our proposals," this is a blind alley.

The third possible way to get out of Vietnam has the weightiest support behind it, both in the Senate and elsewhere; it is to withdraw steadily with a fixed terminal date. Here is the option upon which attention should have been focused. Here is the real challenge to presidential decision making. If the President were to reason with the most reasonable of his critics, he should have spent the bulk of his energies showing why this plan is disadvantageous compared to his; yet the emphasis it receives is minor.

The few swipes he takes at fixed-schedule withdrawal are instructive. "An announcement of a fixed timetable for our withdrawal would completely remove any incentive for the enemy to negotiate an agreement. They would simply wait until our forces had withdrawn and then move in." This attack is curious indeed. Have we not already written off the prospects for negotiation? Under what possible logic would the enemy be more likely to "wait until our forces had withdrawn and then move in" if they have a terminal point for that wait than if they do not? Is this not likely to happen whether the timetable is secret or public? Here is the core of the dispute between the President and his detractors, and he attends to it with a casual and obfuscating logic that defies belief.

The only other attack on the idea of a *terminus ad quem* for withdrawal is based on its alleged inflexibility; Mr. Nixon does not want to be "frozen in on a fixed timetable." One can accept that some flexibility in such an operation might be in order. This seems not to have deterred our officials from setting up, if not a rigid schedule, at least a terminal date for the accomplishment of other objectives. One must strain one's imagination somewhat to conceive Mr. Nixon incapable of extending a deadline for withdrawal in the face of Vietcong attacks which he defined as serious.

Here is the sum total of the President's refutation of the most serious challenge his program faces. It is hardly worth the candle.

So, finally, we come to alternative number four, the plan adopted and defended by the President. This scenario was worked up by Herman Kahn of the Hudson Institute. The July, 1968 *Foreign Affairs* carried an article by Kahn setting forth his plan for deescalation: build up Arvin, withdraw most American combat units, leave behind a reservoir of between 200,000 and 300,000 men to "deter a resumption of major hostilities."[20] This is now Nixon's plan, with the additional proviso that no long-range schedule be announced.

One needs, at this stage, to view the plan as a whole, inspecting the justifications for it, the reasons for preferring it to alternatives, the rhetoric in which it is clothed. A number of salient points need close scrutiny. As with any policy proposal, the payoff stage is the prediction of future consequences: how will the plan work?

Specifically, one needs to know whether it is probable that (1) the Vietcong and Hanoi will tolerate the presence of 450,000, 400,000, or 350,000 foreign troops while the hated Thieu regime attempts to develop combat effectiveness; (2) the Vietcong and Hanoi will beyond that tolerate the indefinite presence in the country of 250,000 or more occupation troops; (3) the shaky regime in Saigon will really develop political support and military muscle sufficient to keep the communists at bay; (4) the American public, including the great silent majority, the Emerging Republican Majority, and all the rest of us, will tolerate this kind of semipermanent occupation even if combat casualties drop to zero; and (5) there will be less right-wing recrimination should this plan fail than if there is a fast, clean withdrawal.

The President's defense on all these points deserves the closest inspection. We need, in a situation where Mr. Nixon admits "that many Americans have lost confidence in what their Government has told them about our policy," some indication of the evidence on which these assumed consequences are based, whether it be from the CIA, the military, the State Department, Sir Robert Thompson, or wherever. We need some assurance that the President is capable of what social psychologists call "tough-minded empathy," or the ability to see this plan as Hanoi sees it, and not just from the compulsively optimistic viewpoint of the Department of Defense.

There is nothing. The plan is there, take it or leave it. There is a warning to Hanoi to go along or else. There is a recognition that "some of my fellow citizens disagree" with the plan he has chosen. There is a rejection of demonstrations in the street, an appeal to the young people of the nation to turn their energies to constructive ends, a call for patriotism, a reference to Woodrow Wilson (at whose desk he spoke). In defense of his plan, there is only a contemptible rhetorical device, "My fellow Americans, I am sure you can recognize from what I have said that we really have only two choices open to us if we want to end this war. I can order an immediate precipitate withdrawal of all Americans from Vietnam without regard to the effects of that action. Or we can persist in our search for a just peace through . . . our plan for Vietnamization." Here it is, all over again, the false dilemma, the black or white position, the collapse of all alternative strategies into the one most offensive and easiest to ridicule. Only two choices: my plan, or the cut-and-run cowardice of the rioters in the streets.

It is, perhaps, a consummation to be expected of the politician who perfected the technique of "The Illusion of Proof."[21]

For the attentive public to accept the Nixon program of open-ended, no-deadline withdrawal, we have got to have answers which he does not provide. Literally dozens of his opponents have protested that he is giving Saigon the best excuse in the world for not broadening its base, for not coming to terms with the Buddhists and General Khanh, for not cracking down on corruption, for not accommodating to the demands of the peasants in the countryside. As Reston put it, "For if his policy is to stick with the South Vietnamese until they demonstrate that they are secure, all they have to do is prolong their inefficiency in order to guarantee that we will stay in the battle indefinitely."[22] No defense of the President's plan could ignore the logic of this argument; yet ignore it is precisely what Mr. Nixon did.

Consequences

The announcement that the President would speak about the war on November 3 had consequences in itself. The October Moratorium was weakened; an attitude of "let's wait and see" may have deterred many would-be-doves from participating. But the significant consequences were of course after the speech.

The stock market, that sensitive barometer of America's morale and business health, dropped. At 10:30 on the morning of the 4th, prices were down 7.72 on the Dow-Jones industrial average. Stocks largely recovered later in the day, and closed mixed; but the people who handle the money clearly didn't think the President had pulled a coup.

One consequence of the speech, given Nixon's past debilitating relationship with the journalistic fraternity, was a serious lowering of his credibility. Reston put it this way: "The result is that the really important men reporting on the Presidency—not the columnists but the reporters and White House correspondents—are now wondering about the President after his Vietnam speech and his partisan reaction to the elections. He invited them to believe that he would not be like President Johnson, that he would be open and candid. But his approach and reaction to the elections have not been open and candid but personal and partisan. Like Johnson he has dealt with the politics of his problem but not with the problem of Vietnam."[23]

The effects in Saigon were electric. As the *Times* headline read on November 10, "Nixon's Impact: Thieu is Helped Through A Tight Spot."[24] The National Assembly had been raising hell, a motion of no confidence was being discussed in the lower house, and a petition calling for a nationwide referendum was being circulated. Nixon stopped all this. His reaffirmed commitment to stay until there was no more challenge to "freedom" strengthened Thieu's hand immeasurably. Not being one to bite the hand that upholds him, Thieu recorded his gratitude for the press: this was "one of the most important and greatest" speeches made by an American President.[25]

The three domestic audiences identified at the beginning of this essay reacted predictably. Nixon's supporters, the hawks and the Emerging Republican Majority, were delighted. Columnist Joseph Alsop rejoiced hugely: "Whether you agree or disagree with its content, this remarkable speech was one of the most successful technical feats of political leadership in many, many years."[26]

The silent majority was impressed. Gallup, who clocked them in by telephone immediately after the speech, found 77% approving. And in his regular survey of presidential performance, taken November 14–16, approval of the President generally rose 12% over the previous month, to a high of 68%.[27] Although as Gallup noted, there was some question as to the durability of this result, the speech did sell; the "terrifying sincerity" was just what the public wanted to see. But the long pull is yet ahead.

The doves were horror-struck. There had been much reason to believe that the speech would be conciliatory, that the rhetoric would be encouraging. One consequence of the toughness of the speech was that registrations for buses to Washington for the November 13–15 events flooded in;[28] and the ultimate crowd in Washington could be said to be a direct result of Nixon's challenge to the dissidents. The effete ones were not going to take it lying down.

The candid conclusion must be that the President cheered his friends and disheartened his enemies. The peace movement is in disarray, planning no more massive marches, resigned to campus and campaign activities—until the President slips, or Hanoi trips him. As of the end of December, Richard Starnes of Scripps-Howard put it succinctly: "Peace Marchers Give Round to Nixon."[29]

Epilogue

The Nixon style in this speech has been characterized as "tough talk." But this is not the same as saying it was rough; Nixon did preserve the amenities. As Reston put it, "He put Spiro Agnew's confrontation language into the binding of a hymn book."[30] But hymn books are not the only score from which the Administration sings. The cruder, more abrasive tunes are coming steadily from the Vice-President; and it is worth inquiring as to whether the Nixon tune must be heard against the accompaniment of his second in command.

The arguments that have raged in Washington as to whether the Vice-President plays the role of hatchet man to Nixon's above-the-battle dignity just as Nixon was once the hatchet man for Eisenhower, has now largely been resolved. Agnew comes up with his own script. His purple-passioned prose is indigenous, and with the exception of his November 13 blast against the television networks, which according to Clark Mollenhoff "was developed in the White House,"[31] the ideas as well as the language are his.

But even when he is doing his own thing, Mr. Agnew represents the President's true gut feelings.[32] The relationship is one of willing supporter, not ventriloquist's dummy. If Agnew were not around to ventilate the President's pique, someone else would have to be commandeered to put out the purple-passioned prose. The President himself, of course, could do it very well; the summer of 1969 he reverted to a former style with his colorful speeches at General Beadle State College and the Air Force Academy; but the reaction to these by the President's staff was less than enthusiastic, and he has since then turned over the rough talk to the Vice-President.

What we have, then, in the President's speech, is the substance of toughness without the rough style. And the President's text is indeed sanitized. What he might have said, what his style would have been were he not consciously trying to retain the old Republican genteel clientele, one can discover by reading Agnew. The visceral language, the blunt insults, the uncompromising hostilities are missing.[33]

But a presidential address must meet higher standards than campaign oratory or the speeches of lesser figures. Nixon's speech did not meet them. Neither his rhetorical strategies nor his substantive argument were sound. Yet the most likely time for healing and realistic rhetoric has passed. The President's personal involvement in Government decisions will grow, his commitment to what we are doing now will increase, his access to noncongruent intelligence will decrease, the youth will become more alienated. Nixon is not LBJ, and the total closing of filters that occurred in the last days of the Johnson Administration probably will not happen again; but the prospect for improvement is slight. One can always hope that another Clark Clifford is waiting in the wings to restore sanity, or another Eugene McCarthy will appear in the hustings to startle a self-deluded establishment.

A fitting summary of the whole business is provided by Anthony Lewis:

> The preeminent task of Richard Nixon's Presidency is to heal a nation torn apart by Vietnam. The President knew that when he took the oath of office, and it is no less urgently true today. Part of the process must be to help the American people know, and accept, the unpleasant truths about the war: that we got into it by stealth and for reasons at best uncertain; that the Government we defend in South Vietnam is corrupt and unrepresentative; that in the course of fighting we have killed people and ravaged a country to an extent utterly out of proportion to our cause, and that, in the old sense of dictating to the enemy, we cannot "win." In those terms, Mr. Nixon's speech to the nation last Monday evening was a political tragedy.[34]

It was not just the speech that was a political tragedy; the speech merely made visible tragic policy decisions—to maintain the goals and propaganda of the cold war, to seek confrontation with those who want change, to go with a power base confined to white, nonurban, uptight voters. Given such decisions, the shoddy rhetoric, the tough talk, the false dilemmas are inevitable. Instant criticism, via the networks, while desirable, cannot begin to do justice to such policies and such rhetoric. They require more searching exploration. As the saying goes, presidential rhetoric is much too important to be left to presidents.

Notes

1. Robert B. Semple, Jr., "Speech Took 10 Drafts, And President Wrote All," *The New York Times*, November 4, 1969, p. 17.
2. *Ibid.*
3. Rowland Evans and Robert Novak, "Nixon's Appeal for Unity" (Baltimore) *News-American*, November 3, 1969, p. 7B.
4. For a candid statement of the pressures operating on politicians, and the hard choices they make in the struggle for survival, see John F. Kennedy, *Profiles in Courage* (New York, 1956), ch. I.
5. November 5, 1969, p. 10.
6. Mansfield has generally been more sympathetic to the President's position than Fulbright; the Majority Leader joined Minority Leader Hugh Scott in sponsoring a resolution expressing qualified support of the President on November 7. See UPI dispatch, "40 Senators Back Cease-Fire Plea," *The New York Times*, November 8, 1969, p. 10.
7. "Nixon's Mystifying Clarifications," *The New York Times*, November 5, 1969, p. 46.
8. "Polls Show the 'Silent Majority' Also Is Uneasy About War Policy," *The Washington Post*, November 5, 1969, p. A19.
9. "One Man Alone," *The New York Times Book Review*, November 23, 1969, p. 10.
10. Luther A. Huston, "Asian Peril Cited: High Aide Says Troops May Be Sent if the French Withdraw," *The New York Times*, April 17, 1954, p. 1. Someone in Paris is alleged to have blown his cover, and Nixon was identified as the "High Aide" the next day. See also Bernard Fall, *Hell in a Very Small Place: The Siege of Dien Bien Phu* (New York, 1966), ch. IX.

11. (New Rochelle, 1969).
12. The categories of Wallace supporters are those of Andrew Hacker in his sympathetic review of Phillips, "Is There a New Republican Majority?" *Commentary,* XLVIII (November 1969), 65–70.
13. Robert B. Semple, Jr., "Nixon's November 3 Speech: Why He Took the Gamble Alone," *The New York Times,* January 19, 1970, p. 23.
14. Rowland Evans and Robert Novak, "Nixon's Speech Wedded GOP Doves to Mass of Americans," *The Washington Post,* November 6, 1969, p. A23.
15. Anthony Lewis, "The Test of American Greatness in Vietnam," *The New York Times,* November 8, 1969, p. 32.
16. All quotations from the speech are from *The New York Times* text, carried November 4, 1969, p. 16.
17. (Garden City, N.Y., 1961).
18. *The Dominican Revolt* (New York, 1968), p. 1.
19. Probably the best source on American violations of the Geneva Agreement on Vietnam is George M. Kahin and John W. Lewis, *The United States in Vietnam,* rev. ed. (New York, 1969).
20. "If Negotiations Fail," XLVI, 627–641.
21. See Barnet Baskerville, "The Illusion of Proof," *Western Speech,* XXV (Fall 1961), 236–242.
22. James Reston, "Washington: The Unanswered Vietnam Questions," *The New York Times,* December 10, 1969, p. 54.
23. James Reston, "Washington: The Elections and the War," *The New York Times,* November 7, 1969, p. 46.
24. Terence Smith, *The New York Times,* November 10, 1969, p. 2.
25. Terence Smith, " 'Thieu Hails the Speech: One of Most Important,' " *The New York Times,* November 5, 1969, p. 10.
26. Joseph Alsop, "Nixon Leadership is Underestimated," *The Washington Post,* December 29, 1969, p. A13.
27. George Gallup, "Nixon Support Soars to 68%," *The Washington Post,* November 24, 1969, p. A1.
28. David E. Rosenbaum, "Thousands Due in Capital in War Protest This Week," *The New York Times,* November 9, 1969, pp. 1, 56.
29. *The Pittsburgh Press,* December 26, 1969, p. 15.
30. James Reston, November 5, 1969.
31. E. W. Kenworthy, "Nixon Aide Says Agnew Stand Reflects White House TV View," *The New York Times,* November 16, 1969, p. 78.
32. Robert B. Semple, Jr., "Agnew: The Evidence is That He's Speaking for Nixon," *The New York Times,* November 2, 1969, Sec. 4, p. 3.
33. But the old debater's syndrome is very much present. A good capsule description of what this means is in Earl Mazo and Stephen Hess, *Nixon: A Political Portrait* (New York, 1968), p. 7.
34. *The New York Times,* November 8, 1969, p. 32.

The Defeats of Judges Haynsworth and Carswell: Rejection of Supreme Court Nominees

Richard E. Vatz and Theodore Windt

In accepting the Republican presidential nomination in 1968, Richard M. Nixon proclaimed: "Let us always respect our courts and those who serve on them. But let us also recognize that some of our courts in their decisions have gone too far in weakening the peace forces as against the criminal forces and we must act to restore that balance."[1]

This thinly veiled attack on the Supreme Court of the United States struck a responsive chord in the electorate of 1968. For fourteen years the Warren Court had been the eye in the hurricane of juridicial and social controversy. Decisions involving desegregation, Bible reading and prayers in public schools, and the rights of those accused of criminal acts had perplexed and angered many citizens. "Law and Order," a slogan that could be interpreted to mean a tougher stand against marching minorities or against accused persons or against demonstrating students became a major, if ambiguous, issue in the campaign. Clearly, the mood of many Americans was not toward greater tolerance or toward more liberal interpretations of civil liberties or civil rights. To many the Supreme Court held the key to reversing the direction, or at least slowing the tempo, of social change.[2]

During the first year of his presidency, Mr. Nixon had the opportunity to fulfill his campaign promise to alter the "liberal" orientation of the Court. Two seats became vacant. Filling those seats with conservatives, especially if one were a Southerner, would keep the campaign pledge, appear to balance the Court ideologically, and perhaps add more Southerners to his constituency.

To Richard Nixon the times and circumstances seemed propitious to name "strict constructionists," as judicial conservatives are called, to the Supreme Court. Weary of "social change," the public appeared to desire a return to old stabilities and a retreat from rapid innovation. Furthermore, senators usually attach great weight to presidential prerogative in such matters; that is, in the right of the President to appoint men whose beliefs are compatible with his. In the twentieth century only one nominee, Judge John J. Parker, was not confirmed by the Senate for the Supreme Court. Finally, the President was

Mr. Vatz is Associate Professor of Speech Communication at Towson State University.
Reprinted by permission of the Speech Communication Association of America from the *Quarterly Journal of Speech* (December, 1974), pp. 477–488.

enjoying the first year in office, the "honeymoon period." Knowing the difficulties that attend the assumption of power and staffing of the Executive branch, senators usually defer to the President by avoiding any head-to-head confrontations during this time.

Despite these advantages, in the short space of only eight months President Nixon failed to win approval from the Senate for two of the four men he nominated to the Supreme Court. This essay is an examination of the rhetoric used in rejecting those nominations.

There are three conventional grounds for announcing opposition to a Supreme Court nominee; philosophy, ethics, and competence. Opposition on the basis of judicial philosophy is usually insufficient to defeat a nominee. To ask that a nominee be rejected because of his political beliefs is, symbolically, to deny him his right to hold such beliefs or to say that his beliefs make him unfit for public office. Moreover, to question a nominee extensively about his politics and then to make that the cause for rejection implies to many the undermining of two vital principles of the American system: the right to hold dissenting opinions and the myth that "justice is blind." If one is ever to oppose a nominee on the basis of his philosophy, he must demonstrate that the nominee's beliefs are so extreme that he could not render justice fairly. This strategy is usually ineffective when attacking potential judicial appointees. Instead, the major arguments center on the man himself: his public ethics and his judicial competence.

1

Background on the nomination of Haynsworth. On June 9, 1969 Warren E. Burger was confirmed as the fifteenth Chief Justice of the Supreme Court of the United States. Two months later on August 18 Mr. Nixon nominated Judge Clement F. Haynsworth of the Fourth Circuit Court of Appeals to fill the seat vacated by Abe Fortas. Judge Haynsworth was 57, a distinguished Southerner from Greenville, South Carolina, and a 1964 convert to the Republican party.

The nomination immediately aroused opposition from labor, civil rights, and other liberal groups. These organizations characterized Haynsworth as anti-labor and, in the words of George Meany, indifferent to the "legitimate aspirations of Negroes."[3] During the long dispute in Prince Edward County, Virginia he had voted against the majority of the Court when it ordered integration of the schools.[4] As obnoxious as such opinions were to civil rights groups, they did not form the major thrust of the opposition to Haynsworth, but rather remained in the background—alluded to, occasionally spoken about, but seldom debated forcefully.

The major issues in the controversy concerned judicial ethics, conflicts of interest, and lack of candor in answering Congressional questions. During the Senate Judiciary Hearings that began on September 16, these facts were made salient. In 1963 Haynsworth participated in ruling on the *Darlington Manufacturing v. NLRB* even though he owned stock in and served on the board of the Carolina Vend-A-Matic Company that held contracts in a subsidiary of Darlington Mills. In addition, other conflicts of interest were alleged.[5] The judge participated in the *Brunswick Corporation, Plaintiff, and Floyd Corporation D/B/A Pleasant Lanes, Defendant v. J. D. Long, Alberta S. Long and Beach Co., A Corporation, Appellants* case in 1967. Before the announcement of the decision that favored Brunswick, Haynsworth's stock broker bought 1000 shares in Brunswick for him. In 1968 Haynsworth participated in several decisions denying extension time for appeals of the pro-Brunswick decision.

These facts did not constitute *prima facie* grounds for refusing to confirm Haynsworth. They did provide the raw materials from which opponents would weave a tapestry of effective opposition. But first they had to confront several difficult problems.

Rhetorical problems. The first problem opponents faced concerned the tone and style of their arguments. The Warren Court had been attacked for usurping the legislative powers of Congress through its liberal rulings and directives. Politicians, including Mr. Nixon, had implied that the Court's concern for the rights of the accused in criminal cases reflected a misplaced interest in criminals to the neglect of law-abiding citizens and law enforcement agencies. Furthermore, the integrity of any institution rests as much on the reputations of the persons who administer it as anything else. The revelations about former Justice Fortas had weakened the *ethos* of the Court. Rumors circulated that the five marriages, as well as the authorship of "radical works," of Justice William O. Douglas rendered him unfit for judicial service.[6]

Given this political climate, opponents could not launch a full scale attack on Haynsworth without risking further erosion of confidence in the Court. If they did attack forcefully and Haynsworth were confirmed, he would join the Court under a cloud of suspicion about his integrity. Were he defeated, he would return to the Appeals Court as a discredited judge. Opponents would have to balance delicate phrasing with reputable evidence if they were to succeed in blocking his appointment, but also to avoid branding him outrightly as a dishonest man.

Second, senators would have to protect themselves against reprisals from voters when they stood for re-election. This problem became particularly important when President Nixon made a major political issue out of each nominee. He transformed the deliberations over Haynsworth and, to a greater extent, over Carswell into a confrontation between the President and the

Senate, between his prerogatives and its, between his "strict constructionist" philosophy and its "permissive" philosophy, between the South and the rest of the country. This problem was further complicated because liberal Democrats, who formed the core of the opposition, had to gain substantial support from Republicans, conservatives, and Southerners to establish a majority that would reject the nomination. Harping on Haynsworth's alleged antagonism toward civil rights would serve no useful rhetorical purpose. Opposition would have to be cast so senators could be persuaded that constituents would not believe that conservatives had voted against a conservative, Southerners against a Southerner, Republicans against a Republican appointee—except for good cause.

Third, the opposition would have to find a suitable leader. Logically, he would come from the Senate Judiciary Committee that holds initial hearings and questions the nominee as well as other interested parties. Since one major charge against Haynsworth involved "ethical insensitivity," the leader of the opposition must have impeccable credentials himself.

There were four Democratic senators on the Judiciary Committee whose political beliefs made each a logical choice to oppose Haynsworth: Senators Edward Kennedy, Philip Hart, Joseph Tydings, and Birch Bayh. Senator Kennedy's involvement in the events at Chappaquiddick quickly eliminated him. Senator Hart had led the abortive fight to replace Chief Justice Warren with Abe Fortas who left the Court in disgrace. Tydings ruled himself out because he had worked with Judge Haynsworth on legal reform programs and was leaning toward voting for him.[7] The choice of Bayh was more than a process of elimination. He had a modest reputation as a muckraker, a positive attribute.[8] Moreover, he appeared untouched by scandal of any sort.[9] Leaders of labor and civil rights groups asked Bayh to lead the fight and supplied him with information about Haynsworth's alleged conflicts of interest.

Attacks on Haynsworth. Senator Bayh's major line of argument throughout the deliberations concentrated on the belief that Haynsworth had displayed an *appearance of insensitivity* toward conflicts of interest, an appearance that would exacerbate the "crisis of confidence" that plagued the Supreme Court. On the floor of the Senate Bayh stated, "I am concerned about the ethical appearance of this whole business and that all the accusations that the Senator [Hollings] quoted were stated and specified and enumerated in that context and only that context. I must say that we can either say we are concerned about appearances or we can say we are not. We can say that the Statute of Justice with her eyes blindfolded is giving us a message or it is not. But I am concerned about appearances"[10] Throughout the entire affair Bayh pursued this line of argument linking each piece of evidence to the alleged appearance of insensitivity.[11]

Bayh relied on the Darlington and Brunswick cases and on Haynsworth's connections with the textile industries to substantiate his claims of untoward appearances. Members of the Judiciary Committee questioned Haynsworth on each of these matters. Neither Haynsworth's sympathies toward textiles nor the Darlington decision greatly aided Bayh's cause. Every politician has "sympathies" toward a major organization or industry. Furthermore, Haynsworth argued with considerable effect that he had a responsibility to sit on the Darlington case. John Frank, a lawyer and legal expert (so acknowledged by Bayh), supported him. At the end of early testimony on these issues, even Senator Tydings maintained that no concrete evidence had been produced to prove Judge Haynsworth guilty of a conflict of interests.[12] Yet, Bayh continued to press the appearance of impropriety. He stressed that Haynsworth remained a Vice President of the company until 1963 and that his wife, Dorothy, served as secretary for the corporation for two years while Haynsworth was on the Federal bench.

The Brunswick case proved more potent. Bayh's initial cross-examination of Haynsworth on this subject was strong enough to bring an immediate reaction from President Nixon who used a press conference to reaffirm his confidence in Haynsworth's integrity.[13] The charges of conflicts of interest gained greater poignancy as Haynsworth admitted he had bought shares in the corporation through his broker before the Brunswick decision was announced. Bayh's handling of these charges impressed several crucial senators, including Robert Griffin, the Republican Whip who had opposed Fortas for ethical reasons, John Williams, often called the "conscience of the Senate," and John Sherman Cooper, a conservative from Kentucky. Even Haynsworth's supporters granted that he had acted unwisely.

To complement his charges of personal impropriety, Bayh alleged that Judge Haynsworth had misrepresented his relationship to Carolina Vend-A-Matic.[14] Bayh referred to this allegation throughout the hearings and debates as a "lack of candor," a delicate euphemism for lying similar to the euphemism "credibility gap." This charge at the height of public sensitivity to governmental deceit was particularly telling. Haynsworth admitted the charges, but depicted them as trivial.[15]

Opposition increased in October when Senator Edward W. Brooke requested in a letter to the President that the nomination be withdrawn. Other Republicans followed, among them Robert Griffin and Margaret Chase Smith. The opponents of Haynsworth had created the nucleus of an effective opposition by gaining support from Republicans and conservatives, thus lifting the attacks beyond a primarily partisan level.

Counter-attack by the Administration. The Administration's defense of Haynsworth in early October was muted, possibly indicating the Administration's surprise at the mounting opposition. An effective counter-attack needed an effective advocate. President Nixon chose Clark Mollenhoff who, like Bayh, boasted credentials as a muckraker. He was also considered the liberal-in-residence at the White House and thus would not be perceived as grinding an ax for a conservative *cause celebre.*

Mollenhoff released several papers in October and November through Herbert Klein's office. In these papers, especially the extensive *Explanation of the Haynsworth Case,*[16] Mollenhoff dealt with each charge brought by the opposition. His persistent line of argument was to *minimize* the importance or value of each charge. Regarding cases in which Haynsworth had an investment in parent companies, Mollenhoff chose to examine the Judge's possible financial gain from the case, instead of the absolute amount of money involved or the question of whether Haynsworth ought to have been involved in such dealings in the first place. He derogated each case by claiming "no substantial interest" was involved. Mollenhoff attacked Bayh to the extent that he claimed Bayh misrepresented Haynsworth's relationship to Carolina Vend-A-Matic in his Bill of Particulars.[17]

President Nixon limited his role in the deliberations to an informal press conference on October 20, his second and last public statement on the nomination before the voting. His intended audience was most likely the undecided or "leaning" senators, especially Senators Percy, Schweiker, Saxbe, and Aiken.[18] In his statement President Nixon sought to praise Haynsworth, discredit his most vocal opponents, and derogate the charges of judicial impropriety by charging that they were masks used to obfuscate the real issue involved. In an oblique reference to Senator Bayh, the president charged that Haynsworth's opponents were guilty of vicious "character assassination." This tactic, Nixon claimed, was exemplified by the opponent's allegation of connections between Haynsworth and Bobby Baker.

Nixon refuted selected charges of conflicts of interest, as Mollenhoff had, by *minimizing* their importance and emphasizing their triviality. But he also added *ad hominem* attacks by stressing that the charges by opponents were a facade for their real concern: Haynsworth's conservative judicial philosophy. That concern, Nixon contended, was an invalid reason for rejection: "I would agree with those Senators, many of whom are now opposing Judge Haynsworth, who, in the [Thurgood] Marshall confirmation, categorically said that a judge's philosophy was not a proper basis for rejecting him from the Supreme Court."[19] The difference between the two cases was that during the deliberations over Marshall, his work in the cause of civil rights was the major argument against his confirmation. Opponents of Haynsworth had not made his philosophy their central issue. Nixon had. In short, Nixon was attempting to shift the focus of debate from Haynsworth's finances and truth-telling, which the judge had admitted were indiscreet, to his conservative judicial beliefs, a stronger place to defend Haynsworth.

The press conference had little effect. The momentum was too great; the Brunswick charge had become too embarrassing. Above all, Nixon's arguments were not credible to many since a number of Republicans and conservatives had joined the opposition. Senator Aiken, who later voted for Haynsworth, doubted the President "made any votes by his statement."[20]

As Senate debate began on November 13, Senator Hollings complained that minds were already made up, implying rejection was certain. Yet, the Administration still tried to grasp victory by "arm twisting." According to James Conmy, press secretary to Senator Richard Schweiker, there was "more pressure on this issue than on any other in his nine years."[21] As it turned out, the pressure was counter-productive. Senator Len B. Jordan of Idaho concluded: "I would be doing my country a disservice if I concurred in this nomination, against the dictates of my conscience, simply on the grounds of party loyalty."[22] The Administration's efforts were too much too late. Haynsworth was defeated in the Senate by a vote of 55 to 45, and he returned to his seat on the Fourth Circuit Court of Appeals in South Carolina.

2

Background on the nomination of Carswell. To oppose the President on two successive Supreme Court nominations is difficult for a Democrat and close to political treason for a Republican. After the Haynsworth defeat President Nixon seemed to have *carte blanche* for appointing whomever he wished. Hence, the nomination of Southern Judge George Harrold Carswell appeared, in James Conmy's words, "unstoppable."[23] In addition to this powerful presumption in his favor, Carswell did not own any stocks or bonds at that time nor did he own any during his tenure as U.S. Attorney or as Judge on the Fifth Circuit Court of Appeals.[24] Senator Bayh stated during the Senate debate, "The Carswell nomination does not involve the ethical questions present in the Haynsworth nomination. . . ."[25]

Thus, to stop the Carswell appointment opponents would have to argue on grounds of judicial philosophy or judicial competence; the former generally considered illegitimate, the latter a vague area for opposition. The prospects were poor indeed. A successful fight on the basis of judicial philosophy would have to prove a disposition so patently extreme that it would attract Republicans and conservatives despite the presumption in favor of the nominee. The possibility for such a case arose with the discovery of a blatantly racist remark made by Carswell in a 1948 speech in his campaign for the Georgia Legislature. At that time Carswell stated:

I am a Southerner by ancestry, birth, training, inclination, belief and practice. I believe that segregation of the races is proper and the only practical and correct way of life in our states. I have always so believed, and I shall always so act. I shall be the last to submit to any attempt on the part of anyone to break down and to weaken this firmly established policy of our people. . . .

I yield to no man as a fellow candidate, or as a fellow citizen, in the firm, vigorous belief in the principles of white supremacy, and I shall always be so governed.[26]

This speech did not constitute a *prima facie* case against Carswell but it legitimized the issue of judicial philosophy and created the confidence needed to build opposition.

The opposition developed more slowly in the Carswell case than with Haynsworth's nomination due to the presumption in his favor and to the absence of significant labor opposition. In fact, much of the evidence presented at the initial hearings was gathered by volunteers.[27] In those hearings Senators Bayh, Tydings, and Kennedy shared the interrogation. Despite the possibility he might be branded an obstructionist, Bayh eventually assumed the most active role of questioning seemingly by impetus from his leadership of the Haynsworth opposition.

Attacks on Carswell. Encouraged by the discovery of the 1948 speech, opponents of Carswell sought out other evidence of the Judge's apparent racism. To legitimize the attacks on Carswell's beliefs, opponents implied that the Judge's judicial behavior did not merely bespeak conservatism but was so extreme as to indicate demonstrable inability to apply laws and legal rights fairly and equally. Though the racial charges would be sustained throughout the deliberations, opponents would emphasize not so much that racism was bad but that it caused Carswell to pervert legal procedures.

To substantiate the charge that Carswell's racial views caused him to interpret laws unfairly when Black people were involved in litigation, opponents used four specific pieces of evidence. First, they persistently referred to the 1948 speech. Second, they accused Carswell of helping to incorporate a private golf course for purposes of avoiding integration, despite Carswell's claim that he was ignorant of that motive. Third, they accused Carswell of selling a piece of land with a restrictive covenant of which Carswell claimed he was unaware. Finally, they accused Carswell of constantly ignoring judicial precedent in civil rights cases and consequently suffering an unusual number of reverses by higher courts.[28]

Each piece of evidence was used to persuade senators and the American public that Judge Carswell's racial beliefs were so extreme or archaic that they influenced his interpretations of the law. To bolster this contention, several witnesses testified that Carswell harassed civil rights lawyers and litigants. Professor Leroy Clark of New York University, who spent six years investigating Southern civil rights litigation, called Carswell "insulting" and "the most hostile Federal district judge I have ever appeared before with respect to civil rights matters."[29]

The complement to the racial charges was the accusation that Judge Carswell was incompetent, a charge which if true implied a new threat to the *ethos* of the Court, a threat from which the Court was presumed immune. This issue—judicial competence—would prove crucial. It provided opponents a non-racial ground for opposing the appointment; it gave conservatives and Republicans a non-political reason for deserting the President.

The attacks on Carswell's judicial ability began in the Judiciary Committee with the testimony of William Van Alystyne, Professor of Law at Duke University. Van Alystyne severely attacked Carswell's competence and opposed his nomination. His testimony gained credibility because he was a Southerner and by virtue of his previous vigorous support for Judge Haynsworth. Thus began the long campaign to depict Carswell as a mediocre judge. The major sources for proof came from those whose *ethos* would indicate a discerning eye for judicial ability. Voluminous mail from attorneys, professors, and judges as well as testimony from legislators—many of them lawyers—pointed disparagingly to Carswell's lack of publishing, his short opinions, and the aforementioned reversal rate.[30]

The short opinions and lack of publications, opponents argued, indicated a lack of intellect. The reversal rate, they added, pointed to a lack of understanding judicial precedent as well as hostility toward civil rights and disrespect for higher courts. Altogether they converged to mark a man unfit for the Supreme Court. By March 31, 1971 several hundred lawyers, academic and political figures had expressed opposition to the appointment of G. Harrold Carswell as a Justice on the Supreme Court.[31]

The attacks concentrated on his competence to judge not only racial issues, but any issue brought before him. On such a non-political charge, opponents hoped to rally liberal Republicans and judicial conservatives to their cause. Was Carswell fit to sit on the Supreme Court of the United States or not?

Senatorial counter-attack. Unlike the Haynsworth case the nomination was not decided before debate in the Senate began. Possibly noting the adverse nature of its efforts on behalf of Haynsworth, the Administration was even more muted in its support for Carswell. Two weeks before the final vote, *The New York Times* noted, "So far there has been virtually no evidence of the White House's attempting to influence votes on the nomination."[32]

Conservative senators, freshman Senator Robert Dole in particular, then Nixon's protégé, led the defense of Carswell on the Senate floor. Carswell defenders dismissed the charges of racism as unfounded and, as was the strategy in the Haynsworth case, described them as a camouflage for a reprehensible bias against Southern conservative judges.

The defense of Carswell's competence was unusual to say the least, and later doomed his appointment. To put it simply, Carswell's supporters admitted he was mediocre. After this admission, the only thing supporters of the

Judge could do was invent reasons for approving a mediocre judge to the Supreme Court. Evidence of senatorial imagination was seldom more apparent than in the means devised to justify mediocrity in government.

Senator Roman Hruska, Republican from Nebraska, argued that mediocrity and representative government are compatible, if not essential. In a televised interview, widely rebroadcast, Senator Hruska said that "even if he [Carswell] were mediocre, there are a lot of mediocre judges and people and lawyers. They are entitled to a little representation, aren't they and a little chance? We can't have all Brandeises and Frankfurters and Cardozos and stuff like that there."[33] This admission by one of Carswell's strongest supporters on national television severely hurt the judge's chances for approval by the Senate.

Several other senators questioned the necessity of intelligence as an essential quality for a Supreme Court Justice. Some recited demagogic tirades linking intellectualism to dangerous convoluted thinking. Senator Russell Long stated: "Does it not seem . . . that we had enough of those up-side down, corkscrew thinkers? Would it not appear that it might be well to take a B student or a C student who was able to think straight, compared to one of those A students who are capable of the kind of thinking that winds up getting us a 100-percent increase to crime in this country?"[34] Senator Long seemed to imply that lack of intelligence would decrease crime.

A third line of defense of Carswell's mediocrity concentrated on *ad hominem* arguments. Several senators impugned the ability of the Senate to judge Carswell's competence and argued that only those on Carswell's Court or those *from his immediate geographic area* could truly judge his abilities. Typical of this argument was Senator Hruska's remarks during the Senate debate: "That this [judicial mediocrity] is the principal objection to Judge Carswell speaks well for him since it proves that there is no valid deficiency in his qualifications and his detractors must rely on their opinion, based on incomplete knowledge since only those who have known Judge Carswell intimately for a long period of time know and are qualified to express a valid opinion as to his innate qualifications."[35] One might also argue that only Chairman Mao's closest associates are competent to judge him.

The most inventive argument justifying mediocrity came from Senator James Eastland. He argued that mediocrity was in actuality a potential mark of excellence. He stated that several other nominees who became Justices on the Supreme Court were once called mediocre but later turned out to be competent and therefore, by implication, so might Carswell.[36]

Other sporadic defenses emphasized that the American Bar Association had endorsed Carswell and that the Senate had twice before confirmed him to Federal Court positions. These arguments were not taken seriously by members of the Senate in view of the perfunctory examination that led to each endorsement.

The public acceptance of Carswell's mediocrity as a judge by his supporters in the Senate was the turning point in the process of rejection. *Supporters had admitted that the major charge against Carswell was true.* The convoluted rationalizations after this admission only added to the perceptions of ridiculousness of the nomination. The public can tolerate mediocrity, even on the Supreme Court, but only if no one admits publicly that a judge is truly mediocre.

The Administration's efforts. The pro-Carswell forces' most potent weapon after the rationalizations of mediocrity was "Presidential prerogative." As the charges of racism and judicial ineptitude fueled the opposition and as the defense against the charges grew more affected and embarrassing, the more Carswell's defenders invoked the claim that the President's right to choose his own Court transcended other issues.

Supporters of Carswell indicated in debate that they believed that to oppose two consecutive nominations was practically unconstitutional. Senator Brooke, who opposed the appointment of Carswell, noted with dismay on the Senate floor: "I have heard colleagues say, 'How can you go against the President twice?' "[37] In his well-publicized letter to Senator Saxbe, President Nixon attempted to make his Presidential prerogative the central issue in the deliberations. He linked his prerogatives as President to his Constitutional duties, claiming that opposition to Carswell endangered the balance of power among the three branches of government. He stated: "The fact remains, under the Constitution, it is the duty of the President to appoint and of the Senate to advise and consent. But if the Senate attempts to substitute its judgment as to who should be appointed, the traditional constitutional balance is in jeopardy and the duty of the President under the Constitution impaired."[38] According to Mr. Nixon, to argue against him, to oppose his nominee was tantamount to subverting the Constitution, to undermining the ostensible balance of powers.

The President's letter, according to *The New York Times,* angered the pro-Carswell forces as well as some of those uncommitted, although the *Times* observed that "there was no indication that the letter had swayed any Senator's vote."[39] The Senate regards its role in the advise and consent process with maternal guardianship. Furthermore, Senators were sensitive about the authoritarian way in which Presidents Johnson and Nixon had handled foreign affairs without the consent of the Senate. Although Nixon's letter did not singularly cause changes in the vote, it was at least another influence working against Carswell's chances. President Nixon seemed to many to be saying that the opinion of the Senate did not matter, only its support. As Senator Fullbright stated following Carswell's defeat, "The Senate has reasserted itself."[40]

To counteract the impact of arguments about Presidential prerogatives, Senator Fred Harris proposed on March 23 to recommit the nomination to the Judiciary Committee. Ostensibly, this tactic was designed to bury the nomination without actually voting against the President. In actuality, it served to allow Senators to cast one vote *for* the President by rejecting recommittal (which the Administration vigorously opposed) and then to vote *against* Carswell, if need be. No senator who voted for recommittal voted for Carswell's confirmation.[41]

The motion to recommit was defeated on April 6 and a final vote on the nomination was set for April 8. Confirmation, according to *The New York Times,* appeared "likely."[42] Yet, the Administration still chose to employ the potentially dangerous political strategy of "arm-twisting." As in the Haynsworth nomination, it appears that this tactic proved counter-productive. According to *Newsweek,* Howard Cannon, Democrat from Nevada, was assured little opposition in the 1970 election if he voted for Carswell. He voted "nay."[43] *The Congressional Quarterly* reported on April 10 that: "Senators reported that White House and Justice Department officials canvassed the offices of uncommitted Republican Senators for possible support the day before the vote."[44] After the defeat of recommittal, there were three undecided senators: Margaret Chase Smith, Marlow W. Cook—a leader of the pro-Haynsworth forces, and Winston L. Prouty who, it was rumored, would vote as Cook and Smith voted.

The President met with Senators Smith and Cook the night of April 7. All three participants refused to disclose the nature of the conversation. Mrs. Smith indicated she would probably vote to confirm Carswell. But on the day of the vote she cast hers against him. There were indications that she was angered by officials of the Administration who presumably announced her vote for Carswell to several other senators.[45] Senator Cook also voted against Carswell as did Prouty. A change in the votes of Smith and Cook—and therefore probably Prouty—would have produced a tie that then-Vice President Agnew could have broken in favor of the Administration.

As was the case with Judge Haynsworth, Carswell's public *ethos* was the central issue. Senator Cook, who may have cast one of the deciding votes, explained his reasons for voting as he did. He later recounted that he made up his mind the day before the vote when he attended a White House ceremony at which the President awarded twenty-one Medals of Honor posthumously. "When I came back from the White House, I thought 'Those were men who did their best and lost their lives.' And all of a sudden I thought that we were going to vote for someone who didn't fulfill the degree of excellence in the legal field that I thought those men deserved."[46]

The President's conclusions. On April 9, the day after Judge Carswell's nomination was rejected, President Nixon spoke in the Briefing Room of the White House and issued a statement regarding nominations to the Supreme Court. Both were bitter and acrimonious. He concentrated on the motives of those who had voted against his nominees rather than the issues involved. He characterized the attacks on Haynsworth and Carswell as "vicious assaults on their intelligence, their honesty and their character."[47] He argued that opponents—apparently both Democrats and Republicans—had voted against the nominees because the nominees shared Nixon's belief in strict constructionism of the Constitution or because they came from the South. He accused those who had opposed his nominees of hypocrisy: "But when all the hypocrisy is stripped away, the real issue was their philosophy of strict construction of the Constitution, a philosophy that I share, and the fact that they had the misfortune of being born in the South."[48] He concluded that he believed that a sitting Judge who believed in strict construction of the Constitution but who, more important, came from the North would be confirmed, and therefore his next nominee would be such a man.

In summing up his bouts with the Senate over Supreme Court nominees, President Nixon ignored the fact that many Southerners and many judicial conservatives had decided against the nominees. He sought to leave the public impression that his opponents had voted against Haynsworth and Carswell mainly because they came from the South and because they shared his view of strict constructionism. His speech and his statement represented a distortion of the debate over confirmations and were perceived by even many supporters as an insult to the Senate.

During an eight month period, opponents of President Nixon's two nominees to the Supreme Court were able to mount successful rhetorical and political campaigns against these two men. This unprecedented feat involved a skillful blend of fact and *ad hominem*. In the case of Judge Haynsworth opponents marshalled evidence and accusation to demonstrate that he appeared to act in ways insensitive toward the relationship between private finances and judicial decisions. In the case of Judge Carswell opponents used evidence and admissions by his supporters to persuade people that Carswell was a mediocre judge unfit for service on the Supreme Court of the United States. In the first case supporters of Haynsworth found themselves in a quandry as to how to refute charges based not on fact, but on appearances. In the second case, supporters of Carswell made the fatal mistake of agreeing about the Judge's mediocrity and thus had to find means for justifying judicial mediocrity on the Supreme Court. In each case neither political issues nor judicial decisions truly influenced the final rejections, but rather the *ethos* of each determined the outcome. Eventually, President Nixon found new nominees whose *ethos* was not vulnerable to attack and whose judicial beliefs were consistent with his own. The nominations of Judges Haynsworth and Carswell may well be treated by historians as the kind of judgments which would lead to the "Watergate Presidency."

Notes

1. Richard M. Nixon, "Presidential Nomination Acceptance Speech Republican National Convention Miami Beach, Florida, Thursday, August 8, 1968," *Six Crises* (1962; rpt. New York: Pyramid Books, 1968), p. x.
2. Cf. Richard Harris, *Justice. The Crisis of Law, Order, and Freedom in America* (New York: E. P. Dutton, 1970).
3. Quoted in Rowland Evans, Jr. and Robert D. Novak, *Nixon in the White House: The Frustration of Power* (New York: Random House, 1971), p. 162.
4. *Ibid.,* p. 161.
5. Many accusations were made, but those made most salient included: *Farrow vs. Grace Lines, Inc.* 381 F2d 380 (1967); *Donohue v. Maryland Casualty Co.* 363 F2d (1966); and *Maryland Casualty Co. v. Baldwin* 357 F2d (1966).
6. On November 7, 1969 then-Representative Gerald Ford threatened to initiate impeachment proceedings against Justice Douglas if the Senate rejected Haynsworth, an act that apparently so smacked of political blackmail that it backfired and was quickly dropped.
7. Robert Sherrill, "Birch Bayh Isn't a Household Word—Yet," *The New York Times Magazine* (15 Feb. 1970), p. 68.
8. Cf. *Congressional Quarterly* (26 Jul. 1968). p. 1908 describing his actions to curb corruption in Vietnam. Also his *Legislative Summary,* distributed by his office, indicated Bayh considers himself a muckraker.
9. Sherrill p. 46.
10. *Congressional Record,* 20 Nov. 1969, p. 35177.
11. Bayh's charge that Haynsworth was guilty of the appearance of financial impropriety rather than of the act of financial impropriety was a rhetorical stroke of genius. On the one hand, he did not have to prove that Haynsworth had used his office to make money. He only had to prove that it seemed he had. On the other hand, he did not violate the unwritten code of the Senate that a Senator does not accuse another public official of personal corruption unless overwhelming evidence exists.
12. *The New York Times* (17 Sept. 1969), p. 1, col. 4.
13. *The New York Times* (27 Sept. 1969), p. 1, col. 3.
14. See Bayh's representation of this relationship in *Hearings Before the Committee on the Judiciary on the Nomination of Clement F. Haynsworth* (Washington, D.C.: U.S. Government Printing Office, 1969), pp. 128–129. Cf. Haynsworth's interpretation of this relationship in *Hearings,* p. 26 and *Congressional Record* 13 (Nov. 1969), p. 34061.
15. Cf. *Hearings,* pp. 73–107, 210–313, *passim.*
16. Released through Herbert Klein's office, 11 Oct. 1969.
17. There were several misrepresentations including an unsubstantiated causal link between Haynsworth's ascension to the bench and the rise in revenue of Carolina Vend-A-Matic. Additionally, Bayh accused Haynsworth of violating the law by not disclosing a pension fund when the law only cites willful negligence as illegal. Bayh admitted during the Senate debate that he did not believe Haynsworth had broken the law.
18. Robert B. Semple, "Nixon Vows Help for Haynsworth Till Senate Vote," *The New York Times* (21 Oct. 1969), p. 1, col. 8.
19. *Ibid. The New York Times* (21 Oct. 1969), p. 34, col. 4.
20. *The New York Times* (21 Oct. 1969), p. 34, col. 5.

21. This information was obtained from a personal interview conducted by Mr. Vatz with Mr. Conmy in Feb. 1970 in Washington.

22. Warren Weaver, "Idahoan Opposes Haynsworth Bid," *The New York Times* (15 Nov. 1969), p. 1, col. 5.

23. Conmy interview. For a full account of the politics of the Carswell nomination, see Richard Harris, *Decision* (New York: E. P. Dutton, 1971).

24. *Hearings Before the Committee on the Judiciary on the Nomination of George Harold Carswell* (Washington, D.C.: U.S. Government Printing Office, 1970), p. 15.

25. *Congressional Record* (16 Mar. 1970), p. 7487.

26. Quoted in Carswell Hearings, p. 22.

27. Harris, pp. 10–57.

28. On 5 Mar. 1970 at a press conference authorities of the Ripon Society revealed that nearly 60% of Carswell's 84 published decisions had been reversed, nearly twice the average rate of other judges on the Fifth Circuit Court-Cf. Harris, p. 101.

29. Quoted in *Congressional Record* (16 Mar. 1970), p. 7504.

30. Cf. Bayh's presentation of evidence on this matter in *Congressional Record* (13 Mar. 1970), pp. 7359–7367.

31. *Congressional Quarterly* (3 Apr. 1970), p. 906.

32. *The New York Times* (27 Mar. 1970), p. 1, col. 2.

33. Quoted in Harris, p. 110.

34. *Congressional Record* (16 Mar. 1970), p. 7487.

35. *Congressional Record* (18 Mar. 1970), p. 7881.

36. *Congressional Record* (17 Mar. 1970), p. 7645.

37. *Congressional Record* (19 Mar. 1970), p. 8065.

38. "Text of the President's Letter to Senator Saxbe Defending His Nomination of Carswell to High Court," *The New York Times* (2 Apr. 1970), p. 28, col. 6.

39. *The New York Times* (3 Apr. 1970), p. 16, col. 1.

40. *Congressional Quarterly* (10 Apr. 1970), p. 945.

41. *The Pittsburgh Press* (10 Apr. 1970), p. 4, col. 8.

42. *The New York Times* (7 Apr. 1970), p. 1, col. 8.

43. *Newsweek* (20 Apr. 1970), p. 37.

44. *Congressional Quarterly* (10 Apr. 1970), p. 944.

45. *The New York Times* (9 Apr. 1970), p. 32, cols. 1–4.

46. Quoted in Harris, p. 204.

47. "Statement by the President Regarding Nominations to the Court," *Weekly Compilation of Presidential Documents,* 6, no. 15 (13 Apr. 1970), 505.

48. *Ibid.*

Pity the Helpless Giant: Nixon on Cambodia

Robert P. Newman

One might, with some justice, entitle this paper "The Two Richard Nixons" because there are, at a minimum, two highly disparate personalities coexistent in the present occupant of the White House. But they are not the new Nixon and the old Nixon; they are the private Nixon and the public Nixon. Many observers believe that one's view of Mr. Nixon depends solely on one's vantage point: those who work intimately with Nixon in the privacy of the Executive offices see him as calm, accurate, intelligent, and considerate, and they trust him implicitly.[1] Such a view was expounded by the sophisticated Pat Moynihan in his encomium taking leave of his White House duties to return to Harvard in December, 1970.[2] Moynihan's view is shared by Finch, Rogers, Shulz, Richardson, and a host of other Nixon intimates, all of sound judgment and unimpeachable character.

But with outsiders, those whose perceptions are confined to the public Nixon, a diametrically opposite opinion prevails; the President is neither calm, nor accurate, nor consistent. Indeed he is, if not as irascible as LBJ before him, almost as treacherous. One would buy neither a used car nor a foreign policy from him. And it is with the public Nixon that we are forced to deal: with his actions and his rhetoric, his policies and the rationale he gives for them. In that apocalyptic address by which he announced to a trembling world that American forces were going into Cambodia, the outsider's perceptions find substantial confirmation.

One finds, for instance, vast discrepancies between his real reasons and his announced reasons, between his real objectives and his claimed objectives, between his rhetoric and his actions. But how does one know what his real reasons are? One is dependent, of course, not only on close attention to what he says, but also upon the testimony of insiders who were involved in the decision process. This testimony is relayed through newsmen with access to White House inner councils. Such evidence has its dangers. One can never forget Arthur Schlesinger's caustic blast at the credibility of journalistic reports of proceedings in White House decision meetings.[3] I am fully aware of the denials of various accounts of how Lyndon Johnson reached his bombing halt decision, and of Jack Valenti's petulant insistence that only LBJ himself can tell the unadulterated truth about that great event. But LBJ has no small investment in a benevolent version of history, an investment far greater than

Address given at the University of Virginia, Radford College, and the University of Richmond in September, 1971. Rejected upon submission in modified form to the editors of *Quarterly Journal of Speech* as too hostile toward President Nixon.

any other memoir-writer or journalistic chronicler. The analysis he makes of his own motives and of who did what to whom is not, *prima facie,* more accurate than that of the other participants or observing reporters. Johnson's memory is subject to the lapses and deflections of all humanity; and most debilitating of all, he has sole custody of his own documentary record, which can be sanitized and purged of inconvenient items.

As I practice history, the analysis of the Cambodia decision, as of the bombing halt decision two years previously, comes to us in basically sound form from the journalistic accounts already available. The opening of what remains of official documents three decades from now may refine, but it will not refute, our present picture of how Richard Nixon came to invade Cambodia.

No one believes that the decision to invade was reached lightly, or without great soul-searching. Coming as it did a mere two weeks after the triumphant reception of our moon-voyagers, and ten days after Nixon's April 20, 1970 cheerful and optimistic announcement of additional withdrawals from Indochina (more light at the end of the tunnel, as it were), the explosive foray across a neutral border could not have been without its personal trauma for the President. As intelligence accumulated about Communist activities in Cambodia, the optimism of the April 20 withdrawal announcement rapidly dissipated. It was a worried and perplexed President who arrived in Washington April 21, 1970; and for nine days thereafter he wrestled with this latest challenge to his Vietnamese game plan.

How and why the decision to invade was taken has been well told by several prominent teams of correspondents;[4] for present purposes, the aspect on which I want to focus is the major television announcement. Nixon spread on the record a rationale which, he hoped, would build support for the decision just as his withdrawal announcement of November 3, 1969, defused the peace movement. Each of Nixon's previous major television addresses was followed by a noticeable improvement in his standing in the polls. Committed to what he knew would be an unpopular decision, what else would avail save to appeal, once more, to the sensible, silent majority?

Thus in an atmosphere of burgeoning rumor and growing tension, Nixon faced the cameras at 9:00 p.m. April 30, 1970. A complete analysis of what the President did in Cambodia, and why he did it, is beyond the scope of this paper. But I share with Theodore Draper in his superlative analysis of the Dominican crisis of 1965 the conviction that "what was done cannot be separated from . . . how it was justified to the American people and the world at large."[5] The April 30 speech was Nixon's prime justification.

The Expectations: To Save Cambodia?

One frequent justification for American activity in Vietnam is to preserve for the Vietnamese the opportunity to select their own government. Presumably under our benevolent tutelage they can do this. Just across the border, in Cambodia, is another state of the old French Indochinese confederation which for many years was led by Prince Sihanouk, a ruler who walked a successful tightrope between conflicting pressures from the Americans and the Communists. Sihanouk was ousted, on March 18, 1970, and Lon Nol took over; immediately the position of Cambodia began to shift toward American wishes and became tougher on Communist desires. Washington waited anxiously to see how the Communists would react.

In April, 1970, it became apparent that the Communists were not willing to lie down and play dead in Cambodia. Precisely what they were up to was much disputed; for every intelligence interpretation there was a counter interpretation. Some captured documents portrayed the Communists as merely trying to re-establish supply lines which had been interrupted by Lon Nol; others indicated that a vast expansion of Communist-occupied territory was underway. But most intelligence reports agreed that there was movement of Communist troops such as to threaten the capital, Phnom Penh. Could Lon Nol, with his miniscule army, hold against a determined Communist threat? Clearly the answer was no.

One of the major expectations of Mr. Nixon's Cambodia speech was that it would broaden our Indochinese commitment to guarantee the non-Communist government of Cambodia. Why not? Even under the Nixon Doctrine, whatever it is, we guarantee the non-Communism of the Philippines, Thailand, Vietnam, Taiwan, and, partially, Laos. Is Cambodia any less deserving? Would Communist tyranny there be any less outrageous? Would the fall of the Cambodia domino somehow be less awful than the fall of the Saigon domino?

Indeed, in his speech, Mr. Nixon did obliquely deal with the fate of the Cambodian government. He noted that thousands of Communist soldiers were invading Cambodia from the border sanctuaries, encircling the Capital, that Cambodia had sent out a call for assistance.[6] But he stopped short of committing the United States to a defense of the Lon Nol government.

Thus one of the most significant things about this speech was what it did not say, namely, "We are going into Cambodia because we cannot tolerate Communist overthrow of a democratic government." And sedulously, Administration spokesmen put the word around Washington that we had no commitment to sustain Lon Nol or his successors, that we would not be drawn into another Vietnam as we were drawn into the first one; that this domino, somehow, was different.

Here the rhetoric and the reality begin to part company. Consider for instance, the logic of our "temporary" invasion. Communist troops in Cambodia are a menace to American forces in Vietnam and to their Saigon proteges—in 1970. Make even highly optimistic assumptions about rejuvenation of ARVN (Army of South Vietnam) in the years to come. If North Vietnamese troops in Cambodia are a menace to us in 1970, will they not also be a menace in 1973 and 1976? It will *always* matter who controls Cambodia, just as it matters who controls Hanoi, and the Plain of Jars, and North Korea, and. . . .

One might resist this logic, by postulating a wholly unlikely surge of strength in Saigon, such that the South Vietnamese could withstand easily any challenge to their armed forces from across the Cambodian border. One then has to come to grips with some of Mr. Nixon's other utterances, not in a public forum where doves and peaceniks might take offense, but to a select group of chauvinists who visited the White House on April 28. To this group, in the best Dale Carnegie style, Nixon said what they wanted to hear. Innocently, one of these auditors let it slip. Vice Admiral W. R. Smedberg III (Ret.), president of the Retired Officers Association, and one of Mr. Nixon's visitors on April 28, printed it in his newsletter. Mr. Nixon said, according to the Admiral, "I am not going to let Cambodia go down the drain as some of my advisors want me to do."[7]

So here is the first blatant gap between public rhetoric and private conviction. "We shall avoid a wider war," he said over television. "I will not let Cambodia go down the drain," he said to a visitation of hawks. We do not know, at this stage, whether he told the truth to Smedberg or to the nation. Or perhaps one should say that we do not know whether his disposition on the 28th not to let Cambodia "go down the drain" or his rejection of a "wider war" on the 30th will win the upper hand in his internal deliberations. But we do know that somewhere along the line he has fudged the truth.

The Tone: White's Misperceptions

It might be thought unnecessary to point out that the language of the Cambodia announcement is almost exclusively that of the classical misperceptions identified by social psychologists. Yet the insistence of the President that we alone are for peace, the reiteration of our moral self-image, our virile self-image, and the diabolical enemy-image, cry out for analysis. This is the President who began his term with a call to move from confrontation with our enemies to negotiation; from such a position, the language of his public discourse has now shifted 180 degrees.

I will presuppose, in this section, some acquaintance with Ralph K. White's excellent work, *Nobody Wanted War: Misperception in Vietnam and Other Wars*.[8] Of the typical misperceptions White delineates, three are particularly prominent in the Cambodia speech. One of them, a canard which has been exposed so often one would think even the John Birch Society would give up on it, is that version of the virile self-image which claims, as both Johnson and Nixon have so often claimed, that we cannot afford to lose in Vietnam because we cannot bear "to see this nation accept the first defeat in its proud 190-year history." Proud we may be; successful at arms we have usually been. But never defeated? Let us pass for the moment the case of Korea, and turn to the description of the War of 1812 written by that bastion of historical rectitude and naval glorification, Samuel Eliot Morison. Madison so mismanaged the War of 1812, he writes, that the Peace of Ghent was ratified by the Administration with unseemly haste despite news of Jackson's victory at New Orleans. Morison concludes: "So ended the most unpopular war in our history. But because of Jackson's victory at New Orleans, the American people came to believe that they had won it, and that whatever setbacks had occurred were the fault of those nasty New England Federalists."[9] Sheer poppycock. We got creamed in 1812, myth to the contrary. This virile self-image is a misperception, and it does no credit to either of our last two Presidents.

Let us now look at our moral self-image, as portrayed in the stirring call to arms of April 30, 1970. There are two major exemplars of this syndrome: the picture of the United States as alone respecting Cambodia's neutrality, and the claim that only we have offered sincere and reasonable terms at the Paris peace negotiations.

Cambodia, noted the President, has been a neutral nation since the Geneva Agreement of 1954. "American Policy since then has been to scrupulously respect the neutrality of the Cambodian people." Excellent. How comes it, then, that Sihanouk, in his period of carefully balancing between the armed forces contending on his soil, charged the U.S. and its allies with more than 7,000 land, sea, and air violations of Cambodian territory?[10] That the North Vietnamese were also operating in violation of Cambodian neutrality is not in dispute; that we were blameless is patently absurd. The President was simply not telling the truth; his moral self-image would not tolerate admission of our infringements of Cambodian neutrality.

The other frame of moral self-image came in Mr. Nixon's discussions of the lengths to which we have gone to bring the war to a peaceful conclusion:

> We have made and will continue to make any possible effort to end this war through negotiations at the conference table rather than through more fighting on the battlefield. Let us look again at the record. We have stopped the bombing of North

Vietnam. We have cut air operations by over 20 percent. We have announced with-drawal of over 250,000 of our men. . . . The answer of the enemy has been in-transigence at the conference table, belligerence in Hanoi, massive military aggression in Laos and Cambodia and stepped up acts in South Vietnam, designed to increase American casualties.

Such a massive self-delusion needs no comment. Would that it were all true. Would that the sensitive, silent majority really understood what carnage yet is wreaked by the mere 80% of our air operations which are still being carried out; or that the silent majority remembered to compare this version of in-creased American casualties with the more common White House claim that we have been winding down the war, and with it the casualties. Ralph White has done a sober, objective job of analyzing such claims, particularly during the Johnson years; I refer the unconvinced to him.

Lastly, there is the diabolical enemy-image. It is the North Vietnamese who have established sanctuaries in Cambodia—but do not mention that we have them in Thailand, the Philippines, and the Gulf of Tonkin. It is the North Vietnamese who have inflicted "slaughter and savagery" on hundreds and thousands of innocent peasants—but do not mention the Mylais, the frag-mentation bombs, the B-52 high explosives, the chemical defoliation and other American savageries. I do not pretend, here, that an American President is going to tell the world about our minor military indecencies; I do pretend that when Dwight Eisenhower found it necessary to talk tough to the enemy, he managed to avoid the sanctimoniousness of the diabolical enemy syndrome. This restraint, unfortunately, seems beyond the powers of Richard Nixon, as it was of Lyndon Johnson before him. The quality of public discourse is the worse for that.

Before leaving the topic of common misperceptions, a word needs to be said about the new vocabulary of war, about the extent to which 1984 and News-peak are already upon us. War is peace, concentration camps are pacification centers, invasions are incursions, bombing is protective reaction, murdering an enemy agent is termination with extreme prejudice, defeating the enemy is winning the peace. It is perhaps a measure of the dishonesty of our age, which the young see through better than those of us who have lived with human mendacity a bit longer, that these euphemisms occasion scant ridicule. The current Government, and its chief spokesman operating on the night of April 30, 1970, was not without evocations of Orwell's Miniluv and Minipax. It is small wonder that the campuses exploded.

The Rejected Options

But let us look at the substance of the President's discourse. In the face of increased enemy activity in Cambodia, various options were available. These were carefully laid out for him by Henry Kissinger, by the Department of

Defense, by the National Security Council. He enunciated only three of them: do nothing, send massive aid to Cambodia, or invade with American troops. Let me quote Mr. Nixon fully on this first option:

> First, we can do nothing. Well, the ultimate result of that course of action is clear. Unless we indulge in wishful thinking, the lives of Americans remaining in Vietnam after our next withdrawal of 150,000 would be gravely threatened. Let us go to the map again. Here is South Vietnam. Here is North Vietnam. North Vietnam already occupies this part of Laos. If North Vietnam also occupied this whole band in Cambodia, or the entire country, it would mean that South Vietnam was completely outflanked and the forces of Americans in this area, as well as the South Vietnamese, would be in an untenable military position.

Think about this statement for a minute. The first clear implication of Mr. Nixon's dire prediction is that we have *already* indulged in some wishful thinking; for the band of Cambodian border territory to which he referred has in fact been in the hands of the North Vietnamese for years, during all the time when the brave talk about the success of Vietnamization has been pouring forth from the White House. If Communist troops in this area precluded the success of Vietnamization in April, then that success was also precluded in January, and the previous November, and all the other times when Mr. Nixon told us about his fool-proof plans for extricating American troops from Indochina. If his plans for withdrawal will not work now without eliminating the Communists from the border sanctuaries, then the previous claims for those plans were a fraud and a delusion.

The second clear implication of his statement is an affirmation of what we have noted before, namely, that Vietnamization will never work if Cambodia falls, if, as he says, "North Vietnam . . . occupied . . . the entire country." In short, if doing nothing will lead to disaster, if the fall of the Cambodian domino will scuttle his entire strategy, then his talk of a merely temporary incursion is misleading. He cannot have it both ways. He must maintain a friendly and non-threatening Cambodia, or he must admit defeat.

The second option was massive military assistance to the Cambodians. This would fail, he said, because it could not be utilized rapidly and effectively. This was no doubt a sound judgment. It also presupposes the judgment which Mr. Nixon was reluctant to make public, that Cambodia cannot be allowed to fall.

Thus the stage is set for the only acceptable option. No action, or only military aid, will not do the job that has to be done. This job, as Mr. Nixon *really* perceived it, was to keep Cambodia lock, stock and barrel, out of the hands of the North Vietnamese.

The Accepted Option and Its Goals

Nixonian rhetoric is nothing if not pitched to what he believes to be the emotions of the electoral majority. Consequently whatever his real feelings about the necessity for sacrifice to save the world from Communism, one can expect the theme of bringing our boys home, protecting American fighting men, and saving American lives to dominate his discourse. In this speech it does. Nineteen separate times in the April 30 speech he hits the theme of saving or protecting American lives.

But the American people are becoming wary of this appeal. As Gallup demonstrated, people realize that the way to save American lives is to get out of Indochina, and a vast majority of them in 1970 advocated precisely that. Nixon, in attempting to sell the idea that his major motivation in extending the war to Cambodia—and later to Laos—was to save American lives, utterly failed. There is even some doubt that many people were persuaded by the officially lower casualties following extensions of the war; they know that casualties are the result of aggressive action on somebodies' part, and that the Administration can reduce casualties at will simply by decreasing offensive action. And not only can we reduce casualties by decreasing our own offensive actions, we can eliminate casualties by removing our troops from zones where the enemy can get at them. Therefore the "reduce casualties" theme rings untrue, and the President's repetition of it must have contributed to the growing disbelief in his integrity.

But there is more in the Cambodia speech to disturb the alert citizen. We are told, in adjoining paragraphs, first that the enemy "is concentrating his main forces in these sanctuaries," and second, "Thousands of their soldiers are invading [Cambodia] from the sanctuaries; they are encircling the Capital of Phnom Penh, coming from these sanctuaries, as you see here." Who would not boggle at this apparent contradiction? How can they be building up the sanctuaries when they are emptying them of soldiers to attack Phnom Penh. And, to the ever skeptical reporters who dogged White House staff about this discrepancy, the more candid answers of Presidential advisors and of the Department of Defense, were clear: the enemy was *not* building up the sanctuaries. He was moving westward toward Phnom Penh. This movement, in fact, was what caused Secretary Laird to give up his original opposition to the invasion; with enemy soldiers scattering from the target area, the danger to American troops was precisely decreasing. Events in Cambodia presented, not a threat, but an opportunity.[11]

The speech of April 30 was something less than candid in this regard. Nixon presents a steady drumfire of claims about the increasing threats to the lives of American boys, when he knew that the immediate picture was one of decreasing danger.

But if the President lied about the immediate threat; surely he was correct in claiming that the long term prospect of North Vietnamese activity in Cambodia threatened his program for Vietnamization? Let us not delude ourselves about this program. Vietnamization is not a program to end the war; Vietnamization is a program to Asianize the war. Perhaps a few Americans might stay on as advisors, or there might be need for residual American air power, and probably a bit of military aid might be needed. Here one recalls Lyndon Johnson's campaign slogan of 1964: he was not about to send American boys to do a job that Asians should do for themselves. Given the present climate of opinion, Mr. Nixon has done well to pay at least lip service to this principle.

And now that massive American intervention has quieted the overt Communist challenge to Saigon internally, we can finally turn over the war to ARVN. Almost, that is; there remains this long-term threat of Communist activity in Cambodia. We had to wipe out the sanctuaries in order to assure the success of Vietnamization. Unfortunately, the President's uneasiness about prospects for Vietnamization was not shared by his field commanders in Vietnam. As Robert Kaiser, *The Washington Post's* man in Saigon, surveyed reaction to the April 30 speech, he found the following:

> President Nixon's prognostication came as a surprise in Vietnam. What he said, in effect, was that all the boasts about Vietnamization in the past were hollow; the program couldn't work because of the enemy's sanctuaries in Cambodia. Those sanctuaries existed before Sihanouk was deposed March 18. Nothing that happened after March 18 made them any more dangerous, according to Mr. Nixon's own commanders in Vietnam.[12]

So there does appear to have been some dissension in the intelligence community about the existence of a long range threat. Let us resolve the dispute in favor of the President; let us assume that whatever the Communists were doing in Cambodia, it might be a threat to Vietnamization; then let us inspect the rhetoric in which he presented his program to deal with it.

We know, of course, that he rejected a do-nothing policy and a policy of massive military aid alone. He also considered and rejected, though he did not publicly acknowledge it, sending South Vietnamese troops in by themselves. He opted instead for a joint U.S.-ARVN operation: "Our third choice is to go to the *heart of the trouble.* That means cleaning out major North Vietnamese and Viet Cong occupied territories, these sanctuaries which serve as bases for attacks on both Cambodia and American and South Vietnamese forces in South Vietnam." *(Italics Supplied)*

There is no point in spending much time on this rhetoric, or in trying to improve on the deadly precision with which James Reston skewered it in the *Times:*

> But the heart of the trouble is not in Cambodia, but in North Vietnam and beyond that, in the Soviet Union and Communist China. This is what we have been up against from the beginning. The real sanctuaries, which Mr. Nixon wisely is not

prepared to challenge, are Hanoi, Peking, and Moscow, and that being so, it is a thunderingly silly argument to suggest that wiping out the enemy's bases in Cambodia will get to the "heart of the trouble."[13]

And having insulted our intelligence by this thunderingly silly argument, he moved immediately to another. It was presented with all the drama which, in World War II, attached to the invasion of Normandy or the Battle of the Bulge.

Tonight, American and South Vietnamese units will attack the headquarters for the entire Communist military operation in South Vietnam. This key control center has been occupied by the North Vietnamese and Viet Cong for five years in blatant violation of Cambodia's neutrality.

Geronimo, here we have it. The jungle Pentagon, nicknamed COSVN, is now going to be eliminated. The nerve center of the whole operation; the Kremlin of the gooks, the Reichskanzlerei of the men in the black pajamas is finally going to be wiped out.

Now it is probable that there are, or have been, various concentrations of command serving Communist forces in Indochina, some of which might justify the solemn acronym COSVN. But COSVN has been destroyed by American forces several times. Contrary to the President's claim, it has not been thought to be in Cambodia for the last five years. In 1966 and 1967, at least, General Westmoreland thought it was in Vietnam.[14] Can we have so soon forgotten operations Cedar Falls and Junction City? Is the public to have erased the memory of Tay Ninh Province and the Iron Triangle? Have the brave men who penetrated the hostile jungle to wipe out this Communist nerve center not once, but twice, now become unpersons? True, there might be reason to repress these memories. Casualties were heavy, and American commanders were never quite sure they had gotten everything. Just eight months after Operation Junction City the Communists were well enough organized to launch the Tet offensive of 1968, whose aftermath even President Nixon cannot have forgotten.

But in 1970 there was a new Commander-in-Chief, and a new field commander, and they were entitled to their crack at decapitating the enemy and rendering him helpless. Unfortunately, it never came off. Somehow COSVN escaped, and the Saigon public relations officers were reduced to questionable body counts and adding up grains of captured rice to make the whole thing look good.

This exaggerated rhetoric with which President Nixon announced the sweep into Cambodia did not sit well with the military. General Abrams was distinctly unhappy with the President's oversell; to him, the Cambodia operation was a tactically desirable chore, and hanging grandiose goals on it was unwarranted. He wanted to "put a dent in the enemy's supply system and not, as Mr. Nixon suggested, to overrun and clean out the Communist headquarters."[15] Eventually, of course, the Pentagon admitted that COSVN wasn't there.

If one can evaluate a speech by the accuracy of its predictions, this one was risible. The President said we were going to do something which he should have known we couldn't do, which his generals in the field didn't expect to be able to do, and which we in fact failed to accomplish.

The failure had interesting consequences. There was the expected gentle sniping in the press, but the only real blast at the President, and at the intelligence system which presumably informed him, came from an unlikely source. Before the Senate Defense Appropriations Subcommittee on May 4, 1970, with Allen J. Ellender, a certified hawk, in the chair, appeared Gen. John D. Ryan, Chief of Staff of the U.S. Air Force, and Robert C. Seamans, Jr., Secretary of the Air Force. Presumably their business did not relate directly to Cambodia, but that subject nonetheless came up. And from an interview with Ellender after the closed hearing, George Wilson of *The Washington Post* reported the following:

> The failure to find the enemy's headquarters in Cambodia looks like the biggest blunder since Gen. Douglas MacArthur failed to predict that the Chinese would enter the Korean War, Sen. Allen J. Ellender (D-La.) said yesterday. "If they don't find that headquarters pretty soon, there's going to be a hell of a stink here in Congress and hell to pay for Nixon politically," Ellender said.[16]

But in the longer run of events, it is hard to see that the President caught hell for having claimed the imminent capture of that permanent floating crap game. Six times since the Cambodian incursion, the President has appeared before the press to take questions. A Presidential press conference is a situation where all participants expect that hard questions will be asked, potentially embarrassing questions, questions which will strip off the veneer of Administration propaganda and expose the truth of what's really going on. One does not expect that a Presidential speech, or a Ziegler news release, will produce anything except what the Administration wants the public to know. The whole point of a press conference is to expose those vital matters which politicians and bureaucrats want to forget. Nixon has publicly recognized this probing, adversary nature of press conferences, and has exonerated various pointed questions by acknowledging that listeners can't be allowed to get the impression that the press is being "soft on Nixon."

The press conference, despite its drawbacks, is the only forum between elections, in which an American President can be called to practical accountability. And yes, in all those times the President has faced the press since Cambodia, none of his questioners has confronted him with the awkward gap between promise and performance in Cambodia. Of all the tough questions which might have been asked of the President since April 30, 1970, the blockbuster of all would be "Mr. President, you told us when you announced the Cambodia incursion that our troops would attack and destroy the key control center for Communist operations in South Vietnam, COSVN. You made this a major objective of that military action. Whatever happened to COSVN?"

That this question has never been asked shows a serious flaw in our public intelligence system. It is inconceivable that no correspondent thought it worth asking. It is impossible that all Mr. Nixon's questioners had forgotten this important rationale for the invasion. To me, the only plausible answer lies in that alarming book by George Reedy, former press Secretary to President Johnson. *The Twilight of the Presidency*[17] exposes for the first time the full extent to which deification of the American executive has placed him beyond ordinary political give and take, has put him on a pedestal where none dare confront him *to his face* with his lies, distortions, and human failings; has, in fact, made it impossible for a reporter to confront him directly and publicly with a question which will expose his nakedness. Loyal citizens are still, even in America, reluctant to tell the emperor that he has no clothes.

There is an alternative explanation. Perhaps the expectation of honesty in political rhetoric is so low that nobody cares. In any case, Senator Ellender's prediction did not hold true. Mr. Nixon got away with it, and with much more.

Threats, Diversions, and Pathos

Since this was a Nixon speech, it is likely to have the standard warning clause directed at Hanoi: We are withdrawing our soldiers, and if you know what's good for you, you better not make things awkward for us. To a revolutionary movement that has fought for almost three decades to expel first the Japanese, then the French, and now the Americans from Indochinese soil, such warnings are not likely to be highly salient. But let us look at one of Mr. Nixon's specific warnings: "Tonight, I again warn the North Vietnamese that if they continue to escalate the fighting when the United States is withdrawing its forces I shall meet my responsibility as Commander-in-Chief of our Armed Forces to take the action I consider necessary to defend the security of our American men."

And what was this challenge to the security of our American men? Attacks on Camranh Bay? Hand grenades in the Caravelle Hotel? Free heroin to all replacements arriving at Saigon airport? Not exactly; the actions which so upset Mr. Nixon as to draw forth this dire warning were precisely movements *away* from American troops, into areas of Cambodia where Lon Nol had recently interrupted the cozy Communist supply source through Sihanoukville.

All this has to be interpreted, remember, in the context of an optimistic withdrawal speech of ten days earlier, when we were told that the end was finally—repeat, finally—in sight. And it has to be seen against a background of steady claims of success for Vietnamization, of repeated boasts that the

Administration had kept every promise it ever made to reduce our casualties and phase out the war, against a background of promises by Mr. Nixon to Republican bigwigs that by the time of the 1972 elections, the war will not be an issue and we will not have "lost" South Vietnam to the Communists.

From this near-euphoria, we come to April 30, when the word from Mr. Nixon is that "the enemy response to our most conciliatory offers for peaceful negotiation continues to be to increase its attacks and humiliate and defeat us. . ." Here a careful listener could hardly believe his ears. Humiliation and defeat? But we have been winning, and taking fewer casualties, and withdrawing! We are now suddenly humiliated and defeated by an enemy charge into *Cambodia?* It is no wonder that Nixon's credibility has been steadily on the downgrade.

The President is, in fact, caught in a terrible bind. His deep-seated, long term anti-Communism, which involves a twenty-year-old commitment to keep Indochina out of the hands of the Vietminh and their successors, is in basic conflict with the political realities of dealing with the American electorate, which has decided that the fall of Saigon is really not the prelude to an invasion of Seattle. Mr. Nixon's internal ideological gyroscope forces him to be tough, determined, persistent in denying victory to the Viet Cong; but his will to domestic power requires that he withdraw from Indochina. The policy of Vietnamization, designed to allow him to have it both ways, is not the easiest scenario to bring off.

One of his tactical beliefs compounded the difficulty; he believes that in dealing with Communists, you must be willing to take risks, to make sudden bold moves that take the enemy by surprise.[18] Cambodia was such a sudden, bold move; and it scared hell out of much of the American electorate. "Now the Administration is caught," in Murray Marder's words. "Simultaneously, in trying to convince its international enemies that the United States cannot be counted on to take only predictable actions, while it is compelled to convince its own alarmed citizens that the reverse is true—that it is on a steady, committed course."[19]

No rhetoric, however sophisticated, could accomplish these two incompatible tasks. And this Administration is not on a steady, committed course. The helmsman is capricious, tortured, insecure. He may, sometimes and in some situations, be disposed to liquidate the war under a veneer of tough talk; but one cannot count on this tomorrow or next year. And at the very moment he is telling the public how we are withdrawing from Vietnam, he may be planning a private speech to the Retired Officers Association announcing a new addition to the list of American protectorates.

If there was bluster and threat in the April 30 address, there was also pathos. "Feel sorry for me," he said in effect, "this may make me a one-term President." And he's right; it may. But it is interesting to consider whether it was his military strategy, or his rhetorical strategy, which did him the most damage in the Cambodian affair.

Given the expectations of the public, let alone the Congress, the change in policy was unsettling enough. But, in strictly military terms, it was not an unreasonable decision. We had lived through many another search and destroy mission during the years of the Westmoreland command. There is no case in international law against crossing an international boundary into territory controlled, not by the nominal sovereign, but by a belligerent. Perhaps the invasion of the Cambodian sanctuaries was reasonable geopolitically.

What was bad, really unbelievable of a professional politician, was the decision to make a big thing of it, to flaunt it, to blow it up into a major rhetorical effort to show how tough we are. Here is where inadequate intelligence crippled the President. Here is where some canny and loyal advisor should have been able to dissuade him from going public. But the President did not consult the Finches, the Moynihans, the Hickels. And of his foreign affairs advisors, only Rogers spoke out against invasion, and none of the others was able to persuade the President to play it cool. The quality of the domestic intelligence available to the President during the decision period is illustrated by the statement of one of his staff that the Kent State aftermath would blow over in 24 hours;[20] from such a seer, no great help in planning information strategy is likely. Had the President sensed the counterproductivity of flaming rhetoric, other strategies for handling developments come readily to mind. A delayed, routine, underplayed Department of Defense announcement, such as those which have kept the resumption of bombing North Vietnam from detonating public opposition, might have done as well here. Or, as in the Laotian case 7 months later, Mr. Nixon might more appropriately have gone off to the Virgin islands, as a signal that nothing big was up at all.

In short, this speech should never have been given. All the objectives of the invasion could have been achieved without a major announcement. Certainly the Communists needed no televised address to know that, from a placid course of disengaging, the United States was capable of a lurch or two in a new direction. Certainly the sanctuaries could be cleaned out whether or not Mr. Nixon ballyhooed the process. Presumably Lon Nol would get the idea that the United States was interested in helping him against Communist invaders simply from the presence of the American expeditionary force. And to the extent that one of the President's aims was to portray himself to his constituents as being bold in the pattern of Wilson, Franklin Roosevelt, Eisenhower and Kennedy, all of whom he mentioned in his speech, perhaps some more muted channel might have served better for this purpose also. The grim television performance of April 30 smacked of protesting too much.

But even were my judgment wrong, even had some Presidential announcement been necessary, fewer great expectations might have gone into it. James Reston puts the matter in sober perspective:

> There is a good case to be made for attacking the enemy's bases in Cambodia— always has been. Some of them are only 33 miles from Saigon. No general with the brains of a corporal would willingly give his opponent a safe haven from which Saigon could be attacked in the night or even destroyed by relatively short-range missiles which Moscow and Peking have the power to provide. But why can't this plain and sensible tactical battlefield case be made honestly? The President explained the move into Cambodia, not as a necessary tactical invasion—which it undoubtedly is—to reduce casualties and save the the staggering Cambodian Government through the coming monsoon season; but he presented it as some kind of magical stroke that would stun the enemy, wipe out the sanctuaries, bring the boys back home quicker, prove our determination to the Russians and the Chinese, and help arrange a just and lasting peace.[21]

It was a clear case of rhetorical overkill. Hedrick Smith, summarizing the Cambodia decision two months later for a team of *New York Times* correspondents, reported "All of Mr. Nixon's senior aides still wince at some of his rhetoric."[22] My prediction is that twenty years from now, they will still be wincing.

Even the public, conditioned as it is to awe of a Presidential television address, winced a little. Immediately after the speech, Louis Harris reported, more people disbelieved that the Cambodia incursion would accomplish its objectives than believed it. However, the rioting students came to the President's rescue, and two months after the beginning of the venture into Cambodia, public concern over campus unrest topped concern over the war. When the President got American ground troops out of Cambodia, this also helped erase the initial public uneasiness. But neither the April 30 speech, nor later Presidential addresses have reversed the long-term trend. The Gallup poll announced March 7, 1971, shows that 69% of the people believe the Administration is not telling the public all they should know about the war (which is a bigger credibility gap than Johnson's in February 1967); further, by 46% to 41%, the public disapproves of the way Nixon is handling Vietnam.

The Denouement: Pity
the Helpless Giant

Students of the Cambodian decision give great weight to the cumulative sense of frustration felt by the President at his inability to meet many of the challenges thrown up to him by the Communists in the first two years of his Presidency. We know from *Six Crises* that Mr. Nixon's sense of manhood demands prompt and firm response to challenges. We know that he was challenged by the North Korean downing of an EC-121 aircraft, but was dissuaded from doing anything about it. We know that he felt challenged by the Communists' Tet shelling of Saigon in 1969. We know that he felt challenged by Russian moves into Egypt. All these challenges built up hair-trigger tension in the Presidential mind; the prospect of Lon Nol's fall was simply the final straw. It was time to demonstrate that the "richest and strongest nation in the history of the world" had the will and the character to respond to challenges.

Consider, now, paragraphs 44 and 45 of the April 30 address:

> My fellow Americans, we live in an age of anarchy, both abroad and at home. We see mindless attacks on all the great institutions which have been created by free civilizations in the last 500 years. Even here in the United States great universities are being systematically destroyed. Small nations all over the world find themselves under attack from within and without. If, when the chips are down, the world's most powerful nation, the United States of America, acts like a pitiful, helpless giant, the forces of totalitarianism and anarchy will threaten free nations and free institutions throughout the world.

"When the chips are down." Nixon has always, as he put it once in a moment of great candor, had the feeling that people wanted to kick him around. Now it was the Communists. Here is the sense of cumulative challenge, the frustration of the President by undealt with crises boiling to the surface. The chips on the Indochinese table are the only ones exposed, in this speech, but we know that he has others in mind. They are real chips, and in a real poker game—the stake in which is nothing less than survival of the human race.

But can Mr. Nixon's apocalyptic rhetoric contribute to playing a rational hand? Can, in fact, one who feels himself kicked around ever play a cool hand? Nicholas von Hoffman does not think so:

> We have palsied the world with our power; we have affrighted ourselves with it. The only head of state on this globe who would use the words pitiful and helpless in regard to the murderous potential of the United States is Mr. Nixon, the President

who moves from mansion to mansion, cogitating about whether he is man enough, whether he is the equal of Woodrow Wilson, Franklin Roosevelt, Dwight Eisenhower and John Kennedy. He who seeks relief from such doubt can never find it and never stops looking.[23]

Only Mr. Nixon can work off his feeling of helplessness. He has to affirm his machismo for himself, respond to the Communists in his own way, nail his own coonskin to the wall. This is what the Cambodia decision, and the rhetoric accompanying it, were all about; it was Mr. Nixon nailing his coonskin to the wall, with Southern California rather than Texas cattle ranch accents.

Months later, when it came time for the Laos decision, history did not quite repeat itself. U.S. ground troops were not sent along with ARVN. No exaggerated claims were made about the scope of the punishment which was about to be dished out to the enemy. There was, in fact, no television speech or any other kind of public announcement; there was even an embargo on the embargo of news. Mr. Nixon went off to the Caribbean.

But he did not entirely neglect the function of public persuasion. Joseph Alsop, whose support for American aims in Vietnam is undiluted, wrote a glowing column about the new operation. The White House distributed copies of the Alsop column liberally to the media and other opinion leaders.

My admiration for Mr. Alsop, who has interred the Peking regime and disembowelled Hanoi monotonously over the last ten years, is something short of ecstatic. But as an alter ego for the President, as a substitute for the type of jingoistic rhetoric Nixon himself put out about Cambodia, this ploy worked very well. This is a conclusion which I share with columnist Joseph Kraft:

> My impression is that Mr. Nixon approached his decision on Laos in precisely the same spirit as he approached the Cambodian decision last year. At that time he called his critics "bums" and announced that he himself was acting to prevent the United States from being a "pitiful helpless giant." This time, instead of blurting our these sentences himself, he lets Alsop do it for him. It is the same ego trip—taken now by proxy.[24]

Does all this sound sacrilegious about the man whom we did, after all, elect as President of these United States? Perhaps so; but let me point out that the revered textbook image of the President, as a kind of superman, is under steady attack by younger scholars.[25] A modern President does indeed command a more fearsome engine of military destruction than his predecessors; but there is no evidence that his wisdom, or the wisdom of his courtiers, has improved with the passage of time. Even a President puts his trousers on one leg at a time. Even a President is capable of believing that he could get away with lying about U-2 flights over Russia; with believing that 1400 men could over-throw the government of Fidel Castro; with believing that bombing could bring Hanoi to its knees. Presidents do have egos, they do have psychological hang-ups, they do make monstrous rhetorical as well as strategic errors.

Conclusion

It is difficult to leave the topic of Nixon's Homeric performance on the eve of the Cambodian invasion without remarking on one of the cheapest shots in the political armory, his final appeal for sympathy. Quote:

> It is customary to conclude a speech from the White House by asking support for the President of the United States. Tonight, I depart from that precedent. What I ask is far more important. I ask for your support for our brave men fighting tonight halfway around the world—not for territory—not for glory—but so that their younger brothers and their sons and your sons can have a chance to grow up in a world of peace and freedom and justice.

I do not judge the probable effectiveness of this appeal. But I do judge its logic, and its hypocrisy. Our brave fighting men are halfway around the world precisely because Johnson saw fit to put them there, and Nixon has not seen fit to bring them home—not yet. An appeal for them is an undisguised appeal for the men responsible for their being there. And as for our brothers and sons growing up in a world of peace and freedom and justice, that is precisely the case to be made for our Indochinese policy, not an outcome which can be as-sumed.

Once again, in recent American history, our military establishment is en-gaged in eschatalogical speculation about the intentions of the Peoples Re-public of China, as our troops are engaged in close proximity to China's borders. Once again the decisions and the rhetoric about probable Chinese intervention are optimistic. Our incursions into Cambodia and Laos seem not to have pan-icked the dragon in Peking. Let us pray that we do not push our luck into North Vietnam. Yet it would be foolish to believe that there will be no more challenges sufficient to stir Mr. Nixon to action.

Just as one of the main results of the Dominican invasion was the creation of Lyndon Johnson's credibility problem, so may the primary outcome of the Cambodian invasion, and of its accompanying rhetoric, be the creation of Richard Nixon's credibility problem.

Notes

1. See, for instance, James Reston, "The President at Age 58," *The New York Times,* January 10, 1971, Sec. 4, p. 15.
2. "Moynihan Sums Up Two Years With Administration," *The Washington Post,* December 28, 1970, p. A18.
3. "The Historian and History," *Foreign Affairs,* April, 1963, pp. 491–497.
4. See especially Hedrick Smith, "Cambodian Decision: Why President Acted," *The New York Times,* June 30, 1970, pp. 1 and 14; David R. Maxey, "How Nixon decided to invade Cambodia," *Look,* August 11, 1970, pp. 22–25; Stewart Alsop, "On The President's Yellow Pad," *Newsweek,* June 1, 1970, p. 106; Chalmers Roberts, "Planning of Asia Thrust Began in Late March," *The Washington Post,* May 26, 1970, p. A14.
5. Theodore Draper, *The Dominican Revolt.* (New York, 1968), p. 2.
6. This and all other citations of the President's speech are taken from the mimeographed text distributed by the Office of the White House Secretary, April 30, 1970. The text is also carried in *Weekly Compilation of Presidential Documents,* May 4, 1970, pp. 596–601.
7. Daniel Rapoport, "Nixon Visitors Get Hint on Cambodia," UPI dispatch in *The Pittsburgh Press,* May 1, 1970, p. 12.
8. (New York: 1970).
9. Morison *et al, Dissent in Three American Wars.* (Cambridge, Mass, 1970), p. 31.
10. T. D. Allman, "The Price of Neutrality," *Far Eastern Economic Review,* February 26, 1970, pp. 25–28.
11. See Hedrick Smith, note 4. On May 21, 1970, Jerry Friedheim, Deputy Assistant Secretary of Defense for Public Affairs, acknowledged officially that the North Vietnamese were evacuating the border areas at the end of April. See Peter Braestrup, "Pentagon Says COSVN Shifted Beyond 21-mile limit for GI's," *The Washington Post,* May 22, 1970, p. A1.
12. "The View From Saigon: No End in Sight," *The Washington Post,* May 31, 1970, p. B1.
13. "Washington: The Heart of the Trouble," *The New York Times,* May 3, 1970, Sec. 4. p. 14.
14. For a brief summary of attacks on COSVN, see Ralph Kennan, "It's Third Strike At Nerve Center." *The Pittsburgh Press,* May 1, 1970, p. 12.
15. Terence Smith, "U.S. Aides in Saigon Question Policy," *The New York Times,* June 3, 1970, pp. 1 and 14.
16. "Ellender Blasts Failure to Find Enemy Center," *The Washington Post,* May 5, 1970, pp. A1 and A14.
17. (New York and Cleveland, 1970).
18. "Washington: President Nixon's Three Theories," *The New York Times,* May 13, 1970, p. 40.
19. "Nixon's Risks Boomerang," *The Washington Post,* May 15, 1970, pp. A1 and A19.
20. Don Oberdorfer, "No Reply by Nixon, Says Hickel," *The Washington Post,* May 13, 1970, p. A3.

21. Reston: see note 13.
22. Smith: see note 4.
23. "Dialectic of Death," *The Washington Post,* May 4, 1970, p. D1.
24. "The Alsop Implications," *The Washington Post,* February 14, 1971, p. C6.
25. See Thomas E. Cronin, "Superman, Our Textbook President," *The Washington Monthly,* October, 1970, pp. 47–54; and James David Barber, "Analyzing Presidents: From Passive-Positive Taft to Active-Negative Nixon," *The Washington Monthly,* October, 1969, pp. 33–54.

Failure of Apology in American Politics: Nixon on Watergate

Jackson Harrell, B. L. Ware and Wil A. Linkugel

During the early morning hours of June 17, 1972, the American phantas-magoria that was to become known as "Watergate" began with the arrest of five employees of the Committee to Re-elect the President in their attempted burglary of Democratic National Headquarters. For the next two years, Americans were treated to a dream-like procession across their television screens. Through their living rooms marched numerous figures acting as either defenders or detractors of Richard M. Nixon's role in the political misdeeds collectively named after the Watergate office complex. Most would, congruent to the nature of phantasms, quickly dwindle into obscurity through resignation, imprisonment, or completion of their assigned functions. To the President, however, fell the task of constructing a sustained defense of his character—a campaign of apologetic rhetoric substantively beginning on March 12, 1973, and ending only with his resignation from the Presidency.[1] Confronted with this complex series of events, rhetorical critics face the task of explaining why in the case of Richard Nixon, who used apologia on a scale unprecedented in the history of American politics, apology failed.

Attached to this task, however, is a significant opportunity. Though the apologetic form of discourse receives considerable attention in critical literature, two gaps appear in its treatment. First, little has been said concerning any unique contribution apologia may make to our political system. Many of the critical works relating to apologies deal with the self-defenses of political agents, but these works have not directly tied apologetic rhetoric to the theoretical assumptions regarding authority bases in politics. There exists, in other words, a paucity of theory relevant to the manner in which apologetics aids politicians in maintaining their authority over the governed, despite the willingness of students to afford apology generic status in rhetoric.[2] Second, little of the critical literature treats the apology generically. Critiques, characteristically of one speech or an analog treatment of two, are normally conducted from a general conception of rhetorical theory, rather than from the theory of the genre itself. Apology is a genre distinguished by the exigency which calls it forth. The theory of apologetics, as detailed by Ware and Linkugel, is

Mr. Harrell is Account Executive with Hill and Knowlton, Dallas, Texas.
Mr. Ware is an attorney practicing in Houston, Texas.
Mr. Linkugel is Professor of Speech at the University of Kansas.
Reprinted by permission from *Speech Monographs* Vol. 42, (November 1975), pp. 245–262.

275

concerned with the strategic, primarily verbal,[3] response which the rhetor fashions to extricate himself from the situation. This essay provides a study of apology from within the theory of the apologetic genre.

With due recognition that much of the early presidential rhetoric stemming from Watergate does not represent true apologetic in the sense of being a *personalized* defense by an individual of his morality, motives, and reputation, discourses issued by Nixon in the spring and summer of 1973 do appear as attempts at such a defense.[4] These addresses apparently shaped Nixon's rhetorical strategy for handling personal charges throughout the remainder of the Watergate scandal in a manner almost entelechial.

The impact of rhetoric, particularly in the political arena, is largely based upon perception rather than clear fact. In the long run, of course, the Nixon administration was destined to leave the White House before "Four More Years" had been completed. The facts of the case, as revealed in 1974 with both the selective and complete release of tapes, can allow no other conclusion. But these facts were not known to the public in 1973. During that year the Nixon apologies were fully dependent upon public perceptions of rhetor credibility, largely because the public had little documentary evidence to use as a basis for judgment. Such evidence as was available was open to interpretation, doubt, and construction to both support and attack the President, depending upon who was doing the constructing and for what audience. Thus the 1973 Nixon apologia present the opportunity to study the strategies of political apology in a relatively pure state.[5] The strategic importance of the Nixon apologies, in combination with their authorship by the nation's most prominent politician, recommends them as likely critical artifacts, albeit as negative examples. Likewise, they provide a sufficient impetus for the beginning of a theory concerning the role of apology in our political system.[6]

The Bases of Political Authority

Central to the successful execution of the office of the Presidency or, for that matter, any political office is support of the governed at a level sufficient to provide enforcement of decisions by the office holder.[7] Though the components of such political support are numerous, David Easton argues convincingly that most important in determining the authority of an office holder is the general approbation, or *diffuse sentiment support,* granted to him by the governed. Diffuse sentiment support is best thought of as a "reservoir" of favorable attitudes or good will held toward a political figure despite the popularity or unpopularity of immediate specific decisions he may have made.[8] It is that type of sentiment that public opinion polls often attempt to measure through questions soliciting either approval or disapproval of the way an individual is handling his office. In greater detail, Easton explains the nature of diffuse support through the key term "legitimacy": "The inculcation of a sense of legitimacy is probably the single most effective device for regulating the flow of diffuse support in favor . . . of the authorities. . . . A member [of the political community] may be willing to obey the authorities . . . for many different reasons. But the most stable support will derive from the conviction on the part of the member that it is right and proper for him to accept and obey the authorities."[9]

The three components of political legitimacy identified by Easton, i.e., structural, ideological, and personal legitimacy, may therefore be considered as the bases of political authority. An examination of these interactive, though conceptually distinct, bases of political authority relative to the Nixon administration provides insight into both the substantive bases available to Nixon in forming his Watergate defenses and the reasons behind the erosion of the President's ability to command authority during Watergate. In addition, such a study indicates the unique potential that apologetic discourse holds in our political system.

Structural Legitimacy

The first authority basis identified by Easton is structural legitimacy. Using this means of building diffuse support the authority borrows from the legitimacy of the office he holds. More specific to the case in point, the office of the Presidency imparts legitimacy to the holder of that office. Nixon's ability to claim structural legitimacy in early 1973 was considerable, as it is for most presidents at most times. An occupant of the Oval Office tends to have automatically conferred upon him the trust and power that Americans give to the office itself. Americans apparently have a great deal of respect for the office and wish to grant its occupant the powers necessary for the performance of presidential duties. Roberta S. Sigel found impressive opinion survey support to the effect that *"voters want strong presidents who know how to lead and how to make their will prevail. They want them to be far more than chief executives. They want them to be people with programs and ideas of their own, with the power to carry them out."*[10]

The public, however, does not grant complete authority to the holder of the office. As Sigel observes, "they admire power and yet they fear it."[11] A president may reap the benefits of structural legitimacy only if he acts within the broad limits of behavior acceptable to the people. Hazel Erskine, reporting an extensive survey of polls regarding presidential power, concludes: "Unsophisticated as the public may be in knowledge of constitutional provisions for the separation of powers, they have systematically given implied consent to the principle of checks and balances or, at the least, have shown majority reluctance to grant too much power to one man, the president."[12]

With respect to Nixon's presidency in particular, his second administration inherited a full measure of structural legitimacy, thus accounting for some portion of his total authority base. According to Sigel, "willingness to delegate decision making to the president stems not only from the public's view of his superior ability to do so because of his better knowledge . . . but also from the public's trust that as a rule presidents are not wont to abuse their decision-making power."[13] Since the early months of the Watergate episode produced little or no evidence of presidential wrongdoing, the American people returned Nixon to the White House in November, 1972, with such a mandate that there is little doubt they expected him to exercise the immense prerogative structurally belonging to both the office and, hence, to himself.

Ideological Legitimacy

To what extent a president is accorded diffuse support in the form of ideological legitimacy sentiments depends upon the degree to which the public perceives his values and principles as similar to theirs.[14] A large measure of Nixon's diffuse support can be traced to public identification with his ideology. Two factors seem to have converged during the 1972 election to undergird Nixon's ideological basis for authority. Not only did the public perceive Nixon as strongly believing in the "real American values," they also drew a sharp contrast between Nixon and Senator McGovern whose perceived liberality and permissiveness led many to fear him and to believe more strongly that Nixon personified America's first principles.

Nixon became strongly identified in 1968 with the "law and order" theme, and much of the strongest rhetoric that issued from his first administration sustained the public's linkage of Nixon and The Law. Even though he did not directly make "law and order" one of his major issues in the 1972 campaign, Nixon retained much the same image. In 1972 Nixon's campaign team broadened the law and order image to emphasize "social order" more than law enforcement. Order, in turn, had been subsumed under the broader category of "patriotism" or "first principles of the republic." Commenting upon the attraction "American flag lapel buttons" held for the "first team" of the Nixon re-election team, Theodore H. White also noted their recognition of the "dynamic of the family of terms that went with 'patriotism'—'family life,' 'neighborhood schools,' 'American values.' "[15]

So the Nixon ideology, grounded in his 1968 law and order theme but broadened out greatly, centered on traditional American values. And in that motif the American public found much with which to identify. People were, of course, tired of Vietnam—but they were equally tired of assaults on the symbols of the Nation. Nixon had been a steadfast defender of the nation's symbols and, in a broad way, they identified with his statements on behalf of the flag and the democratic way.[16]

But a second factor seemed to heighten the degree of public belief that Nixon should be their choice on ideological grounds. Their perception of the policies and beliefs of George McGovern was in direct contrast to their view of Nixon. As Gallup reported, "Blue collar workers feared that McGovern would encourage a permissive society that would fail to provide safe streets and cities."[17] The public identified McGovern with the general state of social unrest which they wished to leave behind. The impact of this, as regards the public's conferral of ideological legitimacy on Nixon, cannot be ignored. In an election involving conflicting ideologies the turning away from McGovern, which would normally be termed a negative action, also entailed a turning to Nixon. At base, Nixon drew a reasonable degree of legitimacy from public identification with his patriotic values, but the move toward Nixon based upon these values was undoubtedly strengthened by the concurrent contrast they saw in his opponent.

Personal Legitimacy

Nixon's personal legitimacy was a much more recently developed phenomenon than was either his structural or ideological legitimacy. Nixon had never attracted voters because of his personality. Throughout much of his political life he was unhappily referred to as "Tricky Dick." Political cartoonists commonly depicted him as akin to the man with a sneaky squint and beady eyes who sell the used car and its engine separately. But for a brief period at least, this image changed considerably. During 1972 and early 1973, the public ascribed to Nixon a kind of public integrity and personal morality; and they came to see in him the kind of independence of personality that characterizes a man of action. Since this view of Nixon was an element new to his voter appeal, it was on the tenuous ground shared by most all newly reformed attitudes and, thus, deserves careful attention.

The qualities attributed by the nation at large to the "New Nixon" are similar to those Sigel discovered in her study of Detroit voters as most important in a president. The sources of a president's personal legitimacy, according to her survey, are found in beliefs regarding his honesty, intelligence, and independence. Of these qualities, the one clearly most important to those surveyed was honesty.[18] The breadth of the honesty concept is important because it emphasizes the personal image the public wishes its chief executive to exhibit: "Inquiring into the president's moral character, seventy-nine percent express themselves in favor of a man whose private and public life is exemplary. . . . When this answer is viewed in conjunction with the strong preference for honesty, one may speculate whether to the public the term 'honesty' is not perhaps a rather all-inclusive term covering a wide spectrum ranging from public rectitude to personal righteousness."[19] The mask of honesty is doubly important in that the appearance of dishonesty could carry with it the direct implication that a leader has been dishonest in describing his ideology to the public. Failure to live up to the expectations of either legitimacy mask could damage the other authority source.

The 1972 Nixon campaign organization worked hard to demonstrate the emergence of the New Nixon, a political figure that embodied the qualities found to be so important in Sigel's study. This new character was dynamic, not tricky; honest, not shifty. Much that Nixon did during 1972 pointed to a new dynamism and forthrightness in the man. His trips to China and to Russia, which Americans shared from their living rooms, had been most successful. Just as importantly, he worked the necessary magic to end the scourge of Vietnam. Largely because of the broad picture drawn by these successes, he came to be viewed by many as a man of action who could accomplish important matters.[20] Beyond these foreign policy successes, Nixon also emerged as a strict moralist. The New Nixon was against amnesty, he was against pornography, he was against liberalizing abortion.

To what extent did this image of a dynamic and honest Nixon contribute to the mandate of 1972? Though opinion polls did not specifically gauge the public's view of these qualities in Nixon, indirect indices of the incumbent President's personal legitimacy suggest its paramount importance in determining the election results. While the President was gathering a victory of landslide proportions, other Republicans running for office were experiencing difficulties. In the Senate, for example, Republicans suffered a net loss of two seats. In the House, they gained twelve seats, but remained in the minority, 192–243.[21] In May of the election year, Gallup polled the public regarding their party preferences for solving selected national problems. He found that forty-four percent of the public believed that the Democrats were the "party best for prosperity", as opposed to only twenty-five percent favoring the Republicans. Similarly, more believed the Democrats were the "party best for peace."[22] Hence, though Nixon enjoyed the advantages of incumbency, other Republicans possessing similar structural legitimacy lost or only narrowly won their races. Furthermore, other Republicans, many of whom voiced ideologies similar to Nixon, did not share in the landslide. Personal legitimacy, as opposed to either structural or ideological, was Nixon's in an amount to which he was not accustomed. Although the New Nixon had forged this fulcrum to turn a victory into a landslide, his personal image was newly attributed by the public and we must consider it susceptible to easy reversal.

The Rhetorical Persona in Political Life

This discussion of the bases of Nixon's political authority suggests a unique role played by apology in our political system. The complete authority of a public figure is a complex yet subtle intermixing of the structural, ideological, and personal bases of legitimacy. This perceptual configuration of a political authority might be most effectively described as the rhetorical persona in political life.[23] The persona concept details a distinction "between the man and the image, between reality and illusion."[24] The persona is not the person, but rather is the auditor's symbolic construction (and implied assessment) of the person. Further, the authority's persona is far broader than Easton's analytic category encompassed by the "personal legitimacy" label. The rhetorical persona in political life represents the public's attribution of preferred personal, ideological, and structural legitimacy sources to the political agent. To the extent that the governed see the appropriate characteristics in the holder of an office they accord him the diffuse support necessary to both retention of the office and effective administration of it. More important to critical theory for apologetic rhetoric, as the political figure comes under attack along one or more of the diffuse support dimensions he is threatened with a recasting of his persona by the public and a resultant decrease in one or more types of support.

As that form of discourse in which a rhetor presents a personal defense of his worth, one distinctly different from a defense of programs and policies, apologia serves the unique role in our political system of being the rhetorical instrument best suited to the maintenance of rhetorical personae against charges that an individual is personally unsuited to wear the public mask and, hence, not fit for public trust and office. The rhetorical persona construct is, in one sense, *impersonal* in that it implies the existence of a "mask that is required by the mythical pattern, the ritual, the plot—the mask that is there before any person turns up to fill it."[25] To some extent, someone is always given sufficient legitimacy to fill the presidential authority role. The role is, however, filled differently by different people at different times. And in this sense the construction of rhetorical personae is an extremely *personal* matter, for it requires the active participation of particular authority figures and audience members in the process. The peculiar mix of desired qualities in any particular authority figure provides a unique momentary blend of supportive sentiments from the audience. A rhetorical persona is a public symbol and therefore wields moral authority over those who receive it. This symbolic quality means that each constituent of the persona, having been present at its creation, identifies closely with and is responsible for it. This identification with the persona is the means by which individuals indirectly identify with and participate in the political system. Any charge, therefore, that implies the incorrect attribution of a persona to an individual office holder is likely to be taken personally by the electorate and, therefore, to require an apologetic—a personal response from the accused. A successful campaign of apology for Nixon during the Watergate scandal, then, needed to be personalized in the sense that his rhetoric should have resulted in an acceptable view of Nixon as an individual possessing the characteristics with which he had earlier filled the legitimacy mask.

A Legitimacy Analysis: Why Apology Failed

In analyzing Nixon's 1973 Watergate messages critical terminology developed elsewhere by Ware and Linkugel specifically for the study of apologetic discourse is useful. In their terms, four primary strategies consistently appear in self-defense rhetoric: denial, bolstering, differentiation, and transcendence. In framing apologies, most speakers assume one of four rhetorical postures resulting from combinations of these strategies. The *absolutive* posture results "from the union of primarily the differentiation and denial factors . . . in which the speaker seeks acquittal" from those charges levied against his character. *Vindicative* apologies are those in which the rhetor depends heavily upon transcendence and denial strategies in hope of not only preserving his reputation but also with the intention of gaining "recognition of his greater worth as a human being relative to the worth of his accusers." *Explanative* addresses are those resulting from a combination of bolstering and differentiation based upon the assumption that if the audience better understands the situation, they will not judge the accused adversely. *Justificative* address is that in which the speaker seeks to gain approval, largely through bolstering and transcendence, for what he has done.[26]

Although we are primarily concerned with the major apologetic statements which Nixon presented during 1973, the events and suasoria preceding Nixon's personal defense on Watergate deserve passing critical attention because of the impressions they began to form in the public mind and the limitations they placed upon him during the height of the scandal. It is important to notice, however, that while these statements exhibit the formal characteristics of apologia they were not delivered in response to a clearly threatened withdrawal of public support for Nixon. Instead, this period is characterized by Nixon's attempt to present apologia-like statements on behalf of the entire White House organization.

Beginning with the Watergate break-in and technically lasting through early March, 1973, this initiation phase of the Watergate apologia consistently exhibits a posture of absolution for the White House Staff. Nixon's chief strategy was to draw a line of distinction between members of the White House and the street-level operatives who had been caught red-handed. This defense took place primarily during the fall months of 1972. The absolutive appeal is exemplified in two Nixon statements. On October 5th he combined the denial and differentiation strategies into one concept: "One thing that has always puzzled me about it is why anybody would have tried to get anything out of the Watergate. Be that as it may, that decision having been made at lower levels, with which I had no knowledge."[27] This strategy was employed in similar fashion in another 1972 statement. Basing his claim upon John Dean's investigation, Nixon told newsmen, "I can say categorically . . . that no one in the White House staff, no one in this administration, presently employed, was involved in this very bizarre incident."[28]

Absolution is a posture designed to clear fully the accused party from any hint of wrongdoing. Nixon's primary thrust was to convince the public that they should not even consider it possible that staff members were in any way involved. By thus wrapping the White House in a blanket with himself, the President risked attaching any past actions of staff members to his own persona. This strategy had detrimental potential for two components of Nixon's authority image. First, the consistent strength for Nixon's diffuse support lay in his strong ideological position, largely perceived by the public as the proper enforcement of laws and the conduct of government along accepted constitutional lines. Second, the new found strength in the Nixon image was that of a strong and independent president acting upon the national scene.

Nixon's fall 1972 position inhered two risks. In the first place, he risked the viability of his ideological stability by failing to assert that all members of the team were subject to investigation and were open to prosecution should evidence be found against them. Further, he risked his tenuous personal legitimacy by basing his early arguments upon it. If he were later proved wrong, it might appear that he had not been honest with the public. Under this circumstance, the spector of "Tricky Dick" could re-emerge all too easily and obliterate the "New Nixon." On top of these risks, we must also consider the personal stance which Nixon exhibited. In failing to cast himself as the great enforcer of the law, he not only risked his ideological legitimacy but he also failed to project an image of the strong and independent leader.

Throughout this early stage of "indirect" apologia, Nixon's popularity and job rating remained fairly high in the opinion polls. This was largely because no definite evidence had emerged to link the White House directly to Watergate.

Personal Apology I: Explanation

The Nixon apologia during 1973 can best be described by noting two distinct phases. During phase one, beginning with his March 12 statement regarding executive privilege, events unfolded in such a way that four members of the White House team eventually were released from service. This eventuality, combined with Nixon's earlier categorical assertion of their innocence, forced Nixon into an explanative posture. Explanation was a necessary choice, as was the abandonment of White House absolution, because it became apparent to the public that blanket claims of White House innocence could not be supported. In addition, when Nixon decided to protect his aides from testimony he needed to explain his reasons. The strategy chosen entailed the significant risk that if he were unable to convince the public to accept his position he would appear to be withholding important evidence from the public eye. Failure, in other words, would undermine his ideological and personal bases of legitimacy.

Nixon explained on March 12 that he refused to allow his staff members to testify before panels inquiring into Watergate in line with the structural principle called "executive privilege." To bolster his position, he referred to American legal tradition: "It [executive privilege] was first invoked by President Washington, and it has been recognized and utilized by our Presidents for almost 200 years since that time."[29] His primary bolstering strategy was an attempt to remind the public of the powers which normally accompany the office, reminding them that the "doctrine is rooted in the Constitution, which vests 'the Executive Power' solely in the President."[30] To emphasize the importance of the principle, he explained that "Without such protection, our military security, our relations with other countries, our law enforcement procedures, and many other aspects of the national interest could be significantly damaged and the decisionmaking process of the executive branch could be impaired."[31] In an effort to dispel the potential public fear that he was invoking executive privilege to prevent relevant facts from coming to light, rather than to protect the Presidency, Nixon differentiated regarding its use: "Executive privilege will not be used as a shield to prevent embarrassing information from being made available but will be exercised only in those particular instances in which disclosure would harm the public interest."[32]

During the period of time the diffuse support that Nixon had enjoyed at the beginning of 1973 began to slowly slip away. By the end of March his job rating had dropped from the January high of 68 percent to 59 percent.[33] In the following week, on April 7, Gallup recorded an additional drop to 54 percent support.[34] These polls seem to reflect a public which increasingly failed to see Nixon as an honest and independent leader acting vigorously to uphold political morality. Because of his failure to project a clear image based upon acceptable ideology, Nixon's personal legitimacy began to erode sharply.

Then, on April 29, came a devastating blow to Nixon's position. As a result of attacks upon key members of the White House staff, top aides H. R. Haldeman and John Ehrlichman resigned. Along with them came the resignation of Attorney General Richard Kleindienst and the dismissal of John Dean from his post as White House counsel. In his announcement, Nixon attempted to remind the public that the resignations did not indicate any involvement by Haldeman and Ehrlichman in wrongdoing,[35] but their very resignations contributed to the public's unwillingness to sustain Nixon's personal and ideological legitimacy. The attempted absolution of his aides was clearly being contradicted by the facts and accusations as interpreted by the public. The two elements of his political persona which derived from nonstructural sources were becoming more and more endangered.

Against this background, with his personal legitimacy coming into potentially severe question, Nixon addressed the nation on the evening of April 30. The President maintained an explanative posture, as he had since March 12. During March, however, he had been primarily concerned with bolstering his image by turning to structural powers as the basis for executive privilege. In this address he sought to bolster his image by both strong structural and ideological appeals. The speech is filled with references to "this great office I hold," and maintaining "the integrity of the White House." In what appears to be a direct appeal to retain the legitimacy which the people grant a president because he occupies the office itself, the President declared, "This office is a sacred trust and I am determined to be worthy of that trust." But he added to this an appeal to basic American values: "I love America. I believe that America is the hope of the world."[36]

Differentiation operated as a secondary strategy in the address. Nixon talked of the difference between what he could have known and what he perhaps should have found out. It must have been apparent to him that the public sensed the inaccuracy of his earlier statements claiming absolution for members of his staff. If he were not to be viewed as having either lied or of having tried to cover up the truth, he needed to establish in the public mind that he could not possibly have known of the involvement of his staff. So, Nixon reminded the public that he had repeatedly asked "those conducting the investigation whether there was any reason to believe that members of my Administration were in any way involved. I received repeated assurances that they were not."[37]

Nixon committed a strategic error during this phase of the Watergate self-defense. As the charges against his close associates became louder and more effective, he was forced to explain away previous statements and was forced into a position of reacting to events instead of leading the crusade for political morality. Thus, not only did it undermine his claim to personal honesty but it also denigrated his ability to fulfill the public expectation of an independent leader. Once more Nixon gave the public an opportunity to drift back toward the belief that his political intelligence was derived from shiftiness and craftiness instead of wisdom and vision. The persona was being resculpted and his own hand held the chisel.

The risk involved in the strategy Nixon used during March and April was a significant one. The Gallup organization found that 40 percent of those polled did not think Nixon had "told the whole truth" in his April 30th address. Only 30 percent thought he did. Additionally, 50 percent thought that he had participated in a "coverup" of the Watergate matter.[38] The risk, however, had seemingly been limited to a reduction in his personal and structural legitimacy. More, it seems, had been at stake. In response to a question concerning advance knowledge of the Watergate bugging or participation in a coverup, a plurality of 30 percent thought that Nixon should be impeached if he were involved in either.[39] Because of strategic errors in the management of the public perception of his image, Nixon entered the second phase of his Watergate apologia fighting for his political life.

Personal Apology II: Absolution

During the second phase of the Watergate apologia, Nixon made only two major public statements. The first of these occurred May 22, 1973, before any major witnesses had testified for the Ervin Committee. It was a response to charges that the President himself had in some way been involved in the Watergate affair. Although his printed statement did not receive the direct public attention a broadcast address might have enjoyed, the statement merits consideration because it is Nixon's first statement in his direct defense against charges of personal Watergate involvement, and it established the Nixon line of defense against which several witnesses would chip away in the ensuing months.

In his statement Nixon chose the posture of absolution. He denied that he had personally been involved in any way in either the Watergate break-in or in any attempt to cover it up; additionally, he differentiated national security operations from the Watergate case. It was important to Nixon that he deny any personal involvement in Watergate events. To accomplish this successfully he needed to draw clear distinctions between covering up the Watergate case and keeping national security operations under cover, since charges had been voiced implying that Nixon was using national security as a blanket term to protect himself from revealing important Watergate information.

In his May 22 statement, Nixon sought to clearly differentiate between the dual roles of persons who had been involved in the Watergate break-in and who had earlier been employed in national security operations. In perhaps the clearest instance of drawing the desired distinction, Nixon remarked:

> I was . . . concerned that the Watergate investigation might well lead to an inquiry into the activities of the special investigations unit itself. . . .
> I wanted justice done with regard to Watergate; but in the scale of national priorities with which I had to deal . . . I also had to be deeply concerned with ensuring that neither the covert operations of the CIA nor the operations of the Special Investigations Unit should be compromised.[40]

This distinction was a critical one to the President's defense, because one could easily imagine that in preventing inquiry into the earlier national security operations, it might be all too easy also to put the lid on a proper investigation of Watergate. The public's willingness to accept the distinction, and to believe that the President had acted in accordance with the distinction as he was now drawing it, depended upon their willingness to trust him to report honestly his actions and motives. Because certain parts of his earlier Watergate statements had probably undermined his personal legitimacy, specifically regarding his perceived honesty, the President was on tenuous grounds.

As for Watergate itself, Nixon denied involvement: "It now seems that . . . there were apparently wide-ranging efforts to limit the investigation or to conceal the possible involvement of members of the Administration and the campaign committee. I was not aware of any such efforts at the time."[41] The denial was short. It occupied only a few paragraphs in a relatively lengthy statement. More important, its veracity depended entirely upon the word of a president whose image was already deteriorating. As with the attempted differentiation, the losses the President sustained during his defense of his aides must have undermined the public's willingness to believe such a position, even though a scant majority still stood in support of his Presidency.

We find three specific weaknesses in Nixon's absolutive statement of May 22nd. As indicated above, Nixon was quite late in undertaking personal absolution and, we believe, the earlier attempts at absolving his aides, followed by attempts at explaining away their involvement, weakened his base of support for this personal apology. Additionally, with the coming of a summer-long television fare of Watergate hearings, Nixon's choice of a press release no doubt reached fewer Americans than would have a television address. Lacking such a broadcast, most of the public had last seen him in an attempt to explain away his attempts to absolve his aides' involvement, and only the diligent readers in the public could have clearly understood the nature of this personal defense. Beyond this, the printed medium is a strangely impersonal way to introduce a personal defense. Finally, we believe that the denial portion of Nixon's appeal was nonspecific, failing to present concrete reasons to believe in his innocence. With the public's receding levels of diffuse support sapping both his personal and ideological legitimacy, he needed to provide more specific backing for his denials.

In the ensuing months, the televiewing public saw numerous witnesses paraded before the Ervin Committee. As the hearings proceeded, two issues became important and distinct: the involvement of the President in the Watergate incident and attempted cover-up, and a more general issue of the manner in which Nixon executed his office. The former increased the assault upon personal and ideological support sentiments, while the latter presented a direct challenge to his right to maintain the powers inherent in his office.

The witness most damaging to the President on the first issue was John Dean. His testimony, more than any other, directly linked the President to the Watergate cover-up.[42] Not only did Dean suggest Nixon's culpability, potentially undermining both the President's honesty and his law and order image, but he also talked openly of Nixon's lies to the public, an even stronger challenge to personal legitimacy. Following Dean's testimony, Gallup reported an additional five-point erosion in support.[43] In addition to these charges, the hearings suggested that Nixon had offered clemency to the Watergate burglars,[44] that he had attempted to use the Internal Revenue Service against political opponents,[45] and that he had authorized the payment of hush money to Watergate defendants.[46]

Added to all these charges was Alexander Butterfield's revelation that Nixon had a taped record of most all matters discussed in the executive offices of the President.[47] Nixon's refusal to release the tapes to the Ervin Committee met with clear public disapproval: Gallup recorded only 23 percent approval of Nixon's refusal and a full 67 percent disapproval.[48]

So, when Nixon spoke to the nation on August 15, his "popularity had plunged to the lowest rating given any American president in 20 years."[49] For many, Nixon was not living up to his professed ideology and he appeared to have been less than honest with them in earlier statements. Additionally, a significant minority, voicing a preference for impeachment, was beginning seriously to challenge his right to maintain his structural powers. The August 15 apology was thus an extremely important speech for the President.

The address Nixon presented to America that evening was far more complex than his earlier statements and speeches. Within the same speech he assumed two separate postures and handled each posture in a distinct manner. Regarding the issue of Watergate itself, Nixon continued his absolutive posture: he denied that he had any part in illegal activities either before or after the break-in and differentiated what he had indeed done from that which he had not. Although Nixon accepted responsibility because "the abuses occurred during my Administration and in the campaign for my re-election,"[50] he drew a distinction between accepting responsibility and admitting personal involvement: "I had no prior knowledge of the Watergate break-in; I neither authorized nor encouraged subordinates to engage in illegal or improper campaign tactics."[51] He backed this denial with his own assertions of what had taken place at several key meetings with his aides during 1972 and 1973. These brief statements, coupled with his expanded explanation, constituted the denial portion of the speech.

An attempt at differentiation immediately followed the denial. In this portion of the address, Nixon tried to indicate that his failure to find the cover-up and act upon it was due to his being misled by trusted aides: "Because I believed the reports I was getting, I did not believe the newspaper accounts that suggested a coverup. I was convinced that there was no coverup, because I was convinced that no one had anything to cover up.''[52]

The second major posture in the address, a justification of his general conduct of the Presidency, began with Nixon's discussion of problems associated with releasing the White House tapes. The President addressed the issue from the standpoint of protecting the integrity and efficient operation of the executive office. As such, he was bolstering his position. The strategy seems to have been to indicate that he could prove his innocence by using the tapes, but that protection of the Presidency was a more important goal. "The principle of confidentiality of Presidential conversations," he said, "is at stake in the question of these tapes. I must and I shall oppose any efforts to destroy this principle, which is so vital to the conduct of this great office.''[53]

Nixon also bolstered his position by expressing his contempt for the sorts of abuses alleged to have occurred in the 1972 campaign. Having previously denied any involvement in them, he promised that he would lead the drive to assure that such events could not recur: "I pledge to you tonight that I will do all that I can to insure that one of the results of Watergate is a new level of political decency and integrity in America.''[54]

Finally, Nixon employed national security as a third means of bolstering the public's conception of his Presidential image. He admitted that some abuses had taken place in the name of national security, but at once suggested the importance of national security and the importance of avoiding excesses in the future: "It is essential that such mistakes not be repeated. But it is also essential that we do not overreact to particular mistakes by tying the President's hands in a way that would risk sacrificing our security, and with it all our liberties.''[55] It is important to notice that Nixon, when speaking of past abuses, attempted to maintain a proper distance by speaking of the culprits in the third person: "abuses resulted from the assumption by those involved.''[56]

The final segment of the address is the transcendence portion of his posture of justification. Nixon turned from the charges against him and, in almost chiding fashion, asked the nation to put Watergate behind them. Vitally needed domestic legislation was going unattended and critical national negotiations were taking place. "These are matters," Nixon told the nation, "that cannot wait. They cry out for action now.''[57] Nixon tried to transcend the Watergate question entirely by portraying himself as the guardian of the public interest and casting his accusers as in pursuit of a small matter at the expense of vital political business. This final section of the August apology seeks to cast an image of a man fit to retain the public trust and the powers of his office. Nixon intended to fulfill the mission of his office, he was assuring the public, despite the petty charges against his personal integrity.

Although Nixon did register a slight temporary improvement in his job rating after the August 15 address, [58] the public remained dissatisfied with his explanation regarding Watergate. This feeling was widespread among Americans, with only two of the 36 Gallup subgroups—Republicans and farmers—failing to show majority disapproval of Nixon's explanation.[59] That the impact of the speech was only temporary is made clear by the next opinion poll, taken in early September: the newly gained support had already slipped by four percentage points, and disapproval had risen back to 56 percent.[60]

Apparently Nixon assumed the August 15 audience would find him more believable than they actually did. He still spoke *ex cathedra* rather than carefully justifying his actions regarding the general conduct of the Presidency. He seemed to believe that he could draw upon structural legitimacy to convince the public that he was innocent, merely because the President proclaimed his own innocence. The polls show that Nixon had long passed the point where such an expression of innocence would prove effective. His personal legitimacy was so low that he needed to offer detailed, and, if possible, objective support for his claims. Nixon's proof consisted largely, if not entirely, of broad assertions followed by a sometimes specific, but personally recollected, detailing of reasons for his claims. The constituency could easily recall that many of Nixon's past claims, based equally upon personal assertion, had been proven incorrect as time passed.

The first issue of the August speech, personal honesty, dictated that Nixon assume an absolutive posture. The second issue, the conduct of the Presidency, carried no such constraint and Nixon shifted to a justificative stance. The charges before the public did not call for an understanding of Nixon's reasons for shielding the tapes from investigative scrutiny. They were, rather, charges that he had consistently abused the privileges of his office to protect himself and to damage his opponents. Nixon's justificative posture on the second issue forced him to remain silent on the central question of guilt or innocence, as it assumed that no one really believed he was guilty of the charges.

Postscript to Failure

Alexander Butterfield opened a hornet's nest when he revealed the existence of the Presidential tapes. Clearly, they had been available all along and Nixon had failed to make them publicly known. This secretive handling cast suspicion upon the contents of the tapes. Nixon again failed to project the image of a strong political actor. He tried to shelter all the tapes under the cloak of executive privilege and national security, both of which had proven to be ineffective appeals throughout much of the Watergate morass. His image in handling the tapes was consonant with his image throughout the entire 1973 period: the Watergate apologia was delivered from a "back-to-the-wall" position. Instead of controlling the scene he constantly let himself get pushed against the wall on all leading issues. Always yielding to the inevitable, he lacked a vital sense of timing and was unable to turn the situation around to create an impression that he was generating the action of the moment. The Nixon decision to withhold the tapes was counted by Gallup as an extremely unpopular one. A large segment of the public must have assumed that the President was guilty and that he was simply engaged in a strategy of buying time.

The final act of the Watergate story as it unfolded in 1973 was the firing of his special investigator, Archibald Cox. Quite ironically, the only time Nixon acted decisively on the Watergate question he fired an investigator rather than a participant. The furor of the Cox firing was considerable and the President announced that he would address the nation. Unfortunately, the Middle East crisis caused a cancellation of the address. He answered a few questions regarding the matter at a news conference, but said little that significantly extended or changed his Watergate apology for the year.

Conclusion

The theatrical component of political leadership is the establishment of a rhetorical persona, the interactive construction by politicians and their constituents of a public symbol embodying an individual's claim to political authority. Apologia, the personal defense by an individual of his own character, is that form of discourse which provides for the maintenance of such personae when they come under attack. Political questions of authority uniquely demand that the authority under attack maintain his public image along personal, ideological, and structural lines of legitimacy. Political research indicates the extent to which these sources of support interact in complex ways. Personal legitimacy is most basically grounded in perceived honesty, largely a moral perception of the rhetor drawn by the public. In the case of Richard Nixon, as with many other political figures, the direct relationship between these judgments and judgments regarding ideological legitimacy are closely intermixed. Perhaps the most bitter irony of the Nixon defense was the extent to which his perceived personal behavior seriously undermined the public's willingness to truly believe that he acted in consonance with his oft-pronounced ideological mask.

Judged instrumentally, Nixon's rhetorical efforts concerning Wategate in 1973 clearly constitute an instance when political apology failed. His enormous backlog of diffuse support dissipated almost entirely in the course of one short year.[61] Our analysis has led us to the following major conclusions as to why Nixon's apology failed.

Nixon was never in control. He never created an image of the strong and independent leader acting upon the scene. The situation called for the President to make full use of the high degree of ideological legitimacy he possessed as a means of strengthening his personal legitimacy. Instead, he began his public handling of Watergate by tying himself inexorably to his aides, risking both his tenuous personal legitimacy and his ideological image.

When his personal legitimacy failed, Nixon erroneously thought that he could hide behind structural legitimacy and continued to believe that he could gain belief through broad personal assertions. Sigel's dictum that the public places limits upon acceptable presidential actions seems important here. Nixon often found himself using structural appeals to justify actions which the public clearly disapproved. Further, the public has made it clear that their chief requisite for an officeholder is honesty. The New Nixon image had been carefully constructed, but he failed to appreciate how quickly the image could fade-out and be replaced by the "Tricky Dick" label. Nixon consistently failed to project the needed image of openness, honesty, and forthrightness. The President eventually assumed his best available apologetic posture—absolution—but he did so only when forced into it. Even then he confused his denials by attempting to appeal in too many directions at once, relying additionally upon structural transcendence to unpopular national security and executive privilege appeals.

After the first phase of Watergate, because of reduced believability, Nixon needed backing for his assertions, but he never offered any because he could not. His knowledge of the facts caused him to perceive constraints, both real and imagined, which directed his attention to the unproductive strategies he chose. Overall, he seems to have taken the matter too lightly for too long. In so doing he produced a complex maze of strategic errors, indicating poor rhetorical judgment in managing both the sources of political legitimacy and the available apologetic postures.

Apologetic discourse involves a rhetor attempting to reconcile a derogatory charge with a favorable view of his character. If this rhetor is a political character he must maintain his persona along personal, ideological, and structural lines. The success of the political apology is largely governed by a skillful management of these legitimacy sources within the constraints of the strategic options in the apologetic genre. When the accused political rhetor ignores or fails to appreciate the dynamics of the legitimacy sources which produce his diffuse support, apology predictably fails.

Notes

1. Texts for all Nixon statements are available in *Weekly Compilation of Presidential Documents*. This source will hereafter be referred to as *Presidential Documents*. The text for the first substantive treatment of Watergate by Nixon during 1973 can be found in *Presidential Documents*, 9 (March 5, 1973), 219–220. The President had briefly dealt with Watergate related questions in three news conferences the year prior: June 22, August 29, and October 5, 1972; but it was not until the spring of 1973 that the Watergate matter reached proportions that required the President to assume a personal apologetic stance.
2. Examples of criticism in the apologetic genre include James H. Jackson, "Clarence Darrow's 'Plea in Defense of Himself,'" *Western Speech*, 20 (1956), 185–95; L. W. Rosenfield, "A Case Study in Speech Criticism: The Nixon-Truman Analog," *Speech Monographs*, 35 (1968), 435–50; Wil A. Linkugel and Nancy Razak, "Sam Houston's Speech of Self-Defense in the House of Representatives," *Southern Speech Journal*, 34 (1969), 263–75; Bower Aly, "The Gallows Speech: A Lost Genre," *Southern Speech Journal*, 34 (1969), 204–13; David A. Ling, "A Pentadic Analysis of Senator Edward Kennedy's Address to the People of Massachusetts, July 25, 1969," *Central States Speech Journal*, 21 (1970), 81–86; Sherry Devereaux Butler, "The Apologia, 1971 Genre," *Southern Speech Communication Journal*, 36 (1972), 281–89; and B. L. Ware and Wil A. Linkugel, "They Spoke in Defense of Themselves: On the Generic Criticism of Apologia," *QJS*, 59 (1973), 273–83.
3. Apologetic discourse, like all other discourse, is influenced by factors other than its instrumental, verbal aspects. Though nonverbal behavior by the apologist, as well as matters not directly derived from his presentation, may influence the outcome of his appeals, the theory of apology is most directly concerned with the messages which the rhetor constructs and implements. This study is limited, therefore, to an analysis and evaluation of Nixon's statements within the limitation of the theoretical superstructure from which it flows.
4. This definition of apology is taken from Ware and Linkugel, p. 274. Two addresses Nixon delivered in 1974 can also readily be classified as apologia. However, for reasons cited in the article, we are limiting ourselves to his 1973 addresses.
5. Certain of Nixon's actions, obviously, led some of the public and some members of Congress to infer Nixon's guilt during 1973. However, the Gallup surveys noted below indicate that the impact of these actions did not become widespread until most of the 1973 apologies had concluded. An analysis of the earlier Gallup surveys suggest that those drawing the early "guilty" inference may have largely been predisposed against Nixon. For the most part, therefore, we conclude that the public was lacking the conclusive, documentary evidence which emerged in 1974.
6. The critical response presented in this study is based upon an investigation into Nixon's instrumental use of communication. It concerns the strategies Nixon employed in pursuit of his goal of clearing his name and image. The question of morality is both interesting and important, particularly given the revelations during the final days of the Nixon Presidency, but it is not a question of central concern to this study. Our concern is with the Nixon statements of 1973, long before the public had the opportunity to judge his morality on any but a speculative, or at best inferential, basis.
7. David Easton, *A System Analysis of Political Life* (New York: John Wiley, 1965), p. 159.

8. Ibid., p. 249.
9. Ibid., p. 278.
10. "Image of the American Presidency—Part II of An Exploration into Popular Views of Presidential Power," *Midwest Journal of Political Science,* 10 (1966), 123. Notice should be taken that in all but three of the years since 1952 the Gallup organization discovered that the president was the man most admired by Americans and that in two of the remaining years a former president was named.
11. Ibid., pp. 123–124.
12. "The Polls: Presidential Power," *Public Opinion Quarterly,* 37 (1973), 488.
13. Sigel, p. 127.
14. Easton, p. 289.
15. *The Making of the President 1972* (New York: Bantam Books, 1973), pp. 291–92.
16. On the specific issue of law and order, which Nixon had attempted to broaden, the public still felt a great deal of concern for the public safety. Even though crime rates had continued to rise in the major cities during the first Nixon Administration, the people still identified him as the candidate who would try hardest to enforce the rule of law. The Gallup organization, in November of 1972, summarized the impact of this part of the "Americanism" ideology in the minds of the public: "Of the two candidates of the major parties, voters thought that President Nixon could deal with this problem of crime and lawlessness far better than Sen. McGovern. Blue collar workers who have traditionally cast their ballots for democratic presidential candidates, by the ratio of 46% to 30% in an October survey, held this view, which is perhaps the most important reason for their high rate of defection," The *Gallup Opinion Index,* No. 89 (November 1972), p. 5.
17. Ibid.
18. Sigel, p. 130.
19. Ibid., p. 131.
20. Each of these, taken individually, indicate the derivation of specific support; taken collectively, however, they draw a picture of a man effectively executing his office and thus indicate the derivation of diffuse support.
21. White, p. 459.
22. *Gallup,* No. 83 (May 1972), pp. 23–24.
23. The term "rhetorical persona" is employed here in a sense somewhat different than the concept of "personae" as used elsewhere in critical literature. See Robert Langbaum, "The Mysteries of Identity: A Theme in Modern Literature," *The American Scholar,* 34 (1965), 569–86. Interesting treatments of the concept of persona in rhetorical theory and criticism are found in Edwin Black, "The Second Persona," *QJS,* 56 (1970), 109–19; and Paul Newell Campbell, *Rhetoric-Ritual* (Belmont, California: Dickenson, 1972), 258–69.
24. Black, p. 111.
25. Langbaum, p. 576.
26. Ware and Linkugel, pp. 282–83.
27. *Presidential Documents,* 8 (October 9, 1972), 1489.
28. Ibid., 8 (September 4, 1972), 1306.
29. Ibid., 9 (March 19, 1973), 253.
30. Ibid.
31. Ibid.
32. Ibid.
33. *Gallup,* No. 95 (May 1973), p. 2.
34. Ibid.
35. *Presidential Documents,* 9 (May 7, 1973), 431.

36. Ibid., pp. 433–38.
37. Ibid., p. 433.
38. *Gallup,* No. 95 (May 1973), 9–10.
39. Ibid., p 11.
40. *Presidential Documents,* 9 (May 28, 1973), 696.
41. Ibid.
42. *The Watergate Hearings: Break-in and Cover-up,* ed. New York Times Staff (New York: Bantam Books, 1973), pp. 307–08.
43. *Gallup,* No. 97 (July 1973), p. 1.
44. *Watergate Hearings,* p 149.
45. Ibid., p. 355.
46. Ibid., pp. 470–72, 480.
47. Ibid., pp. 434–43.
48. *Gallup,* No. 98 (August 1973), p. 5.
49. *Gallup,* No. 99 (September 1973), p. 1.
50. *Presidential Documents,* 9 (August 20, 1973), 985.
51. Ibid.
52. Ibid., p. 986.
53. Ibid., p. 988.
54. Ibid., 989.
55. Ibid.
56. Ibid., 990.
57. Ibid.
58. *Gallup,* No. 99 (September 1973), p. 4. Gallup reported that approval of Nixon's handling of the Presidency rose from 31 percent to 38 percent, and disapproval fell from 57 percent to 54 percent.
59. Ibid., p. 9.
60. Ibid., No. 100 (October 1973), p. 8.
61. Ibid., No. 102 (December 1973), p. 3, registered Nixon's job rating at the beginning of December at 31 percent approval and 59 percent disapproval. This is a complete reversal of the 59 percent approval and 30 percent disapproval recorded exactly one year earlier, as reported in the January 1973 *Index,* and compares even more unfavorably with the job rating of 68 percent approval and 25 percent disapproval recorded by Gallup in January 1973, as reported in the February *Index.*

GERALD R. FORD

Ford's War on Inflation: A Metaphor That Did Not Cross

Hermann G. Stelzner

On August 28, 1974, nineteen days after assuming the Presidency, Gerald Ford held his first press conference and centered his attention on three domestic problems, unemployment, then less than six per cent, energy, and inflation. Forecasting an undefined future, Ford said about the first, "We won't have high unemployment. We'll have ample job opportunities."[1] The second problem had to be met two ways. The "consumer industrial nations" would have to act together to keep the costs of energy, especially the price of oil, within reason, and the United States would have to "accelerate every aspect of Project Independence."

The third domestic problem Ford made strikingly visible, imposing meaning via an explicit hierarchial structure. Inflation, he said, was "Public Enemy No. 1" and the nation had "to win the battle against inflation." Although the three domestic problems were interrelated, if inflation were controlled, "and I think we're going to have a good program, most of our other domestic programs or problems will be solved." As might be expected Ford did not elaborate in his first press conference how the battle against inflation would be fought or how winning it would solve the other problems. He did say that "wage and price controls are out, period," indicating that inflation could be controlled without resorting to an ultimate political weapon and indicating that business and labor were not causes of the problem, but allies in the effort to overcome it. Given the seriousness of the problem and the thrust of the metaphor and anxious to head off divisiveness about his future policies, Ford sought unity: "I don't think making partisan politics out of a serious domestic problem is good politics." With the inflation spiral then in double digits, Ford promised to cut the Federal budget and asked "every wage earner . . . to follow the example of their Federal Government which is going to tighten its belt. And, likewise, for an interim period of time, watch every penny."

For the next five months Ford consistently used the war metaphor in public statements[2] as a way of making comprehensible what was happening.[3] But if the war metaphor appeared suddenly in August 1974, it disappeared equally as suddenly with the beginning of the New Year. In his "State of the Union" address to Congress on January 15, 1975, Ford reported on the progress of

Mr. Stelzner is Professor of Communication Studies at the University of Massachusetts.
Reprinted by permission from *Communication Monographs* Vol. 44, No. 4 (November 1977), pp. 284–297.

the war and said bluntly, "I must say to you that the State of the Union is not good." And he added, "I've got bad news, and I don't expect much, if any, applause." The interrelated problems of unemployment, energy, and inflation were still troublesome, but the President announced that "The moment has come to move in a new direction," signalling a reordering of the hierarchial structure announced in the first news conference: "The emphasis on our economic efforts must now shift from inflation to jobs."[4] The shift in emphasis also signalled the end of the war metaphor as Ford's means of stimulating public and Congressional concern and support. War imagery does not appear in the January 15, 1975 "State of the Union" address and during 1975 was not employed consistently to probe, define, and amplify the domestic difficulties.

Although Ford's shift in emphasis in January 1975 from inflation to unemployment made further use of war imagery categorically inappropriate, his effort to make the metaphor of war salient and dominant between August 1974 and January 1975 was also less than satisfactory. Its failure as a rhetorical resource can be explained in these terms. (1) Appearing as it did closely upon the end of the Vietnam conflict, it asked a public tired of and strained by war language to accept a war metaphor as a valid interpretation of domestic difficulties, especially inflation. Though concerned about inflation, unemployment, and energy, the public resisted Ford's association of ideas. This proposition is difficult to demonstrate (at least, I have been unable to achieve it to my satisfaction), and it remains an assertion, only indirectly supported by the two following propositions. (2) In the popular press and from public platforms, analysts both agreed and disagreed with Ford's analysis and exposition of the problem of inflation. That was surely to be expected, but often they presented their views in imagery which undercut Ford's effort to make the war metaphor dominant and salient. This proposition, too, is difficult to demonstrate directly but images which compete for a public's attention and understanding obviously make cohesion and salience more difficult. Because this proposition is not the central concern of this essay, only a few illustrations of Ford's competition are provided. (3) The central proposition of this essay is that a major reason for the war metaphor's failure to cross to its public and to be accepted by its public lies not in Ford's lack of personal commitment to it, but in his inability to "work it." Though inflation was the clearly designated enemy, Ford could not portray the severity of the crisis and did not propose short term, precise, realistic incentives for engaging the enemy. Within the framework of the war metaphor, Ford stressed volunteerism as the basic approach to inflation, the enemy, but without enforcement the approach lacked certainty and strength. In short, Ford's metaphor of war served only to define a crisis in the American character, and this definition simply did not guarantee the authenticity of the metaphor.

The first section of this essay examines Ford's public efforts to make the metaphor of war dominant and salient, an approach which might loosely be termed "from the inside to the outside." In the second section the approach is "from the outside to the inside," an examination of selected alternatives to Ford's efforts. This division is arbitrary and brittle, but it sharply reflects the efforts of the participants, and sharply juxtaposes images, making possible sharp distinctions.

I

If Ford was content to label inflation "Public Enemy No. 1" at his first press conference, he used the first formal occasion after assuming the Presidency to develop his metaphor and to shape and color it for future use. On September 6, 1974 he spoke in Philadelphia at a dinner honoring the reconvening of the First Continental Congress. The time and place provided examples and comparisons yielding emotional resonances.[5] Using history as his touchstone, Ford described the Then: "I am glad that this period of national rededication, which will extend to July 4, 1976, begins on this almost forgotten date, when the colonial delegates wrestled with their common problems of skyrocketing prices, shrinking purchasing power, shortages, hoarding, and financial speculation." The delegates, described in language consistent with the demands of the scene, previewed Ford's emphasis upon voluntary participation: The "men and women of 1774 were inflation fighters before they took up arms against the British redcoats. Actually, they met voluntarily to wage economic warfare for their future freedom and prosperity, even before the Liberty Bell tolled the birth of a new nation."

No great skill was required to superimpose the resonances of the Then upon the Now, and making the argument via the imagery. The times were similar: In 1774 a sense of "urgency and unity" existed in Philadelphia and there "is the same sense of urgency and unity in America today." So, too, were the men: "In short, the inflation fighters of 1774 were not much different from the inflation fighters of 1974 who started a series of conferences in Washington [the Economic Summit] yesterday." Ford offered an explanation of the similarities between the times and men, but dissimilar causes for them. Whereas early in the address he had stated that the colonial delegates met voluntarily to confront their internal domestic difficulties, he now provided an external agent as their perceived enemy: In 1774 the people were animated by "the tyranny of the British Parliament and Crown" and today the "common enemy" is "the tyranny of double-digit inflation" which "is the cruelest kind of taxation without representation."

Employing clear, crisp, militaristic images, Ford concluded the Now: The internal enemy was isolated. The people were united. The government was committed and energetic. Victory was less than two years distant. Yet because caution and deliberateness were also key terms, tone was tempered:

> I have decided that the first priority for us as a Nation, domestically, is an all-out war against inflation. Like the patriots who met here 200 years ago, we may seem to be moving cautiously and too deliberately. But I hope no one will underestimate the generalship or fighting ability of all Americans today the same way they did in 1774. . . . We are going after, one and all, Democrats and Republicans, we are going after what I term public enemy number one, inflation, in 1974, and we will lick it by July 4, 1976.

To a joint session of Congress on October 8, 1974, Ford delivered a nationally televised address[6] about the economy which opened with testimony from Roosevelt's first inaugural: "The people of the United States have not failed. They want direct, vigorous action, and they have asked for discipline and direction. . . ."[7] Further, said Ford, the Congress responded to Roosevelt's "appeal in five days." In his effort to confront the Depression, Roosevelt early did three things which Ford, whatever the reasons, did not do. First, he obviously did not fault the citizenry for the situation beyond their control. Second, he named an enemy, the business community. Third, he willingly committed the resources of the Government to the problem. Ford admitted that "our economic difficulties do not approach the emergency of 1933," but said that "the message from the American people" was for "leadership" and "action." Tested against the problems of 1933, Ford's description of difficulties in 1974 was only relatively severe. And though Congress was soon to adjourn, he wanted it to act as it did in 1933. But the personal call for action was muted: "Today I will not take more of the time of this busy Congress, for I vividly remember the rush before every recess, and the clock is already running on my specific and urgent requests for legislation."

The wide ranging address to Congress contained ten proposals[8] only two of which are central to this essay. The problem of energy Ford coupled to the problem of inflation and though the former was less important than the latter, discussion of it was also developed in militaristic overtones. For example, Rogers Morton, Secretary of the Interior, was named "the over-all boss of our national energy program" and his "marching orders are to reduce imports of foreign oil by one million barrels a day by the end of 1975. . . ." Further, to create new sources of energy, Ford indicated that he would "use the Defense Production Act to allocate scarce materials for energy development." Thus, a peace time policy was proposed in the language of war-time legislation.

Ford's fifth area of concern, a "very important part of the overall speech," was the unemployed, the "casualties" of inflation who "are jobless through no fault of their own." Assuming this matter to be important, one must wonder why it was fifth among ten concerns; rhetorically the middle in a list of ten is not the most visible place for a "very important" matter.

Ford reported to Congress that in mid-September he had released funds to provide "public service employment for some 170,000 who need work." Further he asked Congress "to augment this action" with a "two-step program": To provide thirteen weeks of special unemployment insurance benefits to those workers whose regular benefits were exhausted, and twenty-six weeks of special unemployment insurance to those who qualified but were not covered by regular unemployment insurance programs. The second step asked Congress to "create a brand new community improvement corps" and support "short-term useful work projects" which would "improve, beautify, and enhance the environment of our cities, our towns and our countryside." This "stand-by program" would become effective whenever unemployment exceeded "6 percent nationally" and "stopped when unemployment" dropped "below 6 percent." Ford's "formula" for this concern revealed his evaluation of its severity. Because "short-term problems require short-term remedies, I therefore request that these programs be for a one-year period."

The term, recession, does not appear in the message to Congress, and on the following day Ford held a press conference.[9] The very first question put to him addressed "a few things . . . left unsaid in your economic message yesterday. I was wondering if you could say now if the United States is in a recession. . . ." Ford's reply: "I do not think the United States is in a recession. We do have economic problems, but it's a very mixed situation." Five weeks after the news conference, and a week after the November elections the mixed situation took on a firmer form. Ron Nessen, Ford's press secretary, announced publicly that the year-long decline in the economy had reached serious proportions, and "it would appear that this month we are moving into a recession," the first time the White House used that term.[10] Thus, by the time of Ford's "State of the Union" address in January 1975, both the people and the government had perceived the dimensions of this new problem and Ford's anticlimactic personal announcement of it was too late to sustain an image of vigorous and active leadership.

In his message to Congress Ford had suggestions for the people and they all stressed volunteerism, e.g., "To help save scarce fuel in the energy crisis, drive less, heat less."[11] To help "increase food and lower prices, grow more and waste less." Voluntary restraint "will strengthen our spirit as well as our economy." To give shape and thrust to the collective voluntary effort Ford announced that he had asked Sylvia Porter, "the well-known financial writer, to help me organize an all-out nationwide volunteer mobilization." And he had "enlisted the enthusiastic support and services of some 17 other distinguished Americans to help plan for citizen and private group participation." To give visibility to the effort and to engage the people in it, Ford displayed "a symbol of this new mobilization which I am wearing on my lapel. It bears the single word, Win."[12] He also announced that a "simple enlistment form" would appear in newspapers through "the courtesy" of "volunteers from the communication and media field."[13] Mobilization would go forward but there would be "no big Federal bureaucracy set up for this crash program."

Although inflation was clearly Ford's primary concern, none of his ten proposals, which both "the executive and legislative branches of government" must address, stood a chance "unless they are combined in a considered package, in a concerted effort, in a grand design."

The substance of the considered package, concerted effort, and grand design was synonymous with the substance of an equally considered image, emphasizing the need for collective effort, a "total" and "massive mobilization," said Ford, the grand design for which was the metaphor of war. To engage the Congressional and national audience with the substance of the packaged metaphor, Ford indicated that in other times of crisis presidents addressed Congress and a few had even "truly inspired the most skeptical and the most sophisticated audience of their coequal partners in government." He didn't "expect this one to be" such a session because his referent for such occasions was World Wars I and II when the enemy was external and conflict a fact. The interpretation is suggested by Ford's illustration: "Only two of my predecessors have come in person to call upon Congress for a declaration of war." An enigmatic statement then appeared: "And I shall not do that." Ford didn't distinguish between the literal and metaphorical. Congress and the people would have been shocked had he literally declared war. Despite the momentary confusion, the metaphor was central to Ford's grand design and he had to reintroduce it and rebuild it quickly so that it would sustain a reality, the identification of inflation with a "well-armed war-time enemy" which would destroy "liberty" and "national pride." Having named the enemy, Congress and the people had "to intercept" it. The time to "enlist" was "now":

> But I say to you with all sincerity that our inflation, our Public Enemy No. 1, will, unless whipped, destroy our country, our homes, our liberty, our property and finally our national pride as surely as any well-armed wartime enemy.
>
> I concede there will be no sudden Pearl Harbor to shock us into unity and to sacrifice but I think we've had enough early warning. The time to intercept is right now. The time to intercept is almost gone.
>
> My friends and former colleagues, will you enlist now? My friends and fellow Americans, will you enlist now?
>
> Together, with discipline and determination, we will win.

In his message to Congress, Ford announced that on October 15, 1974, he would be in Kansas City, Missouri, to address the "Future Farmers of America, a fine organization of wonderful young people whose help with millions of others is vital in the battle." Because the Kansas City address was also televised nationally, the metaphor, embodying the policy, would again be circulated.[14]

Because the people were ahead of the Congress in recognizing the need for action, they were responding: "A great citizens' mobilization has begun and is beginning to roll," and is "already evident here in this eager, up-beat convention. . . ." In the war against inflation, "farmers are the front line soldiers." During the last week Ford had received "inflation fighter enlistments from Americans of every conceivable occupation, economic circumstances, and political persuasion." In the audience before him, he did not see anyone "wearing a button that says 'lose' "[15] The people, unlike the Congress, said Ford, "are hungry for some tough stuff to chew on. . . ." The Congress hadn't "shown much appetite," for example, for his proposal "to postpone for three months a pay increase for Federal Government employees which would have saved $700 million." If Congress wouldn't act, "I may be back with some tough turkey." Congress, apparently, was only concerned, not yet having developed a sense of crisis and not yet having been enveloped by the war metaphor.

For the Future Farmers of America, Ford sketched in some details of the Citizens' Action Committee to Fight Inflation chaired by Sylvia Porter.[16] He had met with twenty-two members just prior to his appearance in Missouri and of course their concern "greatly impressed" him. The Committee, he announced, had "elected four co-chairmen," only one of whom, Frank Stanton, president of the National Red Cross, had national visibility.

Ford emphasized that the group was "a volunteer working committee, a completely non-partisan group dealing with a non-partisan problem," seeking "to mobilize America against inflation and for energy conservation." Further, he told the group that if it "seemed to be merely a front for the White House, it would be doomed to failure." Sylvia Porter, said Ford, responded that if he "tried to manipulate the committee or seek to influence its actions, she and the other members would not participate. We understand each other."[17] But the volunteerism, neutrality, and objectivity do not square easily with the need for leadership and direction from the White House in the face of inflation, "national enemy number one."

Ford' specific suggestions to the national and immediate audiences were largely restatements of suggestions contained in his message to Congress, modified and amplified by the Citizens' Action Committee to Fight Inflation. Many had roots either in the depression or in World War II. For example, Committee recommendation three was "to save as much as you can and watch your money grow. . . ." An example was provided by the Frank Tennants of Climax, Michigan, who reported "they do not use credit cards. They put something in their credit union each week and buy a Government bond every month. They should be applauded." And Ford reported: "I have asked the

Treasury Department to look at the possibility of issuing a new series of WIN Bonds. . . ." Committee recommendation number nine was "do it yourself;" examples were supplied: "Plant WIN gardens for yourself or within your community. Pool other do-it-yourself skills, and you can."

Committee recommendation five called upon business and labor "not to raise prices or wages more than costs or services absolutely require."[18] This "complex subject," said Ford, "cannot be handled on a nationwide basis," though such costs and services ultimately affected all the people. Ford suggested the problem be handled locally. In every community "local citizen action committees" would "interpret this recommendation, set realistic goals . . . and . . . report by Thanksgiving—just six weeks away—which plants, which stores, or other enterprises are doing the best job of holding the line in their community on costs and on prices." There was absolutely no recognition of the complexities of such a task, but there was assurance that it could be performed and evaluated.[19] To those local citizens' groups which did a good job "I will . . . award WIN flags . . . as public recognition of their contribution to the fight on inflation."[20]

In his conclusion Ford emphasized that the battle against inflation defined a crisis in the American character and apparently both the battle and the character could be won only if the people recognized that *they were the enemy*:[21]

> With your help, each new day will bring more good news than bad news for our economy. Yes, there will be some setbacks. We will not be out of the economic trenches by Christmas, but I remind you, if I might, of just one fact: Every battle in history has been won by the side that held on for just five minutes longer. Our enemy in this battle has been called inflation. But perhaps Pogo was wiser when he said, 'I have met the enemy and he is us.'

II

Having set the terms through which to perceive and around which to organize responses to the problem of inflation, Ford obviously hoped that the metaphor would cross to its publics. Though there is no sure test of the proposition, a look at selected responses furnishes reasonable inferences about its ability to form and inform public perceptions, to make them congruent with the thrust of Ford's messages.

The covers of popular journals impinge upon and influence public perceptions simply because they are among the first things seen. Ford's war metaphor did not dominate those covers which said something about economic conditions. For example, the September 30, 1974 issue of *Newsweek* directed its readers to an internal story emphasizing economics: "Special Economic Report: What to Do?" which was supported by a visual message, a dollar bill with Ford's, not Washington's, portrait center forefront. Ford, eyes closed, left hand on brow, lips slightly parted and tense, was, if not worried, reflective.[22] The tonalities of this cover message did not reflect those in Ford's first press conference or his address in Philadelphia on September 6. Shortly after the November elections which returned Democrats to Congress in large numbers, *Newsweek*, November 18, 1974, again emphasized economic conditions, asking on its cover "What Do We Do Now?" and personified the donkey, placing a large red WIN button on its lapel and raising its left arm so that its hand could scratch a furrowed brow. *Time's* cover of October 14, 1974 presented Ford as a pugilist, feet firmly planted, left fist clenched, right hand on left bicep testing the muscle, left sleeve rolled up, and determined facial features. The verbal caption: "Trying to Fight Back, Inflation, Recession, Oil." *Time* thus added to Ford's fight, recession, a problem his metaphor was not designed to absorb. Far in advance of Ford, *Business Week*, November 9, 1974, recognized and portrayed the developing problem of serious unemployment, carrying on its cover a photo of men and women in an unemployment or welfare office and captioning the visual, "Unemployment becomes an explosive issue: The Jobless vs Inflation." The cover of *Business Week*, December 7, 1974 (is the date ironic or symbolic?) featured a large red balloon being squeezed in a closing vise; its caption: "The Modern Paradox: Fighting Inflation and Recession." Both *Business Week* covers suggested that Ford publicly recognize the problem of recession and act forcefully and urgently upon it. *Time*, December 9, 1974, featured on its cover a bedraggled and crest-fallen Santa Claus pulling into the holiday season a patched, tattered and empty bag; an oxymoron made the point, "Recession's Greetings." The week following Ford's "State of the Union" message, *Time's*, January 27, 1975, cover had Carl Albert and Ford wearing green surgical gowns. The latter's had a WIN button on its lapel, caring for an emaciated patient using less than precise political equipment, except for a standard governmental plasma bottle labelled with a dollar sign and containing green economic blood; the caption: "Doctoring the Economy: What Will Work"? In a variety of ways popular magazines failed to support and develop Ford's chosen imagery.[23]

On its October 10, 1974 cover *U. S. News and World Report* directed readers to a major essay asking: "Ford's War on Inflation: A Losing Battle?" and one assumes that the question would not have been put if the magazine's, as well as Ford's, public were united in the face of a common enemy. Others met Ford's imagery head-on and argued that if the metaphor correctly defined the problem, Ford's political recommendations were inadequate to it. In late September 1974, Pierre A. Rinfret wrote: "If we are going to mount a war on inflation, we should mount a war effort. A war requires war effort. It requires an all-out, dedicated effort to achieve victory. Half measures, partial measures, partial commitment and 'business as usual' have never won a war." Soon "stern and drastic measures" would have to be taken, he argued.[24] Responding to Ford's address to the Congress, *Time* adopted his war imagery to editorialize about his proposals, titling its lead economic essay, "Small Weapons for the Two-Front War."[25]

On November 7, 1974 Leo Greenland, Chief Executive Officer, Smith/ Greenland Company, Inc., spoke before the American Association of Advertising Agencies in Detroit. "Advertising 1975: Wartime Measures to Rally a Sick Nation," was the title of his address.[26] His judgment was that "1975 will find us wallowing in one of the worst economic crises in our history" and that wearing buttons saying " 'Whip Inflation Now' is like giving a teaspoon of castor oil to a whale with a stomach ache." Because he felt that the nation needed "wartime action to deal with a national emergency" Mr. Greenland offered four proposals, only three of which need be summarized here. Proposal two was to "appoint a new cabinet position—Secretary of Communications" who would "develop a program to tell the truth and help harness a positive and constructive program to help whip our country back into shape." This Cabinet Officer would develop messages to instruct citizens in "what we as a people have to do to survive," because the Administration "must treat the country as though we're at war." In his third proposal, Greenland argued that the "country . . . adapt the same thinking as that which existed during World War II." Having said that he required but a short jump to implement the metaphor: "I call for wartime mobilization. Not of armed forces, but of attitude and priorities." As examples of the latter he suggested that some old World War II slogans "Spitting in the Fuehrer's Face" be replaced by "kicking hell out of inflation." "Keep silent, the person next to you may be the enemy" could be replaced by "keep the dollar strong—and here's how." In Greenland's view the mobilization of attitudes and priorities needed to be supported by concrete legislative action; thus in proposal four he announced that the "Government should enforce the same kinds of emergency activities programmed for World War II. We had rationing, wartime production, air raid shelters and many other emergency activities set up in the national interest. Why not proceed on a similar basis?"

The September 9, 1974 cover of *US News and World Report* called attention to its lead essay on the economy with the metaphor of illness, "A Sick Economy," thereby offering competition to Ford's war metaphor. The *Newsweek* cover of November 18, 1974 announced its lead story, "The Economy— A Stronger RX," employing yet another image of illness and medicine. Earlier in the year *Newsweek* titled a lead story, "The World's Economic Ills: Any RX?"[27] Such imagery again is not unusual, but it does invite different perceptions of the problem. Only one example need be developed here.

Milton Friedman, one of twenty-eight economic authorities who attended the White House Summit Conference on Inflation in September 1974, was one of the few who stressed the need for tough curbs on inflation. "There is," he said, "one and only one way to cure the disease of inflation: slow down the rate of increase of total dollar spending. Only the Federal government can effect that cure." Friedman agreed with Ford that "wage and price controls are no part of the cure. On the contrary they are one of the most damaging parts of the disease." Because economic difficulties were complex, argued Friedman, care had to be taken to treat the disease as chronic but nonetheless manageable: "A more subtle program is how to devise sedatives to ease the painful side effects of the cure, which will include a temporary period of low growth and relatively heavy unemployment. These effects cannot be eliminated, but they can be greatly eased by sensible policies."[28]

Finally contributing to the undermining of Ford's war on inflation metaphor were commercial interests intent on stimulating the consumer to spend money. Many examples appear in print of the war metaphor, employed by Ford for a public end, turned to private gain. For example, The Coca-Cola Company offered a WIN, Whip Inflation Now, coupon for twenty-five cents on the purchase of TAB or Fresca, headlining the advertisement, "A Refreshing Way To Fight Inflation," and developing it: "For you, it's a great way to watch your budget and your calories at the same time. For both of us, it's a chance to do something about inflation."[29] Chrysler-Plymouth wanted people to look at the new Plymouth Valiant and urged them to "Come in for a Free Inflation Fighter Kit" which was "just loaded with money saving offers, coupons and discounts at leading merchants. . . ."[30] The acronym, WIN, and its referent, Whip Inflation NOW, announced a "special one week only" sale of cameras,[31] and a variant headline, "INFLATION KILLER," was the loss leader for a cook's apron in an ad for a chain of New York City gourmet centers.[32] The East New York Savings Bank announced "The Inflation Survival Kit (*it's crammed with good things* to celebrate the opening of our Oceanside office!)"[33] Examples like these could be multiplied ad infinitum. The commercial world used them to stimulate and provoke appetites. Ford's metaphor intended to restrain them. The commercial world diminished pain. Ford stated it was central to success. The commercial world offered immediate gratifications, Ford only long-range.

The examples and illustrations in Part II were selected from the public arena, the popular press and platform, and constitute less than an organized and unified collection. And they represent only a small sample of materials readily available to different publics. But together they represent images in direct conflict with Ford's dominant metaphor which, if it could not absorb them, had, at least, to reduce the distance and tensions between them.

III

How does one measure with precision the extent to which a public leader's dominant metaphor passes from him to his public and functions consistent with its originator's hopes, assuming that any metaphor in public discourse has at least two important ends: (1) to shape a reality which a public will accept as accurate, and (2) to compel a public to feel the accepted reality in the flesh? Ford, having set the terms through which to perceive the problem of inflation and around which to organize responses to it, must have believed that his dominant metaphor and the variant images which it spawned was negotiable. Yet despite Ford's intense personal commitment to the metaphor, it did not achieve the ends above, i.e., it did not cross, despite public concern with the issue the metaphor addressed.

One gross measure of any public's reaction is statistical, and polls in the fall of 1974 reflected dissatisfaction with the resolution of economic problems. "The business financed Conference Board, which polls 10,000 households on the economy every two months . . . finds consumer confidence at an alltime low," the index having "plummeted 30 per cent in September-October alone," reported *Time* in early December,[34] and in mid-December a University of Michigan Survey Research Center poll "showed consumer confidence at an index figure of 58.4 (1966 equals 100). That is down 13.6 points from May and is by far the lowest figure in 24 years the survey has been conducted."[35] A Gallup poll taken shortly after the November 5 elections reported that public approval of the way "President Ford has done his job . . . slipped to 47 per cent from 55 per cent in late October."[36] A Harris poll in December "indicated that 86 per cent of Americans surveyed had no confidence in the ability of the President to manage the economy."[37]

Although many variables determine why those polled responded as they did, the language of a President must be considered among the influential determinants, even if a precise weighting of degree cannot be measured.

In all of his public messages Ford consistently ruled out wage and price controls for labor and industry. He did not single either out for governmental action or public attention. That is he did not make either the metaphorical enemy on which the public might center its attention as a, if not the, major cause of the difficulties which it experienced. Ford certainly chose an enemy, inflation, but in his public discussions he also had to assign "cause" and he limited "cause" to government and consumer spending.

Government spending was undoubtedly a cause but it was also a political issue. Ford proposed modest cuts and promised no increases in the Federal budget, but the issue itself had to be negotiated with a Democratically controlled Congress, representing many conflicting views. In ordinary circumstances differences of opinion would in time be adjusted. Ford's metaphor made time (NOW!) extraordinary: But Congress still moved slowly, allowing Ford when he chose to blame it for the difficulties the people experienced, but also allowing his public to wonder about his assessment of urgency, assuming that Congress would not dally in the face of urgency. On the matter of government spending Ford would propose and Congress would dispose, each primarily according to its sense of political urgency as distinguished from the urgency demanded by the problem. Ford's metaphor, his association of ideas, should have obliterated that distinction. It failed.

During the fall of 1974, Ford was aware that his proposals for legislative action were limited and restrained, but he publicly applauded himself for his deliberateness and caution. When he spoke before the Business Council on December 11, 1974 he referred to the increasing problem of unemployment and established a tone for his future policies that was consistent with his past actions: "If there are any among you who want me to take a 180 degree turn from inflation fighting to recessionary pump priming, they will be disappointed."[38]

Critics of Ford who used the war metaphor to highlight the weaknesses in his war metaphor were in a minority, but their approach did provoke questions. If the situation was as serious as Ford proclaimed, why was not more risked? If the situation was not as serious as Ford's metaphor proclaimed, then the metaphor, the instrument of definition, was inaccurate and inappropriate to the economic reality, causing one to wonder what reality it did describe. Such analyses were rigid and severe, but they did place Ford in the excluded middle, between the polarities of an extreme war metaphor and no war metaphor. But if any metaphor demands an uncompromising position, a war metaphor surely qualified. Yet in no message did Ford ever publicly address the problem of inflation as Commander-in-Chief, an identification his chosen metaphor made possible. As President, Ford could choose to do much or nothing. He chose to do moderately, but when he chose the war metaphor the substance of the figure demanded much substantive action. Ford raised doubts about the integrity of his position which were intensified by his critics.

When Ford turned directly to his public and asked for it, via the metaphor, to center attention on the enemy, inflation, he had to provide those considering enlistment with some causes. The public learned (1) that it was largely responsible for the enemy's presence and (2) that to fight the enemy was to engage the self. Thus, the metaphor defined a crisis in the American character. Via the metaphor Ford urged the public to voluntarily organize itself to address itself. To war on the private self and the collective public self is not only demanding but downright unhealthy and dangerous. Still a citizenry might be willing, provided they sensed the complex issue of inflation was being addressed and acted on vigorously.

In the absence of clear evidence, the war on inflation could not be fought successfully from the "bottom up," from the "outside to the inside." Yet the metaphor from the "inside to the outside" made unjust demands. To ask the poor in the name of war and survival to cut down on food, heat, and gasoline when budgets were already strained by inflation was cruelly ineffective. To ask the growing numbers of unemployed to work harder was callous, especially when political recognition of, much less political action on, their condition was delayed. To ask the middle-class, spending more merely to maintain and stabilize a standard of living, to practice unusual self-restraint was to ask for more than they would voluntarily give.

One major reason why the metaphor of war had to be jettisoned when Ford's concern shifted from inflation to recession in 1975 was that unemployment could not be described or explained as a test of character. Ford knew that.[39] Could the unemployed whip their condition "now" by practicing self-restraint? Could the unemployed form local unemployed action committees to monitor those businesses and industries which no longer needed their services? Could the unemployed war on themselves? If not, who or what would be the chosen enemy? Before the Business Council on December 11, 1974 Ford seemingly recognized the problem of definition. First, he stated the act: "We are in a recession. Production is declining and unemployment, unfortunately, is rising." But he also drew a distinction between his former major problem, inflation, which he termed "a national crisis" demanding "immediate and drastic action," and recession, his new concern, which he termed "a national problem" that "demands widespread understanding and carefully deliberated solutions. . . ."[40] Thus when Ford addressed the nation via television on January 13, 1975, two days prior to his State of the Union message to Congress which fleshed out the preceeding address, he placed his and the public's problems in a revised hierarchy, "recession, inflation, and energy dependence." "However, he wasn't interested in warring on them, preferring only to tinker with them:[41]

> The danger of doing nothing is great; the danger of doing too much is just as great. We cannot afford to throw monkey wrenches into our complex economic machine, just because it isn't running at full speed.

Critics and supporters of Ford's approach to inflation occasionally used the metaphor of life, images of health and medicine, to make their views clear to their publics. There is nothing unusual about conflicting metaphors in political deliberations, but the metaphor of life also does not ordinarily have as its primary referent a test of character. Of course, citizens can always be careful and prudent, especially when confronted with and caring for minor illnesses. But a serious major illness contracted by an individual or a plague which affects a collective cannot be treated by voluntary measures; expert knowledge is required and vast infusions of money and technical supplies are necessary. To the extent that citizens do not ordinarily associate life—health and illness—with character, this conflicting metaphor may have provoked many to ask why Ford's explication of his war metaphor placed so much of the blame and responsibility on them.

Given Ford's cautious, conservative political instincts, his approach to the problem of inflation through the metaphor of war was inappropriate to him. He would not act politically to guarantee the authenticity of the metaphor which, once invoked, demanded more of him than he was willing or able to give. The public, fatigued by bloated war language and calls to sacrifice during the Vietnam war, probably carried to Ford's messages a residue of suspicion about his dominant imagery. And over time audiences could sense the distance between Ford's imagery and his actions in the name of imagery. Further the popular press presented to its readers conflicting images of the problem. Because Ford's metaphor was inappropriate to him, his lines of argument, and his public, it did not cross. Politically, it was the wrong metaphor for the speaker, the audiences, and the time. Rhetorically, the metaphor was mismanaged causing Ford more losses than gains. Both undoubtedly contributed to the negative evaluations of Ford's performance at the polls in 1974.

Notes

1. All citations are from *New York Times*, 29 Aug. 1974, p. 20.
2. Ford, of course, made many addresses during these months, but those cited herein reflect, with minor variations before specific audiences, his overall approach and, with minor exceptions, were addressed to national audiences.
3. In a discussion of political language, Thomas H.Middleton set Ford's acronym, WIN, within the context of a game metaphor, a judgment which is erroneous as this essay will demonstrate. See Thomas H. Middleton, "Light Refractions," Saturday Review/World, II Jan. 1975, p. 61.
4. All citations are from *New York Times*, 16 Jan. 1975, p. 24. On 13 Jan. 1975, two days prior to his "State of the Union" address, Ford delivered a televised speech to the American people and announced that the country had "suffered sudden and serious setbacks in sales and unemployment. Therefore, we must shift our emphasis from inflation to recession." The metaphor of war does not appear in this address either. See *New York Times*, 14 Jan. 1975, p. 20.
5. Text of this address supplied by the Office of the White House Press Secretary and all citations are from it. Excerpts from the address appear in the *New York Times*, 7 Sept. 1974, p. 10.
6. All citations are from *New York Times*, 9 Oct. 1974, p. 24.
7. William E. Leuchtenburg has carefully described how Roosevelt used the metaphor of war for support of his policies during the depression. See "The New Deal and the Analogue of War," in *Change and Continuity in Twentieth-Century America*, ed. John Braeman, et al. (Columbus, Ohio, 1964), pp. 81–143.
8. Ford's ten topics were: Food, Energy, Restrictive Antitrust Practices, Increased Capital Supply, Inflation Casualties, Housing, Thrift Institutions, International Interdependency, Federal Taxes, Federal Spending. See *New York Times*, 9 Oct. 1974, p. 1.
9. All citations are from *New York Times*, 10 Oct. 1974, p. 38.
10. *New York Times*, 13 Nov. 1974, p. 1. Also see *New York Times*, 29 Nov. 1974, p. 1. It appears that Ford's first public recognition of the recession occurred in a press conference December 2, 1974 and he compared it with inflation, "which is a deadly long-range enemy that cannot be ignored." Recession "is a serious threat that already has hurt many citizens and alarms many more. Hopefully, it is a shorter-range evil—but neither can it be ignored, nor will it be." See *New York Times*, 3 Dec. 1974, p. 28.
11. All citations from *New York Times*, 9 Oct. 1974, p. 24.

12. Curiously Ford did not explicate the acronym. It was left to the popular press to explain what it meant. The story of the creation of the WIN button provides interesting insights about the campaign to organize the American people. See *New York Times*, 9 Oct. 1974, p. 25 and 20 Oct. 1974, sec. 3, p. 15 and *The New Yorker*, 21 Oct. 1974, pp. 32–33. The button was a source of much humor, a sign that the effort to promote inflation as a serious matter was occasionally less than serious even if the fact of inflation was serious. For example, Ron Nessen, the President's Press Secretary, "walked into a White House press briefing . . . wearing a WIN button upside down so that it read NIM," explaining "that the President had warned that there would be No Immediate Miracles in curing the nation's economic ills." In terms of the public's perceptions this question must be asked: To what extent, if at all, does such competing jesting imagery deflate and tarnish the President's imagery? See *New York Times*, 25 Nov. 1974, p. 18, and *Time*, 18 Nov. 1974, p. 73 for examples of the NIM button and discussion of its meaning.

13. The enlistment form carried a reproduction of the WIN button and this message: "Dear President Ford: I enlist as an Inflation Fighter and Energy Saver for the duration. I will do the very best I can for America." It was to be sent to the President's WIN Coordinating Office, The White House, Washington, D. C. A copy of the form appeared in the *New York Times*, 9 Oct. 1974, p. 25 and in other newspapers at "White House request." *Time*, 21 Oct. 1974, p. 41 also carried a copy of the form and reported that "the first 100,000 people to fill out the form and mail it to the White House will get a free WIN button," suggesting that others would receive nothing or have to pay for what they received. An army of 100,000 enlistments is surely small in the face of Ford's emphasis on the serious nature of the enemy. But the Government did not fully commit itself to the campaign. It printed no forms and stamped no buttons. No Federal offices distributed forms and they were not readily available to the public beyond the time of their first appearance in the newspapers. In early December to the Business Council, Ford reported that he had received "more than 200,000 pieces of mail in support of the WIN program, by far the largest amount of favorable public response to anything that I have done since taking office." Text of Address supplied by Office of White House Secretary.

14. Text supplied by Office of White House Secretary and all quotations are from it.

15. But such buttons were in the public domain, "although there is some disagreement among wearers about what the LOSE buttons signify. . . . Some say LOSE stands for Let Our Stockbrokers Eat, an allusion to the statement by Allan Greenspan, Chairman of the Council of Economic Advisors, that stockbrokers are suffering proportionally more than other sectors of society under current economic conditions. Others say it means Let's Omit Spurious Exhortation." *New York Times*, 25 Nov. 1974, p. 18. An Oliphant political cartoon centers on the Win-Lose polarity, showing an official of the Administration at the White House rear entrance emptying box upon box of WIN buttons into trash barrels. See *Newsweek*, 18 Nov. 1974, p. 29.

16. Ford never publicly announced that the White House coordinator of the Citizens' Action Committee was Russell W. Freeburg, "one-time managing editor and Washington bureau chief of *The Chicago Tribune*," and "most recently . . . an executive with Wagner & Baroody, a Washington public relations firm." *New York Times*, 9 Oct. 1974, p. 25. Sylvia Porter's selection undoubtedly reflected her abilities, but it may also have reflected Ford's sense that it would be good politics to appoint a woman. Writing about the Summit Conference, Karen DeCrow, President of NOW, said: "I represented NOW, as a delegate to the Summit, and sadly

must report that it was a male performance. We should be proud that NOW was invited: I was the only delegate of a feminist group, one of the few women present, and the only person speaking for women's representation, or the lack of same. It is certainly a recent development that when the White House invites the 700 leaders of the nation to a meeting that NOW is included. Although there are nearly 40 million women workers, the labor Panel [at the Summit Conference] consisted of 100% white men. How these persons expected to speak for the interests of women and minority men is a puzzle." "From the President," *Do It NOW*, 7 (November, 1974), 16.

17. WIN, the acronym of the Committee, was quietly discarded early in 1975. "It is dead, and God bless it," said Mrs. Porter after the third full meeting of the Committee. "That wasn't our gimmick! You all know what happened—we were left with the job of building the airplane in the air." The President had shifted emphasis from inflation to recession and the Committee shifted emphasis from inflation to energy conservation which "will be the first priority," said Mrs. Porter who also reported that the Committee required government and private funding and assistance for its efforts. *New York Times*, 9 Mar. 1975, p. 32.

18. Ford anticipated and prejudged the Committee's recommendations which were not publicly announced until November 11, 1974 about a month after his speech. The Committee prepared for distribution three different pledges aimed at enlisting citizens in the fight against inflation: Businessman's and Businesswoman's Pledge, Consumer's Pledge and a Worker's Pledge. The text of the business-man and woman's pledge said: "I pledge . . . that . . . I will hold or reduce prices. . . ." The worker's pledge said nothing about maintaining or reducing wage levels, asking only that workers' seek "ways to conserve energy and eliminate waste on the job." For texts of the pledges see *New York Times*, 12 Nov. 1974, p. 28. The Chamber of Commerce of the United States of America, and Arch Booth, its president and a member of the Committee were outraged at lack of equity and the discrimination in the pledges. See *New York Times*, 12 Nov. 1974, p. 1 and the Chamber of Commerce news release, Washington, November 11, 1974.

19. Ford spoke on October 15, 1974. In reality there was absolutely no evidence for believing the tasks could be accomplished by Thanksgiving. Indeed the Citizens Action Committee to Fight Inflation did not announce preliminary plans for any action until November 11, 1974, and then Sylvia Porter indicated that the only action taken by the Committee was to send "letters to the Governors of the 50 states and to 10,000 Mayors and county officials asking them to take the lead in forming the citizens' groups." *New York Times*, 12 Nov. 1974, p. 28.

20. No evidence has been found that flags were ever made up and awarded. Sometime early in the fall of 1974 someone in the White House asked Stanley Adams, President of the American Society of Composers, Authors, and Publishers, for a song with an anti-inflation theme. On October 7, 1974 Adams called Meredith Wilson who reported: "I put the finished words and music in the mail" on "October 16, 1974." "A White House spokesman said in early December the song would be released at the appropriate time." *New York Times*, 1 Dec. 1974, Sec. 1, p. 45.

21. Italics added.

22. This cover was reproduced in a full page advertisement for this issue of *Newsweek* in *New York Times*, 24 Sept. 1974, p. 84.

23. Of course, popular journals compete with one another and thus must present issues differently. The point is that Ford's metaphor was not strong enough to temper the competition and to prevent disparate messages from impinging upon the public.

24. *Newsweek*, 30 Sept. 1974, p. 76.
25. *Time*, 21 Oct. 1974, pp. 41–48.
26. Text supplied to author by Mr. Greenland; excerpts appear in *New York Times*, 8 Nov. 1974, p. 58.
27. *Newsweek*, 30 Sept. 1974, pp. 62–88.
28. Ibid., p. 77. Excerpts from his remarks also appear in *US News and World Report*, 16 Sept. 1974, p. 23. At the conference J. Kenneth Galbraith also stressed the need for tough controls, using less medical imagery but speaking in terms of "sedatives" for the problem of unemployment. *US News and World Report*, 16 Sept. 1974, p. 23.
29. *New York Times*, 25 Nov. 1974, p. 25.
30. Ibid., December 5, 1974, p. 66.
31. Ibid., October 24, 1974, Section 2, p. 38.
32. Ibid., 2 Dec. 1974, p. 25.
33. Ibid., 28 Sept. 1974, p. 9. Italics added. There is irony in such ads. The National Chamber of Commerce, various advertising groups, and business in-general, pledged help to Ford in the battle against inflation.
34. *Time*, 9 Dec. 1974, p. 31.
35. *Time*, 23 Dec. 1974, p. 20.
36. *New York Times*, 12 Dec. 1974, p. 38.
37. *New York Times*, 14 Jan. 1975, p. 20.
38. Text from Office of White House Press Secretary. Excerpts appear in *New York Times*, 12 Dec. 1974, p. 1.
39. The unemployed, said Ford, "are jobless through no fault of their own," in his "State of the Union" message, January 15, 1975. *New York Times*, 16 Jan. 1975, p. 24.
40. Text supplied by Office of White House Secretary.
41. *New York Times*, 14 Jan. 1975, p. 20.

Corrupt Rhetoric: President Ford and the Mayaguez Affair

Dan F. Hahn

In his 1973 Speech Communication Association presidential address, Robert C. Jeffrey complained of our professional complacency with the ethics of Nixon administration discourse, lamenting "It is a sad commentary on the state of rhetoric in the academy when we admit that ethical studies of the Nixon rhetoric are more readily available in the press than in scholarly journals."[1] Sad, perhaps, but understandable. Press critics are somewhat closer to the events in Washington and have private sources of information not easily accessible to the scholar. More important, perhaps, the journalist is expected to comment on current events while the scholar who does so is suspect immediately as partisan, thus unprofessional.

Despite this risk to professional reputation, I propose to discuss a relatively recent rhetorico-political event. I do so because the discourse in question represents an example of corrupted discourse—one that is particularly significant because the quiet acceptance of it ushered us once again into the "Imperial Presidency," which the Nixon impeachment was supposed to have ended.

The broad outlines of the *Mayaguez* affair are familiar: the Cambodians captured the small American vessel; the U. S. government demanded an immediate release; the Cambodian government did not respond; the United States attacked; the vessel was recaptured; the Cambodians released the crew. In this retelling, and in the administration's original tale, the operation sounds simple and straightforward. And that is part of the problem: the discourse was corrupted by a false description of the situation.

The Cambodians captured a small American vessel named the *Mayaguez*. Why? The American press, thus the people, never asked that question—and the U. S. government never answered it. The ostensible reason for the capture was that the boat lay eight miles off the coast of a Cambodian island, well within the 12 miles Cambodia claimed as territorial waters. Let us suppose for a moment that that *was* the reason for the capture. Is it an unreasonable reason? Does the United States recognize the 12-mile territorial limit? Ostensibly, no. The United States recognizes a three-mile limit for some purposes (including, presumably, the purpose that the *Mayaguez* was pursuing) and a 12-mile limit for other purposes. The nine miles of waters between what the U. S. recognized in this situation and what the Cambodians recognized

Mr. Hahn is Associate Professor in the Department of Communication Arts and Sciences at Queens College.
Reprinted by permission from *Communication Quarterly* Vol. 28, No. 2 (Spring 1980), pp. 38–43.

could reasonably be described as "contested" waters. How did our government describe them? In the original release describing the capture, the location was depicted as "on the high seas."[2] That is a phrase normally taken to mean "those seas not under the jurisdiction of any government." But . . . jurisdiction as decided by whom? That we do not know. All we know is that, *for the purpose of this operation,* the U. S. government chose to define eight miles out as "high seas." When the miles are off the U. S. coast rather than the Cambodian, the government utilizes a different standard: "The U. S. Coast Guard regularly seizes vessels that have strayed inside the twelve-mile limit."[3]

Did not the U. S. government consider the 12-mile Cambodian limit valid? Indeed, President Ford acted against the interpretation of his legal counsel, who ". . . cautioned him that . . . the ship's capture was not 'piracy.' Under international law, they said, Cambodia had a legal right to seize the ship after it steamed within the 12-mile limit which Cambodia claims as its territorial waters."[4] That made Ford's description of the location ("high seas") and the act ("piracy") not just "dissembling," but lying. President Ford chose to describe a legal Cambodian action as illegal, and then, on the basis of his own false description, to engage in military action in retribution for that legal action.

Note, also, that his description made it a clear case of good guys versus bad guys. Any citizen who accepted his description had little choice but to accept his action. The situation seemed simple; the resultant action seemed legitimate. The corrupt discourse of President Ford established a climate in which the actions of President Ford had to be applauded.

It should be remembered that the foregoing hinges on the assumption that the Cambodian action was motivated by the infringement of their territorial waters. Could they have had other, perhaps more plausible, motivations? Certainly, in a time when the shenanigans of the CIA were being aired, it was possible to suspect that the boat was not the simple "American merchant ship"[5] described by Ford. Indeed, the *Mayaguez* does seem to have dealt in rather strange merchandise. The trip immediately preceding this one was from Saigon to Hong Kong, and the cargo was, according to White House press secretary Ron Nessen, "some administrative material" from our Saigon embassy.[6] For this trip the boat was under contract to the U. S. army, carrying meat, liquor, coca cola, and the like to U. S. troops stationed in Thailand.[7] Assuming that the Cambodians had good enough intelligence information to know that the *Mayaguez* had recently been and/or currently was in the employ of the U. S. government, could that information have been specific enough for them to have known that the cargo was meat rather than mortars, cokes rather than CIA spys? And could they have known for sure that the supplies were for U. S. troops in Thailand rather than rebels in Cambodia? Indeed, do *we* know that for sure even today?

In short, the U. S. assumption that this was an innocent civilian boat may not have been the assumption upon which the Cambodians were operating when they captured it. Thus, the description of the boat as merely "an American merchant ship"[8] glossed over the important detail that the merchandise of this merchant ship was military cargo and that, without specific knowledge of the nature or destination of the cargo, the Cambodians could have perceived the *Mayaguez* as a dangerous military threat. Again, President Ford chose to overlook these factors in his description of the ship—a description that made a complicated situation look like a simple case of piracy, logically answerable by simple application of military power.

A second major way in which the Ford administration corrupted the discourse surrounding this affair was by not allowing "solution-by-discourse" (i.e., diplomacy) a chance to work—and by talking as though they had.

It is difficult to piece together the sequence of events in order to determine if diplomacy was given a fair chance. The best information available to the public provides the following sequence:[9]

May 12, 5:03 A.M. The U. S. government learned of the seizure of the *Mayaguez*.[10]

May 12, 2:00 P.M. The U. S. government announced the seizure and began diplomatic efforts.[11]

May 13, 6:20 A.M. U. S. aircraft fired warning shots across the bow of the *Mayaguez*.[12]

May 13, evening (exact time unknown) U. S. forces destroyed three Cambodian patrol boats and immobilized four more.[13]

May 14, 1:00 A.M. First U. S. air attacks.[14] (Note: This may be redundant of the May 13, 6:20 A.M. entry; not enough is known about either event to be sure.)

May 14, morning (exact time unknown) The National Security Council decided to utilize military action to recapture the *Mayaguez* and its crew.[15] (Note: the action previously reported was not to recapture but merely to prevent movement of boat and crew to the mainland.[16])

May 14, 5:55 P.M. "Consultation" with Congress begun.[17]

May 14, 8:15 P.M. Cambodian offer to return the *Mayaguez* received.[18]

May 14, 8:20 P.M. "Consultation" with Congress concluded.[19]

May 14, 9:00 P.M. *Mayaguez* recaptured by U. S. forces.[20]

May 14, 9:15 P.M. Ford demanded release of the crew.[21]

May 14, 10:53 P.M. U.S.S. Wilson announced crew was approaching.[22]

May 14, 10:57 P.M. U.S. planes bombed Cambodian airport.[23]

May 14, 11:14 P.M. Ford told crew was safe.[24]

May 14, 11:30 P.M. Crew rescued.[25]

May 14, 11:50 P.M. U.S. planes bombed Cambodian oil refinery.[26]

May 15, 12:27 A.M. Ford announced the successful completion of the mission.[27]

The time schedule is somewhat confusing, and most entries relate to military, rather than diplomatic, ventures. This is not to say that there was no diplomacy, but that the times for these were never indicated. We know, for instance, that the Chinese representative in Washington was asked to deliver a message to the Cambodians and refused formally (although the president believed the message was sent despite the refusal).[28] We do not know when the Chinese representative was approached. We do know that, subsequent to the Chinese refusal, the U.S. Ministry in Peking delivered a message to the Cambodian Embassy in Peking.[29] We do not know when that took place. More important, we do not know if the Cambodian Embassy was able to get the message to the decision makers in Cambodia. Finally, we know that the United States appealed to the U.N. for help sometime after the U.S. attacked the Cambodian boats,[30] but we do not know whether it was after the May 13 warning attack or after the main attack began the evening of May 14.

We do, however, know a few things which impinge upon our assessment of the diplomatic endeavors. We know that from the time Washington heard of the capture of the *Mayaguez* until it started operations to recapture it, approximately 60 hours elapsed. That is the most extensive time schedule that can be deduced. The most contracted schedule, that between the reported begining of our diplomatic efforts and the firing of our first bullet, was 16 hours. Thus, the amount of time devoted to diplomacy was somewhere in the 16–60 hour range.

That leaves a number of imponderables: Were 16 hours enough? Were 60 hours enough? Were sufficient diplomatic channels explored? Were the diplomatic channels that were utilized able to contact the appropriate authorities in Cambodia? Was the first message from Cambodia (May 14, 8:15 P. M.) a response to the diplomatic efforts begun up to sixty hours before or to the military attempt at recapture begun approximately two hours before? Why, when the first communication from Cambodia—a conciliatory one—was received, were the U.S. forces not ordered to cease fire in place (in effect, taking a defensive rather than offensive posture)? The answers to these questions, absent the missing information, require each of us to make value judgments. For me, the answer to the key question whether enough time was devoted to diplomacy before military intervention was employed must be negative. Too few diplomatic attempts are reported, and those few seem too nonpersistent, for me to see them as anything but perfunctory at best, hypocritical at worst (hypocritical in the sense that they seem only to have been undertaken to provide a legalistic screen through which the desired military action could be sifted).[31]

Be that as it may, it is clear that the administration's rhetoric surrounding the capture and recapture of the *Mayaguez* corrupted the discourse by implying that all appropriate diplomatic efforts had been taken when, at best, that is a doubtful proposition. In the official announcements concerning the *Mayaguez* only three references—two direct and one indirect—to diplomatic efforts were located. In the original announcement of the capture, the official press release says, "He has instructed the State Department to demand the immediate release of the ship."[32] In announcing the decision to utilize force to recapture the boat and its crew, the statement of the press secretary began,

"In further pursuit of our efforts to obtain the release . . . ,"[33] implying that diplomatic efforts had been "pursued." Finally, in the letter to Congress explaining and justifying his efforts, President Ford contended, "Appropriate demands for the return of the Mayaguez and its crew were made, both publicly and privately, without success."[34]

The sequence in these three official announcements is simple and clear: we *will make* a diplomatic demand; we *have been* pursuing nonmilitary means; we *did* make the "appropriate demands" but "without success." The simplicity, of course, is deceptive. The government did not deem it necessary to tell us what diplomatic channels were available to it, which of those it chose to utilize and why, or whether any of the messages reached their target within the Cambodian government. Rather, it chose to imply that all appropriate channels had been utilized and that the Cambodians had refused to negotiate. Perhaps that is the case. However, it is not reflected in the public communication surrounding the event. On the basis of that information, I must conclude that the government willingly lied to us about the "failed" diplomacy in order to attain our support for the military operation. For those unwilling to travel that far with me, I submit that at the least the discourse was corrupted by the withholding of information concerning the diplomatic attempts, thus forcing us to evaluate the efficacy of the diplomacy with inadequate information.

The third major corruption of the public discourse was through false claims of authority for taking the military action. These false claims were put forward by President Ford and his legal counsel, Roderick Hills. President Ford contended, "This operation was ordered and conducted pursuant to the President's constitutional Executive power and his authority as Commander-in-Chief of the United States Armed Forces."[35] His counsel added that Ford "acted under his constitutional war powers to protect the lives and property of Americans."[36]

Let us examine the first claim of authority, the president's "constitutional executive power." Such powers are enumerated in Article II of the United States Constitution. Nowhere in that enumeration is found the power to engage in military operations outside a declaration of war. In fact, the only military reference among the enumerated executive powers says, "The President shall be commander in chief of the army and navy of the United States." But this was Ford's second "authorization." Unless authorization number one was identical to authorization number two, President Ford claimed to be acting under "constitutional Executive power," which simply does not exist. If there is additional executive power permitting military action, beyond the commander-in-chief position, it is not *constitutional*. Thus, Ford corrupted the discourse by claiming to have acted under powers delegated by the Constitution, when such powers do not appear in the Constitution.

Ford's second rationale was that he was acting under his authority as commander-in-chief. What authority does the commander-in-chief have? What is a commander-in-chief? Clearly, it is a military title, the highest military title. Logically, it means that the president is the number one general. But no general, even number one, has the right to engage in an act of war without a declaration of war (the power to declare war is specified in the Constitution as belonging to Congress—Article 1, Section 8, paragraph 11). For the president to take that power unto himself, in the name of his military position as commander-in-chief, is as clear a violation of the Constitution as is imaginable.

Yet, it may be argued, presidents have been utilizing such powers for some time. Precisely; and for that reason the Congress passed the War Powers Act of 1973. "The act requires a president, before sending troops into action, to 'consult' with Congress."[37] Thus, it appears that Congress—the war-declaring body—has determined that some military actions can be undertaken without a declaration of war but that such actions must be decided upon in consultations between the president and the Congress.

Did such consultations take place? That depends, does it not, upon what is meant by "consultation?" If your son, Gerry, has one of his friends tell you that Gerry is going to the movies tonight, is that a consultation? I think not. Rather, I imagine "consultation" to mean that the two of you get together and come to a mutual understanding about whether he is going to the movies. The understanding, the decision, grows out of a dialogic process we call consultation.

What was the nature of the "consultation" in the *Mayaguez* decision? We find that the decision to take military action was made on the morning of May 14, while the first "consultation" did not take place until 5:55 that afternoon. Obviously, the consultation could not have been of the "let's decide what to do" type (and since that is the only type of consultation that exists, it must be that this later "consultation" was not a consultation at all).

Other anomalies appear. The "consultations" were not among principals. President Ford did not talk to the congressmen; he had them called by members of the White House staff.[38] Nor was it a "consultation" with the 535 people who constitute Congress; only 18 members of Congress were contacted.[39] The president had some of his friends tell some of Congress, "We are going to war tonight." To call that a consultation that fulfills the requirements of the War Powers Act takes us past credulity—perhaps to an "incredibility gap."

So much for the president's "constitutional executive power" and his "authority as commander-in-chief." What about "his constitutional war powers to protect the lives and property of Americans," the argument of his legal counsel? We must first note that there is no such thing as *constitutional* war powers of the president, above and beyond the commander-in-chief appellation. And, even if there were, they surely would not be "operational" absent a declaration of war. Congress has, during our many wars, conferred special war powers upon the president, but at the conclusion of each war those powers have reverted automatically to the Congress. It is nonsensical at best, dictatorial at worst, for the president to assume these special war powers in peacetime.

But certainly, it may be argued, even if we forget the constitutional argument and the war powers argument and the commander-in-chief argument, the president has the power to which his counsel alluded, the power to protect the life and property of Americans; did not President Johnson utilize such powers to land troops in the Dominican Republic? The answers are: yes, President Johnson utilized such powers; and no, they don't legally exist. The controlling law in this circumstance is still the congressional act of July 27, 1868, which says that when a foreign country deprives a U.S. citizen of his liberty the president is directed "to use such means, *not amounting to acts of war*, to obtain the release, and promptly to report to Congress."[40]

I conclude that President Ford acted unconstitutionally and illegally,[41] in sending troops to recapture the *Mayaguez* and that his false claims for authority to take such action corrupted the public discourse surrounding the event.

President Ford, by his illegal acts, tore asunder the Constitution and emasculated the War Powers Act of 1973. For the society to condone his actions would be, in the words of constitutional historian Raoul Berger, "to undermine the foundations of our democratic society."[42] And for us speech communication scholars to condone the false descriptions, misleading simplifications, and lies of President Ford and his lieutenants would be "an abrogation of our role as protectors of ethical communication."[43] And that role, I suggest, is not just to be concerned about isolated cases of corrupt rhetoric, for such cases can have widespread insidious results. As Edwin Black has argued, we must be alert to discourse that disposes "an audience to expect certain ways of arguing and certain kinds of justifications in later discourses that they encounter."[44] The Ford stance on the *Mayaguez* can be presumed to have done precisely that: by reinstituting the "president knows best" syndrome of the Imperial Presidency, Mr. Ford reinstituted a form of argumentation that the Nixon impeachment hearings had sought to eliminate.

The American Response

Assuming that the foregoing provides a reasonable evaluation of the rhetoric surrounding the *Mayaguez* event, a nagging question remains: why did the American people so overwhelmingly approve Ford's handling of the situation? Are we so imperialistic, nationalistic, chauvenistic, and messianic that we will support any foreign military adventure the president desires? No doubt some people think so, but the evidence here is insufficient to demonstrate such an evaluation. In addition, such a sweeping indictment of the American population is not necessary to explain their positive reactions in this case. A case can be made for understanding their positive response to the *Mayaguez* actions in terms of the historic situation. We had just "lost" Viet Nam and were feeling somewhat abused—tired of being "pushed around" by every "second rate" power in the world. Our historic senses remembered, with some shame, an earlier capture of a U.S. ship, the *Pueblo*, by North Korea. *Mayaguez* gave us an opportunity to flex our muscles, to "reassert our manhood."

While this historic explanation may establish that the administration and people were predisposed toward face-saving actions somewhere in the world, it does not establish why the specific action in question was perceived to be so exemplary. A better explanation of that is implied in the foregoing analysis: the American people responded positively because the Ford administration was able to structure their perceptions. "In the field of foreign affairs, the public is not able to scrutinize an empirical reality. . . . Especially in such cases where . . . [the public does] not have firsthand access to an objective situation, their perceptions are based upon pictures or images constructed through their linguistic interaction with others."[45]

The American people are not conversant with international law, and thus had no reason to doubt the "high seas" and "piracy" descriptions given by President Ford. In similar manner, not knowing much about the possibilities of international diplomacy, the American people had no trouble believing that all possible diplomatic avenues had been explored.

As Richard Cherwitz had demonstrated, "the primary character of a crisis is defined by the President's discourse."[46] The president's definition, then, provides the "terministic screen" through which the population views the event, while at the same time providing him with a "terministic compulsion" to follow the implications of the terminology to their logical conclusions. In this case, Ford's terminology logically required military action. And a population whose perceptions were determined by that terminology had no trouble in accepting and applauding the resulting action.

All of this does not, of course, prove that the action was wrong. But it does demonstrate that corrupt discourse poisons the possibility of evaluating action, and—to the degree the action was taken because of terministic compulsion—it demonstrates that action, right or wrong, can be taken for the wrong reasons if the terminology is incorrect. Corrupt rhetoric corrupts decision making.

Notes

1. Robert C. Jeffrey, "Ethics in Public Discourse," *Spectra*, (December 1973), pp. 15–16.
2. "The White House: Statement by the Press Secretary," May 12, 1975, p. 1.
3. Ron Chernow, "Of the United States, Cambodia and the Mayaguez Affair," *New York Times*, May 22, 1975, p. 38.
4. Jack Anderson, "Veterans' Benefits," *New York Post*, May 28, 1975, p. 41.
5. "The White House: Statement by the Press Secretary," p. 1.
6. "West German Magazine Asserts Mayaguez Carried C.I.A. Data," *New York Times*, May 23, 1975, p. 3.
7. Ibid.
8. "The White House: Statement by the Press Secretary," p.1.
9. All indicated times are EDT.
10. Anthony Lewis, "The Morning After," *New York Times*, May 12, 1975, p. 29.
11. Ibid.
12. Gerald R. Ford, "Text of a Letter to the Speaker and the President Pro Tem," May 15, 1975, p. 1.
13. Ibid.
14. Lewis, p. 29.
15. I. F. Stone, "Conned in Cambodia," *The New York Review*, June 12, 1975, p. 16.
16. Ford, p. 1.
17. Stone, p. 16.
18. Lewis, p. 29.
19. Stone, p. 16.
20. Ford, p. 2.
21. Lewis, p. 29.
22. Ibid.
23. Ibid.
24. Ibid.
25. Ford, p. 2.
26. Lewis, p. 29.
27. Ford, p. 1.
28. Jack Anderson, "Dissension Over Mayaguez," *New York Post*, May 21, 1975, p. 45.
29. Ibid.
30. By comparison, at this writing (February, 1980) the American hostages in Iran have been held for over two months and the administration is still finding diplomatic avenues to pursue.
31. "Waldheim Raps U.S.," *New York Post*, May 20, 1975, p. 5.
32. "The White House: Statement by the Press Secretary," p. 1.
34. Ford, p. 1.
35. Ibid., p. 2.
36. Raoul Berger, "The Mayaguez Incident and the Constitution," *New York Times*, May 23, 1975, p. 37.
37. Stone, p. 16.
38. Ibid.
39. Ibid.
40. Berger, p. 37. Emphasis added.

41. This judgement concerning legality is, of necessity, based purely on the evidence here presented. Through January 1980 no interpretations have appeared in any law journals, domestic or international; no claims have been filed with the World Court; no mention of *Mayaguez* has appeared in any Admiralty case.
42. Berger, p. 37.
43. Jeffrey, p. 16.
44. Edwin Black, *Rhetorical Criticism: A Study in Method* (Madison: University of Wisconsin Press, 1978), p.35.
45. Richard A. Cherwitz, "The Contributory Effect of Rhetorical Discourse: A Study of Language-in-Use," paper presented at the 1979 Speech Communication Association convention, pp. 5–6.
46. Ibid., p. 6.

JIMMY CARTER

The Rhetoric of Jimmy Carter, 1976–1980

Dan F. Hahn

In 1976 Jimmy Carter surprised everybody by moving from the back of the pack to win the Democratic nomination and going on to accomplish the nearly unprecedented task of unseating an incumbent president. Perhaps because communication is such a central component of presidential campaigns, Carter was considered a masterful communicator when he took office. And for a few months, while he engaged in a clever campaign of symbol manipulation, that evaluation continued. But by mid-term his presidency was in trouble and before it ended he was perceived as a poor communicator.

"Communication," of course, is a broader term than "rhetoric," so it is not necessarily the case that a good or bad communicator will concomitantly be a good or bad rhetor. In Jimmy Carter's case, it seems obvious that he was never a particularly effective speaker, although his reputation in this area suffered a diminution as his general reputation fell.

From the very first his ability as a speaker was suspect. As early as October of 1975, R. W. Apple, Jr. characterized his speaking as containing "no applause lines, little detail on issues, no rhetorical flourishes."[1] Three months before the 1976 election, Lewis Lapham lambasted him with this line: "He isn't an eloquent man, and his visions of America the Beautiful have the quality of the gilded figurines bought in penny arcades."[2]

It should be noted that the negative assessments of Carter's rhetoric seem not to be related to political prejudice. Liberals, conservatives, and moderates all saw him as undynamic. Liberal former Senator Eugene McCarthy said, "He's an oratorical mortician. He inters his words and ideas beneath piles of syntactical mush."[3] I. F. Stone, the liberal publisher, complained, "There's no music in him. He just can't lift off. He can fool people for a while, but he really doesn't know how to inspire."[4] From the other end of the political spectrum, Evans and Novak characterized him as "allergic to all efforts at eloquence,"[5] And the more moderate Paul Healy noted, "Carter's natural speaking style is fine for insomniacs."[6]

All of these judgements do not prove, however, that Carter's lack of dynamism drove people away. *The New York Times,* commenting editorially on Carter's inaugural, noted "there was nothing memorable about Carter's words, though we like the melody."[7] Academic analyses tended to be even kinder. J. Lewis Campbell III found Carter's 1976 rhetoric charismatic,[8] while Keith

Reprinted by permission of Center for the Study of the Presidency, publishers of *Presidential Studies Quarterly,* Vol. XIV, No. 2 (Spring, 1984), pp. 265–288.

Erickson concluded, ". . . no other candidate could have so articulately woven together civic piety, religious disclosures, and politics."[9] Chris Johnstone contended that Carter was rhetorically clever in convincing us that a vote for him was a vote for ourselves,[10] John Patton credited him with restoring transcendence to politics[11] and Dan Hahn, in a backhanded compliment, attacked him for manipulating his religious rhetoric to get elected.[12] But the seeming contradiction between politico-journalistic and academic evaluations was more apparent than real. The politicians and journalists were evaluating Carter as a speaker; the academic analysts were focusing on the cleverness of the rhetorical content rather than the effectiveness of the rhetor himself.

Those academics who did analyze Carter's speeches were as appalled as the journalists. Ronald Sudol found that Carter's defense of the "strategic retreat" on the Panama Canal was a failure.[13] William Houser judged Carter's speech at the Camp David ceremony adequate, but also pointed out that Menachem Begin "stole the show."[14] Catherine Collins found enormous weaknesses in Carter's rhetoric justifying the SALT talks[15] and two different analyses of Carter's 1979 energy speech found it deficient.[16] To my knowledge, only one published academic analysis of a Carter speech was laudatory, and its conclusion, that Carter's 1979 energy speech "established his ability to lead,"[17] was belied by subsequent evaluations of Carter in the opinion polls and at the ballot box.

In short, with few exceptions, political, journalist and academic analyses agreed: Jimmy Carter was not a dynamic public speaker. It remains to detail the reasons for that judgement and to attempt to determine if his rhetoric might have contributed to his failure to maintain the relatively positive image he had as he entered the presidency in 1976.

Carter's Messages

A major evaluation of Carter's message during the 1976 campaign, which even became a campaign issue, was that he was "fuzzy" on the issues. His rhetoric was described as one which "generally avoids details,"[18] was "noticeably vague,"[19] made up of "generalized statements"[20] and "amorphous ambiguities"[21] which reflected "general aspirations."[22] Gus Tyler concluded, "He has the skill to be a loquacious sphynx, to keep his meanings silent even when he is sounding off."[23]

This fuzziness, it should be noted, may be endemic to American electoral politics. The large, variegated and non-ideological audience, with its tendency to vote against rather than for candidates, may force those candidates into ambiguities. But whether forced or natural, candidate Carter seems to have been a master—so much so that conservatives perceived him as conservative, moderates as moderate, and liberals as liberal.[24]

Yet, journalist critics found him to be either a liberal with some conservative quirks or a liberal who had added in some conservatism to broaden his appeal. Evans and Novak saw him as combining "a liberal idiom with some hard-line positions . . . ,"[25] while Patrick Anderson characterized him as "a fairly conventional liberal, but one whose views take a conservative bounce now and then."[26] In July of 1976 he was said "to balance a generally liberal speech with moderate qualifications . . . ,"[27] and in August, "Whenever Mr. Carter came close to embracing liberal dogmas . . . he almost always carefully qualified his remarks to satisfy some conservative objections."[28]

So, was Carter an ambiguous politician, a liberal with some conservative tendencies, or a liberal who made some conservative statements to broaden his appeal? Charles Mohr concluded, "His record indicates that Mr. Carter is as conservative—or as liberal—as he needs to be at any moment or in any political situation."[29]

To accomplish his "all things to all people," political strategy Carter utilized a number of rhetorical tactics in 1976. One of these, counterbalancing liberal and conservative positions, has already been implied. For instance, speaking in conservative Alabama in September of 1976, he called for an end to the "welfare mess" and support for a strong national defense; then, to appeal to liberals, "he recommended that welfare recipients who cannot work should be treated with dignity and respect; and he suggested that military budgets are obese and therefore can be cut without endangering national security."[30]

A second method he utilized was to give the policy to one side and the rhetoric to the other. His stand on abortion exemplifies this approach. Anti-abortionists wanted to amend the Constitution to make abortion illegal. Carter opposed such a measure, but in heavy Roman Catholic areas he prefaced the statement of his position with anti-abortion rhetoric, saying, "I think abortion is wrong. I don't think the government ought to do anything to encourage abortion."[31]

Another tactic was to agree to study a proposal or a position which ran counter to his own. Thus, while Carter opposed federal aid to cities, he promised Mayor Beame of New York that he would "study the creation of a Federal municipalities securities insurance corporation . . ."[32] The strength of this approach, of course, is that Carter thereby appeared to be open to rational persuasion without promising any substantive change at all.

This tactic, then, shades into the next: encouraging both sides to believe he was with them. This was usually accomplished through some kind of hedge. "Carter would make general value statements reflecting the sentiments of one sector of his audience and then tack on conditions or operational statements that would satisfy another segment. [For instance, he always combined "imagery of compassion with a line about administrative toughness."[33]] Though such statements might be inconsistent or contradictory, many of the people listening would only hear the part that conformed with their own views and ignore or discount the other material."[34]

A fifth rhetorical tactic he utilized to blur the liberal-conservative question was semantic distinctions. Perhaps the best example of this approach was his position on amnesty for those who had resisted service in Viet Nam. Carter's position was that he opposed amnesty "because 'amnesty says that what you did was right.' But he [added] that, in his first week in office, he would issue a 'blanket pardon' to 'defectors' because 'a pardon says that you are forgiven for what you did, whether it was right or wrong.' "[35] No one has ever located a dictionary which makes such a distinction; in fact, in most "amnesty" is defined as "a general pardon."

No wonder, then, that Mr. Carter's fuzziness on the issues, fueled by his rhetorical tactics, led people from all points of the political spectrum to identify with him. That was the goal all along. As Betty Glad concluded, "Mostly Carter skillfully fudged on the controversial issues. He did this by sending out complex messages that various listeners could interpret according to their own predispositions. From the multitude of signals—a word, a condition, a posture—Carter was able to send different people different signals about his positions."[36]

This conclusion is even true concerning one of his central positions in the campaign—his anti-Washington stance. To distance himself from the capitol he emphasized that he had not been a part of the group in Washington that had created the mess; in fact, he wasn't even a lawyer. Further distancing was created by dressing casually, carrying his own suitcase, sometimes staying in the homes of supporters rather than in hotels and, in general, picturing himself as an outsider. Thus he came to be seen not only as non-Washington but anti-Washington.

However, that was mostly facade, the image-message. Substantively, he didn't run against Washington at all. "Carter never said that government should be reduced or should do less. He said that the number of agencies should be reduced, but not that they should deliver fewer services or employ fewer people."[37] At the same time, it should be pointed out that both his rhetoric and his symbolism were seen, and were meant to be perceived, "as a cryptic way of saying that we need *less* government without actually having to alienate those who directly benefit from government."[38]

The foregoing analysis of Carter's fuzziness, liberal-conservative confusion and anti-Washington image assumes that substantive issues are significant. That is never a safe assumption,[39] and may be especially misleading when applied to the 1976 campaign. In what I find to be the most persuasive of the analyses of that campaign, Chris Johnstone argues that the election turned not on issues but the broader theme of faith, "in particular the faith that

Americans need to have in their government and, most especially, in themselves if the democratic system is to function properly."[40] Both candidates, says Johnstone, recognized the significance of this theme, but Carter won because he either understood or treated it better. "Whereas both Ford and Carter told us that *they* were honest, competent, compassionate, etc., Carter carried the idea further. He told us that *we* were. Beyond this, he told us that he derived his own wisdom, compassion, and competence *from us*. *We* became the subject-matter of Jimmy Carter's discourse, and we were persuaded to reaffirm our faith in ourselves by acting for him."[41] In a sense, we voted for ourselves. And Carter became President. So we now turn to an analysis of his messages in office, seeking lines of continuity to his campaign rhetoric as well as signs of weakness which might have contributed to his declining popularity through the four year term.

Weaknesses emerge immediately, literally moments after his taking the oath of office. For his inaugural address was "a themeless pudding, devoid of uplift or insight, defensive in outlook and timorous in its reach . . ."[42] Carter presented five major subjects in the address—religiosity, the American Dream, presidential responsibility, citizen's duties, and international affairs. And each topic was undermined by the way Carter presented it.

James Reston referred to the Inaugural as "revival meeting,"[43] Hedrick Smith said it was "less rallying cry than sermon,"[44] and Anthony Hillbruner entitled his analysis of it, "Born Again: Carter's Inaugural Sermon."[45] Certainly these commentators noted the most obvious subject in the speech.

In defining the world as two distinct parts, physical and spiritual, and then emphasizing the latter, President Carter set a religious mood for his inaugural address. In the very first sentence, when Carter thanked President Ford for "all he has done to heal our land,"[46] he implied that one of the Presidential responsibilities is that of "healing," a job which can be seen either in medical terms or, metaphorically, as a divine responsibility.

Carter specifically referred to his faith by talking of the TWO Bibles before him and by quoting the prophet Micah. And, throughout, the speech was sprinkled with religious language. He declared that the inauguration attests to the "spiritual" strength of the nation, that there is "a new spirit among us all," that "ours was the first society openly to define itself in terms of . . . spirituality," etc. By my count, he used the word "spirit" seven times and other clearly religious words—"pray," "moral," "religious," etc.—an additional twenty-seven times.

In addition to his Christian faith, Carter assessed his faith in the nation and in the American people. He seemed to ask the citizens to have that same faith in him. In this manner he became a missionary with his own church of political believers. He had made a commitment to America; in return, he sought a commitment from the people. Again, the religious overtones drowned out the political ones.

At the end of the speech the President listed six goals. Although they were stated in the past tense, the aphoristic form made them resemble the Ten Commandments. One statement followed another without explication, each with its own ideology, each pertaining to moral and spiritual issues. Any could be converted from aphorism to commandment by replacing "that we had" with "Thou Shalt." "That we had strengthened the American family" would become "Thou Shalt strengthen the American family."

Clearly, there was a religiosity theme running through the speech. How was it undermined? By overkill. We Americans don't like to be preached to; the descriptive phrase for somebody who does so is the negatively-toned "preachy."

We do expect a little religion to be interspersed in our political addresses— "God" has been defined as a word in the final sentence of a political speech— but we get nervous about unbending fanaticism. And a good portion of the overweening piety could have been excised from this speech. For instance, "while he could have called for a resurgence of *belief* in the nation and in ourselves, with the religious theme dominant over the secular one, Carter asked instead that we have 'full *faith* in our country—and in one another.' "[47]

Not only was the religion over-emphasized in and of itself, but it interfered with the secular messages by casting them in a non-political light. For instance, Carter was undoubtedly right in claiming that "our *moral* sense dictates a clearcut preference for those societies which share with us an abiding respect for individual human rights," (emphasis added) but that affinity is not exclusively morality-based. It is also political and economic. The stressing of his religious standpoints meant that his discussion of political topics seemed to float in a state of limbo outside any point in political history. The resultant tone was that of a Southern preacher's eternal moralistic generalization rather than that of a presidential policy-maker.

Carter's second subject, the American Dream, is almost inherently related to the first. The religio-political analog draws one myth into the presence of the other in a way not unusual in the American experience. Both function, amongst other ways, to provide hope to their audiences, although Carter's Dream rhetoric seemed less hopeful than his religious, perhaps because he introduced it negatively: "the bold and brilliant dream which excited the founders of our nation still awaits consummation. I have no new dream to set forth today, but rather urge a fresh faith in the old dream."

Perhaps it is too much an overstatement to call that a "negative" introduction to the dream. But it did suggest an aura of stagnation. In saying that he had no "new dream," Carter indicated his conservatism, his willingness for things to remain pretty much the same. Perhaps "he appeared . . . reluctant to define his own version of the American dream lest he lose support."[48] At any rate, given the concomitant discussion of "recognized limits" of the government, he "seemed content to go along with the revolution of sinking expectations."[49]

Further, he gave conflicting testimony to the state of the Dream. First he said it "still awaits its consummation;" then that it "endures," and finally that it is "undiminished" and "ever-expanding." For something to endure and expand while it still awaits consummation seems, at best, confusing.

And when he moved beyond the dream to generalized principles and ideals, the confusion continued. When he said, "we have already found a high degree of personal liberty" he undermined the meaning with his word choice. True, liberty is sought for, thus "found"; but more importantly, it is created and fought for, processes more active than mere "finding."

Another misunderstood historic principle was revolution. In saying, "if we despise our government we have no future," Carter indicated that revolution is outside the pale. Did we not despise our government in the time of George III? Did we then assume that we had no future? Or did we discover a moral duty, a religious calling, a God-given right to revolt? Again, we find Carter passivity.

Throughout he offered only a comforting sameness. As long as we believe in the nation's hallowed symbols such as freedom and democracy, he seemed to say, we cannot only maintain the status quo, but return to a past, even a better, one. Thus, instead of offering a threat of change which might alienate or worry the average American, Carter held out a glorious vision of a past to be revived. The times they may be "achanging," but with Carter in office our values wouldn't be. "All this raises a couple of important points: Is the new President's appeal to the noble principles of the American past relevant to the challenges of the present and the future? And are the American people, with their broken families, their spectacular divorce, crime and drug rates ready to respond to the new President's appeals to austerity, discipline and sacrifice?"[50]

Obviously, Carter realized that such questions were central. Having grounded his address, however maladroitly, in religious and patriotic hopefulness, he sought to identify his duties and those of his countrymen.

At only one point did Carter explicitly talk of presidental responsibility: "You have given me a great responsibility—to stay close to you, to be worthy of you and to exemplify what you are." But at other points in the address other responsibilities are implicitly recognized—to be a healer, to urge us to faith, to take on moral duties, to avoid drift, to be competent and compassionate and bold, etc.

While staying close, being worthy and exemplifying others *may* be great responsibilities, Carter immediately undermined his role by saying, "Your strength can compensate for my weakness, and your wisdom can help to minimize my mistakes." As William Safire commented, "After campaigning for three years on the theme that Government must be as good as its people— promising strong leadership to match the national character—he now changes that into an apology that he's no better than us, and therefore we can't expect much."[51]

Democratic theory suggests that leaders shouldn't get too far ahead of their followers, but Carter, perhaps influenced by the popularity of Schlesinger's analysis of "The Imperial Presidency,"[52] overdid it. There was no establishment of himself in the speech except in the most humble and subservient context. His projection of his image as a common man worked against him in his desire to be perceived as a leader. He did little to project leadership qualities or to extend to the people the security which a strong, charismatic president provides.

Even his explicit listing of his duties worked against him, for they did not include the duties we normally associate with leadership, thus raising the question of whether he knew the full extent of his duties. For instance, what about the powers of the office? What about specific actions? It is a widely held belief that unity comes through action, but Carter's view of unity (which he called for in several passages) was totally passive.

The overall impression of the secular portions of the speech was passivity. Carter even justified inaction when he said, "even our great nation has its recognized limits and . . . we can neither answer all questions nor solve all problems." The unstated addenda was, "so we won't even try."

And the language the President utilized elsewhere in the speech reinforced this image of passivity. For instance, he relied on negatives to describe the positive. Rather than calling on us to face the future boldly, he said, "nor can we afford to lack boldness as we meet the future." Since the negative was used to state the positive, the logical assumption was that Carter was more passive than active. Another clue indicative of his passiveness is found in the verbs he used to describe action: "to help shape" and "a step forward" both indicate gradual change and moderating action.

So Carter undermined his leadership theme with his unctuous humility and his (explicit and implicit) passivity, the latter of which was to dog him throughout his presidency.

Just as it is axiomatic that if leaders are to lead followers must follow, so it is true that no politician talks about his responsibilities without speaking of the roles of citizens.

With Carter, the references to the citizens, like "A President may sense and proclaim that new spirit, but only a people can provide it," seemed selected to make the American people feel they were an integral part of the decision-making process. It was a ritualistic reaffirmation of the government's dependence upon the people, of the role the people play in government. As such, it is standard fare in inaugural addresses. Woodrow Wilson's inaugural (the one Carter studied most closely while preparing his own[53]) included a call for returning government to the people, in these words: "The great government we loved has too often been made use of for private and selfish purposes, and those who used it had forgotten the people."[54]

Beyond the specific identifications of citizen roles, Carter relied on plural pronouns to suggest their involvement. He used "we" forty-three times in the speech and "our" thirty-six times. By contrast, he employed the personal pronoun "I" only six times. Of the thirty-five paragraphs of the speech, twenty-five began with "we," "our," or "let us."

Perhaps because he undermined his role of leader so badly by overstating his dependence on the citizens, the undermining of the roles of citizens was relatively tame. But at least a modicum of damage was done. For instance, in attempting to mute the call for sacrifice while avoiding the discussion of specific policies, he may have produced discomfort. It is not comforting to hear the president ask for "individual sacrifice" without an explanation of what that might entail, or even the necessity for it.

In a similar manner, when he said we would "fight our wars against poverty, ignorance and injustice," he may have conjured up negative feelings. "Wars against poverty" remind one of the Johnson era and, while containing possible evocative meanings, may also suggest images of a sprawling bureaucracy rather than the controlled one he had promised in the campaign.

One stylistic weakness in his discussion of citizen roles should be mentioned. When he said, "Your strength can compensate for my weakness, and your wisdom can help to minimize my mistakes," he lost the desired balance. "Strength" vs "weakness" works, but he obviously could not find a suitable opposite of "wisdom." And while our strength could *compensate* for his weakness, all our wisdom could do was *help to minimize* his mistakes—whether that was to be because of limitations on our wisdom or the egregiousness of his mistakes was not discussed.

While the speech "was addressed primarily to the spirit of the American people, rather than the intractable problems of foreign affairs,"[55] there was a thread of international concern running through the speech. As compared to the absence of concern for substantive domestic problems, Carter stressed international policies and the importance of respecting human rights. He set forth "a new role for the country as an international symbol of decency, compassion and strength."[56]

It was here that his tone best reflected his message, for he was calm and controlled rather than frenetic and aggressive. We were reminded, in subdued terminology, of the armaments race and the threat of nuclear weapons. But the competition remained unnamed; it was the world which suffered the danger, not us alone. Even enemies seemed to share the problems as much as provoking them. Carter preferred words over weapons and suggested that perseverance in this preference would lead to peace.

Throughout the discussion of foreign affairs, Carter evinced a quiet patriotism. But the caution created by his consideration of reality undermined his pathos. Each inspirational idea was balanced with probabilities. Each potentially powerful statement was diluted with a drop of realism. For instance, near the end of the speech he said, "I would *hope* that the nations of the world *might* say that we had built a lasting peace . . ." (emphases added). His credibility would not have been destroyed if he had employed a more assertive language. This conditional approach unsettled more than refreshed, for it robbed him of emotive force.

He continued to dribble in probabilities with statements like, "we urge all other people to join us, for success *can* mean life instead of death." (emphasis added) When speaking of the rising passion for freedom, he weighed down the impact by starting the next sentence with the words, "Tapping this new spirit . . ." "Tapping" is a control word; the implied mechanicalness emasculates the zeal of the passion, as if the furies could be dispensed from a water cooler.

In short, Carter's foreign policy discussion was undermined by his cautious approach, preventing him from stirring the audience with the desired emotional force. His logos weakened his pathos.

The major image of Carter which emerged from his inaugural was passivity. At a later point in his tenure that would come to be called weakness, and would be blamed on his actions, or lack of actions. But the seeds of that judgement were already revealed in the inaugural address.

Two weeks later, on February 3, 1977, President Carter presented his first Fireside Chat—and again demonstrated rhetorically the weakness which would eventually destroy his presidency. This can be demonstrated by examining his treatment of problems and solutions in that speech.

The problems were introduced as emergencies but the solutions were hardly described as panaceas:

problem: "One of the most urgent projects is to develop a national energy policy."[57]
solution: it "started before this winter and will take much longer to solve."
problem: "the worst economic slowdown of the last forty years."
solution: "It will produce steady, balanced, sustainable growth."
problem: "we must reform and reorganize the Federal Government."
solution: the system "will take a long time to change."
problem: the tax system is "a disgrace."
solution: "The economic program . . . will . . . be just a first step."
problem: "The welfare system also needs a complete overhaul."
solution: We have "begun a review."

Finally, speaking generally about all of his proposals, he said "Many of them will take longer than I would like . . ." How one reacts to all of these identifications of emergencies followed by slow and partial solutions depends somewhat on political orientation. A sympathizer might say that Carter was just being realistic about how long solutions take, while an opponent might contend that Carter was trying to demonstrate a commitment to promises on which he had no intention, or chance, of delivering.

A more rhetorical assessment would take as its point of departure Murray Edelman's claim that every government engages in a "cycle of anxiety and reassurance" to provide a "supportive following."[58] All citizens of this country should be familiar with the process: first we are told that somebody (usually Russia) is a great danger; then we are assured that our government can cope with the situation. In this speech, then, Carter's problem was that he oversold the anxiety part of the formula by elevating problems into emergencies. Naturally, then, the world of political reality being as slow as it is, he could not promise to solve the emergencies immediately.

Assuming that he continued this rhetorical approach throughout his presidency, it may give us a clue to his declining fortunes. That is, any leader who oversells problems without overselling his solutions is bound to be perceived as incapable of coping with the problems.

Another early problem which continued throughout his presidency was his penchant for taking conflicting positions . . . or taking forceful positions and then retreating. Neither of these tendencies projects competence, and both may be related to the fuzziness found in the campaign rhetoric—in two ways. First, the "something for everybody" aspect of fuzziness appears to be a first cousin to the "conflicting positions" approach. Second, the fact that his fuzziness allowed him to avoid taking any position in the campaign left him free to adopt any position he favored later, and he often did so without considering political implications. Then, faced with political reality, he had to retreat.

The conflicting positions taken during his presidency neared legendary proportions. He opposed the Cuban military intervention in Angola and Zaire at the same time that he was talking of restoring diplomatic relations with Havana.[59] He preached against inflation and protectionism, but paid off the maritime members for their support with inflationary and protectionist subsidies.[60] "He proclaim[ed] a new policy of reducing American arms sales abroad. Then, in the four months following the proclamation, he approve[d] sales of more than $4 billion."[61] Faced with the discovery of a Soviet brigade in Cuba he first announced its existence there as unacceptable and summoned several special sessions of the Security Council. But when he subsequently reported to the nation he hinted that the whole affair was overblown and claimed the brigade was not a "clear and present danger," thus downgrading "the significance of the drama in which he was supposed to be the central character."[62]

Nearly equalling his conflicting positions, both in regularity and in damage to his tenure, were his retreats. He retreated from his $50 tax rebates and his cancellation of 30 expensive water projects,[63] from defense cutbacks and the human rights test in foreign affairs.[64] He proclaimed "the moral equivalent of war" on energy, then retreated to a position which held that no real sacrifice was necessary.[65]

While the reasons for all these retreats are still not clear, several hypotheses have been advanced. A *New York Times* editorialist claimed they suggested "an excessive haste either in the embrace of policy or withdrawal from it."[66] James Reston, calling it a penchant for "passing long on first down," suggested the positions were taken before considering the politics of the situation: "He advocated a 'homeland' for the Palestinians without checking it out even with his own State Department. He announced his energy and welfare programs without analyzing the opposition in Congress, and he called for support of his Panama treaties before the text was published or both sides agreed on what it meant."[67] Herbert Klein more simply attributed the retreats to Carter's tendency of "shooting from the hip."[68] And Joseph Kraft concluded that Carter just didn't know what he was doing, saying he was reminded of "the old image of a small figure in deep seas whose idea of governing is to lash the waves."[69]

C. Vann Woodward, rather tongue in cheek (I think), marveled at "Carter's remarkable propensity—gift, flair—for fusing contradictions and reconciling opposites. The political consequences have been an unusual assortment of unified ambiguities and ambiguous unities. He once described himself as 'a populist in the tradition of Richard Russell.' Which is rather like conjuring up 'an anarchist in the tradition of Grover Cleveland,' or 'a socialist in the tradition of Herbert Hoover.' "[70] But to the rest of us, Carter's contradictions and retreats were not seen as gifts or flairs. We saw weakness or, when charitable, a man "hesitant in his exercise of power."[71]

And just when Carter's popularity had reached a devastatingly low point, history played a bad trick on him. Iranian "students" took over the U.S. embassy, taking our employees there hostage. It looked like a political opportunity for Carter to appear a strong leader and achieve the national unity he had been seeking throughout his presidency. So he played it to the hilt. And it did help for a while, long enough for him to wrap up his renomination on the Democratic line. But it ultimately defeated him, and it did so in part because of the way he approached it:

Jimmy Carter played into Khomeini's hands by blowing up the political value of the hostages . . . In his withdrawal from campaigning during the Presidential primaries, so that he could handle the "crisis," Jimmy Carter helped create a feeling of emergency in the United States which suggested that the holding of the hostages was a national security threat, comparable to that posed by major powers in the past. The only president in the twentieth century who had not campaigned on national security grounds was Franklin Roosevelt in 1944, during World War II. In his dramatic refusal to turn on the Christmas lights at the White House until the hostages should be returned, a symbolic refusal which had not been employed even during World War II, Carter suggested that the whole nation had been dimmed by this assault on its integrity. In his calls for a moratorium on all 'criticism' right after the hostages had been taken, and in his subsequent suggestions that his critics were unpatriotic, he reinforced the view that the U.S. was in a great battle, where the contribution of each and every American, somehow, would make a significant difference in the outcome. But, saying that each and every life was so important to all Americans, and putting their safety at the top of his agenda, he created a domestic political climate in which it would be very difficult for him to employ American's military power, even in the form of threats, to salvage American prestige. In effect, President Carter, with the collaboration of the mass media, helped turn the American hostages into a symbol of the entire nation. Like the individuals imprisoned in Iran, the American nation as a whole had been captured—with few options open to it, but to implore with its captors to let it go.[72]

But did Carter have any choice? That is, did he define the hostage situation as a crisis or did the media do so? The executive producer of ABC's World News Tonight, Jeff Gralnick, contends that "If the government had nothing public to say, except that it would run things as if no crisis existed, the media would not have been able to do anything with the Iran story."[73]

In a sense, then, the "crisis" was of Jimmy Carter's making. Yet, because he lacked either the will or the ability to solve the problem, escalating it into a crisis was a mistake. "Moreover, his many public attempts to exercise influence—in political circumstances where failure was likely—helped diminish American 'power' on the world scene. For power is based on prestige, and prestige has always been protected by avoiding public attempts to exercise it when one cannot do so. Indeed, the mobilization of such strong emotions, when the situation did not permit him to transform those emotions into effective action, contributed to American feelings of impotence . . ."[74] and, along with the other weaknesses of the Carter messages, contributed to the assessment of Carter as too weak to continue to inhabit the White House.

Carter's Style

Style is a nearly ineffable subject. Almost all agree that language, voice and physical components, all of which we will return to later, are components. But there is something else, less easily defined, that is also included—perhaps "tone" or "mode of approach" hint at it. Or better yet, although impossibly imprecise, "feel," as in "the feel of the man," gets at it.

This "something else," this "feel," is partly the result of the cumulation of the other components of style, but it also is composed partly of other elements nearly impossible to identify. Or perhaps these other elements vary from observer to observer to observer, come from the interplay of the characteristics of observer and observed. At any rate, people who can agree on assessments of language, voice and movement can still come to differing judgements of style, so some attempt must be made to understand these nearly mystical elements if assessments of style are to move beyond the banal.

And such an examination is especially important in attempting to understand Jimmy Carter, for he was from the beginning a candidate of style, or, in the more popular parlance, an image-candidate. Countless references could be dredged up from his early days on the national scene, in which people said they didn't know what he stood for but they liked him, or they didn't know why they liked him, they just did.

Obviously, such unreasoned acceptance made his opponents nervous, so Max Lerner cast his discussion of Carter's style in the form of an answer to the hypothetical question, "What has Jimmy Carter got that I don't have?" "Maybe the answer is: an engaging smile, a soft voice with an ingenuous look, a cool mind, a steel will, a Southerner's roots, a moderate's instincts, a liberal Georgian's connections with a black constituency, a rural evangelical religion, a capacity to fudge issues, a politician's antipolitician stance, a fair amount of cheek, a profile that can be made to look like Jack Kennedy's and a set of morals that can't."[75]

It will be noted that Lerner's list includes some traditional style categories—voice, appearance, language—as well as political assets. But it also includes some estimates of unmeasurable qualities—mind, will, roots, instincts, cheek—which made up, for him, the "feel of the man."

Of especial interest during the 1976 campaign was the impact of what Lerner called a "Southerner's roots." Beyond the political fact that Carter was expected to carry the South, his Southern heritage was presumed to be a component of his style, explaining his success in small gatherings, his first-name-basis orientation, his avoidance of issues, and even his smile. His campaign, so invigoratingly fresh to much of the country, was found to be the style of traditional Southern politics:

> It is still a style in which issues are not discussed in the campaign. It is still a very personal style. It is still a style in which the candidate spends most of his time and energy trying to convince the voters that he is a Good Ol' Boy. It is still a style that reduces the constituency to friends and neighbors who cannot, after their votes are counted, argue that the candidate for whom they used their franchise stands for anything more specific than, say, God.
>
> It was inevitable that some Southern politician would do what Carter is doing today, try the Southern style of politics on the national electorate.
>
> It seems that Carter has found the exact moment when the national electorate is ready for the Southern style, when many of us prefer that the energy crisis, detente, the economy, busing, assassination conspiracies and Watergate be left undiscussed.
>
> Carter is not the man to remind us of these perplexing and often painful problems, certainly not as long as his smile works.[76]

So Carter's style was traditional Southern. Or was it? The author of that piece was not talking so much of Carter's personal style as the design of his campaign. At a more personal level, there is evidence that his years away from Georgia made him something of a Yankee. William Miller argued against the Southern style analysis, saying, "he is no Southern talker, orator or writer. He writes and speaks without embellishment. Though verbally agile, he uses words as instruments only, to convey facts, points, arguments. . . . His formal speeches . . . are not particularly well-written. His spontaneous talk is not eloquent. In a particularly un-Southern way, his speeches have no rhythm. Big words pop out in unexpected places. Complex formulations intrude when he is trying to be simple. Parallels don't parallel. . . . He is a long way from either the verbosity or the eloquence of the 'Southern' use of language."[77]

The conclusion, then, is that Carter ran his campaign in the Southern style (i.e., manner) but without the eloquence (bombast?) which has been presumed to be a part of the personal style of Southern politicians.

Rather than offering himself as a Southerner, Carter presented an average American persona, often saying in 1976 that he wasn't the best qualified man for the job, by training or experience. However, he claimed to be the best because his values and beliefs perfectly mirrored those of his audience. At a time when memories of "The Imperial Presidency" still haunted the public, the idea of a commoner in the White House was attractive. Indeed, it was Arthur Schlesinger, Jr. who most clearly delineated Carter's common man approach: "Mr. Carter's tone is direct, colloquial, engaging, often flat but sometimes oddly moving. His faith in work, discipline, education, character recalls an older and better America. He speaks without embarrassment about deeply personal things—trust, truth, the family, love and, when pressed, the Almighty. He rarely goes in for rhetorical pretense or flourish. It is the tone of a plain, homespun American talking seriously to his neighbors or his Sunday School class."[78]

The "averageness" Schlesinger noticed was carried into the White House, where Carter's early symbolic activities (walking "home" after the inauguration, refusing to set up an elaborate vacation retreat a la San Clemente, removing the gold braids of the "palace guards," enrolling Amy in a public school, etc.) stripped the presidency of some of its accumulated royalist trappings and returned "the office to a more normal, less immune to criticism, status."[79]

The "averageness" of Carter led him to demystify the office. That reassured the populace, as did his "cool" or "soft" approach. He was calm, organized and ready to negotiate rather than impulsive, excitable and ready to fight. A public tired of frenetic politics was ready for this approach.

But these same characteristics eventually became liabilities when the audience began once again to desire active, forceful leadership. For instance,

Terence Smith complained that in his Panama Canal appeal "His tone was subdued, as though he was trying to convince his audience of the merits of the treaties more by gentle persuasion than exhortation."[80] Note that the change was not in Carter but in the audience expectation. In 1976 gentle persuasion was desired; by 1978 we wanted exhortation.

By 1979 Carter's calmness had become a real liability, and what had been called calmness was now attacked as detachment: "Carter has seemed a man detached from the message he was delivering. In part the impression is a product of the even level of his recitals; a less charitable description would be monotony. There are rare intervals when any statement seems to achieve precedence over another. One can almost imagine him announcing the start of a fateful nuclear collision and the appointment of a new ambassador to an obscure country without noticeably altering the decibel count."[81] Indeed, Murray Kempton worried that "alarmed serenity" was "his highest pitch of style."[82]

So, once again, we find that Carter's rhetoric contained a weakness that undermined his presidency. This time it was less that he didn't turn out to be the kind of person we wanted than that he did, but we had changed our minds about what we wanted. From cheering his walk down Pennsylvania Avenue on inauguration day, we had moved to an anti-pedestrian stance. The common man in the White House no longer fulfilled our expectations.

Language

As befitted his cautious man personality and image, Jimmy Carter normally was careful and precise in his use of language. This was especially true of the mechanics. After Carter's first presidential press conference, James Wechsler noticed, "There are no unfinished sentences, rambling detours, embarrassing stammerings, rarely even a dangling participle."[83] James Reston apparently was the journalist who was most appreciative of and impressed by this facet of Carter's language, as he mentioned it in three different columns in 1977: "he speaks in sentences, thinking between commas, without a subject or predicate out of place";[84] "In good times and bad, he faces his critics with more regularity, more precision of fact and language, and more patience and courtesy than any other president of the television age";[85] "More than any other Chief Executive since the last World War, Mr. Carter respects and uses the English language carefully and accurately."[86]

This careful handling of language, so lauded at the grammatical level, occasionally got Carter into trouble at other levels, as it did during the 1976 Florida primary:

> Asked if he had promised to nominate Governor Wallace at the 1972 Democratic convention (as Mr. Wallace has often said he did), Mr. Carter denied that was true and said there was proof of that denial in a telegram he had sent to the Alabama Governor.

"I told him I'd have to decline the honor of nominating him," he said as the television cameras whirred and the tape recorders registered his every word.

Did he use the word "honor" in his telegram? He was asked.

"No, I'm using it now," he said.

Sincerely or sarcastically?

"I used it deliberately," he said.

But sincerely or sarcastically?

"Well, if it had been an honor to nominate him," he said curtly, "I would have nominated him. Does that answer your question?"

His apparent intention, before the questions became so insistent, was to leave the impression that although he had not nominated Governor Wallace . . . it was not an entirely unacceptable idea.[87]

So in this case his attempted careful use of the language to tint an issue was unsuccessful, but we saw earlier that he was able to utilize language to create a fuzzy impression, defusing some of his more unpopular stands by mastering "the art of presenting liberal positions in conservative language and conservative positions in liberal language,"[88] or, as James Reston called it, the art of "being precisely imprecise."[89]

None of this criticism should be taken to imply that Carter was in any way an unusual politician in attempting to make his language work for him, although the fact that he promised never to lie to us made it seem that his language-based "hedges" were more reprehensible than the same thing from other politicians.

Sometimes Carter was attacked for handling language not only as others do, but as is required in the political world. A case in point was his preference for the subjunctive mood. Marshall Frady, hinting darkly of unpalatable manipulation, charged that Carter "had learned over the years that his purposes were better served by the subjunctive than the declarative . . ."[90] And in a *New York Times* editorial it was suggested that "Careful scrutiny of a candidate's phrases often reveals deliberate hedging. 'I would never give up full control of the Panama Canal,' Mr. Carter said, adding 'as long as it had any contribution to make to our national security'—a conditional note which opens a wide realm of judgmental freedom."[91]

We will never know, of course, whether Carter really was hedging on the Panama Canal in 1976, saying what his audience wanted to hear, or if his "conditional note" was the careful language of a realistic politician who understood that the political world is a probabilistic world, best dealt with through hypotheses, contingencies and possibilities, i.e., with the subjunctive. As George Will has noted, "Most of what a President says is politically, if not grammatically, in the subjunctive mood because he can do little alone. A President's principal power is the highly contingent power to persuade Congress. And Congress hears a discordant clamor of other voices."[92] From this perspective, the subjunctive only brings the rhetoric into realistic alignment with the political world.

Unfortunately for Carter, his language-based problems stemmed less from his carefulness and use of the subjunctive than from carelessness and the fact that "As a man and as a wordsmith, Mr. Carter likes absolutes and superlatives . . ."[93] We recall that his autobiography was not titled "Why Not Competence" but "Why Not the *Best,*" that he promised *never* to lie to us, that he characterized the Federal bureaucracy as "*totally* unmanageable."[94] In 1976, offering to shake hands with each contributor at a fundraiser, Carter said that "they should take the handshake as something that would 'cement a lifelong friendship between us.' "[95]

To see how this penchant for hyperbole continued, and was bothersome, in his presidency, consider Carter's 1980 State of the Union Message.[96] While we expect exaggeration from politicians, in this speech the absolutes and superlatives were magnified by the poor fit between his announcement that henceforth we're going to "face the world as it is" and statements like "the United States will remain the *strongest* of all nations" or "our nation has *never* been aroused and unified so greatly in peacetime," or the U.S.-U.S.S.R. relationship "is the *most critical* factor in determining whether the world will live at peace." (emphases added.)

But his most famous superlative in the address was his contention that the Soviet invasion of Afghanistan was "the most serious threat to the peace since the second world war." His primary opponent, Senator Kennedy, took issue with that one, asking, "Is it a graver threat than the Berlin Blockade, the Korean War, the Soviet march into Hungary and Czechoslovakia, the Berlin wall, the Cuban missile crisis, or Vietnam?," and concluding, "Exaggeration and hyperbole are the enemies of sensible foreign policy."[97] They were also Carter's enemies, as in this speech they undermined his assertion of fealty to the facts and brought into question his ability to assess the world.

Two specific favorite words in Carter's vocabulary—"comprehensive" and "reform"—are difficult to categorize. Surprisingly, both can be seen as either cautious or hyperbolic locutions. A comprehensive program may be one put together carefully, covering a multitude of problems . . . or a rag-tag melange of ideas thrown together almost haphazardly and mislabeled "comprehensive." Likewise, "reform" may suggest a cautious, non-revolutionary improvement or may be employed to provide a patina of acceptability to an otherwise undistinguished proposal. Thus, whether one perceives Carter's legislative drafts as "comprehensive" or "reforms" may depend somewhat on the observer's ideology. But the fact that Carter preferred those descriptions is undeniable. He proposed "a comprehensive strategic arms limitation agreement, a comprehensive Middle East peace settlement, a comprehensive national energy program, comprehensive welfare reform and comprehensive tax reform."[98] He used the word "reform" so often that the *Wall Street Journal* started quarantining the word by encasing it in quotation marks.[99]

There is a chance that these two favorite words were more expressive of Carter's hopes than they were descriptive of his programs. All along, Carter seemed as concerned with how he felt about actions as with the actions themselves, which explains his excessive use of adverbs as well as permitting his feelings to rise to the surface in other comments, sometimes inappropriately, as in his promise to "whip Kennedy's ass."[100]

In a strange kind of way, Carter's use of language as self-fulfilling prophecies seems to have been related to his whole desire for and promise of trust. That is, we are what we think we are; our feelings capture reality; our programs are as we describe them. We must trust ourselves, our feelings, our solutions. Then, as we see how well everything works, we will be able to trust each other and, eventually, even our government. Somehow, the key to his whole political approach was revealed and reflected in his language. It was, in a sense, the politics of biofeedback wherein trust and confidence flowed from actions, but successful actions flowed from trust and confidence. So the "logical" point at which to begin to repair the damage to public confidence was the rhetorical. Hence the "trust me" campaign, the symbolism of his first year, the 1978 presentation of the liberation of the Panama Canal as an act of atonement,[101] the malaise speech of 1979 and perhaps even his overall preference for the straightforward and banal rather than the eloquent.

Unfortunately for Carter the end result was merely that he was seen as lacking eloquence and his "plain" style one that reduced "great phrases into banalities. Lincoln's 'we must think anew and act anew. We must disenthrall ourselves' degenerated into Carter's 'we must change our attitudes as well as our policies.' And the Founding Fathers' ringing pledge of 'our lives, our fortunes and our sacred honor' became, in Mr. Carter's pallid paraphrase, 'their property, position, and life itself.' "[102]

Voice

It is obvious to anyone who ever heard Carter speak that "soft-voiced"[103] and "low-pitched"[104] describe his voice accurately. But our concern is less with phonics than functions. How did this soft voice affect his audiences? The evidence, assuming journalistic listeners are somewhat representative, is that, as in so many other of his rhetorical characteristics, Carter's voice was a plus in the 1976 campaign and a hindrance thereafter.

In January of 1976, James Wolcott, in an otherwise highly critical piece, praised Carter's voice: "As a speechmaker he's articulate and expressive, quietly softly expressive, as if straining his voice would tear into the delicacy of his mood."[105] "Carter is cool, very cool, yet his emotional tonalities surface. The most impressive remark Carter made . . . was when he said that more than being disappointed by Watergate, the American people were 'hurt,' and his voice curved around the word, as if curving around the pain of a hard truth . . . the word was laid on the plane of the sentence like a bruised apple upon a still-life table."[106]

Six months later, David Halberstam's coverage of the Democratic Convention included these reflections on Carter's voice: "Watching him again and again on television I was impressed by his sense of pacing, his sense of control, very low key, soft, a low decibel count, all this in sharp contrast to the other candidates who, getting free television time, tried to get the maximum number of words in. Carter, by contrast, even when he was getting (and knew he was getting) only a minute and a half on the network news shows, used the pauses. The pauses were reassuring: they seemed to echo his own self-confidence, the lack of rush, his strong sense of his own roots among a people less and less sure of theirs."[107]

Carter's voice, clearly, was a positive factor in 1976. But by mid-term the assessment had changed. Marshall Frady hinted at the new evaluation: "For all his commendable gameness and earnestness, yet there still lingered about him some sense of slightness, a quality of balsa wood. It may have been merely the light wisping of his voice—some sound of thin grasses in that drawl with its muted fogs—or the fine and almost mincingly polite effect he maintained, an unrelenting niceness and diffidence . . ."[108] "His voice still has that faint, shrill, reedy strain and an odd off-syncopation—it's as if, however further he has ranged now in eminence and self-certainty, his voice were still left somewhere back about at the point of his high-school graduation."[109]

Frady didn't come right out and say that Carter's voice made him appear weak. But that was his message—slight, light, thin, muted, mincing, diffident, faint, out of tune with the world, as naive as a high school graduate.

Again, it will be noted that the change was not in Carter but in the public desires. In 1976 his soft voice calmed us and we liked that, seeking surcease from the frenetic world; but by 1978 we had decided that we wanted a tough leader and Carter's soft voice sounded to us like weakness.

Physical Aspects

As befitted a non-dynamic speaker, Carter rarely gestured. When he tried to improve his image in 1980 by clenching his fist during one of his speeches, everyone realized that it was an artificial attempt to appear more resolute and discounted it accordingly.

Carter's physical attributes apparently helped him in 1976, especially on television. "The camera is kind to him, it heightens his strengths—a strong sense of himself, a good smile, a face wonderfully American, born of a thousand Norman Rockwell covers; we know him if not from our past, then at least from what we were told was our past. Similarly, the camera minimizes his

potential weaknesses: he is said to be short, but he does not *look* short, therefore he might just as well be tall. He is said to be cold and aloof, but he does
not *look* cold and aloof, therefore he might just as well be warm."[110] However,
though no critic seems ever to have mentioned it, there is a possibility that his
slight physique added to the perceptions of him as weak during his presidency.

As to the judgements of his stage movement, the only assessment I have
found is the minor complaint of William Safire that he "looks to both sides
too quickly, as if at a fast badminton match . . ."[111]

There are, however, several critiques of his movements off stage, one positive and one negative. Wolcott found that "his movements have a dancerly
wholeness, suggesting not only a campaigner who knows how to proportion
fatigue equally throughout his body, but somehow so assured, so serenely confident, that doubts and fears don't manifest themselves as bodily neuroses but
are consciously objectified."[112]

Almost diametrically opposed to that assessment, as though he were talking
of a different person, Frady found a "peculiar awkwardness": "He slumped
slightly forward with his head thrust out and slightly lifted, giving him rather
the look, with his pink chapped skin, of an unshelled terrapin. He went swooping
along corridors and down main street sidewalks with a kind of marionette's
tight, dangly slap and flop in his movements, a strange flimsily hinged loose-
ness in his wrists, his hands flapping at his sides as he eagerly forged on."[113]

I can not solve the Wolcott-Frady disagreement; they neither seem to be
describing the movements of the Carter I saw. That Carter walked precisely—
not as stiffly as Richard Nixon, rather more like a child who had mastered
walking and was proud of it. Likewise, his lack of gestures when speaking
reminded me of a child reciting a piece rather than an engaged personality
involved in persuading an audience.

There were also, I found, differences in his rhetorical movements depending
upon his attitude to the subject. In his 1980 debate with Reagan, when he
spoke on a subject he seemed comfortable with (domestic programs for the
poor, the Camp David accord, his energy conservation proposals) he rested his
hands on either side of the podium, halfway between top and bottom. His weight
was evenly distributed on both feet and he spoke either into the camera or to
his questioner. He rarely faced Reagan when he was in his comfortable stance.
He also smiled slightly more, blinked less and squinted not at all.

When he appeared uneasy (discussing the economy, the hostage situation,
the SALT treaty and the Soviet invasion of Afghanistan) he placed his hands
at the top of the podium, shifted his weight nervously from one foot to the
other, reared back slightly and turned his head toward Reagan significantly
more often. He also smiled less, squinted noticeably, and blinked approximately 17% more often.

Without hard empirical data it is difficult to know how all of this was translated by the public. Yet what we know in more general terms would lead us to assume that his lack of gestures contributed to the perception that he lacked dynamism, his physique may have suggested weakness, and his nervous stage movements may have undermined his ethos. While these conclusions must remain highly tentative, it can be said with assurance that there is nothing in our literature to suggest that any of the physical characteristics here identified might have helped his image.

So, with the possible exception of this last category, we have found that all the components of style examined here—feeling, tone, language, voice and physical aspects—contributed to the perception of Carter as a weak man, a weak president. It is doubtful if even an objectively strong president could have overcome the image of weakness portrayed in Carter's rhetorical style.

Characteristics

Keeping in mind the image of the man which emerged in his style, we turn now to an examination of personal characteristics of Carter's which were embedded in the content of his rhetoric—if you will, his implicitly-revealed ethos.

Religious

The most obvious characteristic of Jimmy Carter, revealed in his rhetoric as well as in other ways, was that he was a deeply religious person. Despite the obviousness of the religious overtones in his speeches, which James Naughton said were "moral sermons" rather than "political speeches,"[114] some analysts found religiosity of negligible importance in 1976: "Patton dismissed Carter's explicit expressions of fundamentalist faith as an issue in the campaign; Swanson classified religious disclosures as 'junk news'; Rarick *et. al.*, investigating his 'persona,' ignored piety as an element of character; and Hamilton Jordan, the candidate's campaign strategist, labeled in the 'weirdo factor.' "[115] Nonetheless, Erickson has persuasively demonstrated that "Carter's references to his spiritual faith and use of religious-political discourse . . . were not inconsequential. Carter's religious-political discourse reaffirmed our civic piety and faith in America: his religious discourses communicated trustworthiness, served as a source of identification with evangelicals, and generated media attention."[116]

Furthermore, an analysis of his pre-presidential rhetoric by Brooks Holifield, professor of religious history at Emory University, demonstrated that Carter was not inconsistent in his religious references, and suggested that the religion was deeply ingrained rather than added on for electoral advantage. For instance, as Governor of Georgia, "Carter rarely used the word 'God' in his official speeches, 'but when he did the term functioned generally in two ways: the poor should have the right and means to develop their 'God-given talents,' and the powerful have the responsibility to share their 'God-given blessings' for the common welfare.' "[117]

As I suggested earlier, in discussing his inaugural address, Carter's religious orientation was not an unmixed blessing when he reached the White House. The reasons for that are not entirely clear, but several suggest themselves. One is that there was an inherent contradiction between his religious and political appeals: "To audiences consumed with impotent rage Mr. Carter used the language of Christian piety to convey a sense of the Lord's vengeance. Thus the paradox implicit in his success. He presented himself as the candidate of hope and new beginnings, but he floated to the surface on a tide of despair. In place of a vision of the future he offered an image of the nonexistent past, promising a safe return to an innocent Eden in which American power and morality might be restored to the condition of imaginary grace."[118] Once he became President then, the hoped-for transformation did not materialize and the rage and despair were turned against him.

A second explanation suggests that religion is a private affair, so the public display of it creates doubts about the displayer. "When the language becomes moralizing, and the speaker begins to whine, the listener is overcome with a sense of phoniness and will respond with embarrassment and/or the impulse to flee. . . . When piety is pursued privately, it evokes humility. But when piety is made public, it becomes obsessive and suffused with self-serving righteousness. The more Mr. Carter protests against the sin of pride, the more he communicates his enslavement by it. At best, the piety proclaimed here communicates heroic egomania, at worst, an egomania joined by hypocrisy. The first quality accounts for Mr. Carter's failures during the first two years in the White House: his incapacity to learn anything of the subtleties and nuances of governance. What is there to learn for a man who is in constant touch with God?"[119]

Whereas the second explanation suggests that Carter's religion underwent a subtle change, a third holds that it was Carter who changed. More specifically, the God-Carter-people relationships changed. During the campaign Carter's religion was used to suggest to the people that Carter's godliness could help him be a good president, that because of the God-Carter relationship the Carter-people relationship would be close. That is, because we are all equal in the sight of God, Carter would not be an imperial president.

But once he became president the equality ceased. Carter became the mediator between the people and God, at best a minister, at worst a pope. The quotation from Micah which Carter utilized in his inaugural, "He hath showed thee, o man, what is good; and what doth the Lord require of thee, but to do justly, and to love mercy, and to walk humbly with thy God," perfectly portrayed the pre-presidential attitude: the leader and the people together should do good, be just, show mercy and display humility.

The scriptural quotation which he wanted to use in that address,[120] but was talked out of by his advisors, II Chronicles 7:14, suggests a different relationship: "If my people, which are called by my name, shall humble themselves, and pray, and seek my face, and turn from their wicked ways; then will I hear from heaven, and will forgive their sin, and will heal their land." Here is implied a quite different God-leader-follower relationship; namely, the leader must get the people to turn from their wicked ways. Question: why would a candidate who had argued that we needed a government as good as the people want to open his presidency with a quotation highlighting their "wicked ways?" The answer suggested here is that the people's goodness was not seen as accomplished but as potential. That potentiality required a leader who could mediate between them and God and bring goodness to fruition. The equal who was going to run the office with our help suddenly became the superior who was going to cure us of our evil ways and thus bring God's blessing upon us. That change in Carter's mission, and the people's role, was sensed by the people, leading them to distrust him. His 1979 "Energy Sermon,"[121] then, did not display any new negative attitude about the people . . . it just made explicit the attitude that Carter had been struggling to sublimate since his inauguration.

By 1980 his religiosity could not save the presidency for him. In addition to the problems it had caused with the electorate in general, he even lost ground amongst the evangelicals. In part that was because he had been a disappointment to them, for instance with his refusal to support an anti-abortion constitutional amendment; more importantly, however, his opponent was also a born-again evangelical Christian . . . and one whose conservatism was more appealing to the evangelical movement than was Carter's moderation.

Inflexible and Mean

A second Carter characteristic displayed in his rhetoric was inflexibility and meanness. It may be surprising to some that such attributes coexist with religiosity. It shouldn't be. If religious fanatics are absolutely intolerant of opposing creeds, it stands to reason that non-fanatic but nonetheless deeply religious people might be relatively inflexible.

Whether Carter's unyielding nature came from his religious orientation or some other cause(s), he brought from his Governor's experience "a reputation for being stubborn and inflexible, a moralist with little appreciation for the art of political compromise."[122] Early in the 1976 campaign he was described as "single-minded,"[123] and that perception of him as a driven man, coupled with his born-again religious emphasis, suggested to many that he might be some kind of fanatic.

The first direct evidence of Carter's inflexibility came in his response to criticism of his campaign rhetoric. As Charles Mohr noted at the time, "It is not easy, perhaps not even plausible, for Mr. Carter to admit simple error or a mistake or an ordinary political vice such as telling one audience what it seems to want to hear and trimming those remarks for a different forum."[124]

So how did Carter respond when caught out in an error? "He tend[ed] to explain that his staff did not follow up or that an aide wrote a letter which Carter did not see or that Carter had forgotten an incident from the past or that he was unaware of some tactic in his campaign,"[125] or, if no answer seemed possible, he flashed his "mules eating briars smile" and pressed on.[126]

Perhaps part of the reason he was seen as inflexible was his seeming lack of humor. Charles Mohr reported that Carter had "about the same attitude toward humor as that of a simple meat-and-potatoes cook towards garlic, hot peppers and herbs. A little, he seems to believe, goes a long way."[127] He employed only two pieces of humor during the campaign. In the first he would point out that he might not be the most qualified person in the country, or even in the immediate audience, for the presidency, then thank all his audience members for choosing not to run. In the second he talked of his family, saying his third son was 22 years old and that following his birth Carter and his wife had a fourteen year argument which he won, and their youngest, Amy, is now eight.

Others, closer to Carter, claimed that he did have a sense of humor, but that, since it entailed attacking others with a series of zingers, it was inappropriate for the campaign. As one 1976 aide described Carter's humor, "Jimmy's idea of self-deprecating humor is to dump . . . on his staff."[128] Clearly, such "funnyness" would be perceived by most as meanness. To avert that perception Carter chose to avoid humor and be perceived as dull instead.

Another Carter rhetorical tactic which might have had some alleviating affect on the charge of inflexibility was his constant attempt to find a way to identify with his audience. However, he was so inflexible in insisting that that component be in every speech that he sometimes seemed to be trying too hard, as when he told voters in Boise, Idaho that "he felt a 'special kinship' for the people of Idaho because 'potatoes and peanuts are the only major crops that grow underground.' "[129]

By the 1980 campaign Carter's many policy vacillations had erased the charge of inflexibility, but he was still occasionally considered mean, especially in terms of his attacks on Reagan. The New York Post talked of the attacks on Reagan as "savage tactics,"[130] "the politics of extremism,"[131] going "for the jugular,"[132] "fighting dirty,"[133] and a "crude attempt to smear"[134] by a "compulsively nasty little campaigner"[135] who "has an attraction to opponents' groins and eyeballs."[136] The *Daily News* somewhat less vitriolic but still upset, said, "The whole tone of the President's campaign . . . has been ugly, mean-spirited and dirty. His tactics are a disgrace to the Presidency and a disservice to the country."[137] Even the *New York Times,* which supported Carter, said his 1980 campaign was "vacuous,"[138] "negative"[139] and "whiny,"[140] and that he had "overstepped the bounds"[141] and made "unworthy cracks,"[142] not recognizing that "there is a difference between hard blows and low ones."[143] Carter probably would have been happy to have returned to the days of being perceived merely as inflexible.

Cautious (The Engineer Mentality)

Despite the fact that he sometimes "went overboard" in his rhetoric, especially during campaigns, Carter generally was a cautious president. Elected as a centrist, he clung tenaciously to centrist positions and moderate language. His watchwords, hence approach, emphasized stability, predictability, efficiency, caution.

An examination of his 1978 address on inflation at the annual meeting of the American Society of Newspaper Editors[144] will exemplify this approach. He used words denoting "increase" ten times, "holding the present course" twelve times and "decreasing" twenty-one times. That is, at forty-three points he utilized words of caution, but not once in the address did he employ more absolutist words like "solve" or "stop." Three times he emphasized that the programs should be coordinated with others; another three times he demonstrated the gradualism of his approaches by referring to them as "steps toward," and on seven occasions he underlined the fact that his program could not be enforced by referring to the necessity for government to set a good example.

Discussing his goals and programs he said he wanted to keep the inflation rate at a "reasonable and predictable level," develop "very carefully targeted initiatives," adopt "measures that avoid . . . extremes," use "our existing . . . output more efficiently," and make sure that all programs are "economically efficient and consistent with sound budget policy." Even this modest approach might have been perceived as too hopeful so Carter emphasized that there are "no easy answers," and that "it is a myth that government itself can stop inflation."

Throughout, his cautious approach emphasized reasonable and efficient programs put forward by a rational and prudent man. The resultant image was less of a dynamic leader than a competent administrator.

This emphasis on administration may have been one of his great weaknesses as president. As early as April of 1977 Hedrick Smith complained that

Carter "has not yet projected a clear vision of the American future," but rather "has seemed more like a problem-solving engineer intent on making both Government and society work better than a social reformer articulating a philosophy of social justice or coming down hard early in his term on a cluster of programs that would give his Administration a clear-cut political definition."[145]

By the start of 1978, the President's press secretary, Jody Powell, was conceding Carter's thematic weakness: "If there is one area that I see the biggest failure, it is exactly in that area. We haven't clearly enough articulated that overarching, unifying theme or presentation of what we're about or the way we're approaching things."[146]

Despite Powell's implication that the problem was lack of communication, there are indications that it went deeper than that. James Fallows, one of Carter's speechwriters, said "I came to think that Carter believes fifty things, but no one thing. He holds explicit, thorough positions on every issue under the sun, but he has no large view of the relations between them, no line indicating which goals (reducing unemployment? human rights?) will take precedence over which (inflation control? a SALT treaty?) when the goals conflict. Spelling out these choices makes the difference between a position and a philosophy, but it is an act foreign to Carter's mind."[147]

Fallows' position was echoed by another close aide: "I'm not sure there is a generalized political philosophy. If you want to know where Jimmy Carter stands, tell him what the problem is and what needs to be solved."[148]

But whether because of lack of communication or Carter's inherent orientation, it is clear that his Administration was themeless and that Carter plunged himself into "a preoccupation with the details of program and policy, for which a more confident President would have been willing to rely on hired thinkers . . ."[149]

This concern for detail was one of the primary pieces of evidence that critics pointed to when charging that his orientation was too reliant on his engineering outlook. James David Barber said he was a "technocrat" with "a sort of hydraulic worldview."[150]

The values associated with this engineering approach, Jimmy Carter's values, have been labelled "clean" virtues. Sheldon Wolin explains:

Consider what is absent from his list: the basic political virtues of justice and equality. These are 'dirty' virtues, the despair of any society that tries to realize them. At best there are approximations, always there are anomalies and imperfections. The crucial point about the clean virtues is how profoundly congenial they are to the 'values' and mode of thinking represented by administrative and organizational thinking: rationality, efficiency, straight lines of authority, choosing among priorities which have been rendered homogeneous so that they can be treated as commensurable, and depersonalized job descriptions.

The commandments of managerialism are the analogue to purifying rites: clean it up, get it straight, cost-account, organize, rationalize, one column for costs, another for benefits. Administration is the baptismal rite for a political world that has to be cleaned of disorder and mutiny.[151]

Thus, there is a link between Carter the engineer and Carter the born-again Christian. But for our purposes there is a more important linkage—between the engineer and the ineffective rhetor: "The engineer believes that political problems must, ultimately, have objective solutions, beyond controversy—solutions with which everyone will agree. Indeed, he is inclined to believe that political argument and controversy represent something discreditable and unreasonable in men, a vulgar inheritance of a pre-scientific age. To indulge them, he thinks, is to show indifference to mankind's higher interests. It is to fail to be truly serious."[152]

So Carter did not really try to persuade the country. Rather, he tended to give dry and boring reviews of the needs, merely listing his solutions. "This habit of listing his proposals rather than arguing for them is one of the reasons which prevented Carter from being an effective rhetor, since one of the basic rules of public speaking is to present one's audience with viable arguments which support one's assertions."[153] Yet, as Tom Wicker has said, "Presidents are elected fundamentally to carry the country," and Carter's refusal to do so showed him to be "recoiling from the first duty of a political office."[154]

Thus, just as his messages and his style undermined his standing as a strong leader, so too did his basic characteristics. His religiosity, inflexibility and engineer's cautiousness all led to the perception that Carter, while basically a good man, was deficient in leadership capabilities.

Changes in Office

Beyond the relatively unchanging nature of his messages, style and personal characteristics, it remains to be asked if there were any changes in Carter, or his rhetoric, during his term which led to the debilitating shifts in our perceptions of him.

We have already hinted at the changed perceptions which came from changes in our expectations, and have noted several ways in which he seemed to change once in office. But there is one additional alteration in his rhetoric, and perhaps in his outlook, for which he alone must bear the responsibility. That change was from Carter the commoner, the man of the people, who by relying on us would accomplish things with us to Carter the President who was above us, who relied on himself and his Georgia staff and did things for us.

This change first surfaced in his 1978 State of the Union speech. In that speech he addressed the problems of an unfeeling government, too oriented toward lawyers, accountants and lobbyists and too little concerned with the people. " 'We must have,' he asserted, 'what Abraham Lincoln sought—a government for the people.' In selecting that particular phrase . . . the President effected a distortion in Lincoln's original that was as revealing as it was radical. Lincoln's formulation . . . recognized that a democratic conception required that the first two prepositional phrases had to control the third and that, by itself, government 'for' the people was inconsistent with democracy. Carter, in contrast, omitted the crucial references to government 'by' and 'of' the people. The effect was to set democracy against itself, to use it to legitimate an essentially bureaucratic conception of government and to redefine the president as a manager. . . ."[155]

Every president, of course, comes to be seen as an "insider," but that was an especial problem for Carter because he had run on the rhetoric of an outsider in 1976. To offset the changed circumstances, the 1980 campaign plan was to utilize an "insider-outsider" approach: to run as "the same man, with the same instincts and concern for ordinary citizens as the Jimmy Carter of 1976—but with four years of practical experience, the outsider who now knows how Washington works, but is still prepared to take on the oil companies, the special interest groups."[156]

However, Carter was unable to shake off his new orientation and return to his 1976 emphases. For instance, in the three 1976 debates with Ford he had employed the word "people" over seventy times,[157] but in the 1980 debate with Reagan he "referred to 'the people' only nine times . . . while invoking references to the presidency twenty-seven times."[158] Furthermore, when he did mention the "people" in 1978, it was clear that his perception of their role had changed. "Rather than providing the source of wisdom and knowledge for his presidency, the people are subjects, to be commanded by the president. For example, in discussing energy, Carter said, 'We have demanded that the American people sacrifice and they've done very well.' "[159]

Not only did the change in his rhetoric undermine his attempts to depict himself as a man of the people, but the paternalism of his new stance fed into Reagan's theme of getting the government off our backs. Faced with a choice between a father and a champion the people opted for the champion. Carter's changed orientation undermined his reelection bid as well as his presidency.

Conclusion

When I began this study I expected to find an occasional place where President Carter's rhetoric contributed to his political demise. But I was surprised by the extent to which that turns out to have been the case. In every component I examined, message, style, personal characteristics, changes in office, I found that his rhetoric undercut his position, either inherently or because citizen expectations had changed. The conclusion, then, seems unavoidable: just as he talked his way into the White House from 1972–1976, once there he talked himself out of it.

Notes

1. R. W. Apple, Jr., "Carter Seems to Hold Big Lead in Iowa as Caucuses Approach," *The New York Times,* October 27, 1975, p. 17.
2. Lewis H. Lapham, "The Wizard of Oz," *Harper's Magazine,* August, 1976, p. 11.
3. Quoted in James T. Wooten, "The President as Orator: His Deliberate Style Appears to Run Counter to the Inspiration He Seeks to Instill," *The New York Times,* January 26, 1978, p. A 15.
4. *Ibid.*
5. Rowland Evans and Robert Novak, "Carter's Blind Spot: The Shifting of World Power," *New York Post,* January 31, 1979, p. 23.
6. Paul Healy, "Carter, the Born-Again Orator," *New York Daily News,* July 17, 1979, p. 4.
7. "From Micah to the New Beginning," *The New York Times,* January 21, 1977, p. A 22.
8. J. Lewis Campbell, III, "Jimmy Carter and the Rhetoric of Charisma," *Central States Speech Journal,* 30 (Summer, 1979) 174–186.
9. Keith V. Erickson, "Jimmy Carter: The Rhetoric of Private and Civic Piety," *The Western Journal of Speech Communication,* 44 (Summer, 1980) p. 235.
10. Christopher Lyle Johnstone, "Electing Ourselves in 1976: Jimmy Carter and the American Faith," *The Western Journal of Speech Communication,* 42 (Fall, 1978) 241–249.
11. John H. Patton, "A Government as Good as Its People: Jimmy Carter and the Restoration of Transcendence to Politics," *Quarterly Journal of Speech,* 63 (October, 1977) 249–257.
12. Dan F. Hahn, "One's Reborn Every Minute: Carter's Religious Appeal in 1976," *Communication Quarterly,* 28 (Summer, 1980) 56–62.
13. Ronald A. Sudol, "The Rhetoric of Strategic Retreat," *Quarterly Journal of Speech,* 65 (December, 1979) 379–391.
14. William Evan Houser, "The Camp David Ceremony and the Genre of the Presidential Parasocial Broadcast Announcement," paper presented at the Eastern Communication Association Convention, Pittsburgh, April, 1981, p. 18.
15. Catherine Ann Collins, "Justificatory Rhetoric Surrounding the SALT Talks," paper presented at the E.C.A. Rhetoric and Public Address Conference, Altoona, PA., October, 1980.
16. Jill Birnie, "A Rhetorical Look at Jimmy Carter's 1979 Energy Speech," paper presented at the E.C.A. Rhetoric and Public Address Conference, Altoona, October, 1980; Dan F. Hahn, "Flailing the Profligate: Carter's Energy Sermon of 1979," *Presidential Studies Quarterly,* 10 (Fall, 1980) 583–587.

17. Robert A. Francesconi, "Preparing the Ground: Carter, July 15, 1979," *Exetasis,* 6 (January 9, 1980), p. 30.
18. Christopher Lydon, "All the Candidates Fall Short on Defining Issues," *The New York Times,* January 11, 1976, p. E 4.
19. Tom Wicker, "Going After People," *The New York Times,* January 25, 1976, p. 17.
20. Thomas W. Ottenad, "Jimmy Carter: A Smile and a Shoeshine," *The Progressive,* May, 1976, p. 24.
21. Gus Tyler, "The Rites of Jimmy Carter," *The New Leader,* May 10, 1976, p. 14.
22. James T. Wooten, "As Carter Moves Into the Limelight, He Becomes Highly Visible and Vulnerable," *The New York Times,* February 4, 1976, p. 15.
23. Tyler, *op. cit.*
24. David E. Rosenbaum, "Carter's Positions on Issues Designed for Wide Appeal," *The New York Times,* June 11, 1976, p. A 16.
25. Rowland Evans and Robert Novak, "Carter in Florida," *New York Post,* November 20, 1975, p. 41.
26. Patrick Anderson, "Peanut Farmer for President," *New York Times Magazine,* December 14, 1975, p. 82.
27. Charles Mohr, "Carter Qualifies Pledge to Cities," *The New York Times,* June 30, 1976, p. 20.
28. Charles Mohr, "Labels Won't Stick on the Democrats' Nominee," *The New York Times,* July 11, 1976, p. E 3.
29. *Ibid.*
30. James T. Wooten, "Carter, With Wallace at His Side, Hails South's Basic Conservatism," *The New York Times,* September 14, 1976, p. 26.
31. Rosenbaum, *op. cit.,* p. A 16.
32. *Ibid.*
33. Lydon, *op. cit.,* p. E 4.
34. Betty Glad. *Jimmy Carter; In Search of the Great White House.* New York: W. W. Norton and Co., 1980, p. 306.
35. Rosenbaum, *op. cit.*
36. Glad, *op. cit.,* p. 306.
37. Tom Bethel, "The Need to Act," *Harper's,* November, 1977, p. 36.
38. *Ibid.,* pp. 36–37. If this analysis is correct, a strong case could be made that Carter's 1976 rhetoric and symbolism helped lay the groundwork for the successful substantive anti-Washington campaign of Ronald Reagan in 1980. To the degree that Carter's campaign encouraged anti-government sentiment, he may have undermined his own efforts in office as well as his chances for re-election.
39. Dan Hahn and Ruth Gonchar, "Political Myth: The Image and the Issue," *Today's Speech,* 20 (Summer, 1972) 57–65.
40. Johnstone, *op. cit.,* p. 242.
41. *Ibid.,* p. 245.
42. William Safire, "Pedestrian Inaugural," *The New York Times,* January 24, 1977, p. 23.
43. James Reston, "Revival Meeting," *The New York Times,* January 21, 1977, p. A 23.
44. Hedrick Smith, "A Call to the American Spirit," *The New York Times,* January 21, 1977, p. A 1.
45. Anthony Hillbruner, "Born Again: Carter's Inaugural Sermon," Speech Communication Association convention paper, Washington, D.C., December, 1977.

46. Jimmy Carter, "In Changing Times, Eternal Principles," *The New York Times,* January 21, 1977, p. B 1. All subsequent quotations of the inaugural from this source.
47. Hillbruner, *op. cit.,* p. 8.
48. Safire, *op. cit.*
49. *Ibid.*
50. Reston, *op. cit.*
51. Safire, *op. cit.*
52. Arthur M. Schlesinger Jr. *The Imperial Presidency.* Boston: Houghton Mifflin Company, 1973.
53. William Safire, "The Inaugu-Writers," *The New York Times,* January 20, 1977, p. C 37.
54. Woodrow Wilson, "Inaugural Address," *Inaugural Addresses of the Presidents of the United States from George Washington, 1789 to John F. Kennedy, 1961.* Washington, D.C.: United States Government Printing Office, 1961, p. 200.
55. Reston, *op. cit.*
56. James T. Wooton, "A Moralistic Speech," *The New York Times,* January 21, 1977, p. A 1.
57. Jimmy Carter, "The Text of Jimmy Carter's First President Report to the American People," *The New York Times,* February 3, 1977, p. 22. All subsequent references from this speech are from this source.
58. Murray Edelman, "On Policies That Fail," *The Progressive,* May, 1975, p. 22.
59. James Reston, "Carter's Best Week," *The New York Times,* April 24, 1977, p. E 19.
60. James Reston, "Mr. Carter's Balance Sheet," *The New York Times,* August 3, 1977, p. A 19.
61. Anthony Lewis, "Meaning What You Say," *The New York Times,* October 10, 1977, p. 29.
62. James A. Wechsler, "Another Presidential Bombshell Fizzles," *New York Post,* October 3, 1979, p. 29.
63. Reston, "Carter's Best . . . ," *op. cit.*
64. "The First Quarter of Mr. Carter," *The New York Times,* April 27, 1977, p. A 22.
65. Hedrick Smith, "Problems of a Problem Solver," *The New York Times Magazine,* January 8, 1978, p. 34.
66. "The First Quarter . . . ," *op. cit.*
67. James Reston, "Carter and the Lobbies," *The New York Times,* October 9, 1977, p. E 15.
68. Herbert G. Klein, "Again, 'Credibility,' " *The New York Times,* February 9, 1978, p. A 21.
69. Joseph Kraft, "The New Carter Image," *New York Post,* May 12, 1978, p. 17.
70. C. Vann Woodward, "The Best?" *The New York Review of Books,* April 3, 1980, p. 10.
71. Hedrick Smith, "A Changed Man, A Changing Office Not Yet in Step," *The New York Times,* May 21, 1978, p. E 4.
72. Betty Glad, "Jimmy Carter's Management of the Hostage Conflict: A Bargaining Perspective," paper presented at the American Political Science Association convention, New York City, August, 1981, p. 17.
73. *Ibid.,* p. 38.
74. *Ibid.,* pp. 71–72.
75. Max Lerner, "Victors and Losers," *New York Post,* May 3, 1976, p. 43.

76. George McMillan, "Grins and Grits," *The New York Times,* April 9, 1976, p. 37.
77. William Lee Miller, "The Yankee from Georgia," *The New York Times Magazine,* July 3, 1977, p. 18.
78. Arthur Schlesinger, Jr., "Jimmy Carter, an Original," *The New York Times Book Review,* June 5, 1977, p. 1.
79. Amitai Etzioni, "Carter's Symbolism," *Human Behavior,* July, 1977, p. 10.
80. Terence Smith, "Carter in TV Talk, Asks Canal Backing," *The New York Times,* February 2, 1978, p. A 1.
81. James A. Wechsler, "Presidential Smile and Style," *New York Post,* April 11, 1979, p. 31.
82. Murray Kempton, "All Things Considered, a Modest Success," *New York Post,* July 26, 1979, p. 2.
83. James A. Wechsler, "Born Again," *New York Post,* February 24, 1977, p. 29.
84. Reston, "Carter's Best . . . ," *op. cit.*
85. James Reston, "Don't Sell Jimmy Short," *The New York Times,* September 30, 1977, p. A 27.
86. James Reston, "High-Risk Politics," *The New York Times,* October 14, 1977, p. A 27.
87. James T. Wooten, "Carter's Drive From Obscurity to the Front," *The New York Times,* March 15, 1976, p. 36.
88. Ottenad, *op. cit.,* p. 24.
89. James Reston, "Carter's Mideast Strategy," *The New York Times,* January 6, 1978, p. A 21.
90. Marshall Frady, "Why He's Not the Best," *The New York Review of Books,* May 18, 1978, p. 27.
91. "Mr. Carter's World . . . Under Scrutiny," *The New York Times,* June 25, 1976, p. A 26.
92. George F. Will, "Jimmy Draws His Sword," *New York Post,* April 27, 1977, p. 35.
93. Charles Mohr, "Carter as 'Man of Integrity' Is in a Classic Mold," *The New York Times,* May 30, 1976, p. E 3.
94. Charles Mohr, "Carter and Audiences," *The New York Times,* June 2, 1976, p. 20.
95. Charles Mohr, "Reporter's Notebook: Enigmatic Side of Carter," *The New York Times,* July 1, 1976, p. 12.
96. Jimmy Carter, "Transcript of President's State of the Union Address to Joint Session of Congress," *The New York Times,* January 24, 1980, p. A 12. All quotations from the speech taken from this source.
97. Edward M. Kennedy, "Transcript of Kennedy's Speech at Georgetown University on Campaign Issues," *The New York Times,* January 29, 1980, p. A 12.
98. Charles Mohr, "Carter's First Nine Months: Charges of Ineptness Rise," *The New York Times,* October 23, 1977, p. 36.
99. Tom Bethell, "The Liberal Carter," *Harper's,* August, 1978, p. 20.
100. Michael B. Grossman and Martha J. Kumar, "Carter, Reagan, and the Media: Have the Rules Really Changed?," paper presented at the American Political Science Association Convention, New York, September, 1981, p. 13.
101. Carter's defense of the Panama Canal treaties has not yet been analyzed as a case study in atonement. But it is clear that there was that thrust—both in the theological sense of an act which would bring reconciliation between God and sinner (to put us "right with God") and the secular analog of reparation for past wrongs (to put us "right with the world").

102. William Safire, "The New Foundation," *The New York Times,* January 25, 1979, p. E 21.
103. Evans and Novak, "Carter in Florida," *op. cit.*
104. Apple, "Carter Seems to Hold . . . ," *op. cit.*
105. James Wolcott, "Presidential Aesthetics: You've Seen the Movie ('Nashville'), Now Meet the Candidate—Jimmy Carter," *The Village Voice,* January 19, 1976, p. 77.
106. *Ibid.*
107. David Halberstam, "The Coming of Carter," *Newsweek,* July 19, 1976, p. 11.
108. Frady, *op. cit.,* p. 18.
109. *Ibid.,* p. 23.
110. Halberstam, *op. cit.*
111. Safire, "The New Foundation," *op. cit.*
112. Wolcott, *op. cit.*
113. Frady, *op. cit.,* p. 18.
114. James N. Naughton, "Reporter's Notebook: Ford Resembles Carter at Times," *The New York Times,* October 20, 1976, p. 29.
115. Erickson, *op. cit.,* p. 222.
116. *Ibid.*
117. Clayton Fritchey, "Religion and the White House," *New York Post,* June 29, 1976, p. 32.
118. Lapham, *op. cit.*
119. A. Lawrence Chickering, "Extreme Unction," *Harper's,* August, 1979, p. 86.
120. James and Marti Hefley. *The Church that Produced a President.* New York: Wyden Books, 1977, p. 223.
121. Dan F. Hahn, "Flailing the Profligate: Carter's Energy Sermon of 1979," *Presidential Studies Quarterly,* 10 (Fall, 1980) 583–587.
122. Anderson, *op. cit.,* p. 80.
123. Wolcott, *op. cit.,* p. 77.
124. Mohr, "Carter as 'Man of Integrity' . . . ," *op. cit.*
125. Ottenad, *op. cit.,* p. 27.
126. Wooten, *op. cit.*
127. Mohr, "For Carter, a Dash . . . ," *op. cit.*
128. Eleanor Randolph, "The Carter Complex," *Esquire,* November, 1977, p. 184.
129. Mohr, "For Carter, a Dash . . . ," *op. cit.*
130. Max Lerner, "Reagan Tackles the Peace Issue," *New York Post,* October 22, 1980, p. 38.
131. "Carter's Campaign Rhetoric: Debate or Desperation," *New York Post,* October 8, 1980, p. 38.
132. *Ibid.*
133. Mary McGrory, "Carter is Acting Mean and Fighting Dirty," *New York Times,* September 27, 1980, p. 9.
134. " 'Warmonger' Fraud: The Politics of Desperation," *New York Post,* September 25, 1980, p. 30.
135. Joseph Sobran, "Carter Blew His Image—To No Gain," *New York Post,* September 25, 1980, p. 31.
136. *Ibid.*
137. "Going Down the Low Road," *New York Daily News,* September 28, 1980, p. 45.
138. Anthony Lewis, "Carter Against Himself," *The New York Times,* October 16, 1980, p. A 31.

139. *Ibid.*
140. *Ibid.*
141. "What's Fit to Say in a Campaign," *The New York Times,* October 12, 1980, p. E 20.
142. *Ibid.*
143. *Ibid.*
144. Jimmy Carter, "Transcript of the President's Address on Inflation," *The New York Times,* April 12, 1978, p. A 16. All references to this speech taken from this source.
145. Hedrick Smith, "Carter and the 100 Days," *The New York Times,* April 29, 1977, p. A 16.
146. Smith, Problems of a . . . ," *op. cit.,* p. 44.
147. William Safire, "The Secret of Carter," *The New York Times,* April 26, 1979, p. A 23.
148. Smith, "Problems of a . . . ," *op. cit.,* p. 45.
149. Tom Wicker, "Carter at the Precipice," *The New York Times,* July 10, 1979, p. A 15.
150. James David Barber, "An American Redemption: The Presidential Character from Nixon to Ford to Carter," *The Washington Monthly,* April, 1977, p. 32.
151. Sheldon Wolin, "Carter and the New Constitution," *The New York Review of Books,* June 1, 1978, p. 18.
152. William Pfaff, "Mr. Carter's Slide Rule," *The New York Times,* June 22, 1979, p. A 27.
153. Birnie, *op. cit.,* p. 6.
154. Wicker, "Carter on the . . . ," *op. cit.*
155. Sheldon Wolin, "The State of the Union," *The New York Review of Books,* May 18, 1978, p. 31.
156. Terence Smith, "Jimmy Carter, Now the Insider, Dusts Off the Outsider Appeal," *The New York Times,* April 29, 1979, p. E 4.
157. Steven R. Brydon, "Outsider vs. Insider: The Two Faces of Jimmy Carter," Western Speech Communication Association convention paper, San Jose, CA., February, 1981, p. 3.
158. *Ibid.,* p. 8.
159. *Ibid.,* p. 16.

Leadership, Orientation, and Rhetorical Vision: Jimmy Carter, The 'New Right,' and the Panama Canal

Craig Allen Smith

Leadership, whether presidential or otherwise, must orient potential followers. The issue of orientation—the would-be leader's ability to cogently define, for self and others, their common situation—underlies questions of leadership style, effectiveness, responsiveness, and accountability.[1] This process of orientation is highly dramatistic in nature, as the leader shares a vision of past, present, and future, of heroes and villains, of golden ideals and imminent dangers. When the would-be leader's orienting vision speaks to the potential follower's private concerns, i.e. when the listener or reader sees himself or herself *in the drama* the leader-follower relationship has been forged. But when a would-be leader fails, despite significant resources, to orient potential followers, the other aspects of leadership cease to matter.[2]

As the sole elected leader of the nation, a president enjoys certain orienting advantages over his competitors (e.g. the trappings of the office, press coverage, his role as titular head of his party, and the very fact of an elected president's victory). But presidents do not, of course, lead in a vacuum. Because aspiring leaders are, themselves, orienting their own followers, presidential leadership periodically entails a defense of his orienting vision. The stakes are high, since disorientation undermines the very foundation of the president's leadership.

This essay examines a recent case of orientational conflict—Jimmy Carter's conflict with the emerging "New Right" over the 1978 Panama Canal Treaties.[3] Specifically, it contrasts the orienting visions offered by the pro-treaty and anti-treaty forces as developed, respectively, in President Carter's February 1, 1978 address to the nation and in Congressman Philip Crane's (R.-IL) *Surrender in Panama* (100,000 copies of which were distributed by the "New Right" in January of 1978).[4]

Mr. Smith is Assistant Professor of Speech Communication, University of North Carolina at Chapel Hill.
Reprinted by permission of Center for the Study of the Presidency, publishers of *Presidential Studies Quarterly* Vol. XVI, No. 2 (Spring, 1986), pp. 317–328.

The Importance of the Canal Issue to Carter and the New Right

The Panama Canal treaties of 1978 were not a Carter initiative. President Johnson authorized negotiations in 1964, and Presidents Nixon and Ford continued efforts to complete satisfactory agreements. The first skirmish in the controversy occurred when Ronald Reagan used it to gain ground on Gerald Ford in their contest for the 1976 Republican Presidential nomination. Reagan's victory in the North Carolina primary convinced many conservatives that the Panama Canal issue had demonstrated its explosive potential.[5] The emergent New Right continued to use the issue to orient supporters in 1977.[6]

When he began campaigning for the presidency in 1974, Jimmy Carter was surprised by the frequency and intensity of canal-related questions. But because Carter and Ford essentially agreed on the need for the new treaties, the issues that had helped Ronald Reagan in the primaries was allowed to lie fallow during the 1976 general election. Whether because of this calm or despite it, President Carter's first Presidential Review Memorandum concerned his administration's canal position.[7]

Public opinion on the canal issue was divided during 1977; but precisely *how* it divided remains unclear. Although New Right organizer Richard Viguerie and Carter concur that 70–80% of the public opposed the treaties, the Gallup poll puts the figure much lower than that (47% in August of 1977).[8] Although the treaties passed the Senate by a two-vote (68–32) margin, ratification can be a misleading index of *rhetorical* success. As Viguerie explains:

> Our campaign to save the Canal gained conservative converts around the country—added more than 400,000 new names to our lists—encouraged many of the movements leading figures . . . to run for public office—and produced significant liberal defeats [by defeating 20 treaty supporters while losing only one treaty opponent]. The New Right came out of the Panama Canal fight with no casualties, not even a scar. Because of Panama we are better organized. We developed a great deal of confidence in ourselves, and our opponents became weaker. That November [1978] the New Right really came of age.[9]

The Panama Canal treaties, then, provided a vehicle through which the emergent New Right believed it was reorienting potential followers. Whether the controversy actually affected individual voters or not, the New Right believed it had. Believing that the issue had helped Ronald Reagan take his campaign all the way to the convention floor, anti-treaty forces provided a unifying vision which, in turn, generated mailing lists, campaign funds, and a clear criterion for electoral targetting. President Carter later described the Panama controversy his "most difficult political battle" and mused:

> If I could have foreseen early in 1977 the terrible battle we would face in Congress, it would have been a great temptation for me to avoid the issue—at least during my first term. The struggle left deep and serious political wounds that have never been healed; and, I am convinced, a large number of members of Congress were later defeated for reelection because they voted for the Panama treaties.[10]

The Panama Canal had proven to be, as Viguerie had predicted, "a 'no-loss' issue for conservatives."[11]

Competing Worldviews

Both supporters and opponents of the treaties argued the canal question in terms of orienting rhetorical visions. Our decision either to relinquish or to retain the canal, they agreed, would demonstrate to the world the kind of nation America has been, is, and will be for the foreseeable future. Each scenario involved three issues and time-frames: the legitimacy of America's claim to the canal (past), the state of Panama specifically and of Pan-American relations generally (present), and the kind of world power to which America aspires (future).

America's Claim to the Canal

President Carter stressed the "Ethics of Fairness" in his televised address supporting the treaties. The Panama Canal, he said, was a source of "some continuing discontent" in Panama because of the unfair Hay-Bunau-Varilla Treaty of 1903:

> [The treaty] was drafted here in our country and was not signed by any Panamanian [but by American John Hay and the French canal engineer Philippe Bunau-Varilla representing Panama]. Our own Secretary of State who did sign the original treaty said it was "vastly advantageous to the United States and . . . not so advantageous to Panama."[12]

Because the original treaty was unfair to Panama it was, in Carter's view, morally wrong. Carter implicitly argued that the new treaties provided a vehicle for the purification of our national soul by allowing us to demonstrate our innate sense of fairness. Carter says that "This agreement is something we [Americans] want because we know it is right." And he concluded by explaining that ratification "is what is right for us and what is fair to others."[13]

But Congressman Philip Crane provided a very different basis for our claim to the canal—a legalistic account of our proprietorship grounded in the "Ethics of Self-Interest" rather than Carter's "Ethics of Fairness." Crane recounted the legal chain: the 1901 Hay-Pauncefote Treaty with Britain permitted American involvement in any Central American Canal, the Colombian Senate unanimously rejected the 1903 Hay-Herran Treaty which would have granted the United States complete control over the Panama canal area for purposes of building and operating a canal, the Panamanian secession from Columbia

in 1903 with American assistance playing "a secondary role," and the negotiation of the Hay-Bunau-Varilla Treaty by which newly independent Panama
granted America the right to build, operate, maintain, and defend the canal,
relinquishing claims of sovereignty over the newly designated Canal Zone.[14]

America's claim to the canal, according to Crane, was a legal one based
upon our shrewdness and opportunism:

> When any nation goes to the bargaining table it does so with the determination to
> act in its own best interests and to derive as many benefits as possible from the
> ensuing negotiations. Our 1903 agreement with Panama was no exception. There
> is no doubt that the Hay-Bunau-Varilla Treaty was very favorable to the United
> States, a shrewd bargain.[15]

Crane's recognition of the original treaty's imbalance was shared by Secretary
of State John Hay who negotiated the treaty. Crane quotes a letter from Hay
to Senator Spooner which warned that American failure to ratify the Hay-
Bunau-Varilla Treaty could mean the failure of any American canal effort:

> As it stands now as soon as the Senate votes we shall have a treaty in the main very
> satisfactory, vastly advantageous to the United States . . . not so advantageous to
> Panama. If we amend the treaty and send it back there [to Panama] some time next
> month, the period of enthusiastic unanimity, which . . . comes only once in the
> lifetime of a revolution, will have passed away, and they will have entered on the
> new fields of politics and dispute . . . If it is again submitted to their consideration
> they will attempt to amend it in many places, no man can say with what result.[16]

In short, Philip Crane argued that America's claim to the canal was legally
derived from a succession of treaties culminating in the Hay-Bunau-Varilla
Treaty of 1903. But neither Hay nor Crane argued that the American claim
to the Panama Canal derived from an *equitable* treaty. Both readily conceded
that the treaty was advantageous to America, disadvantageous to Panama,
and likely to have been rejected by Panama upon reconsideration. Carter
maintained that the unfairness of the treaty invalidated American claim to
the Canal Zone. But Crane held that, in diplomacy, the ethics of self-interest
transcend the ethics of fairness. The treaty was unfair because the Panamanian negotiators were simply less skillful than the Americans. The treaty was
substantively unfair to Panama, but more importantly it had been derived from
a fair procedure—the only valid ethical consideration in diplomacy. For Crane,
then, the treaty's unfairness to Panama constituted not a moral transgression
but a fulfillment of our moral obligation to fairly negotiate in our own interests.

Thus, while Carter and Crane both discussed the fairness of the original
treaty, only Crane discussed the ethics of self-interest. This omission is curious
since Crane's book was written and distributed prior to Carter's address. The
omission was damaging because the President's discussion of fairness was easily
accommodated within the framework of self-interest constructed by Crane—

a framework to which Carter offered no compelling alternative. Crane's scenario allowed his audience to simultaneously embrace fairness, shrewdness, pride, and self-interest, while Carter's scenario forced a choice between fairness and shame on the one hand and cleverness and pride on the other.

Pan-American Relations

Not only did Crane and Carter disagree about the legitimacy of America's claim to the canal, but they also disagreed about the nature of contemporary Panama and the state of current Pan-American relations.

First, Carter described Panama as one of our "historic allies and friends" headed by a stable government which has encouraged the development of free enterprise in Panama and which will hold democratic elections to "choose members of the Panamanian Assembly."[17] Crane described, a "banana republic" dominated by "forty influential families" in which "poverty is abysmal." General Omar Torrijos runs a "corrupt, vicious police state he has built . . . with the help of his Marxist allies" and is only kept from bankruptcy by "the New York banking community."[18]

Second, Carter and Crane advanced contrasting views of Pan-American relations. Carter saw understandable disaffection in the hemisphere. He noted that the canal was a "source of continuing discontent" among Panamanians and referred to the canal as "the last vestige of alleged American colonialism."[19] Carter spoke of defending the canal with the Panamanian Forces "joined with us as brothers," and he eagerly anticipated this "new partnership."[20] The Carter vision thus had an egalitarian theme counterpoised by legitimate Panamanian resentment of America.

But where President Carter saw our exploitation and injustice as contributors to Panamanian resentment, Crane saw only childish ingratitude:

> The United States did for Panama what the Spanish, Simon Bolivar, the French company, and the Colombians had all failed to do: built and operated a magnificent interoceanic canal that pumped commercial vitality and opportunity into the stagnant economic bloodstream of Panama. We also rid the country of the scourges of malaria and yellow fever, brought good jobs and opportunity to thousands of needy Panamanians, and promptly paid increasingly large subsidies to the Panamanian government—all after helping Panama to win independence in the first place. To the extent that Panama exists and is a viable state today, it is because a strong America, which could have taken what it wanted without giving anything in return, has been a generous friend of Panama from the moment of ratification of the 1903 treaty. But . . . gratitude soon grows old. All of us know . . . [people] who find it harder to forgive a favor than an injustice.[21]

Crane's view of Pan-American relations was distinctly paternalistic: the American parent has bestowed countless favors upon its Panamanian child only to encounter resentment. Crane's response was predictable: since ingratitude is a sign of unfitness for favor, Panama should be taught a lesson. Metaphorically, Crane seemed to argue that Panama should be sent to bed without its canal.

Against this backdrop, Carter saw the Canal as central to Panama's survival, while Crane saw the threat of *closing* the canal as the key to their future. President Carter reminded his audience that in seventy-five years "no Panamanian government has ever wanted to close the canal." He suggested that "Panama wants the canal open and neutral—perhaps even more than we do" because "Much of her economy flows directly or indirectly through the canal." For this reason "Panama would be no more likely to neglect or close the canal than we would be to close [our] Interstate Highway System." Any danger to expeditious American use of the canal would come "not from any government of Panama, but from misguided persons who may try to fan the flames of dissatisfaction with the terms of the old treaty."[22]

But in Crane's account it was General Torrijos whom we need fear will seize the canal. According to Crane:

> Violence, and the threat of violence, underlay all of Torrijos's negotiations. It was hinted, and sometimes stated, that if Americans did not go peacefully, and pay a sufficient ransom by way of penance for our supposed past sins, we would be driven out by force.[23]

Referring to a speech in which Torrijos predicted that he would die a violent death fighting for the canal, Crane warned that:

> it is precisely the kind of incendiary appeal that has sent thousands of Latin American rioters into the streets in the past, and might very well do so again in the future—especially in the face of a passive, docile America that has demonstrated a pattern of yielding to threats instead of dealing from a position of strength.[24]

Crane warned that it would be a "criminal blunder" to turn the canal zone over to a "corrupt dictator" who is "a flagrant violator of human rights" and is "surrounded by criminals and Marxists," "an intimate friend of Fidel Castro, a rabid anti-American, and a seeker after advice, technicians, and aid from the Soviet Union" because we would risk both blackmail and closure of the canal.[25] "The real threat of violence to the canal," writes Crane "would crest *after* the departure of American security forces, not while they were in place to protect the zone."[26]

As they examined Pan-American relations, then, Jimmy Carter and Philip Crane saw divergent rhetorical visions. Carter described an emerging hemispheric unity based on partnership with a stable government actively promoting free enterprise. Crane saw a threat from a corrupt, ruthless dictator

facing national bankruptcy and enticed by Marxism who threatens to humiliate America, thereby destroying our international prestige.

The Kind of Power We Wish to Be

Both President Carter and Congressman Crane agreed that the canal decision would signal the kind of world power America would be in the years to
come. Carter invoked Theodore Roosevelt's support for the treaties "because
he could see the decision as one by which we are demonstrating the kind of
great power we wish to be."[27] Specifically, Roosevelt "would join us in our
pride for being a *great and generous* people, with the *national strength* and
wisdom to do what is *right for us* and what is *fair to others*.[28] By ratifying
the treaties, said Carter, "We will demonstrate that as a large and powerful
country, we are able to deal fairly and honorably with a proud but smaller
sovereign nation . . . [because] We believe in good will and fairness, as well
as strength."[29] He spoke of the "new partnership" as a "source of national
pride and self-respect."[30] Panama was to be transformed from "a passive and
sometimes deeply resentful bystander into an active and interested partner"
who will "[join] with us as brothers against a common enemy" should the
canal need military defense.[31] The treaties would not create a "power vacuum"
but would "increase our Nation's influence in this hemisphere, . . . help to
reduce any mistrust and disagreement, . . . [and] remove a major source of
anti-American feeling." Indeed, Carter noted that "Between the United States
and Latin America there is already a new sense of equality, a new sense of
trust and mutual respect that exists because of the Panama Canal treaties."[32]
In the Carter vision the United States was a powerful, fair, generous neighbor
ready and willing to demonstrate those admirable traits by sharing the canal
with the Panamanians.

But Congressman Crane saw a different future based upon the centrality
of property and its defense. A decision to *Surrender in Panama* would be "one
more crucial American step in a descent into ignominy—to the end of America's credibility as a world power and a deterrent to aggression."[33] The issue
was not generosity but cowardice, according to Crane:

> Edmund Burke warned that, "the concessions of the weak are the concessions of
> fear." There can be no question but that, in the eyes of a Soviet Union engaged in
> a massive naval and military build-up, and in the eyes of third-world countries en-
> vious of America's affluence, surrender in Panama would appear as not a noble act
> of magnanimity, but as the cowardly retreat of a tired, toothless paper tiger.[34]

Lest there be any doubt that he and Carter saw different visions, Crane warned
that, "The world is not a Sunday school classroom in Plains, Georgia . . . It
is a violent, conflict-ridden place where peace and freedom only survive when

they are protected . . . Peace comes only to the prepared and security only to the strong."[35]

Carter and Crane advanced sharply contrasting worldviews. Crane saw danger, Carter security. Crane wanted superiority, Carter partnership. Crane implied force and punishment, Carter generosity and kindness. Crane thought America weak, Carter thought us strong. Crane saw shame in "surrender," Carter in continued imperialism. Each believed that the other indirectly helped America's enemies.

Summary

The Carter and Crane worldviews are mutually exclusive. Yet each worldview presented an *internally consistent logic* which justified its respective canal decision. Carter's scenario was based on the ethics of fairness, the justifiable resentment of a stable capitalist democracy against colonial exploitation, an egalitarian alliance with our hemispheric siblings, and a conception of America as a gentle giant respected for its magnanimity. Crane's scenario was based on the ethics of self-interest and shrewdness, the inexcusable ingratitude of an unstable Marxist dictatorship against American beneficence, a paternal orientation toward our hemispheric neighbors, a conception of America as an increasingly timid and gun-shy power in a world where only the strong survive.

Conclusion

In 1964 Senator J. William Fulbright voiced his concern that foreign policy debates not become a struggle over images. The divergence between perception and reality, he wrote, was both dangerous and unnecessary:

> dangerous because it can reduce foreign policy to a fraudulent game of imagery and appearances, unnecessary because it can be overcome by the determination of men in high office to dispel prevailing misconceptions through candid dissemination of unpleasant but inescapable facts."[36]

But with two decades' hindsight, it appears that foreign policy debates can be conducted either *within* a worldview or *between,* in Nimmo and Comb's terms, two (or more) competing worldviews.[37]

Just as scientific knowledge, according to Thomas Kuhn, develops within a prevailing paradigm until an anomaly suggests the wisdom of adopting a new paradigm, so foreign policy is conducted within emergent worldviews.[38] Where Senator Fulbright advised us to abandon the reflexive Cold War vision for a more thoughtful, pragmatic, and less moralistic vision, Congressman Crane and the New Right used the Canal issue as a vehicle for challenging the Fulbright-Nixon-Ford-Carter "Post-Cold War" vision and for restoring the dominance of the Cold War scenario.[39] As Fulbright had urged us to exchange "Old Myths" for "New Realities," Crane urged us to abandon "New Myths" in favor of the "Old Realities."

When a foreign policy debate is between conflicting rhetorical visions the struggle over images, heroes, villains, values, and motives is more than a distraction—it is central. This symbolic struggle becomes critical—as it did for both Fulbright in the 1960's and Crane in the 1980's—because it provides a way for Americans—whether policymakers or ordinary citizens—to make sense of the world around them. A vision provides the transcendent framework within which specific incidents are interpreted.

The debate over the Panama Canal treaties was conducted primarily between, rather than within, rhetorical visions as advocates advanced their mutually exclusive worldviews. The Senate votes on the canal issues resolved the formal question of ratification. But as Viguerie observed, the ratification vote was simply a springboard for New Right activism. *Treaty ratification did not end the debate because the central issue was not ratification, but the choice between rhetorical visions.*

But the choice between worldviews was left unresolved by the treaty votes. Because President Carter and the treaty supporters were unable to excite public imagination with their vision, the Canal issue was left for the New Right as a dramatic 1978 election issue.

Indeed, the long-term choice between visions may have been decided less in terms of Panama than Iran. The seizure of the American hostages and the apparent failure of the Carter Administration to secure their expeditious release undercut his "respected, gentle giant" vision. The spoils of the New Right's battle included a return to Cold War imagery, issues, and criteria for decision-making: a substantial and significant change of course.

In the final analysis, the emergent spokespersons of the New Right fixed upon the proposed Panama Canal treaties as a means to "realign American politics, reinvigorate a weakened spirit of nationalism, and if lost, do for those who surrendered the Canal what Yalta did for the Democratic Party."[40] They pursued this objective by discussing the canal treaties in terms of a transcendent rhetorical vision: the ethics of self-interest and shrewdness, the inexcusable ingratitude of an unstable Marxist dictatorship against American beneficence, a paternal orientation toward our hemispheric neighbors, and a conception of America as an increasingly timid and gun-shy power in a world where only the strong survive. When they lost the vote as expected they continued to argue for the worldview. Subsequent developments (especially in Iran) seemed to support their arguments.

The two rhetorical visions provided outlets for distinctive audience fantasies. Crane dramatized nationalistic pride, Carter shame. Crane pointed to legality, Carter morality. Crane emphasized superiority, Carter equality. Crane alarmed, Carter reassured. In each case Crane seemed to offer the more dramatic and self-serving fantasy. For his part, President Carter failed either to generate a dramatic rhetorical vision or to undercut the new Right's dramatic vision. This apparently derived from his administration's inability to apprehend the dramatistic orientational dimensions of the debate.[41] And behind the difficulty of Carter's task looms President Carter's calm, reasonable, reassuring, but uninspiring rhetorical style—a poor match against the Crane, and in the 1980 election the Reagan, dynamism.

The struggles of foreign policy are often struggles over perceptions. While this is true of politics in general, it is especially pertinent for foreign policy where our understandings of Panama, Angola, El Salvador, and Lebanon are so imperfect. The Panama Canal debate of 1978 provided a vehicle by which the emergent New Right could force a President of modest rhetorical skills to defend (on behalf of the Democratic party and the defense establishment) the operative rhetorical vision which oriented American foreign policy. Their rhetorical vision provided the framework for Viguerie's mailings, television programs, and lectures. And although they narrowly lost the ratification battle, the New Right effectively challenged the president's orienting vision and contributed to his defeat in the 1980 election.

Notes

1. The importance of orientation to leadership is evident in most studies of leadership. It is consistent with Burns's definition of leadership as "leaders inducing followers to act for certain goals that represent the values and the motivations—the wants and needs, the aspirations and expectations—*of both leaders and followers.* And the genius of leadership lies in the manner in which leaders see and act on their own and their followers' values and motivations." James MacGregor Burns, *Leadership* (New York: Harper Colophon, 1978), p. 19. This view of orientation is implicit in at least three recent essays on presidential leadership: Sen. Nancy Landon Kassebaum, "The Essence of Leadership," *Presidential Studies Quarterly,* 9 (1979), p. 239: "The essence of leadership is the identification of mutual values, needs and goals."; Nicholas D. Berry, "The Foundation of Presidential Leadership: Teaching," *Presidential Studies Quarterly,* 11 (1981), p. 99; "If the aim of leadership is to attain and maintain the welfare of a group, then the first task consists of establishing goals which define the welfare of the group. Essentially leaders must know the group's morals, values, and interests. The second task revolves around convincing the group that the desired goals are possible. . . . The third task entails outlining a program of action or strategy which utilizes available resources, fits circumstances, and explains why a certain sequence of actions will result in the goal."; and Mark Steven Gordon's award-winning student essay, "The American Presidency in the 1980's: The Challenges of Four Core Problems," *Presidential Studies Quarterly,* 10 (1980), p. 611: "A link must be forged in the minds of

Americans between their common past and their collective present. . . . It is imperative, then, that the Presidency, with its resources and power, be thrust into the paths of this trend for until Americans once again feel good about their 'Americanness' they will not grant either legitimacy or complicity to the activities of their government or its leadership."

2. See Ernest G. Bormann, "Fantasy and Rhetorical Vision: The Rhetorical Criticism of Social Reality," *Quarterly Journal of Speech,* 58 (1972), and Dan Nimmo and James E. Combs, *Mediated Political Realities* (New York: Longman, 1983), esp. pp. 1–20. "Rhetorical visions," wrote Ernest Bormann, are "the composite dramas which catch up large groups of people in a symbolic reality." (p. 398) These visions arise through communication and provide themes, heroes, villains, values, and motivations which are invoked in later communication. Bormann's own analyses of the communicative behavior of small groups benefitted greatly from social psychologist Robert Bales's discovery of the dynamics of "group fantasizing". As Bales and his followers moved toward psychohistorical analyses of the group fantasies, Bormann and his students moved toward the investigation of fantasizing and group cohesion and, ultimately, fantasizing in the public domain. In small groups or large, one hears thoughts which resonate with one's own privately-held thoughts. The hearer contributes his/her example and builds upon the theme—another follows, and another as the individual fantasy "chains out" to the group. While the group fantasy provides its members with a reinforced view of "reality", the sense of participation derived from the act of building the fantasy contributes to group cohesion.

3. Nimmo and Combs argue that *all* political "realities" are created through communication (p. 4). Even short of their position, rhetorical visions seem especially relevant to foreign policy debates where clear explanations are usually illusive. Bormann observed: "When the authentic record of events is clear and widely understood the competing visions must take it into account. . . . [But] Whenever occasions are so chaotic and indiscriminate that the community has no clear observational impression of the facts, people are given free rein to fantasize within the assumptions of their rhetorical vision (p. 405)."

4. Philip M. Crane, *Surrender in Panama: The Case Against the Treaty* (New York: Dale Books, 1978); and Jimmy Carter, "Panama Canal Treaties," *Public Papers of the Presidents of the United States: Jimmy Carter, 1978* (Washington, D.C.: U.S. Government Printing Office, 1979), pp. 258–263. According to "New Right" activist Richard Viguerie, "Phil Crane, [his political advisor] Rich Williamson and I decided that we needed a good readable book on the Panama Canal. I agreed to publish it. And so in January 1978, 100,000 paperback copies of *Surrender in Panama* . . . came out. Copies were sent to just about every important media person and political leader in the country. It was another example of how the New Right goes into high gear." Richard A. Viguerie, *The New Right: We're Ready to Lead* (Falls Church, VA: The Viguerie Company, 1981), p. 68.

5. The Canal issue became important in the North Carolina primary. Ford recalls that he wanted to leave Reagan room to withdraw from the race and save face, so he eased his attacks in North Carolina. Reagan countered with fierce attacks built around the canal and detente in general. Ford viewed Reagan's approach to the canal issue "inflammatory and irresponsible." Strategically, however, Ford had to choose between responding to Reagan (and thereby losing much of conservative support) or leaving the issue to Reagan. Ford chose the latter course. Whether for this reason or, more likely, a combination of other reasons, Ford fell from a 10%

lead to a loss in the North Carolina primary. But the important point is not whether the canal issue hurt Ford's candidacy; instead, it is that conservative Republicans *believed* that the canal issue had proven potent enough to defeat an incumbent president. See Gerald R. Ford, *A Time to Heal* (New York: Harper and Row, 1979), pp. 374–380; and Alan Crawford, *Thunder on the Right* (New York: Pantheon Books, 1980), p. 8, and Viguerie, p. 66.

6. Crawford reports that the American Conservative Union, spending 1.4 million dollars and sending some 2.4 million letters, spearheaded the New Right's anti-canal effort in 1977, and benefitted greatly (p. 8). In his memoirs, *Keeping Faith* (New York: Bantam Books, 1982), President Carter recalls opposition from the American Conservative Union, Ronald Reagan, the John Birch Society, the Liberty Lobby, and others (pp. 160–161). The organizational keystone seems to have been Richard Viguerie, the mass-mailing specialist.

7. Carter, *Keeping Faith,* pp. 155–157.

8. An exhuberant Richard Viguerie claimed in 1981 that "No political issue in the last 25 years so clearly divided the American establishment from the American people as the Panama Canal treaties." As Viguerie saw it, the proposed treaties were supported by six American presidents, the Democratic leaders in both house of Congress, all members of the Joint Chiefs of Staff, "Big Labor, Big Business, Big Media, the big international banks, and just about every liberal political and cultural star you could name (p. 65)." Opposed to the treaties were "the American people—about 70% of them . . . probably 85% of registered Republicans" and a coterie of conservative spokespersons who would become known as the "New Right": Senators Paul Laxalt, Jake Garn, and Bill Scott, Congressmen Philip Crane, Larry McDonald, and Mickey Edwards, and organizers Paul Weyrich, Howard Phillips, William Rhatican, Terry Dolan, and Viguerie (pp. 66–67). Gallup reported 47% (not 70%) of those who had heard of the treaty opposed it in August, 1977 and 39% in January 1978 (only 17% of those hearing of the treaty from the interviewer opposed it). Viguerie seems to have counted as "opposing" the treaty both those announcing opposition and those claiming no opinion. The data for Republican opposition is similarly divergent: rather than Viguerie's 80%, Gallup found 58% of the Republican respondents opposed the treaties in August, 1977, which grows to only 69% if "no opinions" are counted as non-supportive of the president. But the Gallup poll in January, 1978 revealed surprising trends: more previously uninformed Republicans supported the treaties than opposed them (35%–26%) while Republicans who qualified as "informed" about the canal supported the treaties 49%–48%. See American Institute of Public Opinion, *The Gallup Poll: Public Opinion, 1972–1977* Vol. 2 (Wilmington, DE: Scholarly Resources, 1978), pp. 1181–1183; and *The Gallup Poll: Public Opinion, 1978* (Wilmington, DE: Scholarly Resources, 1979), pp. 44–50.

9. Viguerie, pp. 70–71.

10. Carter, *Keeping Faith,* p. 184.

11. Viguerie, p. 65.

12. Carter, "Panama Canal Treaties," (hereafter referred to as PCT) p. 258.

13. Carter, PCT p. 262 and p. 263.

14. Crane, pp. 23–33.

15. Crane, p. 41.

16. Hay's letter quoted by Crane, p. 38.

17. Carter, PCT p. 262.

18. Crane, pp. 56–57, 71, and 66.

19. Carter, PCT p. 258 and p. 261.
20. Carter, PCT p. 260 and p. 262.
21. Crane, p. 41.
22. Carter, PCT p. 262.
23. Crane, p. 93.
24. Crane, p. 93.
25. Crane, p. 82.
26. Crane, p. 102.
27. Carter, PCT p. 262.
28. Carter, PCT p. 263, emphasis added.
29. Carter, PCT p. 259 and p. 262.
30. Carter, PCT p. 262.
31. Carter, PCT p. 260.
32. Carter, PCT p. 261.
33. Crane, p. 113.
34. Crane, p. 112.
35. Crane, pp. 113–114.
36. Fulbright, p. 4.
37. Nimmo and Combs, pp. 1–18.
38. Thomas Kuhn, *The Structure of Scientific Revolutions*, 2nd ed. (Chicago: University of Chicago Press, 1970).
39. John F. Cragan argues that American foreign policy from 1948–1972 was conducted within a "Cold War Rhetorical Vision" created by the Truman Doctrine. Because events in the post-war period underwent the "One World of Wendell Wilkie" vision, the Truman Administration combined elements of the "Walter Lippmann Power Politics" and "Karl Mundt Red Fascism" visions into a rhetoric of East-West confrontation. It was this vision which Fulbright attacked in *Old Myths and New Realities*, fostering disparate interpretations of American policy in Vietnam. Cragan argues that the team of Nixon and Kissinger moved to a more pragmatic, less ideological, "Power Politics" vision with the 1972 trips to China and Russia. It may be that the New Right's emphasis on Marxist influence and danger rekindled the "Red Fascist" fantasy while President Carter's emphasis of fairness and gentle strength reminded people of the long-discarded Wilkie vision. See "The Origins and Nature of the Cold War Rhetorical Vision 1946–1972: A partial history," in John F. Cragan and Donald C. Shields, *Applied Communication Research: A Dramatistic Perspective* (Prospect Heights, IL: Waveland Press, 1981), pp. 47–66.
40. Viguerie, p. 66 quoting columnist Patrick Buchanan.
41. In *Keeping Faith*, Carter's account of the canal controversy is devoted almost exclusively to his jawboning of individual senators. He mentions his pleasure when polls showed that pro-treaty forces took the lead in public opinion polls (p. 167), but does not discuss his "Big Picture" orienting vision.

Flailing the Profligate: Carter's Energy Sermon of 1979

Dan F. Hahn

In July of 1979, President Jimmy Carter cancelled a planned speech on energy (his fifth on that topic), retreated to Camp David for ten days of consultation and meditation, and returned to Washington to give two speeches in one—a sermon on the American loss of confidence and a presentation of his "new" energy policy.

The *St. Louis Post-Dispatch* said the speech "mixed morality with energy, being in some respects a sermon and in others a call to action."[1] And the two portions of the speech were greeted differently by various elements of the audience. The *Richmond News Leader* hailed the sermon portion as containing "a good deal of good sense," while rejecting the energy policy as merely "more government, more of what we already have too much."[2] Alternatively, the *Buffalo Evening News* dismissed the sermon portion as "the talk about all the insights the President gleaned from every Tom, Dick and Harry," but applauded Carter's "resolute determination to stop our increasing dependence on foreign oil."[3]

Why did Carter leave himself open to this kind of mixed response? Was he unable to decide which speech to give? Indeed, did Carter himself perceive the exercise as two speeches or as one? It seems from the available evidence that the latter is the case. This article will demonstrate how it can be perceived as one speech and why Carter deliberately structured it in that way.

The thing to keep in mind is that this was a speech by Jimmy Carter. That is, the President is a person who, like all of us, "tries to cope with an environment by using techniques he has found effective. For all the complexities of personality, there are always regularities, habitual ways of handling similar situations, just as the demands and opportunities of the Presidency are complex, but patterned. Thus, the President-as-person interacts with the set of recurrent problems and opportunities presented by the Presidency; the pattern of this interaction is his political style. He copes, adapts, leads, and responds not as some shapeless organism in a flood of novelties, but as a man with a memory in a system with a history."[4]

The characteristic which most typifies the President-as-person insignia of Jimmy Carter is his born-again Christianity. The influence of that evangelical experience pervades—symbolically, structurally, and ideologically—the very

Reprinted by permission of Center for the Study of the Presidency, publishers of *Presidential Studies Quarterly* Vol. X, No. 4 (Fall 1980), pp. 583–587.

foundation of the Energy speech. And so, in order to understand the person-President mix, we must also understand the interaction of the man and his faith.

As a devout Christian, Carter undoubtedly remembered that "Whenever a nation in the Bible faced a crisis, its leader, like Moses, went up to Mount Sinai and came down with the Ten Commandments; or like Jesus went into the wilderness for 40 days and 40 nights."[5] While Carter laughingly dismissed the idea that he could be a modern Moses descending from Camp David in the Catoctin Mountains[6] (for one thing, his energy program had six points, not ten), the retreat, decision, pronouncement syndrome was not new to Jimmy Carter. It is the typical sequence of the born-again experience: identification of problem, retreat to meditation, decision to commit, announcement of re-birth.

It is also typical of Carter's past political experience. When his campaign was sputtering in the fall of 1976, candidate Carter "convened his staff, along with outside advisors, for several days of self-analysis at an isolated retreat; afterward, it was publicly announced that Mr. Carter, having somehow strayed from the path that had led to his nomination, would retrace his steps. His Administration floundering in the Spring of 1978, the . . . President convened his staff, along with outside advisors, for several days of self-analysis at an isolated retreat; afterward, it was publicly announced that the President, hav-ing strayed from the path that led to his election, would regroup his Admin-istration."[7]

Retreat, decision, pronouncement—was that not the familiar "mountain-top" strategy for decision-making of Richard Nixon? The question arises—is such a decision-making style really endemic to the Oval office rather than the office-holder?

The answer is no; obviously there have been modern Presidents who es-chewed such a style—Kennedy and Johnson, for examples. Then in what ways are Carter and Nixon similar that such resemblance should produce a similar decision-making style? While a professed Quaker, Nixon apparently was in-fluenced more by his father's Methodist teachings than by his mother's Quak-erism.[8] Furthermore, Nixon had an evangelical awakening at the age of 16, when, at a pentacostal meeting, he was baptized a Christian and committed his body and soul to Jesus.[9]

But to return to Jimmy Carter: the retreat, self-analysis, rededication ac-tivities were vintage. How such a pattern influenced the Carter person-Pres-ident mix has yet to be explored.

Carter's understanding of government and society emerged out of his ex-perience as a born-again Christian. A basically good man, he arrived at a point in his life when he needed only to *re*adjust his life and *re*commit himself to

God. Likewise, in 1976, he told us that what government needed was a *re*-organization and the people would then *re*commit themselves to society, resulting in a *re*birth of patriotism. The government would then be as good as the people and we would *re*establish a political Eden. But the play did not follow the script, so the 1979 Energy sermon was Carter's attempt to redirect our energies to achieve that utopia.

In broad outline, the first part of the speech was a listing of our sins—the chief among them being the worship of mammon: "human identity is no longer defined by what one does but by what one owns."[10] "Consuming" and "owning" will not "satisfy a longing for meaning." "Piling up material goods cannot fill the emptiness in our lives," Carter concluded.[11]

It is an article of faith in Carter's religion that one can not be saved until one's sins have been publicly confessed and repented. And so Carter articulates for us all of our sins; besides mammon, there are disunity and disarray, adherence to special interests, disloyalty, lack of discipline among disciples, and, most important, loss of faith.

Once articulated, the sins are washed away. Only then can the born-again Christian profess his faith. But, Carter avers, we cannot have faith in Washington—it is gripped in "paralysis and stagnation and drift." It is "isolated."[12] And we no longer have faith in ourselves as individuals—that is where our crisis of confidence had its origins.

Then what? Where shall we put our faith? Carter answers, "we simply must have faith in each other; faith in our ability to govern ourselves and faith in the future of this nation."[13] And how can we who have lost faith in ourselves develop such renewed faith in each other? Carter's path to faith lies in the solution to the energy problem: "On the battlefield of energy we can win for our nation a new confidence, and we can seize control again of our common destiny."[14] So, the President-cum-preacher concludes, "let us commit ourselves together to a rebirth of the American spirit. Working together with our common faith, we cannot fail."[15]

To see how the speech works as an exercise in societal rebirth, we can compare it to the born-again religious experience: While it is obvious that the process for societal rebirth recommended by Carter is not *exactly* parallel to the Christian experience of being reborn, it is close enough to suggest that Carter's religious background could very well have had a major influence on the construction of the speech.

Religion[16]

1. *Belief.* You must recognize what God did: that He gave His Son to die on the cross.
2. *Confession.* You must confess your sins. Only then can God wash your sins away—and only if confessed.
3. *Repentence.* You must repent for your sins—through prayer and fasting.

4. *Salvation.* You must choose to be saved.
5. *Baptism.* You must receive Jesus as Savior and Lord; you must live in the Body of Christ, derive strength from the Body.
6. *Witnessing.* You must show evidence of Salvation by confessing Christ publicly—witnessing Christ to others.

Carter's Speech

1. *Belief.* You must recognize that Government cannot solve your problems.
2. *Confession.* You must see that the very meaning of our lives is in doubt because of our loss of unity of purpose.
3. *Repentence.* You must quit worshipping self-indulgence and comsumption. "There is no way to avoid sacrifice."[17]
4. *Salvation.* There are two paths to choose from—one leads to chaos (secular sin), the other to "control over our common destiny."[18]
5. *Baptism.* You must have faith in each other (and gain faith by solving the energy crisis).
6. *Witnessing.* "Whenever you have the chance, say something good about our country."[19]

Not only is Carter's religion apparent in the broad outline of the rebirth motif holding together the substance of the speech, but it can also be found in the style of the speech as well. For instance, it is common in Christianity to speak of "drawing strength from God." In the speech, it is not God from whom strength is being drawn (although Carter does request His "help"[20]), but others; yet this belief in drawing strength from outside oneself is at least faintly religious, whether it is our drawing it from each other or Carter saying he is a President who "draws his strength and wisdom from you."[21]

Specific word choices reinforce the religious message—faith, vision, disciples, God's love, spiritual, soul, spirit, proverb, worship, agony, deep wounds, sacrifice, praying, creation, create, and rebirth are all found in the text.

And the specific message of rebirth is reinforced by numerous "re-" words: resolve, restore, regain, rebuild, reverse, replace, rekindle, and renew, as well as rebirth itself.

Even the war metaphors— battlefield of energy, we will mobilize American determination, fighting the moral equivalent of war with BB guns, our energy battle, to conquer the crisis, this struggle for freedom, an all-out effort—can be seen as influenced by Mr. Carter's religious heritage, assuming his Church gives him such melodic reinforcement as "Onward Christian Soldiers," "A Mighty Fortress is Our God," "The Son of God Goes Forth to War," etc. Indeed, the mid-Victorian penchant for the military in religion emerges in evangelical Christianity as a struggle against the satanic forces of evil, a war waged at times with vicious enthusiasm.[22]

Thus, I conclude that President Carter perceived his 1979 Energy Sermon as a single piece. The preparations for it—retreat, decision, pronouncement—followed traditional Carter steps, and the content paralleled to a large extent his Christian heritage and past political actions.

Two questions remain unanswered: first, does Carter believe all of this rebirth business, and, second, did Carter deliberately structure the speech in his unusual two-part fashion?

The answer to both questions seems to be yes. Yes, Carter believes all of this rebirth business—because it derives from his Christian upbringing, because it is familiar, and because no amount of convincing to the contrary was successful in removing it from the speech, even though at least two advisors cautioned him that it might weaken the energy proposals themselves.[23]

And yes, Carter structured the speech deliberately in this fashion, because no other structural style successfully linked his two speech purposes—to set forth a policy of energy conservation, and to reduce the crisis of confidence in the future.

During the 1976 campaign, Jimmy Carter promised to make the government as good as the people. In 1979, having failed to change the government substantially, President Carter discovered that the people were self-indulgent, materialistic, and morally dispirited—in short, profligate. He could have concluded that the government and the people were a perfect match; instead, he chose to flail the profligate. As President he had had, he said, "just mixed success,"[24] now he hoped for more as a preacher in the Bully Pulpit, as the chosen vessel to lead the people to a societal rebirth.

Notes

1. "Nation's Newspaper Editorialists Split over Carter's Energy Talk," *The New York Times*, July 17, 1979, p. A13.
2. *Ibid.*
3. *Ibid.*
4. James D. Barber, "Adult Identity and Presidential Style: The Rhetorical Emphasis," *Daedalus*, 97 (Summer, 1968) 938–939.
5. Leonard Levitt, "The Gospel According to Jimmy," *New York Post*, July 16, 1979, p. 4
6. Hedrick Smith, "Carter, Conscious of Risks, Seeks Wider Audience," *The New York Times*, July 14, 1979, p. 6. Interestingly enough, a letter was sent to Jimmy Carter early in his Presidency by David Wilkerson, a well-known evangelical preacher, outlining the steps necessary for successful spiritual leadership. In the letter, Wilkerson outlined leadership examples from the Bible to demonstrate success and failure. A portion follows:

The Bible speaks of another time and society that was vexed with turbulence. The whole world was sick. "And in those times there was no peace to him that went out, nor to him that came in, but great vexations were upon the inhabitants of the countries . . . and nation was destroyed of nation, and city of city; for God did vex them with adversity." (II Chronicles 15:5,6 kjv.)

God, in His mercy, destined a great leader to bring people together. His name was Asa, a leader the Bible says "who did that which was right in the eyes of the Lord his God." This chosen man was confronted by the prophet Azariah with this warning, "The Lord is with you, while you are with him; and if you seek him, he will be found of you; but if you forsake him, he will forsake you." (II Chronicles, 15:2 1b, paraphrased.)

King Asa, in a troubled and turbulent hour, led all of Israel back to the God of their fathers. The Bible says, "He commanded them to seek the Lord of their fathers, and to obey the law and the commandments. . . ." The people gladly responded. The result? They rebuilt cities. They prospered beyond all that could be imagined. The country had peace. They grew powerful and strong. All because "We sought the Lord our God, and He has given us rest on every side. So they built and prospered." (II Chronicles 14:7 1b, paraphrased).

Here is Wikerson's example of failure:

King Jehoram came into power during a time of great prosperity and peace in Israel. But "he did that which was evil in the eyes of the Lord." He led his people into compromise, dishonesty, and bribery. Suddenly, a nation that enjoyed peace and prosperity was threatened with war by the Philistines and Arabians. Enemies "carried away all their substance." And this man died with an incurable disease, for "God smote him" after only eight years in office. And he was buried with no public mourning, having become very unpopular. (II Chronicles 21,1b, paraphrased.)

See David Wilkerson, *Racing Toward Judgment* (New Jersey: Fleming H. Revell, Co., 1976), pp. 157–158.

7. Victor Gold, "The Politics of Repentence," *The New York Times*, July 22, 1979, p. E19.
8. James D. Barber, *The Presidential Character* (New Jersey: Prentice-Hall, 1972), pp. 406–409.
9. Bruce Mazlish, *In Search of Nixon* (Baltimore: Penguin Books, 1972) p. 31.
10. Jimmy Carter, "Transcript of President's Address to Country on Energy Problems," *The New York Times*, July 16, 1979, p. A10.
11. *Ibid.*
12. *Ibid.*
13. *Ibid.*
14. *Ibid.*
15. *Ibid.*
16. Judith A. Burns, "The Rhetoric of the Born Again Christian: An Exigence for Irrational Discourse," *The Pennsylvania Speech Communication Annual*, 35 (July, 1979) 24. The Model used here is an adaptation of Burns', plus additions suggested by the following evangelical works: David Wilkerson, *The Vision* (New Jersey: Fleming H. Revell, Co., 1978); Norris Cerullo, *The New Anointing* (Calif.: World Evangelism, Inc., 1975); New Testament Missionary Fellowship, *Gleanings* (New York: Thomas E. Lowe, Ltd., 1972); Leroy Jenkins, *How I Met the Master* (Ohio, L. J. Evangelistic Association, 1971); and Rex Humbard, *The Prayer Key Family Book* (Ohio: Rex Humbard Foundation, 1979).
17. Carter, *op. cit.*
18. *Ibid.*

19. *Ibid.*
20. *Ibid.*
21. *Ibid.*
22. Susan S. Tamke, *Make a Joyful Noise Unto the Lord: Hymns as a Reflection of Victorian Social Attitudes.* (Athens: Ohio U. Press, 1978) pp. 150–155.
23. Department of Energy White House source, in conversation, April 8, 1980.
24. Carter, *op. cit.*

RONALD REAGAN

Presidential Rhetoric and Presidential Power: The Reagan Initiatives

Theodore Windt
with
Kathleen Farrell

During the first six months of his administration President Ronald Reagan scored a stunning series of rhetorical and political successes. He got the first set of budget cuts in social programs through Congress, even as he pushed through a dramatic increase in spending for national defense. Equally, if not more important, Reagan initiated the largest tax cut in American history, a 25% reduction in federal taxes to be phased in over three years. Commentators have called him a "master communicator," and so he is. He speaks plainly and directly. His speeches have none of the stylistic soaring that occasionally set President Kennedy in flight. They show little of the social concern for the downtrodden that made some of President Johnson's domestic speeches moving. And they hardly exhibit the logical or psychological complexities that made Richard Nixon's addresses intriguing. On the other hand, in delivery alone, Reagan is refreshingly attractive after the dull dog days of Presidents Ford and Carter.

In this essay we intend to examine President Reagan's rhetoric during the early months of his first year, limiting ourselves to his Economic Renewal Program. We propose to give tentative answers to several pertinent questions. First, how well did President Reagan exploit the rhetorical opportunities available to him? Second, what meaning can be assigned to the fundamental substantive and strategic rhetorical efforts he used to get his economic programs passed? And finally, we need to make some early assessment of his *ethos*: is President Reagan an authentic political voice or is he practicing the "politics of nostalgia" as his critics have claimed?

1.

The Presidency—or at least the modern electronic Presidency—runs in cycles. Fresh from election or re-election, a President holds advantages over Congress. The first months of a new administration provide an especially unique opportunity. An aide to Reagan incisively described this period as the "rhetoric stage" of the administration.[1] And so it is. It offers a new President, if he

Ms. Farrell is completing her doctorate in Rhetoric and Communication at the University of Pittsburgh.
A shorter version of this paper will appear in a 1982 issue of *Speaker and Gavel*.

387

seizes it, the opportunity to impress his agenda, his perspectives, his language upon the American public in such a way as to galvanize public support for his programs.

However, these opportunities are not unlimited. Political realities impinge upon and circumscribe the President's range of actions. The first such reality lies with a President's choice of whether he will concentrate on domestic issues or foreign affairs. In the foreign realm the President is Commander-in-Chief and has a variety of constitutional powers available to him to act. On the domestic side, he has few comparable powers. In a slim volume appropriately entitled *Congress Against the President*, Richard M. Pious pointed out that real legal power in domestic affairs resides with Congress and proposed describing the President as "Initiator-in-Chief," for he can only initiate new policies or request power from Congress to act.[2] President Franklin Roosevelt realized this impotence of power in his first Inaugural Address. He declared he would "*ask* the Congress for the one remaining instrument to meet the crisis [of the depression]—broad Executive power to wage a war against the emergency, as great as the power that would be given one if we were in fact invaded by a foreign foe."[3]

The second influence on a President's ability to exercise power is the margin by which he was elected. If a candidate is barely elected (as Kennedy was in 1960 by only .1% of the popular vote) or is elected by a minority (as Nixon was in 1968 with 43.4% of the vote), he has no "mandate" to act upon his campaign promises. He may, instead, have to spend his rhetorical energies courting a constituency or constituencies so as to expand his power base with the electorate. On the other hand, if he is elected by a wide majority as Lyndon Johnson was in 1964, he will be perceived as having that elusive "mandate" and his ability to act will be much greater.

The final major influence on a President's power in domestic affairs during this initial period is control of Congress. If the President's party controls Congress, then obviously the President stands a much better chance of getting legislation passed than if the opposition party controls one or both Houses of Congress.[4] But if the opposition party is in control of the Senate or House of Representatives, the President must necessarily go over the head of Congress to appeal directly to the American people for support even as he and his legislative aides attempt to forge an ideological majority from dissident members of the opposition party.

Even with these contraints on Presidential power, the President still has distinct advantages over Congress in this initial period. He is *the* national leader and *the* voice of the country. Elmer Cornwell pointed out the strength this gives a President:

> The President's prime weapon for influencing policy-making is his ability to command and influence a national audience. Since little is likely to be done constitutionally to strengthen the President's hand, his ability to lead and mold public opinion, for all its inherent limitations, remains his prime reliance.[5]

After this unique period passes, his speeches will become repetitive, familiar, and may lose vitality except in moments of crisis. But at the outset, a new President has the opportunity to mobilize public opinion as a weapon to persuade Congress to grant him authority to act or to pass the legislative bills he has given priority to.

The second year of a Presidency is one of policy results and electoral politics. Attention shifts from promises to performance. Part of this change is due to the "rise of the rhetorical Presidency."[6] To get elected, a candidate has to promise as much as possible. During his first year the newly, democratically elected President is given a rather wide path in which to propose legislation and to predict results. But by the second year he is expected to have his policies begin producing results. If he has raised expectations too high, as seems to be a defect among recent Presidents, he will be vulnerable to attacks from the opposition party for the failure of his programs. Usually, a President finds himself on the defensive in his second year. His problems are further compounded by the fact that it is an election year. As each party looks toward the election in November, partisan criticism increases, and issues tend to be cast in terms of the forthcoming election.

The second period of the Presidency ends with the off-term elections in November. This election is perceived as symbolic, as a referendum on the President's popularity. In the twentieth century the Presisdent's party has lost an average of thirty seats in the House of Representatives and three in the Senate in these elections. Voters apparently blame the President's party for his failure to solve problems as rapidly as they believe they ought to be solved or perhaps voters who deserted their party in the Presidential election return to the party fold two years later. What is important, however, is the symbolism. If the President's party loses between 15 and 30 seats, it is thought to be typical. But if the party loses more than 30 seats—as Democrats did in 1966 under Lyndon Johnson—the President is perceived to be unpopular and vulnerable. Partisanship intensifies, and the President finds himself increasingly on the defensive and his powers in other areas greatly diminished. Conversely, if the President's party loses less than 15 seats, he is perceived as a popular President whom Congress should treat with greater deference so far as his programs are concerned or risk the political consequences. The most dramatic example of this kind of victory in recent times occurred in 1962 when the Democrats did not lose any net seats. The public, politicians, and pundits saw this as a smashing victory for President Kennedy. More important, it allowed Kennedy to move away from many of his conservative policies on civil rights and in certain areas of foreign affairs to propose the public accomodations civil rights bill and to negotiate the limited nuclear test ban treaty.[7] Thus, in many respects, the President's fortunes and ability to exercise power are dependent upon the results of this election and how it is interpreted in this third period, the third year.

The fourth period of an administration, of course, is the election year. At this time much of legislative politics, except in moments of crisis, almost ceases. If a President chooses not to seek re-election, he becomes a lame-duck President and usually contents himself to doing administrative work. If he seeks re-election, his policies and bills tend to become campaign issues to be placed before the public rather than bills to be negotiated with Congress.

Let us return then to the initial period—the rhetoric period— of the Presidency. Soon after Mr. Reagan's election, a team of advisors began working on a study of what Presidents since Franklin Roosevelt had done in the first 100 days of their administrations. According to David R. Gergen, chief of this project, they came to three conclusions:

> One, the first 100 days is the time during which the President establishes his Presidential persona. Two, the general character of the Administration is established and lasts at least the first term. And, three, the President is vulnerable to making a big mistake, the obvious example being the Bay of Pigs or Carter's energy program . . . .[8]

Furthermore, they advised the President to concentrate solely on the economic issues and to develop a thematic approach to speaking on those issues. In so doing, they created a classic example of how a President may exploit to his fullest advantage the "rhetoric stage" of a new administration.

2.

President Reagan set his priorities firmly. He would stress domestic affairs, not foreign affairs. He would concentrate on economic problems, not social issues. These choices—limited and concentrated—gave coherence to his programs and direction not only to his subordinates but to the public as well. Furthermore, he acted swiftly, putting together a rhetorical package of three major speeches (a fourth would be added after the assassination attempt), each intended to function as a different part of the over-all rhetorical effort. By advancing it quickly, he caught Congress (and especially Democrats) still in its organizing state of disorganization.

Beginning with the Inaugural Address in which he encouraged the nation to embark with him on a "New Beginning," Reagan began his massive rhetorical and media campaign. He rejected the constraints President Carter had voiced in his Farewell Address and instead called for a return to American greatness:

> We have every right to dream heroic dreams. Those who say that we're in a time when there are no heroes, they just don't know where to look. You can see heroes every day going in and out of factory gates. Others, a handful in number produce enough food to feed all of us and then the world beyond. You meet heroes across a counter. And they're on both sides of that counter. There are entrepreneurs with

faith in themselves and faith in an idea who create new jobs, new wealth and opportunity. They're individuals and families whose taxes support the government and whose voluntary gifts support church, charity, culture, art, and education. Their patriotism is quiet but deep. Their values sustain our national life.[9]

The Inaugural emphasized traditional, individualistic values and reaffirmed the belief—so often voiced in his campaign—that Americans can act decisively to solve their problems. The President pledged to fulfill his campaign promises: to do something about Big Government, to solve the country's economic problems, and to restore America to her rightful place as leader of the western world. In sum, he sought to restore confidence and optimism to the nation. On that same day, he acted by issuing an Executive Order freezing government hiring. Probably, Reagan did not have the legal power to order the freeze, but that was less important than the symbolism of the act. He had promised to reduce the size of the federal bureaucracy, and this act—minor though it was—symbolized that he meant what he had promised.

In his second nationally televised speech of 5 February, Reagan sought to build public momentum and support for the detailed economic programs he would present to Congress two weeks later. He called the situation "the worst economic mess since the Great Depression."[10] The speech dwelt on two topics: (1) a detailed examination of how different segments of American society are effected by this "economic mess;" and (2) an exposition of the causes Reagan believed created this situation. It is a classic "problem" speech with emphasis on the extent of the problems and their causes. In the speech Reagan gave short shrift to the solutions by only mentioning them, leaving those topics for his speech to Congress.

At the outset Reagan cited figures about the extent of the problems facing the Federal Government as well as some facing Americans in general. He said:

> The Federal budget is out of control, and we face runaway deficits of almost $80 billion for this budget year that ends September 30th. That deficit is larger than the entire Federal budget in 1957, and so is the almost $80 billion we will pay in interest this year on the national debt.
>
> Twenty years ago, in 1960, our Federal Government payroll was less than $13 billion. Today it is $75 billion. During these 20 years our population has only increased by 23.3 percent. The Federal budget has gone up by 528 percent.
>
> Now, we've just had 2 years of back-to-back double-digit inflation—13.3 percent in 1979, 12.4 percent last year. The last time this happened was in World War I.
>
> In 1960 mortgage interest rates averaged about 6 percent. They're 2½ times as high now, 15.4 percent.
>
> The percentage of your earnings the Federal Government took in taxes in 1960 has almost doubled.
>
> And finally there are 7 million Americans caught up in the personal indignity and human tragedy of unemployment. If they stood in a line, allowing 3 feet for each person, the line would reach from the coast of Maine to California.

Reagan continued to examine various economic problems with this kind of specificity.

Woven throughout his narration of economic problems was an exposition of four causes that created this situation: (1) excessive taxation; (2) excessive government spending; (3) excessive regulations of business, and (4) the lack of a consistent and stable monetary system. Throughout the speech Reagan brought back each of the various problems to one of these four causes. Thus, a thematic consistency as well as repetition was created. It does not come as a surprise to the audience that near the end of the speech Reagan outlined four solutions to eliminate these causes: (1) a tax cut; (2) a curb on government spending; (3) a reduction of Federal regulations; and (4) a stable monetary policy.

Of course, this speech was aimed at the American people, to prepare them for the details of his economic renewal program to be presented to Congress, to dispose them favorably toward that program by impressing upon them the imperative to act swiftly. Hedrick Smith observed: "The political strategy that he and his inner circle have devised counts on his celebrated skills as a political communicator and educator to build enough public momentum for his programs to persuade Democrats as well as Republicans to go along with them."[11] It was also intended to motivate them to let their Congressmen and Senators know they wanted action. David Stockman pointed out: "To win this fight the President is going to have to generate a million cards and letters a month to Congress."[12]

On 18 February before a joint session of Congress President Reagan presented his economic renewal program. Reagan briefly recounted the problems facing the country and their causes, a summary of his previous speech, and concluded: "We can no longer procrastinate and hope that things will get better. They will not. If we do not act forcefully, and now, the economy will grow worse."[13]

President Reagan, then, gave the details of his program: $467 billion of Federal spending cuts and $709 billion of Federal personal and corporate tax cuts over the next five years (including a 10% reduction in personal taxes for each of the next three years), a Task Force on Regulatory Relief, and a stable monetary policy.

In presenting his programs President Reagan used two basic arguments to gain support for them. First, he contended that the entire package rested on fairness to all. Everyone would get an equal tax cut of 10%, no one getting more, none getting less. In describing cuts in benefits provided by the Trade Adjustment Assistance program to employees who are unemployed because of foreign imports, Reagan stated: "There's nothing wrong with that, but because these benefits are paid out on top of normal unemployment benefits, we wind up paying greater benefits to those who lose their jobs because of foreign competition that we do to their friends and neighbors who are laid off due to domestic competition. Anyone must agree that this is unfair."

Second, the President argued that the cut in social programs would be aimed at eliminating waste and fraud. He stated the government could save $1.8 billion from the Food Stamps program by "removing from eligibility those who are not in real need or who are abusing the program." The school break- fast and lunch program would save $1.6 billion by "cutting back on meals for children of families who can afford to pay . . . ." He concluded that the major problem in social programs resided in waste and fraud: "One Government estimate indicated that fraud alone may account for anywhere from 1 to 10 percent—as much as $25 billion of Federal expenditures for social programs. If the tax dollars that are wasted or mismanaged are added to this fraud total, the staggering dimensions of this problem begin to emerge." To complement this argument, Reagan insisted that these cuts in social programs would never hurt the truly needy and promised a continuing "safety net" for them.

President Reagan thus portrayed his flat-rate tax cut and his across-the- board cuts in social spending as inherently fair since everyone would be af- fected equally. Furthermore, he would provide a "safety net" for the truly needy and eliminate only waste and fraud from government spending. If the rhetoric took hold in the public consciousness, then anyone opposing him would be perceived as being unfair or as one willing to perpetuate waste and fraud to save some special interest program.

Further anticipating his opposition, President Reagan presented two re- futative arguments. He persistently laid the blame for current economic prob- lems on the New Deal-Great Society excessive spending of the past and asked rhetorically: "Are we simply going to go down the same path we've gone down before . . . ?" His second refutative device and by far the more effective came near the end of the speech:

> I would direct a question to those who have indicated already an unwillingness to accept such a plan: Have they an alternative which offers a greater chance of balancing the budget, reducing and eliminating inflation, stimulating the creation of jobs, and reducing the tax burden?

This argument would be used repeatedly and potently against Democrats in weeks to come.

Two major themes undergirded the program: (1) the persistent fear that if we do not act, our situation may grow hopeless; and (2) the persistent confi- dence that if his programs were enacted, our present distress would be alle- viated. These observations may seem commonplace, typical arguments used by a politician. But after 18 months of drift and disarray under President Carter, the decisive rhetoric of Reagan may have convinced many that once again they could master their own fate, that they could become the heroes he had spoken about in his Inaugural. The image of confidence was intended to spawn a real confidence that would be essential if Reagan's programs were to have any chance of passage in Congress. Indeed, the Senate Budget Committee members had been surprised when the Treasury Secretary openly acknowledged that the highly optimistic administration forecasts for economic recovery were dependent on expected positive responses from citizens.[14]

Moreover, representatives from the administration ushered forth carrying Reagan's message through the media to the public and before Congressional committees to legislators. The week-end following the speech before Congress, administration officials appeared on each of the nationally televised news conferences: Meet the Press, Face the Nation, and Issues and Answers. They seemed to repeat Reagan's message verbatim.

The 18 February speech had been aimed at Congress to get action, but more than just the package of speeches was needed. *Time* reported one source as saying:

> Reagan's allies are also preparing to lobby Congressmen in their home districts. Charles Wick, former co-chairman of Reagan's Inauguration committee, plans a closed-circuit TV program during which the Administration economists will explain the plan to perhaps 15,000 Reagan loyalists around the country, who will then be expected to evangelize their Congressmen. Says one: 'If a Republican doesn't vote for us, he will have one hell of a time getting us into his district to campaign for him in 1982. And if a Democrat votes against us, he just might see a lot of us in his district when he runs for reelection.'[15]

The President was acting decisively to fulfill his campaign promises. Opponents knew this. One Democratic Senator said: "We all read the same election returns. It is Reagan who has the mandate to try something different and has left the other side at least temporarily in rout."[16]

The March 30th assassination attempt on the President's life underscored his important rhetorical role in maintaining public support. As one adviser put it: "Nobody can replace the President as a salesman for his package."[17] But within a month the President regained the initiative. On 28 April, President Reagan appeared before a joint session of Congress in another nationally televised speech to thank the nation for its outpouring of sympathy and to re-enforce support for his economic proposals. The speech was a repetition, at least as far as arguments were concerned, of the others he had given. What was more important was that the President was recovering and was again in rhetorical control. The assassination attempt that had initially seemed to rob the Reagan program of its momentum had turned into a rare rhetorical and political opportunity. The appearance of the wounded President brought an overwhelming response and four standing ovations. As Representative Robert Michel of Illinois observed, the speech brought "the kind of reception that makes a few of the waverers feel 'Gosh, how can I buck that?' "[18]

All in all, President Reagan seized the rhetorical opportunities available to him in his first 100 days in a masterful manner. Congressional opponents quickly found themselves on the defensive, and Reagan's Presidency had that mysterious, elusive ingredient for effectiveness—"momentum." James Reston summed it up well: "On domestic policy, there has been no hesitation. Mr. Reagan has been as definite as a punch in the nose. He promised in the campaign to cut the budget, cut taxes, and slaughter every fat Democratic cow in the corral, and he has kept his promise."[19]

3.

But how do President Reagan's efforts compare with those of other recent Presidents? Neither President Kennedy nor Nixon nor Ford nor Carter used this "rhetoric stage" of a new administration as effectively.

From a rhetorical standpoint, Kennedy stands out as one of the least effective. Within three months of his inauguration he destroyed his "honeymoon" with Congress by approving the disastrous Bay of Pigs invasion. For the next two years Kennedy found himself on the defensive, defending policies in place rather than effectively advancing the programs he had so vigorously advocated during the 1960 campaign. Furthermore, after his stirring Inaugural Address, he practically abandoned oratory for the televised press conference. Certainly, press conferences are a worthwhile means for explaining disconnected policies and even clearing up occasional misunderstandings, but they are not an effective substitute for speeches in marshalling support. They are unfocused, for the most part, and too many issues are discussed in short, disconnected fashion. Nor, until after the mid-term elections of 1962 did President Kennedy begin to creep forward with the most important items on his domestic agenda. But by that late date, the list of items had been severely curtailed.

More concerned with foreign policy and building a workable constituency, President Nixon waited until June, 1969 to begin his rhetorical offensive. Most of these efforts were spent expanding his constituency and trying to quiet the protests that haunted the land instead of pressing for domestic legislation. Indeed, with the notable exceptions of environmental legislation and some crime-fighting bills, one is hard-pressed to think of much significant domestic legislation in connection with the Nixon administration.

President Ford, that accidental President, never had a chance. The pardon of Nixon—one month after the resignation—destroyed the era of good feeling Ford's ascension to the Presidency had created. And he was rhetorically inept. William Safire said of him that he was the only President in the twentieth century not to utter one memorable phrase during his administration. His "WIN" campaign attests to his rhetorical ineffectiveness.

President Carter had opportunities similar to Reagan's, but he squandered them. He waited three months before presenting his comprehensive energy program. By then, Congress was organized and waiting. So too were special interest groups. Carter attempted the same thing as Reagan: first, a fireside chat to the people on the need for an energy program; second, an address to a joint session of Congress outlining his programs in detail; finally, a press conference intended to clarify any points not covered by the speeches. But all these efforts were squeezed into a single week. Congress ate him alive. Thus, his rhetorical efforts were rather like a skyrocket that burst beautifully against the dark night, then fizzled and fell to ground silent. It took President Carter nearly three years to get major portions of his energy package passed.

Only President Lyndon Johnson realized the advantages of the "rhetoric stage" and exploited them fully. Five days after the assassination of President Kennedy, Johnson used the collective grief of the American people to urge passage of Kennedy's tax cut bill and the civil rights bill. On January 8, 1964 Johnson declared war on poverty. Once he was elected overwhelmingly in his own right he was able to solicit from Congress a variety of programatic weapons with which to wage the poverty war. Johnson so seized the advantages of his unique "rhetoric stage" that both his ideological opponents and the Congress found themselves on the defensive for the next two years. During that time Johnson compiled a domestic record of legislation that only a few Presidents in American history can match.

President Reagan made an equally auspicious start. He has done about all he could do rhetorically to gain passage of his programs. Ideological, partisan, and special-interest opponents discovered that the rhetorical *blitzkreig* of Reagan had swept them aside. When the Democrats finally came up with some alternatives, their proposals—though differing in emphasis and purpose—still accepted basic premises set forth by Reagan and some of their bills were strikingly similar. In late March the Senate Budget Committee voted to cut spending even deeper than the President had requested, and the lack of an effective opposition took its toll. In August the final victory of Reagan's economic program was achieved when Congress voted the largest tax cut in history with many Democrats joining Republicans. President Reagan had achieved what he promised, and his rhetoric played no small part in that achievement.

4.

Now, to our second question: What meaning can we assign to the fundamental substantive and strategic efforts Reagan has initiated? Since this essay is principally an over-view of Reagan's early rhetoric, we shall leave it to our colleagues and others for a detailed and intensive analysis of that rhetoric. The substantive issues turn on two points: (1) the package itself of tax cuts, budget cuts, monetary stability, and regulation reform; and (2) Reagan's conception of the responsibilities of the Federal Government. The first is well-known and need not detain us long. The emphasis in Reagan's rhetoric has been on the programs and their promise of relief rather than on the ideological principles that guide them. He appears to believe that promises of a tax cut and budget cuts will be more attractive to voters than the recitation of conservative dogma that originally gained him a following. The election mandate had been a specific one: to bring prosperity back to the economy. Reagan's political philosophy has been disguised by the repetition of what some regard as simplistic slogans: "Government is not the solution to our problems; government is the problem." "We've got to get government off the backs of people." These statements strike a responsive chord among those burdened by taxes, suffocated by what they consider excessive regulations, frightened by high interest rates and the inflation rate. They serve as rallying points to alleviate frustration by promising individual relief. But Reagan has been after something more substantive.

In his 18 February speech before Congress Reagan stated: "The taxing power of government must be used to provide revenues for legitimate government purposes. It must not be used to regulate the economy or bring about social change. We've tried that, and surely we must be able to see it doesn't work. Spending by government must be limited to those functions which are the proper province of government."[20] These statements succinctly summarize Reagan's political thinking. Federal money should not be used to regulate the economy. Federal money should not be used to bring about social change. The first suggests a modern *laissez faire* economic system, and few Reaganites have denied that interpretation. The second is more ambiguous. Denying the use of federal money for social change implicitly means bringing forth another kind of social change. For skeptics of Reagan, it means a retreat from social justice, human rights, and equal opportunity. For rabid Reaganites, it means a return to basic American values which translates into returning prayers to public schools, an anti-abortion amendment, and an end to school busing. But there is another layer of meaning beneath this one. If Reagan limits government involvement in economic and social matters and if he is able to return Federal revenue sources to the states, he will be undermining the uniformity with which the Federal Government has enforced laws for the last fifty years. Such a change in Federal responsibilities may eventually dwarf the changes wrought by the New Deal.

Reagan's revolutionary vision of Federal responsibilities seems to be accompanied by a political revolution. A careful reading of his speeches reveals a distinctive strategic approach to the public. The primary and persistent argument repeated in speech after speech is that all of us must sacrifice now so that all of us may benefit in the future. There is a not very subtle shift in appeals from clearly defined constituencies to a more general constituency.

Every American President makes appeals to his "fellow Americans." But if Reagan means to change the direction of American government, as we believe he intends to do, and if he is successful in his programs, this strategy portends a move away from traditional coalition politics to the outskirts of ideological politics.

Reagan's proposals mark a historic departure from national priorities that have prevailed for decades. Anthony Lewis noted that "President Reagan's economic speech to Congress marks the turn of a long historic tide in American federalism. However successful he turns out to be in getting the details of his program enacted, we know we are at the end of the age in which Americans looked to Washington to meet their every public need."[21] And such a shift, if successful, would mean a radical change in both the institutions of Government and our political parties as well.

5.

Finally *ethos*: the most potent instrument of persuasion. Is Reagan's voice authentic to our times or merely an echo from the days of Calvin Coolidge? Thomas Cronin compared Reagan to John Kennedy in the sense that each could recognize a morale problem, simplify it, and make it interesting enough for people to listen to.[22] Certainly, his ready smile, his joking manner, even his jellybeans contribute to the image of a truly sincere politician who would never knowingly hurt anyone, let alone the truly needy.

But is Reagan simply a "nice guy" with no clear vision for the country beyond echoing the past that may never have been? We tend to believe he is an authentic voice of today speaking from the vast reaches of the Southwest and West. It does not seem to be one we in the East are accustomed to, what with its concern for the 55 mile an hour speed limit, the need to be born again not only in our private lives but our public lives as well. In an insightful book, *Power Shift: The Rise of the Southern Rim and Its Challenge to the Eastern Establishment*, Kirkpatrick Sale detailed the characteristics of this new "establishment" emerging to challenge the old: a "cowboy" era buttressed by agribusiness, extensive defense contracts, expanding high technology, real-estate conglomerates, and a leisurely life-pattern. It is a voice, rambunctious and full-throated shouting the age-old cry of Westerners: "Don't fence me in!" Ronald Reagan is no sedate nostalgic throw-back to the days of Harding and Coolidge. He is an authentic representative of the rising new establishment of the Southwest. The Cowboy Era is upon us. And it may be ushered in more forcibly by that authentic voice—smooth and sincere—than by all the elaborate rhetorical strategies and arguments his advisers have devised. Whether it is the prophetic voice of the future, however, will ultimately rest on the success or failures of the economic policies President Reagan has now gotten enacted. He turned an election that was to a large extent a rejection of President Carter into a mandate for widespread changes in economic policy. He proposes major changes in the role of the Federal Government and in its responsibilites. The American public will wait to be persuaded ultimately by the results these changes produce.

Notes

1. *The New York Times* (March 8, 1981), p. 4E.
2. Richard M. Pious, "Sources of Domestic Policy Initiatives," *Congress Against the President*, ed. by Harvey C. Mansfield, Sr., Vol. 32, No. 1, *Proceedings of the Academy of Political Science* (Montpelier: Capital City Press, 1975), pp. 98–111.
3. "First Inaugural Address," *The Roosevelt Reader*, ed. by Basil Rauch (New York: Holt, Rinehart and Winston, 1957), p. 94. Emphasis added.
4. Richard Nixon, a President elected by a minority, became the first President in the twentieth century to face, as he entered office, both Houses of Congress controlled by the opposition party.
5. Elmer Cornwell, Jr., *Presidential Leadership of Public Opinion* (Bloomington, Ind.: Indiana University Press, 1965), p. 303.
6. James W. Ceaser, Glen E. Thurow, Jeffrey Tulis and Joseph M. Bessette, "The Rise of the Rhetorical Presidency," *Presidential Studies Quarterly* Vol. 11 (Spring, 1981), pp. 158–171.
7. Cf. Theodore Windt, "John Fitzgerald Kennedy," *Presidential Rhetoric: 1961–1980*, ed. by Windt, 2nd ed. (Dubuque: Kendall/Hunt, 1980), pp. 7–9.
8. Sidney Blumenthal, "Marketing the President," *The New York Times Magazine* (September 13, 1981), p. 110.
9. "Inaugural Address of President Ronald Reagan," *Weekly Compilation of Presidential Documents* (January 26, 1981), p. 3. All subsequent quotations from the Inaugural are from this version.
10. "The Nation's Economy. Address to the Nation, February 5, 1981," *Weekly Compilation of Presidential Documents* (February 9, 1981), p. 93. All subsequent quotations are from this version of the speech.
11. Hedrick Smith, "Blunt and Simple," *The New York Times* (February 6, 1981), p. A 12.
12. Quoted in *Newsweek* (February 16, 1981), p. 20.
13. "Program for Economic Recovery. Address Before a Joint Session of Congress. February 18, 1981," *Weekly Compilation of Presidential Documents* (February 23, 1981) p. 130. All subsequent quotations are from this version of the speech.
14. *The New York Times* (February 18, 1981), p. A 16.
15. *Time* (March 2, 1981), p. 13.
16. *Newsweek* (March 2, 1981), p. 23.
17. *The New York Times* (April 12, 1981), p. E 5.
18. Quoted in *The New York Times* (April 29, 1982), p. A 22.
19. James Reston, "Reagan's First Three Months," *The New York Times* (April 12, 1981), p. E 1.
20. "Program for Economic Recovery," *op. cit.*, p. 137.
21. *The New York Times* (February 19, 1981), p. A 17.
22. *The New York Times* (January 21, 1981), p. B 2.

Trying to "Stay the Course": President Reagan's Rhetoric during the 1982 Election

Beth A. J. Ingold and Theodore Windt

In the first full flush of President Reagan's legislative victories in the summer of 1981, some of his aides were saying they anticipated major Republican victories in the 1982 mid-term elections. Some predicted they would not only increase Republican control of the Senate, but might even capture control of the House of Representatives for the first time in a generation. They appeared to have reason to rejoice.[1]

The President had been successful in getting Congress to enact the largest tax cut in American history, controversial budget cuts in essentially non-entitlement social programs, and a hefty increase in defense spending for the military. These triumphs seemed to signify a "new beginning" for American government, a real change in direction from the New Deal-Great Society concept of expanding federal responsibilities to a much more conservative approach of a limited government. The President had been so dazzling in persuading the public and Congress to adopt his programs that his aides warned representatives who might vote against Reagan's Economic Renewal Program that to do so would risk the "Master Communicator" campaigning against them in 1982. *Time* quoted one such aide as threatening: "If a Republican doesn't vote for us, he will have one hell of a time getting us into his district to campaign for him in 1982. And if a Democrat votes against us, he just might see a lot of us in his district when he runs for reelection."[2] This threat along was sufficient—given Mr. Reagan's popularity at the time—to keep many legislators in line even though they might harbor private, heretical doubts about this economic program that Vice President Bush had once called "voodoo" economics.[3]

The disarray of the Democrats also worked to the President's advantage. Conservative "boll weevils" deserted the Democratic party in enough numbers to assure passage of the economic bills in the House. Liberal Democrats fumbled around trying to come up with an alternative to Reagan's proposals and failed miserably.

But, above all, stood the President's rhetorical effectiveness. *"The whole issue of running the Presidency in the modern age,"* Richard Beal, one of Reagan's advisors, said, *"is control of the agenda."*[4] Indeed, at the heart of

Reprinted by permission of Center for the Study of the Presidency, publishers of *Presidential Studies Quarterly* Vol. XIV, No. 1 (Winter, 1984), pp. 87–97.

President Reagan's politics is his belief that to be effective he must stay on the offensive by defining and controlling the major issues he wants placed before Congress and the public. In this respect, the President has certain advantages over other branches of government and over other advocates:

> The President's prime weapon for influencing policy-making is his ability to command and influence a national audience. Since little is likely to be done constitutionally to strengthen the President's hand, his ability to lead and mold public opinion for all its inherent limitations, remains his prime reliance.[5]

Television has become the technological means for a President to enhance this power. It provides a President with instantaneous communication with a national audience and is "the most effective communicator of ideas and images . . . that political man has yet developed."[6] In this age of the "rhetorical Presidency," few Presidents have been as bold as Ronald Reagan in exploiting these advantages.

But advantages do not assure success. Even though a President may enjoy initial advantages over Congress, in the long run Congress with its legislative and budgetary powers still holds sway eventually over the Presidency. And television is a two-edged sword. Though television provides the President with direct access to the public, it also serves as the rhetorical balance to the President:

> Television news not only carries the messages of governing officials to the people; it also selects the issues that are presented to the government for 'action' of some sort. 'Real' expressions of mass opinion . . . are replaced by the news' continuous 'sophisticated' analyses that serve as a surrogate audience, speaking to the government and supposedly representing to it what the people are saying and thinking. Driven by its own inner dynamic to find and sustain exciting issues and to present them in dramatic terms, news creates—or gives the impression of creating—national moods and currents of opinion which appear to call for some form of action by the government and especially by the President.[7]

Thus, the modern era has created a new "checks and balances"—one never dreamed of by the Founding Fathers—in government. Congress now serves as a legislative check on the Presidency, and the media news as a rhetorical balance to Presidential pronouncements. Therefore, election campaigns have taken on greater significance as a guide to public desires and wishes. And in the absence of a Presidential election, the mid-term elections have assumed the symbolic role of telling officials what the public "truly" desires and wants, a kind of preliminary report card on the first two years of an administration.

This essay is an examination of President Reagan's rhetoric during the 1982 election campaign. It is divided into two sections: (1) the political context in which the rhetorical strategies had to be developed; and (2) an analysis and criticism of those rhetorical strategies, as President Reagan hoped to control the political and rhetorical agenda of the nation.

1.

Looking back on the first year of Reagan's administration one can see how effectively the President controlled the national political agenda. Soon after his election, a team of advisors began working on a study of what Presidents since Franklin Roosevelt had done in the first one hundred days of their administrations. According to David R. Gergen, chief of the project, they came to three conclusions: "One, the first 100 days is the time during which the President establishes his Presidential Persona. Two, the general character of the Administration is established and lasts at least the first term. And three, the President is vulnerable to making a big mistake, the obvious example being the Bay of Pigs or Carter's energy program. . . ."[8] To achieve these ends, Reagan's aides put together a rhetorical package of speeches to the public and before joint sessions of Congress. These worked magnificently well and resulted in August in the passage of his Economic Renewal programs.[9] They also established a genial Presidential persona and a decidedly conservative character for the administration. They also avoided making a big mistake.

In retrospect, we can see that they not only scripted the first one hundred days, but the first twenty-two months as well. As best we can make out, they divided these months between the Inaugural and mid-term election into three distinct rhetorical periods.[10]

The first period, of course, extended from the Inaugural to August, 1981, when the Economic Renewal programs were passed. Once Congress voted on these issues, the President and his people apparently sought to give Congress a "breather" between September and January so Congress could act upon its own agenda and do its house-keeping chores.[11]

The second rhetorical/legislative period began with the State of the Union message in January and was intended to continue control of the agenda as well as to introduce the second phase of Reagan's New Federalism. James A. Baker III, White House Chief of Staff, explained it well: "This [State of the Union address] represents the fifth installment on the President's mandate. Last year, he cut spending, he cut taxes, he cut regulations and he strengthened defense. The fifth thing he wanted to do was return power to the states. This fundamental realignment of the Federal system is a dramatic and bold initiative, and I think it's going to allow us to dominate the debate."[12] In his address President Reagan called for the transfer of some forty Federal programs to state and local governments and the gradual transfer of funding for these programs from Federal to state and local responsibility. The President apparently believed that his popularity and the momentum of his successes during the first year would cause Congress to enact these proposals quickly.

The third period was intended to begin in September, 1982, as a prelude to the mid-term elections. Actually, the groundwork for this period was to be laid in the spring and summer when the social issues—prayers in schools, abortion, school busing, and the constitutional amendment mandating a balanced Federal budget—would be introduced into Congress. Social conservatives would be mollified by these initiatives. They had watched during the first year as Reagan concentrated on economic issues, but by mid-1982 they would want action.[13] President Reagan would give it to them by endorsing some of Senator Helms' social bills and amendments. Of course, the practical purpose was *not* to get these bills and amendments passed, but to force votes on them. Then, these volatile issues could be used as major campaign issues against liberals and Democrats in the House and Senate.

All these strategies were to culminate in Republicans gaining seats in the Senate and having only minor losses, if losses there must be, in the House.[14] Media pundits would interpret these results as a clear victory for the President and his policies. The President's party usually loses seats in the mid-term elections. That is commonplace. What is important is how many seats his party loses and what symbolism is attached to those losses. If the President's party loses less than fifteen seats, analysts consider it a Presidential victory. If they lose more than twenty-five seats, analysts consider it a defeat and the President politically vulnerable. The administration intended on making the 1982 mid-term election a victory.

But, alas, for much of the 1982 campaign, the President was unable to control the agenda. Life is not a movie; real people sometimes refuse to play their reel roles; and events are not subject to rewrites. By September, 1982 the political climate had changed dramatically.

First, "voodoo" economics had cast its spell over Congress, but for many segments of society it had spelled only "bubble, bubble, toil and trouble." Even though inflation had been cut in half and interest rates had begun to drop, the Federal deficit threatened to double the previous record of $66 billion set during the final year of President Ford's administration.

Second, Republicans were unable or reluctant to bring the social issues to a vote in the Senate. These issues—prayers in public schools, abortion, and the tuition tax credits for private schools—had President Reagan's endorsements. But by the beginning of the campaign in September, the Senate had voted only on the constitutional amendment requiring a Federal balanced budget, and the House had defeated this amendment.

Finally, even though the President remained personally popular, his job approval rating had dropped significantly. The major problem appeared to be his image as a "rich man's president" who had been unfair in cutting social programs for the poor while giving tax breaks to the wealthy.[15] Two strategies were developed to confront this problem. First, the President frequently appeared at backyard barbecues, ethnic festivals, and at home at his ranch. One aide explained that they wanted the President to be seen as "boots and saddles," "kielbasa and beer,"[16] Furthermore, the President's campaign developed a seventy-five page briefing book, entitled *Fairness Issues,* that marshalled facts and figures to demonstrate that Democrats had caused current economic problems, that the President's programs would eventually work, and that the public should continue to support him.[17] Nonetheless, as unemployment continued to rise, the issue of fairness would persistently haunt the campaign of President Reagan.

Thus, it was within this political milieu that President Reagan launched the most vigorous campaign of any modern President in an off-term election.[18] However, due to the changing economic climate the President had to alter his strategy and tactics several times during the campaign.

2.

The campaign strategy team, assembled by James Baker III, decided on the theme of "patience" or "staying the course" as the central theme of the campaign. They knew that Franklin Roosevelt had successfully used that theme in 1934 by arguing that his New Deal programs needed time to work and that he needed more Democrats in Congress to carry through those programs. In that election Democrats gained nine seats in the House, only the second time since the Civil War that the President's party had gained seats in an off-term election.

The theme of staying the course became the unifying theme in President Reagan's rhetoric. Richard M. Teeter, a pollster within the campaign strategy team, said the theme told voters: "We've made some big changes. The question is do you want to stay the course and see them through or go back to the policies of the past?"[19] This theme was amplified consistently by dividing it into two topics of past failures and future hopes. Every campaign speech by President Reagan emphasized the severe economic problems he *inherited* when he entered office:

> Now I know that there are some whom I've referred to as 'Rip Van Winkles,' who seem to have forgotten that America even existed before 1981. They subscribe to the Big Bang Theory—a whole universe suddenly came into being through a great explosion. The only difference is, in their vision, the Big Bang was on January 20th, 1981. And according to them, our economic crisis emerged full blown by spontaneous generation just a few seconds after I took office. Up until then, we didn't have any troubles at all. . . . The problems of overspending, big taxing, and runaway bureaucracy that have sapped our economic strength did not begin 20 months ago. They'd been building for 20 years, leading us to higher and higher levels of inflation and unemployment. And it was in the four years before we took office that those problems became so acute, they nearly brought America down.[20]

His speeches also contained promises of future relief and prosperity based on the economic accomplishments of his administration in reducing inflation, interest rates, and taxes. These arguments remained stable throughout Reagan's campaign.They were consistent with the theme of staying the course, and they allowed him to avoid the *present* danger of facing the issue of unemployment.

The President sought to use the theme of staying the course to control the agenda of the campaign. However, the President also had to adapt to other issues and to circumstances. Thus, the President's campaign divided itself into four rhetorical periods, as the President made major adjustments in rhetorical strategy and tactics: (1) *attacking on the social issues;* (2) *defeating on the fairness of his programs;* (3) *confronting the issue of unemployment;* and (4) *asking the electorate to vote its hopes, not its fears.*

The social issues. President Reagan sought to place Democrats on the defensive by stressing the social issues which he and his aides believed would allow them to control the issues of the campaign. Thus, President Reagan opened his part of the 1982 campaign in Manhattan, Kansas with his speech at the Alfred M. Landon Lecture Series on Public Issues on September 9, 1982. He took as his theme the need to recapture traditional American values. He stated:

> We must restore to their place of honor the bedrock values handed down by families to serve as society's compass. Our time-tested values have never failed us when we've had the courage to live up to them. Speaking here 15 years ago, I was asked, following the speech, a question from the audience: if our young people of that day were not turning away from our traditional values? And I replied that maybe those young people just didn't think *we* were living up to them. There was a roar of approval from the students present that indicated agreement. They hadn't abandoned those values; they just didn't think that our older generation cared any more. So, it's up to us to make sure they realize we do.[21]

The remainder of the speech concentrated on two sets of values—social values and economic values—that when embraced would help the President reach the "ultimate and overwhelming positive goal" of his administration of putting "limits on the power of government."

President Reagan recounted four social values that Americans must strive for: returning prayers to schools, protecting the innocent life of the unborn child, reducing crime, and volunteering private services for public social needs. He wrapped these in the cloak of traditional morality and individual initiative.

On economic values the President told how he had concentrated his efforts to lift "the yoke of economic oppression that has penalized hard-working families, weakening our strength, threatening our security. . . ." The economic values he stressed coincided with the policies he had pushed through Congress the previous year. He recalled how his administration had brought down inflation, reduced interest rates, and initiated "tax reform" through the ninety-eight billion dollar tax decrease. He promised to continue to work for a balanced budget and for further reduction of taxes. He gave the problem of unemployment only passing mention.

In subsequent speeches during his first week of campaigning, President Reagan continued (with varying emphasis) to stress the social issues within the framework of the persistent theme of his campaign. However, this strategy was soon scrapped. The social issues did not take hold as an attractive campaign issue. One aide explained: "There is only one issue to talk about out here, and that's the economy. Social policy and foreign policy don't make a blip. . . ."[22] Indeed, the public seemed more interested in the abortive economy than in abortion. The President's aides thought voters saw his use of the social issues as a means for diverting attention from the state of the economy, and such a perception might weaken his claim to being a forthright and decisive leader. But most important, the failure of the Republican-controlled Senate to force votes on these issues weakened, if not destroyed any attempt by the President to make them partisan issues against Democrats. The collapse of this strategy became clear on September 23 when the Republican Senate voted to table proposed legislation that would have allowed prayers in public schools.[23]

Fairness. By late September, the President had dropped the social issues, except before selected audiences, and focused instead on the economy. He gave his standard speech asking the public to stay the course and repeated that he had inherited the worst economic situation since Roosevelt. However, the demise of the social issues as a topic exposed the essential weakness of the theme of staying the course: it was defensive because it involved admitting that the promised economic recovery had not fully occurred. This admission left the President open to attacks that his economic program generally had been unfair and that he had done little specifically to alleviate unemployment. Thus, in this second rhetorical phase of the campaign the President found himself on the defensive, struggling to control the agenda and not faring well.

To cope with the issue of fairness the President developed two distinct rhetorical strategies. First, he charged that Democrats offered no real alternative to his policies except to "tax and tax, and spend and spend" which would have disastrous consequences for Americans:

> But this is an election year, and the air is filled with liberal voices talking big talk about fairness and compassion. They would urge the American people to turn their backs on everything that we've accomplished together. And to listen to their horror stories about budget cuts, you'd have to like horror movies.
>
> When they talk about fairness, I have to ask them, where have they been? It was just less than two years ago . . . when they turned over control of the Government to us, and we were left to cope with the worst combination of high inflation and high interest rates and taxation in more than 100 years, and we didn't hear any words about fairness then.
>
> The other question is, where would they take us now? And the answer is right back to the same swamp that we're trying to get out of. They're not promoting fairness; they're selling the same old snake oil. They honestly can't see that their policies brought us to the brink of disaster. And yet, they want another blank check to spend more money. They resist a constitutional amendment against red-ink

spending, even though 80 percent of the American people think it's a good idea. And they want to take away the third year of the tax cut and indexing—two provisions which benefit low and middle-income families the most.[24]

This set of arguments fits neatly with his repeated charges of past failures by the Democratic party.

His second argument charged that because his administration had begun to solve the problems of inflation, people on social welfare programs were actually better off today than previously.

> Now, as to fairness, Aid for Dependent Children in the decade of the seventies— their benefits were increased by one-third. In that same decade, because of the inflation that was brought on by the irresponsible government spending, those people actually . . . had a one-third decrease in their ability to buy food and the necessities of life, because of inflation. Now, not only those people who are on Aid for Dependent Children find they have increased purchasing power because of the change in the inflation rate, people at the poverty level have about $600 more in purchasing power. . . .
>
> Now, what is more fair. . . .[25]

Such arguments were not as effective as the attacks on Democrats because this second set of arguments were still defensive.

Unemployment was a more difficult issue and one of growing influence. For the most part during this phase of the campaign, President Reagan sought to ignore it or to spend as little rhetorical energy as possible on the subject. On the few occasions when the President addressed the issue of unemployment, he used three different strategies to deal with it. First, he argued that even though unemployment had risen, more people than ever—ninety-nine million or more—now had jobs. He added that these workers were actually better off than before because he had brought inflation under control.[26] Second, he argued that more people constitute today's workforce thus increasing the percentage of unemployed, but stated that Americans now have "safety net" benefits to protect them when they become unemployed. Frequently, the President would draw upon his personal experiences of searching for a job during the Depression to introduce this line of argument:

> In those days, of course, there weren't any provisions as there are now for unemployment insurance or anything for quite some time. It is possible we might touch 10 percent [unemployment]. I hope not, but, if we do, I would also like to point out that there is a higher percentage of the eligible workers in the land—that is considered to be over the age of 16, men and women—that there is a higher percentage employed today than has been true even in the past in times of full employment.
>
> I've used the 1953 figures when unemployment was 2½ percent. They didn't have as big a percentage. So, it isn't all recession. What has happened is a greater percentage of adult Americans have entered the work force, are in the work force than ever before.[27]

Needless to day, such complicated figures and convoluted reasoning offered little solace to laid-off auto workers or steel workers where unemployment had stretched to nearly forty percent.

His third line of argument was not very subtle and was short-lived. President Reagan blamed the unemployed themselves for being unemployed. In his remarks to employees of the AccuRay Corporation in Ohio, he said:

> Every time I find myself in a city on a weekend I'm away. . . . I look in the Sunday paper at the help-wanted ads. And you look at them in the great metropolitan centers, and you count as many as 65 pages of help-wanted ads. And you say, 'Wait a minute, you know, 9.8 percent unemployment, but here are employers. They're advertising for people, and they can't get the jobs filled.[28]

However, neither these rhetorical strategies nor the de-emphasis on unemployment would make the issue disappear. Indeed, it only became a more powerful weapon for Democrats on October 8 when the Bureau of Labor Statistics announced that unemployment had reached 10.1 percent, the highest level since 1940.[29]

Thus, another mid-course correction was needed in campaign rhetorical strategy. The unemployment issue loomed darkly on the political horizon. Equally important, control of the campaign agenda had slipped away from the President. The issue of unemployment had taken hold with much of the electorate, and Democrats used it as their prime issue in the campaign. Control of the agenda, moreover, had shifted from the President to media. Speaking primarily to regional audiences, the President did not command a national audience, *except* as journalists reported sections from his speeches. That shift contradicted the fundamental rule of Reagan's politics and therefore dictated a shift in rhetorical strategy.

Unemployment. President Reagan decided to face the issue of unemployment squarely by going over the heads of journalists to speak directly to the American people. He asked for national television time to give a "nonpartisan" speech on the economy on October 13. Two of the three national networks obliged him.

In the speech President Reagan reiterated many of the arguments he had previously used to demonstrate that his policies were working. But the emphasis he placed on arguments changed considerably. He abandoned his stress on past failures and future hopes to concentrate on present fears. His whole discussion of unemployment changed as he sought to defuse the issue of unemployment.

The President noted that he had inherited five major economic problems when he entered office: high taxes, high inflation, runaway government spending, high interest rates, and unemployment. Using visual graphics, he checked off the first four problems as having been brought generally under control due to the policies of his administration. Only rising unemployment remained.

To put the best light on a dark subject, President Reagan tried to explain away the highest unemployment rate since 1940 by relying on three major arguments. First, he cited inflation as the principal cause of unemployment and called for patience:

> But remember, you can't solve unemployment without solving the things that cause it—the out-of-control government spending, the skyrocketing inflation and interest rates that led to unemployment in the first place. Unless you get at the root cause of the problem—which is exactly what our economic program is doing—you may be able to temporarily relieve the symptoms, but you'll never cure the disease."[30]

The argument is skillfully constructed. If people can be convinced that inflation (caused by excessive government spending which results in high interest rates) is the major cause of unemployment, then they will have patience with the President's program because inflation has only recently been brought under control. This argument also fits easily into the unifying theme of the campaign—staying the course—thus giving a pervasive consistency to his campaign and places this speech properly within the context of his previous speeches.

The second and third lines of argument are complementary, the first explicitly stated, the second inherent in the first. The President described unemployment as a disease and prescribed treatment that will require sacrifice and pain to cure it. This economic approach to the problem may be called the "deep root canal" theory of economics. It was Arthur Laffer's belief, embraced by Reagan, that an "economics based on the theory that like deep root-canal oral surgery, economic austerity *must* be good for you if it is truly painful."[31] In this speech, this metaphoric appeal was made specific:

> Again, as with unemployment, the old quick fixes simply did not work. Each time they were applied, they gave a little temporary relief to the patient, but left him weaker than he was before.
>
> It's a consistent pattern. Each time inflation has shot up since 1969 there has been a deadly, delayed reaction of rising unemployment. Inflation is like a virus in the economic blood stream, sometimes dormant and sometimes active, but leaving the patient weaker after every new attack.

Reagan's cure—controlling inflation—performs surgery on the root cause. But as in any surgery, it has the temporary side-effect of also causing suffering and pain. In speaking about the pain of unemployment, Reagan tried to turn this liability into an asset. He recited the other achievements of his administration and stated that unemployent is always the last condition to be reversed. Since his policies had begun solving the other problems, so too unemployment would eventually be solved. This argument might be called argument from success by association.

President Reagan's televised address was an effective defense of his economic programs. But therein lay the weaknesses of the speech. It was a *defense.* By responding vigorously to the Democrats' major issue, President Reagan gave greater legitimacy to it thereby further losing control of the agenda to Democrats.[32] A final shift in rhetorical strategy became necessary.

Hope, not fear. In the final phase of the campaign Reagan did not drop the theme of staying the course, but added a new theme of asking voters to vote their hopes, not their fears. In a major campaign speech in Raleigh, North Carolina, he claimed his administration had changed the course of America:

> America has a future of courage and hope—hope that grows brighter as more people respond to the drop in inflation, tax rates and interest rates. Not every statistic is strong yet, but look at the trend. Real wages, adjusted for inflation—real wages are up. Retail sales are up; housing starts and permits are up; the value of the dollar is up; productivity is up; research and development spending is up; venture capital in small business near a record.[33]

He charged his Democratic critics with "playing with people's fear, trying to scare them into believing that things will get worse, so their own political fortunes will get better." This "hope-versus-fear" theme dominated the final week of the campaign. Furthermore, Reagan portrayed the Republican party as the party of the common good while castigating the Democrats as the party of partisan ambition. This theme allowed Republicans to appear as the positive party while painting Democrats as the negative—an adroit strategy because many voters by this time had begun complaining about the negative quality of many campaigns. Above all, this strategy highlighted the prime weakness of Democrats: their lack of specific alternatives to Reagan's programs. To associate the hope offered by his administration with the future, Reagan included in each speech in these final days a message from the *Psalms* that accommodated his positive outlook.

> There's a passage in the Psalms which says: 'Weeping may endure for a night, but joy cometh in the morning.' America has endured a long, terrible night of economic hardship, but now we're seeing the first welcome burst of sunshine, the dawn of a new day for our country. America is entering a new season of hope, a genuine hope which springs from the vitality of the American spirit. We will put strong wings on weary hearts.[34]

Thus did President Reagan conclude the final phase of the 1982 election campaign.

3.

President Reagan made the 1982 off-term elections a referendum on his Presidency at mid-point. The results of the election were mixed. Republicans lost no seats in the Senate, but Democrats gained twenty-six seats in the House of Representatives. It was not an overwhelming defeat for Republicans, nor was it a mandate for a return to traditional Democratic liberalism. Nonetheless, certain conclusions can be drawn about President Reagan's rhetoric during the campaign and from the results of the election.

First, unemployment emerged as the major issue of the campaign. The President and his advisors sought to avoid it through much of the early campaign by concentrating on the problems they had inherited and the solutions they had initiated. But eventually they had to face the issue and were unable to overcome its political explosiveness. Unemployment and the sluggish economy remain major rhetorical/political dangers to President Reagan as he enters the third year of his Presidency.

Second, the President was unable to use the social issues effectively in the campaign either to rally single-issue supporters to Republicans or to place Democrats on the defensive. The President acted quickly in September to drop them from his rhetoric. In this rhetorical change President Reagan demonstrated that he is more politically pragmatic than President Nixon was in the 1970 mid-term campaign when Nixon persisted in using social issues as principal topics of that campaign.[35] If the 1982 campaign was any indication, the social issues are probably "dead" politically for the next two years, or at least until the national economy improves.

Third, President Reagan demonstrated an ideological consistency throughout the campaign in his attempts to get Americans to "stay the course" he had mapped out for them. Though he changed central topics for his speeches—from the social issues to unemployment—he did not change his thinking about how to cure economic problems. He insisted that controlling inflation and cutting government spending as well as reducing taxes would eventually cure our other economic ills.

Finally, President Reagan was unable to control the political agenda of the 1982 campaign. Institutional and political reasons prevented that dominance. Since it was a campaign, media journalists had to abide by the equal time provisions. Thus, news stories that carried the President's speeches were balanced with contrary stories and opinions. In addition, the President did not have direct access to the American people, except for his speech of October 13 and his radio addresses, as he had during non-campaign periods of the administration. Media reports, through the selection and emphasis of reporting the President's speeches, became as much an agenda-setting institution as the President.

On the political side, the President had to respond to events as they occurred in the campaign. The most damaging to him was the announcement that unemployment had exceeded ten percent. That rise in unemployment required the President to readjust his rhetorical strategies for the campaign and put him further on the defensive in answering issues instead of developing them on his own terms.

The experiences and results of the 1982 elections create a new rhetorical situation for the President. With the addition of twenty-six new Democrats to the House of Representatives, President Reagan will no longer be able to count on southern Democrats to give him the majorities he had during the first year of his administration. Also, the Republican losses—in a campaign in which the President campaigned vigorously—meant that the rhetorical magic of his administration has diminished considerably. But above all, the political agenda for the next two years is no longer dominated by the President. How President Reagan adjusts to this new rhetorical situation may well determine how effective and successful the second two years of his administration will be.

Notes

1. Cf. Rowland Evans and Robert Novak, *The Reagan Revolution* (New York: E. P. Dutton, 1981), pp. 1–20; 59–246.
2. *Time* (March 2, 1981), p. 13.
3. For a description of some of the concerns held by the President's advisors and Congressional Republicans about Reaganomics, See Steven R. Weisman, "Reaganomics and the President's Men," *New York Times Magazine* (October 24, 1982), pp. 26–29, 82–85, 90–92, 109.
4. Quoted in Sidney Blumenthal, "Marketing the President," *New York Times Magazine* (September 13, 1981), p. 110. *Emphasis added.*
5. Elmer E. Cornwell, Jr., *Presidential Leadership of Public Opinion* (Bloomington: Indiana U. Press, 1966), p. 303.
6. Newton N. Minow, John Bartlow Martin, and Lee M. Mitchell, *Presidential Television* (New York: Basic Books, Inc., 1973), p. 5. See also, Bernard Rubin, *Political Television* (Belmont: Wadsworth, 1967) and Dan Nimmo and James E. Combs, *Mediated Political Realities* (New York: Longman, 1983).
7. James W. Ceaser, Glen E. Thurow, Jeffrey Tulis and Joseph M. Bessette, "The Rise of the Rhetorical Presidency," *Presidential Studies Quarterly* XI (Spring, 1981).
8. Blumenthal, p. 43.
9. For one analysis of the rhetoric used by President Reagan to have his Economic Renewal programs passed, see Theodore Windt with Kathleen Farrell, "Presidential Rhetoric and Presidential Power: The Reagan Initiatives," *Essays in Presidential Rhetoric,* ed. by Theodore Windt with Beth Ingold (Dubuque: Kendall/Hunt, 1983), pp. 310–322.
10. Over-all these periods are consistent with the rhetorical periods of an administration as described by Windt and Farrell in "Presidential Rhetoric and Presidential Power," pp. 311–313. These periods are also consistent with making the best use of the media's treatment of recent Presidents. See Michael B. Grossman and Martha Joynt Kumar, "The White House and the News Media: The Phases of Their Relationship," *Political Science Quarterly* (Spring, 1979) pp. 37–53.

11. President Reagan's control of the political agenda slipped away three times during this first period. First, the assassination attempt on his life robbed the administration of its most effective spokesman for more than a month. Second, statements by Secretary of State Haig and the news media's focus on El Salvador diverted attention from economic matters. Finally, the growing anti-nuclear movement in Europe required President Reagan to give a major speech on foreign policy in November, 1981.
12. *The New York Times* (January 27, 1982), p. A17.
13. For one such conservative attack on Reagan, see the July issue of *Conservative Digest*.
14. The Republicans believed they had the advantage in the election because 19 Democrats and only 13 Republicans were up for re-election in the Senate.
15. *Washington Post* (August 30, 1982), p. A3.
16. *The New York Times* (September 2, 1982), p. 12.
17. *Washington Post* (October 3, 1982), p. B5.
18. In 1954 and 1958 President Eisenhower did little campaigning as he gave that responsibility to Vice President Nixon. In 1962, President Kennedy cut short his campaigning to confront the Cuban missile crisis. President Johnson hardly campaigned at all in 1966 because he underwent a gall stone operation prior to the campaign. Vice President Agnew did most of the campaigning for Republicans in 1970 although President Nixon joined in during the last two and a half weeks of the campaign. In the aftermath of the pardon of Nixon, President Ford campaigned relatively little in 1974. In 1978, not very many Democrats wanted President Carter to campaign for them, and he did little.
19. *The New York Times* (September 3, 1982), p. 1.
20. "Remarks at a meeting with Republican candidates, October 6, 1982, *Weekly Compilation of Presidential Documents* (October 11, 1982), p. 1268. Hereafter, the *Weekly Compilation* will be referred to as *PD*. During the campaign President Reagan rarely referred to the Carter administration, but instead talked about the problems from the "four years before we took office." This was an attempt to capitalize on an unspoken current among the electorate. Richard Wirthlin's polls for the President showed that three times as many people blamed Carter for the current recession as they did Reagan. One of the authors of this essay worked for Democratic candidates in several states during the campaign. The private polls of those campaigns confirmed Wirthlin's figures about the strong anti-Carter sentiment among voters.
21. "Remarks at the Alfred M. Landon Lecture Series on Public Issues, September 9, 1982," *PD* (September 20, 1982), p. 1116.
22. *The New York Times* (September 24, 1982), p. 1.
23. *Ibid.*
24. "Remarks at the Fundraising Reception for the Republican Candidate for the U.S. Senate from Maine, September 21, 1982," *PD* (September 27, 1982), p. 1188.
25. "The President's News Conference of September 28, 1982," *PD* (October 4, 1982), p. 1223.
26. Charles T. Manatt, Chairman of the Democratic National Committee, charged that the President's contention that unemployment averaged over seven percent during the last seven years was true only because of the "steep increase in unemployment which has resulted from the Reagan recession." *The New York Times* (September 30, 1982), p. 1.
27. "The President's News Conference of September 28, 1982," pp. 1225–1226.

28. "Remarks at a meeting with Employees of the AccuRay Corporation, October 4, 1982," *PD* (October 11, 1982), p. 1255.

29. President Reagan sought to soften the bad news about unemployment exceeding ten percent by using a rhetorical strategy of "inocculating." One aide explained: "It's a classic political technique: Warn the people of bad news, warn them so much that when it finally happens, it loses steam and credibility." *The New York Times* (October 5, 1982), p. 15. Furthermore, on his weekly radio broadcast that week, President Reagan did not mention unemployment but sought to revive briefly the social issues by devoting his short address to the need for more legislation to combat crime.

30. "The Nation's Economy," *PD* (October 18, 1982), p. 1306.

31. Evans and Novak, p. 69.

32. The Democrats pointed out that Reagan really had no *program* to help the unemployed in their effective counter-offensive. The President was on the defensive again. In his weekly radio broadcast of October 23, President Reagan defended himself against "six big myths," as he called them, put forward by Democrats.

33. "Remarks at a State Republican Party Rally, October 26, 1982," *PD* (November 1, 1982), p. 1392.

34. *Ibid.,* p. 1394.

35. See Rowland Evans, Jr. and Robert D. Novak, *Nixon in the White House. The Frustration of Power* (New York: Random House, 1971), pp. 303–346; and William Safire, *Before the Fall* (New York: Belmont Towers, 1975), pp. 316–340.

Ideology, Rhetoric, and the Shooting Down of KAL 007

Beth A. J. Ingold

In the third year of his administration, President Reagan abruptly changed the political agenda for the nation. During his first two years, the President concentrated on domestic issues, especially his controversial budget and tax cuts. For the most part, he placed foreign affairs on the rhetorical back-burner. The first and only major address on Soviet-American relations between his election and the 1982 midterm election was given on November 18, 1981. This speech, delivered at 10 A.M. at the National Press Club (instead of the Oval Office), announced the President's START proposal. Reagan made the speech as the nuclear freeze movement was gaining strength in Europe and on the eve of Chairman Brezhnev's highly publicized trip to Western Europe.[1] Once it was over, the President returned to domestic issues as the central topics for major speeches.[2]

But after the midterm elections, Reagan shifted national attention from domestic matters to defense and foreign affairs. On November 22, he delivered a nationally televised address on arms reduction and deterrence. In December, he toured Latin America. Later that month and on into January, 1983, he pushed for production of the MX missile and greater defense spending. But it was in a speech on March 8, in Orlando, Florida before the National Association of Evangelicals that he expressed views about the Soviet Union most forcefully, views quite contrary to those voiced in his "START" speech. Calling the Soviet Union the "focus of evil in the modern world" and explaining the "crisis" the Western world faced as a "spiritual one, at root," the President urged his listeners:

> to beware of the temptation of pride—the temptation of blithely declaring yourselves above it all and label both sides equally at fault, to ignore the facts of history and the aggressive impulses of an evil empire, to simply call the arms race a giant misunderstanding and thereby remove yourself from the struggle between right and wrong and good and evil.[3]

Although the speech was not televised, the phrase, "evil empire," immediately caught the attention of journalists and political opponents alike who interpreted it as evidence that the President was not sincere in his arms reduction proposals.

Actually, the speech was the second part of a two-track campaign the President was waging for control of public opinion in terms of Soviet-American

This paper was presented at the 1983 Pennsylvania Speech Communication Association convention in Pittsburgh, and has been revised for publication in this volume.

relations and arms negotiations with the Soviets. On the one hand, the President talked tough about the inherent evil of Soviet communism—and communism, in general, for that matter—and how the Russians could not be
trusted. On the other hand, he advanced with much less fanfare a variety of
arms reduction proposals, such as START, Zero-Option, and the Interim
Agreement, aimed at reaching some kind of agreement with the Soviet Union.

By the summer of 1983, each of these proposals had been rejected by the
Soviets. The Soviets rejected the terms of START because those terms would
cut deeply into their land-based missiles, the most valuable part of their nuclear arsenal, while leaving the American triad of nuclear forces generally
intact, and exempting American strategic bombers of which the United States
has a ten-to-one advantage over the Soviet Union. The President's Zero-
Option offered to cancel the deployment of the Pershing II and cruise missiles
in exchange for the withdrawal behind the Ural mountains and the eventual
dismantling of all Soviet SS-4, SS-5, and SS-20 missiles. The President's Interim Agreement placed an equal limit on each government on the number of
medium range missile warheads deployed by each side. The Soviets rejected
both proposals as imbalanced because they did not count British and French
missiles targeted at the Soviet Union, but did count Soviet missiles deployed
against American weapons in the Far East. By the summer of 1983, these
proposals and their rejections had produced a deadlock in arms negotiations.
The major remaining hope was that a summit meeting might be arranged
between the President and the new Soviet leader, Yuri Andropov, that might
lead to progress out of the stalemate.

At the same time, there was a deadlock on the domestic front. Political
opponents fired away at the President for the lack of progress on arms control,
and they stalled funding for the MX as well as his newly proposed increases
in defense spending for the 1984 federal budget. Journalists questioned his
commitment to arms control, and opponents cited the "evil empire" speech as
evidence of the President's insensitivity to the danger of an unlimited nuclear
arms race. Additionally, liberals ridiculed the President's Star War project,
unveiled to the public in late March. Even some Republicans joined in by
questioning the President's priorities in calling for extravagant increases in
defense spending while continuing greater reductions in domestic spending.
As the end of summer neared, the President's 1984 budget was in trouble, the
nuclear freeze movement was growing not only in Europe but in the United
States as well, and the President was under attack from a variety of sources
for what appeared to be simplistic, exaggerated, and out-of-date positions on
the threat posed by the Soviet Union to American national interests. Indeed,
by this time the President's proposals on arms control and defense spending
appeared to need serious revision due to political pressures, and the future of
his foreign policy, especially in regard to the Soviet Union, seemed bleak.

The shooting down of the Korean jetliner 007 on September 1 changed both the national and international political environment completely. Immediately, there were calls for retaliation, especially because an American Congressman, Larry McDonald, died with the other 268 victims aboard the plane. In the three days that elapsed between the attack and President Reagan's formal speech on the matter, fears arose that war might break out between the two superpowers. The Soviets contributed to the growing concerns by disassembling, lying, and evading when it came to explaining their reponsibility for the tragedy.

The KAL 007 tragedy constituted an international crisis that President Reagan, the nation's voice in foreign affairs, had to address. Whether the President would respond was never in question. It was only a matter of the form and the degree of severity the response would take.

On September 4, Labor Day, the President spoke and forcefully condemned the Soviet Union in ringing terms reminiscent of his "evil empire" speech. This "crime against humanity," as he described it, "was an act of barbarism borne of a society which wantonly disregards individual rights and the value of human life and seeks constantly to expand and dominate other nations."[4] He devoted the entire first half of the speech to comparable denunciations. The second half outlined the retaliatory actions the United States intended to take against the Soviet Union, including: limitations on cultural, scientific, and diplomatic exchanges; efforts to restrict Soviet civilian aviation in the West; suspension of the Soviet-American agreement on cooperation in transportation; continuation of the 1981 suspension of Aeroflot flights into the United States; and demands for reparations for the families of victims.[5]

The President's speech was a curious mixture of moral outrage and moderate retaliation, a contradiction both in style and response. It seemed to match the differences between his public and his private moods, as George Skelton of the *Los Angeles Times* pointed out: "The rhetoric has been tough—Reagan has called the Soviets barbarians, liars and terrorists, but his private manner with advisers has been relatively calm and unemotional, matching the generally mild retaliatory actions he has taken."[6] Some would say that the President's speech was the only realistic response he could make to the Soviet Union in a nuclear age, and many expressed praise for the President's moderate action, for his ability to forego his strident anti-Soviet ideology and behave in a responsible, statesmanlike manner. But that same anti-Soviet ideology had raised expectations among some and fears among others that if he were ever confronted with a crisis in Soviet-American relations, such as the very one he now confronted, he would respond much differently. Therefore, Democrats and liberals congratulated the President on his even-handedness, even as they criticized him for the "strong rhetoric" as well as his attempt to turn the crisis into a plea for support of his defense spending plans. Conservatives, on the other hand, approved the condemnation of the Soviets, but criticized the "symbolic sanctions"—once more, as so often in the past—and questioned the President's real commitment to his ideology. Richard Viguerie described Reagan as "Teddy Roosevelt in reverse. He speaks softly but carries a small stick."[7] His handling of the incident—severe condemnation and harsh language combined with mild retaliatory action—seemed as inconsistent as his previous pattern on arms control of combining confrontational rhetoric with cooperative proposals.

The immediate critiques and interpretations of Reagan's speech and actions miss the mark, I believe, in understanding not only Reagan's response to the Korean jetliner incident, but in understanding his presidential style of leadership as well. And that leadership style is what must be addressed first if we are to understand how his speech on the KAL 007 incident was indicative and typical of Reagan.

President Reagan is the first President to successfully combine and incorporate ideology and campaigning as a means of governing. This combination is the key to understanding his leadership. The question is not whether he has abandoned his idealogy. He has not. The question is not whether his actions are designed *solely* to respond to the mood of the public as gauged by his pollsters. They are not. Instead, the essence of his style of leadership is the constant reconciliation and adjustment of his hardline ideology to the fluctuations of public opinion in which public approval for his actions is a foremost prerequisite for maintaining the major features of that ideology. Precisely because these two activities—campaigning and governing—seem incongruent, most analysts and commentators on Reagan do not blend the two and thus usually classify his actions as predominately ideological or political.[8]

To understand how this form of governing operates, one might study the Reagan decision-making processes, the public policies, or the rhetoric of the first three years of his administration. Each would reveal the ideological nature of his presidency, which provides the substance of his leadership, and the series of never-ending campaigns targeted by persistent pulse-taking pollsters, which provides the techniques of his leadership. But such a wide-ranging survey is beyond the purpose and scope of this essay. Instead, I will briefly describe how this form of leadership operates through the Reagan presidency and demonstrate how the response of Reagan to the Korean jetliner incident was typical of this leadership and rhetoric.

I. The Ideological Component of Reagan's Leadership

Ronald Reagan is, first and foremost, an ideologue. He exalts principles over pragmatism, and he has little use for pluralism in American society. The beliefs comprising his ideology are the primary determinants of his thinking.

Edward Shils defined ideology as "the product of man's need for imposing intellectual order on the world." Ideology provides a "cognitive and moral map of the universe," which forms the disposition of a person. This cognitive and moral map is the means by which events are interpreted and information is understood. An ideology, and the fundamental propositions that comprise it, brings to the political ideologue the belief that he is in possession of what is "ultimately right and true."[9] For the political ideologue the ideology becomes a guide to interpretation and action by simplifying the complexities of the political world to fit the ideology. The policies and action of the ideologue are an attempt to realize the ideology in action by imposing this normative force upon society. Reagan's overriding ideology manifests itself most clearly in his obsession with the Soviet regime as an evil power. Although sometimes clothed in a different language, Reagan's beliefs represent a return to the simplicities of the 1950's cold war thinking. There are three significant principles or beliefs that make up Reagan's ideology in regard to the Soviet Union and Soviet-American relations.

First, peaceful coexistence, he believes, is impossible. The United States and the Soviet Union have two mutually exclusive worldviews, and the Soviets' views are inherently evil. The cause of any conflict, then, stems from this inherent nature of Soviet communism. As Reagan once stated in an interview: "we have a different regard for life than those monsters [the Soviets] do."[10] The intrinsic goodness of the United States compels it to oppose the evil system, and that opposition makes any real or lasting peaceful coexistence impossible. In his fiery address to the evangelical preachers, he stated: "There is sin and evil in the world, and we're enjoined by Scripture and the Lord Jesus to oppose it with all our might."[11]

Reagan's second principal belief is that the Soviets seek world conquest. In his 1982 Memorial Day Address, Reagan warned that we must never "underestimate the seriousness of their aspirations to global expansion. The risk is the very freedom that has been so dearly won."[12] Not only does Reagan believe that the Soviet Union is expansionist, a view many others share, he also believes that almost every international conflict is either caused by Soviet communism's aggressive nature or creates the potential for the Soviet Union to act to feed its insatiable hunger for expansion and conquest of the rest of the world.

A third principal belief is that the United States must confront the Soviet Union on all fronts to prevent its domination of the world. Since every international conflict or potential conflict is either caused by the Soviet Union or presents an opportunity for the Soviet Union to expand its dominion, the United States—as defender of the Free World and Western civilization—must thwart Soviet ambitions. The goal is ideological victory over the enemy. The means to attaining that goal in place of nuclear conflict are a public enlightened about the real nature of the struggle and increased military spending that preserves American strength. In his speech in Orlando, President Reagan expressed his confidence in the nation's ability to triumph over and eventually vanquish communism: "I believe we shall rise to the challenge. I believe that communism is another sad, bizarre chapter in human history whose last pages even now are being written. I believe this because the source of our strength in the quest for human freedom is not material, but spiritual. And because it knows no limitation, it must terrify and ultimately triumph over those who would enslave their fellow man."[13] Thus, speeches such as this one demonstrate the evil nature of the Soviet system by viewing it through the properly ground theoretical lens of the ideology. Such speeches are intended to enlighten the civilized public to the real nature of the struggle. And once enlightened, the public will support a strategy to counter Soviet military superiority.

These three principal beliefs comprise the anti-Soviet ideology that Reagan holds steadfast. They combine to inform his decisions, policies and rhetoric. The ideological component of governing supplies the content—the substance—of his leadership style, but the campaigning component supplies the form and the techniques.

II. The Campaigning Component of Reagan's Leadership

Campaigning, in the sense used here, is not a pursuit for office, but the pursuit of public support for a particular policy, program, decision, or worldview. The techniques of campaigning serve as a model to be used in governing. This component guides the process, rather than the content, of governing. The concept of campaigns setting the tone of governing is not new to the Reagan administration. It is a distinctive mark of the modern presidency. The intrusion of television into the political processes provided recent Presidents with direct access to the public and thus the opportunity to guide, mold, and perhaps change the public's beliefs and attitudes. Pollster Pat Caddell advised President Carter at the beginning of his term that "governing with public approval requires a continuing political campaign."[14] In the third year of the Carter presidency, Caddell again advised that: "Carter should return to the style that had marked his campaign for the presidency. . . ."[15]

The difference in the Reagan administration is that it has been quite skillful in following the campaign model of governing whereas other administrations were not. Reagan has perfected the art of government by campaign. He has the knack of using his incumbency as a tool or vehicle for knowing when to seek public support, what message is most appropriate, and timing the message for maximum impact. One Reagan enthusiast described this as "an aspect of his great communicator role. This is a gifted sense of when to choose his issues and when to make a direct appeal to the people instead of becoming immobilized by the Oval office's trappings and contradictory advice."[16]

However, that he is skilled in campaign-governing in no way implies an abdication of the basic principles of his conservative ideology. Reagan has been able to use the campaign component in furthering his ideology at selective moments by choosing his issues and his moments carefully. The ideology, based on unshakeable principles and beliefs, is instinctive. Thus, one would surmise that Reagan's first response in a crisis would be a tendency to respond ideologically, according to his Russophobe instinct. The evidence in the incident involving the Korean jetliner seems to bear this out. In one of his first public statements in California, following the incident, Reagan implied he was considering ending discussions and possibly even negotiations on arms control with the Soviet Union. He asked: "What can be the scope of legitimate mutual discourse with a state whose values permit such atrocities?"[17] However, once back in Washington after a series of weekend meetings with his top advisers, it became clear that severe sanctions would not be imposed. What this change in attitude suggests is that Reagan's sophisticated team of advisers deserve some credit in maintaining the balance between the ideological and campaign components of his style of leadership. All those who work for Reagan agree that attempting to change the President's mind is a complex and tricky business. Reagan advisers have explained that the key is to argue that a new position is compatible with his fundamental beliefs: "Then Reagan can justify a switch [in policy positions] as a mere tactical adjustment rather than a reversal of his conservative philosophy."[18]

A response to the shooting down of KAL 007 based solely on Reagan's ideological instincts could possibly have included not only ending negotiations on reductions of arms, but perhaps even included taking action against the sale of Vodka as eighteen states did or reprogramming video games throughout the United States to feature Soviet targets, as did one arcade operator, who identified one of the video targets as "Andropov, Communist mutant from outer space."[19]

A more serious response, however, dependent upon the ideological component, most likely would have included economic sanctions, such as canceling grain and technology sales, actions advocated by Walter Mondale, John Glenn, Thomas (Tip) O'Neill and Edward Kennedy as well as Republican hardliners. From the perspective of the campaign component, though, such actions might be like a straw vote in a Maine caucus. It sounds great, but it would do very little. The ultimate purpose, in terms of the ideology, is to defeat communism. That will be the real victory. Economic sanctions probably would cause little substantial harm or pain to the Soviet Union (the Carter experience is instructive in drawing that conclusion), would not stop communist expansion, and would most likely result in the loss of support from much of the farm and agrobusiness vote—not a wise move in light of another campaign, this one very tangible, approaching in 1984. Therefore instead of seeking support for overt punishment through economic sanctions, President Reagan sought to turn the incident into an appeal for support for his floundering proposals to increase defense spending. Thus, the campaigning mentality modifies the ideological mentality.

The campaigning component of Reagan's style of leadership encourages opportunism in the pursuit of ideological goals. Yet, because its very nature is to find the best opportunity and means for enlisting support, the campaign component also serves as a buffer between those from whom support is sought and the raw ideology. By viewing Reagan's response in light of these two components of governing, there is no real inconsistency between his words and deeds.

III. Reagan's Response

On September 4, 1983 President Reagan spoke to the American people and indeed the world about the shooting down of KAL 007. In following a basic rule of the campaigning component, Reagan sought to use the crisis to put his opponents on the defensive while seeking public support for his policy goals.

A primary strategic objective of the speech was to isolate the Soviet Union from the rest of the world as a truly evil empire that commits inhumane crimes against innocent people. He used the word "massacre" six times in his speech to describe the Soviet action. Through this deed, he said: "the Soviets reveal that, yes, shooting down a plane, even one with hundreds of innocent men, women, children and babies, is part of their normal procedure if that plane is in what they claim as their airspace." To exemplify the validity of his accusations, he played a brief segment of the Soviet pilot's radio transmissions to demonstrate the unemotional attitudes of the pilot as he relayed to ground control, "I have executed the launch. The target is destroyed." Picturing the Soviet Union as a callous nation was no difficult task because most nations had reacted with revulsion and denunciation upon learning of the incident. Nonetheless, for strategic purposes as well as the rhetorical requirements of the moment, Reagan necessarily began his address with a harsh condemnation of the Soviet action. Furthermore, this condemnation was consistent with the harsh anti-Soviet ideology he maintains.

Achieving this primary objective required avoiding the Americanization of the issue. To do so would focus attention on the conflicting worlds of the superpowers, thereby deflecting attention from the immediate incident. And consistent with his ideology, the incident was not representative of a conflict between the United States and the Soviet Union, but an example of the over-arching ideological conflict between the Soviets and the rest of the civilized world. This belief was directly stated in unmistakable language: "And make no mistake about it: This attack was not just against ourselves or the Republic of Korea. This was the Soviet Union against the world and the moral precepts which guide human relations among people everywhere. It was an act of bar-barism, born of a society which wantonly disregards individual rights and the value of human life and seeks constantly to expand and dominate other na-tions." According to one person who was present at the National Security Council meeting on September 2, President Reagan saw the rhetorical occa-sion as an opportunity "to focus world attention on Soviet culpability."[20] Reagan exploited this advantage to the fullest allowing the Russians no room for admissions of error or apologies and at the same time carefully avoided describing the incident in terms of the Soviet-American rivalry. Instead, Reagan stressed the need for cooperative reactions among other nations in the world. He stated: We are cooperating with other countries to find better means to insure the safety of civil aviation. . . ." And again: "We have joined with other countries to press the international civil aviation organization to inves-tigate this crime. . . ." And finally: "We intend to work with the 13 countries who had citizens aboard the Korean airliner to seek reparations for the fam-ilies of all those who were killed." Thus, while the ideological language de-scribed the act and worked to separate the Soviet Union from the rest of the world, the campaign language described the response and worked to seek co-operation and support from other nations.

Successfully isolating the Soviet Union would also help achieve Reagan's second objective: to minimize criticism of his plan to deploy the Pershing II and cruise missiles in Western Europe later that year. To that end, Reagan sought to differentiate between the two superpowers, a distinction that was essential to weaken European criticism.[21] Consistent with his ideology, he per-sistently portrayed the Soviet Union as aggressive and the United States as peaceful. He pointed out that the United States has never nor would it ever under similar circumstances resort to such barbaric violence: "Commercial aircraft from the Soviet Union and Cuba on a number of occasions have overflown United States military facilities. They weren't shot down. We and other civilized countries believe in the tradition of offering help to mariners and pilots who are lost or in distress on the sea or in the air. We believe in following procedures to prevent a tragedy, not to provoke one." This objective of making our European allies more receptive to the deployment of new mis-siles also explains, in part, Reagan's decision not to end arms negotiations. Suspending the arms talks in Geneva or any other comparable dramatic re-taliatory action would damage and undercut the image of the United States that Reagan was attempting to create. Instead, Reagan went to extraordinary lengths to reaffirm his commitment to arms reduction even in this dark hour: "[W]e can not, we must not, give up our effort to reduce the arsenals of destructive weapons threatening the world. . . . We are more determined than ever to reduce and if possible eliminate the threat hanging over mankind. We know it will be hard to make a nation that rules its own people through force to cease using force against the rest of the world, but we must try." Seen in this light, his "small stick" response as conservatives called it is neither inconsistent with his ideology, nor surprising given his style of leadership. Placing the missiles in Europe met Reagan's ideological requirements and continuing negotiations met his campaigning requirements of building support for his actions. As one State Department official explained: "If we had halted the Geneva talks on missiles a lot of Europeans would be saying that Reagan is a warmonger and there would be demonstrations against us and the Flight 007 would be forgotten."[22] Not breaking off the negotiations, then, became a politically strategic decision.

Furthermore, continuing the negotiations not only weakened European opposition to the missiles, it also aided in achieving Reagan's third objective of the speech: weakening Congressional opposition to his defense budget and to the passage of his MX spending plan. As I remarked earlier, Reagan's defense proposals, especially funding for the MX missile, were in serious trouble with Congress prior to the Korean jetliner incident. Now, the incident could be used to justify the defense budget:

> There's something I've always believed in which now seems more important than ever. The Congress will be facing key national security issues when it returns from recess. There has been legitimate differences of opinion on this matter, I know, but I urge the members of that distinguished body to ponder long and hard the Soviet aggression as they consider the security and safety of our people—indeed of all people who believe in freedom.

And to insure that Congress received his message, Reagan invoked the memory of Senator Henry Jackson:

> Senator Henry Jackson, a wise and revered statesman, and one who probably understood the Soviets as well as any American in history, warned us, 'the greatest threat the United States now faces is posed by the Soviet Union.' But Senator Jackson said, 'If America maintains a strong deterrent—and only if it does—this nation will continue to be a leader in the crucial quest for enduring peace among nations.'

The late Senator Jackson had made these remarks on the Senate floor during the debates on the MX missile. President Reagan used the jetliner tragedy as confirmation of the Senator's wisdom and the need for passage of the funding. The message was not lost on Congress. Representative Joseph Addabbo remarked: "I imagine Congress will go along with the President on the MX after this. These things will give people a big visible vote to say, 'Well, I got back at the Russians.' "[23] Representative Addabbo summarized the attitudes of

Congress and the American people accurately. In the week following the President's address, Congress approved the $188 billion spending plan for 1984. The bill gave Reagan every major weapons system he requested including the $4.9 billion for the MX missiles, $408 million for Pershing II missiles and $144.6 million for poison gas weapons.

In soliciting support for the MX President Reagan described the MX as necessary in order to achieve peace through strength, but he also emphasized that the United States would never give up efforts to bring "peace closer through mutual verifiable reduction of the weapons of war." Thus, the ideological requirements join with the campaign requirements to accomplish his rhetorical and policy goals. It is ironic that continuing the Geneva negotiations that were designed, in Reagan's words, to "reduce the arsenals of destructive weapons threatening the world," was used as the very reason for supporting increases in "the arsenals of destructive weapons threatening the world."

Conclusion

The KAL 007 tragedy produced both a crisis and a turning point in President Reagan's foreign policy toward the Soviet Union.[24] Prior to the incident, the President's critics had denounced his harsh anti-Soviet rhetoric, especially as expressed in his address to the Evangelicals, as unduly antagonistic toward the Soviet Union, out-dated in an era of détente, and counter-productive in the pursuit of arms control. But the senseless shooting down of KAL 007 and the loss of 269 innocent lives appeared to give concrete substance to Reagan's charge that the Soviet Union was an "evil empire," and muted those criticisms at least temporarily. Indeed, not only conservatives but liberals and Democrats as well denounced this venal act and advocated strong reprisals against the Soviet Union. When President Reagan delivered his formal response in his speech on September 4 condemning the Soviet action, but invoking only wrist-slapping sanctions while reaffirming his commitment to negotiating with the Soviets, his reply satisfied neither his supporters nor his critics. Liberals contended that the anti-Soviet rhetoric was still too harsh, especially given his commitment to the continuation of negotiations, and conservatives thought his sanctions much too moderate in proportion to this monstrous act. Even such perceptive rhetorical critics of Mr. Reagan as Craig Allen Smith and Kathy B. Smith concluded their introduction to the speech: "But unfortunately for Reagan, heinous crimes demand severe punishment. Thus his full-scale condemnation of the Soviet 'massacre' rendered his various sanctions mild by comparison. . . ."[25] Truly, the speech was *internally* inconsistent in this sense, but such criticism misses the mark in understanding the political ingenuity and brilliance of the speech and of Reagan's unique style of presidential leadership.

President Reagan's leadership is a combination of rigid ideological commitments and adroit campaigning techniques. He demonstrates consistency on the ideological level even as he constantly searches for public support through these campaigning tactics to achieve his policy objectives.[26] In his address on KAL 007, the President joined the harsh condemnation of the Soviets, which expressed the generally wide-spread moral outrage, with a statesmanlike refusal to rush into equally severe reprisals, which demonstrated his ability to see even this violent incident as a part of a larger world nuclear picture. Thus, viewing the speech in this context, it manifested the President as a man of moral sensibilities *and* as a statesman with a responsible and broader vision of what the incident meant.

Furthermore, his critics were short-sighted. Most seemed to see the incident as one that required American retaliation of some sort against the Soviet Union. Thus, the mild sanctions were seen as woefully insufficient by hardliners. But President Reagan apparently recognized that any retaliation would be symbolic, at best, and would probably do very little to achieve any tangible result. After all, President Carter's much more substantive sanctions following the invasion of Afghanistan had had very little effect on subsequent Soviet action and had, for the most part, been repealed after Reagan assumed the presidency. Instead, the President saw the incident as an opportunity to press forward with his defense spending programs and with the MX missile. In responding in this fashion, the President achieved tangible results: passage of his previously floundering defense budget proposals which gave him a domestic victory and further military build-up which contributed to his policy of negotiating with the Soviets from a position of strength, as he called it, instead of a position of weakness.

Finally, President Reagan's response helped to position him for the forthcoming presidential campaign. His condemnation of the Soviets demonstrated his continuing and unwavering commitment to his anti-Soviet ideology. Beyond that, the incident provided an example of substance to his charge that the Soviet Union is an evil empire. On the other hand, his refusal to cancel the Geneva negotiations demonstrated his commitment to arms reduction and the pursuit of peace in the world. And later, when the Soviets walked out of those negotiations, the President could reply that it was they—the Russians—who really did not want fruitful talks or concrete agreements, not he. Thus, the President could present himself as a staunch anti-communist for his conservative supporters as well as a statesman committed to the pursuit of peace, which his detractors had questioned in the past. Indeed, his measured response to the tragedy made it much harder for opponents to portray him as rigid and intractable on Soviet-American relations.

The shooting of KAL 007 was a tragedy. But President Reagan turned it into a political triumph through his strategic management of the crisis. Although the speech appeared to be internally inconsistent, it was in actuality quite consistent with President Reagan's style of leadership of combining an unswerving commitment to ideology with the flexibility of campaigning tactics intended to achieve the central policy goals of that ideology. And in this context, the President's speech of September 4, 1983 serves as prime example of that leadership, one in which the speech is not inconsistent nor his action merely symbolic.

Notes

1. Most commentators believe that the speech was principally directed at the European audience, instead of the domestic American audience. The timing of the announcement about START, choosing 10 A.M. to deliver the address so it could be carried on prime time news in Europe—all these suggest the primary audience as European. Furthermore, it appears that Reagan chose to make this public announcement of an important proposal on arms reduction to give Western European leaders ammunition to counter Brezhnev's call for a nuclear freeze.
2. The two exceptions to this trend were his speeches on the crises that erupted in the Middle East.
3. "Remarks at the Annual Convention in Orlando, Florida," March, 8, 1983 *Weekly Compilation of Presidential Documents* (March 14, 1983), p. 369. All subsequent excerpts of the speech are taken from this transcript.
4. "Transcript of President Reagan's Address on Downing of Korean Airliner," *The New York Times* (September 6, 1983), p. 9. All subsequent excerpts are taken from this transcript.
5. A "Fact Sheet" distributed at the White House briefing prior to Reagan's speech described further limitations on cultural, scientific and diplomatic exchanges. The Soviet-American agreement on transportation included restrictions on exchanges of information on: urban research and development, bridge construction and tunneling, railroad transportation, air traffic control and noise pollution from aviation, highway safety, and the transportation of hazardous materials. Soviet-American cultural and scientific exchange included restrictions on: exchanges of performing art groups, museum exhibits, and scholarly presentations. Also cancelled were discussions aimed at establishing consulates in Kiev and New York City.
6. Quoted in the *Pittsburgh Press* (September 11, 1983), p. B 3.
7. Quoted in *Time* (September 14, 1983), p. 15.
8. On the differences between the form and rhetoric of campaigning and governing, see Theodore Otto Windt, Jr., "Presidential Rhetoric: Definition of a Field of Study," *Central States Speech Journal* (Spring, 1984), pp. 32–33.
9. Edward Shils, "The Concept and Function of Ideology," *The International Encyclopedia of Social Science, p. 69.
10. Quoted in Robert Scheer, *With Enough Shovels: Reagan, Bush and Nuclear War* (New York: Random House, 1982), p. 140.
11. "Orlando Speech," p. 368.
12. "Remarks at Arlington National Cemetery," May 31, 1982 *Weekly Compilation of Presidential Documents* (June 7, 1982), p. 724.
13. "Orlando Speech," p. 369. See also, Paul D. Erickson, *Reagan Speaks: The Making of an American Myth* (New York: New York University Press, 1985), especially pp. 72–94.

14. Quoted in James Ceaser, *et al*, "The Rise of the Rhetorical Presidency," rpt. in *Essays in Presidential Rhetoric* ed. by Theodore Windt with Beth Ingold, 1st ed. (Dubuque: Kendall/Hunt, 1983), p. 16. On the development of the campaigning or rhetorical component of governing, see the entire essay by Ceaser *et al*, and Sidney Blumenthal, *The Permanent Campaign* (New York: Simon and Schuster, 1982).

15. *Ibid*.

16. *The New York Times* (September 18, 1983), p. E 5.

17. *The New York Times* (September 6, 1983), p. 9.

18. *Time* (December 13, 1982), p. 15.

19. *Time* (September 19, 1983), p. 15.

20. The *Pittsburgh Press* (September 11, 1983), p. B 8.

21. Many West Europeans were skeptical about Reagan's proposals for arms reductions and peace. He appeared to many of them as a right-wing, anti-communist fanatic who had little understanding of the terrors of nuclear weapons. Reagan's 1981 answer to a reporter's question about the likelihood of a limited exchange of nuclear weapons in Europe and whether it would directly involve the United States and the Soviet Union had angered them. Reagan had replied: "I could see where you could have the exchange of tactical weapons in the field, without it bringing either one of the major powers to pushing the button." Quoted by Christopher Hitchens, "Minority Report," *The Nation* (September 18, 1982), p. 230. His reply seemed to convey little sensitivity toward what would happen to Europe if such a battle with tactical weapons occurred. Thus, in the minds of some Western Europeans, there was little difference between the United States and the Soviet Union when it came to sacrificing Europe for their own interests.

22. *The New York Times* (September 6, 1983), p. 8.

23. Quoted in *The New York Times* (September 11, 1983), p. 4 E.

24. The most balanced and complete account of the shooting down of KAL 007 is now provided by Seymour Hersh, *The Target Is Destroyed* (New York: Random House, 1986).

25. Craig Allen Smith and Kathy B. Smith (eds.), *The President and the Public* (Lanham: University Press of America, 1985), p. 268.

26. For an analysis of the President's uses of strategic management of domestic issues using these same techniques, see Hugh Heclo and Rudolph G. Penner, "Fiscal and Political Strategy in the Reagan Administration," *The Reagan Presidency: An Early Assessment,* ed. by Fred I. Greenstein (Baltimore: Johns Hopkins University Press, 1983), pp. 21–47.

MisteReagan's Neighborhood: Rhetoric and National Unity

Craig Allen Smith

"The Question" invariably arises. It may come at a family reunion or a political science meeting. It may surface at a faculty tea or a communication convention. It may come from students or nextdoor neighbors. But invariably, it arises. "You study presidential rhetoric," it begins. "How does he do it?" The "he" is, of course, President Ronald Reagan, the "Great Communicator." The "it" refers to the presidential style that has helped him to achieve two of the greatest electoral landslides in history, to escape blame for policy failures while receiving credit for even marginally successful policies (the "Teflon Presidency" phenomenon), and to continually fare better in the opinion polls than do the policies he supports.

"The question" demands more serious attention from academically based students of presidential rhetoric than it has thus far received.[1] While there are several useful studies of individual Reagan speeches or campaigns, we do not yet have a coherent answer to "The Question." This essay is a step in that direction. It is devoted to President Reagan's ability to unify the nation (relative to his recent predecessors) behind his leadership.

Specifically, this essay examines five dimensions of community that permeate the President's 22 first-term televised addresses to the nation.[2] What I shall term "MisteReagan's Neighborhood" is a powerful rhetorical creation that unifies the country, impels action, and insulates the president from damaging criticism. To the extent that his rhetoric draws upon the myths, symbols, and beliefs previously referred to as the "American Civil Religion," the "American Public Philosophy," the "Priestly Functions of the Presidency," and "Populist Argument," President Reagan's themes are not unique; and indeed, that familiarity is undoubtedly responsible for much of its appeal.[3] But the Reagan rhetoric distinctively weaves these themes together into a seamless tapestry that pre-empts the argumentative grounds of morality, heritage, boldness, heroism, and fairness. His depiction of the American Neighborhood left little basis for cogent opposition arguments. Let us turn to a discussion of the five dimensions of community before evaluating President Reagan's rhetoric of community.

Reprinted from a manuscript by permission of the author and to be published in the *Southern Speech Communication Journal*, 1986.

The Extraordinary Ordinary Americans

The America of Ronald Reagan is populated by "extraordinary 'ordinary' Americans who never make the headlines and will never be interviewed."[4] "The greatness of America doesn't begin in Washington," he said, "it begins with each of you."[5] This identification of the essential goodness of the nation with the little people is classic Populist argument.[6]

In MisteReagan's Neighborhood, these common people are consistently identified economically. "We the People" are the "men and women who raise our food, patrol our streets, man our mines and factories, teach our children, keep our homes, and heal us when we're sick—professionals, industrialists, shopkeepers, clerks, cabbies, and truckdrivers."[7] According to Mr. Reagan, Americans historically have built for the future through "our vision of a better life for farmers, merchants, and working people."[8]

The State of the Union involves the state of "autoworkers in Detroit, lumberjacks in the Northwest, steelworkers in Steubenville who are in the unemployment lines . . . black teenagers in Newark and Chicago . . . hardpressed farmers and small businessmen . . . [and] millions of everyday Americans who harbor the simple wish of a safe and financially secure future for their children."[9] The confusing array of economic facts and figures are to be understood in human terms: "how they're affecting the everyday lives of our people . . . young couples struggling to make ends meet, teenagers looking for work, older Americans threatened by inflation, small businessmen fighting for survival, and parents working for a better future for their children."[10] Government regulations, he says, are imposed upon "the shopkeeper, teacher, the craftsman, professionals, [and] small industry";[11] and the "basic energy problem" can therefore be solved by removing such "undue interference" from the "ingenuity of consumers, business, producers, and inventors."[12]

President Reagan stressed that his early economic initiatives were possible only because "millions of you Democrats, Republicans, and independents, from every profession, trade, and line of work, and from every part of this land . . . sent a message."[13] And "together we took control of a rudderless ship."[14] People began to invest "from small investors on Main Street to those who manage billions of dollars, including our workers' pension funds."[15] And the president continued to hear from these people "in meetings . . . at the White House; on visits to schools, meeting halls, factories, and fairgrounds across the country; and in thousands of phone calls and letters."[16]

Even as the recovery progressed into 1983 it remained a "painful period" for "farmers, steel and auto workers, lumbermen, black teenagers, [and] working mothers." Nevertheless, "the big story about America," in January of 1983, was that "From coast to coast, on the job and in the classrooms and laboratories, at new construction sites and in churches and community groups, neighbors are helping neighbors. And they've already begun the building, the research, the work, and the giving that will make our country great again."[17]

The familiar inventory of cliched but divisive demographic identities (e.g., rich and poor, east and west, north and south, black and white) is absent from the Reagan rhetoric. It is replaced with *functionally interdependent* economic identities (e.g. producers, consumers, farmers, and shopkeepers). This emphasis of economic identities meshes beautifully with his efforts toward economic reform. If his discussion of constituents sounds more Democratic than Republican, it may well derive from his own early experience as a liberal Democrat.

The Absence of Domestic Adversaries

Although President Reagan's American community faces hard times, he creates no domestic adversaries. This is accomplished by attributing America's economic travails to the inherent deficiencies of government and by absolving people from any responsibility they may have had for governmental policy.

The victimization of government theme was articulated in the first inaugural address. "In this present crisis," said the President, "government is not the solution to our problem; government is "the problem."[18] Two weeks later his first economic address continued the strategy: "the audit presented to me found *government policies of the last few decades* responsible for our economic troubles."[19] He then differentiated government policy from people: "We forgot or just overlooked the fact that *government—any government—* has a built-in tendency to grow."[20] With blame attributed to government and government separated from the people in the neighborhood, it remained only for President Reagan to firmly but gently admonish us for our thoughtlessness, "Now, *we all* had a hand in looking to government for benefits as if government had some source of revenue other than our earnings."[21]

The victimization of government and the absolution of people was most clearly evident during the 1982 Congressional elections. While others followed the usual practice of personalizing policies and responsibility, President Reagan magnanimously depersonalized and absolved. Referring to this "blame game," the President said that:

> the accusing finger has been pointed in every direction of the compass, and a lot of time and hot air have been spent looking for scapegoats. Well, there's plenty of blame to go around. [But] The problems we face are bigger than any one party or group of people. They're the result not of weeks or months, but of years, even decades of past mistakes. *The problem isn't who to blame: it's what to blame.*"[22]

And "what to blame," throughout Reagan's economic analysis, is government.[23] In his 1984 re-election eve speech he depicted the alternatives as "whether we go forward together . . . or turn back to policies" that failed.[24] Semantically, we are asked to choose between explicit people with implicit policies, or implicit people with explicit policies.

The threat to the community, then, is not human but governmental—the tendency of government to grow and to extravagantly spend *individuals'* dollars. This happens because "It's easy to lose touch with reality when it is other people's money that you're spending."[25] But Mr. Reagan is magnanimous. "In a way I guess I can understand why so many of our political leaders fell into this trap [of taxing and spending]. I'm sure they did it with the best of intentions."[26] But then he discloses the basis for his magnanimity. "Indeed, like many others, for a time I accepted government's claim that it was sound economics. But there came a day when I and millions of other Americans began to realize the terrible consequences of all those years of playing politics as usual while the economic disaster lines crept higher and higher."[27]

This confession is essential Reagan. Nobody in the neighborhood brought about our troubles (except through carelessness and the very best of intentions). While identifying himself with those laudable intentions, Reagan transcends possible criticism through reference to a higher economic consciousness to which his tax-and-spend critics are, by definition, not privileged. This transcendence is evident in a forcefully vague passage from a 1981 address. Noting that "some of those who oppose" his plans had "participated" in the "extravagance", he "grant[s] they were well-intentioned" but argues that "in their objections to what we've proposed, they offer only what we know has been tried before and failed."[28] His policies are both justified and insulated from criticism by the higher economic consciousness that his critics simply cannot attain.

The well-intentioned but misguided people who created and sustained these policies are never specified. There are, in the community, cynics and "doubting Thomases" whose lack of optimism undercuts the community's spirit of renewal. Characteristically in Reagan's national economic speeches, "you" are well-meaning and hard-working, while "they" are the cynics and the profiteers. "You" never need to be chastised, and "they" rarely have reasonable reservations. Importantly, "we," "you" and "they" are non-partisan. Notice how he semantically transformed his adversaries to disassociate the Democratic Party from the notions of both leadership and strength:

Now, when I first proposed this . . . the *Democratic leadership* said a tax cut was out of the question. It would be wildly inflationary. And *that was before my inauguration.* And then your voices began to be heard and suddenly, in February, *the leadership* discovered that, well, a 1-year tax cut was feasible. Well, we kept on pushing our 3-year tax cut and by June, *the opposition* found that a 2-year tax cut might work. Now it's July, and *they* find *they* could now go for a third year cut provided there was a trigger arrangement that would only allow it to go into effect if certain economic goals had been met by 1983.[29]

In this paragraph the "Democratic leadership" loses its partisanship and becomes "the leadership" before melting into an obstructive and authority-less "opposition" and ultimately into two mentions of an amorphous "they." Through this transformation the Democratic party is reduced to insignificance, opposing arguments are dismissed as simple orneriness, and the President, his ordinary Americans, and their Congressional voices are merged into the dominant "we."

The diminution of the Democratic Party and the victimization of government resurfaced in combination on re-election eve. Even here, where one would expect partisanship, his scorn is directed not at Democrats but at "Professional politicians":

As you worked harder to keep up with inflation, they raised your taxes. When our industries staggered, they piled on more regulations. When educational quality slumped, they piled on more bureaucratic controls. They watched crime terrorize our citizens and responded with more lenient judges, sentencing, and parole. When the Soviets invaded Afghanistan, they punished our farmers with a grain embargo and neglected to rebuild our defenses.[30]

Not surprisingly, the good intentions formerly attributed to Mr. Reagan's opponents are absent at the moment of decision (magnanimity does have its limits where votes are concerned). And yet the threat posed by the Democratic Party and its candidates is too slight to warrant recognition.

But if MisteReagan's Neighborhood is characterized by a lack of domestic adversaries, it is not devoid of foreign enemies. The most troublesome foreign enemies are, of course, the Soviets. Robert Ivie identified eight depictions of the Soviets in Reagan's speeches, all of them unsavory. The Soviet Union is depicted as "a Natural Menace," as Animals, Primitives, Machines, Criminals, as Mentally Disturbed, as Fanatics and Ideologues, and as Satanic and Profane.[31] Moreover, the Russians are implicitly behind every unfortunate turn of events. The inflammatory condemnation of the "Korean Airlines Massacre" provided an appropriate opportunity to advance these depictions. But his decision to introduce the discussion of the terrorist attack on the Beirut Marine barracks and the Granada invasion with a reference to this earlier unrelated Russian atrocity is indicative of the pervasiveness of the Soviet threat.

The lack of domestic adversaries is a dimension of the Reagan style that is strikingly different from his recent partisan predecessor, Richard Nixon. Where Nixon personalized, Reagan depersonalizes.[32] Where Nixon maintained an enemies list, Reagan absolves domestic opponents as misguided. Where Nixon focused his opposition on prominent Democrats, Reagan ignores his political rivals and thereby keeps them from the national limelight and diminishes their roles in our ongoing political drama. The Reagan focus on "what to blame" rather than "who to blame" undercuts his political rivals, bolsters his ethos, directs attention to laws and processes, and reaffirms his conservative principles.

The Proud Heritage

America has a proud heritage because of our moral purpose and good people. President Reagan discusses the meaning of America in almost every televised address. The essence of America is commitment to abstract moral qualities and beliefs. "For us," he said in the 1984 State of the Union address, "faith, work, family, neighborhood, freedom, and peace are not just words; they're expressions of what America means, definitions of what makes us a good and loving people."[33]

Foremost among these principles in President Reagan's rhetoric is freedom.[34] We are a community unique in all history because "we unleashed the energy and individual genius of man to a greater extent than has ever been done before." Consequently, "Freedom and dignity of the individual have been more available and assured here than in any other place on Earth."[35] Everything in our heritage centers around the pursuit of freedom:

> Our struggle for nationhood, our unrelenting fight for freedom, our very existence— these have all rested on the assurance that you must be free to shape your life as you are best able to, that no one can stop you from reaching higher or take from you the creativity that has made America the envy of mankind.[36]

This central principle of freedom has fostered important national character traits. We have, for example, "a proud tradition of generosity,"[37] and "We've always reached for a new spirit and aimed at a higher goal. We've been courageous and determined, unafraid and bold."[38]

Because of its commitment to the principles of freedom, generosity, courage, and boldness, the American community *always* wins. It does not simply survive—it emerges from every crisis as a stronger community. "Back over the years," President Reagan recalls:

> citizens like ourselves have gathered within these walls when our nation was threatened. . . . Always with courage and common sense, they met the crises of their time and lived to see a stronger, better, and more prosperous country. . . . Time and again, they proved that there is nothing we Americans cannot achieve as free men and women.[39]

But notice that the community has survived and prospered not through the *government's* commitment to freedom and principle, but through the acts of "citizens like ourselves." "I've not taken your time this evening to ask you to trust me," said the president in the tradition of decentralized freedom, "Instead, I ask you to trust yourselves. That's what America is all about."[40]

The proud heritage of the American community is based upon individual freedom and the energy, generosity, courage, faith, and determination that it fosters. This heritage is almost anarchistic in nature, as government never does anything laudable. Indeed, even kind and generous acts performed by people through their government are dangerous because we once did these things "voluntarily, out of the goodness of our hearts and a sense of community pride and neighborliness."[41] In the Reagan community the sole legitimate function of national government is national defense. Everything else is properly accomplished by those "extraordinary ordinary Americans" in the community.

Heroism, Faith, and "Can-Do Americanism"

If the Reagan view of limited government leaves much for individuals to do for themselves, that is as it should be. The people who live and work in President Reagan's community can accomplish anything because they are heirs to the proud tradition. This tradition is characterized by enduring principles and committed people:

> We Americans have always been sustained, through good times and bad, by a noble vision—a vision not only of what the world around us is today but what we as a free people can make it be tomorrow. We're realists; we solve our problems instead of ignoring them, no matter how loud the chorus of despair around us. But we're also idealists, for it was an ideal that brought our ancestors to these shores from every corner of the world.[42]

This heritage of realistic idealism enables Americans of all generations to accomplish great feats.

Specifically, President Reagan refers to five kinds of heroes, each of which serves a rhetorical function. References to Former Presidents abound (the 25 references in 22 speeches include six to John Kennedy, four to Franklin Roosevelt, three each to George Washington, Thomas Jefferson, Abraham Lincoln, Harry Truman and Dwight Eisenhower). The second most frequent heroes were "Service People" (nine references to generic military people, three to astronauts, two to secret service personnel, and one each to five specific individuals.[43] The third category of heroic references consisted of ten references to Founding Fathers (3 references each to Washington, Jefferson, and Joseph Warren, and one to Thomas Paine).

The fourth category of heroic references consisted of six references to the heroism of the "extraordinary ordinary Americans" going about their daily business. These references are curious, since they tend to strain the traditional meaning of "heroism." Yet they serve to glorify duty and service to America much like the references to uniformed heroes. Indeed, five of these ordinary people were cited as specific object lessons:

> people like Barbara Proctor, who rose from a ghetto to build a multimillion-dollar advertising agency in Chicago; Carlos Perez, a Cuban refugee, who turned $27 and a dream into a successful importing business in Coral Gables, Florida. . . . A person like Father Ritter is always there. His Covenant House programs in New York and Houston provide shelter and help to thousands of frightened and abused children each year. . . . [Paralyzed in a plane crash] Dr. Charles Carson . . . still believed nothing is impossible. Today in Minnesota he works 80 hours a week without pay, helping pioneer the field of computer-controlled walking. He has given hope to 500,000 paralyzed Americans that some day they may walk again.[44]

There was also rescue worker Lenny Skutnick who "when he saw a woman lose her grip on the helicopter line, dived into [the icy Potomac] water and dragged her to safety."[45]

Finally, the fifth category of heroes consisted of seven references to Celebrities. Interestingly, all of these individuals were celebrities several decades ago: Joe Louis, Bernard Baruch, Will Rogers, Walter Lippman, Al Smith, John Wayne, and Winston Churchill. There are no references to either current or recent celebrities.

President Reagan's emphasis of heroism serves him well in several respects. First, his frequent references to former presidents reinforced the traditional ethos of the American presidency and therefore enhanced his own stature. Second, his frequent references to uniformed service people, "everyday heroes," and both self-made and selfless citizens highlighted the roles of dedicated service, duty, sacrifice, patriotism, and inspiration in his community. Third, his references to celebrities from another age (quite specifically 1920–1960) and his omission of more recent celebrities subtly remind us that his America is a community *returning* to its *former* greatness.[46] Fourth, his invocation of unsung, ordinary individuals who overcame apparently insurmountable difficulties reveals the latent greatness to be found in each American. Finally, his references to the Founding Fathers conforms to other presidents' and politicians' proclivity to draw upon the Framers as a means of identifying with the "true spirit and purpose of America."[47]

Not all of these tendencies are unusual—we can expect any American president to invoke the Founders and his presidential predecessors; but the abundance of uniformed heroes in peacetime rhetoric, the nostalgia of a fairly specific Golden Age (ironically characterized by Depression and World War), and the references to everyday heroes who dared to find their innate greatness are strikingly Reaganesque.

But, *for President Reagan, it is faith in our heritage and the willingness to act boldly upon that faith that provide the real keys to our omnipotence.* When truly *believed,* the tradition itself enables us to regularly accomplish heroic feats. The first inaugural address suggested that the economic crisis required effort and a:

> willingness to *believe in ourselves and to believe in our capacity to perform great deeds,* to believe that together with God's help we can and will resolve the problems which now confront us. And after all, *why shouldn't we believe that? We're Americans.*[48]

Two months later he promised that "We can restore our economic strength, and build opportunities like none we've ever had before." To reach this goal, he said, *"All we need to have is faith, and that dream will come true."*[49]

Sufficient faith in the American tradition of inevitable triumph through courgeous action leads to the glorification of boldness. President Reagan's 1984 remarks about the space program, for example, were clearly metaphoric:

> America has always been greatest when we dared to be great. We can reach for greatness again. We can follow our dreams to distant stars, living and working in space for peaceful, economic, and scientific gain.[50]

Thus, the wisdom or prudence of any course of action is often valued less than the boldness with which that course is pursued. Caution is equated with timidity, and timidity with betrayal of our heritage. Whatever their benefits, discussion and debate are not interpreted as signs of faith in our heritage.

While it is important to President Reagan that faith in our heritage enables Americans to accomplish anything, that alone would be a small and selfish manifestation of a noble heritage. Instead, he sees it as an ongoing or living heritage. Like other organisms, it must grow:

> Throughout our history, we Americans have proven again and again that no challenge is too big for a free, united people. Together we can do it again.[51]

In order to grow, the America of today is *obliged* to perform great deeds in the name of that heritage. In a Yuletide address about Poland he referred to this obligation four times in one sentence:

> [our] blessings bring with them a solid *obligation,* an *obligation* to God who guides us, an *obligation* to the heritage of liberty and dignity handed down to us by our forefathers and an *obligation* to the children of the world, whose future will be shaped by the way we live our lives today.[52]

Mr. Reagan's commitment to a living heritage is nowhere more evident than in his 1982 State of the Union address, when he compares contemporary economic reform to the issue of secession:

> Let us so conduct ourselves that two centuries from now, another Congress and another President, meeting in this chamber as we are now meeting, will speak of us with pride [even as we now speak of Lincoln] saying that we met the test and preserved for them in their day the sacred flame of liberty—this last, best hope of man on Earth.[53]

Those economic reform efforts are not simply equal in importance to secession, they are to be remembered twice as long as the Civil War.

Our Self-Evident Morality

Amidst his discussions of our proud heritage and the ability of Americans to accomplish great feats, President Reagan emphasized the innate moral and spiritual strength evident in the community's behavior. At the most basic level, he vigorously defended the community's heritage on the basis of individuals and their acts.

> Well, sick societies don't produce men like the two who recently returned from outer space. Sick societies don't produce young men like Secret Service agent Tim McCarthy, who placed his body between mine and the man with the gun simply because he felt that's what his duty called for him to do. Sick societies don't produce dedicated police officers like Tom Delahanty or able and devoted public servants like Jim Brady. Sick societies don't make people like us so proud to be Americans and so very proud of our fellow citizens.[54]

The community's spiritual health is also evident in the Reagan program. "Economic recovery, better education, [and] rededication to values," for example, "all show the spirit of renewal gaining the upper hand."[55] This rededication to values not only unifies the community but proves that the heritage is healthy and morally sound:

> The heart of America is strong; it's good and true. The cynics were wrong; America never was a sick society. We're seeing rededication to bedrock values of faith, family, work, neighborhood, peace, and freedom—values that help bring us together as one people, from the youngest child to the most senior citizen.[56]

But if individual heroes, economic reform, and community unity reveal our fundamental morality, so does our international behavior.

In foreign affairs, America is always more concerned with right and generosity than with our own strategic interests. "The defense policy of the United States," he says, "is based on a simple premise: The United States does not start fights. We will never be an aggressor."[57] This selflessness is especially evident in Lebanon and the Middle East, where "Our involvement in this search for Mideast Peace is not a matter of preference; *it's a moral imperative.*" While strategic considerations are not unnoticed, Reagan subordinates them to moral considerations:

> The strategic importance of the region to the United States is well known, but our policy is motivated by more than strategic interests . . . our traditional humanitarian concerns dictated a continuing effort. . . .[58]

The innate morality evident in American acts of courage and selflessness is especially poignant in his account of a young marine wounded in the 1983 truck-bombing of the American Marine barracks in Beirut:

> That marine and all those others like him, living, dead, have been faithful to their ideals. They've given willingly of themselves so that a nearly defenseless people in a region of great strategic importance to the free world will have a chance someday to live lives free of murder and mayhem and terrorism.[59]

Indeed, it is our community heritage, our selflessness and faith in freedom have brought us our unsought stature as world power:

> America's leadership in the world came to us because of our own strength and because of the values which guide us as a society: free elections, a free press, freedom of religious choice, free trade unions, and above all, freedom for the individual and rejection of arbitrary power of the state. These values are the bedrock of our strength. They unite us in a stewardship of peace and freedom with our allies and friends in NATO, in Asia, in Latin America, and elsewhere.[60]

The notion of America's world leadership as moral stewardship is evident to the world. "Through times of difficulty and frustration," he says,

> America's highest aspiration has never wavered. We have and will continue to struggle for a lasting peace that enhances dignity for men and women everywhere.[61]

Our selfless dedication to peace is so self-evident, in fact, that President Reagan seemed incredulous that some were skeptical of our involvement in Central America: "Can anyone doubt the generosity and good faith of the American people?"[62]

In summary, President Reagan finds evidence of the community's moral strength in the accomplishments of individual astronauts, secret servicemen, police, and wounded marines and aides; and in the selflessness of our foreign policy. Individual acts of heroism and generosity prove our innate morality and validate our heritage.

Conclusions

President Reagan's first-term national addresses were built upon the bedrock of community. MisteReagan's Neighborhood is populated with ordinary people who are economically identified. It is these pedestrian individuals (never corporations) who bear the brunt of taxation, high prices, unemployment, and government regulation. It is also these people who make things happen in the *polis* by speaking out. Heroes abound in the neighborhood, although most of them lived some time ago. None of the individuals who have ever lived in the neighborhood are directly to blame for the neighborhood's problems. If today's problems result from earlier decisions, those decisions were government's, not people's, decisions. When individuals made unwise decisions, those individuals are not specified, and their choices were always based on good intentions. Today, however, the neighborhood faces two adversaries: the Soviet Union (the "Evil Empire" that is the direct or indirect source of all that is wrong in the world) and the neighborhood's own government. The spirit of MisteReagan's Neighborhood is constituted from a proud heritage based on freedom and all that it fosters (i.e. initiative, determination, idealism, realism, generosity, and courage). Through faith in that heritage, Americans can do anything. If or when we should ever fall short of our goals, it will be because we had insufficient faith in our heritage to act boldly. This timidity is seen as the tragic flaw in our national character. We must always be bold enough to act, because our individual and community actions are self-evidently moral and necessary for the betterment of both our community and the world outside.

The central point to be made here is that the rhetoric of "MisteReagan's Neighborhood" neatly interweaves these five themes into a seamless tapestry. The American community of which Reagan speaks is a special place with a proud heritage, a sense of moral purpose, and good people who can accomplish anything. All of these elements intertwine to create a series of perfect tautologies: we have a proud heritage because of our moral purpose and heroic ordinary people; we can accomplish anything because of our heritage and moral purpose; our moral purpose is evident in our proud heritage and the otherwise inexplicable accomplishments of humble people; our people are great and heroic because they are heirs to a great moral and heroic tradition, and so on.

The interweaving of these communitarian themes is so thorough and adroit that criticism of any one policy necessarily constitutes an attack upon our good people, our proud heritage, our morality, and our commitment to accomplishments. Let us briefly consider two particularly skillful cases.

After the sneak attack on the Marine barracks in Beirut there was widespread questioning of both the policy stationing our Marines there and of our ability to protect them. In his speech on the incident, however, President Reagan reduced the attack to an extraordinary ordinary marine's heroic personal story. Notice how the following passage reduces policy questions to (a) attacks on the moral qualities of heroic young men, (b) attacks on our proud heritage of selfless heroism, and (c) signs of timidity that betray our bold heritage, before (d) calling for us to live up to our heritage by standing tall in Lebanon:

> I think that young marine and all his comrades *have given every one of us something to live up to.* They were *not afraid* to stand up for their country or, no matter how difficult and slow the journey might be, *to give to others* that last, best hope of a

better future. *We cannot and will not dishonor them now* and the sacrifices they've made *by failing to remain as faithful* to the cause of freedom and the pursuit of peace as they have been.[63]

The wisdom, feasibility, and propriety of the original policy decision sending American marines into Beirut, as well as the wisdom and competence of the Administration, are insulated from scrutiny by the honor of the young marines and by the implicit equation of caution with cowardice. The seamlessness of the Reagan scenario of good, heroic, simple people who can do anything because of their faith in a proud heritage and their self-evident morality renders any kind of criticism a potential attack upon the essential meaning of America.

Similarly, the 1984 State of the Union cleared the path for re-election by depicting national policy as a test of Will and Courage. Whether the economic reforms, foreign policy, and social agenda were well-conceived or not, we are told that we must pursue them or betray our heritage:

> After all our struggles to restore America, to revive confidence in our country, hope for our future, after all our hard-won victories earned through the patience and courage of every citizen, we cannot, must not, and will not turn back. We will finish our job. How could we do less? We're Americans.[64]

It is little wonder that Messrs. Mondale, Jackson, and Hart had great difficulty focusing attention on the wisdom of the Reagan policies in 1984.

Community is an essential element in American political rhetoric. Without a strong sense of community the society may fragment (as it did for Lincoln, Johnson, and Nixon) or lose its cohesion (as it did for Ford and Carter). President Reagan's communitarian rhetoric unifies the country by drawing upon our significant myths and symbols and by depersonalizing blame for current troubles. No American need be his adversary. These communitarian themes impel support and action on Reagan's initiatives because all actions are rendered as duty to our common heritage—a heritage which demands faith, courage, and bold action rather than debate. Finally, the communitarian themes insulate President Reagan (and to a lesser degree, his policies) because he renders criticism of policy as criticism of our proud heritage and our heroic people; it renders cautious debate cowardly and timid, and it forces anti-Reagan spokespersons to claim the mantle of well-intentioned but misguided and faithless cynics.

It is obvious that any president as both Head of State and Head of Government has a responsibility to foster a sense of national community. President Reagan has fulfilled this responsibility through his handling of the community motif. The inspirational nature of his addresses, his patriotic challenges (e.g. "Why shouldn't we? We're Americans"), and his grassroots identification, have fostered a greater sense of national unity and pride among more people than we have witnessed in many years.

Nevertheless, there are several innate dangers in the kind of rhetoric that President Reagan uses so well. Foremost among them is the fact that the Reagan version of America's proud heritage is not the only one. We also have a proud heritage of democratic debate, of recognizing and correcting our mistakes, of government of, by, and for the people, and of a moral fiber sufficient to scrutinize the ethical implications of our behavior. President Reagan's emphasis of a tradition of bold and decisive action encourages rash acts that could jeopardize both our long- and short-term interests and thus ultimately disgrace our heritage and its heirs. Insistence upon the self-evident morality of our acts is the surest way to avoid consideration of their moral implications. The exhortation to "stand tall" in honor of our heritage and our brave people leads us toward sacrifice and martyrdom for their own sake.

The communitarian themes of President Reagan's first term national addresses are not the whole answer to The Question. Although equally important, an examination of his ability to simplify complex matters and the vividness of his language must await another day. But the emphasis upon neighborhood is pivotal because of the way that it skillfully unifies the country by identifying pragmatic policies with the essential meaning of America.

Notes

1. See for example Ernest G. Bormann, "A Fantasy Theme Analysis of the Television Coverage of the Hostage Release and the Reagan Inaugural," *Quarterly Journal of Speech,* 68 (1982), 133–145; Bert E. Bradley, "Jefferson and Reagan: The Rhetoric of Two Inaugurals," *Southern Speech Communication Journal,* 48 (1983), 119–136, and "A Response to 'Two Inaugurals: A Second Look' " *Southern Speech Communication Journal,"* 48 (1983), 386–390; Richard E. Crable and Steven L. Vibbert, "Argumentative Stance and Political Faith Healing: 'The Dream Will Come True'," *Quarterly Journal of Speech,* 69 (1983), 290–301; Sarah Russell Hankins, "Archetypal Alloy: Reagan's Rhetorical Image," *Central States Speech Journal* 34 (1983), 33–43; Robert L. Ivie, "Speaking 'Common Sense' about the Soviet Threat," *Western Journal of Speech Communication,* 48 (1984), 39–50; Martha Anna Martin, "Ideologues, Ideographs, and 'The Best Men': From Carter to Reagan," *Southern Speech Communication Journal,* 49 (1983), 12–25; Martin J. Medhurst, "Postponing the Social Agenda: Reagan's Strategy and Tactics," *Western Journal of Speech Communication,* 48 (1984), 262–276; Gregg Phifer, "The Two Inaugurals: A Second Look," *Southern Speech Communication Journal* 48 (1983), 378–385; C. Thomas Preston, Jr., "Reagan's 'New Beginning': Is it the 'New Deal' of the Eighties?," *Southern Speech Communication Journal,* 49 (1984), 198–211; Henry Z. Scheele, "Ronald Reagan's 1980 Acceptance Address," *Western Journal of Speech Communication,* 48 (1984), 51–61; Gary C. Woodward, "Reagan as Roosevelt: The Elasticity of Pseudo-Populist Appeals," *Central States Speech Journal,* 34 (1983), 44–58; and David Zarefsky, Carol Miller-Tutzauer, and Frank E. Tutzauer, "Ronald Reagan's Safety Net for the Truly Needy: The Rhetorical Uses of Definition," *Central States Speech Journal,* 35 (1984), 113–119.

2. This study relied upon the official transcripts as published in the U.S. Government Printing Office's *Weekly Compilation of Presidential Documents* (hereafter referred to as *WCPD*). For the reader's benefit, citations will refer to the date of the speech rather than the date of the weekly issue. The speeches studied were the "[First] Inaugural Address of President Ronald Reagan," *WCPD*, 17 (January 23, 1981), 1–5; "Address to the Nation on the Economy," *WCPD*, 17 (February 5, 1981), 79–83; "Address to a Joint Session of the Congress on the Program for Economic Recovery," *WCPD*, 17 (February 18, 1981), 108–115; "Address Before a Joint Session of the Congress on the Program for Economic Recovery," *WCPD*, 17 (April 28, 1981), 391–394; "Address to the Nation on Federal Tax Reduction Legislation," *WCPD*, 17 (July 27, 1981), 664–668; "Address to the Nation on the Program for Economic Recovery," *WCPD*, 17 (September 24, 1981), 831–836; "Address to the Nation About Christmas and the Situation in Poland," *WCPD*, 17 (December 23, 1981), 1185–1188; "The State of the Union," *WCPD*, 18 (January 26, 1982), 76–83; "Federal Tax and Budget Reconciliation Legislation," *WCPD*, 18 (August 16, 1982), 1035–1039; "United States Policy for Peace in the Middle East," *WCPD*, 18 (September 1, 1982), 1081–1085; "The Situation in Lebanon," *WCPD*, 18 (September 20, 1982), 1182–1184; "The Nation's Economy," *WCPD*, 18 (October 13, 1982), 1305–1310; "The State of the Union," *WCPD*, 19 (January 25, 1983), 105–112; "National Security," *WCPD*, 19 (March 23, 1983), 442–448; "Central America," *WCPD*, 19 (April 27, 1983), 608–614; "Soviet Attack on Korean Civilian Airliner," *WCPD*, 19 (September 5, 1983), 1199–1202; "Events in Lebanon and Granada," *WCPD*, 19 (October 27, 1983), 1497–1503; "Soviet-American Relations," *WCPD*, 20 (January 16, 1984),40–45; "The State of the Union,"*WCPD*, 20 (January 25, 1984), 87–94; "1984 Presidential Election," *WCPD* (January 29, 1984), 114–115; "United States Policy in Central America," *WCPD*, 20 (May 9, 1984), 676–682; and "1984 Presidential Campaign," *WCPD*, 20 (November 5, 1984), 1798–1802. This list includes televised addresses to Congress, but excludes the President's weekly radio addresses.
3. See Robert N. Bellah, "Civil Religion in America," *Daedalus*, Vol. 96 (Winter, 1967); Dante Germino, *The Inaugural Addresses of American Presidents: The Public Philosophy and Rhetoric*, (Lanham, MD: University Press of America, 1984); James David Fairbanks, "The Priestly Functions of the American Presidency," *Presidential Studies Quarterly*, 11 (1981), 214–232; and Woodward.
4. *WCPD* (January 25, 1983), p. 112.
5. *WCPD* (November 5, 1984), p. 1798.
6. Woodward, p. 47. The other four characteristics of the Populist style, according to his essay, are the "portrayal of bureaucratic or corporate malevolence against 'the ordinary guy'," the "use of appeals centered predominantly on self interest rather than the public interest," a "reliance on a producer-user dualism" and the "use of an 'equal' idiom with constituents and supporters."
7. *WCPD* (January 20, 1981), p. 2. These 'people' were later condensed into "neighbors and friends, shopkeepers, laborers, farmers and craftsmen" *WCPD*, April 28, 1981, p. 393.
8. *WCPD*, (January 25, 1984), p. 92.
9. *WCPD*, (January 26, 1982), p. 76.
10. *WCPD*, (October 13, 1982), p. 1305.
11. *WCPD*, (February 18, 1981), p. 109.
12. *WCPD*, (September 24, 1981), p. 833.
13. *WCPD*, (July 27, 1981), p. 664.

14. *WCPD,* (November 5, 1984), p 1798.
15. *WCPD,* (October 10, 1982), p. 1309.
16. *WCPD,* (October 13, 1982), p. 1306.
17. *WCPD,* (January 25, 1983), p. 105, 112.
18. *WCPD,* (January 20, 1981), p. 2.
19. *WCPD,* (February 5, 1981), p. 80.
20. *WCPD,* (February 5, 1981), p. 80.
21. *WCPD,* (February 5, 1981), p. 80.
22. *WCPD,* (October 13, 1982), p. 1306, emphasis added.
23. Tom Preston contrasted the first inaugurals of Reagan and Franklin Roosevelt and concluded that the role of government emerged as a significant difference. "Reflected in Roosevelt's address was a government that solves economic ills and serves the social good while in Reagan's speech we saw a government that shared with the Democratic Party the notoriety of "scapegoat" (Preston, p. 205).
24. *WCPD,* (November 5, 1984), p. 1798.
25. *WCPD,* (October 13, 1982), p. 1308.
26. *WCPD,* (October 13, 1982), p. 1308.
27. *WCPD,* (October 13, 1982), p. 1308.
28. *WCPD,* (September 24, 1981), p. 834.
29. *WCPD,* (July 27, 1981), p. 666.
30. *WCPD,* (November 5, 1984), p. 1798.
31. Ivie, p. 42.
32. In an article published more than six months prior to the Watergate break-in, Gonchar and Hahn discuss Richard Nixon's predictable proclivity to personalize criticism. Ruth M. Gonchar and Dan F. Hahn, "The Rhetorical Predictability of Richard M. Nixon," *Today's Speech,* 19 (1971), 3–14.
33. *WCPD,* (January 25, 1984), p. 90.
34. Medhurst argues that Reagan entered office with a clear hierarchy of programs ranging from the Economy through Defense, Federalism, and Social Issues down to Crime (p. 263). He further argues that Reagan was able to sustain interest in the social agenda while concentrating on economic and defense matters, in part, through the use of two transcendent god terms: "freedom" and "liberty" (p. 270). The present essay is more inclined to regard the essential Reagan god terms as "freedom" and "faith."
35. *WCPD,* (January 20, 1981), p. 3.
36. *WCPD,* (July 27, 1981), p. 688.
37. *WCPD,* (September 24, 1981), p. 836.
38. *WCPD,* (April 28, 1981), p. 394.
39. *WCPD,* (January 25, 1983), p. 112.
40. *WCPD,* (July 27, 1981), p. 688.
41. *WCPD,* (September 24, 1981), p. 836.
42. *WCPD,* (January 25, 1983), p. 111.
43. The individual heroes cited were World War I private Martin Treptow, Gen. Douglas MacArthur, POW Jeremiah Denton, General Paul Kelley, and Sergeant Stephen Trujillo.
44. *WCPD,* (January 25, 1984), p. 88, 93.
45. *WCPD,* (January 25, 1982), p. 82.
46. Bormann has discussed the first Reagan inaugural as an example of the fantasy theme of "Restoration." This essay affirms the restorative nature of the inaugural and finds considerable evidence of a restorative vision throughout Reagan's first

term address. A fascinating sidelight to the restoration question is President Reagan's ironic insistence that America is renewing itself and "on the way back," while vigorously denying that any of our greatness was ever lost.

47. Invocation of the Founding Fathers, our national purpose, and heroic figures from our past is hardly unique to Ronald Reagan (cf. Bellah, pp. 1–21). Hankins approached the question of Reaganesque heroism differently, suggesting that much of his appeal comes from his ability to play the role of hero.

48. *WCPD*, (January 20, 1981), p. 5 (emphasis added).

49. *WCPD*, (April 28, 1981), p. 394. Crable and Vibbert have suggested that this sort of rhetorical faith-healing produces three results, two of which are good. If the patient improves, the faith-healer can claim a pivotal role in the cure. If the cure does not revive the patient, the failure can be attributed to the patient's lack of faith. The only risk is that the faith-healer will be held accountable for a predicted recovery that does not occur. As they summarize the point "If the 'You shall be . . .' is interpreted as a prediction, the healer is held responsible for any error and victimage of the healer may result. If, in contrast, the 'You shall be . . .' is interpreted as a command, the unhealed is at fault and mortification may be the more reasonable immediate response" (p. 297). But again, appeals to faith are not unique to Ronald Reagan. Fairbanks (p. 217) reminds us of Will Herberg's observation in *Protestant Catholic Jew* (Garden City, NY: Anchor Books, 1960) that the American faith is faith in faith (p. 265); and Germino (p. 20) refers us to Harry Truman's inaugural discussion of the "essential principles of the faith by which we [Americans] live."

50. *WCPD*, (January 25, 1984), p. 90.
51. *WCPD*, (October 13, 1982), p. 1310.
52. *WCPD*, (December 23, 1981), p. 1188.
53. *WCPD*, (January 27, 1982), p. 82.
54. *WCPD*, (April 28, 1981), p. 391.
55. *WCPD*, (January 25, 1984), p. 92.
56. *WCPD*, (January 25, 1984), p. 88.
57. *WCPD*, (March 23, 1983), p. 443.
58. *WCPD*, (September 1, 1982), p. 1082, emphasis added.
59. *WCPD*, (October 27, 1983), p. 1502.
60. *WCPD*, (January 25, 1983), p. 110.
61. *WCPD*, (January 16, 1984), p. 41.
62. *WCPD*, (April 27, 1983), p. 610.
63. *WCPD*, (October 27, 1983), p. 1502.
64. *WCPD*, (January 25, 1984), p. 93.

About the Editors

Theodore Windt is Associate Professor of Political Rhetoric at the University of Pittsburgh where he teaches courses in "Presidential Rhetoric" from Kennedy to Reagan. More than 1,000 undergraduates enroll for his lectures each year.

Mr. Windt received his B.A. degree in English from Texas Lutheran College, his M.A. in Theatre Arts from Bowling Green State University, and his Ph.D. in Rhetoric and Philosophy from Ohio State University. He is the editor of *Presidential Rhetoric: 1961 to the Present* and the author of a number of scholarly essays. He is a member of the Center for the Study of the Presidency and of the Speech Communication Association's National Task Force on Presidential Rhetoric.

Mr. Windt is also a practitioner of rhetoric. He is a professional speechwriter and political consultant as an associate of Matt Reese Communications and Methane and Walsh. Currently, he is the presidential analyst for KQV radio and political commentator on national politics for "Weekend Magazine" for KDKA-TV, both in Pittsburgh.

Beth Ingold was born in Pittsburgh and attended both parochial and public schools in Pittsburgh. She received her B.A. degree in Rhetoric and Communications and her M.A. degree in Political Rhetoric at the University of Pittsburgh, where she is currently completing her Ph.D. Ms. Ingold has presented papers at scholarly conventions, is a member of the Center for the Study of the Presidency and the National Task Force on Presidential Rhetoric.

Ms. Ingold is Assistant Director for Project SCOPE of the Allegheny Intermediate Unit in Pittsburgh, Pennsylvania.